PRODUCTION CONTROL

THIRD EDITION

FRANKLIN G. MOORE
PROFESSOR OF INDUSTRIAL MANAGEMENT
SCHOOL OF BUSINESS ADMINISTRATION
THE UNIVERSITY OF MICHIGAN

RONALD JABLONSKI
ASSOCIATE PROFESSOR OF MANAGEMENT
THE UNIVERSITY OF MICHIGAN

McGRAW-HILL BOOK COMPANY
NEW YORK   ST. LOUIS   SAN FRANCISCO
TORONTO   LONDON   SYDNEY

PRODUCTION CONTROL

Library of Congress Catalog Card Number 68-28418

07-042921-9

567890KPKP7987654

PREFACE

Since the second edition of *Production Control* several trends have combined to make it more difficult to treat the subject of production control in a textbook. All of these trends have made greater the difference in practices between large and small companies, and in the degree of sophistication of the procedures used.

As a result, it has become increasingly difficult to make any general statements at all about production control. In many companies, mostly small ones, the procedures, methods, alternatives, and reasons why are just about the same as they were when the second edition, or even the first edition of this book, was published. In several instances, when preparing this edition, letters to companies asking for newer pictures or copies of printed forms for use as illustrations, produced answers that the old one was still in use. Perhaps this should be expected since the procedures for making mature products in mature industries don't change much in any short span of years.

Yet against this we have seen great changes in the 1960s. Differences in size between large and small companies are greater than ever. Computers are now used almost everywhere and they do a good bit of the detailed work of controlling production. Today's efficient and economical copying machines have changed many production control procedures. The "systems" conceptual scheme for viewing information flows has caused changes. Microminiature film reproduction of drawings and documents has changed other procedures. And further developments in operations research techniques are allowing them to be used in more places.

In our largest companies probably all of these trends have had their impact and have changed the way today's production is controlled. Most of these trends have had at least a limited impact on small company procedures as well. Yet the effects are uneven and spotty. We find places where what was done in 1950 is still done today, whereas in other places, everything has been revolutionized and the procedures of 1950 have disappeared.

It is this mixture of old and new that makes our problem difficult. So much of what we said in earlier editions still applies that it should not be discarded. Yet it no longer applies in as many places.

And the new shiny procedures are so much better and applicable in so many places that they need top billing. The danger is that we will paint a picture of all new and no old and so do an improper job.

We have, therefore, tried in this edition to keep up with advances, to present a proper perspective, and to present an appropriate blend between old and new. Descriptive material has been reduced in order to allow room for including more quantitative material. The text is now more oriented to managerial decision making. Materials and techniques are presented so as to show managers the alternatives available and to show them how to calculate answers so that they will know the most economical and most effective courses of action to take.

Gaps in the second edition have been filled in two major areas. A new chapter has been added on forecasting procedures as part of the greater attention given to coordinating sales demands with production. A new chapter has also been added on statistical quality control since this work is so closely related to production control.

Operations research techniques come in for considerably more attention. Simulation, economic lot quantities, queuing, assignment problems, and other methods are described. In each case the discussion goes into how these tools can be used to help managers make better decisions.

Problems and case materials, published separately for the second edition, have now been incorporated into the textbook itself so that no separate booklet is needed. Text type case materials have been replaced to a considerable extent by problems which call for the student to use the quantitative materials discussed in the text.

FRANKLIN G. MOORE

RONALD JABLONSKI

CONTENTS

TYPES OF PRODUCTION

chapter three

MINOR KINDS OF PRODUCTION

chapter four

PRODUCTION CONTROL PROCEDURES

chapter five

THE PRODUCTION CONTROL ORGANIZATION

chapter six

FORECASTING

chapter seven

FORECASTING (CONTINUED)

chapter eight

ESTIMATING

chapter nine

ESTIMATING (CONTINUED)

chapter ten

AUTHORITY TO MAKE

chapter eleven

EARLY PLANNING—ENGINEERING ASPECTS

PLANNING—ENGINEERING ASPECTS

MASTER PROCESSING INSTRUCTIONS

chapter fourteen

IDENTIFICATION SYSTEMS AND CALENDARS

MANPOWER PLANNING

CONTROLLING INVENTORIES IN ORDER CONTROL

chapter seventeen ✓

INVENTORY CONTROL (CONTINUED)

chapter eighteen

PLANNING—PRODUCTION CONTROL ASPECTS

chapter nineteen

LINEAR PROGRAMMING

chapter twenty

SCHEDULING

chapter twenty-three

PREPARING FOR PRODUCTION

chapter twenty-four

DISPATCHING

chapter twenty-five

KEEPING PRODUCTION MOVING

chapter twenty-six

QUALITY CONTROL

chaper twenty-seven

OTHER SHOP PROBLEMS

chapter thirty

FLOW CONTROL—II

chapter thirty-one

FLOW CONTROL—III

chapter thirty-two

INFORMATION PROCESSING

chapter one

PRODUCTION CONTROL FUNCTIONS

INTRODUCTION

Production control is the factory's nervous system. Almost all factories can perform a tremendous variety of operations and turn out a varied array of products. Yet nothing happens, not one wheel turns, until you tell the factory what you want it to do. Nor can you tell the factory to make a locomotive, or an automobile. True, the factory ends up making completed products but its directions have to be minute and specific. These directions tell it to perform individual operations on all kinds of component parts and to put them together into finished products.

Production control sends the necessary continuous stream of directions to all parts of the factory. These the factory has to have if it is to perform the many operations required to make parts and produce finished products of the kind you want when you want them.

A factory's nervous system is quite a lot like that of a human being. Consider, for a moment, the amount of conscious control you put into walking down the street. It is so little that you never think of it. Your movements are repetitive. It is different, though, when you try to learn to swim, or to play golf or basketball. You have to pay attention to how you use your hands, legs, and body. You have to try to control your every movement.

Factories are much like this. They too need fewer directions when they perform the same operations over and over than they do when they produce nonstandardized products. The production control system has to be appropriate for the job to be done. Furthermore, a factory's nervous system, just as a human system, has to do more than just transmit a one-way series of orders. If you had a perfect mechanism, whether an industrial plant or a human body, you could expect that all orders would be carried out exactly as planned and they would not need further follow-up and control. Such a system where the output would have a known relationship to the inputs could be represented as shown in figure 1-1. In the case of factories, the transformation of inputs into outputs is the production function.

Unfortunately, things never work smoothly. There are always disturbances that enter into the system. Orders are misunderstood, purchased parts don't arrive when scheduled, machines break down, workers call in

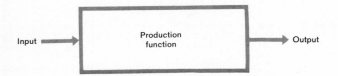

FIGURE 1-1

sick (or just fail to show up for work), and countless other things happen to upset the system.

Production control must therefore also receive signals or reports telling it the condition or state of things. And production control needs to take appropriate action to modify the inputs so that the desired output is achieved. A system to accomplish this would be an elementary form of feedback control system and can be represented as shown in figure 1-2.

When we consider the time element in this model, the dynamic nature and complexity of production control become evident. Each of the above elements will vary with respect to time, and each one will vary in a different manner. Workers' attitudes and skills change with the passage of time and because of turnover; disturbances of one day may disappear the next, probably to be replaced by other new disturbances; and even standards or desired outputs change to meet the fluctuating demand for products. One must plan and then constantly replan.

The methodology of production control has wide application even outside of manufacturing operations. There is no basic difference between scheduling hospital patients into an operating room and scheduling parts

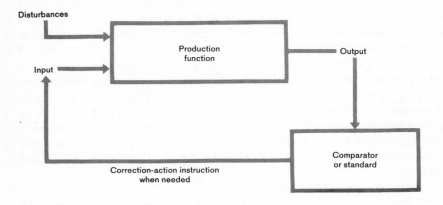

FIGURE 1-2

through machine operations, except that the latter is generally more complex. The determination of the number of hotel rooms to hold in reserve is no different from the determination of the safety stock to be held in inventory. Forecasting and planning of manpower requirements are the same whether one is supplying a manufactured part or a service.

Our subject is, however, production control in manufacturing companies and our emphasis is going to be on metalworking companies even though companies making products out of metal make up only one-third of all American industry. The textile and food industries together employ more men than do all metal fabricating companies combined. And the paper, printing, and lumber products industries together are fully half as large as all metalworking companies.

Nevertheless, because metalworking companies have more complex production control problems than companies in other industries we will, in this book, talk almost wholly about how to control production in metalworking companies. Metalworking companies make a tremendous variety of products. The Link-Belt division of FMC Corporation, for example, a maker of materials handling conveyors, lists over 150,000 items in its catalog. Crane Company, maker of plumbing products, makes over 8,000 varieties of pipe fittings alone. And every one of automobile's big three could make automobiles all year long yet not make two cars alike, so many are the possible combinations of different details.

Furthermore, putting together finished products is only a small portion of the work. Making the parts is a far bigger job. A typewriter contains over 2,000 parts, an automobile over 13,000, and a diesel locomotive nearly 50,000. Small airplanes may require 50,000 parts. Jet airplanes go over 200,000 parts. Moon missiles are more complex. And these figures are just for one model. The numbers skyrocket if your product line contains much variety. Delco-Remey, for example, makes mostly relatively simple products (automobile ignition wiring systems, coils, etc.) yet it makes 10,000 varieties requiring 50,000 subassemblies and parts.

To complicate the matter further, component parts are made by having individual operations performed on them. If you made such a trivial item as paper clips you would start off with a coil of wire. Then you would cut off pieces of wire from the coil. Then you would bend these pieces of wire into shape. It takes two individual operations on each piece of wire, cutting and bending, to make it into a paper clip. But a door hinge is more complex. It must be made in several operations. Most component parts of factory-made products are far more complex. It takes, for example, over 50 operations to make an automobile crankshaft. Directing the performance of all of the operations required to make parts is production control's biggest job.

FIGURE 1-3   Many products are made in limited quantities but in countless variety. The gears shown here illustrate a few of the varieties. Most companies making this type of product are in job lot work and use order control. (Grant Gear Works)

Production control also has to contend with subassemblies. You don't put a bicycle seat together after you fasten its frame onto the bicycle. You first put the seat together as a seat and then attach it to the bicycle. And you do the same with the wheels, the footpedals, the drive chains, and with other components. Most individual piece parts of all metal products go first into subassemblies which then go into the final products. Jet airplanes probably contain over 10,000 subassemblies and moon missiles even more.

Purchasing adds another dimension to controlling production. Everything you make is made out of the materials, parts, and manufactured components that you buy. Some companies buy as many as 50,000 items, all of which have to be ordered from thousands of vendors several or many times a year.

Inside the factory, every operation on every part has to be carried out, and every subassembly and every product has to be made according to directions. A big company might easily have 50,000 processing orders in

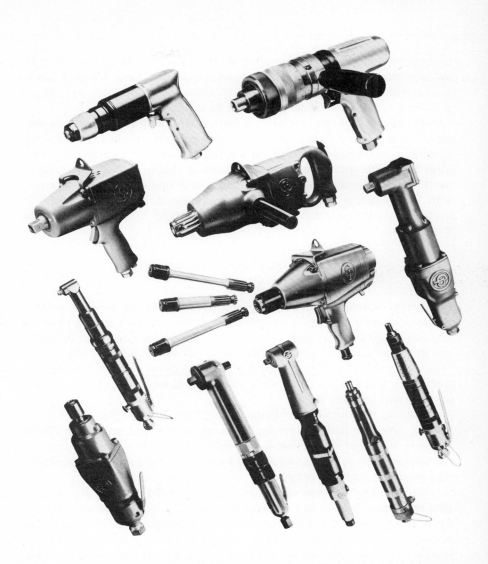

FIGURE 1-4 Assembled products which are made in considerable quantity must frequently be made up on an order basis because of the many varieties made to suit different customers' needs. The pneumatic tools pictured above illustrate the varieties made. (Chicago Pneumatic Tool Co.)

process in just one of its factories all the time. Similarly, the continual inflow of bought materials rests on detailed analysis of the needs of future production and inventories on hand. A company might well have 10,000 purchase orders outstanding all of the time.

Production control problems in nonmetalworking companies are simpler. There is less variety and there are fewer parts. It takes relatively few operations to make grains of wheat into bread, pieces of leather into shoes, strands of wool into suits of clothes, bales of rubber into tires, grains of sand into milk bottles, or pieces of wood into chairs. So we will stay largely with metalworking industries. If you understand production control in metal industries, you can more easily understand production control in the others.

NATURE OF PRODUCTION CONTROL

Production control is an on-going activity designed to strike a balance between several conflicting objectives or goals. To focus too narrowly on any one single objective will lead to a suboptimal situation. If, for example, you minimize inventory control costs, customer service will probably suffer. Costs will be higher than if optimal balance of all factors is attained. Admittedly this is not an easy state to attain but one must keep it in mind and constantly strive for it.

Holding down inventory costs is one goal. Ideally, you try to finish making products just in time for them to be sold but no sooner. Thus, ideally you should never lose a sale because you do not have what the customer wants, yet you should never have to carry any finished inventories and incur the cost this entails.

But you can't escape carrying some inventories because still another goal is to have the factory operate economically. To do this you need to make large volumes of a limited variety of products. If the volume is big enough, you can make products continually at a steady rate and thus hold inventories down in situations where customers buy at a steady rate. Doing this usually reduces unit costs to a minimum. But smaller volume items must be made in lots, several or many at a time, after which you make no more until your supply runs low. Then you make a repeat lot. In this case you have to carry bigger inventories, and besides this, you can never get your unit costs down to match continuous production unit costs.

Unfortunately, it takes time to make products and this fact also keeps you from ever achieving theoretical minimum costs. In both continuous production and lot production, you have to decide ahead, usually months ahead, how many of each product to make. Since it is impossible to guess perfectly what customers will buy and when, you end up running out of some products and having too many of others. You don't wholly accomplish your sales goals, since you will lose some sales by being out of stock from time to time. Also, and even if you didn't plan it that way, you will end up carrying inventories of some items from time to time. Once again you try to be as efficient as you can but there are limitations to how far you can go.

EMPHASIS ON CUSTOMER SERVICE   To complicate matters, customers change their minds. They want more products than they first ordered, or they want fewer. They want their orders sooner, or they want them later. They want frills. They want you to turn handsprings and, of course, all of this at no extra cost. And not unnaturally, the sales department wants to keep customers satisfied even when their demands seem unreasonable.

We should note that in American companies, taking care of the customer's demands, particularly meeting delivery dates, is almost a religion. Reasons that to *you* are good reasons for not delivering on time are *not* good reasons for your customer. Customers sometimes are other companies whose orders are large and who are carrying almost no inventory of parts because they depend on you to supply them. Failure to deliver may close down their plants or may delay their introducing their new models, for lack of your parts.

Companies which don't recognize customers' whims and which don't deliver on time lose their customers. So it is small wonder that companies try very hard to meet all customer demands, including difficult to meet delivery dates. If, in order to deliver on time, you have to work overtime, thereby boosting costs, you may well choose the overtime even when you can't pass the added costs on to the customer.

Of course if a delay is in prospect, you should tell your customer. Sometimes if he knows that you are going to be late, he can rearrange his own work schedules so that it won't matter. But whether he can or not, an expected failure seems to cause much less anguish to customers than an unexpected one.

ACHIEVING PRODUCTION CONTROL OBJECTIVES—THE DILEMMA   Not only is production control usually unable to do a perfect job as the sales department sees it, it also misses satisfying production goals wholly. If you plan to produce continuously, there will always be interruptions to production and sometimes sales forecasts will prove wrong. When sales boom unexpectedly you try to boost production on a forced draft basis with costly overtime. Or if sales lag you have to go on short hours. Neither of these choices lets you operate the factory economically.

It isn't much different if you produce in lots. Again variations in sales result in your having made too few or too many of specific kinds of products to get the lowest factory costs. Rarely do sales happen to generate a factory work load that is exactly the optimum for lowest factory costs.

Nor do you escape diseconomies by building up inventories in slack periods and using them up during sales peaks, because carrying inventories costs money too. Nonetheless, carrying nominal sized inventories usually helps ease both sales and factory problems without causing prohibitive inventory carrying costs.

Usually the job of trying to mesh these diverse goals that we have been talking about and resolving them into a workable production schedule rests in part on the production control department's shoulders.

Closely related to production control's finished inventory obligations is its responsibility for keeping inventories in process moving. Whenever materials or merchandise stop moving they begin to accumulate expenses for storage, insurance, idle capital, extra handling, and other causes. And since most manufacturing companies have more money tied up in inprocess inventories than in raw materials and finished products combined, keeping the inventory in process moving becomes a most important function of production control.

Actually, in one sense, the production control department doesn't really control production. It only tries to. The point is that plans are never carried out wholly and completely. Always things, big or little, go wrong so that a good bit of production control work deals with finding out what actually goes on and then making new plans to replace the old.

PROBLEMS THAT PRODUCTION CONTROL TRIES TO SOLVE

Production control has to try to remedy many problems, among which are: raw material or finished parts aren't on hand when you want them; production levels jump up and down; the plant is all clogged up with materials in process; too many men spend their time hauling things around; you have too much finished goods inventory on hand, yet you can't always make deliveries when you promised because you don't have the right things on hand; you frequently have to use crash programs in the shop in order to deliver on time; you lose sales because of being out of stock of certain items in the plant or certain warehouses; or you ship products to wrong customers too often. Although we won't try to enumerate them all, there are still more problems besides these.

You can minimize most of these problems by doing a more thorough job of controlling production. Generally, the more thorough your control procedures, the more effective they are, yet the more costly they are. This being true, you get to choose: to go in for fairly thorough control, hoping that the value of fewer slip-ups will more than offset the cost of more paper work. Or you can spend less on control, knowing that things will go wrong more often. Many companies prefer not to have elaborate controls, choosing instead to let occasional slip-ups occur. Slip-ups, if they are only occasional, don't cost too much. Furthermore even elaborate controls don't prevent quite all the slip-ups.

FUNCTIONS OF PRODUCTION CONTROL

The production control staff has to carry out a long list of individual functions. These are basic and have to be performed in all manufacturing companies.

In all companies, the production control department gets orders to make certain numbers of specified, completed products. Then it has to figure out what and how many parts are needed, and what raw materials are needed; also how to make the parts, and what operations to perform on them. Production control needs, too, to be sure that there are enough machines to do the work. This means considerable advance checking up, planning, and preparation. Then production control has to make up and issue instructions to the factory to go ahead and perform the necessary operations for making parts and assembling them into complete products.

Once operations are under way, production control has to get reports of production so that its staff can check and see where things are going wrong, get rid of the causes of hold-ups right away, and then replan and reschedule everything.

Some people like to classify production control work under six headings: (1) materials control, (2) planning, (3) routing, (4) scheduling, (5) dispatching, and (6) progress control. This list doesn't help very much though, because the terms are too general and don't tell enough about what production control really does. Here is a more specific, detailed list of the things that production control departments do:

1 Help make forecasts of future sales for scheduling purposes

2 Help make estimates of costs of new jobs

3 Receive orders for products from sales department

4 Translate future schedules into manpower requirements

5 Translate future schedules into machine requirements

6 Determine finished parts needed

7   Determine materials requirements

8   Maintain raw materials stock room

9   Determine operations required

10   Determine machines and machine attachments required

11   Place tooling orders for tooling made inside

12   Operate the tool storage activities

13   Determine the sequence of operations

14   Make up requisitions authorizing issuing materials

15   Make up production orders

16   Make up production schedules

17   Make sure that all facilities for production will be available

18   Distribute and file copies of engineering drawings at appropriate locations

19   Assign jobs to particular men and machines

20   Issue orders and instructions to produce

21   Direct materials transportation in the factory

22   Receive reports of work done and evaluate performance

23   Put design changes into effect

24   Put quantity and schedule changes into effect

25   Replan when original plans are not carried out

26   Expedite all late orders

27   Prevent recurrence of plan failures

28   Control finished parts stock room

29   Control finished products stock room

30   Keep sales department posted on delivery dates

31   Control finished parts stocks in company owned warehouses

Before going on to talk about these functions we want to point out that you can't turn the job of controlling production over to a computer. Computers can handle a good bit of the routine clerical work needed to control production but they can't handle very many of the functions in our list and they aren't up to handling situations when things go wrong. And as we have said, something, big or little, is always going wrong. Computers aren't good at improvising.

We should also note that production control isn't all inventory control and mathematical formulas. Computers do a good job on this part of production control work, so good, in fact, that whole books have been written explaining how they do it. Often the books are entitled *Production Control* or *Production and Inventory Control* yet they cover only the aspects of inventory control that are susceptible to mathematical treatment and leave out all of the rest of the work involved in controlling production. But you can't get production through a plant by inventory control formulas alone. There is much more to the job than that. Also there are times when, for the best interest of the whole organization, you should sacrifice inventory management economy, in order to realize other bigger economies.

We will devote several chapters to inventory control but we will also talk about the other aspects of production control.

ASSIGNMENT OF FUNCTIONS TO DEPARTMENTS

Our list of 31 duties covers just about the whole production control job. These duties are basic, no matter whether they are assigned to the production control department or to some other department. Probably few production control departments are assigned every job in this list, but they get most of them. Several years ago the American Production and Inventory Control Society surveyed the duties of the production control departments in which its members worked. The total list was long, with the following duties listed most often:

ACTIVITY	PERCENTAGE OF PRODUCTION CONTROL DEPARTMENTS RESPONSIBLE
Production planning:	
Levels of production	77
Plant capacity studies	50
Release new products for production	50
Levels of inventories for:	
Work in process	88
Production materials	81
Finished goods	70
Customer service:	
Delivery schedules	76
Delivery promises	76
Answers for customer follow-ups	48
Order records	46
Instructions to ship	44
Shipping department:	
Control of physical quantities of finished goods	65
Production control:	
Product routing	55
Production orders:	
Preparation and issue	91
Order frequency (number of runs)	90
Quantity determination	90
Scheduling product through factory	87
Estimating manufacturing lead time	87
Machine loading scheduled products	77
Scrap allowances	68

ACTIVITY	PERCENTAGE OF PRODUCTION CONTROL DEPARTMENTS RESPONSIBLE
Dispatching:	
Schedules and instructions	91
Follow-up reporting	87
Expediting in plant	87
Control quantity of work in process	82
Intra-plant traffic	66
Controlling raw material inventories:	
Control quantity of production material	78
Placing purchase requisition	77
Record keeping	75
Determine item inventory level	75
Determine order frequency	73
Determine inventory reserves	71
Determine order quantity	70
Control operating supplies inventory	53
Control operating supplies quantities	48

Among duties assigned to from one-quarter to one-third of the production control departments were: participation in the sales forecast, deciding to make new products, make or buy decisions, traffic in and out, and determination of purchase lead time.

The production control department sometimes gets still other minor jobs (in addition to those in our list) to do. A common one is to set the working hours for each factory department (since this depends on the work loads provided by the jobs scheduled). Sometimes this means notifying the power plant of power needs and notifying the cafeteria what meals it will need to serve.

There are also other production control odds and ends duties. Production control sometimes runs a duplicating department or a printing shop to print job orders, identification tags, package labels, and possibly all the forms the company uses as well. Some production control departments operate the plant mail service. Then there are special small-scale cost analysis assignments, including finding answers to such questions as: Have we standardized parts as much as we should? Or, are we using palettes as much as we should?

Our list of production control duties is impressive yet it covers only part of what goes on in a factory. The production control department has, for example, little to do with accounting, personnel, worker supervision, product design, the machinery the company owns, plant maintenance, and many other areas.

TERMINOLOGY

So many people like neat, concise definitions that it is too bad we can't supply them—that is, we can't if we want to be realistic. Industry hasn't standardized on terms, so the best we can do is to tell you what some of the usages are. You need to know certain terms and the several meanings industry gives to them. Here are a few important ones:

PRODUCTION CONTROL DEPARTMENT   The usual name for the department which carries out most of the production control functions. Sometimes this department is called the "production department," in which case you may find that its subordinate section dealing with scheduling is called the production control department.

PRODUCTION DEPARTMENT   A common title for the whole big department doing production control work. If this is the big department title, then you will often find that it is divided into two main sections called the "planning department" and the "scheduling department." Don't confuse the production department with the factory departments that make products. The production department does not make products.

PLANNING AND SCHEDULING DEPARTMENT   A third term which may be applied to the department doing production control work.

PLANNING   usually includes *original planning*—work that must be done before any product can be made the *first* time. It includes determining how to make products and parts of products, deciding what operations, machines, and tooling to use, and often seeing that the facilities are available or are made available. As a rule original planning is done by the planning department, which may or may not be a part of the production control department.

The word "planning" usually also covers *routine planning*, the work you have to do for repeat orders. Ordinarily routine planning requires only the copying of operation lists, figuring the quantities of raw materials needed, seeing that materials are on hand, etc. This is nearly always a production control job. In big companies this work is nearly always computerized.

ROUTING   in some companies means almost everything described above as original planning, although, generally, it does not include seeing that facilities are made available. Specifically, routing covers the making up of original lists of operations needed to manufacture each item. This is a "master" list. Such lists usually show the materials, machines, tools, and attachments required. Sometimes instead of "routing" it is called "processing" or "laying out" a part. Making up shop orders is sometimes called routing.

BILL OF MATERIALS   The list of parts needed to make an assembled product. Sometimes abbreviated as B/M. Also known as a parts list, drawing list, assembly list, material requirement list, group sheet, and other names. Assemblies which go into the final product as units are shown as single items (they have their own bills of material listing their parts).

SHOP ORDER   A directive to the factory to make products or parts. Shop orders are of two main kinds: those directing products to be assembled (usually called assembly orders) and those directing parts to be made (usually called shop orders). Shop orders for parts include all of the information on master route sheets plus other information (quantities, dates, etc.) relating to the order. There are also others, such as repair orders and rework orders. Any order may be special or stock, rush or nonrush.

SCHEDULING   sets the times when activities should take place. Scheduling may be "order scheduling" or "machine scheduling."
   Order scheduling is concerned with when certain lots of products will have specific work done on them.
   Overall order schedules, often called "master schedules," show the quantities of products to be finished within specific weeks or months. The production control department often receives its instructions covering what to make in the form of master schedules.
   The production control department puts schedules (dates for doing things) on all the shop orders it issues to the factory. Usually the schedules show the wanted *completion* dates for individual operations. They may also show *starting* dates for individual operations. Or they may simply list the wanted completion date for the finished product or part, with no specified times when the individual operations should be done.
   Machine scheduling relates to the planned future apportionment of machine time to the various orders. Rarely would you make up machine schedules except for bottleneck machines. You don't have to make up such schedules for machines which can readily handle all of the work you have for them.

DISPATCHING   The issuing of production orders to the factory, thus authorizing and instructing the factory to make the products called for on the orders. Usually "dispatching" also implies obtaining reports of completed production.

JOB LOT SHOP   A factory which produces largely and directly to customers' orders. It is characterized by its handling of many orders, often for small quantities, for a large variety of products.

MASS PRODUCTION SHOP   A factory which makes large quantities of a limited variety of products. The products are usually made to stock rather than to customers' orders.

PROCESS INDUSTRY   An industry which converts bulk materials (liquid, powder, granulated, or irregular chunks) into workable form. The materials are usually moved mechanically, and processing takes place inside mixing tanks, heating or pressure vessels, etc.

A further word of warning about terminology: Men in a particular company often think that their company's usage of these terms is the only right one, all others being wrong. They simply don't know that there are other usages.

RELATIONSHIPS BETWEEN PRODUCTION CONTROL AND OTHER DEPARTMENTS

Production control men must, first, do their own work (preparing directives) and, second, get other departments to do their work (carrying out the directives). Yet the production control staff doesn't have direct authority over other departments.

When we say that production control men have to get other departments to do the work planned, we don't mean that it is a strong authority relationship. Rather it is a service situation even though it is not a service which foremen can reject. Factory departments depend on production control to tell them what to do.

When things in production go wrong, as they frequently do, production control has to make new plans and issue new directions right away. And as we said earlier, many things upset first plans and make replanning necessary. A customer wants to change the quantity he ordered or to change the delivery date. Or bought materials don't arrive on time or when they arrive don't pass your receiving inspection. And you always have to contend with some of the parts that you yourself are making not passing inspection. Then there are tool and machine breakdowns, absent operators, and other causes of delays that make new directions necessary.

In such situations, where one department has to issue directions covering the work of other departments, trouble sometimes arises. Minor frictions and frustrations are common.

Managers should therefore be careful what kind of men they put on production control jobs. Ideally, these men should have an unusual combination of abilities. First, they should be capable of doing their own work well. You can't afford to have them making mistakes.

Second, production control men must be tactful. If they aren't they will get into arguments with men from other departments. And they won't get much cooperation from men who are mad at them.

Third, production control men need to have a sense of responsibility. They need to want to see that the factory operates smoothly and to do everything they can to accomplish this. You don't want them to have a "don't care" attitude, because if they do they won't try very hard to keep things moving and to get orders out on time and at low cost.

This is particularly important in production control work because every time another department fails to do its work well or on time, the production control staff is the one that has to try to straighten things out. If purchasing doesn't get materials, if the toolroom doesn't get tools ready on time, if engineering bills of material, route sheets, and drawings are in any way inaccurate, it is the production control department that runs into trouble. It is the production control department that has to do all of its work over again. The production control department should even prod the others to get them to fix things up. You might call these things the "inherent irritations" in production control work. To keep friction to a minimum you should put men in production control jobs who don't get irritated easily and who don't irritate others.

Fine though it may be to have cooperation and teamwork between departments, this doesn't mean that you want never to have differences of opinion. Having no differences would be almost as bad as having too many. If no one cares how things are done and if no one ever questions how things are done, you'll never change poor practices. If no one cares enough to be annoyed by high scrap losses, production delays, or wrong methods, then your men have the wrong attitude. You want your workers to be interested enough to take issue with things that are done incorrectly.

You even want them to be interested enough to be irritated a little when someone else's mistakes make extra work for them. If this sounds contradictory to what we said earlier about needing tactful men in the production control department, it isn't intended to be. A certain amount of irritation is good when it is justified.

COMPUTERS AND DEPARTMENTAL RELATIONSHIPS   Computers accentuate departmental relationship problems because computers cost so much and handle data so fast that one computer serves several departments. Only in very large companies does the production control department get to have its own computer. In other companies production control has to share the computer's time with other departments. Because of the importance of accounting and cost records, the computer is often under the direction of the controller. Once in a while, however, it is under production control's direction because getting out shop directives and controlling inventories is a big job. In this case the production control department has to take care of its own work and also do the computer work of other departments.

Because computers can be so effective in handling data if the whole information flow system is computerized, companies are often virtually forced to integrate all subsystems into one large information flow system. It may take years for a control systems group to develop such an integrated system and to develop new subsystems which are compatible with each other and with the whole system. When this is not done there is a tendency, because of the speed and ease of data manipulation, to print out every conceivable type of report and too many in total. In order to keep this problem under control, the department which operates the computer has to have close relationships with many other departments.

STUDY MATERIALS

1-1   Describe the input and output characteristics and the nature of the production control function for various production systems. What are the major similarities and differences between systems providing manufactured products and those providing services?

1-2   Characterize the various types of disturbances which might affect the systems defined in your answer to problem 1. How might the system cope with these disturbances?

1-3   What factors might cause changes in the standards established for judging or comparing outputs from the system? Think of some situation where standards may be in conflict with each other and how these might be resolved. What is the role of the production control department in these disputes?

1-4   Can all inventories be minimized by careful scheduling? Justify your answer.

1-5   The Autoswitch Company, 350 employees, makes a line of electrical switches, sockets, plugs, condensers, etc. Business has been booming so much that the factory can't keep up. Deliveries are falling behind promise dates. You (the company's chief industrial engineer) have been asked to see what can be done to improve the situation.

Sales contracts are negotiated almost entirely by the president (who owns 40 per cent of the company's stock). He has been in the business for 20 years and knows both his products and his company well. His wide acquaintance in the industry helps get contracts, particularly with big customers.

He makes his own cost and delivery estimates and when he gets an order he gives it to the factory manager and tells him the required delivery date. If the item is new, the engineers, who work under the factory manager, make up parts lists and operation lists for making parts.

A copy of the order and, for new items, the lists of parts and operations go to the foreman of the department where the first operation is to be performed. (For old items, the foreman has in his file a copy of parts lists and operation lists.) The foreman checks his stock of raw materials (which is stored in the department where it is used), and if he needs more of anything he writes out a purchase requisition and gives it to the purchasing agent. There is no trouble getting materials quickly from nearby sources.

When the foreman of the first department finishes his work on an order his men take the order to the department where the next operation is to be performed. If a foreman runs out of work he goes to the department which performs preceding operations and is usually able to bring back some jobs that are ready. If there aren't any jobs ready he first tries to transfer his men to other departments which may be busy and which need them. Failing that, he sends them home. There has been no trouble of this sort for a long time, however. The trouble is keeping up and getting out all of the orders that are coming in, and not how to keep the men busy.

If an order becomes overdue, the sales manager notifies the factory manager. Such orders are then traced down and pushed through their final processes. Because business has been so good, a good many orders have been getting the pressure treatment. Consequently some other orders keep getting pushed aside. Some nonpressure jobs have been in process for six months. Many of them have now also become hurry-up jobs.

You find that the president frequently "jumps on" the factory manager because he doesn't meet promise dates. The factory manager tells you that he didn't have this trouble in the old days when they manufactured to stock and not to order.

What suggestions do you make?

1-6 The sales department of the Northern Tire Company receives frequent calls from dealers all over the country for special inner tubes for trucking companies. There are many kinds of valves used in these tubes, and dealers do not always stock the complete line. Quick service on such orders is important.

When such calls come in, the sales department relays the requests by telephone to the production control clerk in charge of scheduling the manufacture of inner tubes. The written order verifying the telephone request is forwarded by company mail. Such requests are generally filled in the producing department by removing regular valves from inner tubes of the needed size and inserting the special one wanted. The work is carried on in a small tube repair section of the tube manufacturing department. The work of the repair section is not scheduled by the production control department, since most of it is devoted to reworking tubes rejected because of minor flaws.

The production control clerk relays, by telephone, the request for special tubes to the foreman and as soon as possible takes a written order to him. Sometimes, instead of telephoning, he takes the order directly to the department himself. Often the foreman is not in the repair area, so the directions are given to the operator, who lays aside his other work and immediately fills the request. On more than one occasion the foreman has returned to the repair area to find work he has counted on still undone and the operator working on a job the foreman does not know about. This the foreman does not like at all.

Comment on the above situation from the organizational point of view and from the point of view of customer service.

chapter two

TYPES OF PRODUCTION

In order to understand the job of controlling production, we need to look into the various manufacturing situations being controlled. This chapter and the next are devoted to that end.

There are so many differences in products and in how they are made that we can't talk about them all individually, so we have to consider classes or groups of manufacturing situations. Most manufacturing falls reasonably well into two groups: (1) companies in job lot work (those in "intermittent" production) and (2) mass production companies (those in "continuous" production). The first group makes a wide variety of products, each in limited quantities, while the second group makes big volumes of a limited variety of products.

To find out how prevalent each kind of operation is, the American Management Association some time ago asked a large number of manufacturing companies what kind of operation they carried on. Twenty per cent said that they were in job lot work and rarely made a second order of anything. Thirteen per cent said that they made things in job lots which were not usually reordered. Forty-six per cent said that they made products in lots and that many products were made over and over again. Only 13 per cent of the companies produced on a mass production basis. The final 10 per cent processed materials in batches. Perhaps we should consider both of the last two groups together as being in highly repetitive production. Roughly then, three-quarters of the factories surveyed were in job lot work and one-quarter were in mass production.

Some people divide industries into other groupings, such as: "unique production," "mass production," and "process production." Another classification divides companies into four groups: "jobbing or specific order," "rate or mass production," "load or available equipment," and "time schedule or coordinated effort." We will discuss all kinds of manufacturing in this chapter but we will spend most of our time on intermittent and continuous production.

DISTINCTION BETWEEN INTERMITTENT AND CONTINUOUS PRODUCTION

Intermittent and continuous production differ in the length of time during which equipment setups can be used without change. Industry and product are not important so far as this distinction is concerned. If you use a machinery setup for only a short time and then change it to make a different product, you are in intermittent production. Perhaps you are able to use the machine setup for only a few minutes or possibly hours before the required quantity is produced. But if you set up equipment and use it without change for months, we call that continuous production.

The distinction between intermittent and continuous production has nothing to do with the regularity of a company's operation. A tomato cannery is an example of continuous manufacturing even though it operrates only a few weeks each year. Railroad freight car factories operate continuously when they have orders and then close down completely when there are no orders. The whole plant operates irregularly, but this is still an example of continuous production. On the other hand, a job lot machine shop and a custom-made furniture factory, both intermittent, may operate throughout the year.

CHARACTERISTICS OF INTERMITTENT PRODUCTION

MOST PRODUCTS ARE MADE IN SMALL QUANTITIES   Parts and assemblies are made in lots, usually small lots. If the total of all products for a company in intermittent production is large, it is distributed over many kinds of products, none of which is made in large quantity. If any of the products reach large volume, the company will probably change to continuous production for them, even though the rest of the factory stays on intermittent production.

SIMILAR EQUIPMENT IS GROUPED   Similar kinds of machines or machines performing the same work are located together in single work areas or departments. A factory department is a place that does a certain kind of work, not a place where a certain product is made. This arrangement is called "process controlled layout."

WORK LOADS ARE UNBALANCED   Departmental work loads are usually unbalanced. You may find some departments working overtime while others are on short hours. Or within a department you may find some machines working overtime while others are on short hours or are idle. This isn't because anyone wants it that way. It happens because the machines you own reflect your usual need for the work they do, but day-to-day and week-to-week variations in the product mix result in different demands for specific machines. Which machines are idle and which are overloaded change all of the time, depending on the variations in the product mix.

GENERAL PURPOSE MACHINES ARE USED The term "general purpose" is relative, because all general purpose machines are, to some extent, specialized machines. You can't use a band saw to drill holes and you don't use a drill press to polish a flat surface or to apply paint. We call a drill press a general purpose machine, however, because by changing drill bits, it can be used to drill holes of various diameters and depths. The important point is that you can use it for different jobs. You have to drill each hole separately and you can drill big or little holes, shallow or deep, and you can drill them wherever you want them.

MACHINE OPERATORS ARE HIGHLY SKILLED When you have short runs, as you usually do with general purpose machines, you must often set up machines for new jobs. The setup man has to select the proper tools and fasten them on the machine in exactly the right way. He must figure out and install holding and fastening arrangements for the product. Finally, the operator has to put the products themselves into or fasten them onto the machine and do the operation. Both setting up and operating take skill and experience. Foremen, too, need to be skilled operators because you expect them to be able to step in and show even their best workers how to do difficult jobs.

NUMEROUS JOB INSTRUCTIONS ARE NECESSARY You have to give machine operators, truckers, and others specific instructions, usually in writing, telling them what to do on every new job. You have to tell them what materials to use, what quantities to process, what operations to perform, and when and where to perform them. And you have to tell them how good the products have to be in order to pass inspection. Such instructions have to be given over and over again, for every lot of materials and usually for every operation on each lot. Also you need reports of performance. All this makes for much clerical work.

RAW MATERIALS INVENTORIES ARE HIGH The use of any particular raw material is somewhat irregular, so you have to keep a relatively large stock of standard raw materials on hand. Materials are usually kept in enclosed stock rooms and are issued to workers in the plant only when materials requisitions are presented. Nonstandard raw materials are not stocked but are ordered specially when needed.

IN-PROCESS INVENTORIES ARE HIGH Almost always you finish one operation on every item in a lot of products before you start the next operation. The first items finished lie around until all the rest are done. Then the complete lot waits for a trucker. If, when he delivers the order to the next machine, it is busy, he parks the lot nearby. There it waits until the machine is free. Other orders may already be waiting, so the newly arrived order may have to be stored for days before its turn comes. Other delays, caused by shortages of tools, inspection delays, etc., slow things down still more. Job lot work means that materials move through production slowly and that you always have big inventories in process.

MATERIALS MOVE BY TRUCK   Conveyors are conspicuous by their absence. Few orders require the same sets of operations, so there is great variety in the paths followed by materials through the plant. Power-driven or hand trucks are used to move materials. Trucking is a highly flexible method of transportation and is well suited to move things through diverse paths.

WIDE AISLES, AMPLE STORAGE SPACE, AND NUMEROUS ELEVATORS ARE NEEDED   When materials are moved by trucks, enough aisle space is needed for two-way traffic and for maneuvering space so that loads can be put down or picked up at machines. Temporary storage space is needed next to machines so that workers can unload materials directly from the truck or mobile rack to the machine and back again afterwards. Large permanent storage areas should be available in order to store jobs between operations. Elevators, used to move items to other floors, should be large enough to carry trucks, and there should be enough of them so that the trucks don't have to wait long.

Wide aisles and ample storage space, though needed, aren't always found because space is often scarce. But if you don't have them, you will waste a lot of time and money moving things around in crowded areas.

PROS AND CONS OF INTERMITTENT PRODUCTION
The best thing about intermittent production is its flexibility. It is well adapted to producing numerous orders for small quantities of a wide variety of products. In intermittent manufacturing it costs very little more to make up an order of entirely new products than it does to make up a new lot of products that you have made before. You get flexibility from the plant layout, the types of machines used, the transportation system, the skills of the workers, and the procedures used to direct their work.

Flexibility goes beyond the ability to handle varied orders. You can even take unusual events and interruptions in stride. One machine breaking down is usually not serious. Often the work planned for that machine can be shifted to other similar machines. And if the orders requiring that machine can't be shifted, only the orders requiring it are held up. Orders using other machines are not delayed.

Nor is the hold-up or even the loss of one order serious. True, *that order* is in trouble, but others aren't. Intermittent production also allows you to push emergency rush orders through ahead of regular orders.

The flexibility of intermittent manufacturing is even a kind of insurance against heavy losses if the market demand changes unexpectedly. It doesn't matter if products you make in the future are quite different from those you made in the past; the machines and men can turn them out all right.

Most general purpose machines cost less than special purpose machines. The first investment in intermittent manufacturing is, therefore, usually lower than in continuous manufacture. Also, using general purpose machines does not necessarily keep you from getting low production costs on large orders. If you get a few big orders you can realize some of the savings that ordinarily go with special purpose machines. Just put some special purpose attachments on your general purpose machines. They let you speed up production and cut unit costs.

You can also, for long runs, group your general purpose machines with their special tooling into little "product groups" and let them produce that product only. Doing this lets you get rid of nearly all of the production control paper work that goes with job lots. Move orders and other instructions can be cut out.

Intermittent production's bad features are bad only when you compare them with continuous production. Remember, continuous production requires high volume and nearly complete standardization. If you don't have these two conditions, intermittent production is the only practical method.

CHARACTERISTICS OF CONTINUOUS PRODUCTION

Continuous production factories make a limited line of products in large quantities. Plants are usually large, and production, which is often partly mechanized, is to stock or to large continuing customers' orders.

In the mid-1950s the word "automation" caught the public fancy. It sounded new and revolutionary and there was considerable concern about machines taking jobs away from men and creating mass unemployment. Actually, automation was largely a continuation of the longtime trend toward more mechanization whenever mass production was possible. Cigarette manufacturing, glass bottle making, and several other industries have long been largely automated.

The mid-1950s were, however, characterized by several changes that made the general public more aware of technological innovation. The most dramatic innovation that got people worried was computers, but there were also other important changes. One was the development of solid state transistors used in electronic circuitry which allowed the integrated systems idea to develop, and this in turn allowed the development of machines which ran themselves automatically.

Another important change was the growth of operations research. Operations research formulas for optimizing processing decisions were developed, and their calculations were carried out automatically by computers. In oil refineries, for example, you can tell computers the kind of crude oil available and the prices and demands for various petroleum products and the computer will then tell you what kinds of gasoline and oil to make from the crude. Not only that, the computer will also transmit its decisions to the refinery equipment and direct the making of the gasoline and oil.

Automation has not, however, created mass unemployment. With the possible exception of flow process industries such as petroleum refining and chemicals, very few products are made by anything approaching a fully automated process. As the mid-1960s passed, employment was at record breaking levels and the automation scare was past.

LARGE VOLUME AND SMALL VARIETY ARE ESSENTIAL   In continuous production the quantity you make of a product must be great enough to allow you to use the same equipment setup for weeks or months. You could almost say that continuous production plants are gigantic, single purpose, even automatic, machines. Years ago, Charles F. Kettering of General Motors said, "We don't manufacture automobiles, we publish them." Continuous manufacture in fabricating industries is a duplicating process. You decide on the original model, set up the equipment to make it in quantities, and then run off hundreds of thousands or millions of copies.

Not often, though, do even large companies have such complete standardization and enough market to absorb the output of a continuous production plant for very long. Even large companies have to change now and then. Or, more commonly, they have to provide for minor variations in style or design of products while at the same time maintaining a high rate of output. A few variations, if the differences are minor, don't cause serious problems.

Many companies have continuous production in only part of their production processes. Assembled product manufacturers, even giant companies, commonly operate continuously in assembly work but not in their parts-making departments. We say that they manufacture continuously because their products' final assembly is continuous. Processing industries (chemical, petroleum, etc.), on the other hand, often operate continuously throughout all stages of production.

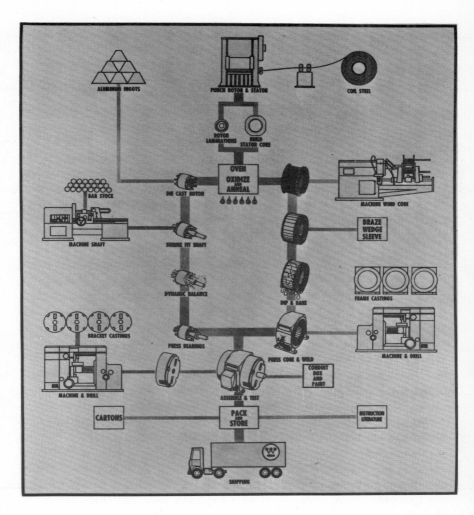

FIGURE 2-1 Schematic diagram of an electric motor assembly line. (Westinghouse Electric Corp.)

PRODUCTION LINES ARE USED Machines required for successive operations on the product are placed side by side. Whether the operations and machines are alike or unlike you line them up next to each other according to the sequence of operations required on the product. This arrangement allows the product to move through the plant in a direct manner. We call this "straight line" production or, because the movement of the product dictates the layout, "product-controlled" layout.

In parts making, production lines sometimes take the form of transfer machines such as the one pictured in figure 2-2. The machinery pictured in figure 2-2 is actually 13 separate machines, each performing several operations on a steel casting for use in diesel trucks. Individual machines are placed next to each other and are synchronized to work on identical time cycles.

The casting is fastened down tightly on the conveyor at the lower left. The conveyor, which is an integral part of the transfer machine, moves a fixed distance every few seconds on a stop and go basis. Its stops are so spaced that one unit of the product is located in front of the working head of every machine along the line. When the conveyor stops, the working heads of every machine along the whole line advance and perform their operations on the casting. Then these heads and their tools recede and the conveyor moves its products to the next work stations. Transfer machines are very costly (usually costing half a million dollars or more), but since they turn out many times the output of similar but separate machines, their cost per unit of product is low.

MACHINE CAPACITIES ARE BALANCED   Because, in continuous production, materials move from operation to operation in a steady stream you need to have the capacity for performing successive operations in balance or nearly so. If one operation takes longer than the others it will be a bottleneck if you don't, in some way, equalize their production capacities. You have to smooth out differences in operation times as much as you can.

If one job takes two minutes and others take one minute, you have to put in two machines to do the two-minute operation. Then you can use each machine for every second product, and the two together will turn out one unit per minute. Sometimes parts of a bottleneck operation can be transferred to other jobs. Sometimes "banks" or extra supplies of parts can be made up in off-hours to help establish balance. There should be few idle machines in continuous manufacturing; either all are in use or all are closed down.

SPECIAL PURPOSE MACHINES ARE USED   Special purpose machines are literally what the term suggests. They are designed and built to do one specific operation. A special purpose machine will do one operation rapidly and almost perfectly, and requires little skill on the part of the operator. In the hole-drilling example used when discussing general purpose machines, a special purpose machine would be very useful. You could design a special purpose drill press that would drill all the holes you want at one time. The holes could be put anywhere and they could be of any size. Your special purpose machine would "spot" or locate the material

FIGURE 2-2 Transfer machine for performing finishing machining operations on cast iron converter housings for automatic transmissions for Ford Motor Company. This machine drills, bores, counter-bores, reams and taps threads. Sixty-eight machining operations and 14 probing and gaging operations are performed. There are 22 stations which carry 18 machining units, 3 probe units, and 1 air gaging unit. The 18 machining units mount a total of 72 spindles or individual word heads. Output is 120 housings per minute. The cycle time (in seconds) goes as follows: conveyor moves 3, clamp 3, rapid advance of tool 2, machining 16, stop 1, rapid withdrawal 2, unclamp 3. (Buhr Machine Co.)

exactly and then drill all the holes at the same time, in exactly the right locations, and to the needed depths. Special purpose machines have a limited use, but for their special jobs they turn out excellent work at a low unit cost.

MACHINE OPERATORS ARE NOT HIGHLY SKILLED AND FEWER OPERATORS ARE NEEDED FOR A GIVEN VOLUME OF OUTPUT   Most machines used in continuous manufacture are almost fully automatic. Once the operator puts the material in the machine, it will change the material's form in the intended way. Pre-set holding devices hold the material in exactly the right position for work. All that there is left for the operator to do is to load and unload the machine. He becomes a machine tender or a machine feeder, although at times even feeding is done automatically.

Continuous manufacturing requires relatively unskilled men. Machine feeders and equipment tenders make up the bulk of the employees, and they are relatively unskilled. Since special purpose machines are fast and automatic, often only one man is needed to tend several machines. Thus, fewer men are needed for any given amount of output than in intermittent manufacturing.

Foremen don't have to be able to set up or operate the equipment under their supervision. In fact, there is no setting up of jobs in the usual sense.

HIGH SKILL IS NEEDED BEHIND THE SCENES Although specialized machines require little operator skill, they require a very high degree of skill on the part of the machine designers and machinery makers. And they require highly skilled maintenance men. Some of the machinery is so complicated that maintenance men need special training, perhaps given at the machinery maker's plant, in order to know how to repair the machines. The ordinary maintenance man is hopelessly out of his depth. Often, engineers from the engineering department work closely with the maintenance men, who sometimes need specific and complicated instructions.

FEW JOB INSTRUCTIONS ARE NECESSARY In continuous production, few changes occur after the first instructions are given. Workers need almost no day-to-day instructions. But the first instructions telling workers how to do their jobs are sometimes given in great detail. Once the men learn their jobs, no more instructions are needed.

Now we have to back up a little and talk about the minor differences in the products that you want from a production line. How do the workers know what variations you want? You do have to give them instructions covering these variations. Some of the television sets made today in a television factory are to go into light-colored cabinets and others into dark cabinets. You have to tell this to the assembly line workers who put the sets into cabinets, and also to the workers making cabinets. Few workers, however, are affected by such changes.

RAW MATERIALS INVENTORIES ARE LOW Raw materials are used at a steady rate and in large quantities. This allows you to set up raw material delivery schedules so that you keep getting new supplies and don't need to carry much on hand. Replenishments are small and frequent. Raw materials should be scheduled to flow into the plant at a rate which equals the rate of their use. Some companies carry so little raw material that when new supplies arrive they are delivered directly to the first operation and not to a stockroom. Storage space may be provided for only one or two days' supply. Automobile companies sometimes work with only one or two hours' bank if their supplier is located nearby.

Occasionally, companies producing continuously carry large inventories of raw materials. This occurs in companies using tin, rubber, burlap, or grain because their source of raw material is sometimes 10,000 miles away and is not wholly dependable. Besides, they have to contend with seasonality. Someone has to carry rubber, burlap, and grain inventories after the harvesting season until they are used. Also, the prices of these commodities fluctuate a good bit. When prices go down, therefore, companies often lay in big supplies. Except in such cases, however, continuous manufacturing companies rarely carry big inventories.

IN-PROCESS INVENTORIES ARE LOW   The inventory of materials going through the factory is almost eliminated in continuous manufacturing. As soon as an operation on a piece of material is finished, the piece goes right on to the next operation, which is performed almost immediately. Machines performing successive operations are only a few feet apart, and not often will you find more than one or two units of a product between operations.

PREVENTIVE MAINTENANCE AND QUICK REPAIR ARE MUSTS   Because there is so little "float" (material moving down the line), if one machine stops, all stop. As you tie successive operations together you increase the line's downtime unless you do a good job of preventive maintenance and of quick repair.

The best way to reduce line downtime is to use preventive maintenance. Inspect machines and overhaul and repair them during off-hours before anything happens. Tool wear, in particular, needs watching. If a drill or a thread tapper gets dull from wear, it will cut improperly. Nonetheless, it will try to do its work and the result will be either nonstandard work or a broken tool. Either is bad.

Tools are individual items; they wear out at different rates and almost always they get dull and need resharpening long before the machine itself needs maintenance. Knowing how many items come off the line doesn't tell you when a tool was put into use and hence how long it has been used. You need to put a counter on the machine to tell you how many pieces the tool has been used for. Also keep, at each machine, a record of the probable life of each tool. This tells the men who watch for these things how long it is safe to use tools before taking them out for resharpening or replacement. Also keep extra tools at tool stations right along the line. Then when a tool needs taking out, the man can put in a replacement and not hold up the line. And, last, design tools so that replacements can be installed quickly. Quick replacements and quick repairs keep stoppages from hurting much.

MATERIALS MOVE RAPIDLY THROUGH THE PLANT   Materials in process keep moving. Ideally, except for small emergency stocks in a few places, partly processed materials never pile up ahead of operations. Each machine can handle the output of the machine before it. Once started into the first operation, materials keep moving and soon emerge as finished products. An automobile frame starting down the assembly line comes off the line as part of an automobile in less than two hours. Even the engine block in an automobile is an unfinished casting for only a few days before it is driven away in a finished car.

We must admit though that the ideal of perfectly balanced capacity between successive operations is by no means always achieved. Some machines are faster than others. This occurs most often in parts making, not in assembly. When it occurs you have to work the slow machines more hours than the fast machines. This requires keeping banks of parts between such machines. In assembly, however, lack of balance is usually just too expensive and the banks would take up too much space. Here you try to do everything possible to equate the capacities of successive operations so that you can cut out storage banks and keep products moving.

MATERIALS MOVE BY CONVEYOR Mechanical conveyors are the cheapest way to move things whenever large quantities follow the same paths. In continuous manufacture large quantities do follow the same paths so conveyors are a natural. Their initial high costs are spread over so many units that the materials end up being moved at low cost.

Not all conveyors are expensive. Some are nothing more than smooth table tops across which workers push products to the next machine. Simple chutes are sometimes used for short moves. But when the material has to be moved long distances you have to turn to regular conveyors, usually monorails hanging from the ceiling. You can never move everything by conveyor, though, so you see some hand trucks, power-driven trucks, and storage racks on wheels in continuous manufacture. But the main bulk and flow of products is by conveyor.

MEDIUM OR NARROW AISLES, LITTLE STORAGE SPACE, AND FEW ELEVATORS ARE NEEDED The utilization of floor space by machines and conveyors is nearly complete in continuous manufacturing. Since trucks are not often used, the aisles can be narrower than they are in intermittent manufacturing. Though many continuous manufacturing plants are laid out with wide aisles, continuous production doesn't require them.

You won't find sizable spaces for the temporary storage of materials next to machines nor large general storage areas where materials are kept for long periods. Elevators are scarce because conveyors take things up and down almost as readily as they move them horizontally. The inside appearance of many continuous manufacturing plants is one of closely packed machines placed in rows or lines. The overhead space, too, is used, since conveyors often hang from the ceiling. Machines should not be so closely packed, however, as to keep maintenance men from being able to get to them when they need repair.

PROS AND CONS OF CONTINUOUS PRODUCTION

The best thing about continuous production is its low unit cost when you have large volume and nearly complete standardization. Special purpose machines, though their original cost is usually high, speed up the job and cut labor costs. They usually multiply several times over the output both per machine hour and per man-hour. In rare cases they turn out 100 times more work than could be done on general purpose machines. The United States mint has, for example, a special purpose penny stamper that makes 10,000 pennies a minute. It would probably take hundreds of general purpose machines to match this output.

Continuous production cuts man waste half a dozen ways. There is no waste of a man's time going after materials, or in handling materials; no machine setups, nor time spent getting out tools or putting them away. Continuous manufacturing cuts transportation costs because distances are reduced almost to the vanishing point and what little transportation remains is mechanized. Learning time is cut to the bone because people can quickly become skilled as machine tenders or bolt tighteners.

You could also realize a big savings in labor costs because you use only semiskilled workers whose hourly rates could be less than that of skilled operators. Actually it doesn't work out that way. Line production semiskilled operators get just about as much per hour as do skilled operators in intermittent manufacturing. You make your savings from the higher output per worker, not from lower hourly pay rates.

How about bad features? Does continuous production have any? Yes, four. First, work stoppages are serious; second, you can't change the output rate easily; third, you can't change products easily; and fourth, you are locked into a big investment.

VULNERABILITY TO WORK STOPPAGES   The first serious weakness of continuous production is its high vulnerability to work stoppages. Since all operations are linked together more or less as one gigantic machine, a stoppage at any point for any reason is a serious matter. The whole plant may have to stop within a matter of minutes. Stoppages are very expensive in terms of idle men, idle machines, loss of output, and in some cases, spoiled materials.

Stopping the whole line when any part stops is so serious that some companies have introduced "segmented" continuous production. In segmented continuous production, the whole line of operations is cut up into segments between which banks of products are stored. Segmented lines reduce delays to the whole line.

Another way to reduce delays is to fix out-of-order machines quickly or to replace them with standby, ready-to-go replacement machines. Some companies mount each machine on its own separate foundation and only bolt it down rather than mounting it permanently, so that it can be taken out quickly for repair.

In some continuous plants you have to perform a whole sequence of operations once you have started the first operation or the material and the machines will be ruined. This is true in a continuous steel-rolling mill. Once you start steel through the successive rolling mills it has to continue without interruption through to the end. Any stop before that point probably would ruin the mill rolls and cause substantial loss in material reprocessing costs. Any company working with heated material, whether it be steel, rubber, glass, food, or any other, suffers loss if operations are interrupted mid-cycle.

RIGIDITY OF OUTPUT RATE   A second weakness of continuous manufacturing is the relative rigidity of the rate of output. All operations are linked together, and the machines are designed to produce at one rate. It is hard to get more output except by working the whole line more hours. Reductions work the same way; you can't get less output except by cutting hours.

This isn't always true of continuous assembly lines. In the radio and electronics industries and many others, assembly is largely hand work. It is a matter of placing wires, soldering connections, fitting pieces together, placing screws, riveting, etc. The employees use hand tools. You can increase or decrease the line's production simply by changing the number of workers along the line. But in order to do this you have to redistribute all of the little bits of work along the line into new work package sets to suit the new lineup of workers.

PRODUCT CHANGING DIFFICULTIES   Specialized machines and specialized plants are relatively inflexible. If your product changes or if the market demand changes, that means costly machine and equipment changes. You couldn't, for example, change an incandescent lamp factory into one making fluorescent lamps without redoing it almost completely.

Products do change, though. The best that you can do is to hold down the costs of changing as much as possible.

We are talking about the second of two kinds of change. The first kind has to do with your being able to handle day-to-day minor variations in products. You change from blue automobiles to red and from two-door models to four-door and back again. Or you make six-, eight-, and ten-transistor radios. This kind of change goes on every day and makes no serious problem.

The difficulties in changing that we are referring to are those that occur when you stop making this year's products and change to next year's. Changing from old products to new means changing machines (mostly they are machines used to make parts since fewer machines are used in assembly work). Special purpose machines cost so much that it would be very expensive to discard all of the old ones every time a new model came out.

You can save some of the changing cost by making such machines in sections (some people call this the "building block" approach). Machines are made with standard bases, tool heads, and indexing tables. You can keep on using most of these component sections in combination with other new component sections instead of junking whole machines. Product design changes will outdate one or more sections, but not the whole machine. For example, stamping presses used to make fenders for last year's car can be kept. Just fit them with new dies. Then they will make different shaped fenders for this year's cars. Of course you have to discard last year's dies but not the presses. You can do this, however, only because the press is designed to allow your changing dies.

Using sectional machines makes special purpose machines more flexible but never as flexible as general purpose machines. They can't be changed drastically and even new sections for them are costly.

The layout in continuous manufacturing is also relatively inflexible. Changes in the product's design might mean putting in two new machines in place of one old one. But the line is already set up and often there is no room for an extra new machine. Lines of machines and the fixed-path conveyors that go with them are also expensive to change.

Sometimes changes in operations affect the operating times. Unless all operations are affected alike, changes upset the work balance between machines. Some machines do their new work faster or slower than others. Thus some machines become bottlenecks while others work only part time.

Inflexibility can also affect the purchase of raw materials or parts used on the assembly line. Automatic machinery for the assembly of electronic printed circuit boards requires that the wire leads of component parts be cut to a specific exact size. And they have to be cut much more exactly to fit than is necessary for hand assembly. A man can compensate for irregularities more readily than can special purpose machinery.

THE INVESTMENT COMMITMENT   Line manufacture costs so much to install and so much to change that you don't change without good reason. The big investment tends to lock you into a given design for a good while. This means that you need to have good forecasts so that you won't need to change. But equally important, you must be realistic and change, even at high cost, when you ought to change. If it is time to redesign your product, you should do it even if this means buying new specialized machines and throwing out old ones which may be far from worn out.

Most companies can't get away with following Volkswagen practices. The Volkswagen beetle design lasted over 20 years and yet the car sold well the whole time, allowing ample time to wear out and get full value out of special machines. Actually, when the final chapter is written, we may find that Volkswagen's no-change policy was not altogether good. In the mid-1960s the more attractive German Ford and German General Motors cars gained sharply on Volkswagen. Probably Volkswagen should have changed designs long before they did in 1965.

In summarizing the pros and cons of continuous production, we should emphasize that management is not really a free agent when it comes to deciding whether to produce continuously or intermittently. If you have volume and standardization you practically must go to continuous production. It is the only way you will get your costs down low enough to compete with other companies using continuous methods. It takes courage to sink so much money into machines when you can't be positive that the volume will materialize, but failure to do it may mean that you can't compete cost-wise.

PROCESS INDUSTRIES
Process industries are those handling bulk materials, liquids, powders, granular materials, and chunks of materials. Their products are petroleum, chemicals, cement, flour, and many processed food items, such as breakfast foods, sugar, salt, and liquor. The first operations in the manufacture of paints, glass, plastics, ceramics, and rubber are of the same nature.

Process industries are characterized by almost fully automatic manufacture. The things done to materials are done in mixing tanks and heating and pressure vessels. You move materials by pipe, duct, chute, or conveyor. They may pass through the processes either in a continuous stream, as in the manufacture of paper, or in "batches." When a fixed quantity, perhaps a mixing tank load, is processed as a unit it is called "batch" production. The appropriate quantities of raw materials to make up a tank-ful are put into the tank and mixed for a specified time. Then the whole batch is passed on to the next operation and a new batch is put into the mixing tank. The batch is the unit of control in this form of production.

As a rule, factories in processing industries are large, or they at least require a high investment of capital per worker. In the usual metal fabricating plant the investment in machinery ranges from, say, $7,000 to $20,000 per employee, but in process industries it is more likely to run from $40,000 to $75,000.

Processing industries have all the advantages and disadvantages of continuous production except that they are present in more extreme degree. As in continuous production, a breakdown anywhere in processing stops everything. Worse, there is almost no possibility of cushioning the effects of breakdowns by carrying banks of materials between segments of the total process. Also, the rate of output is more rigidly fixed in process industries than it is in continuous production. You can change the quantity of output only by changing work hours or by opening up or closing down additional processing lines.

Often, processing industries work with the products of nature, performing only the first few operations required to transform them into semi-processed form suitable for later further processing. Being products of nature, usually they vary in chemical and physical properties. This makes you do three things. First, you must check often: run continuing physical and chemical analyses of the incoming raw material to see what its properties are. And second, after you find out, you have to change mixing formulas, processing temperatures, or processing times to compensate for the variations you find. Third, you test your end products to see if you compensated enough for nature's variations and make more extensive adjustments if they are needed. Only by doing this can you turn out homogenous products.

Most of this surveillance work can be done electronically, so it is not surprising that process industries have been in the forefront in the development and application of automatic sensing and control devices. They were also the earliest users of linear programming and other mathematical techniques for maximizing an output under a series of constraints such as variable input materials.

SIMILAR–PROCESS INDUSTRIES
Similar-process industries are not quite like process industries nor are they like continuous manufacturing. Their products all go through the same processes or operations but the flow of products is not a continuous

stream; it is a series of slightly differing lots or batches. Similar-process industries include shoe manufacture, textiles, clothing, books, and newspapers. Probably steel rolling mills and large foundries should also be included in this group, although certain of these industries are sometimes referred to as "load" or "available equipment" industries.

Since all products in these industries pass through the same processes you find them using product layout. They arrange the equipment so that the product can flow quickly through the usual set of operations. Materials movement is largely mechanical, very little trucking being required. So far similar-process industries sound like both the process and continuous industries.

They differ greatly, however, from process and continuous production industries in that the products being made must be made in lots or batches. Differences in size, type, color, issue (newspapers and books), thickness, etc., mean that they must be kept in different lots as they pass through the processes. Exactly the right number, or at least a certain minimum (and overruns sometimes are waste), of each kind must be made. You can't use extra pages of one book to make up for pages short in another book.

As a rule, the equipment used in similar-process industries must be reset slightly between runs of different products. Rolling mill rolls must be set either closer together or farther apart, depending on the separate orders for steel strips. Large foundries using mold loops have to change the pattern, and sometimes the metal being made into castings must be changed when enough castings of a certain kind have been made. Book manufacturers must change the plates on their presses after each run is printed. Shoe factories produce different styles, each in the quantity ordered (appropriately distributed among sizes). After one order is made, the next one may call for different leather, lasts, color, or finish.

SPECIAL PROJECT MANUFACTURE

Special projects of gigantic size are made by some companies. In this category belong ships, automatic freight car unloaders, bridges, special coal and ore strip-mining equipment, and turbo-electric generating equipment. These projects have problems resembling those of the construction industry. Sometimes it is hard to draw a line between manufacturing and construction. Often the final assembly of such products is done at the job and not at the manufacturing company. Heavy, large-size industrial equipment is often made up in sections in the factory and then moved to the point of installation. There the sections are assembled under the direction of the manufacturer's fieldmen.

Special projects are usually unique; you want only one, or a very few of a kind. The product is of gigantic size, contains thousands of parts, takes months to produce, and involves large sums of money. This kind of manufacture is intermittent manufacturing carried to its extreme.

AIRPLANE AND MISSILE MANUFACTURE

In 1967, the airplane and missile manufacturing industry employed over 825,000 people, making it one of the largest industries in the United States. Not only is it a large industry, but airplane and missile manufacturing companies have the most complex manufacturing and production control problems to be found anywhere.

Airplane and missile companies buy many of their products' major component sections. Still other components are furnished by the government. Such government-furnished items include jet engines, landing gear, and radar equipment. This would seem to simplify the production control problems of airplane companies as indeed it does. But modern airplanes and missiles are so complex that, even after being relieved of making many components, these companies still have the most complex production control problems found anywhere.

FIGURE 2-3 Final assembly department in an airplane factory. (Boeing Aircraft Co.)

UNLIKE PRODUCTS   Military and commercial airplanes are costly and both the government and the commercial airlines want certain unique features built into the airplanes they buy. Making slightly different airplanes for every customer is one thing that complicates production control in these companies.

STARTING BEHIND SCHEDULE   A second complicating factor is that airplane and missile manufacturing, like special project manufacturing, is almost always behind schedule before contracts are signed. Because so much money is involved and so many details have to be settled, negotiations invariably continue past the time when the manufacturer should start the order if he is to meet the original promised delivery dates. By the time production control gets to work on a contract, trying to get back on schedule is a rat race.

A FEAST OR FAMINE BUSINESS   A third reason why production control work in airplane and missile manufacturing is unusually difficult is that sales contracts are large and few rather than small and many.

   Both commercial airline customers and the government place contracts irregularly and this makes problems. Many individual contracts represent over 1 million man-hours of work. This is enough work to employ 500 men for one year. Some contracts are 10 times this big. Sometimes a company will have several such contracts all at the same time, yet only one or two big contracts at other times. During the feast period the company may have to hire thousands of workers. Then at other times, when contracts are scarce, it may have to lay off thousands of men. Airplane companies are often in a feast or famine situation.

LONG LEAD TIMES   The fourth factor which complicates production control in airplane companies is the long lead time required. It takes from two to four years to get a prototype product into the air. And follow-up regular production airplanes and missiles also take a year or two to make.

   But why so much time? It takes time to design the details and parts, to decide production methods, to develop tooling and jigs for parts making and assembly, to determine material requirements, to get tools, jigs, and fixtures, to determine worker job assignments, to decide on plant layout, to arrange physical facilities, to process materials, and to purchase parts. It also takes time to make parts and subassemblies, and to assemble the end products. It also takes a long time to get some of the purchased components, such as engines. Finally, in the case of airplanes, they must fly before the customer will accept them.

But doesn't every manufacturer of assembled products do nearly all of these things we have just listed? Why does it take longer for airplanes and missiles? It takes longer because the whole job is more complex. For example, it takes *millions of engineering man-hours* to design an airplane and to develop production methods. And it takes hundreds of thousands of man-hours to make each airplane or moon missile. Of course, many parts of the work can be done concurrently and this saves time, but not enough of the work can be done concurrently to cut down the total time very much. The landing wheels of an airplane can't go on until the fuselage is assembled.

The fact that production takes a long time means that parts are needed at various times and not all at once. You may want certain parts in January, yet certain other parts for the same airplane aren't needed until July or even November. The scheduling problems are complex.

DESIGN CHANGES   The unending race to make better and still better airplanes and missiles forces these companies to put innovations into their products as soon as they are reasonably well perfected, even into airplanes already half manufactured. On large airplanes it is normal to have *thousands of design changes* between the start and completion of each individual airplane. Lockheed had over 100 design changes *per day* in the early period of manufacture on one contract, and this was only one of several contracts in production.

In making airplanes and missiles, design changes after production has started are not just the usual thing—they *always* occur. Sometimes purchased items are involved, so orders to change the design must be sent to suppliers and the production orders in their factories must be changed. Tooling and assembly jigs and fixtures may have to be remade. The time when the changes will be "zeroed in" (meaning which airplane or missile going down the line will be the first one to receive the change) has to be decided. The units already past the zero point will be unchanged. Those not yet up to it will incorporate the change.

LEARNING CURVES   The "learning curve," too, makes production control's work harder. The more airplanes you make, the fewer man-hours it takes to make each one. Production schedules have to recognize this. In a limited way, learning curves operate in other industries too but they are more pronounced in the case of airplanes and missiles. We will discuss how the learning curve operates in Chapter 9.

STUDY MATERIALS

2-1   What are the characteristics of intermittent production and in what way do they affect production control?

2-2   Consider a typewriter and its parts. In which stages of its manufacture should you use intermittent production? Which work should be done by continuous production? Why? Could you use other methods? Describe them.

2-3   In problem 2 above suppose that you have been making 10,000 typewriters a year but that your new model catches on and you have to plan for making 200,000 a year. What work will you change from intermittent to continuous production?

2-4   How complicated and how important is production control work in each main type of production? In which kinds of production would production control work require the greatest proportion of workers? In which the least? Why?

chapter three

MINOR KINDS OF PRODUCTION

In Chapter 2, we described the principal types of production. Besides these there are always quite a few "odds and ends" products and activities which need control. These odds and ends are usually not at all like the main products and the main activities. The jobs are small and rush jobs are common. Consequently, odds and ends take more than their share of production control's time and it is man time, not computer time. Usually they are too varied for computer handling.

SHORT—RUN MANUFACTURE

Factories always have a certain amount of "short-run" work, orders for one and two items instead of big quantities. Such orders are annoyances. They waste both man and machine time because they make so many setups. Workers, particularly those on piece work, don't like short runs because they can't get into the swing of production and earn bonuses. Short runs are costly to make and, when you put them through regular production channels, take an undue amount of production control effort.

But you have to take care of such orders sometimes. What can you do about them? You can: (1) run them through regular production, (2) put them through a miniature short-run factory, (3) put them through the company's "experimental" shop, (4) put them through the toolroom or the maintenance department's machine shop, or (5) subcontract them outside (if your labor contract allows this). A short-run department is usually the best choice.

Short runs may be for products or parts. If they are for assembled products they are particularly wasteful. It takes almost as long to get together two of everything to make two assembled products as it does to get together the parts for 100 products. Not only do you have to get the parts together, but if the product is an old model, some of the parts may have to be made specially. You have to get out old drawings and assembling instructions and study them over and then actually make the parts you don't have and can't buy, and finally get the product put together.

Doing such short-run work in regular production areas is inefficient and clutters up the assembly areas. It is better to keep this work, for just one or two products, apart from regular assembly work. If possible, you should assign certain employees and set apart a space in the assembly department for short-run assembly work.

Short runs in parts manufacture come from: (1) replacing shortages on parts orders (in regular manufacture) where scrap losses have been high, (2) repairing parts rejected in regular manufacture, particularly when the repair operations differ from regular operations, (3) making repair parts for the machines and equipment in the plant, (4) making parts to be sold as repair parts for products you made years ago, (5) making parts for experimental models or for apparatus for engineering and research, (6) making regular products where the volume of sales justifies only occasional short runs, (7) making up a small rush lot of a part that the assembly department needs desperately (to keep the line going until the regular production lot comes through), (8) making tooling, jigs, and fixtures within the plant, and (9) putting through small pilot lots of new products to show the engineering or research departments what production difficulties will arise.

Sometimes in the case of making up parts shortages you can avoid short runs because such orders are repetitive. Today's regular order can go through short. Then you can boost the quantity on the next order. You can't do this, though, on shortages of parts not to be made again. You will probably have to send the small quantity needed to make up the shortage through regular production. You do this instead of making up the shortage in a short-run shop because of the tooling. The tooling you used to make the original order fits the regular machines and you still have both the tooling and the machines.

If, however, the setup costs are extremely high, perhaps you'd better make up the shortage in the short-run shop, doing the work on general purpose machines even if this doesn't let you use the tooling you used before for the original order. Similarly you may perform repair operations on rejected parts in a short-run shop. Then you can perform whatever operations the repairs call for. If, for example, a steel shaft got bumped and has a dent in it, you can fill in the dent by welding on some more metal and then machine it down to size again. Shoe companies do something like this with shoes. Rejects go to a "cripple" section where they get individual treatment.

Situation 2 above has you making repair parts for your producing machines and equipment. It would seem that you should not do this but instead order these parts from the machinery maker. The reason you make your own is that, in many cases, you can't buy the parts (they don't make them any more). Or if you can buy them, they are costly or take a long time to get. If you make them yourself, you usually do the work in the maintenance department's machine shop.

We are going to talk more later about short runs being made to supply parts for your obsolete products out in the hands of customers. These parts for old products are usually made in a short-run shop.

Parts for experimental products and for apparatus are always special and, in many companies, are made in the engineering department's experimental machine shop. If there is no such department, then most likely these will be made up in the same way as repair parts for old machines. Similarly, tooling, jigs, and fixtures are usually made in a department for that purpose. Only occasionally are such items made in the regular manufacturing departments.

Short runs to see how certain materials fare in production are, of course, always put through the regular production departments. If you think that a plastic gear will be better than a metal gear or if you think that a stainless steel part will be better than a cast-iron part you should always make up a few of the proposed kind using your regular production processes to see if they make any production difficulties. The production control department and the manufacturing departments must endure these pilot runs.

To sum up: Short runs can be handled in one or more special departments. When you have such departments, it is better to keep short runs out of regular manufacturing departments and assign them to these special departments. Regardless of the main work which a special department (as for example, a model shop) is set up to do, it is likely to have to do other short-run jobs now and then.

Short-run shops have several advantages. You don't have to develop detailed shop instructions. They keep short runs out of regular factory departments where production costs would be high. This lets you accept orders that you should not otherwise consider and lets you give good service to customers on old repair parts.

A short-run shop can also, at times, act as a subcontractor to the main factory, taking over tricky jobs from it. Short-run shops do, however, cost something to operate, and they also occupy space, sometimes as much as one-tenth of your whole production area. The shops are little job shops using general purpose machines which are manned by highly skilled employees. Production costs are therefore high, sometimes as much as ten times the costs of products made in large lots in the regular production departments. Even so, the costs are often less than the costs of short runs in regular departments.

SERVICE PARTS

Manufacturers of machinery and equipment have to make "service" parts (repair parts) for their customers. Long-established companies that have been selling machines for years often find that parts sales make up a substantial portion (up to one-third) of their business, so spare parts sales isn't a back-alley operation. In the case of wearing parts, you will often end up selling more parts for repairs than you ever used making new products.

Service parts make inventory problems, however. If you have 10,000 live parts for current models you'll likely need 20,000 dead parts for old models. And most of the dead items are slow movers.

You start to sell spares or service parts as soon as your product goes on the market. Dealers have to stock parts right away in order to give service to the few customers who need replacement parts right away. Sometimes you make repair kits containing replacement parts, and supply them to dealers or sell kits as extras with the products. Selling spares in this way makes few problems. Since the parts are in current production all you have to do is to boost your quantities enough so that there are enough extras to make up the kits.

Service "parts" often means "components" rather than individual piece parts. An electric motor or an automobile engine or a door is a "part" in that you think of it as a unit and not as a collection of subparts. Sometimes component subassemblies to be sold as units make problems in the factory because the component, for service purposes, isn't quite like the one for your own regular assembly. Automobile engines to be sold as components, for example, are "short" engines and don't have on them all the parts that an engine needs. This is because not often do buyers want a complete engine. Some of their old parts will do. In automobile companies short engines actually have to be made in a separate service department because they are different enough from regular engines that they upset the regular heavily automated engine assembly lines.

SERVICE PARTS FOR OLD MODELS   Service parts for old models make real problems. As we said, your dead parts far outnumber your live parts. The problem starts with parts for recent but not current models. These you can usually handle all right because you have a carry-over stock of parts made when the item was current, or you need enough such parts that it pays to set up your machines every now and then and run off a new lot of them. You can run off several years' supply of them whenever you have to make up a lot. Of course, you have to get the old tooling out of your dead storage, but you usually keep old tooling for 5 or 10 years. If you sell to the government, you probably have to guarantee to supply parts for 10 years.

The real headaches, however, come from parts for products that you haven't made for years. Customers want only one or two of an old part and nearly always they want it right now because their machine is out of operation and standing idle until your repair part arrives.

Repair parts for old products cause much of the short-run department's work. These old parts may have to be made almost by hand because you no longer have the machines and tooling that you used years ago when you made the item regularly. Even if you have the machines, you may have long since thrown away the tooling, it may have rusted beyond use, or you may have cannibalized it and used its parts to make other tooling.

Sometimes customers send in broken or worn parts from old machines and order replacements without identifying them. You may have to go around among your older employees to see if any of them recognize the parts. A replacement part can be made only after the part has been identified.

So far as production control is concerned, repair parts orders are nuisances. But, from the company point of view, they are profitable nuisances and in any case are important in maintaining customer good will. Machinery makers such as Cincinnati Milling, Bullard, and others guarantee to furnish parts for 25 years. And usually they keep on filling requests long after that.

Although most companies try to give good service and get a good price for old parts, this isn't always true. Minor parts, those costing 50 cents or $1, might be given away free. You can't charge much money for screws and other minor items without making customers mad. Besides, if you go to the expense of sending out bills for 50-cent and $1 items, it costs more to handle the records than the item is worth. So you keep the customer happy and save money at the same time by sending him minor parts free.

Service parts also have to be packaged whereas you don't have to bother doing this for the same items used in production. This adds one more thing that production control has to get done.

REPAIRING CUSTOMERS' PRODUCTS

Machinery manufacturers always have to do a certain amount of repairing and overhauling of the machines they have sold to their customers. And the older your company gets, the more of this work you will have to do. In fact, over the years, some companies become more service companies than manufacturing companies. This has actually happened in the case of

FIGURE 3-1 Production line for repairing coffee makers sent in by customers. (*Dun's Review*)

diesel electric locomotives. Diesel electric locomotive companies are, today, more in the repairing and overhauling business than in the manufacturing business.

Some companies, however, don't have much repair business of this sort. Machinery sold to other companies seldom comes back to the manufacturer for repairs because the customer repairs it in his own repair shop. And consumer items such as watches, sewing machines, typewriters, refrigerators, radios, automobiles, etc., are generally repaired locally and are not sent back to the factory. It would cost too much in shipping costs to justify sending such products back to the factory.

On the other hand, small, portable, and reasonably expensive products, such as cameras, guns, automatic coffee makers, or in a factory, testing equipment, are often different. You do sometimes send these items back to the factory for repairs. Repairmen have to be expert, and since the products have high value, it is worthwhile to pay the postage or express to send them back to the factory for repair.

Although the amount of customer repair work is usually small compared to regular operations, it may be large at certain times. The Daisy Company, maker of air rifles for boys, sells over 1 million rifles a year. Christmas is its big season. Then, during the first few weeks after Christmas, Daisy gets back over 1,000 rifles a day for repairs. It isn't that the rifles are badly made but that the boys who get them for Christmas are so hard on them. Rifles aren't made to be used as crowbars.

CUSTOMERS' AUTHORIZATIONS COVERING REPAIRS   As products returned for repair are received, you need to identify each one with a tag showing the owner's name. Don't do anything to the item, though,

FIGURE 3-2   Repairing pens. (*Dun's Review* and Parker Pen Co.)

until you hear from the owner lest you run up a bigger repair bill than he is willing to pay. You might look over the item and make a note of its condition, but don't repair it until you get the owner's instructions. Then look over the product again to see if his instructions cover the work needed. If they do, go ahead and fix it.

But if the customer's instructions don't authorize you to do enough work to put the product into good operating condition, you should write to him and tell him what it really needs before you do any work. Give him an estimate of the cost of the needed repairs. It is important to do this because customers often feel that the company should repair its products at a very low cost regardless of how they used or abused them. You can lose a lot of customer good will by sending customers big repair bills. Companies often lean over backwards trying to hold down repair costs so that they won't lose customer good will. On the other hand, you shouldn't carry this so far as not to make money on repairs. The repair work you do for customers should be billed at a price that includes a profit.

REPAIRING TRANSPORTATION EQUIPMENT   Transportation equipment requires a separate and unique kind of repair work. Railroads, bus companies, truck lines, taxicab companies, air transport lines, and ocean and inland-water shipping companies all operate transportation equipment which must be kept in repair. For the most part customer companies maintain centralized repair shops and do the work themselves. Sometimes, though, they limit themselves to only light repairs. For heavy repairs they depend on the manufacturer. Having the manufacturer do it has the double advantage of getting the job well done and improvements incorporated at the same time.

Most users of transportation equipment operate complete repair shops, doing heavy as well as light repairs. These shops are factories in almost every sense of the word. They sometimes employ thousands of workers, and make parts and assemble products. Even larger, however, than most private transportation repair shops are those operated by the Armed Forces of the United States. Airplane overhaul and repair stations and naval ship repair yards are equal in size to large factories.

Large-scale repair work on equipment is more difficult than regular manufacturing. So is production control in such shops. Most of the equipment being repaired is old, and you can't buy replacement parts. Sometimes the equipment has been in a wreck. You just don't know how much repairing you have to do until you get the product apart. You have to clean and inspect all parts before deciding whether you can use them again. On many parts there is no identifying part number, and on others it may be worn off, or defaced beyond recognition.

Under such circumstances it is a hard job to make up a list of the new or repaired parts that you need for reassembling the product. Some of the parts taken out can be used without repair; others are repairable. Still other parts are beyond fixing and you have to replace them. For parts that need replacing, you have to make up drawings and shop orders covering their manufacture. For repairable parts, you have to decide what rework operations have to be done and then make out shop orders to cover the work. Of course, both the shop orders for the parts you are making new and those you are reworking have to have operations lists and, for the newly made parts, raw materials requisitions. If you are lucky enough to be able to buy repair parts, make out purchase requisitions for the purchasing department. Repair orders, manufacturing orders, and requisitions must all show the assembly order number so that they will reach the correct reassembly station at the proper time.

Fortunately, you can stock some repair parts. Wearing parts have to be replaced so often that you can make them in quantity and use them as needed. Sometimes you get parts by cannibalizing products that need too much repair. Take them apart, save whatever usable parts they still have, and add those parts to your stock. Of course, such additions to your parts stock are irregular and they complicate your record keeping. And of course you can't sell them as new parts.

Although large-scale repair shops have problems before they get down to actually making repairs, the work is like regular job lot work once shop orders to repair or make parts have been issued. There is one difference though. Individual products (even identical products) require unlike sets of repaired or replacement parts, so you have to gather together on the assembly floor exactly the right parts for each unit. In regular manufacturing, one parts list serves for a whole order for assembled products of the same kind.

If you don't have too many types of equipment in use, you can simplify your control of repair by making "periodic" repairs or by using "class" repairs. Perhaps you can give all equipment light repairs every three months and a thorough overhauling annually. This would be periodic repairs.

Class repairs operate differently. You set up "degrees" of repairs. A class A repair might be a quick overhaul of one part of the equipment. It is like getting your automobile ignition system gone over before winter. A class B repair might be a motor overhaul. Classes C and D would mean heavier repairs.

When equipment comes into the shop, inspect it to see what it needs and assign it to a class. It will then get the standard repairs that all equipment in that class gets. All products designated as needing class B repairs are disassembled to the same extent and all get the same repairs. With class repairs you don't always put every one of the item's own parts and components back into it. Whole rebuilt units, such as electric generators and starting motors, are installed. The removed components are inspected and repaired later and put into repaired parts stock for use in future repairs.

MODIFICATIONS

Manufacturers of large expensive products sometimes have to remodel, rebuild, or "modify" their older models owned by customers. Diesel electric locomotive manufacturers sometimes even have to remodel and change over a competitor's locomotive. When they do, they put in their own electrical and mechanical parts.

It is in the materiel of the Armed Forces, however, that modifications are the most important. Airplanes, ships, guns, tanks, in fact, almost every kind of durable materiel is at one time or another remodeled to embody the latest improvements.

Modifications differ from regular repair work. As a rule, the products to be modified haven't failed in any way. Instead, some innovation has made new products work so much better that old models can't compete without a face-lifting job. Customers wanting their products remodeled send them to your factory. You may have enough change-over work at times to justify setting up a special department just for change-overs. This lets you set up production lines to take apart, to the proper degree, the old products. And you can set up other lines to reassemble them as you incorporate the improvements.

Although modification isn't repair, you always do some repairing along with modifications because it is easy to do when you have the product apart. Some of the units coming in for modification are in good condition, needing only the modification; others need small repairs, while some need extensive repair. In all such cases you combine repairs and modifications.

When several slightly different models are to be modified the job becomes complicated. Airplanes, for example, need to have the latest radar equipment, yet probably no two airplanes come off the assembly line exactly alike in every minor detail. Every airplane coming off the line contains the latest improvements as of the time of its manufacture. June's airplanes are a little different from May's airplanes, even though they started down the line intended to come out the same. Although the differences are usually small, they affect any modification work done later. The last made airplanes need less modification than those first off the line.

Besides, some improvements which are part of the modification have, you discover, already been made out in the field on some of the products. "Spares" (extra parts) and "modification kits" sent out into the field for that purpose have already been installed.

You end up with every unit needing individual treatment. When each product comes in, you have to inspect it and decide the extent of repairs and modification needed. Production control has then to make up work orders covering the specific work to be done.

RETURNED REJECTED PRODUCTS

Customers sometimes reject the products you send and return them to you. When they arrive, you should identify them as to the customer and sales order on which they were shipped. Don't do anything to them until you hear why they have been returned. Then inspect them to see if the customer's claim is justified and report your finding to the sales department, which handles all correspondence with the customer.

Assuming that the returned items are not to be sent back again to the customer, the question is what to do with them. Do just about what you would do if your own inspectors had rejected them before they were shipped. See what repairs they need and make out work orders to cover the work of disassembling, repair, and reassembling. If the products are beyond repair you may have to scrap them or sell them as damaged products. But if they are assembled products, and if you decide not to repair them, you can still take them apart and put the good parts back in stock.

Sometimes a lot that is returned because the percentage of defectives is too high can be combined with a lot that has a lower percentage of defective so that both lots will meet the minimum standards of the purchaser. Although this practice might seem to be a bit underhanded, it is usually justified by arguing that the purchaser is only paying for some stipulated level of quality and that as long as it is met, no breech of good faith occurs.

FINISHING RUNS

When an order for an assembled product ends, it is quite a trick to have enough parts to finish the last product and yet have no parts left over. If any parts are short you can't finish the last unit of the product. Yet leftover parts may be waste. Probably you will be able, later on, to sell some leftover parts as repair parts but leftovers aren't always "wearing" parts. They don't wear out and almost never need replacing. One year Oldsmobile had 150,000 door handles left over after it had finished making the model using them. These door handles were probably all waste because door handles hardly ever need replacing.

Production control orders very close on the last parts orders, sometimes giving orders for only one or two pieces. Making one or two of a part is expensive but you may have to do it in order not to have one or two incomplete products. Yet there is no point in ordering more than your bare needs when the extras are going to be worthless.

MODEL CHANGE–OVERS

New model change-over periods are periods of low production and schedule headaches for production control. Sometimes machines are redesigned and rearranged. Sometimes you get new machines. But you can't move machines around and put in new ones and take out old ones while you are still working on this year's models. Of course you go ahead and make all of the changes you can without interrupting production. But some of the changing has to wait till after you have finished making the old models. Then you may have to close the plant down completely to make the remaining changes in machines and layout.

Besides causing assembly line problems, change-overs increase parts making work. During a change-over you have to make parts for both old and new models for a period of several weeks. Right up to the end of making old products, production control has to get old parts made in order to finish all the old products scheduled. And at the same time, it has to order new parts for new models.

Manufactures of refrigerators, stoves, radios, television sets, and such products have less trouble changing their assembly lines to new models than do many other manufacturers. This is because their assembly work is largely hand work. Often even changing from old to new parts isn't a big job because the new models continue to use a good many old parts.

Large companies operate several assembly lines making the same products. Changing is relatively easy for the manufacturing departments because they can change one line at a time. But, as we said, production control has to get double sets of parts made during the change-over period and this nearly doubles production control's work.

There are still more troubles, however, even after the change-over is complete. As new models come into production there are always at least a few minor difficulties with the new tooling. This holds up the production of certain parts or certain products.

By being fast on your feet you can often compensate and avoid losing production. If you can't make one model, step up the production of another. Then later switch back again. One year, for example, at the start of its new model year, Chrysler had production difficulties making 8-cylinder engines for Plymouth cars but no trouble with its 6s. The production control department quickly boosted the schedules for 6-cylinder cars so no production at all was lost. As soon as the 8s were coming through all right, production control boosted the number of 8s and cut down on 6s until the schedules of both models were back in balance.

On new models, you should expect to have to change schedules back and forth. You can be ready if you carry, at the start, more than normal inventories of parts for the models that are the least changed and hence least likely to give trouble. Then you can swing over to them if the most changed products run into trouble. You should also warn parts suppliers that you may have to jump orders up and down until things go smoothly.

RUNNING IN NEW PRODUCTION LINES

You always have to "run in" new production lines. Your engineers can't lay out everything perfectly in the drafting room and have production lines run smoothly the first time. You just can't go directly from drawings to mass production, without having "bugs" crop up. New tooling and machines don't work just right. Sometimes parts don't fit because the tools aren't shaped quite right, or because the metal doesn't work just right, or for other reasons.

A run-in period is not actually a preproduction period but rather it is the first week or two of regular production of a new production line. During this period you plan for less production than you expect later. This lets you "shake down" the equipment and find and fix trouble spots so that later production will go smoothly. Because run-in periods are periods of low production, but not no production, you have to make parts to keep the line going but your quantities are way below what they'll be later.

RESEARCH DEPARTMENT MANUFACTURING

Research departments always have to fight off the tendency to become manufacturing departments. There are two situations always tending to put them into manufacturing. The first, we might call "accidental" manufacture and the second "incubation" manufacture.

Accidental manufacture happens because the research department needs special apparatus for its experiments and tests. Often this apparatus is so special that it can't be bought, so the research men design and make it themselves in the small machine shop they operate for this purpose. The next thing, they are also making special test equipment for the factory, perhaps not as a regular thing, but from time to time. And from time to time they make special apparatus for factory jobs other than test jobs.

From here on it is but a short step to selling such testing and special production apparatus to customers who want these items too. Soon you are running a little manufacturing company inside your research department. So long as the outside market is small, the research department may continue to make the items. But if sales go up you transfer their manufacture to a manufacturing department.

Incubation manufacture is different. Research departments of electronics, chemical, pharmaceutical, and many other companies are always developing new materials, processes, or products. At some point they are perfected to the point where you can sell them outside. Then the testing and experimental work dwindles and regular manufacture begins. During the long experimental period the research department makes products on a small scale, enough for their experiments but no more. Some products never get out of the experimental stage, because they prove to have weaknesses. Successful items, though, do emerge. This brings up a transition stage. For a short time the research staff may operate a small-scale processing facility, producing small quantities of products for sale. Later, you set up regular production facilities and take the job away from research.

For the research department the time probably never comes when it gets rid of all accidental and incubation manufacturing, because it is always developing new products. Nor does it ever get rid of regular manufacture of products for sale if their manufacture requires a high degree of technical knowledge and if their volume stays low.

MODELS, PROTOTYPES, AND NEW PRODUCTS

Model and prototype manufacture is important in many companies. It is part of research work, yet it is actual manufacturing. Sometimes models are the immediate predecessors to items produced in quantities. In other cases models are purely experimental, made to test the performance of certain equipment or designs. If you made refrigerators, you might, for example, make up several sample refrigerator doors with different kinds of insulation and of different designs to see which insulation works best and to see how the doors fit and which look best.

Sometimes models are made up more to test the market than anything else. They are put on display at machinery shows and the amount of customer interest is noted. And, of course, if you build an operating model you learn what it will cost to make and you can test its performance.

Models may be of full size or reduced size and may be performing models or mere "mock-ups." Prototypes are full size and are intended to perform. Sometimes more than one of a model is made—even 50 or 100.

How and where should you manufacture models and prototypes? Some companies run them through regular production. Large companies invariably make them in separate model shops—at least if they are made in only ones or twos. Some companies have manufacturing facilities in the research department that are complete enough so that they can make prototypes there. You can also have models made on the outside, although most companies would rather do this inside. Parts for models are sometimes made in the model shop, in regular factory departments, in the toolroom, or even in the company's maintenance department machine shop.

Models and prototypes are made almost altogether by hand and so are quite costly. Sometimes, as in the case of airplanes, they are intentionally made different from the production models that are expected to follow. They are loaded down, for example, with equipment to test stresses, strains, etc., during trial runs. Other equipment, which will go on regular products later (such as seats in airplanes), is not attached. The information collected on test runs is used to modify the final design before the item goes into production.

Your company will always be developing new products but you don't always have to make up models or prototypes. In the machinery industry, for example, the customer often wants a machine specially designed for his work. Often the machine he wants is similar to one of your regular machines. Your engineers, working with the customer's representatives, are nearly always able to design such a machine wholly on paper and then go directly into manufacture. Unless the machine is quite unusual, you can just make up the drawings, and sign the contract without building a model. When you get the order, ordinarily you produce such machines, even when one of a kind, in the factory and not in a model shop.

DEMONSTRATION, DISPLAY, AND PASS-OUT SAMPLES

Automobile companies, office machines manufacturers, and some others often put on shows at which their products are demonstrated. Sometimes these companies make up special products with cut-away sections to show how the parts operate. Motors and other parts are nickel-plated and dressed up in other ways to make the most attractive appearance. Transparent plastic parts are sometimes substituted for metal parts to permit their internal workings to be observed.

Makers of cloth, paint, paper, and wallpaper have to make up and send out large numbers of sample pads. Some processers of food, notably breakfast food, as well as soapmakers, produce small packages to pass out as free samples. Shoe manufacturers make up sample shoes in their new styles in advance. Colored pictures of the new styles are made for salesmen and customers, and salesmen are also supplied with sample shoes. They are specially made since regular production of the new styles will start only after orders begin to come in.

Salesmen for companies making small portable products are often supplied with sets of samples or "kits" of sample products. Getting the samples together into sets usually makes a little extra work but even more work goes into making sure that they are of the highest quality which is why these items are manufactured with particular care. Demonstration, display, and pass-out samples all require special handling either in the manufacturing process, packaging, or both. And they require special shop directives from production control. Usually too they are rush jobs because the top brass wants them out as fast as possible after they settle on designs.

TEST MODELS
New products should be put through exhaustive tests before they are announced for sale. They should even be tested under extreme conditions of use and abuse because customers sometimes use them that way. You want to know the limits of your product's performance.

Test models will probably have to be made in your short-run shop even though later products will be made in regular factory departments. You have to do this because you do most of your testing before regular production starts. You should try *not*, however, to build extra high quality into test models because you want to test normal or average products.

Sometimes the customer wants you to make up several test models so he can try out more than one. The United States government, when buying small arms, is likely to want up to 100 models for testing. If the quantities become that large, you make them in the regular production departments.

TOOL, JIG, AND FIXTURE MANUFACTURE
Most companies make some of the tools, jigs, and fixtures that they use. Tooling is costly whether you make it or buy it, but if you make your own it usually costs less and usually you have it when you want it.

Try, though, if you make your own tooling, to give the tool-making department a steady load of work, because it is costly to have the highly skilled men and expensive machines in the toolroom idle part of the time. If your tool-making work load varies, probably you should operate only a small department that you can always keep busy. Then when your load is big, send the excess work outside for manufacture.

An alternative is to operate a large toolroom and keep it busy during slack periods by transferring to it some of the factory's special close tolerance production jobs. Occasionally you find a factory that makes some of its tooling in regular factory departments. But you can't do this unless your regular production departments are able to do close tolerance work.

SUPPLIES MANUFACTURE

Large companies buy such enormous quantities of some supplies that they can, and occasionally do, make some of their supply items themselves rather than buying them. Many companies buy boxboard and make their own cartons and shipping containers. Often they make (or at least print) their own labels and identification tags. They do the same with printed forms. Also companies making liquid products sold in bottles sometimes make their own bottle caps and stoppers. Companies whose products are sold in cloth sacks may make and print the sacks.

Except for printing labels, tags, and forms, however, most companies don't make a practice of making supply items. You can usually buy supply items cheaply and not often does it pay to make them.

FOREIGN SALES

Most companies sell some of their products in foreign markets. Some companies own foreign subsidiaries which need products from their sister plants in the United States to round out their lines. Some foreign subsidiaries make assembled products from parts of their own manufacture plus other parts sent from the United States.

Today there are many more sister plant relationships between plants located abroad and those in the United States than there used to be. Almost all big American companies now have plants all over the world. Sometimes they are just assembly plants but lots of them make parts too; in fact, electronic parts such as transistors are just about as likely to be made abroad as not. Many are imported into the United States. Sister plant relationships are more complex than ever, considering the added dimensions of distance, language, customs, different monies, and all kinds of local government regulations. Automobiles sold in Mexico, for example, now have to have 60 per cent of their value made in Mexico. In Spain, however, where the figure is 90 per cent there are fewer sister plant relationships because almost all of the parts have to be made in Spain.

Products sold abroad usually differ from their domestic counterparts. In the case of machinery, the electrical voltage of the motors and the calibration scales on all gages, control lever designations, etc., are different for almost every country. The product has to be made to suit the country in which it is going to be sold. Even nameplates showing the machine's size, capacity, electrical voltages required, etc., must be different. Linear measures, weights, and liquid measures are different. Think, for example, of cash registers. National Cash Register makes them to handle dollars, pesos, pounds sterling, lira, francs, marks, yen, and many other currencies. Or consider typewriters whose characters are in Chinese, Arabic, Hindi, French, German, and other languages. Even nuts and bolts have to be made differently. Several systems of threads are used around the world. Automobile tires and storage batteries for foreign markets are smaller because foreign cars are smaller. And last, products sold abroad are always packaged and labeled differently to suit the language and foreign government packaging regulations and to withstand rough handling in transit.

Sales orders from foreign customers are likely to be rush orders, partly because they have to be shipped so far that products take a long time to get there. A different reason for rushing shipment is that you don't ship products abroad to unknown customers without knowing how you are going to be paid. The customer won't send money ahead but he does send a "letter of credit." This is a letter, addressed to you, from a well-known foreign bank. In it the bank says that it will pay for the order when it is shipped. *But* the credit guarantee in letters of credit often expires in one or two months. If you don't ship within that time the customer will have to get a new extension of credit. Maybe he can and will get it. Since you can't be sure, you rush his order through production so as not to lose it.

Individual orders for products to be sold in foreign markets are usually small, but if you get enough of them, they add up to big volume.

STUDY MATERIALS

3-1 The production manager and the marketing manager have been unable to resolve their differences concerning the necessity, or advisability, of (1) producing "specials" such as major modifications to customers' orders, (2) producing promotional items for salesmen, and (3) guaranteeing replacement parts for the lifetime of certain parts of your major products. As president of the company, how would you resolve these differences? What factors would you take into consideration?

3-2 If you decided to engage in the types of production discussed in this chapter, should the added expense be considered a production cost or a marketing cost? Or would there by any added expense?

3-3 What factors would govern the decision as to when production should start to be involved in an engineering development? At what point should the development be turned over to production?

3-4 In each of the following cases, where should the repair of products needing repair be done?

1 Machinery that you use in your factory

2 Portable laboratory equipment

3 Hoisting trucks used to move materials around the plant

4 Caterpillar tractors

5 Airplanes

6 An electric shaver

7 A diesel locomotive

Consider also other likely alternatives which you have rejected in your choices and explain why they would be less suitable than the departments you have chosen.

3-5 For over 50 years the Erskine Conveyor Company has made many kinds of conveying equipment. Parts for current and recently discontinued models are regularly stocked. Customers are guaranteed that parts will be available for 10 years at the current list price. But on still older models, stocks are maintained of only the most commonly used replacement parts. Most parts for old equipment are not stocked but are made up on regular production orders whenever they are ordered by customers. The prices quoted for these items are high enough to yield a good profit.

Such orders are characteristically for one or two pieces. Both the production control department and the shop find that these frequent small orders cause considerable difficulty. It is hard to make schedules when so much setup time is used for small orders, and sometimes the old tools needed for the job are missing.

It is proposed by the production control manager that all this business be removed from regular production departments and that one department be set up in the shop for just such orders. Discuss the merits of the proposal. Have you any other suggestions as to how to handle this situation?

3-6 Scott and Company made instruments which were assembled from wood and metal parts. The engineering department released the drawings for a special instrument, and production on the order started. The foreman of the woodworking department reported to the production control department and to the project engineer in the engineering department that he thought certain of the wood parts would warp. He suggested that these parts be made from metal, although metal would be more expensive. A member of the staff of the production control department also spoke separately to the project engineer about the foreman's views. The project engineer said he thought there was no danger of the wood warping, and since it was cheaper, to go ahead but to let him know if any trouble developed in processing. Accordingly the wooden parts were made up and no trouble was encountered in making them. But by the time they were assembled many were warped, and they cracked when forced into position in the assembly.

The chief engineer heard about it and immediately took the production control manager to task for failing to report it to him. He was told that it was reported to his project engineer, who was not receptive. The chief engineer said that the production control department's responsibility should not end with getting the parts made but should include a responsibility for seeing that the parts will work or at least informing him ahead if the parts are not going to work.

How should such a situation be handled? Is it wise to economize on materials in the manufacture of special instruments? Should the staff member of one department go directly to the staff member of another department? Should he go only to the head of his own department? Should he go to the head of the other department? Does the production control department have any responsibility beyond having the parts made as specified?

chapter four

PRODUCTION CONTROL PROCEDURES

Whatever the kind of manufacturing you are in, you still have to perform all the basic production control functions listed in Chapter 1. But there are differences in how often you have to do certain work, when and where it is to be done, and who does it. So there are different kinds of production control systems.

"Order control" and "flow control" are the two main types of production control although not always does a company use only one and not the other. Sometimes one department uses one kind of control while another department uses the other. Some companies too use combination methods, of which "block" and "load" control are two.

ORDER CONTROL

People usually refer to job lot manufacture as manufacture "to order," and to the production control method as "order control." Manufacturing to order means that the factory gets separate directions to produce each lot of products. Often this means that you already have a sales order on hand. You could say that you "make what you sell." Examples of companies that manufacture to order include these which make industrial machinery, locomotives, and electric power generators.

You can, however, order, in lots, replacement supplies of products that you stock, so manufacturing to order does not always mean "to the customer's order." In either case, though, whether you already have a sales order or are just making to stock, you use order control.

Details of order control are given in Chapters 23 to 25. Here we merely want to "rough it in." In intermittent production you produce many small lots of products. Orders vary in quantity, in form, in materials, in operations called for, and in many other respects, so you have to perform most or all of the functions of production control for almost every order. Because so many orders are for new items you have little opportunity to use old plans over again. Old parts lists and old operation lists are no good for new products. The information about how to make yesterday's products, how long operations take, and so on doesn't apply to today's products.

Order control gets its name because each lot of goods must be kept separate from every other order. Each lot gets an order number that belongs to it alone. In the cost accounting department all materials costs, direct labor costs, and machine costs incurred in producing the order are collected in its own account. After the products made on an order are finished, all the amounts charged to the order are added up. To this figure is added an appropriate overhead assessment to get the total cost of manufacturing the order.

Outside the accounting department, the order number is used in all work relating to manufacture. It identifies and segregates every lot from every other lot of materials in process. It is also a name or title for the particular lot of goods. All instructions and report forms relating to the lot bear this number.

CENTRALIZATION AND DECENTRALIZATION OF CONTROL   Order control may be quite centralized or somewhat decentralized. Since manufacturing instructions for all departments need to be coordinated, the making out of instructions is usually done centrally. Yet the instructions finally have to be passed out to departments and to the men who work on the product. The difference between centralized and decentralized control is in the way the instructions filter down to the operators.

Typically, centralized control operates as follows: Shop directives are prepared ahead (by the production control department) and held in dispatch offices until time for the work to be done. Dispatch offices are branch offices of the production control department and are located in each of the manufacturing departments. When a worker finishes a job, he gets his next work assignment from the dispatcher, who is a production control department employee, and not from his foreman. Truckers and materials movemen also get their instructions for moving materials through the plant from the dispatcher.

Centralized control is usually an effective way to get coordination but the extra paper work (from keeping central records of where everything is and of everything done) costs money. Centralized control is also not as flexible as decentralized control—in spite of the dispatchers being located in the shop where they are in close touch with operations.

Decentralized control still keeps order writing, scheduling, and routing centralized; but after the orders are prepared they are turned over to the foreman, who controls the operations of his department in his own way. The foreman chooses what jobs to do next and decides which workers work on which jobs. He knows about the little things that make one decision better than another. Also in decentralized control you can save paper work by dispensing with written move orders since the foreman can tell truckers where to take materials.

There are even some advantages for the workers in a decentralized operation. The most important of these is that they receive orders from a single supervisor. A potential conflict exists whenever a worker is being directed from more than one source. When the dispatcher works for the foreman, the orders to the workers go out in the foreman's name and the unity of command is preserved.

Centralized and decentralized control aren't greatly different, however, because within manufacturing departments, both methods work about the same way. The work to be done is the same and the shop directives still have to be sent to the factory operatives. In decentralized control, departmental dispatch offices are often set up in almost the same way as they are under a centralized arrangement, except that the dispatchers are responsible to the foremen and not to the production control department. The foreman retains his responsibility for running his department.

One very real difficulty with decentralized control is that foremen will be foremen. Many of them are poor planners and are careless. Copies of shop orders get lost. Foremen rarely check up in advance on the availability of materials, tooling, or machine capacity. Things go wrong more often than need be. Worse yet, foremen won't tell you when an order gets behind. Often they don't know it themselves. You end up not getting all of the expected gains from decentralization.

We needn't, however, be too hard on foremen. They have to spend time on labor matters, product quality, machine repair, and other matters. Work scheduling and production control can't always come first in their thinking. Sometimes the foreman turns this work over to his department clerk who gives it only casual attention. Perhaps too it is unfair to tar all foremen with the same brush because some of them are good foremen who do meet their work schedules. Decentralized control therefore ends up being spotty—it works well in departments where you have good foremen and poorly in departments with poor foremen.

PRODUCTION CONTROL BY EXCEPTIONS   Production control's directives "push" production through the plant. You tell the plant which operations to do and when to do them. When the plant follows the directions, production results. There is, however, also a "pull" that you might overlook. The pull comes from the factory departments, not from production control. The pull is merely the factory's need to keep busy. When a factory worker finishes a job, he needs another one. So you give him another job.

He finishes it and needs another and so on for all factory workers in all departments. Their need for work "pulls" jobs through. Once materials or job orders start into production there is a strong tendency for them to keep moving through the factory and on to the shipping room.

This pull can sometimes be used to simplify production control work. If production will truly pull itself through why do all the paper work that is needed to keep track of where everything is all the time? Why have production control figure out exactly when each operation will be done if it will be done at about the same time anyway? The answer, of course, is that you should cut out all of this work if production really will come through on its own.

You can do this if you don't have too many unusual products. Foremen and their workers don't need to be told again how to do jobs they have done before. Production can be controlled by "exceptions." You assume that, say, 95 per cent of the production will come through without trouble. So you make out just the minimum of directives. And cut out reports telling that operations have been performed. Don't keep progress records showing how orders are moving through the plant.

You still need to be concerned, however, with the 5 per cent of the orders that won't pull themselves through. Whether your plant is busy or not, some orders will be delayed because bought materials don't arrive on time, or tools and machines break down, or for other reasons. Your procedure needs to tell you about the few orders that do have trouble. This is where the exception idea comes in. You get no reports of orders moving along as they should but those that have trouble are exceptions. Set up your procedure to get full reports on them. Make your foremen report daily all orders not moving as they should. Make foremen tell you why certain orders are held up. And make them tell you how they plan to speed them up. Some companies call these "trouble" reports. Send copies of trouble reports to the superintendent as well as to production control. Doing this will make foremen more active in getting roadblocks removed.

Airplane companies have so many parts orders to keep track of that they use this method. They make out quite complete reports on orders delayed. They have so many orders in process (perhaps 20,000 all the time) that only summary reports go to higher officials. These show how many orders there are in the plant and how many are held up. And they show what percentage of orders are behind schedule. Those held up are shown in groups according to how far behind they are. The reports also show how many orders are critical (for items already short on the assembly floor), how many were behind last week, how many of those are now caught up, and how many new ones have fallen behind.

How, though, does a foreman know when an order is behind schedule? Actually, you shouldn't make your minimum directives so minimum as to leave him in doubt. Put on your shop orders not only the lists of operations to be done but also a desired completion date for each operation. With this wanted completion date, a foreman can tell when a job gets behind in his department.

Production control work, when based on exceptions, is relatively inexpensive but you don't get full control. It is strong on correction but weak on prevention. As a rule, orders have to get behind schedule before they get special attention. This is a bad feature because you don't start fixing trouble until after it happens and you find out about it. If you had known it sooner often you could have fixed it and kept orders from getting delayed.

Some companies, in spite of its extra cost, prefer more complete and more certain control than control by exceptions can provide. They want a system where the performance of each individual operation is separately directed by production control and its completion reported. This gives them tighter control but makes more paper work, much of it wasteful because the factory would do most jobs on time anyway. Generally, with tighter control you find out about delays and prospective delays sooner so you can do something about them earlier than you can with control by exceptions. Whether fewer schedule failures outweigh the extra costs of detailed control is a matter which each individual company has to decide.

CONTROL OF MINOR PRODUCT MANUFACTURE All the minor kinds of production that we talked about in Chapter 3 have to be controlled. Yet when minor manufacturing goes on in the research department, the short-run shop, or any place other than regular factory departments, the production control department doesn't have to issue many instructions. The departments themselves usually decide how to do the work, which work to do first, and so on.

FLOW CONTROL
Repetitive or mass production companies usually "sell what they make." Most of the time they make products before they are sold and fill customers' orders from stocks of finished products. These companies use "flow" or "rate" control to control production. The factory's orders to manufacture are to keep on making more of the products which are selling. In this group are makers of television sets, electric light bulbs,

canned foods, door hinges, typewriters, medicines, soap, matches, shoes, and a host of other items.

Not all mass production, however, is manufacture to stock. Coca-Cola bottles, for example, are made to the customer's order, but an order to make Coca-Cola bottles would be a big order. Making storage batteries for Chevrolet automobiles or picture tubes for Zenith television sets is manufacturing to order, but again the orders are for large quantities. These companies all use "flow control."

Flow control, like order control, is too complex to discuss fully here. Again we are only "roughing it in." Details will come in Chapters 29 to 31.

In continuous production, you make large quantities of identical or nearly identical products. You try to maintain a *constant rate* of output. All materials and parts *flow* through production at this rate, and there is no change in the kind of products (other than minor variations) from hour to hour and from day to day.

Production control doesn't have to tell workers what jobs to work on, what materials to use, what parts to make, what operations to perform, how to do the work, how long the jobs should take, what machines to use, nor where to take the materials next. Neither does it have to get reports on the production of every little quantity of every item made at every operation.

In a sense, these production control functions have been eliminated in continuous production. Nearly all of them are actually, however, very carefully performed during the planning of production processes. The plant's layout embodies most of the production control functions that seem to have disappeared. The materials, parts, operations, methods, machines, time of operations, instructions to workers, and transportation of materials all have been carefully analyzed and decided upon *before* the machines are designed and installed. Once done, these things stay done. You don't have to figure out again and again what operations you need, how you will do them, and so on.

By the time production gets under way, about all you see of production control is "run" sheets, a fairly simple kind of directive for production. Run sheets are lists showing the quantity and sequence of each variety of part or product to be made. You need them only because your products aren't quite fully standardized, and you need them only at first operations and at a few key spots farther along.

Production control in continuous production is not a snap job, however. Almost all of the work is centralized and most of it is "ahead-of-time" work. The big job is to work out the hundreds or thousands of schedules for parts and subassemblies needed to keep them flowing into the final assembly line at rates matching their use.

Production control tells the manufacturing departments the planned rate of production and receives reports showing the actual rate accomplished. Production control then compares the planned and actual totals. This comparing is very important because discrepancies make trouble. You can't make automobiles faster than engines or the other way around. If their two rates differ, you will quickly be in a jam.

Variations in products, minor though they are, add to production control's job. If automobile number 51 on the assembly line is to be green, then the men on the supply line for wheels must know this so that they can put green wheels into the number 251, 252, 253, 254, and 255 positions in the wheel line. If you had completely standard products, you wouldn't need even these instructions. All the wheel supply line would need to know is how many wheels per hour you need.

LOAD CONTROL

Some industries are like continuous industries, but their control problems are like those in intermittent production. "Load" control is suitable in many such situations. It is described more fully in Chapter 28, but again a brief explanation is appropriate here.

Load control gets its name from the emphasis that it puts on key machines. It *allocates the time of large key machines* to certain orders or products. In the book printing business, for example, these are the printing presses. Operations before and after the presses usually have enough capacity to handle all that the presses can turn out so they don't need close control.

In load control companies, production operations don't go on as smoothly as they do in continuous manufacturing. Partly this is because you have to stop the machines when you change from one lot to another. And since the downtime for changing is different on different machines, it upsets any perfect balance that you might have been able to work out.

Load control differs from order control in that you issue no *processing* instructions for individual lots, and all products go through the same processes. All you have to do is to send lists showing the quantity of each size and type of products. Your list divides up the machine time between the various lots. The lists also show the lot sequence on the machines. The material in process almost always carries identification tags or marks similar to those in order control.

BLOCK CONTROL
The men's clothing industry uses a variation of load control called "block" control. Instead of a key machine, however, the control is based on the capacity of the cutting department.

Men's suits are cut from cloth by men working on piecework. A "block" is a half day's work for these men. Orders for suits are sent to a factory in groups or blocks, whose total cutting piecework cost equals what the cutters normally earn in a half day.

Every suit in each block not only carries its block number, but has an individual suit number as well. As each suit passes out of the cutting department (and from department to department thereafter) the department check-out station checks it off. When the last one has gone on, the block is "cleared." The foreman must clear each block in sequence but a block can't be cleared if even one suit hasn't come through. Foreman then get after the laggard suits. Block control is a good method for keeping all orders moving through production.

Airplane and missile manufacturers use a different kind of "block" control. Final assembly is a continuous operation but parts and subassemblies are almost always made in lots and are made well ahead. Orders are released to cover the parts for a block (a given number) of airplanes, say 20 airplanes, at a time. These releases, made several months before final assembly, authorize the release of all shop orders for parts and subassemblies for this block of airplanes.

SPECIAL PROJECT CONTROL
Special projects, or giant products, were mentioned in Chapter 2. For them you use order control but it is not as simple as the order control used in ordinary job lot shops. Some people have used the term "time schedule" or "coordinated effort" to describe this kind of control.

Giant products, for production control purposes, are thought of as being made up of major sections or segments. First, you have to set up an overall master schedule for completing the major components. Then you make detailed plans for getting each of the major sections manufactured. Schedules for subordinate activities are set so that the overall schedule can be met. For each major section of the product you will probably want to keep track of such things as when drawings and job tickets are complete and when all of the other shop instruction forms are ready.

If you manufacture sections of the project in different plants you will have to check the work loads of all of the plants concerned and get promise

FIGURE 4-1 A product of unusual type and proportion. It is a spherical valve now in a hydroelectric plant in Missouri. To get an appreciation of its size, notice the man below the valve in the center of the picture.

dates from each one covering its share of the work. Otis Elevator, for example, makes elevator cages in one factory, power and hoisting equipment in a second plant, and up-and-down tracks in a third factory. For any one elevator project these schedules have to be coordinated.

Because special projects always require tremendous amounts of engineering work, one of the first things to do is to estimate the total number of engineering man-hours the job will require. Next, divide by the number of engineers you can assign to the job and find out how long it will take to prepare the drawings for the factory. This gives you a schedule for the completion of drawings after which you can proceed to set up schedules for manufacturing. Some of the newer mathematical techniques such as PERT, PERT/COST, and the Critical Path Method have proved to be quite helpful in this type of scheduling. In fact, their use is required on some large military contracts. Usually you have to do all of this scheduling before you even get contracts for special projects. You have to furnish schedules to the sales department because, when bidding, it has to quote delivery dates.

Detailed engineering work on special projects starts with drawings of the customer's facilities. Your engineers will probably have to make a trip to the customer's plant in order to make up drawings of the area where he wants to put the machine, conveyor, turbine, or whatever the project may be. Your engineers will have to design it to fit that location and so must consider any limitations (walls, posts, other machines, and so on) which the surroundings impose.

Almost always, too, you will need considerable special tooling for big jobs. You need to figure out what tooling you need, and then design it and order it as quickly as possible so that it can be produced while the remaining engineering work is being done. Special tooling is often very expensive, tending as it does to be extra large machines or equipment capable of doing precise work. These special items may cost up to 20 per cent of the cost of the whole job.

Once the engineering department releases drawings to the factory for the major sections of the big product, you can start on their manufacture. Here you save time by making the various sections of the product in different parts of the factory at the same time. Hence the name coordinated effort.

DESIGN CHANGES DURING PRODUCTION   You are always in such a hurry on these projects that you start making some parts before they are fully designed. Of course this is somewhat wasteful. It is a little like starting to build a house before you decide on all the details. There will be times when you have to undo or tear out or throw out something you have just put in. But costly though it is, this method gets on with the project. Normally you don't have to undo very many things, so almost always you save time.

There are other reasons for starting a product before its design is complete. Sometimes the special project (say it is an atomic reactor) is so new to you that you don't really know just how you will work out every minor detail. The whole thing is different enough from your past experience that you can't foresee just how everything will work. So you design the item as fully as possible and leave some details to be worked out as you go along. You need to decide as many details as you can, however, before going ahead because changing is so expensive. Close cooperation among engineering, production control, and factory foremen is essential.

SUBCONTRACTING

The study referred to on page 11 found that the production control depart-ment was responsible for subcontracting in 34 per cent of the companies reporting. Although this figure seems to be on the high side, this is a produc-tion control responsibility in some companies.

Production control probably has little say about which items are to be bought outside except perhaps to farm out temporary overloads. Nor does it play much part in contract writing.

Instead, its part comes into play as the subcontracts are carried out. If special tooling has to be sent to the supplier, the production control staff might have to do all of the arranging to have the special tooling made and sent to the subcontractor. And, in particular, production control is active in making out supply schedules. It usually works directly with the subcontractor in setting delivery schedules so that final production needs can be met.

It is here that long lead time problems are at their worst. Sometimes your subcontractor buys certain components from someone else who gets parts from another company which buys its materials from still another company. Long lead times build up in chain fashion. Here, for example, is an instance. Lockheed is the prime contractor for the C-141 military air-plane, which it makes at Marietta, Georgia. It buys jet thrust reversers from Rohr Aircraft of Chula Vista, California. In these reversers is a hy-draulic control system made by Borg-Warner in Chicago. One component of this system is made by the Fluid Regulator Co. of Painesville, Ohio. One item in this component is a casting made by Solon Industries of Solon, Ohio. This 5-lb. casting travels 4,700 miles before it reaches Marietta.

By dollar volume, 62 per cent of the C-141 is subcontracted out. By weight, 60 per cent is subcontracted. On this contract Lockheed has placed major contracts with 33 companies and other direct contracts with 1,200 companies. Some 6,000 suppliers are finally in on supplying its parts. In the case of Rohr, 49 per cent of its contract with Lockheed is further sub-contracted. The next layer subcontracts 40 per cent to still another, more remote layer of subcontractors. In each company, the production control department has to work closely with the next subcontractor below on all matters of scheduling the deliveries of the bought components.

DATA PROCESSING METHODS

Although computers have been moving in on manual methods for han-dling production control data, manual methods are by no means extinct.

The following table shows what an American Production and Inventory Control Society survey found so far as computer use in 1966 was concerned.[1]

TYPE OF INFORMATION	PERCENTAGE OF PLANTS USING THESE METHODS			
	MANUAL SYSTEMS	PUNCHED CARDS	PROGRAMS STORED IN COMPUTER	CONTROL BOARDS
Customer delivery schedules and order backlog	53	16	23	10
Production orders:				
Quantity and timing	59	13	24	12
Preparation	69	11	17	3
Detailed schedules for production departments	58	10	12	12
Follow-up reporting of progress on schedules	57	11	14	8
Inventory records for:				
Finished goods	40	18	27	2
Work in process	44	15	21	3
Raw materials	50	14	20	1
Order entry	41	24	27	5
Machine loading	45	8	11	9

USE OF OPERATIONS RESEARCH IN PRODUCTION CONTROL

In recent years operations research techniques have come of age, and they are now sometimes used in production control work. Several of the most applicable operations research techniques are described in later chapters of this book. Considering that these techniques sometimes are most helpful, it is surprising that they are not in more general use.

Yet the APICS 1966 survey showed little general use of operations research. Several long-established procedures, now thought of as operations research techniques, are the most popular. Economic order quantities were used in inventory control by 50 per cent of the companies and in production control by 30 per cent. A B C classifications were used by 50 per cent in inventory control and 20 per cent in production control.

[1] A survey of the production control practices of 573 plants, made by the American Production and Inventory Control Society and based on 626 answers from its members. Reported in "Exclusive Survey Shows New Directions in Production and Inventory Control," *Factory*, October, 1966.

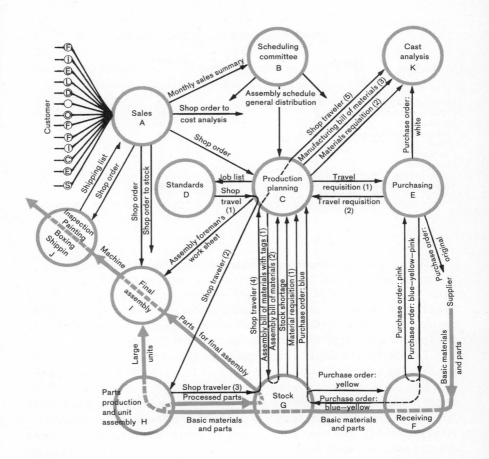

FIGURE 4-2 Flow of production control and related activities at Warner & Swasey Company. (Case Western Reserve University)

Two-bin systems were 25 and 5 per cent respectively. PERT was used in inventory control work by 4 per cent of the companies and in production control by 18 per cent.

Except for PERT, all of these procedures have been used for at least 50 years, long before the term operations research developed, and so are hardly part of the new science. Nor was PERT considered to be an operations research technique when it appeared in the late 1950s.

More specifically, operations research procedures were found by the APICS study to be used as follows:

| TECHNIQUE | PERCENTAGE OF COMPANIES USING TECHNIQUE | |
	FOR PRODUCTION CONTROL	FOR INVENTORY CONTROL
Line balancing	14	4
Exponential smoothing	9	18
Simulation	8	6
Linear programming	8	4
Queuing theory	8	1
Probability theory	7	10
Correlation	6	5
Game theory	4	4
Servo-mechanism theory	3	3

The nonuse of operations research was highlighted by the report of the widespread use of "plain judgment." Seventy per cent of the companies were reported to set inventory reserves by plain judgment. Fewer than half used reorder points. And although 90 per cent of the answering companies made assembled products, fewer than one-third of them used the requirements explosion process described in Chapter 32.

The merits of operation research seem to justify its more widespread use. Yet the APICS research study reported that in half of the companies that had done operations research, no improvements resulted. From answers it appears that in most companies a lack of communication exists between the operations research technicians and the men responsible for plant operations. The operations researchers are not where the problems are and the plant men don't know what the operations researchers can do for them.

STUDY MATERIALS

4-1   What factors should you consider when deciding whether to make or buy a part or component? Who is in the best position to evaluate the pros and cons and to decide? Would a committee be useful and, if so, who should be members?

4-2   What changes will the advent of "real time" computers have upon production control procedures? Will the effect be the same on both small and large companies?

4-3   Indicate how the various types of production control procedures discussed in this chapter might be applied to nonmanufacturing activities.

4-4   The plant manager is on the telephone calling you, the purchasing agent, about production hold-ups. He says that several jobs are being held up in the factory from lack of purchased parts arriving. He has just called the supplier who has told him that there is no reason for the delay. The supplier could easily have gotten the parts delivered if he had only known that you wanted them.

    What happened was that because of production trouble with materials, an unusual number of items were spoiled in process and more were needed. The factory's production control department, being forbidden to call suppliers direct, had called the buyer in the purchasing department asking for a rush shipment. But the buyer was out sick with a cold for two days and didn't get the call and missed learning about it when he came back.

    Should the factory's production control department ever call suppliers direct? What reasons are there for and against their doing this?

4-5   The Superior Sheet Metal Company (100 employees) makes heating and ventilating equipment. The manufacturing activities are confined to the manufacture of sheet metal pipes, ducts, etc., and of supports and attachments to hold the ducts in place. Items such as motors, dust collection tanks, cloth dust collection sacks, fans, and other accessory items are bought.

    Manufacturing is segregated into two departments. The "fabricating" department includes shears, brakes for bending sheet metal, punch presses, and die presses. The "assembly" department includes assembly and erection of the equipment. Operations performed include assembly, welding, grinding, painting, and crating for shipment. Large items are assembled with nuts and bolts to be sure that they fit and are then disassembled for shipment. During final assembly on the job the nuts and bolts are replaced by rivets and welding.

    The company is troubled with frequent shortages of parts on the assembly floor and occasionally at the point of installation. The short materials are generally purchased items.

    The following production control procedure is used: Upon receipt of a customer's order it is first sent to the engineering department where it is given a number. Usually the order is accompanied by drawings and specifications from the customer. The engineering department checks these and clarifies or supplements the instructions received and sends them to the superintendent. He looks them over and sends them to the foreman of the fabricating department, who makes up a list of the materials required. Upon completion of the parts, he sends them to the assembly department, where they are held until all are received.

    No parts lists are made up, nor are any operation tickets of any sort used. The foreman issues instructions to the workers by showing the lead man of a group the drawings and telling him the quantity and kind of pieces wanted. For parts to be purchased, he tells the storekeeper what is needed. The storekeeper then orders these items. Supply items and small parts, such as welding rods, paint, nuts and bolts, rivets, etc., are stocked regularly and reordered by the storekeeper when the supply gets low.

    Sometimes he runs out of certain items because of failure to order or, more frequently, because certain jobs require unusual quantities of one or two items. These shortages, of course, hold up production. At times, too, he does not order special items required to be purchased. Invariably when this happens the foreman of the fabricating department has not told him to order them but claims that he has. Occasionally the foreman tells him to buy certain items and then decides to make them in the department after all, with the result that duplicates are on hand. Only once has the superintendent heard of this happening, but he suspects that it has occurred more often.

How complex a production control system can you afford in a small company? Can you afford to do without a production control procedure even in a small company? Where would you start if you were told to put a production control system in at the Superior Sheet Metal Company? Would you make up bills of materials? Operations lists? Would you schedule jobs on individual machines? How would you handle the shortage of parts problem?

chapter five

THE PRODUCTION CONTROL ORGANIZATION

PRODUCTION CONTROL IN SMALL COMPANIES

Small companies sometimes have so little production control work to do that there is no department; possibly not even one full-time person is assigned to it. Most companies with fewer than 100 employees, for example, have no full-time man assigned to production control. But somewhere in the 100 to 200 employee range, it usually becomes necessary to assign one or more employees to full-time production control work.

In small companies making standard products, incoming orders usually come to an order receiving man in the sales department. Normally he orders the items that can be shipped out of stock to be sent. For items not in stock he issues manufacturing orders directly to the factory superintendent. He also issues manufacturing orders directly to the factory superintendent for new supplies of any products whose stock is running low. The superintendent passes on the orders to the foremen who get the products made. There is no production control department as such.

In some companies making "engineering type" products (dust collecting and ventilating systems for industrial buildings, for example), the engineering department actively assists in getting contracts and in discussing design features and prices with customers. When you receive an order in such a company, the engineering department checks it over and makes up final drawings showing the product's contours, dimensions, wiring diagrams, etc. The orders and the accompanying drawings go directly to the plant superintendent who after looking them over sends them on to the foreman. Questions concerning details or methods are worked out by the foreman and superintendent, and when necessary, the engineering department.

In small companies, procedures for transferring information can be simple. The few established routines can be changed easily. Problems are handled by personal discussion among those concerned, so paper work is kept to a minimum. This works quite well in small companies.

On the other hand, this very lack of formal procedures in small companies is a weakness. Small companies let their customers down more often than big companies. Often they are careless about meeting delivery promise dates. They depend on foremen to do most of the planning but some foremen don't do it well. They are either too busy or incapable of planning well. Nearly complete jobs are sometimes held up for lack of a minor part which has been overlooked. More formal procedures, although more costly clerically, would improve this situation. Sometimes small companies keep so few records that they can't tell customers how their jobs are coming along without going out in the shop to see.

PRODUCTION CONTROL IN MEDIUM–SIZED COMPANIES

You don't have to be very big to make formal production control procedures necessary. Certainly you arrive at this point long before you get up to 1,000 employees. In medium-sized companies (say those with 1,000 to 3,000 employees), production control work (including stock-room operation and internal transportation) requires from 25 to 100 employees, perhaps more. By this time you are so big that you divide the production control group into several specialized small groups, each with limited functions to perform. And you have to pass information around on written forms. In medium-sized companies, however, you still have considerable personal contact between groups performing different functions. Minor problems can be handled quickly, so coordination is ordinarily easy to achieve.

As companies grow in size certain functions are split off from the production control department. The *finished products* inventory is usually controlled by the production control department in small companies but not in large ones. Somewhere, as a company grows, control over the finished products inventory is separated and taken out of the hands of production control.

Control of *raw materials* stocks, too, is more likely to be under production control in small companies than in large. But this function is not separated out so soon nor so commonly as is the finished products inventory. It stays in the production control department even in some large companies.

Original planning for production (figuring out how to make products for the first time) also tends to emerge as a separate function. In many medium-sized companies original planning is done by a separate group within the production control department. In others it is outside the production control department altogether.

Production control procedures of medium-sized plants of multi-plant companies tend to be more formalized than they are in independent plants of equal size. One reason is that the officials of medium-sized captive plants have worked in the company's larger plants and they like the greater degree of control that usually comes from more fully developed procedures.

ORDER DEPARTMENTS   Medium-sized companies which make mostly standard products largely to stock but partly to order often have an "order department" or "order desk." Manufacturers of nuts and bolts, for example, often use this arrangement.

All incoming orders come to the "order desk" where there is a record of all finished stocks on hand. There a clerk checks the customers' orders against the stocks of the items on hand and makes out shipping orders for those that can be shipped out of stock.

Orders for regular items whose stock is too low to allow their filling are held up until the factory replenishes their stocks. Requests to the factory to make replenishment stocks normally come to the production control department, however, from the finished stock supervisor, and not directly from the order desk.

Orders for nonstandard products are usually handled differently. By

FIGURE 5-1 Incoming order receiving file at Bethlehem Steel. The rotary arrangement allows quick access to the orders by the order handling clerks, which results in their quick shipment. Orders to make special steel can get to the mill and often it can be made and shipped the same day if the order arrives before 1 p.m. (Bethlehem Steel Corp.)

"nonstandard" we mean that the item is a little different from regular items that the company normally makes. They may not be truly non-standard. If you made nuts and bolts of steel but not of brass, a request to make some of brass would be nonstandard to you.

The order department supervisor would decide whether you should go ahead and make the items or not and at what price. If the variation from standard is only slight, the order desk supervisor would estimate its cost himself and decide whether to accept the order and what price to quote to the customer. But if the item were noticeably different, then he would check with the engineering department and with the sales department to see how the product would be made, what it would cost, and whether the company ought to get into making such products.

PRODUCTION CONTROL IN LARGE COMPANIES

Large companies (say 10,000 employees and up) are invariably multi-plant companies, sometimes operating 50 or more separate plants. Certain parts of their production control work are done at the central office, but other parts of production control are done at major divisional headquarters, and some is done at individual plants.

Most of the time these companies are organized into major divisions, each of which makes and sells a whole product line. Here are a few of General Electric's many divisions: Motor and Generator, Switchboard and Control, Locomotive, X-ray, Chemical, Carbaloy, Construction Material, Measurements and Industrial Products, Lamps, Air Conditioning, Electronics, GE Appliances, Aircraft Gas Turbines, and Ordnance Systems. There just isn't any connection at all among most of these divisions so far as production control is concerned.

Giant companies are usually like GE. There are almost no production control relationships *between* divisions. Even when one division buys parts from another, its orders are often scheduled and handled just about the same as are the orders of outside customers.

INTERDIVISIONAL RELATIONSHIPS   But before we conclude that there are no production control relationships between divisions of multi-plant companies, let's look at General Motors. Chevrolet is one of GM's divisions. Chevrolet does have some relations with other GM divisions. Chevrolet bodies are by Fisher, ignition systems come from Delco-Remy, spark plugs from A-C, transmissions from GM's transmission division, and so on. In GM, giant though it is, there are many interdivisional production control contacts.

Whenever you find sister plants in a seller and buyer relationship with each other, the needs of one plant become the production schedules of the other. The interrelationships sometimes become quite complex. Parts-making plants usually supply *several* sister plants, not just one. A-C spark plugs go in *all* GM cars, not just Chevrolets. The same is true of Delco wiring systems. The needs of all sister plants, not just one, become the production schedules for parts-making plants. A-C's and Delco's schedules have to mesh with those of all GM's automobile factories.

The problem is, in fact, more complicated. Parts-making plants often sell on the outside too. A-C sells spark plugs to any number of outside dealers who sell them to you and me for replacement in our cars. And A-C sells spark plugs to other companies which make such items as farm tractors, power lawn mowers, and motorboats. So A-C's production schedules end up being only partly set by the needs of its sister GM plants. Production schedules must consider sister plant needs and other needs as well.

Also, on the using end, multi-plant relationships are not simple. Chevrolet and Buick plants get parts from everywhere. They make some of their own parts, they buy other parts from sister plants, and they buy still other parts from outside GM. Placing the orders and setting delivery schedules gets to be a big job.

LOCKHEED'S PRODUCTION CONTROL ORGANIZATION   Production control organizations in large companies are too complex to show on any chart small enough for us to show here. Yet we can get some idea of the operation from an oversimplified chart. Figure 5-2 shows such a greatly simplified chart of the production control organization at the Lockheed-California Company in Burbank.

At Lockheed-California, the several production managers direct all in-plant fabrication of parts, assembly of aircraft, and the production control work associated with these activities. Each of the subordinate duties listed under a department heading on figure 5-2 is the work of one or more subordinate departments.

Master schedules are set by a master schedule department, which reports directly to the president. The master schedules it sets are the basis for the work of the operations control department. This department is a staff department reporting directly to the director of operations. An unusual feature is the way this department connects up with lower echelons. Notice in figure 5-2 that the main upward chain of command in manufacturing goes from the directors of operations to production managers, on to works managers, and then to division managers.

Each type of airplane is assembled by a separate division under its

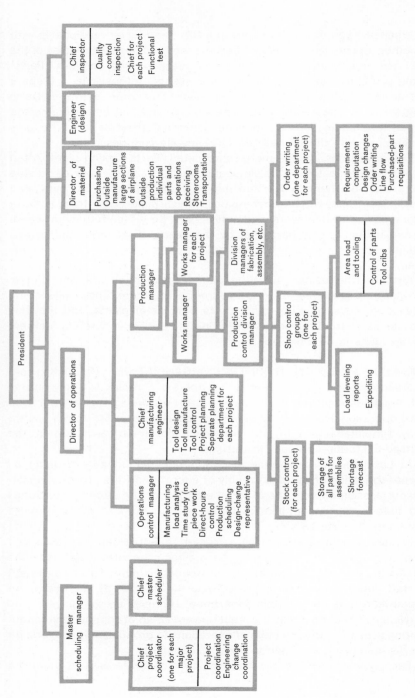

FIGURE 5-2 Organization chart of the production control department at Lockheed Aircraft's Burbank plant. (Lockheed Aircraft Corp.)

own works manager. Each has its own production control department and its own fabrication division. Production control directs and controls all fabrication and assembly operations on its product. But no assembling division makes its own parts.

The operations control department deals with overall department work loads. It sets programs which give the departments reasonable work loads and which will meet the master schedule's requirements. Schedules are set by means of the "indent" system described in Chapter 20.

Orders are released well ahead of the time the products are to be made. The shop control groups can then plan their work force size and hours of work for the various shops several weeks ahead. This method allows considerable flexibility in starting orders through the shop. If certain orders which are supposed to be started cannot be worked on for some reason, other orders can be pushed ahead to keep the shop busy. Meanwhile, extra effort can be exerted to get the held-up orders into production, and once in production to hurry them through so that they will be finished on time.

Original work routing at Lockheed is done by the manufacturing engineering departments and not by the production control department. Purchasing is the responsibility of a director of materiel who also has charge of receiving and storing of all raw materials and procured parts.

INTERNATIONAL HARVESTER COMPANY   International Harvester has a central production control department which serves the whole company as a means for controlling supplies and inventory. Within this department are four subordinate departments: estimate and order review, order and distribution, materials control, and divisional supply and inventory.

The first three are company-wide staff organizations which establish procedures, methods, and standards for company-wide supply and inventory operations. Divisional managers of supply and inventory have to carry out company-wide policies at the plant level.

The estimate and order review department makes sales forecasts and estimates for the whole company. The materials control department, through the divisional supply and inventory organization, converts sales estimates into production programs and sees that they are carried out. This department also controls all factory inventories except finished products. The order and distribution department is responsible for the distribution of finished products and for finished products themselves.

Each plant has a stores and production department under the direction of materials control. Each plant also has its own materials controller who sees that the plant schedules meet the overall program set by central materials control.

OTIS ELEVATOR COMPANY   Like International Harvester, Otis Elevator has a central department which does certain production control work.

Elevator components are mostly standard assemblies. Planning starts at Otis as soon as a contract is signed. An abstract summarizing the contract's requirements is made out and sent to the master scheduling department. The department lists the major components and adds them to the order load for the plants where the components will be made. The projected loads are called "forecasts" but they don't authorize manufacture. The master scheduling department schedules the engineering and "specifying" work.

Otis's specifying department is a little unusual. Its work is normally done in planning departments (or in "preplanning" departments) in other companies. It receives from sales the contract and all the drawings and details agreed upon. These are the parent documents from which all other documents are made. The specifying department takes the contract and translates parts descriptions into the Otis company terminology. (Some companies call this "dressing the order.") Then they make up "order forms" listing the subassemblies and parts needed.

All of this is done in the central office. The "specified" contract then goes to the factories to their "order and distribution" desks. The order desk man "calls out" (gets from engineering) the drawings. He also makes up orders for special items to be made. Drawings for standard components are held until their release to the factory is indicated on the weekly schedules issued by the central office. Once on this schedule, the factory goes ahead with making the assemblies. Thereafter, production control follows the usual order control procedures required to get products pushed through the factory.

CENTRAL PRODUCTION CONTROL WORK IN LARGE COMPANIES
Although the specific work done by company-wide production control staffs varies a great deal between companies, here are four activities they would normally carry on:

1 A central production control department serves as a functional overseer of production control departments in lower echelons, even in divisions making unlike products. It sees that lower groups get help when they need it and that they use good procedures. Men from the central office visit the different divisions and plants and go over their problems with them, making suggestions for improvement. Central production control may also run training classes and it may recommend promotional transfers of production control men across departmental or divisional lines.

2 Central production control meshes together the proposed schedules of different divisions and sees that master production schedules of all the divisions concerned are feasible and workable, particularly when one division supplies another.

3 Central production control keeps track of work loads of various divisions and plants and, when necessary, shifts orders around to balance out operations. This work is more a matter of shifting work between plants of a division than it is of shifting work across divisional lines. An exception is where you have set up your divisions geographically, instead of by product line. You can shift orders from one geographical division to another but not from X-ray machines to dishwashers. Normally your divisions make such different products that you can't shift work back and forth between divisions.

4 You also need a central office to handle big multi-plant customers. Suppose that Alcoa sells a big order of sheet aluminum to Lockheed or to Boeing for airplanes. Lockheed wants some of its aluminum sent to Los Angeles, some to Atlanta, and the balance to other locations. Boeing wants its purchase sent to Seattle and other locations. You can allocate such orders to your plants better if you have a central department to watch plant loads and decide where to send particular orders.

HOME PLANTS   Many large companies have a "home" or "mother" plant. (General Electric at Schenectady, Westinghouse at East Pittsburgh, Eastman Kodak at Rochester, National Cash Register at Dayton, Caterpillar Tractor at Peoria, International Business Machines at Endicott.) The home plant is their oldest and biggest plant and it is where the company's home office is located. The mother plant production control department sometimes has to double in brass and serve as both the production control department for the main plant and also as the company-wide production control department on matters that need such a department. Particularly, you are likely to find the mother plant department serving in both capacities if it, the mother plant, supplies some parts to several or all other plants.

PRODUCTION CONTROL IN LARGE INDIVIDUAL PLANTS
Production control in large individual plants, whether they are independent companies or individual plants of multi-plant companies, is a big undertaking, usually requiring hundreds of employees. The production control department is divided into several major and minor departments, each with specific functions to perform.

All directions, instructions, agreements, schedules, schedule changes, and design changes have to be in writing. You must set up and follow formal procedures. Some large companies prepare instruction manuals explaining their procedures. Such manuals sometimes are hundreds of pages long and may even run into several volumes. Special printed forms are designed to convey information through regular channels. Before schedules can become effective, they must be approved by the heads of all the departments that will have to work on them.

Production control departments in large companies are usually lim-

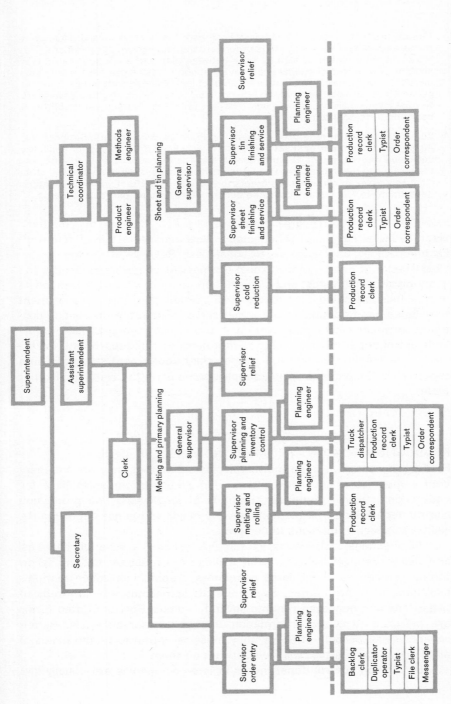

FIGURE 5-3 Organization chart of the production planning department of U.S. Steel's Fairless Works at Morrisville, Pa. (U.S. Steel Corp.)

ited strictly to production control functions. They rarely have any responsibility for cost estimating, ordering tools, or original planning. Nor do they operate the raw materials stockroom or have anything to do with purchasing.

Production control's policing function—keeping after engineering, purchasing, and other departments—is usually not as important in large companies. Instead, whenever two departments have to fit their work together, they meet and go over the work to be done and agree upon dates for completing each one's share of the work. The dates they agree upon are regarded as *promise dates and are binding*. Top management expects every department to meet its promise dates.

If engineering agrees to get drawings out by a certain date, it tries very hard to do it. If purchasing promises to have certain materials in the plant on definite dates, those materials are supposed to be there. The tool department is supposed to have tooling ready on time. In large companies, production control is not supposed to keep after other departments continually lest their work not be done. If departments don't meet their promise dates, *they have to answer to top management* for their failure. Top management knows that every time one department doesn't get its work done, all of the departments that depend on that work are held up.

Plant "loading" becomes an important production control function in large companies. Loading, discussed later, means seeing if the products to be made will keep the plant busy. The load of work in prospect for the plant and for individual departments may be too much or too little. Production control translates tentative schedules into their plant capacity requirements. If too much or too little work is in prospect, management is told. Usually the schedules are adjusted before master schedules are approved. Sometimes, though, management tells you to adjust the capacity and let the tentative schedule stand.

After master schedules are approved, production control makes up detailed plans of each department's manpower needs. These plans are used for budgeting and hiring new employees. A section of the production control department devotes its time to loading of this sort.

Large company production control departments are likely to have two main groups. One group *receives orders* to make things and the other *passes out shop directives*.

ORDER RECEIVING GROUPS IN THE PRODUCTION CONTROL DEPARTMENT   The order receiving group is subdivided by product line. Each product line has its production control staff. For example, an electrical appliance manufacturer might make dishwashers and washing machines in the same factory. Orders to make dishwashers go to one group in the production control department, orders for washing machines go to another group. Each specialized group in the production control department makes out parts and materials requirements lists for its products and sets schedules for getting parts made. If whole factory departments are devoted to making their line, they issue their directives to their shop departments.

Assembling is often done in departments specializing in one product line. But *parts* for several product lines are usually made on one or two large parts-making departments. When that is so, orders to make parts do not go directly to the parts-making departments. Instead the various product line staff groups (in the production control department) turn their parts-making orders over to a second kind of subordinate group in the production control department.

MANUFACTURING DEPARTMENT GROUPS IN THE PRODUCTION CONTROL DEPARTMENT This second group specializes by *manufacturing* departments. The control group for automatic screw machines, for example, gets shop orders and parts requirements lists from several product line planners. It meshes them together and comes up with a work schedule for the automatic screw machine department—a schedule that will make all the parts the different final products need.

A company making electrical accessories for home use might have several product lines but only one sheet metal shop. Orders for the sheet metal parts of cake mixers, roasters, waffle irons, coffee makers, and toasters are made up by the men in the product sections dealing with those items. The orders do not go directly to the sheet metal shop but rather to the production control section that makes up orders for the sheet metal shop.

The production control sheet metal group coordinates its orders and makes shop schedules. If the orders from product line sections call for too much work at certain times the shop control section will have to get the other groups to change their schedules.

PRODUCTION CONTROL GROUPS IN MANUFACTURING DEPART-MENTS Besides the two kinds of production control groups in the plant's central production control department, you need a production control group in every *manufacturing department*. These shop control groups normally work for the central production control department. But not in all companies. Sometimes they report to each shop's superintendent. That gives him more direct control over his shop and makes for efficient operations. But doing it this way leaves it up to the superintendent and his foremen to get jobs out. The foreman decides which orders to work on next, which specific machine will be used, and who will do the work. Foremen *must* get things done on time. Unless this is firmly impressed on them, they will not meet schedules and the operations of other departments will suffer.

PRODUCT LINE MANAGERS

Product line managers are common in large companies, particularly those making consumer products. Such companies make many related products in great volume and almost always, products are made to stock—not to order.

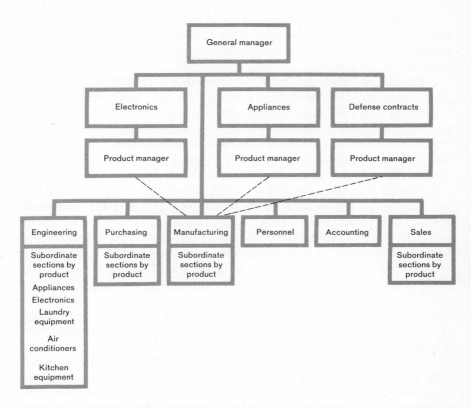

FIGURE 5-4 Chart showing how product line managers function in the electrical appliance division of a large electronics company.

A product line is a group of products serving the same or related purposes. Usually they are sold through the same marketing channels. Product line managers are common in companies making household appliances. A typical set of product lines might include refrigerators, kitchen ranges, water heaters, home freezers, radios, television sets, automatic washers, driers, air conditioners, kitchen cabinets, sinks, disposals, and dishwashers. One product line manager would have charge of all models and types of each of these product lines.

Product line managers are expected to see opportunities for developing new products in their lines. Working with the engineering department, they ask it to design new products which can be made for a cost that allows a reasonable selling price. Of course, management's approval must be obtained if very much money is to be spent for developing new products or tooling up for their production. Product line managers should also simplify their lines, avoiding too many grades, sizes, models, or other varieties.

Product line managers keep track of the inventories or products in their lines both at the factory and in the company warehouses around the country. They watch the sales and make out orders for more products when their stocks run low.

Product line managers plan and schedule the production of their finished products. At this point these are only "desired" schedules, not actual schedules. They pass these desired production schedules on to the appropriate order-receiving sections of the production control department. The production control group then breaks these schedules down into their parts and subassemblies requirements after which it passes the requirements lists to other production control groups serving the factory departments.

Product line managers do not coordinate their demands on the factory with each other. The manufacturing department groups in the production control department do this as they coordinate and develop work schedules for their factory departments. It is therefore possible for the total work load to be too much for factory departments to handle. If so, one or more of the product managers won't get all he asks for. This can cause friction because each manager is responsible for getting *his* product made. If such conflicts do arise the production control department tries to smooth things out and get everyone's orders out as fast as it can. Only after the desired schedules have been made to mesh with the possibility of meeting them do they become actual schedules.

You will recognize in this discussion the typical big plant arrangement of having two main groups in the production control department. The first group receives lists of products wanted from product line heads. This is the group we have been talking about above. The second main group, the men who pass out orders to the factory to make parts or to assemble products, has little to do directly with product line managers, unless the sum total of everyone's production orders is too great.

PROJECT DIRECTORS

Airplane companies have found that they need to appoint "project directors" to be responsible for each of their large contracts. These men, in a sense, have the right to operate a small company within the company so far as their project (usually a single multi-million dollar contract) is concerned.

The project director has the right to build up a small project staff of men who watch over the production of the contract. He can draw men out of other departments to set up this staff. During the existence of the contract they have overriding authority to push their contract's work through all departments concerned. While it might appear that this would make problems when two or more different contracts were being pushed and not all could be handled, this method seems to be very effective in securing the coordination necessary in making complex products. When conflicts arise, as they do occasionally, top management rules on priorities. At the conclusion of the contract the project director and his staff disband and return to other work.

THE PRODUCTION CONTROL DEPARTMENT'S SIZE

How big ought the production control department to be? There is no good answer. Of course it depends on the department's efficiency but it also depends on how many functions you assign to the department and how much variety there is in the work. In the author's experience, the ratio of production control workers to all employees has varied from 2 to 33 per cent.

The company with 2 per cent of its employees doing production control work assigned to the department only a few of the functions listed on pages 9 and 10. In the 33 per cent example, the department included almost every function listed and more. It even included tooling, plant maintenance, and industrial engineering. Another company with only 3 per cent of its employees in production control work (including industrial engineering) has 8 per cent of its employees in its purchasing department (an unusually high figure). But the purchasing department includes receiving, operation of the stock rooms, and shipping.

Every few years someone makes a survey of the number of people doing production control work. Usually the numbers vary a great deal, partly because of the different functions covered. A survey made in 1966, however, showed a considerable consistency, at least so far as size of company is concerned.[1] In small companies over 4 per cent of the employees did production and inventory control work. Many large companies got the figures down to 3 per cent.

SIZE OF PLANT, NUMBER OF EMPLOYEES	PERCENTAGE OF PRODUCTION AND INVENTORY CONTROL PEOPLE NEEDED
50–99	4.3
100–499	3.2
500–999	3.0
1,000–4,999	3.0
5,000+	4.1

Actually, ratios of from 4 to 8 per cent are common. If fewer than 4 per cent of the employees are engaged in production control, one of three things is indicated: (1) production control is being very efficiently done, (2) it is being done inadequately, or (3) very few functions are covered. If the production control department includes over 8 per cent of the employees the reverse of one or more of the above conditions applies. In the airplane and missile industries, for example, ratios of 10 to 15 per cent are the rule because of the extremely difficult problems which make so much extra production control work. High ratios are also found where product designs or schedules are changed often. Nonstandard parts also increase the ratio since their production takes more paper work than is needed for standard parts.

Sometimes business levels go up or down enough to vary the amount of production control work. Nonetheless most companies try not to add to or cut down on the size of the production control department to any great extent. When the staff gets swamped with orders, it works longer hours and puts aside all but today's work. Then when things lighten up they work normal hours and catch up on postponed jobs.

North American Rockwell handles such variations differently. It limits its production control staff to the needs of its minimum work load. Then during busy periods it transfers certain direct hourly paid workers (who have been trained for this work) to the production control department on a temporary basis. Later they go back to their regular production jobs.

[1] See "Exclusive Survey Shows New Directions in Production and Inventory Control," survey of American Production and Inventory Control Society, reported in *Factory*, October, 1966.

CONTROLLING PRODUCTION CONTROL COSTS

You should be careful about pressing too hard for low production control costs or you will cut costs at the expense of good control. Poor production control costs money in several ways that don't show directly. You get low production, high inventory of materials in process, and high setup costs due to unnecessary setups. You will often lose orders in process, miss meeting promise dates, have too many rush orders, and end up with your people being mad with each other and with disappointed customers.

Maybe this sounds as if we mean that you shouldn't even try to control production control costs. We don't mean this; we mean that economy-minded managers should watch to see that on-the-surface savings are not more than canceled out by under-the-surface losses. Production control costs money for salaries, office equipment, computer rental, printed forms, communication systems, and office space. Its costs, like those of other staff departments, need to be controlled because they tend to go up when business goes up and then not to come down when business falls off.

Budgeting seems to be the best way to control production control costs. Yet the production control work load doesn't fluctuate with business volume changes. Some of the bits and pieces of the work increase and decrease with changes in business volume but some don't.

Less volume, for example, usually means fewer and smaller orders, orders for one and two items. Fewer orders means less production control work, but orders for small quantities make almost as much production control work as orders for large quantities. Usually when business is bad you try to keep both raw materials and finished goods inventories as low as possible. The amount of production control work might actually increase because you make out frequent orders for small quantities of products.

Both IBM and McDonnell Douglas Aircraft, among others, try to set intelligent budgets by looking into the bits and pieces of the work. They find which are variable and go up and down with work loads, which are semivariable, and which are reasonably fixed. Then from future work schedules they can set good budgets.

Such attempts to control the costs of production control will undoubtedly become more widespread in the future because of the increase in the number of all office people, including production control. When 60 per cent of your work force is on white collar jobs (as is the case already at IBM's Poughkeepsie plant) you just must try to set reasonably accurate budgets for indirect labor. And since the proportion of office workers is growing everywhere, the IBM–McD-D method will surely become more common.

Most companies try to judge whether or not the production control staff is doing a good job by using various ratios. One such ratio is "performance against schedule," meaning the ratio between orders behind schedule and total orders. Sometimes this ratio is refined to show also how late the orders are. One order behind schedule 20 days is more serious than 10 orders each behind 1 day. Other ways to try to judge the effectiveness of production control work include keeping overtime down and machine utilization ratios.

Besides these measures of the effectiveness of production control there are several measures of inventory management, such as inventory turnover, dollar investment, volume of dollars of obsolete items, return on investment in inventories, and volume of dollars in surplus items.

Besides these there are several measures of delivery performance. These include percentage of items delivered on time, age of past due items, percentage of volume delivered on time, percentage of dollars delivered on time.

None of these measures is a wholly accurate measure of the effectiveness of production and inventory control. Yet they are better than no measures at all and are commonly used.

STUDY MATERIALS

5-1   What are the advantages and disadvantages of having the production control organization a part of the manufacturing organization? Where else might it be placed on the corporate organization chart?

5-2   Would your answer to problem 1 be the same no matter whether the company was organized on a functional basis or on a product line basis?

5-3   Select one of the production types discussed in Chapter 1 or Chapter 2, and indicate the information flow necessary for the system to function properly. What information is needed? Where does it come from? What has to be done with it? What use is made of it? What is the role of the production control department in this work?

5-4   For the system you picked when answering problem 3, what should be the goals of the production control organization? Are there any potential areas of conflict with the goals of the engineering, marketing, or other departments of the whole corporation? Indicate possible solutions to any areas of conflict.

5-5   You are an industrial engineer and the plant manager has asked you to develop some kind of a report which will help him to judge the effectiveness of the way production control work is done in your company. He proposes that you set up a series of indexes for each of the following:

1   Value of inventory
    a   On hand
    b   On order

2 Number of orders placed in a period
   a Purchase orders
   b Shop orders
   c Assembly orders
3 Number of orders outstanding
4 Number and value of:
   a Current purchases
   b Stock shortages or "outages"
   c Behind time orders

Go ahead with your assignment. Reject any or all of his suggestions, giving reasons why. Or add others and justify them. In your answer don't overlook the main problem: How can the manager judge the effectiveness of the production control work being done?

5-6 The Sylvester Products Company made small but complex accessories for machinery used by other metalworking companies. For years the company followed a policy of employing only graduate engineers in production control work as well as designing work. There were occasional differences of opinion between staff members of the two departments concerning how products should be made.

The attitude on the part of the production control staff was often expressed in such remarks as: "Why don't the engineers design it so that we can make it the best way?" "Why don't they design it so it will work?" "Why do they want such a close tolerance?" The engineers in the engineering department countered with "Don't you fellows have enough of your own work to do? Why don't you just make it the way it says and never mind about how it will work?" "If you make it right it will work."

How would you suggest improving this situation? Would your answer be any different if the production control staff members were not engineers by training but had had considerable experience in production control work?

5-7 The cost accounting department of Greenway, Inc., manufacturers of stamped sheet metal products, asked the production control department to change its forms so that they would provide cost accounting information. The change requested called for providing spaces on job tickets for reporting the time spent setting up jobs and tearing down setups. Setup and teardown work was done by the machine operators themselves and was paid for at a rate approximating 90 per cent of the operators' piecework earnings.

The job tickets were changed accordingly, although it made extra work for the production control department's dispatch clerks. It also interfered somewhat with the scheduling of jobs, since the operators rang off the job and in on machine teardown time at clocks close to their work places without reporting immediately to production control that the job was done. Only after the teardown was complete did they ring out and report the job completion to the dispatch office. The production control department consequently did not receive immediate notification of jobs completed.

The cost accounting department was, however, well pleased with the arrangement. Soon it requested another change. It was suggested that the production control department enter its estimate of the proper time for machine setup and teardown time on the tickets. It was suggested also that the dispatch clerk subtract clock ring-in times from ring-out times and record the time taken on all jobs and machine setups and teardowns. And lastly, it was suggested that the production control department collect all job tickets and materials requisitions, extend the costs, and sum them up before forwarding them to the cost department.

What responsibility does the production control department have to cooperate with the cost accounting department? Which department should do each part of the work referred to in the paragraph above? Would a combination of the cost accounting department and the production control department be illogical? Why?

chapter six

FORECASTING

THE NEED TO FORECAST

Good forecasts are important in controlling production because missing the mark costs money. If you underestimate you run out of stock and lose sales. If you overestimate you are caught with big inventories which cost money to carry or which may have to be sold at marked-down prices.

Forecasts give you a preview of your income and profit so that you can set budgets. They provide a basis for inventory planning and for financial planning. Maybe they will show that you should expand your company. If so, you may need to plan to secure money for more machines and more working capital.

Production control starts when you decide how many of each product to make. If you manufacture only to order you don't have to do a great deal of forecasting of what to make because you make what your customers order. Nonetheless you still need to do some forecasting of your future level of activity so you will be prepared for future ups and downs.

Many companies, however, make almost everything to stock so they must forecast in considerable detail. Such companies make products before they are sold, before knowing whom they will be sold to, or indeed before knowing how many of them it will be possible to sell. And because it takes a long time to get materials and make them into parts and assemble them into products, these companies have to decide in February what products will be completed in August for sale in September. So, in February they try to figure out what their September sales will be.

Curiously, many companies don't consider that they are forecasting when they decide what to make months before the products will be finished. If you ask them whether they forecast, many will say no. The American Management Association some time ago surveyed the forecasting practices of 45 companies: 25 of them said that they watched economic trends and did a thorough job of forecasting; the other 20 were vague and didn't claim to do any forecasting at all. Yet answers to other questions showed that they did forecast although some did it only roughly. Some companies just try to reduce inventories when the business horizon looks cloudy. Others rely largely on the consensus of the opinions of their top officials—"the jury of executive opinion."

Still another survey, this one by the American Production and Inventory Society,[1] showed the following:

TECHNIQUE	PERCENTAGE OF COMPANIES USING
Sales manager's estimate	67
Past sales projected but adjusted by latest sales information	50
Executive opinion	49
Marketing analysis	28
Trend and cycle analysis	25
Expected share of the market	23
Correlation with economic indicator	22
Exponential smoothing	12
Charts with control limits	11

The relatively small use of sophisticated techniques is difficult to interpret. Survey results indicate that in some companies certain such techniques have been tried and then discarded. But there is much more evidence that a great many companies just have never tried them. The APICS study, for example, found half of the respondents recommending the use of better techniques, more education and training for their production and inventory control staffs, and the need for more accurate and dependable forecasts. Three-quarters of the respondents said that their company's production and inventory control procedures were not as good as they should be. In summary, therefore, it seems that sophisticated techniques merit more common use than is found.

Perhaps such methods would improve the reliability of forecasts so that there wouldn't be so many poor forecasts. Then everyone could have more confidence in them and you wouldn't get results such as those shown in figure 6-1. Figure 6-1 shows the near-future forecasts made by machinery companies in the United States of their sales from 1956 to 1965. Section 1 of figure 6-1 shows their forecasts for the next quarter ahead. The dotted lines and dots at the ends show where the forecasts made at the time expected sales to be for the next quarter. Section 2 is the summation of forecasts for two quarters ahead. Sections 3 and 4 look ahead three and four quarters, respectively.

Notice how wrong the year-ahead forecasts in 1963, 1964, and 1965 were. Every forecast said, "A year from now we'll have the same amount of business we have now." Yet the orders of these companies went up by 75 per cent in these three years. Even the forecasts for one and two quarters ahead were always considerably too low during these three years.

Several years ago when frozen orange juice caught on, the whole tin can–making industry was caught napping. Not one company foresaw it in its forecasts. Yet cans for frozen orange, lemon, and other juices grew

[1] Reported in "Exclusive Survey Shows New Directions in Production and Inventory Control," *Factory*, October, 1966. A report of the practices of 573 plants, as reported in a survey made by the American Production and Inventory Control Society.

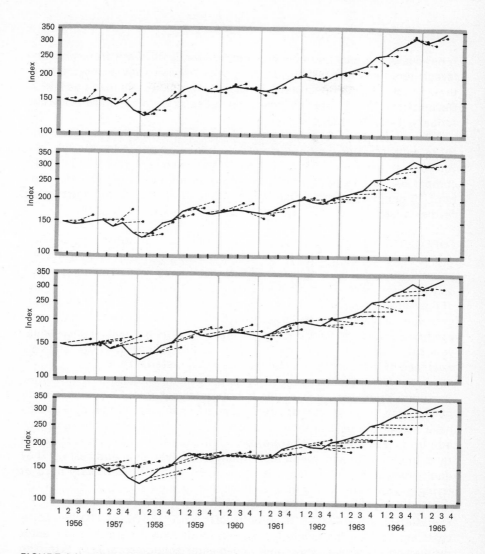

FIGURE 6-1 Ten-year record of machinery companies' forecasts of their near future business. (Machinery and Allied Products Institute)

quickly to a $35 million a year business. And several years ago one can company wrongly forecast a heavy consumer demand for cone-topped beer cans. Its competitor who banked on flat-topped cans ran away with the business.

Why are forecasts not better? Why are they not more reliable? Probably the most important reason is just the unpredictability of customers.

What customers buy and how much is frequently different from what the forecasters think they will buy. In 1965, color television set sales were more than double the manufacturers' forecasts, even forecasts made as late as December of 1964. Yet in 1967 television set sales were one-third below the January, 1967, expectations.

The hazards of forecasting don't, however, mean that you shouldn't try to do it. Most of the time you will be better prepared for the future if you rely on an imperfect forecast than if you have no forecast at all. Most companies are able to forecast their business for a year ahead within perhaps 20 per cent of the actual figure although individual items are often farther afield.

FORECASTS AS GOALS   Forecasts are previews of future sales. But they are more than previews; they are sales programs and sales goals. An approved forecast is an objective. It is a goal that you can sometimes reach only by trying hard. Rarely is it so easy to reach as were the 1965 forecasts of the sales of color television sets. Normally you won't achieve the forecast goal without advertising and sales effort. Nor will you get there unless your product designs and your prices are right. And if, as the season goes along, your sales lag behind the forecast, you redouble your sales effort. The very existence of sales forecasts helps make sales materialize.

Manufacturers of automobiles, soap, household appliances, and other consumer products use forecasts to help them set goals. Automobile companies know to the hundredth decimal point what share of the market they have had in the past. If their forecasts, built up from within the company, add up to less than that share of the total market for next year, they just raise the forecast and spend more money on advertising and selling. They don't always get the added sales they want, but they work very hard at trying to reach the high goal they have set for themselves.

FORECASTS AS BASES FOR PRODUCTION CONTROL ACTIONS   Forecasts are the starting points for making production programs and master production schedules. Programs and master schedules are, in turn, the bases for placing purchase orders, planning the factory production, and providing the men, machines, and tooling accessories needed.

You may have to place certain purchase orders a long time ahead, sometimes even before you make up factory schedules. And when you do have to place orders far ahead you do it on the basis of the forecast since you can't wait until you have firm factory schedules.

There are three reasons why you might have to place orders very early. First, if the vendor has to do much special work on your order he has to design and get special tooling and that takes time. Placing orders well ahead is particularly important for bought components being made for the first time because it takes so much time for your suppliers to decide on, obtain, and install the machinery and tools to make them.

Second, if your supplier has to order special components from his suppliers, this takes time too, maybe months. Notice, in figure 6-2, how lead times stretch out when you buy from a supplier, who buys parts from someone else, who buys raw materials from someone else. Remember, too, the example given on page 71 of the travels of the casting in the jet reverser for Lockheed's C-141 airplanes.

Third, maybe your supplier is swamped with orders. Your order has to wait its turn. During the first half of 1964, you had to wait three months for rolled steel. Steel-using companies that didn't order way ahead found their production being held up from lack of materials.

So, as we said, although forecasts for distant months are somewhat tentative, *they must be used to authorize all long lead time activities.* Only those activities which must be started early are, however, authorized on the basis

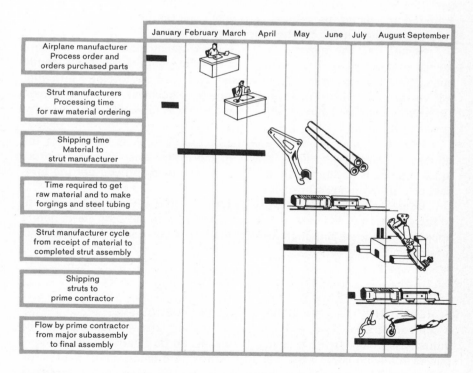

FIGURE 6-2 Chart of activities that go on during the long lead time that it takes to get some parts, in this case, part of an airplane's landing gear.

of tentative forecasts because they usually change at least a little before they firm up into factory schedules.

Actually, placing orders way ahead for long lead time items doesn't always mean that you will make very many changes. In February, General Motors can order sheet steel for automobiles to be made in August, and can do it with reasonable safety even though it doesn't know in February exactly how many of each model of car it will build in August. The quantity of sheet steel used isn't affected much by normal variations in the product mix. Nor does it hurt much not knowing exactly how many cars in total will be made. The steel mills are willing to adjust your order quantities up or down within reasonable limits.

GENERAL PATTERNS OF FORECASTING
There are two quite different ways to make sales forecasts for business use. One is to go from the general to the specific and the other is to go from the specific to the general. You might call the first "top-down" forecasting and the second "bottom-up" forecasting.

Going from the general to the specific (going down from the top) means that you first make a forecast of future general business conditions, then develop an industry forecast. Next you try to figure out what will be your company's share of the industry's business. Lastly, after you get a company total figure, you fragmentize it into forecasts of the sales of specific products.

The other way, from the specific to the general, is going from the bottom up. You first make forecasts of the future sales of specific products. Then sum up the individual product forecasts and you get the forecast of your company's business.

Probably it is better not to use either method, top-down or bottom-up, to the exclusion of the other. Most companies try to get both views before adopting a forecast, although most of their attention goes to using internal information.

FORECASTING THE INDUSTRY'S FUTURE BUSINESS
A company's sales, in any short period, depend largely upon how well its industry is doing. If the industry flourishes, so do nearly all of the companies in the industry. If the industry suffers hard times, so do most of the companies. Most companies, therefore, are much interested in forecasts of their industry's future.

Unfortunately you can't always get industry figures with which to compare your own because there isn't really any "industry." General Electric, for example, makes light bulbs, but there isn't any light bulb industry. Minnesota Mining makes Scotch tape but there isn't any cellophane tape industry.

Giant companies also have problems from being in many industries each of which needs to be forecast separately. General Electric is in the household appliance, railroad locomotive, electrical machinery, jet engine, and other industries.

Whenever a company (or a division of a giant company) is in a specific industry there may be industry figures available. For many industries you can get forecasts from the U.S. Department of Commerce and other government departments. Also, many private organizations, particularly trade associations, continually publish their views on the future of certain individual industries. Business magazines, too, predict the future of individual industries.

Moreover, a company's forecasters can keep informed through personal contact with others in the industry. They can attend association and trade group meetings and conferences—both to hear experts speak and to exchange views about the industry's future with executives of other companies.

A few industries have a little easier job. Their business tends to follow, in a predictable way, some other industry's sales. Manufacturers of plumbing supplies can, for example, expect that the ups and downs in residential construction will be reflected in their business. By checking on the number and value of building permits being issued today they get a preview of their sales a few months ahead. They also watch the total value of contracts awarded for new commercial and industrial buildings and get a preview of sales in those areas.

In other cases there is a close correlation between an industry's business and some other economic indicator. Automobile sales, for example, move up and down with changes in the gross national product and consumers' spendable income. Such correlation may not help you as much as you might think. If your industry moves up and down with the GNP you still have to forecast the GNP in order to know where your industry is going. The gain that you may get stems from the fact that a lot of high-calibered men are making their living (in the government and in other agencies) trying to forecast the series you are interested in.

Certain industries' business is "derived" business. It ties in with, and is dependent on, another industry's business. The plumbing supply business mentioned above, in so far as it applies to new construction, is an example. Companies manufacturing automobile parts are another example. They make parts for new cars and repair parts for old cars. Their new car business depends upon new car sales. Plate glass manufacturers, another example, depend upon both the construction industry and the automobile industry. Industries whose business derives from that of other industries can look at the sales forecasts for their customer industries when making their own forecasts.

FORECASTING INDIVIDUAL PRODUCT DEMAND

Companies making hundreds or thousands of kinds of products individually forecast only the sales of their very highest volume items. The sales of all other products are forecast by class of product using dollar or tonnage figures. You would spend too much money on forecasting if you tried to forecast individually the future sales of thousands of products.

In spite of what we have just said, however, many companies which do their inventory control work on computers do a crude sort of forecasting for many or even for all of the items which are controlled by computers. We describe how they do this in Chapter 16 on inventory control. It is only one-, two-, and three-month ahead forecasting and it is not very sophisticated forecasting but the computer does it at low cost and where it is applicable it has proved to be quite worthwhile.

When forecasting individual product sales (or when forecasting the sales of classes of products) you could use statistical procedures such as are described in Chapter 16. But even if you did, you would surely also want to use whatever added information you can get.

You would surely look at your records of past sales figures by product groups, by sales territory, by type of sales account, by type of outlet, and by "end-use" customer groups. By studying carefully the trends in past figures, you can eliminate the effects of "one-shot" windfall sales or of materials shortages or other things that keep past sales figures from being valid as indicators of future sales.

You ought also to pay attention to the "grass-roots" information coming in from salesmen and distributors. You can learn a great deal from your men out in the field about conditions in their territories and the buying plans of customers in their areas. Of course, you have to discount what they tell you somewhat because salesmen are usually too optimistic, but you can still learn a lot about local conditions from them.

STATISTICAL FORECASTING TECHNIQUES

Several statistical techniques are available to aid forecasters as they make their projections of future business. Forecasters may be able to develop a conceptual scheme, or model, which takes into account the various forces at work. Such procedures may be used to forecast the industry's future or even the sales prospects of a company's big bread and butter product lines.

Actual results in every industry are the result of the interaction of longtime trends, of cycles, of seasonal patterns, and of random factors. It is sometimes possible, by analyzing past data, to "decompose" them and to separate out each of these underlying forces and see how each one operates. If you can, from past data, isolate out the way these factors operate, you can then make projections of each into the future and then recompose them into a composite total projection. So long as the underlying causal factors continue unchanged, such projections produce fairly good forecasts.

TREND ANALYSIS   Whenever you are forecasting the sales of products for which you have data for five years or more in the past you can calculate a trend line which often is helpful in making projections of future business. The "least squares" method is perhaps the most satisfactory method for calculating the trend.[2]

THE LEAST SQUARES METHOD: FIRST DEGREE LINES   The least squares method is one which allows for computing trend lines (or lines of "best fit"), either straight or curved. If the original data seem to follow a straight line, then the least squares formula for a straight line should be used, but if the data tend to follow a curve, then the formula for a curved line should be used.

The formula for any straight line is

$$Y = a + bX$$

where Y = the variable we wish to predict or the "dependent variable"
   a = the intercept of the equation of the Y axis
   b = the slope of the line, or the amount of change that occurs every year
   X = the year, the "independent variable"

When using least squares to calculate a straight line trend, the Y series is the sales volume and X is time in years (or months). The two constants in the formula for a straight line, a and b, have to be calculated by solving the following two simultaneous "normal" equations:

I $$\Sigma Y = Na + b\Sigma X$$
II $$\Sigma XY = a\Sigma X + b\Sigma X^2$$

[2] An alternative procedure, the "moving average" method for studying the directional movement of a series, is less satisfactory in trend analysis because the averages always lag behind. You have to extrapolate just to bring moving averages up to the current period and then extrapolate again in order to get figures for future periods.

In these equations ΣY is the total sales for all of the years concerned and N is the number of years. ΣX is the sum of the year numbers which, in order to simplify the calculation, are usually called years 1, 2, 3, etc., and not 1966, 1967, 1968, etc. ΣXY is obtained by multiplying each year's sales volume by its year number and then summing up these products. ΣX^2 is obtained by squaring each year number and then getting the total of these squares.

Although it is not hard to calculate the values of a and b from these equations, the job is made easier if you number the years from the center. Years before the middle year become years number -1, -2, -3, etc., and the years after are years $+1$, $+2$, $+3$, etc. The middle year is year 0. Technically, this is permissible only because the X-axis intervals, which are years, are always equal to each other and there are no sales volume figures for in-between points.

Should you have an even number of years, there is a complication because the middle 12-month period of your time series includes one-half of each of the two center years. The easiest way to handle this complication is not to use the data for the oldest year. Then you will have an odd number of years and there will be a middle year. Rarely will discarding a way-back year be of much consequence. If you don't drop off the early year you have to carry on your calculations in terms of half-year periods, which makes a little more work. How to do this is explained in statistics books.

Numbering the years from the middle makes ΣX become 0. and the normal equations become

I $$\Sigma Y = Na \quad\text{or}\quad a = \frac{\Sigma Y}{N}$$

II $$\Sigma XY = b\Sigma X^2 \quad\text{or}\quad b = \frac{\Sigma XY}{\Sigma X^2}$$

To show how this works we will use new car production for the years 1960 to 1966 as shown in Figure 6-3.

Using the equations given above, we find

$$a = \frac{\Sigma Y}{N} = \frac{52.8}{7} = 7.54$$

$$b = \frac{\Sigma XY}{X^2} = \frac{+15.4}{28} = +.55$$

Once you get the a and b values, you calculate the trend line (the "regression" line) by using the formula $Y_c = a + bX$. Y_c means the computed value of Y for a particular year. You can calculate a Y_c figure for every year, but to establish the regression line you need to calculate only

FIGURE 6-3

YEAR	YEAR NUMBER X	X^2	MILLIONS OF NEW PASSENGER CARS PRODUCED IN U.S. Y	XY
1960	-3	9	6.7	-20.1
1961	-2	4	5.5	-11.0
1962	-1	1	6.9	-6.9
1963	0	0	7.6	0
1964	$+1$	1	7.8	$+7.8$
1965	$+2$	4	9.3	$+18.6$
1966	$+3$	9	9.0	$+27.0$
$N = 7$	$\Sigma X = 0$	$\Sigma X^2 = 28$	$\Sigma Y = 52.8$	$\Sigma XY = +15.4$

two points since any two points on a line determine the line. The regression line point for 1960 is $Y_c = a + (-3)b$ or $7.54 - 1.65 = 5.89$. For 1963 it is $Y_c = a + (0)b$ or $Y_c = 7.54$.

Figure 6-4 shows actual car production with the trend line plotted in. The trend line's dotted extension for 1967 and 1968 represent the forecasts for those years by this method. According to this trend line, car production in 1967 and 1968 should have been 9.74 million and 10.29 million cars, respectively. Actually, with 1967 behind us, we can compare its actual factory production to this projection. The actual figure was 7.6 million cars, a very disappointing year.

In our example (as in all trend line analyses) the actual figures for individual years differ to some extent from the Y_c values along the line. This raises a question of how far away from the line to expect that the 1967 and 1968 figures might reasonably be. Although we don't go into it here, there are statistical procedures that tell you where to draw lines parallel to the trend line above and below it that will set off zones of probability. If, for example, you would like to know the limits for 1967 and 1968 between which half (or any other fraction) of the probable actual figures will fall, these can be calculated.[3]

Although using least squares to get a trend line for extrapolation into future years is generally a reasonable practice for the near future, it is dangerous to extend it very far ahead lest the underlying causal factors no longer operate as they did in the original data period. This is often true

[3] In order to do this, you would need to calculate the "standard error of estimate" which is explained in statistics books.

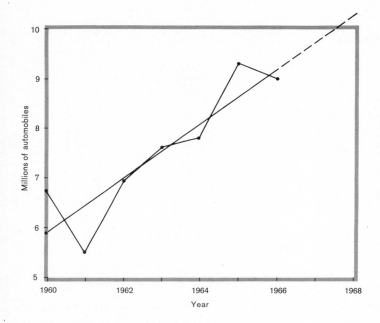

FIGURE 6-4   New automobile sales, actual and trend projection,
1960–1968.

during a period when a new product catches fire. Color television sets, for
example, sold extremely well in 1965 and 1966, as black and white viewers
went for color. It would be wrong, however, to project the 1965–1966 trend
very far into the future to get forecasts for future years because after
almost everyone gets a color set, then sales will be largely only to newly
established families plus replacements as today's sets wear out. In fact,
although the sales of color sets in 1967 were above 1966, they were far
below expectations. The big rush to color slowed down.

THE LEAST SQUARES METHOD: SECOND DEGREE AND HIGHER DE-
GREE LINES   It is a good idea, before deciding to use a least squares
straight line as a trend indicator, to plot the original data and look at the
pattern of dots. Maybe they follow a curved line instead of a straight line.
If so, you should use the formula for calculating a curved line and not the
formula for a straight line. If the data follow a regular curved pattern much
like a half moon, then the formula for the line becomes

$$Y_c = a + bX + cX^2$$

But if the data appear to follow an S shape curve, then the formula

$$Y_c = a + bX + cX^2 + dX^3$$

will produce a more appropriate regression line. You could calculate curved lines with more changes of direction ("higher degree" curves) but almost never should you do this because it is highly unlikely that the data you are dealing with fluctuate as a result of the interaction of five or six or more factors whose past interrelationships will all hold true into the future.

To calculate a "second degree" regression line (which is the simplest curved line), you need to solve the following three equations simultaneously:

I $$\Sigma Y = Na + b\Sigma X + c\Sigma X^2$$
II $$\Sigma XY = a\Sigma X + b\Sigma X^2 + c\Sigma X^3$$
III $$\Sigma X^2Y = a\Sigma X^2 + b\Sigma X^3 + c\Sigma X^4$$

Solving these equations simultaneously will give values for the constants a, b, and c. The somewhat lengthy calculations in prospect are reduced materially by continuing to use the simplification device of calling the middle year 0. The sums of all odd powers of X become zero and the three equations are reduced to

I $$\Sigma Y = Na + c\Sigma X^2$$
II $$\Sigma XY = b\Sigma X^2$$
III $$\Sigma X^2Y = a\Sigma X^2 + c\Sigma X^4$$

Using new car sales figures and solving, we get

I $$52.8 = 7a + 28c$$
II $$15.4 = 28b$$
III $$215.2 = 28a + 196c$$

From equation (I) we find that

$$a = \frac{52.8 - 28c}{7}$$

Substituting in equation (III), we get

$$215.2 = 28\,\frac{52.8 - 28c}{7} + 196c$$
$$215.2 = 4(52.8 - 28c) + 196c$$
$$215.2 = 211.2 - 112c + 196c$$
$$c = +0.01$$

Returning to equation (I),

$$a = \frac{52.8 - 28(+0.01)}{7} = \frac{52.8 - .3}{7} = 7.50$$

FIGURE 6-5

YEAR	YEAR NUMBER X	X^2	a 7.50	bX .55X	cX^2 +0.01X^2	Y_c
1960	−3	9	7.50	−1.65	+0.1	5.86
1961	−2	4	7.50	−1.10	+0.0	6.40
1962	−1	1	7.50	−0.55	+0.0	6.95
1963	0	0	7.50	0	0	7.50
1964	+1	1	7.50	+0.55	+0.0	8.05
1965	+2	4	7.50	+1.10	+0.0	8.60
1966	+3	9	7.50	+1.65	+0.1	9.16

From equation (II) we find

$$b = \frac{+15.4}{28} = +.55$$

These values for a, b, and c give us a formula for the regression line as

$$Y_c = 7.50 + .55X + 0.01X^2$$

Since we have a curved line we have to compute a Y_c value for every year rather than just two points, which was sufficient for a straight line.

In our example the amount of curvature of the data is almost negligible, as is shown by the very small value for c. The curvature begins to show a little, however, as the line is extrapolated. 1967 and 1968 would be years +4 and +5. X^2 would be 16 and 25. So the cX^2 factors are +0.2 and +0.3, respectively. The Y_c figures for these two years are 7.50 + 2.20 + 0.20 = 9.90 million cars for 1967 and 7.50 + 2.75 + 0.30 = 10.55 million cars for 1968.

EXPONENTIAL CURVES In some cases data appear to grow at a constant percentage, just as money left in a bank at interest and compounded annually grows. When this is so an exponential growth formula ($Y_c = a + bn^x$) for the line is appropriate. Not often should you use the exponential curve since it "explodes" too rapidly. If you extrapolate it for very many years into the future the Y_c figures rise very rapidly for every added X year. Usually, in rapidly expanding economic series, market saturation soon occurs, and the trend lines don't go up by increasing amounts for very long.

GROWTH STAGES Many industries follow a three-stage growth pattern. They grow slowly during a first stage when technological difficulties are being remedied and markets are being established. Then, in stage 2, the product catches on and sales go up fast, as color television did in the mid-1960s. This is followed by stage 3, a period of slow growth as market saturation becomes a factor. If you fitted a second degree curve (or an exponential curve) to the data midway through stage 2, you would get a curve that, when extrapolated, would go up more and more steeply forever. Your forecasts for even the next two or three years based on such a line would be much too high. A straight line projection would probably be better. Still better, however, would be a third degree least squares line which approximates an S curve. Statistics books explain how to calculate third degree lines.

CYCLICAL CHANGES Some industries undergo wavelike transitions with crests and troughs 5 to 10 years or more apart. Longtime figures show, for example, that the building industry tends to follow a 17-year cycle. The machinery industry, too, tends to experience pronounced ups and downs although not on a regular basis.

Rarely do forecasters try to treat cyclical patterns by statistical measures because the basic data are unavailable and cycle patterns usually change during the lengthy period for which you need data in order to study several successive cycles. (You would need figures for 50 years or so in order to be able to study several cycles.) Not often do you have a 50-year record of an industry for analysis. And, furthermore, in some industries the amplitude of cyclical ups and downs is relatively small and so it doesn't matter much. Forecasters usually try to incorporate the effects of cyclical movements into forecasts on a judgment basis and not by using statistical measures.

SEASONAL CHANGES Automobile sales tend to be concentrated in the spring; sales of television receivers are higher in the fall and winter months; while February, because of Valentine's day, is a big month in the sale of boxed candy. Sales of candy bars, in contrast, are more uniform throughout the year. Every industry has its own pattern of seasonal variations and these are usually susceptible to statistical analysis.

In order to project monthly figures into the future you have to measure the seasonal variation for each month. Then you can superimpose it onto trend projections and get some idea of the expectations for each month in the near future.

The most sophisticated procedures for calculating seasonal changes are those used by the United States Federal Reserve Board when it "adjusts for seasonal changes" (eliminates the effects of seasonality) its monthly indexes of industrial production for the United States. The FRB method, a refinement of the moving average method, is too lengthy for general use. For most uses simple comparisons of actual monthly data to moving averages suffice.

To calculate the seasonal pattern by using moving averages you need to have monthly figures for five years or more in the past. Start by adding the first 12 figures, from January through December, and dividing by 12. This gives you the average for the first year. Then drop out the original January and add the figure for January of the next year. Again divide by 12. You now have another average but for a more recent set of 12 months. Next drop the original February and add the February from the following year, etc. You will end up with a series of averages called the moving average.

You aren't yet ready, however, to compare these averages to actual monthly figures. The calculated average for 1967 for any series, for example, can't properly be compared to either the June or the July, 1967, figure, because the average is appropriate to use as the figure for the middle 30 days of 1967 (for this purpose all months are assumed to be 30-day months). The middle 30 days of 1967 begin on June 16 and end on July 15.

An additional step is required in order to arrive at a moving average for the 30-day period which is fully comparable to July. As we said above, in the calculation you treat the 1967 average as being applicable to the 30-day period between June 15 and July 15. Then the next average (the one that includes data for February, 1967, through January, 1968) is treated as being applicable to July 16 to August 15. When you add these two averages together and divide by 2, you get the moving average figure which is comparable to the month of July. The process is called "recentering" and has to be done for the whole set of averages.

Once the recentering has been done, you have a moving average figure for every month and you have an actual figure for each month. So, next, divide the actual July, 1967, figure by its recentered moving average and get a ratio. Suppose that this ratio is .90. This means that so far as 1967 is concerned, July's figure was only 90 per cent of the average month. Continue this dividing process for the whole series and you get a ratio for every month (except for the first six months at the beginning and the last six months at the end).

Next, consider the several ratios for July (one for each year) and pick out the most typical one. You could average the several July ratios or use the median or pick the ratio you judge to be representative. Your choice becomes the seasonal index for July. Do the same for other months and you end up with a set of seasonal indexes, one for every month. Before using them, however, examine them to see if they themselves average to

100 because all seasonal ups and downs should even out in a year. The ratio-to-moving average method does not ensure that the ratios you first select will average exactly 100, although rarely will they be off more than a point or two. If they don't average to 100, adjust them all proportionally so that they do average to 100.

To use seasonal indexes in conjunction with trend analysis you would calculate a projected trend figure for near future months and then multiply this number by the seasonal index for this month. If the trend projections for January, February, and March of next year are 780, 785, and 790, respectively, and the seasonals for these months are 90, 95, and 110, then the forecasts would be $780 \times .90 = 702$, $785 \times .95 = 746$, and $790 \times 1.10 = 869$, respectively.

CORRELATION ANALYSES, LEADING AND LAGGING SERIES We said earlier that sometimes an industry's sales move up or down in accord with some other important industry or with economic conditions. Such relationships are particularly helpful in case the industry you are interested in moves in delayed parallel with some main series. By "delayed parallel" we mean that the main series moves first and your industry follows it by a few months.[4]

Before doing any calculating to see how much correlation exists between two series, you might want to plot the two series together on one chart to see what relationships seem to exist. Suppose, for example, that you worked for Crane Company and wanted to find out how closely your plumbing supply business correlated with building activity. You could start by plotting the value of building permits issued month by month for several years back. Plot also, on the same chart, your sales of plumbing supplies. You could see if they seem to move in a parallel fashion.

Probably they wouldn't fit too well because as we said earlier, the sales of plumbing supplies should lag behind the value of permits. So plot these two series again with the building permits series advanced one month (plot January permits and February plumbing supplies sales on the same vertical line, and February permits with March sales, etc.). Then make another chart with plumbing supplies sales plotted against permits advanced two months, then try three months, and so on. Probably, since building permits come before the buying of house materials, the closest agreement between these series will be found to exist with sales lagging by four or five months.

[4] To be of practical value for forecasting a lagging series, the leading series must lead by three or more months because usually it takes that long to gather statistics and publish reports. You won't learn until October how the leading series performed in August.

FIGURE 6-6

MONTH X		MONTH Y		XY	X^2	Y^2
January	29	January	57	1,653	841	3,249
February	31	February	59	1,829	961	3,481
March	37	March	54	1,998	1,369	2,916
April	32	April	62	1,984	1,024	3,844
May	30	May	77	2,310	900	5,929
June	35	June	68	2,380	1,225	4,624
$\Sigma X =$	$\overline{194}$	$\Sigma Y =$	$\overline{377}$	$\Sigma XY = \overline{12,154}$	$\Sigma X^2 = \overline{6,320}$	$\Sigma Y^2 = \overline{24,043}$
$\bar{X} = 32.3333$		$\bar{Y} = 62.8333$		$\bar{Y}\Sigma X = 12,190$	$\bar{X}\Sigma X = 6,273$	$\bar{Y}\Sigma Y = 23,688$
				$\Sigma xy = \overline{-36}$	$\Sigma x^2 = \overline{47}$	$\Sigma y^2 = \overline{355}$

$$r = \frac{-36}{\sqrt{(47)(355)}} = \frac{-36}{\sqrt{16,685}} = \frac{-36}{129.2} = -.28$$

By inspecting the charts you can tell which leading and lagging relationship seems to be most valid. Probably, however, you ought not to rely on visual inspection to decide which combination is the best to use. Instead you should calculate the correlation "coefficients"[5] for various lead and lag combinations and find out more certainly which is the proper one to use. The highest positive coefficient would tell you which combination to use.

Figure 6-6 illustrates how to do this. In figure 6-6 the numbers in the X and Y columns are hypothetical monthly figures for the time series whose relationship we might be investigating. (In actual practice you would always use figures for more than six months because six months is too short a trial period on which to decide relationships. But six months is enough to illustrate the procedure.) All of the other columns in figure 6-6 are needed in order to calculate the correlation coefficient. Because of

[5] A correlation coefficient (denoted as r) is a statistical measure of the closeness of movement between two series. Correlation coefficients range between the limits of +1.00 to −1.00. Perfect positive correlation is shown by a coefficient of +1.00. An hourly paid man's hours are perfectly correlated with his wages in a positive way. If you know his hourly rate and either the number of hours he worked or his pay, you can calculate the other. Spending money out of a $10 bill is an example of perfect negative correlation (shown by $r = -1.00$). The more you spend, the less you have left. A coefficient of 0 shows no correlation at all. An electric utility company would, for example, probably find little or no correlation between the age of its customers and the amount of electricity they use.

Coefficients of .50 or so show some correlation between the two series but not enough to help much in forecasting. Even .75 still isn't very helpful. But as you go above .85 the correlation between the two series is high. The two series generally go up and down together.

FIGURE 6-7

MONTH X		MONTH Y		XY	X^2	Y^2
January	29	February	59	1,711	841	3,481
February	31	March	54	1,674	961	2,916
March	37	April	62	2,294	1,369	3,844
April	32	May	77	2,464	1,024	5,929
May	30	June	68	2,040	900	4,624
June	35	July	60	2,100	1,225	3,600
$\Sigma X =$	194	$\Sigma Y =$	380	$\Sigma XY = 12,283$	$\Sigma X^2 = 6,320$	$\Sigma Y^2 = 24,394$
$\bar{X} = 32.3333$		$\bar{Y} = 63.3333$		$\bar{Y}\Sigma X = 12,287$	$\bar{X}\Sigma X = 6,273$	$\bar{Y}\Sigma Y = 24,067$
				$\Sigma xy = -4$	$\Sigma x^2 = 47$	$\Sigma y^2 = 227$

$$r = \frac{-4}{\sqrt{(47)(227)}} = \frac{-4}{\sqrt{10,669}} = \frac{-4}{106.7} = -.04$$

space limitations we will show how to calculate r but will not explain the mathematics that lie behind the calculation.[6]

The formula for calculating the correlation coefficient is

$$r = \frac{\Sigma xy}{\sqrt{(\Sigma x^2)(\Sigma y^2)}}$$

In this calculation, it is important to carry out the arithmetic mean (the $\bar{X}$ and $\bar{Y}$ figures) of both X and Y to several decimals of accuracy and not to round them off to two or three place numbers. The correlation coefficient of $-.28$ shows that there is little correlation between the movements up and down of the two series.

We have, however, only started on our analysis of the lead and lag relationship. Next, we repeat the process with X leading Y by one month as in figure 6-7.

Again, there is no correlation at all between the two series, as the $r = -.04$ shows.

But the analysis process goes on. Next try January X paired up with March Y, then with April Y, etc. (In order to do this you will have to bring into the calculation the Y figures for August, September, and October which are 67, 75, and 90 respectively). We won't go through the calculation here but the coefficients turn out to be $+.93$, $+.32$, and $-.16$, respec-

[6] A good explanation of this procedure is given beginning on page 276, in Dick A. Leabo and C. Frank Smith, *Business Statistics for Business and Economics*, rev. ed., Richard D. Irwin, Inc., Homewood, Ill., 1964.

tively. Clearly, in our example, the X series leads the Y series by three months. (Before concluding this, however, you should also try out having Y lead X).

Back on page 107 we said that statistical trend line projections were far from absolute as predictors and that it is well to consider the probable limits between which future actual figures might fall. And we said that in order to do this, you would have to calculate the "standard error of estimate." You can, in a similar way, calculate confidence intervals for correlation coefficients. Again, however, because of space limitations, we aren't able to explain the procedure here.

MULTIPLE CORRELATION   The United States government economists and statisticians use correlation when they analyze the various economic data series in order to forecast the GNP. But the simple two-series kind of correlation that we have been talking about won't do the job needed. The GNP is tied in with several series. The government actually uses 21 series of data. As it happens, 7 of these lead the GNP. Business failures, industrial stock prices, new orders for durable manufacturers goods, and residential construction contracts are among the seven. Seven other of these series move up and down with the GNP on a concurrent basis. Included are employment, bank debits, freight car loadings, and industrial production. And 7 are lagging series. These include retail sales, consumer installment debt, and manufacturers' inventories. Only the first group is helpful in forecasting. The second group reflects what is occurring concurrently. And the lagging set of 7 series, though of no use in forecasting, is of value in that it tends to confirm the previously indicated state of events.

Private companies rarely get into such complex correlation analysis as this but they do sometimes analyze the interrelationships between three or four or even more related series. Multiple correlation can be used here. The calculation, however, gets to be quite complicated. If, for example, you were to use four series to see whether, collectively, they caused movements in a fifth series, you would have to solve five simultaneous equations with five unknowns. Not only that but the number of cross relationships among the variables also increases. As you add factors, the calculation job tends to increase exponentially rather than linearly.

Fortunately there are several short-cut methods available for solving the equations that reduce the work load considerably.[7] And computers lessen the remaining load. Computer programs are available to do all of the calculation called for by the formulas swiftly, accurately, and com-

[7] See, for example, Samuel Richmond, *Statistical Analysis*, 2d ed., The Ronald Press Company, New York, 1964.

pletely. For example, in the University of Michigan Analog Decoder (MAD) Language Executive System one program both examines the linear relationships between the variables and searches out various families of nonlinear functions to determine the best fit between the variables within the specified set of constraints.

In order to find out the correlation that may exist among several variables it is necessary to determine regression line constants a and b. Since several factors are involved the regression equation is quite different from the ones we used for two variables. In its generalized form, this equation is

$$X_1 = a_{1.23 \ldots m} + b_{12.3 \ldots m}X_2 + b_{13.2 \ldots m}X_3 + \cdots + b_{1m.23 \ldots (m-1)}X_m$$

In this equation X_1 is the dependent variable or series we wish to predict and all of the other Xs are independent variables, which bear upon X_1 and cause it to be what it is.

As in the case of the two-item time series analysis, $a_{1.23 \ldots m}$ is a constant and the b values represent the relationship between the dependent variable and the particular independent variable to which it is attached, all other independent variables being held constant. The subscript notation indicates the dependent variable by placing it to the left of the decimal, with all independent variables to the right. The value taken on by m is equal to the number of the independent variables. When two numbers appear to the left of the decimal, as is the case with the b values, this indicates that the calculation is to discover if there is a relationship between these two variables with all other variables being held constant.

We will use as an example a case where three independent variables are being used to predict a value of a fourth variable. The three independent variables are X_2, X_3, and X_4, and the dependent variable, the one we want to predict, is X_1. This makes the regression equation become

$$X_1 = a_{1.234} + b_{12.34}X_2 + b_{13.24}X_3 + b_{14.23}X_4$$

In order to find the value of a and of the three b's, we have to solve the following four normal equations (in equation (I), N is the number of sets of data):

$$\begin{array}{ll}
\text{I} & \Sigma X_1 = Na_{1.234} + b_{12.34}\Sigma X_2 + b_{13.24}\Sigma X_3 + b_{14.23}\Sigma X_4 \\
\text{II} & \Sigma X_1X_2 = a_{1.234}\Sigma X_2 + b_{12.34}\Sigma X_2{}^2 + b_{13.24}\Sigma X_2X_3 + b_{14.23}\Sigma X_2X_4 \\
\text{III} & \Sigma X_1X_3 = a_{1.234}\Sigma X_3 + b_{12.34}\Sigma X_2X_3 + b_{13.24}\Sigma X_3{}^2 + b_{14.23}\Sigma X_3X_4 \\
\text{IV} & \Sigma X_1X_4 = a_{1.234}\Sigma X_4 + b_{12.34}\Sigma X_2X_4 + b_{13.24}\Sigma X_3X_4 + b_{14.23}\Sigma X_4{}^2
\end{array}$$

We need all of these values (the one for a, and those for the three b's) in order next to calculate the standard error of estimate using this formula:

$$S_{1.234} = \sqrt{\dfrac{X_1{}^2 - a_{1.234}\Sigma X_1 - b_{12.34}\Sigma X_1X_2 - b_{13.24}\Sigma X_1X_3 - b_{14.23}\Sigma X_1X_4}{N}}$$

Then we will need still one more figure before we can go on to calculating the degree of relationship between the several series that we started with. The standard deviation of the dependent variable, the one that is the result of the action of the others, is calculated as follows:

$$S_1 = \sqrt{\frac{\Sigma X_1{}^2}{N} - \left(\frac{\Sigma X_1}{N}\right)^2}$$

Now we are finally ready to calculate the multiple correlation coefficient R, using the formula

$$R_{1.234} = \sqrt{1 - \frac{S_{1.234}{}^2}{S_1{}^2}}$$

An example will illustrate this method. Suppose that we wish to see if the volume of new orders for freight cars is closely related to industrial production, freight carloadings, and steel production. The actual figures for one 12-month period for these four economic series are shown in figure 6-8.

In order to solve the four simultaneous equations all of the following sums are needed:

$N = 12$

$\Sigma X_1 = 371$ $\Sigma X_2 = 1,419$ $\Sigma X_3 = 28.7$ $\Sigma X_4 = 98.3$

$\Sigma X_1{}^2 = 13,041$ $\Sigma X_2{}^2 = 167,897$ $\Sigma X_3{}^2 = 69.69$ $\Sigma X_4{}^2 = 827.75$

$\Sigma X_1 X_2 = 43,795$ $\Sigma X_1 X_3 = 874.4$ $\Sigma X_1 X_4 = 3,021.9$

$\Sigma X_2 X_3 = 3,400.5$ $\Sigma X_2 X_4 = 11,609.8$ $\Sigma X_3 X_4 = 234.24$

FIGURE 6-8

MONTH	X_1 NEW ORDERS FOR FREIGHT CARS, THOUSANDS	X_2 INDEX OF INDUSTRIAL PRODUCTION (1957–1959 = 100)	X_3 FREIGHT CAR-LOADINGS, AVERAGE PER DAY, THOUSANDS	X_4 STEEL PRODUCTION, THOUSANDS OF TONS
January	53	113	2.0	10.3
February	15	116	2.1	9.7
March	16	118	2.7	10.6
April	24	119	2.3	9.2
May	32	118	2.3	7.5
June	34	120	2.9	6.7
July	31	114	2.0	6.2
August	28	118	2.3	7.1
September	16	122	2.9	7.3
October	43	123	2.4	7.8
November	36	121	2.3	7.8
December	43	117	2.5	8.1

Putting these figures into the four simultaneous equations makes them become

I $\quad 371 = (12)a_{1.234} + (1,419)b_{12.34} + (28.7)b_{13.24} + (98.3)b_{14.23}$

II $\quad 43,795 = (1,419)a_{1.234} + (167,897)b_{12.34} + (3,400.5)b_{13.24} + (11,609.8)b_{14.23}$

III $\quad 874.4 = (28.7)a_{1.234} + (3,400.5)b_{12.34} + (69.69)b_{13.24} + (234.24)b_{14.23}$

IV $\quad 3,021.9 = (98.3)a_{1.234} + (11,609.8)b_{12.34} + (234.24)b_{13.24} + (827.75)b_{14.23}$

These four simultaneous equations were solved by a computer which produced the following values:

$$a_{1.234} = 81.3524$$
$$b_{12.34} = -0.0753917$$
$$b_{13.24} = -12.8909$$
$$b_{14.23} = -1.30498$$

This would make the regression equation become

$$X_1 = 81.3524 - 0.0753917X_2 - 12.8909X_3 - 1.30498X_4$$

We are not really interested, however, in the regression equation but in using the a and b values in the calculation of the standard error of estimate:

$$S_{1.234} = \sqrt{\frac{13,041 - 81.3524(371) + .0753917(43,795) + 12.8909(874.4) + 1.30498(3,021.9)}{12}}$$
$$= \sqrt{114.69676}$$
$$= 10.71$$

Next we need the standard deviation of the dependent variable:

$$S_1 = \sqrt{\frac{13,041}{12} - \left(\frac{371}{12}\right)^2}$$
$$= \sqrt{130.9097}$$
$$= 11.44$$

And finally we get the correlation coefficient:

$$R = \sqrt{1 - \frac{(10.71)^2}{(11.44)^2}}$$
$$= \sqrt{.1239}$$
$$= .35$$

The .35 in our example shows that although there is indeed some relationship between the independent variables and the dependent variable, the correlation is not high. If you knew all three independent variables you still could not do a very good job of predicting the orders for new freight cars.

The method we used in this example could also be used to establish lead and lag relationships. You could try out having certain of the series leading the others. There are of course a large number of possible combinations of leads and lags available to us, too many to work through without a computer. But with a computer you could have it try out many combinations and calculate correlation coefficients for each one. If there were any reliable lead and lag relationships the computer could find them.

Actually, although the correlation coefficient indicates the closeness of the relationship between the independent and the dependent variables, another measure, the coefficient of multiple determination, is more useful in forecasting. The coefficient of multiple determination (which is R^2) is more helpful because it indicates the degree to which the variation in the dependent variable is statistically explained by variations in the independent variables.[8]

STUDY MATERIALS

6-1   Can you plan without forecasting? When, if ever, should you? Why?

6-2   What similarities and differences are there in forecasting for intermittent and continuous operations?

6-3   Suppose that your company makes stoves. Your superior tells you to see if general nationwide economic measures will help in forecasting the company's business. Go to the library and see what is available. Such figures might include gross national product, disposable personal income, steel output, freight carloadings, and housing starts. Typical data sources are the *Statistical Abstract*, the *Survey of Current Business, Business Week*, and various trade publications.

Before going ahead with any calculations, you are to report to your superior. Are the figures you find usable in the form you find them? If not, what would you have to do to make them usable? How accurate were the forecasts of "the experts" of these various series? If you used such series in your company's forecasts, how much reliance would you place upon your forecast?

6-4   Assume that your company makes ceramic floor and wall tile and you have been told to develop an industry forecast by calculating the seasonal and trend (disregarding cyclical movements) from the following figures.

[8] Coefficients of multiple correlation and of multiple determination are not shown as plus or minus since one independent series might be correlated positively with the dependent series at the same time that another independent series is correlated negatively with the dependent series.

MONTH	FLOOR AND WALL TILE INDUSTRY SALES, MILLIONS OF SQUARE FEET YEAR						
	1	2	3	4	5	6	7
January	19	15	18	20	21	21	23
February	18	15	18	19	21	21	22
March	20	19	21	21	25	26	26
April	19	18	20	22	26	24	25
May	20	20	23	24	24	24	24
June	22	21	22	24	26	26	26
July	19	18	21	23	26	24	22
August	21	23	25	25	25	25	24
September	20	21	21	23	24	25	22
October	19	21	24	25	24	23	21
November	18	20	21	22	22	22	20
December	17	17	18	19	21	22	19

MONTH	PERSONAL INCOME, ANNUAL RATES IN BILLIONS OF DOLLARS YEAR						
	1	2	3	4	5	6	7
January	396	404	429	454	479	515	560
February	396	403	432	453	481	515	565
March	397	407	435	455	483	518	569
April	402	410	438	457	487	520	571
May	404	413	441	460	488	525	573
June	404	416	442	463	489	535	577
July	405	420	444	464	491	535	580
August	405	418	445	465	495	538	585
September	406	420	446	469	498	553	590
October	406	424	448	473	499	547	594
November	406	428	450	474	507	553	599
December	404	431	452	477	512	558	602

MONTH	PRIVATE HOUSING STARTS, ANNUAL RATES IN MILLIONS OF UNITS YEAR						
	1	2	3	4	5	6	7
January	1.37	1.13	1.27	1.34	1.72	1.44	1.61
February	1.37	1.17	1.15	1.38	1.66	1.48	1.37
March	1.12	1.30	1.43	1.58	1.66	1.49	1.57
April	1.33	1.17	1.54	1.62	1.53	1.55	1.50
May	1.33	1.29	1.58	1.62	1.52	1.52	1.32
June	1.28	1.38	1.43	1.57	1.62	1.57	1.29
July	1.23	1.34	1.44	1.60	1.50	1.47	1.09
August	1.36	1.33	1.49	1.48	1.51	1.43	1.11
September	1.09	1.38	1.36	1.75	1.45	1.45	1.08
October	1.27	1.44	1.54	1.86	1.52	1.41	.85
November	1.22	1.37	1.58	1.58	1.51	1.55	1.01
December	1.00	1.30	1.56	1.57	1.61	1.77	1.09

After you present your forecast for the next year to your superior he asks what are the reasonable high and low limits of the figures for the next three months. (You are still to disregard all factors other than the figures above. For this purpose you need not calculate possible variations in the seasonal itself, just the extrapolated trend with the seasonal superimposed on it.) What are these figures for the next three months?

6-5 Your superior now asks you to see, for the seven years for which you have data, if there is any correlation between the sales of tile and housing starts and personal income. (He believes that if there is the published forecasts of these two series will improve the company's forecast of tile sales.) Note, however, that the data given here for housing starts and for personal income have been seasonally adjusted. You must therefore remove (by dividing each month's actual tile sales by its seasonal index) the seasonal factor from the tile sales figures.

chapter seven

FORECASTING (CONTINUED)

THE FORECAST PERIOD
As we have said, production control is concerned almost wholly with fore-casts for the near future months. For these months, the approved fore-cast is quite detailed, showing quantities of individual products. Some com-panies keep their detailed forecasts as much as six months ahead. They make them into "rolling" forecasts. Each month they review and revise, where necessary, the forecasts for the next five months and add a new sixth month. More distant months are less detailed, showing only dollar totals for groups of products.

Revising the close months' forecasts causes many changes in produc-tion control's schedules because parts orders are already in production in the shop. But whenever reports show that current sales and the sales in the next few months are likely to be different from earlier forecasts, you need to change the forecasts, even though doing so causes changes in production schedules which have already been issued and on which the factory is working. Otherwise you will end up with too many of items which aren't selling well and too few of items which are moving.

Actually, most companies, in the fall of the year, prepare a forecast covering the next calendar year. Then they revise this forecast monthly or quarterly as the next future period is added.

MODEL YEARS AND MODEL PERIODS   Companies whose produc-tion involves annual models (automobiles and, sometimes, refrigerators, stoves, television sets, etc.) differ, however, from others in that their fore-cast is not a rolling 12-month forecast. Instead, it is a forecast for the model year (or for the model period if it is longer than one year).

This forecast, which shows specific quantities of the main products for the full model year, is made several months before the new model year starts. The model year, from a production point of view, often starts in November (so that the new models can be in dealers' hands on January 1) and runs through the following October. At first, though, only the first four months are considered firm. Later on, additional months' forecasts are firmed up as they are added.

New tentative months are not, however, added on beyond the end of the model year. This is because in companies with annual models, it is not very helpful to the production control department to have, say in June, a forecast for the twelve months ahead beginning in July and running through June of the following year. The products involved would include two different models but would show only part of the total volume of either this year's or next year's models. This would be of little help to production control and would be of no help at all in planning tooling and capital expenditures. Admittedly, though, such a forecast would be of some use in the general planning of the company's future.

Some companies, those making cameras, moving picture projectors, electric irons, and any number of other items, come out with new models now and then but by no means annually. Perhaps one model will sell for years. Here you need a sales forecast covering the full sales life of the model or at least its sales for two or three years ahead. You might not need to go beyond that because long-range volume is too problematical.

You need this forecast not for production control purposes but to let you decide on "depth" of tooling. The larger the expected volume, the greater the "depth" of tooling that is appropriate. Depth of tooling is the extent of mechanization. Mechanization requires large investments but, with high-volume production, results in low unit costs. You just must try to be right on your depth of tooling. If your forecast is too low and you undertool, you may never get your unit costs down to competitive levels. If your forecast is too high and you overtool, you'll never recover all the money you put into tooling.

Sometimes you don't have to worry about forecasting the total volume of a product. This is when you work on big continuing contracts for customers. On such orders the customer decides how much tooling he wants and usually pays you separately for the tooling in which case he may own it himself.

Forecasts of sales of products made to stock are forecasts of sales at a specific price. When you are thinking of new products you need to get the sales, engineering, tooling, and cost estimating departments together to develop a product that you can sell at a price low enough to attract quantity sales.

TRANSITION PERIODS   When you make sales forecasts of new models of products, don't forget that the transition period needs special attention. During the transition period last year's unsold models will be sold, at a discount, in competition with the new models. Until they are cleared they will cut the volume of new models sold. Against this factor tending to depress new model sales is the need to "fill the pipeline." All your dealers will order a stock of new models for display and inventory. So your new model sales usually start off strong (in spite of competition from last year's leftover products) after which they settle down to quantities approximately equal to consumer sales.

You have to forecast also the market for new *products*, as distinguished from new *models*. This is harder to do since you don't know as much about how the public will take to them as you do with new models of established products. Difficult though it is, you have to make forecasts for new products and provide the necessary new production facilities that they need. It is well not to commit yourself too heavily for machines to make new products, Instead, buy more parts and use more general purpose machines than you normally would. Your costs may be higher but your loss will be much less if the new product doesn't catch on. You won't have to scrap so much expensive special machinery.

STANDARD VOLUME

Automobile manufacturers call their conservative expected volume for a model year the "standard volume." This is the quantity which they really try hard to reach. It is the quantity used for overhead cost allocation and for pricing. Prices are set to cover all costs, including machinery and tooling depreciation as well as all other overheads and a normal profit if this volume is reached. If by the end of the model year, sales exceed the standard volume, the company earns high profits because all overhead costs were covered when the standard volume point was passed. Additional cars cost only the added variable costs, largely materials and labor.

The standard volume is also the volume used to decide on tooling depth. If the standard volume is 1 million cars, then special machines whose cost can be absorbed by this quantity will be bought. But machines which will pay out only at the 2-million-car level will be bought only if they will last through a second model year.

Standard volume is also used to plan plant capacity and employment. If the standard volume is 1 million units and is expected to be reached in 10 months, the output will have to average 100,000 a month. Because of seasonal variations in sales, this will mean that April, May, and June will go up to, say, 120,000 a month, with other months being lower. Because of the costs of hiring new workers, and the costs of laying off men, such as unemployment insurance, most automobile companies plan to man their plants with only enough men to handle average production. Then they rely on overtime to care for the high months and short hours or a few layoffs to take care of the low months.

FORECASTS OF BASICS

Complex assembled products should always be made by putting together major assemblies, minor assemblies, and parts. You would never put whole products together piece by piece. Instead, you first put sets of pieces together into assemblies, then put the assemblies together in finished products.

Some kinds of assemblies are standardized and go into two or more types of finished products. Such standard subassemblies are sometimes called "basics." They may be assemblies that go directly into the final products or they may be subassemblies used in other assemblies. An automobile carburetor is a basic, as is an automatic transmission. They are standard and can be used in any model car.

Basics are often "component families" rather than being unique. Carburetors, for example, come in several kinds and sizes, as do transmissions. And so do electric motors, storage batteries, and many other items.

Basics are often made, in part, from other basics. Automobile bodies are major basics. Most kinds of bodies use the same kinds of doors. Doors are lesser basics. Most of the doors use the same kind of door latch. Door latches are still lesser basics, and so on.

Many industries use the basics ideas. The electronics industry calls basics "black boxes" because most of them are put into black metal boxes. When Hughes Aircraft makes a radar detection unit or an automatic airplane pilot, it is made mostly out of black boxes connected together with electric wires. Black boxes may be transmitters, receivers, generators, differential computers, resolvers, integrators, etc. There are several standard sizes or types of each. They can be combined differently into thousands of different finished products.

Adding machines, cash registers, sewing machines, refrigerators, elevators—these and many others use standard subassemblies in different models of products. Most of the inside components of different models of Burroughs adding machines are the same whether they are six-column or eight-column, and whether they are operated manually or electrically. Many of the parts in a Dodge automobile are the same as those in a Plymouth. Most Otis elevator parts are the same whether the elevator is in a New York hotel or a Pittsburgh factory.

Companies making many types and sizes of products design them to use basics and families of basics wherever possible. It is economical to make completed products mostly of basics, combined in different ways, plus or minus certain individual parts.

Basics which are not too likely to change in design can be regarded as "shelf" or stock items. You can forecast their need and manufacture them

ABC Company
Electronic Manufacturing Division
Radar Unit Manufacturing Schedule
250 KW System

Into Finished Goods Inventory	B/M No.	April 2	9	16	23	30	May 7	14	21	28	June 4	11	18	25	July 2	9	16	23	30
446001-100 Mounting (A)	501	10/29	10/39	10/49	15/64	15/79	15/94	15/109	15/124	15/139	12/151	15/166	15/181	15/196	15/211	12/223	15/238	15/253	15/268
433-52-0001 Mtg Pow Sup (A)	452	30/2829	30/2859	30/2889	30/2919	30/2949	25/2974	25/2999	25/3024	25/3049	16/3065	20/3085	20/3105	20/3125	20/3145	16/3161	20/3181	20/3201	20/3221
446-52-0001 Mtg Pow Sup (A)	552	0/726	s/c																
446-58-0001 Servo Roll	458	0/1471	s/c																
446-58-0001-1 Servo Roll	358	40/2612	40/2652	40/2692	40/2732	40/2772	40/2812	40/2852	40/2892	40/2932	32/2964	40/3004	40/3044	40/3084	30/3114	24/3138	30/3168	30/3198	30/3228
446-59-001 Mtg Servo Roll (A)	559	10/1296	10/1306	10/1316	10/1326	10/1336	10/1346	10/1356	10/1366	10/1376	7/1383	8/1391	7/1398	8/1406	7/1413	7/1420	8/1428	7/1435	8/1443
446-60-0001 Servo Time	460	0/345	s/c																
446-61-0001 Accelerometer	461	43/3828	43/3871	43/3914	48/3962	48/4010	48/4058	48/4106	48/4154	48/4202	38/4240	48/4288	48/4336	48/4384	48/4432	38/4470	48/4518	48/4566	48/4614
446-64-b001 Mtg AF Amp (A)	564	0/780	s/c																
446-65-0001 Mtg Amp Pow Sup (A)	565	0/785	s/c																
446-69-0001 Comp Elev	569	0/695	0/695	0/695	0/695	0/695	5/700	5/705	5/710	5/715	s/c								
446-75-0001 Mtg Elev Comp (A)	575	4	s/c																

FIGURE 7-1 A forecast of basic "black boxes" for radar assemblies.

without reference to specific sales orders for finished products. You can start to make basics even before you get orders for the finished products that you will put them in. Otis Elevator does this with elevator parts. So does Burroughs with adding machine parts. So does Hughes with radar parts.

Actually, few basics ever get stocked because, while they are being manufactured, they are assigned to newly received assembly orders. Assigning them while they are being made speeds final assembly because orders don't have to wait for their basics to be made. Or if you assemble continuously, you set the rate of production of basics to match assembly's requirements.

You can speed up the delivery of customer special orders by using basics. As sales orders are received, you analyze them into their needs for basics and for special items. You need to pay particular attention only to the special components because they will set your final assembly schedule. Basics are coming through production all the time so that normally they present no problem. You can allocate to each new order the basics it needs in the time period when it needs them.

Basics can be slightly different for different assembly orders without causing much trouble. The shaft of a motor for one job may, for example be $\frac{1}{2}$ inch longer than the shaft of a motor used for a different job. Or one job may need a different number of teeth on a gear. Such differences make a little extra production control work but they don't upset the idea of using basics.

PARTS SETS OR "PACKAGES"   Basics don't have to be assemblies. They can be sets of parts, used as alternatives in end products to make slightly different end products. At the Cincinnati Milling Machine Company certain "sets of parts" for finished products are handled the same way as basics. CMM, for example, makes dual milling machines in sizes 2, 3, 4, 5, and 6 and in plane, vertical, or universal style. Different sets of parts make the product into one or the other. It takes 207 such sets of parts at CMM to make the fifteen varieties of dual milling machines. Any particular milling machine requires over 100 parts sets. These are parts that go into the product directly as piece parts, not as parts of subassemblies.

Landis Machine Company makes machines that put threads on nuts and bolts. It, too, uses the parts sets idea. The Landis line covers 90 different threading machines, 120 size and styles of thread cutting die heads, 30 of tap bodies, 123 of tap heads, 17 of solid adjustable taps, and hundreds of special attachments. It takes hundreds of parts sets to cover all of the variety Landis deals with.

The need for sets of parts is forecast apart from sales orders. The

		PART NUMBER	NAME		NO. REQ'D
1	B	89455	Sub-Assy, Piston Rod & Bearings		9
2	B	89489	Piston	1	
3	B	89490	Rod - Piston	1	
4	B	89491	Bearing - Piston Rod	1	
41	B	89483	Key - Univ. Link Flex. Brg. Ret.		1
42	C	89484	Knuckle - Univ. Link		4
43	E	89485	Shaft - Drive		1
44	B	89487	Ring - Bearing Thrust		1
45	B	93619	Snap Ring - Bearings		1
46	B	114822	Spring - Cylinder Bearing		1

DATE _____ PARTS LIST 127165

NAME Sub-Deck - Basic (Common Parts) SHEET NO. 1 OF 1 SHEETS
PV-2050-10 & PF-2050-10 Series E.O. _____
MV-2050-10 & MF-2050-10 Series

W.O. NO. _____

FIGURE 7-2   A bill of materials for common parts which are used for several varieties of machines.

parts are made in quantities that will complete a certain number of sets. Like assembled basics, they are allocated to assembly orders before they are actually finished. Ford Motor does the same with automobiles. Certain sets of trim or accessories are called a "package." Packages are forecasted and their production is scheduled on their own.

FORECASTING WHEN MANUFACTURING TO ORDER

Companies making expensive machinery, made only to order, don't need to do much near-future forecasting because their order backlogs are forecasts. They can't do very much to regularize production. If orders call for more than can be produced, some customers have to wait. This, in effect, does regularize production at a high level. But if customers' orders call for less than enough to keep your plant busy, and this in spite of your sales department pushing sales all it can, even to price cutting, you have to go on short hours or lay off employees.

ORDER BACKLOGS   The explanation above is, however, an oversimplification. It implies that there is no need for forecasting when you manufacture to order, whereas there really is. You need to know whether to expand or contract your plant. You need to know how you ought to take care of your order backlog. If it is building up, maybe you should expand capacity or subcontract more work outside. Or possibly you expand your capacity by going on overtime for a while instead of quoting more distant delivery dates when bidding for new jobs.

Central Manufacturing Co. Work Load in Thousands of Hours								
Machining	Jan.	Feb.	Mar.	Apr.	May	June	July	Aug.
Own	66.4	79.9	81.1	64.6	48.7	50.4	38.6	32.2
Contract	51.7	31.7	57.2	40.3	34.0	49.5	14.6	13.5
Total	118.1	111.6	138.3	104.9	82.7	99.9	53.2	45.7
Assembly								
Own	29.4	25.4	36.9	22.8	15.9	19.4	29.2	14.3
Contract	6.0	9.6	16.0	14.3	9.7	7.8	7.2	4.3
Total	35.4	35.0	52.9	37.1	25.6	27.2	36.4	18.6
Total								
Own	95.8	105.3	118.0	87.4	64.6	69.8	67.8	46.5
Contract	57.7	41.3	73.2	54.6	43.7	57.3	21.8	17.8
Total	153.5	146.6	191.2	142.0	108.3	127.1	89.6	64.3

FIGURE 7-3   Projection of work load expressed in man-hours.

The rate at which incoming orders are received is a good clue to future business. Is the backlog swelling or shrinking? Also, the customers' delivery request dates are clues to the future. If orders are coming in but the customers are not asking for early delivery, lower future business levels seem likely. Most companies watch the rate of incoming orders very carefully and keep up-to-the-minute records of the backlogs of orders ahead.

If backlogs shrink you don't just accept this as evidence that business will slide off in future months. Instead you react to this expectation by going harder after additional orders. This is where you might cut prices to get business.

You know, too, that order backlogs always have some "fat" in them (customers sometimes cancel orders) and you know that the fat swells when backlogs grow bigger. When customers find that they have to wait longer than usual they react by placing orders sooner than they normally would and by ordering more than they want. Sometimes they even place duplicate orders with two or more companies. When one order is received, they cancel the others. Backlogs may, therefore, be big because they contain some orders that really belong to more distant months and they contain protection orders which are bound to be reduced or canceled.

You can express order backlogs in many ways. You can list the number of orders, or their dollar value, or the dollar value of basics, or tonnage, or man-hours, or other measures. You can also use two or three such measures. The main thing is to express the load in a way that reflects the factory's capacity for turning out work. If the factory turns out $1 million in value of products every month, a $4 million backlog is about four months' work. Actually, such a backlog probably includes some work which will take up to seven or eight months to finish, so the plant has some open capacity within the next four months. Figure 7-4 shows how the backlog can be projected. Often the work loads for different departments differ so that you need to calculate each separately.

When forecasting for manufacture to order, allow room for rush jobs. Don't give promise dates for early delivery for enough orders to use up all of your capacity. If experience shows that rush jobs will average 10 per cent of your business, set schedules for all other jobs to use up only 90 per cent of your capacity.

In order to quote tentative delivery promise dates on new jobs being bid for, all prospective jobs have to be translated into work load equivalents and checked against the plant's open capacity. TRW's automotive division translates all prospective new business into man-hours at a fixed rate of one man-hour of direct labor for each $24 of business. Then it compares the man-hours needed to those available.

In most companies many jobs are bid for but only a few are obtained. The promise dates finally agreed upon for jobs obtained depend upon the plant's open capacity when the order is received. If business is picking up, it may be better, as we suggested earlier, to expand the plant's capacity or subcontract more work to outside companies rather than keep customers waiting for lengthy periods.

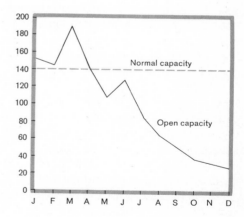

FIGURE 7-4 Chart showing graphically the load of work called for in figure 7-3. Notice that the distant future is largely open capacity. This does not mean that slack times are ahead, only that some of the work to be done from May on will be on orders which Central has not yet received and which will fill up most or all of the unallocated capacity.

But this doesn't always occur. "Heavy" industry, such as steelmaking, uses very expensive equipment and cannot expand quickly, nor would it want to expand unless it were sure that the order level would stay high. Plant capacity as of any given moment has a distinct upper limit. If sales orders in the steel industry exceed that amount, the steel companies just have to let customers wait because it costs so much and takes so long to add new capacity.

Most companies can, however, be more sales minded and can expand production without increasing their costs or decreasing their efficiency very much. And even companies in heavy industry don't work at capacity very much of the time. Most of the time even they can respond to customer demands.

FORECASTING INDIVIDUAL PLANT SALES
Giant companies are always in many businesses and have many plants. As we have said, most are organized on a "divisional" basis, with each division specializing in a product line. And in many cases, divisions have few connections with each other so far as production control is concerned. There are, however, occasional interdivision deals. At General Foods, one plant makes Log Cabin Syrup, Jello Pudding, and Kool-Aid for other divisions. And we have mentioned in Chapter 5 that in General Motors the AC Spark Plug division makes spark plugs and the Fisher Body division makes bodies for all of the auto divisions. In each of these cases the products of one division go to one or more other divisions. The manufacturing schedules of the supplying division depend on the schedules of the using division.

NEED FOR CENTRAL FORECASTING   So far as production control is concerned, giant company divisions usually do their own industry forecasting at divisional headquarters. Forecasts of all large contracts that affect several plants are handled there. Besides this, each local plant forecasts its local business and sends the forecast to the home office where all forecasts are summed up and correlated.

It is necessary for the divisional office (or even the corporation's central office) to be active in the picture because some contracts are with giant customer companies. Often they involve enormous quantities of products and run into millions of dollars. The buying company has many plants all over the country and so does the seller. The buyer wants the products he buys to be delivered to several plants, not just one. As a rule the order will be divided up inside the vendor company or division and portions of the total order will be assigned to the plants nearest the customer's plants.

Individual plants have little to say in all of this and have no forecasting to do in connection with the amount of this kind of business they get.

Actually, even the central office has more trouble forecasting big customer orders than would seem necessary. It would seem that all that they would need to do would be to get from the customer the delivery schedules that he expects you to meet in the weeks or months ahead. It isn't this simple, however. Ask your customer for such a schedule and probably he'll give you one. But he won't hold to it. If his business goes up or down, he'll boost or cut his release orders. You aren't much better off than if you had to forecast unknown business. Not only this but the typical contract doesn't even say how many in total the customer will contract to buy. The contract assures you only that you will get the agreed percentage of his total requirements of the item.

Sometimes, very expensive production lines have to be set up (or have already been set up) to do this work in one or two plants. When this is so, these plants may make the products involved for the whole nation and not just for customers in their normal territory. Again, though, the home office tells you what to produce. Individual plants do what they're told. Some companies (Whirlpool for one, Eaton, Yale and Towne, for another), however, let rival sister plants capable of making the same products bid for jobs. Again, the winning plant may get a contract to serve customers outside of its normal territory.

Forecasts for individual plants of multi-plant companies are sometimes changed as time goes along if one plant gets very busy while another is on short hours. When this happens, the home office sometimes shifts orders from one plant to another. The Aluminum Company of America's home office in Pittsburgh has, for example, at all times, a record of the load of work ahead for each division in each of its factories. It knows the load of the Los Angeles factory's aluminum foundry, its aluminum ingot department, its magnesium foundry, and its extrusion department. It also knows its loads in similar departments at Alcoa, Tennessee, and its other plants. Regardless of original forecasts, orders are shifted among plants by the Pittsburgh office whenever individual plant loads get out of balance. This practice reduces the importance of individual plant forecasts.

HOME PLANTS   In Chapter 5 we spoke of some companies having a home plant. Usually it is the company's original and largest factory. It is a large producer of regular products and is the only producer of some items. It supplies certain parts to all sister plants, domestic and foreign. Its forecasts differ from that of the other plants in that it must include the total company needs for many items. Besides it must pay attention to lead times and get parts to sister plants in time to meet their assembly needs.

SISTER PLANTS AS CAPTIVE CUSTOMERS   Most multi-plant companies require customer plants to buy parts (at least when much money is involved) from sister parts-making plants. Normally they don't admit this. They say that any division manager is free to buy parts anywhere. But can you imagine GM letting Chevrolet buy Briggs bodies, made by Chrysler, for its cars? Or can you imagine GM letting Chevrolet buy its ignition systems from Eltra (an outside company) thereby putting GM's Delco-Remy division on short hours?

A parts-making plant's forecast of its business for sister plants depends upon sales forecasts of the parts-using plants. Many parts-making plants, however, have business of other kinds and sell some products to outside customers. Forecasts of sales to outsiders would be made in the usual way.

Quite a few multi-plant companies, possibly the majority, don't require customer plants to buy *everything* they can from sister plants. Except for the big items, vendor plants in these companies really do have to compete for and bid for sister plant business in the same way as outsiders. Each plant is, from an accounting point of view, on its own and has to earn its own profit. When you quote a price to a sister plant, you figure it just like prices to outsiders. Set the price to cover costs plus a profit. If the buying plant thinks the price is too high, it buys elsewhere.

Companies *requiring* you to purchase from sister plants often determine prices the same way as they do for outsiders. But they sometimes get into arguments about what is a fair price, especially when there is no regular outside market price for the item. Some companies avoid this trouble by transferring products from vendor to customer plants at cost or near cost. At such a price the customer plant is not likely to be able to go elsewhere and get a better price even if it were permitted. Selling plants don't like this, though, because their margins are so low that they don't appear to make much money.

But our subject at the moment is forecasting. How do these policies affect forecasting? These policies have to do with the products you (in the vendor plant) make. *Plants having to compete for sister plant business don't always get it.* You have to forecast sister plant business just the same as outside business because you do not know for sure whether you will get this business or how much of it you will get.

FORECASTING REPAIR PARTS VOLUME

In Chapter 3 we listed several kinds of "incidental" manufacturing which must be carried on along with the main production activities. Normally you don't forecast the volume of products made in incidental manufacture. But sometimes some of the items run into enough volume so that their forecasting becomes necessary.

This is particularly true of repair or "service" parts. Often these are quite important in total volume and two markets, rather than one, exist for them. You need to forecast each market separately. The first market is the customer, the user of the product. He will need repair parts. If he is in some far corner of the world, he may want to buy a kit of commonly needed repair parts when he buys the product.

If you sell repair kits you may end up selling almost as many kits as the customer needs for whatever part wears out the fastest. Once a kit is opened and a repair part used, the repairman sometimes throws away the leftovers from the kit, or he is careless with the remaining parts from opened kits, especially when they are individually small, low-cost items. Then if the same failure occurs again and the part can't be located in an opened kit, a second one is opened and the cycle repeats.

Whether you make up standard kits of parts or not, customers will from time to time order repair parts from the factory. These orders will be few when models are new, will grow as products get older, and will taper off as that model finally wears out and is discarded.

The second market is your dealers. Dealers who sell and service products need stocks of repair parts. Their orders will be heavy at first as they lay in supplies.

Probably you will have to estimate how much extra to allow for repair sales whether you make finished products directly to customers' orders or products for your own finished stock. Company customers sometimes tell you how many extras of each part they want for their repair parts stock. The United States Armed Forces does this on orders for parts for guns, airplanes, and other items. However, most customers don't know, as well as you do, which parts of your products will wear out and how often. Probably they'll expect to carry very few repair parts themselves but they will also expect you to keep a supply and to give them good service. You will have to decide on how many extra to make up to take care of repairs.

Teletype Company, a Western Electric subsidiary, doesn't forecast its need for service parts for current products at all. Instead it just "robs" its current stock. At the end of each month, it sums up the robberies and adds the quantities on to the requirements for the fifth month ahead. (Teletype uses a five-month rolling master schedule.) Experimental needs for regular parts are handled the same way at Teletype. Doing this cuts out a rather difficult forecasting job.

Optional accessories to the main product also need separate forecasts. Often they are substantial products in themselves. Some customers want radios and heaters in automobiles but other customers don't want them. A farmer buying a tractor may buy a power scoop with it or he may not. Accessory products of such value need to be forecast in the same manner as main products.

When optional accessories are actually alternatives you have a different problem. In this case you do want one kind of product and you do not want the alternative. Automobile buyers may order tinted glass, automatic gear shifts, or foam rubber cushions. If they do, then you will not only want more of these special items but fewer regular items. If you don't forecast such accessories separately, you might end up with a correct total forecast but a wrong mix of accessories. And you usually can't shift production from one accessory to another. You can't shift machines for making spring seat cushions to foam rubber seat cushions.

EVALUATING CURRENT SALES
Companies selling products through dealers to the consuming public have a hard time evaluating their sales accurately because they are several stages removed from the consumer. Factory sales go up sometimes when it is largely accounted for by an increase in inventories held by wholesalers and retailers. The company knows what it has sold and what its remaining inventories are but its sales are to wholesalers and their inventories are unknown. Wholesalers, in turn, sell to retailers whose inventories are also unknown. Retailers almost never bother to answer requests from manufacturers about their stocks, and the same is largely true of wholesalers. The point is that you don't know for sure whether a sales increase today means that you should increase production or not.

There is a real danger that changes in consumer demand may, because of the way retailers and wholesalers order, reach the factory in wavelike convolutions. If a sales pickup depletes a retailer's stock, he orders the usual number of replacements plus more. This reorder may be double what he usually orders. His increased orders quickly deplete the wholesaler's stock so the wholesaler places a big order with the factory. The factory gets lots of big orders so it steps up production. By the time the orders are filled the consumer demand bulge is past and everyone has too big a stock, so orders to the factory almost disappear.

Jay Forrester developed a simulation technique for studying the effects of changes in sales levels as they relate to delays in the flow of reports of sales.[1] Such a model of the distribution system allows you to experiment with different ordering policies and, through simulation, to determine

[1] See Jay W. Forrester, *Industrial Dynamics*, The M.I.T. Press, Cambridge, Mass., 1961.

the best policy. Forrester called his investigation a study in "industrial dynamics."

Some manufacturers get help on their problem of estimating the size of dealer stocks by using "warranty" cards. They are put on such items as electric blankets, electric irons, and window air conditioners. The card explains the manufacturer's guarantee and shows the product's serial number. The customer is asked to send in the card showing his date of purchase to establish a date from which the company guarantee runs. A good many customers fill out the warranty cards and send them in to the manufacturer, thus telling him how many of his products have been sold to customers. From this the manufacturer can estimate the number remaining in dealers' hands. This knowledge helps him interpret dealer orders, and tells whether they are ordering more or less than they are selling.

Evaluating the size of dealers' stocks is by no means the only problem in evaluating your current sales. Suppose, for example, you have just put on a successful sales campaign. Maybe part of your sales gain has come merely from advancing your customers' buying. Some of next month's customers were persuaded to buy this month. If this is so, you can expect lower sales next month. Or maybe you have temporarily gotten some of your competitor's business. Can you keep it? Or maybe you have, for the moment, stimulated consumer consumption. Will it last? You have to answer these questions before you know whether to change production schedules or not.

Seasonal changes also require interpretation. If sales in March, for example, are usually 10 per cent above February, what if they are 20 per cent up this year? Was March unusually good? Was February unusually poor? Did you get part of April's business in March? Or is business going to be better from here on? You have to decide the meaning of the results you get. Parenthetically we want again to note that this is another part of production control work that you can't turn over to a computer.

An industrial dynamics simulation model might be helpful here. You could construct a model which would let you see what course of action would be best considering your interpretation of the reasons why your current sales are what they are.

TENTATIVE AND APPROVED FORECASTS

Before talking about tentative and approved forecasts we should note that the distinction between them applies only to companies making products *to stock* or to longtime continuing customer orders, and not to job lot companies.

In companies making products to stock, forecasts are always both tentative and approved at the same time. Distant months (6 to 12 months) are tentative; close months (1 to 3 months) are specific and approved. Approved forecasts are supposed to be firm or fixed and not subject to change. You make your factory production schedules from them. But actually even the factory schedules you make from firm forecasts never stay wholly unchanged.

Before you firm up a sales forecast you must translate it into factory capacity requirements. Investigate its machinery and manpower requirements, inventory requirements, and new equipment requirements. Do these things for each department and for each type of equipment. Wherever you find that the forecast calls for more capacity than you have, something has to change. Maybe you will have to cut down the forecast. Maybe you will end up buying more machines. Maybe you will decide to run two shifts in some departments. Or maybe you will buy more items outside.

Suppose that the forecast won't keep the plant busy. Then you have to plan to cut work hours, buy less on the outside and make more items inside, or raise the forecast and either sell more or build up inventories. If you raise the forecast, that isn't quite what you do. You raise the quantity that you will *manufacture* above the forecast. But if you do that, remember, if the forecast proves to be a correct forecast of sales, you will be building up inventory. Better be sure that this inventory will be sold before too long. Don't build up inventories unless sales upswings are in the offing. On the other hand, you may want to build up inventories in slack periods ahead of sales peaks both to give steady employment and to avoid having to go on overtime later in the year.

Everyone should be quite sales minded when thinking about whether the factory can or cannot produce the tentative sales forecast requirements. Never cut back sales forecasts calling for more than you can produce without good reason. Consider both hiring more men and buying new equipment before you cut a forecast. Don't invite customers to go to your competitor because you are out of stock if you can help it.

At the same time, don't overlook economical production. Meeting forecasts by having a lot of "stand by" labor or equipment most of the time is costly. Production men are sometimes "out-talked" in schedule-making meetings by sales and engineering representatives. The sales department talks them into accepting forecasts that result in irregular operations. Or sales and engineering together talk the production men into accepting difficult and costly designs without enough objection. Important though sales is, don't let it dominate schedule making so much that costs are pushed into the background.

Never approve a forecast until you know its money requirements. In-

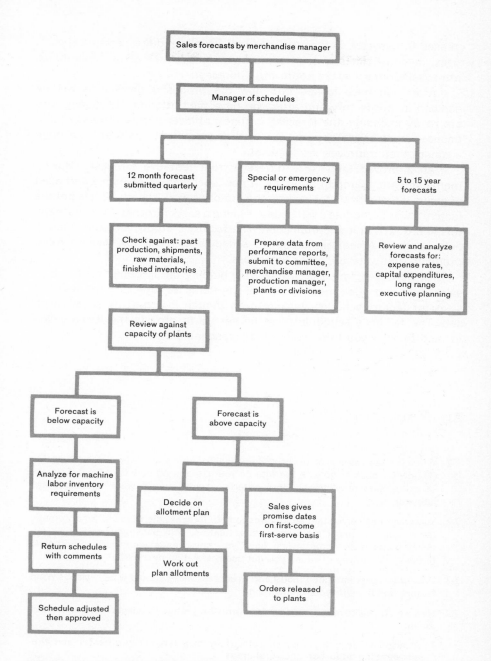

FIGURE 7-5 Johns-Manville's procedure for making up preliminary estimates and translating them into plant production schedules. (Johns-Manville Corp.)

creases in capacity, if they are needed, usually require capital expenditures. Inventory fluctuations, too, involve money. Take all of these things into consideration before approving a forecast.

After you have looked into how the proposed production will be handled in the factory and after you have paid attention to money, you are ready to change the forecast so that it reflects sales, production, and finance needs as well as you can work them all out together. Top management then approves the forecast.

An approved forecast is different from tentative forecasts. Having management's stamp of approval, it now becomes an objective and a set of goals. It is the basis for making the factory's work schedule. It is not the factory's work schedule itself because being a sales forecast it has too many ups and downs in it for production. The factory's production schedule will be smoother. At certain times its schedule will call for making more products than you sell, other times less.

An approved forecast is, however, binding on all departments. It is sales' goal and sales must try to sell the items as forecast. And it is the *basis* for factory schedule making even though it is not the schedule itself. The factory's schedule must be set up to provide the items called for and to allow you to make them at reasonable cost.

STUDY MATERIALS

7-1 When you use regression or correlation techniques in analyses you need to decide (1) how far back to go with the figures you use and (2) how far ahead it is safe to extrapolate projections. What criteria would you use when making these judgments?

7-2 You could use correlation techniques to help forecast the demand for automatic transmissions, power steering, radios, heaters, trim packages, and other optional features of automobiles, once you have made your basic automobile forecast. Would you or would you not use correlation here? Why?

7-3 Once a forecast has been made and accepted, when should it be revised? What factors would justify your changing it?

7-4 How would you go about making short- and long-range forecasts if this were your job in:

1 A large public utility supplying electricity to a large urban center and the surrounding suburban and rural areas

2 A major automobile company

3 A parts-making division of the above company

4 A medium-sized company manufacturing machine tools

5 A major commercial airline

7-5 How can you forecast sales very well when changes in customer demand result in convolution-like waves of reordering? Such a change first depletes the retailer's shelves, so he reorders heavily to replenish his low stock and to take care of the new level of demand. The wholesalers and jobbers find their stocks dropping rapidly so they double or triple their reorders and the factory is swamped. By this time the sales bulge has passed and the retailer is heavily stocked so he cuts his orders. Wholesalers and jobbers stop ordering altogether and the factory goes from overtime to short hours.

Is there anything at all that can be done about this?

7-6 Why not fight back at demand changes with parallel price changes? When business is slack, cut prices; when there is too much business, raise prices. Would this let you keep orders coming in more or less equal to capacity?

7-7 In your industry you use the "standard volume" idea and price products so that all tooling overheads are paid for when standard volume is reached. What, if anything, should you do with prices if (1) it appears that standard volume will not be reached, (2) you surpass standard volume?

7-8 Suppose that you expect to sell 100,000 units of product A at $300 each if you spend $1 million on advertising. This would yield a $4 million profit. Fixed costs are $10 million.

Since the market is responsive to both price and advertising changes you might earn more money if you changed these factors. Assume that price elasticity is 0.5, meaning that for every 2 per cent change in price there is a reverse change of 1 per cent in the number of units sold. And assume that advertising is effective on a 1:5 basis, meaning that if you added 100 per cent to the advertising budget, you'd increase sales 20 per cent. Because of capacity limitations you can produce no more than 130,000 units of product A. You may neglect all other factors.

What should be your price and advertising budget? How many units would you sell and what would your maximum profit be?

chapter eight

ESTIMATING

Estimating is a special type of forecasting. You try to figure out how you will make a product, how much time and how much materials it will take, how much it will cost, and when you will be able to deliver the job if you get the order. Most of the emphasis is on the cost of the product. The delivery date, however, is also important on special products. On engineering projects, when a product can be delivered is often more important to the customer than small differences in price.

Predicting what new things will cost before they are made is partly guesswork. No engineer can foresee every detail in making a new product nor can he or anyone else know beforehand what its exact cost will be. But when new products are similar to old products he can come close.

ESTIMATING DEPARTMENTS   Companies manufacturing to order usually assign estimating to a separate estimating and contract writing department which works mostly with sales and engineering but also with production control, purchasing, and the plant superintendent. Some companies making engineering-type products to order have a "preplanning" department which helps make cost estimates. Its principal duties are to decide on the tooling needed in order to turn out unusual jobs, and after contracts are signed, to obtain whatever special tooling is required. It also orders all purchased parts that take a long time to get. This department does these things before detailed planning for making the order starts. This way the factory is not held up when it starts to plan the order's production.

PRODUCT LINE MANAGERS AND PRODUCT ENGINEERS   Companies manufacturing to stock often have no estimating department as such. Product line managers are responsible for seeing that the company has the right products in their lines. They are responsible, in their lines, for getting new products developed, for making long-range forecasts of the market for new products, and for investigating the prospective manufacturing costs for making new products.

Product line managers (primarily marketing men) may feel that certain new products will be needed two or three years hence. They sketch out the product's outlines, its features, cost, and price—but only as targets. Then the design department makes up tentative designs and product engineers in the engineering department look them over to see how they should be made and to calculate the cost.

There is no separate work set apart and called estimating yet the estimating gets done in the general process. The product engineer usually ends up doing most of the cost estimating for product line managers. Companies manufacturing to stock which do not use product line managers usually have new product committees to pass judgment on new products. Again, the engineering department does most of the actual cost estimating.

Actually only engineers can do the estimating in such situations because only they can know how the new product should be made, what machines will be used, and what the cost of operations will be. Within the engineering department one engineer will probably be assigned the job of putting together all of this information and coming up with the estimate. He is called a product engineer, a project engineer, or a manufacturing engineer. If the new product is approved and put into production he will be assigned to "father" it. He has the responsibility for getting production facilities to make the product set up and he oversees them until production is running smoothly.

Estimators sometimes have to work both sides of the street. On the one hand, they are *making estimates.* Yet since most special jobs require the buying of certain components and new tooling, the estimators have to ask outside companies for estimates on such items in order to complete their product cost estimates. Here they are *asking for estimates.*

COST ESTIMATES AS GOALS
Cost estimates should always be goals as well as forecasts. They should represent the result of efficient production and so really ought to be set a little on the tight rather than the loose side. You want the goal to be tight enough to make everyone buckle down and do his best. The factory is more likely to try hard to meet a tight cost estimate than it is to try hard to get costs down below a loose cost estimate. You can be pretty sure that workers will take it easy on high-estimate jobs and you don't want that.

In estimating you can sometimes be wrong and not know it. Workers and foremen adjust their pace to high or low estimates so that you may never find out that your estimating is poor. Because the cost records verify the estimates, they may look good when really they are not. Workers occasionally go so far as to "protect the estimator." When the work takes considerably more or less time than the estimate, they deliberately misreport their time. They may, with the foreman's tacit approval, charge their time to projects in accord with the estimates. This makes the estimator look good and helps the foreman live up to the budget for each job.

Such practices are not limited to the factory. Design and drafting work is particularly hard to estimate. Engineers often do not ring in and out on separate job cards but estimate their time on different jobs and report the distribution of their time at the end of the day. It is easy for them to cover up for deficient estimating of the amount of engineering time needed for jobs. Actually, misreporting of time is not much of a problem in most companies but in any case you should make every attempt to eliminate it. Pay particular attention to getting accurate reports on all new jobs.

After every job's completion (and assuming correct reporting), you should check its actual costs back against its estimate. This shows you the places where you went wrong and helps you spot production inefficiencies. And having learned where you were off on past cost estimates helps you make more accurate ones in the future.

THE ESTIMATOR'S RESPONSIBILITY FOR DESIGN

An estimator's job goes farther than mere cost estimating. Estimating cost is actually the *last* thing that he does. First, he tries to arrive at the most economical way of making the product so that he can estimate the cost of making it that way. To do this, he needs to know what work the machines you own can do and the costs of alternative methods. He needs to know what methods you ought to use for small orders, what methods are best for large orders, and the cost you'd end up with in each case. He even needs to know about methods that you do not use but which might be best if you were to buy some new machines. Then he can tell you which way is really best.

Figure 8-1 gives some idea of what we are talking about. Four companies bid on a large government order to make a bolt for an Army rifle. This part (not a "bolt" as in "nuts and bolts") helps hold the cartridge in place. One company decided to make the part out of bar stock; the other three decided on a forging. Notice the difference in machines to be used by the four companies. They reflect the machines the companies had available and the different preferences and backgrounds of the engineers. Estimators should be aware of different ways to do work and should choose the least costly way, considering the volume to be made.

The estimator should not rely wholly on his own knowledge of methods used in the company, but should talk to engineers, planners, tool designers, and even foremen. Maybe they'll have good ideas that never occurred to him. Or perhaps they will see ways to change the product's design a little here or there to allow it to be made at lower cost. The estimator should also check with production control to see if the ma-

FIGURE 8-1   How four companies make a gun part.

| | COMPANY AND STARTING MATERIAL | | | |
| | A
BAR STOCK | B
FORGING | C
FORGING | D
CLOSED DIE
FORGING |
	NUMBER OF MACHINES			
Screw machines	8	7		
Numerical control center: boring, milling	. . .	. . .	. . .	4
Multiple drill presses	1	3	8	
Drill presses	15	8	2	
Lathes	3	3	5	
Speed lathes	. . .	2		
Single-spindle automatic lathe	. . .	. . .	. . .	4
Power mills	19	13	21	
Hand mills	15	5	3	1
Spline mills	. . .	1		
Profilers	8	6	3	7
Grinders	1	. . .	2	2
Marking machines	1			
Power saws	1			
Centering machines	1			
Deep hole drill	. . .	. . .	3	
Total	72	48	47	18

chines best suited for the work are overloaded or if he can count on using them for the job. If they are overloaded and will stay overloaded, the estimator better count on less efficient machines and a little higher cost.

Estimating often is a matter of figuring out how to make a product for a stated cost instead of first figuring out how to make the product and then seeing what it costs. This raises the question of the estimator's right to change proposed designs.

Do you want estimators doing design work? No, not exactly. But you certainly don't want to close the door on the estimators' cost-saving ideas. Design should result from the joint efforts of the engineering and sales departments working with the estimator and, on big contracts, the customer. The customer is just as interested in low costs as you are. Product designers must design to a cost and the estimators must estimate to a cost. Often it takes considerable ingenuity on the part of everybody to give the customer what he wants at his price.

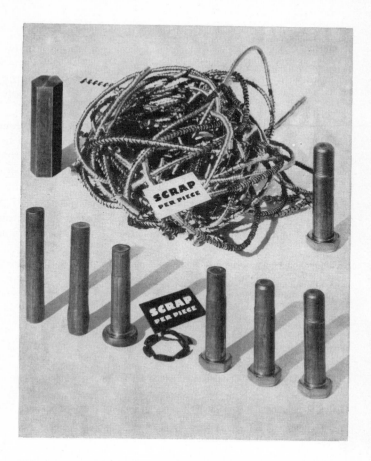

FIGURE 8-2   Here we see the results from making a bolt two ways. At the top, it is made from hexagonal bar steel, a costly procedure in both work and amount of waste steel. At the bottom are the stages a bolt goes through when it is made by the "cold heading" process, a less costly process and much less wasteful of material. It also produces a stronger bolt. (Lamson & Sessions Co.)

ROUGH ESTIMATES

Cost estimating is one kind of forecasting and, like other forecasting, can never be altogether accurate. Sometimes production workers get jobs out in less time than usual; sometimes they take longer. Machine and tool breakdowns may or may not occur and scrap losses vary. Even the time needed for paper work connected with jobs varies. All of these variations keep costs and schedules from working out as planned.

These difficulties are not usually serious, though. They tend to aver-age out so that, on an average basis, you can predict them rather well. Particularly is this true in estimating the costs of new products that are like old ones. And conversely, the greater the difference between new and old products the less reliable the estimates.

When manufacturing is to order, you may have to estimate for 5 to 10 or more jobs for every one you get. If you have to do that much esti-mating you have to pay attention to how much it costs to make estimates. What it amounts to is that every job you get has to bear the cost of esti-mating from 5 to 10 jobs. Look at figure 8-3. It shows the business volume that Danly Machine Corporation bid for over a 12-month period as well as the business it received. A much more dramatic example of the risks in bidding was the Lockheed-Boeing-Douglas bidding competition for the C-5A airplane contract which is described on page 167.

Customers sometimes want estimates made quickly. Both the cost and time factors limit the amount of effort that you can put into esti-

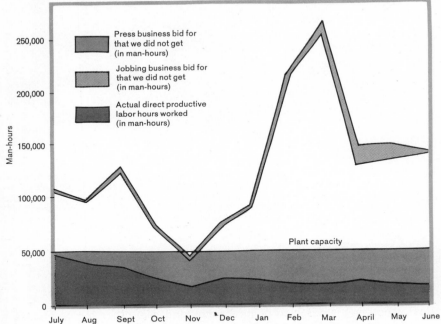

FIGURE 8-3 Desirable though it may be, it is not always possible to make thorough estimates on all prospective orders. Shown above is a comparison of the volume of business bid for (plotted according to the month in which the work might have been done) by Danly Machine Corporation to the business obtained. Under competitive situations it is normal rather than unusual to bid on several times the volume of business obtained. (Danly Machine Corp.)

mating. Often you have to choose between estimating thoroughly at considerable cost or estimating less thoroughly, getting less reliable estimates, but doing it at low cost.

Estimating never needs to be as accurate on small jobs as on big jobs because less money is involved. Machine setup costs are, however, high proportionally on short runs, so they may need to be estimated apart from machine operation costs.

OVERALL MEASURES You can often get reasonably accurate low-cost estimates by using overall measures such as are used in the construction industry. Building costs of houses tend to be somewhere near the same amount per square foot for given types of houses. Multiply the square foot cost by the square feet in a house that you are thinking of building and you will get a pretty good approximation of its cost.

In manufacturing you can use the same idea. Use a new product's weight times your usual cost per pound, or the area times the cost per unit of area. Foundries often estimate using weight. Sheet metal shops do the same, only they use the square feet of sheet metal times their usual cost per square foot.

Rough estimates are about the only kind that most small job lot shops use. Small machine shops, for example, sometimes estimate costs by first estimating the direct labor man-hours a job will require. The labor cost of these man-hours is multiplied by, perhaps, 4 to get a figure which is ample to cover all other costs except materials. Materials costs are then added. On fussy, exacting jobs and on rush jobs the multiplier may be 5 or even 6 instead of 4.

Job lot foundries follow a little different method in estimating. They lump all costs into two or three per pound rates. Simple castings requiring little labor are estimated at one cost figure per pound. More complicated castings have a higher cost figure per pound. The specific needs of individual jobs are not considered unless they are extreme.

Estimators frequently must take estimates of cost without being given the details of the product to be made. The prospective customer sends only a "schematic" drawing giving an overall idea of how the product is to work and what it is to do. There are no drawings of parts because no one has figured them out yet.

The estimator has to figure out what kind of mechanism the product will be, its "configuration." Then he decides on its parts. He figures out how they can be made and what tools will be required. Lastly, he estimates the costs of everything. If he were to make up drawings for the product and all its parts, the cost of estimating would be skyhigh. He must, therefore, try to visualize the whole thing and make his estimates as well as he can with nothing more concrete to go on than the schematic drawing. probably he will base his figures on ratios, of the kind we discussed earlier, for some parts of his estimate.

CAREFUL ESTIMATES

Figure 8-4 is a summary cost estimate form used by TRW. This is the end result when TRW makes up estimates for orders for values.

Careful estimates, thoroughly done, usually give you fairly accurate figures but they are costly to make up unless the new product is very much like some of your old products. Careful estimating requires that the estimator do almost as much work as the planning department does after it gets orders. He has to make up parts lists and decides (with, for big items, the help of a committee which includes purchasing) whether the parts should be bought outside or made inside. He must estimate the cost of purchased items. For things to be made inside he has to decide how they are to be made, what machines and tools will be needed, their cost, and the cost of doing the various operations. He will need to make process sheets for each part. Then he must list every pattern, die, tool, gage, and accessory needed and estimate its cost. The estimator has to keep in mind the costs of the design and manufacture of any special tools. Perishable tools, those which wear out, should be listed in the quantity appropriate to the size of the order.

The estimator needs to calculate how long it will take to set up machines and how much machine time and man time are needed for locating work on the machine, clamping it down, measuring it, performing the operation, and removing the product. Again, he has the help of other departments, in this case the time study department. And he needs to allow for normal lost time and machine maintenance costs.

Accurate estimating must also consider the productivity rate of workers but you don't have to go so far as to estimate whether Jones or Smith will do the job faster and how much faster. True, men work at different rates but you can neglect these differences both in cost estimating and in setting delivery promise dates because they will average out. Sometimes, though, whole departments differ in their rates of performance. You should take this under consideration if your estimates are going to be right. If your business is expanding and you're hiring lots of new men, it would be a good idea to expect a reduction in the plant's overall efficiency until the newcomers learn their new jobs well. But if business is slowing down and you are laying men off, your efficiency is likely to go up because the laid-off men

Form 377-8 TPM

COST ESTIMATE SUMMARY   N⍛ 61571

DIVISION _____

Customer's Name _____   Date Completed _____

Customer's Part No. _____ Part Name _____
Date Required _____ Delivery Promised _____

Customer Quantity Requirements _____
Total Quantity this Order _____ Tool Design Flow Time _____ Tool Design $ _____
Quantity for Tool Recovery * _____ Tool Mfg. Flow Time _____ Tool Mfg. $ _____
Quantity per Set-Up _____ Production Flow Time _____ Tool Purch's. $ _____
Material - Purchased ( ) Furnished ( ) TOTAL FLOW TIME _____ TOTAL $ _____
MATERIAL _____ Add ___% _____
_____ TOTAL TOOL $ _____

No.	DEPARTMENT NAME	STD. D.P.L. HRS. PER 100	DEPT. COST PER 100 PCS.	SET-UP HOURS	SET-UP COST
301	Automatics				
302	Turret Lathes				
303	Milling Etc.				
304	Drill Presses				
305	Surface Grinding				
306	Cylinder Grinding				
307	Bench Work				
308	Punch Presses				
309	Vane Wheel				
310	Assembly				
311	Heat Treat				
312	Plating				
313					
314	Inspection				
315	Packaging				
316	Pre - Production				
317	Piston Pins				
318	Tie Rods				
319	Hydraulic Coupling				
	TOTALS	$		$	

SET-UP CHARGE SUMMARY

Set-Up Cost (without Scrap) _____
____ Pcs. Set-Up Scrap - Mat'l. _____
____ Pcs. Set-Up Scrap - ½ Labor _____
           SUB - TOTAL _____
Add ____% G and A, Div. Adm. _____

          TOTAL _____

COST ESTIMATE SUMMARY

Manufacturing Cost /100 _____
Add ____% G and A, Div. Adm. _____
          SUB - TOTAL _____
Royalties _____
_____
_____
          SUB - TOTAL _____
Profit ____%

          SALES PRICE _____

Add ____% Variance _____
Add Material Cost per 100 _____
Add ____% Scrap Allowance _____
         SUB - TOTAL _____
Add Tooling Recovery per 100 _____
Manufacturing Cost (without Set-up _____

QUOTATIONS TO CUSTOMER:
Date _____ _____
Price per ____ Pieces $ _____ $ _____
Separate Tooling Charge _____ _____
Set - Up Charge _____ _____

Notes on Quotation _____
_____
_____
_____
_____

✳ Total Quantity of Sales expected before Major Design Change OR Total Quantity which Tools will Produce whichever
is smaller is to be used.

FIGURE 8-4 Cost estimate summary showing the items which must be included.
(TRW, Inc.)

are the newest and least efficient. Those you keep are your most experienced and best.

In estimating you do quite a bit of work for bidding purposes. For regular production you have to do these same things for production purposes. The difference between making estimates and planning for production ends up being more a difference of purpose than a difference in what you do and how you do it. If you can do a good job of planning for production you can do a good job of estimating for bidding.

The costs you incur in making a careful estimate are not lost if you get the order. Parts lists and operation lists, made up for estimating purposes, can be used just as they are as the basis for shop orders. This saves new planning and routing work and makes sure that the factory uses the processes you figured on during bidding. Comparing actual costs with estimates is also made easy.

RELATION OF VOLUME TO ESTIMATES

The proper way to make anything depends upon how many you are going to make and how good they have to be. High quality costs more than low quality, usually disproportionately more, so both quality and volume are important in estimating.

Of the two, though, volume is usually more important, particularly if the volume is large. Volume is of top importance because it sets the proper depth of tooling. If you have enough volume to justify special tooling you can usually design the tooling so as to take care of both quality and quantity problems at the same time. As we said in Chapter 7 on Forecasting, when you look at a product's prospective volume while deciding the proper depth of tooling, be sure to look at its prospective total volume, not the volume in the next few months, or even the first year. Give your estimator forecasts beyond this year so he can base his cost estimate on the depth of tooling appropriate for the total volume expected. If the tooling engineer chooses the wrong depth of tooling he will not come up with the lowest price for the quantity to be made.

For volumes of up to 100 of any small product, rarely will it pay to set up any special purpose equipment at all. Do the work on general purpose machines with standard tools. But if you get up into the 500 range or more, you can probably justify some special tools and holding fixtures. For 1,000 or more it usually pays to design and make at least some special tools, fixtures, magazine feeds, or other product-handling devices for the order. Still higher volumes, say 25,000 and up, usually justify machines and tools being specially made just for the job, even if they cost thousands of dollars.

Customers know, of course, that their large orders reduce the company's costs. They often ask for separate bid prices for each of several different quantities. The estimator plans for the tooling appropriate for each volume in his quotations. Incidentally, if the customer has asked for prices for both large and small quantities, for safety's sake file both bid prices in the order-receiving department. Customers sometimes make "mistakes" on their orders. They may order a small quantity but show the low large-quantity unit price on their order.

DOLLAR VOLUME ESTIMATES   Some companies don't give estimators much to go on in the way of long-range volume figures. As we said in Chapter 6, some companies make their forecasts only in dollar volume figures for classes of products for next year. Estimators get no lists of individual products and quantities. Working with the production control department, the estimators translate the dollar volumes into their ideas of what the quantities of each product will be. Then they have to work with the tool engineer to see what facilities will be needed and what it will cost to make the product.

CAPITAL EXPENDITURES   Prospective tooling and machine costs should be reported to management for approval before going ahead because they are capital investment items. If considerable money ($10,000 or more) is involved, the treasurer, controller, and vice president in charge of production probably should approve the order before you can buy new tooling and machines. Management will approve most reasonable requests for equipment because it knows that new products usually require some new machines. But management has to think of the whole company and channel its money to places where it will bring the greatest return. You may not get to buy new machines for every place you want them.

It may be necessary to allocate to each division less than the optimal funds it seeks in order to optimize the rate of return on invested funds in the company as a whole. Whenever you want to optimize any function, such as profits, under a given set of constraints, such as limited funds and available capacity, linear and related programming techniques often can be applied. These are described in Chapter 19.

INITIAL AND ULTIMATE OPERATING COSTS   In arriving at prospective costs estimators need also to consider whether new kinds of machines or newly mechanized production lines are to be used or whether you will do the job on old equipment. With new equipment there are nearly always many bugs to be worked out, and at first you won't get as much production as you will later on. This runs up production costs in the early period of use.

Frequently the time necessary to develop a smooth running operation is underestimated. With new, highly integrated operations, the actual debugging time often is more than double the time originally estimated. The problem is often complicated by the need to have the equipment produce some output before it is fully tuned and operating at maximum performance. In one case involving computerized steel-rolling mills, over a year was needed to get up to maximum production.

Some years ago one of the "big three" automobile companies mechanized its foundry where its engine blocks were cast. The cost of mechanizing ran into millions of dollars. Enough machinery was installed to make all the engine blocks for the company's popular priced car. Two eight-hour shifts were planned, and it was expected that the foundry would work at an 80 per cent utilization rate during the two shifts.

Everything went wrong: operations took longer to do than originally planned; the sand stuck to the patterns; the sand in the molds did not stick together; the castings came out with lumps on them, or holes or cracks in them. After several weeks of frantic effort to get production up, the foundry was still operating at only 40 per cent utilization. On top of it all the company's sales forecast proved too low; more engines were needed. Ten-hour shifts and Saturday production helped, but at high costs. Design engineers, industrial engineers, foremen—everyone was thrown into the breech to try to solve the production difficulties. Most of them were ultimately solved and the utilization ratio was brought up but it was a very expensive experience. The company thought it so serious that a few people lost their jobs.

This example is not typical although neither is it unique. New production facilities usually produce poorly at the start but not so poorly nor for so long as in this example. Most new machines in a new production line are improved models of familiar machines. For the most part they produce as planned. TRW set up several automatic production lines to make automobile parts. Its investment per employee, which had been $7,500, went up to $30,000. But its automatic lines were very successful; they turned out much more output than was expected. Besides, as an extra, quality improved too, in fact quality improved so much that this gain alone was enough to justify the investment.

In addition to figuring on the extra costs during the debugging period, the estimator needs to be realistic about the new equipment's ultimate output rate and its maintenance and operating costs. Many times companies have mechanized certain operations and found to their sorrow that they never fulfilled their promise. They got too little output and had too much maintenance, tool, and other expense. Cost estimates for production from new continuous production lines are so important to the company that the engineering department and the company's high officials make the final decisions so the responsibility is not that of the estimating department alone.

MACHINE USE RATIOS   The costs of operating mechanized production lines are greatly influenced by their use or utilization ratios. The use ratio is the machine's output divided by what it could possibly have turned out. If, during eight hours, a machine could turn out 500 pieces and it does turn out 300, its use ratio is 60 per cent. Machine-use ratios reflect man productivity, machine downtime, absences of operators, scrap work produced, etc. Sometimes men hold up machines, sometimes machines hold up men. Failure to estimate accurately the use ratio of new production lines can be tremendously costly in large-scale production.

It would seem that the production control department has to accept machine use ratios largely as they find them. But this is not so. Fast reaction by production control to delays reduces them and keeps machine-use ratios up. Woodward Governor gets 70 to 80 per cent from its general machine shop (where other companies doing similar work get 45 to 55 per cent) by using real-time control. Quick reporting of hold-ups in the factory coupled with quick reaction by production controllers and computerized order correcting keep machine-use ratios high.

When people talk about the output that can be expected from a machine or a line when it operates at a certain utilization rate, they are usually referring to its output *during normal working hours*. If a plant works only one shift a day it can always get additional production by working more hours or shifts. It is planned this way with expensive machines. Only a few of them are bought and they are used for two or three shifts, even when the rest of the plant works only one shift.

Doing this boosts output from expensive machines but it does make a few problems. It limits expansion because output can't be increased since these key machines are already being used day and night. Another trouble is that other departments, working only one shift, must build up large banks of products during the day to keep the expensive machines busy during the night. The next morning these machines will have built up large banks of products for the one-shift machines which perform the operations that follow. Storage space and extra handling costs may limit the possibilities of this solution.

Some operations, such as oil refining and certain chemical processes, must be on a three-shift, seven-day-a-week basis and the hourly output is almost rigidly fixed. In such cases, expected output and plant capacity are almost the same. In the steel industry, a slightly different situation occurs. Steelmaking operations are on a continuous basis, while the steel-finishing operations are done on a one- to three-shift basis depending on the demand for the various steel products.

OVERHEAD COSTS AND ESTIMATES

"Overhead" or "indirect" costs are those incurred not specifically for any one order or product. You can't charge them directly to orders or products. Fire insurance on a building is an overhead expense. "Direct" costs, in contrast, are incurred for individual orders or products and can be charged directly to those orders or products. The costs of materials used in products are direct costs, as are the wages of factory employees making the products.

In most manufacturing companies the overhead expenses are greater than the costs of direct labor. In some departments they are three or four times as much. Die cast shops and heavily mechanized departments go higher yet. Remember, though, that high overhead cost departments are often *low* cost per product departments because the high mechanization cuts direct labor costs.

ALLOCATING OVERHEAD COSTS   All cost estimates for jobs must include a share of the overhead costs. But since overhead costs are incurred for the benefit of all jobs, not for any particular job, it is necessary to prorate overhead to jobs.

One way to prorate indirect costs is to start by comparing last year's total indirect costs to last year's total direct labor costs and get a ratio of one to the other. Once this is done, assess this year's jobs with overhead at last year's ratio of direct labor. If last year's ratio was 2:1, you assess this year's orders with $2 for overhead for every $1 of direct labor that the orders incur.

Another way is to first allocate last year's overhead costs to machines and machine centers. This gives an overhead cost for operating the machine or machine center for the past year. Dividing this by the number of hours the machines were used last year gives you an hourly machine charge. Each machine and machine center has its own overhead charge for each hour that it is used for a job. Actually, many companies add in the operator's hourly rate and come up with one single rate per machine hour for each kind of machine. Estimators use this charge in estimating the costs of new jobs. There are other ways of allocating indirect costs to jobs but these two (basing it on direct labor dollars or machine hours) are the most common.

OVER- AND UNDERABSORPTION OF OVERHEAD Most overhead expenses are relatively fixed and stay about the same regardless of the company's scale of operations. Applying last year's ratio between overhead and direct labor will prove to assess the right amount of overhead *only* if this year's business about equals last year's business. But if there is more business this year, direct labor costs will be higher, as will overhead *assessments* to jobs. Although *actual overhead expenses* will increase a little, your assessments will "overabsorb" the overhead, and costs will be overstated. This year's jobs actually will cost less than claimed all year long.

If business drops off to less than last year's level the reverse occurs. You will "underabsorb" overhead and not all of it will get assessed to jobs. This problem is the same no matter how you allocate overhead.

It is important to note two facts about the amount of overhead charged to a product. First, *it is not a very accurate figure.* The total overhead that you assess in a year almost always proves, at the year's end, to have been too high or too low. Second, *the overhead assessment is a big part of the total stated cost of a product.* Consequently, the claimed cost of any product is only an approximation—regardless of how accurate some of the figures are that go into an estimate. And this is true whether you are talking about cost estimates for future jobs or the calculated costs of past jobs.

What we have just said becomes very important when you are bidding for jobs. *Since overhead goes on whether you get jobs or not* and since you don't know exactly how much overhead to assess to a job, you don't know exactly what a job will cost. True, you have a cost estimate—carried out to the penny. But the appearance of accuracy is specious.

OVERHEAD AND PRICING Everyone in the company knows this. So the sales department is usually allowed considerable freedom in setting prices when bidding for jobs. Of course, it tries to get business at prices that cover all the calculated costs (including overhead assessments) plus a profit. If it succeeds, fine and good. But if price cuts are needed in order to get jobs when your plant isn't busy, then let sales cut prices.

Of course, you don't like to cut prices and when you can get orders without doing it you don't cut them. But in bad times it is better to cut prices and get business than not to cut and have to close down. This can be demonstrated mathematically. We can say that profits, or earnings, are equal to revenue less total costs, or

$$E = R - C_t$$

But revenue is the price per unit P times the volume, or number of units sold, V. And total costs are the sum of the "out-of-pocket" costs, or variable costs, and the overhead, or fixed costs, C_f. Total variable costs are the product of the variable cost per unit C_v and the volume V. Thus the formula above can be written as

$$E = PV - (C_v V + C_f)$$

which then can be rearranged to read

$$E = V(P - C_v) - C_f$$

So long as some units are sold at a price per unit greater than the out-of-pocket cost per unit, the earnings will be greater than if no units were sold at all. If no products were sold the earnings would be negative, that is, a loss would occur, equal in size to the overhead costs. The volume at which the earnings or contribution exactly equals the fixed costs, and profits are zero, is called the break-even point.

$$V = \frac{C_f}{P - C_v}$$

This point can also be expressed as a percentage of plant capacity K, where K is the ratio of the volume to the plant capacity U.

$$K = \frac{V}{U} = \frac{C_f/(P - VC_v)}{U} = \frac{C_f}{U(P - C_v)}$$

ESTIMATES AND PRICES

The production control manager of one large company said that in his company he thought that estimating was not very important because most of its prices were set (too low, of course) by its competitors. Most companies probably find that many of their prices are, in the last analysis, set by competitors.

This actually *increases* the need for good estimating, however. With good estimates you know just how far you can go in shaving prices to meet competition. Bids, particularly for industrial buyers, may have to be shaved. You want to know what to do when you ask $7.50 each and the buyer says that Jones and Co. has already quoted $6.50. You'd better have good estimates so that you can see if and where you can cut costs more. Also, you will know when to drop out of the bidding and let someone else take on jobs at losing prices.

ESTIMATES FOR UNUSUAL PRODUCTS   Sometimes estimators are called upon to make estimates for items which differ considerably from the usual products. During a war, for example, automobile companies make tanks and other items foreign to their experience and for which their equipment is not well adapted. Naturally, you can't estimate very accurately on such completely different products. Estimating jobs of this nature are especially difficult for the estimator.

When a company has a new product which it wishes to buy outside, it sometimes has an "announcement" meeting at which it explains what it wants to buy to as many vendor company representatives as care to attend. Everybody gets a chance to bid for it. Sometimes prototype products or parts are made up and displayed at such shows. Normally such meetings are uncommon but during war periods and on war products they are common.

CONTRACT PRICES Companies making unusual products occasionally take contracts on a "cost-plus" basis. Cost-plus contracts are of two forms, cost plus fixed fee (CPFF) and cost plus fixed percentage (CPFP). The latter were quite popular in government contracting during the World War II. The difficulty with them is that there is a built-in incentive for inefficiency. As costs rise so do profits. There may be some justification for CPFP contracts during a war because of the uncertainty of the costs of making new kinds of products, but close policing and renegotiation become necessary in order to curtail abuses. In recent years CPFP contracts have fallen into disfavor.

CPFF contracts, on the other hand, tend to reward efficient performance. As costs are reduced, the percentage of profit on the sales dollar (and also on the investment) rises since the actual profits earned under the contract remain the same. Many government contracts today are CPFF contracts but with still further incentive provisions. If you beat the cost date of delivery, and performance targets, you get bonuses. Missing the targets brings penalties which reduce profits.

In writing contracts be sure that you, the vendor, protect yourself around the fringes. Spell out the quality of materials to be used, the accessories to be furnished, the free services to be offered, and such details. Otherwise you may get the contract and find that the customer will claim more than you figured on.

Jobs that you, as the successful low bidder, get sometimes cost more than you thought they would and you stand to lose money. You can tell the customer about your troubles. He may be willing to let you change the design in minor ways to save costs. He might (but don't count on it) even be willing to pay you more for fear quality will suffer a little if he doesn't.

Occasionally companies bid very low on a "one-shot deal" to get the contract. After they get it and work on it for a while, they tell the vendor that they are having trouble and try to get the price raised. They may even claim that they can't deliver it unless more is paid. By that time the customer can't place the order anywhere else because it is too late. This, obviously, is not the way to keep customers. At the same time most customers don't want their vendors losing money on their jobs lest corners be cut and quality lowered, so they may agree to a higher price.

A variation of this practice is to bid low on a contract with the expectation that the customer company will want to make changes in the delivery dates, quality, or equipment specifications during the life of the contract. The successful bidder then charges high prices for the changes and so boosts his overall profits. Of course you can't do this with regular customers and you probably wouldn't do it in bad times to any customer lest he not come back.

Similarly, you might bid low on a research and development contract with the expectation that this will be followed by production contracts where the profits can be made up. At least you would expect that the "know-how" accumulated during the research contract would give you an advantage in bidding on the production contract.

SEPARATE PRICE QUOTATIONS FOR ENGINEERING AND TOOLING
Vendors usually like to quote prices for the whole job and not to quote prices for parts of jobs, as for example, development and tooling. If you quote prices for tooling and for other parts of the job separately, customers sometimes are willing to agree to your prices wherever they think that you are low but they will object to the part of your bid that they consider high. By this method they try to get you to whittle down your overall bid.

This is not a problem on big contracts because everything is always out in the open. You always show separately the part of the price charged for engineering and for each part of the product. You may even show separate price figures for each operation, and the amount estimated for materials, direct labor, and overhead.

You expect to bargain over each item and to handle it the way the customer wants it. He may want, for example, to furnish his own foundry patterns and tooling for machines. Or he may want your company to design and make the tooling, particularly machine accessories. He may want to pay for special accessories for his jobs and to own them himself. Houdaille-Hershey finds that its auto company customers want to own their own tools. So does Dryden Rubber Company. Or your customer may let you handle tooling costs as you see fit, realizing that he pays for them when he pays his bill even though their costs are not shown separately.

Sometimes you have to pay for tooling yourself out of your own pocket. When automobile companies use two sources for a part, they usually pay for the tooling of only one supplier. If you, a second company, want to get part of their business, they may give you some orders but they will not pay extra for your tooling. Nor will auto companies pay even the first company directly for replacement tooling. You'll somehow have to squeeze its cost into the product's price.

Many large customers prefer to own the special tooling (including special machines) used for making their products so that, if they wanted to, they could transfer the job to another company. If you have a strike, or if he is dissatisfied with your work the customer can take his tooling out and get his product made elsewhere. If either of these situations seem likely, the customer may want you to mount the machines in some way so that they can easily be detached and moved. Your customer does not want to be too vulnerable to your strikes.

Sometimes you, the vendor, have patents on certain processes or tools used on a contract. In that case the customer would not own the tooling. Not owning it leaves him vulnerable to strikes in your plant should they occur. And often taking his tooling out of your plant wouldn't solve his problem. He'd need a whole factory to replace yours. Often you will have to give a customer "shop rights" to make and use tools covered by your patents used in making his products in case your plant is closed for any reason.

Regardless of how the customer pays for tooling and regardless of whether, technically, he owns it or not, rarely does he ever ask for it to be sent to his plant. A minor disadvantage in having tooling owned by the customer is the need to get his permission to scrap it in the future. He may hold back and make you keep it for years.

In estimating, you ought to think of customers individually. Some customers are more particular than others in ways that don't show on specifications. One of the "big three" automobile manufacturers, for example, has the reputation of rejecting more products than its competitors. The United States government, as a purchaser, is also a fussy customer. Maybe you need the business of difficult customers but your estimator might as well be realistic. Have him make your estimate high enough to cover the extra costs which such demands cause.

Customers often want hurry-up jobs done. If you accept orders on a hurry-up basis, have your estimator increase his expected costs by enough to cover overtime and other extras caused by rushing things. If the customer really is in a rush, quick delivery is worth something extra to him and he ought to be willing to pay for it.

STUDY MATERIALS

8-1 Under pressure from the Gigantic Mail Order Company buyer, the Little Miss dress company quoted a lower price on a lot of dresses. But upon delivery the dresses were found to be somewhat less attractive than the samples because they were made from poorer quality cloth than had been in the samples. Upon being taken to task, the Little Miss manager said that his company always made up samples and quoted as low a price as they reasonably could considering the quality but that at whatever price they got the contract, they used the best materials that they could afford for the price; the lower the price, the lower the quality.

Isn't this essentially what all suppliers do? To what extent does the estimate determine the price which in turn determines the quality?

8-2 A member company of the American Production and Inventory Control Society wrote in asking for ideas about how to set up a short-cut method of estimating labor for machine shop, mechanical assembly, and electric assembly work. His company is seeking "ball park" figures and a nomograph, chart, or sliding calculator method. What suggestions do you have?

8-3 Let us assume that a road scraper and a hi-fi set contain 1,000 and 300 parts, respectively. Each part requires from 1 to 20 operations, averaging about 5. Each operation has a setup time, an operating time, and usually some inspection time. Making up estimates for next year's models is a big job. Couldn't you get reasonable estimates for each of these products by putting last year's costs on a per pound basis, comparing this year's weight to last year's, and assuming that the same cost per pound would carry over?

8-4 The Hunsaker Company installed time clocks throughout the factory departments and instituted a system of job tickets for all direct labor and products. Workers were required to ring in and out on all jobs. They were paid by the hour. Before the policy of ringing in and out on time clocks was instituted, the employees had kept their own record of starting and stopping times on jobs. At the end of the day they copied these figures onto job slips and turned them in to the foreman, who approved them and sent them to the cost department.

A short time after the clock system had been installed, the chief cost accountant noticed, while out in the planer department, a man ring out on a job and in on the card for the next job while the first job was incomplete. The operator then returned to his machine and continued to work on the first job, although his job card now showed that he had finished it. A question was raised with the foreman, who said it was all right, that he had told the man to protect the estimator on that job. The job was taking longer than had been estimated, and the foreman was trying to see that the record was not too far from the estimate. This had been going on for years.

Who should know the estimator's estimate, job by job? How can you schedule production without using the estimate? How can you prevent a situation such as the one described? Or does it matter? Is it any concern of the production control department?

8-5 The Patterson Products Company has been asked to bid on steel washers for an automobile company. The washers are to be $\frac{1}{16}$ inch thick, $\frac{7}{8}$ inch in diameter, with a $\frac{5}{16}$ inch hole in the center. You are to estimate for 1,000, 10,000, 100,000, 250,000, and 500,000 per month.

You can make them on engine lathes, hand-screw machines, or an automatic single-spindle screw machine from $\frac{7}{8}$ inch bar steel. Or you can punch them out of steel strip, by hand feeding, mechanical feed progressive die, mechanical feed compound punch and die, or mechanical feed five-gang punch press and progressive punch and die. Thus there are seven methods in all. To simplify the problem you may omit setup time from consideration.

You find the following cost figures:

	METHOD						
	1	2	3	4	5	6	7
Production per hour	15	150	375	375	3,000	2,500	15,000
Tool cost per year	$10	$10	$50	$100	$200	$300	$600
Machine cost per year	$400	$600	$2,500	$400	$400	$400	$400
Labor cost per hour	$3.50	$3.50	$3.50	$3.00	$3.00	$3.00	$3.00

1 Find the lowest-cost method for each of the 5 volumes.

2 At what volume do you change from any one method to another method?

8-6 You are to decide how to make an order for heavy-duty brackets which have to have a hole through them to support a steel bar. You can make these brackets as steel castings or you can make them out of pieces of steel welded together. Since there are two alternatives in casting, you actually have three methods from which to choose. The methods available are:

1 Casting: using a wooden pattern which would cost $200 to build in the pattern shop. Only one cast bracket (which will weigh 2 lb.) can be produced per mold using this method. Direct labor cost per bracket is estimated at $1.20 and direct material at 30 cents per pound. The burden rate for foundry operations is 100 per cent of direct labor cost.

2 With an aluminum pattern it would be possible to produce six brackets per mold and effect other economies which would reduce the direct labor cost to 20 cents per pound. The material cost and burden rate would remain unchanged. An aluminum pattern would cost $340.

3 Component parts could be prepared from steel tubing and steel plate. These parts would be welded together to form the completed bracket. While the unit would weigh 2 lb., an additional 1 lb. of scrap would be produced for every satisfactory bracket turned out. Material cost will be 20 cents per lb. for the

steel stock as delivered from the local warehouse. The brackets will require approximately .5 hour of direct labor each. The labor rate is $3.40 per hour. The cost of "fringe benefits" for these workers is about 60 cents per hour, however, so that the company uses $4 per hour for their direct labor cost in estimating jobs. The burden rate for their department is 120 per cent of direct labor.

1 Assuming that you are to recover the full cost of the patterns on the first order, compute the total order cost and cost per unit using each of the three manufacturing alternatives for the following order quantities: 60, 120, 200, 320.

2 Plot the total order costs for question 1 on graph paper. Use dollars as the vertical scale and lot size as the horizontal scale.
   a What is the cost equation for each of the three methods?
   b Compute the order quantity at which it becomes economical to change from (1) method 3 to method 1; (2) method 1 to method 2.
   c Draw in the cost curves for each method on your graph, and show that the graph verifies the answers of 2b.

3 Explain the effect of the cost recovery policy outline in question 1 on the cost estimate for (a) initial orders; (b) repeat orders (assuming that the patterns may be used again).

4 Suppose that your company is in a bad slack period and the sales manager has asked you what "our lowest possible bid to get the job" should be. What costs would you consider in this case?

5 Do you agree with the company's position that "fringe benefits" are a direct labor cost?

6 How "exact" are cost estimates anyway? What are some of the factors which tend to make them approximations?

8-7 The Evans Manufacturing Company has recently bought the patent rights to Exhausto, a device to control exhaust fumes of automobiles. Evans expected to sell 5,000 units the first year, 10,000 units the second, 30,000 the third, 60,000 units the fourth, and 100,000 the fifth. Its engineers were given these figures to use for figuring the tooling and other facilities needed to produce Exhausto fume control devices.
   Here are three specific jobs that the engineers needed to calculate.

1 Welding two pieces of curving contoured steel castings together: With present machines this would take about 2.4 minutes for one man but making Exhausto parts would also require a new holding fixture costing between $2,000 and $2,500. To set up for automatically positioning, clamping, welding, and discharging the part, tooling costing between $50,000 and $75,000 would be required. Such tooling should do the operation in about 30 seconds. One operator would be required to tend the machine.
   Choose between these two alternatives (you may have duplicate facilities if you choose). Count interest on investment at 20 per cent of each year's starting investment. Don't forget to consider how much each method would turn out in a year and so arrive at how many sets of tooling you would need. Assume a 40-hour work week and an 80 per cent machine utilization ratio.

2 Welding the base. Present machines (using two men) plus $750 worth of new tooling would do the operation in about 5 minutes. Here an automatic machine

(using one man) would cost some $75,000 and do the operation in about 1 minute.

3 One casting requires several holes. To drill, tap, counterbore and face the parts with present machines would require a $1,500 jig and would take 8 minutes to do the work. A high-production drilling machine which would not need the jig would do the job in 1 minute and 30 seconds. One man is required in either case. Such a machine would cost $20,000.

What kind of tooling should Evans put in for each of these cases? Assume labor to be $3.50 an hour and all other factors equal. Use a life expectancy of five years for tooling.

Consider all these examples together and as being representative of other operations. What should Evans' decision be with respect to tooling up for Exhausto fume control devices?

chapter nine

ESTIMATING (CONTINUED)

ESTIMATES FOR GOVERNMENT CONTRACTS

In 1965, Lockheed received a $2 billion contract from the United States government to make 58 mammoth C-5A transport airplanes. It took a specially hired force of 2,000 men plus 500 experts at a cost of $11 million to develop the proposal. Charts, graphs, and blueprints weighed 10 tons. Douglas (cost of making its bid: $12 million) and Boeing (cost of bid: $16 million) failed to get the contract.[1] (The three companies were all reimbursed by the government in large part for their bidding costs.)

Not very many government contracts are so big as to justify million dollar estimation costs, but even bidding for small government contracts is a costly business. The government wants so much information and you have to fill out so many forms that it costs more to estimate and bid on government jobs than on others. Rarely would such costs run into millions of dollars as they did in the C-5A case but often they run into tens or hundreds of thousands of dollars. Not only that but the risk is great too. A company that gets 25 per cent of the jobs bid for is doing well and by no means always does the government pay even part of the estimating costs.

One thing the government is particularly interested in knowing is how much profit you will make on a contract. It insists on knowing many details about expected costs, how your books are kept, and so on.

OVERHEAD CHARGES

A problem arises in assessing overhead charges to government contracts as part of their costs. The government won't let you assess its contracts with the costs of any expenses that don't benefit the contract. Usually, for example, you can't charge any part of advertising costs to a contract.

Research costs too are scrutinized as are many other items. Particularly, the government does not want to pay for research you did before the contract was signed or for research not related to or authorized by the contract. The government's view is that it should not pay for research which it hasn't ordered done. You may, however, have had to do certain research specifically for certain contracts. Attempts by companies to get separate contracts to pay for doing such research are not always success-

---

[1] For an account of this bidding contest see Thomas J. Murray, "The Billion Dollar Proposal Industry," *Dun's Review and Modern Industry*, January, 1966, p. 40.

ful. Sometimes this is because you have no end product, no product which you complete and deliver as fulfilling the contract. (The end product of much research is just more knowledge, and not a tangible product.) Sometimes, though, you can get separate contracts to cover research but the estimating job is difficult.

The government's policy of insisting on low overhead charge ratios also makes problems. What do you do if your overhead charge is 300 per cent of direct labor when the government will allow you to assess only 200 per cent? One thing you can do is not to bid on the job. Some companies do just that. Other companies, however, change their accounting practices. They classify everything possible as direct costs rather than as indirect or overhead costs. Doing this reduces the charges that go into overhead accounts and increases direct costs. Maybe using regular accounting practices, you'd have $2 of direct labor and $6 of overhead. Overhead is 300 per cent. Look over the overhead expenses carefully. Call your research men direct workers. Engineers, tool designers, industrial engineers, the production control staff—call them all direct workers. Now you have $4 of direct costs and $4 of overhead. You have reduced your overhead ratio to 100 per cent! By using such accounting practices you may be able to reduce your ratio of overhead to direct labor enough to be acceptable to government contract writers. They know of course what is going on but they are often bound by restrictions and can't approve contracts that don't meet their rules.

The government's insistence on low overhead ratios can have one very undesirable and unwanted effect. We said above that with $2 of direct labor cost and $6 of overhead you had a 300 per cent ratio. If, by using labor inefficiently, the same work cost you $4 you would reduce the overhead ratio to 150 per cent. In fact, by being even less efficient you might get your direct labor costs up to $6. Now your ratio is 100 per cent! Certainly here inefficiency is a great temptation. (But of course your bid price has to be low or you won't get the contract so you can't be very inefficient and still get the contract.)

QUALITY AND COST CONTROLS   Not only are government contracts exacting in the estimating stage but the government is very particular about quality. As a rule, the government will reject more of your shipments than will regular customers. The government also wants to audit your accounts at the close of a contract to verify the charges you claim. Maybe this sounds unreasonable at first, but as we said in Chapter 8, some government contracts are cost-plus contracts. Even a private company paying you this way wants to see your books. The government also needs to see your books if the price is fixed although renegotiable.

Government contracts are sometimes for huge projects such as airplanes or ships. Such products take a long time to make and tie up large amounts of your money for long periods. The government will help you carry the investment in goods in process by making partial payments as successive stages of production are completed. Your estimating department has to calculate the proportion of completion at the end of each stage of production. Both the stages of completion and the amounts to be paid are spelled out in the contract.

If you are heavily in government business you probably operate using certain government-owned facilities. These may be buildings or equipment and machines, or both. Airplane and missile companies often own less than half of the facilities that they use. Furthermore, the government will furnish many of the component parts of your product. The government is almost a partner in your company and is itself so heavily involved that it is only appropriate that it look after the taxpayer's interest.

"CHECK" QUOTATIONS

Companies sometimes are asked to bid for jobs normally done by a customer in his own plant. He may or may not have any real intention of placing an order. Maybe all he wants to do is to check on his own inside manufacturing costs. If your bid is less than his cost you still may not get an order but he goes to work on cutting his production costs. But if his inside supplier is a sister plant rather than a separate department, he might give you an order rather than buy from the sister plant.

Don't waste much time on such estimates if you know them for what they really are. However, you can't be absolutely certain so you have to estimate as usual, and you can never tell, you might get a contract for business that normally doesn't come your way.

Actually, it is a good idea to reverse the procedure and ask for check quotations now and then for products you normally make yourself. Better yet, place a trial order with an outside source now and then. This gives you a real check on costs and provides "educational" orders. You have an established second source if anything happens to your usual source of the item.

Sometimes you make "check" estimates within the company. You do this with items that have been bought outside. They can cost too much but you won't know it unless you ask your estimator what it would cost to make them inside. You may even ask him too how much it ought to cost to make bought items, not because you are thinking of making them yourself but because you want, if the purchase prices proves high, to put pressure on the vendor to cut his price. If he doesn't, you can invite other bids. In this way you can check on the prices you are paying.

LARGE–VOLUME STOCK PRODUCTS

Estimating for products made to stock instead of directly to customers orders is different from estimating customer jobs. Your estimator is not competing with outside competitors who are submitting unknown competing bids.

Ideas for new products usually start in the sales department or the research department. The "new products committee" discusses it and if the committee likes the idea, it asks for both a sales volume forecast and a cost estimate. At McCulloch Motors (a chain saw manufacturer) new designs start with a discussion of the idea by a new products group. Approval of the idea carries with it approval for spending money for design. The product is designed in complete detail even though the design is still tentative. Even parts lists and operation lists are made up. In fact a separate sheet of paper is made to explain in detail every operation of every part. The proposed procedures are discussed with foremen. Doing all of this gives McCulloch a very close estimate of the cost of new products.

Union Special Machine Company, a sewing machine manufacturer, gets most of its ideas for new products from customers. Customers are always asking if they can get products specially designed for their work. If the sales department thinks there is much of a market for a particular kind of machine, it asks top management for an appropriation to pay for its design. Having gotten approval, the design department makes up a pilot model. Then the sales department makes a market survey and forecasts its probable annual sales. The project goes to production control where the manufacturing cost is estimated using the indicated volume to set depth of tooling and probable costs. Then it goes back for administrative review to see if sales can be realized at the costs in prospect.

Usually when you are estimating for new stock products, you must figure out how a product can be made within the confines and limitations of a *predetermined cost*. You don't work from the idea of here is how the product will be made, what will it cost? Instead you start with here is how much the product can cost, how can we make it for that amount? Estimating is almost as much a designing problem and engineering problem as it is a cost estimating job.

Maybe the estimator will find that a new product will cost more than the allowed limit. Then what? Then you try to cut costs by changing design or processes. Probably the changes will produce an item of lower quality.

If that happens, reconsider the market and determine how many you can sell of the lower quality at the price you first set.

There is one situation in which you don't have to do much cost estimating. This is when you are thinking of making a new product that you can make in quantity on machines you already own. Don't estimate. Just make up a few of the new products and see what they cost to make. If it is too much and if you can't cut their cost, don't make any more. Even here, though, cost estimates might be helpful as cost goals. Without goals, costs are likely to be higher. With them, everybody will try harder to hold costs down.

Most new products, though, require at least some new equipment. Then you need to make up careful estimates. One auto company's experience with a new model (of a low volume car) shows how big this problem can become. Ninety per cent of the operations required on a new model were to be done on existing equipment. Even so, this company had to buy 164 new machines, 1,650 new dies, and 805 new fixtures for its new model car! It made 2,615 new tools in its toolroom, installed 13 miles of conveyors, and moved 979 old machines and presses to new locations!

Westinghouse Electric, in its Columbus, Ohio, plant, turns out two refrigerators a minute. In order to do this it takes 2,613 machines and tools and 27 miles of conveyors! Such extensive tooling is so costly that you don't go into it and spend money without careful cost estimating. Millions of dollars worth of tooling are used in each case.

LARGE–VOLUME MADE–TO–ORDER PRODUCTS

When you make products to order for large buyers, such as large manufacturers, mail-order houses, or retail chain stores, you need to estimate your costs very carefully. They all drive hard bargains. Your profit margins will be low and yet because of the big volume, you have to go in heavily for mechanization and your initial tooling costs are high. Parts makers for the automobile, radio, and television industries are also often high volume, low profit margin producers.

Cost estimating for such contracts is a little different from estimating the costs of your own large volume items. You don't even get to do it all yourself. The customer's purchasing representatives and, if it is a manufacturing company, even its engineers will come in and work with your designers, process engineers, and estimators in developing details. They, the customers' men, will study design and cost alternatives and the cost of tooling. It is almost as if all of you worked for different departments of your company.

Although large customers drive hard bargains and insist on prices that contain only a small profit per unit, you still want their contracts. You want the business because the volume is large and the total profit is substantial. Sometimes the contract price on large contracts is "cost-plus," the buyer agreeing to pay for direct labor and material plus an agreed upon overhead rate plus a stated profit margin. The contract may even specify how you are to set up your accounts so that the customer can check and see what you charge to the contract. And, as we said earlier, he may also insist on the right to go over your books, to verify your statement of costs.

We haven't emphasized the importance of careful *materials* cost estimating. But remember that in most companies more than half of the sales dollar goes for materials. It is *very* important on big contracts that you estimate materials costs as well as you can. Big contracts let you mechanize and keep your labor costs low, but at the same time this merely reemphasizes the importance of material costs. Your profit or loss may depend on it.

Curiously, the biggest contracts are sometimes the easiest to get, maybe not the first time but the later reorders. Frigidaire has bought all its clocks and timers for stoves from one maker for years. Sears, Roebuck buys all of its washing machines from Whirlpool without even having a written contract. Once a large buyer has dealt with a seller on one contract and gotten along well, the next contract may be given on a purely verbal basis. The vendor is told that he will get all (or a stated fraction) of the orders for a bought item for the next model. He can go ahead and tool up with confidence even though the contract and all minor details will be settled later.

LARGE ENGINEERING–TYPE JOBS

Every large engineering-type job has to be separately estimated. Often there are only two or three companies that can make the product. This means that if the customer goes ahead with his project, you, as one of two or three, have a good chance of getting it. Thus, you may be willing to incur the high costs of estimating for such jobs. Sometimes, though, it costs so much that it is necessary to ask for engineering fees. Otherwise it would be unwise to take the chance.

As mentioned previously, production control work on large engineering jobs is particularly difficult. In part that is so because you finish some of the designing work after production had started. This common practice makes estimating far from exact.

Perhaps the hardest part of all to estimate on engineering type jobs

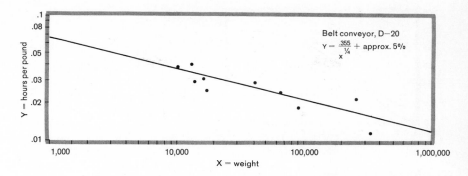

FIGURE 9-1 Engineering man-hours estimating chart used by Link-Belt division of FMC Corporation.

is the designing and drafting work. Link-Belt division of FMC Corporation tried to solve this problem by setting up estimating charts, one of which is shown in figure 9-1. The company grouped its products into a series of classes and analyzed its experience with each class. It found that there was, for each class, a relationship between the weight, in pounds, of a job and the amount of engineering time required for it. As can be seen in figure 9-1, the time, on a *per pound* basis, decreased with the weight of the job. When estimating a job it is necessary only to estimate the job's weight after which the engineering hours per pound can be read from the chart.

Link-Belt has a series of charts, one for each class of product. Estimates of engineering man-hours made from the charts have proved very good on the average but they are not foolproof. The weight of a job is a good but not perfect indicator of the engineering man-hours that it will need. Complex jobs that use less than the usual amount of steel need to be estimated at higher than chart figures.

One result of estimating from the charts at Link-Belt has been to reduce the engineering man-hours required. At first the actual hours ran above the estimate on about half of the jobs and below on half of the jobs. Later the actual hours stayed under the estimate more often. Having goals to shoot at seems to have increased the efficiency of the department.

THE LEARNING CURVE

Practice makes perfect. Nearly everyone knows that there is something called a "learning curve" yet you don't hear much about it in production

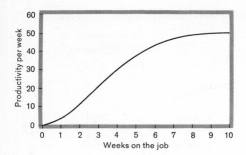

FIGURE 9-2 Typical learning curve showing
the increase of productivity with the passage
of time.

control or in cost estimating except in the airplane, missile, and their
related electronics industries. There they use it for cost estimating, manpower loading, scheduling, purchasing, and final pricing of products.

A learning curve is the line on a chart relating the amount of a man's
production to his time on the job. With practice most people improve their
ability to do almost any manual task. They do the work with fewer motions
and make the remaining motions more quickly. As they gain experience
their productivity goes up until they master the job. You can plot this on
a chart. This line, shown in figure 9-2, is known as the learning curve.
In its usual shape the curve rises rapidly in the early period. Then it
rises less rapidly and flattens out. The "curve" then becomes a horizontal line representing continuing high productivity. Sometimes, before the
final level is reached, there is a temporary leveling off period (called a
"plateau") after which another period of increase occurs which carries
production up to a permanent high level. The curve could also be plotted
as a *cost* curve, in which case it would go down to the right; the more you
produce, the lower your unit costs. In its usual form the learning curve is
shown as a decreasing cost curve.

Airplane manufacturers more than any others have studied this phe-
nomenon in their companies very carefully. They have found that the
reduction in the cost of airplanes, as additional quantities are made,
follows a definite pattern which can be used in predicting performance.
The increase in efficiency proves to be of the learning curve type except
that *there are no plateaus nor is there a final leveling off* beyond which no
further gains in efficiency can be achieved.

Winfred Hirschmann studied several industries to see if there was any
tendency for the learning curve to apply outside of the airplane industry.
He found that it did indeed apply to the industries he studied: oil refining,

electric power production, and steelmaking.[2] At the same time he found that managers in these industries were unaware of its operation in their industries.

LEARNING CURVES AS USED BY AIRPLANE COMPANIES   The main users of the learning curve idea are, as we said, airplane companies. Airplanes cost a great deal of money (millions of dollars each) and take a long time to make (up to two years, longer if you count designing time). Airplane prices, like those of most other products, need to be based on costs, but it is hard to forecast costs a year and more ahead, and it is particularly difficult when you consider that efficiency will increase on successive products.

Nonetheless, airplane companies have to forecast costs. Labor is much the biggest part of an airplane company's own cost (by this we mean to exclude the cost of bought materials and components) so it is important for airplane companies to forecast labor costs as accurately as they can.

These companies have found that for each type of airplane certain amounts of direct labor, *per pound of weight*, are required for the first airplane. They know, too, that the second airplane will require less labor per pound, the third still less, and so on. The rate of increase in efficiency is not absolutely regular but it is consistent enough to be used in estimating.

The industry has found that every time the number of airplanes produced is doubled, the average number of man-hours per pound goes down about 20 per cent. The first 50 planes will average only 80 per cent of the direct labor required for the first 25 planes. By the time you reach 100 airplanes, the average number of man-hours per plane for all 100 will be only 80 per cent as much as it was for the first 50 by themselves.

This relationship holds true for both the labor cost *per airplane* and for the cumulative *average* labor cost of all airplanes. The same ratio of reduction holds. True, the *individual* cost of the fiftieth plane and the *average* cost of the first 50 planes combined are not the same. The individual airplane cost of the fiftieth plane is only 68 per cent (for an 80 per cent cost reduction curve) of the average cost of the first 50 planes. This is always true after the first few planes are made. In all cases where an 80 per cent curve operates, the last unit always costs about 68 per cent of the average up to that point.

Actually, the airplane industry has found that not all types of airplanes, at the start, take exactly the same number of man-hours per pound of weight. They have also found that the reduction ratio differs a little, depending on the type of airplane, and it is also different for missiles. The

[2] See Winfred B. Hirschmann, "Profit from the Learning Curve," *Harvard Business Review*, January–February, 1964, pp. 125–139.

reduction in man-hours for small planes, for example, is not quite as great as for big airplanes. Doubling the quantity produced reduces their average direct labor cost between 15 and 20 per cent. On the other hand, reconnaissance airplanes have a higher increase in efficiency. Doubling their output reduces their average direct labor cost between 20 and 25 per cent.

Before showing how the 80 per cent curve works we should show our first learning curve (the one in figure 9-2) as a cost reduction curve rather than a productivity curve. Figure 9-2 shows how production goes up as a man learns his job. Naturally, the costs per unit go down. Figure 9-3 uses the same productivity figures as were used for figure 9-2, but this time we see how the costs per unit come down. This is the focal point of our interest in learning curves.

The decreasing cost curve is the one we use in our discussion of the learning curve, not the increasing productivity curve. We will work through an example later but first a little more on learning curves.

Looking at figures 9-2 and 9-3 you will see that neither one has the type of plateau that you would sometimes find in the curves for individual workers. This smooth curve without plateaus is the proper one to use for overall purposes because even if there were plateaus in the increased productivity of individual employees, they would occur at different quantities of production on different jobs. The overall effect would produce a smooth curve rather than one with plateaus.

A more important reason, however, for the smooth curve is that it is only in small part a worker learning curve. It is largely a management learning curve. All emphasis on the first one or two airplanes or missiles is to make them so that they will function and fly as they are supposed to do. Saving production costs is a secondary consideration at first. On the

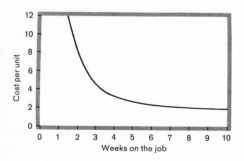

FIGURE 9-3 The same learning curve as that shown in figure 9-2 except that it is plotted as a cost curve showing how costs go down as productivity goes up.

first airplane, too much assembly work is done in the final assembly stage where it cannot be done economically. On the later planes, more and more of the assembly work is pushed back into subassemblies where it can be done more economically.

Also you would find, if you were making airplanes, that you make the first airplanes before all of the tooling you expect to use is on hand. As new tooling arrives and you put it into use, efficiency increases. And as you solve one production difficulty after another and make further improvements, production becomes still more efficient and costs keep going down. You don't make all of these gains at once so your efficiency keeps on improving. Since the most obvious improvements are made first, later gains are harder to achieve so the rate of efficiency increase slows down.

THE LEARNING CURVE IN AIRPLANE COST ESTIMATING AND PRICING

We are going to illustrate using the learning curve by an example from the airplane industry. Our example will show how to use the learning curve in estimating costs and in price negotiations. The object is, of course, to find out how many man-hours it will take to make the airplanes. Once we find this, we can use it also for scheduling and manpower loading, both of which we talk about in later chapters.

We will assume that we are negotiating on contracts for thirty-two large airplanes. We will also assume that each one will weigh 30,000 pounds (the largest airplanes weigh much more than this).

From past records, when making similar airplanes, we know that it will take about forty direct labor man-hours per pound to produce the first airplane. An order for thirty-two airplanes means that the quantity will double five times, (1, 2, 4, 8, 16, 32). By using the 80 per cent learning curve, we know that the first two airplanes, considered together, will require about $40 \times .8 = 32$ direct labor man-hours per pound. By the time we reach four airplanes the average will be $32 \times .8 = 25.6$ hours, etc. The thirty-two airplanes combined will require 13.1 direct labor man-hours per pound weight. Multiplying by 30,000, we find that the thirty-two airplanes will average some 393,000 direct labor hours per airplane. Multiplying this by the thirty-two airplanes, we find that the contract calls for about 12,576,000 man-hours or 6,300 man-years of direct labor.

The figures used in the example are hypothetical but not altogether unrealistic. Airplanes and missiles are terrifically costly in labor and money. In our example, the direct labor cost (at $4 an hour) for fulfilling the contract would be about $50 million, or about $1.6 million per airplane. You can see that both the government representatives and the airplane manufacturer are vitally interested in the validity of the cost projections.

Before we go on with our example we want to look at figures 9-4 and 9-5. Figure 9-4 shows how the man-hours required to make the airplanes used in our example go down. It is plotted on regular arithmetic coordinate paper. Notice the two lines. The lower shows how many man-hours are required for *each* airplane by itself. The upper shows the *average number* of man-hours per airplane for all airplanes up to any given number.

Figure 9-5 shows the same pair of lines plotted on double logarithmic paper. As you see, this makes the lines straighten out and become parallel once the first few airplanes have been made. As straight lines they are useful in letting you see where you'll be if you keep on making more and more of the same product.

Because we have used an example that stops at thirty-two airplanes, the left side of the learning curve (the curved part that related to the first few airplanes) shows up more than it would if we had been talking about 1,000 airplanes. The important part of the chart is the right side, not the left. On the right side, we are getting more into the future and big quantities.

Returning to our example, one way to find out exactly how many man-hours it will take on the average to make any particular number of airplanes is to read it off figure 9-5. Or you can compute it by using this formula:

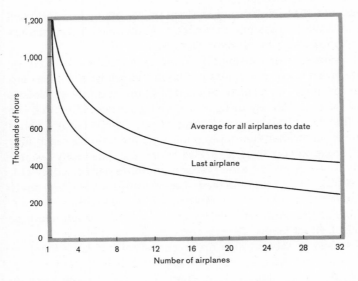

FIGURE 9-4   Eighty per cent learning curves plotted on an arithmetic scale.

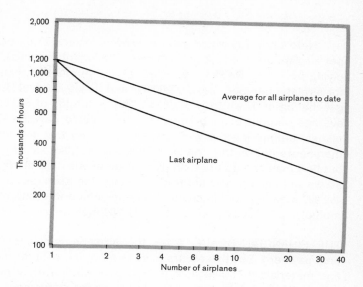

FIGURE 9-5 Eighty per cent learning curves plotted on double logarithmic paper.

Log $Y = -n$ Log $X +$ Log C. Y is the answer you are trying to get; $-n$ is the slope of the line on figure 9-5. For an 80 per cent curve the slope of the line is .322 and since our curve goes down, n is minus and $-n$ is $-.322$. X is the number of airplanes you want to find out about. C is the man-hours needed to make the first airplane.[3]

[3] The slopes for various learning curves and the relationship of the last item to the average are as follows:

LEARNING PERCENTAGE	SLOPE OF CURVE	RELATION OF LAST UNIT TO AVERAGE	LEARNING PERCENTAGE	SLOPE OF CURVE	RELATION OF LAST UNIT TO AVERAGE
70	.515	.485	83	.269	.731
71	.494	.506	84	.252	.748
72	.474	.526	85	.235	.765
73	.454	.546	86	.218	.782
74	.435	.565	87	.201	.799
75	.415	.585	88	.185	.815
76	.396	.604	89	.168	.832
77	.377	.623	90	.152	.848
78	.359	.611	91	.136	.864
79	.340	.660	92	.120	.880
80	.322	.678	93	.105	.895
81	.304	.656	94	.089	.911
82	.286	.714	95	.074	.926

Here's how you would find the expected average number of man-hours per airplane for the first six airplanes. The logarithm of 6 is 0.778151. Multiplying by −.322, we get −0.250565. C, the number of man-hours needed for airplane number one, is 1,200,000 and its log is 6.079181. By adding, we get the log of Y which is 5.828616. This is the log of 673,900 which is the average number of man-hours that you should have on the first six airplanes. Multiplying this average by 6 tells you that the total direct labor man-hours put on the first six planes will be 4,048,400. If you want to find out how many hours the sixth plane itself needs, find the five airplane total as we did for six and subtract. Actually the sixth plane should require 469,900 man-hours. You could also approximate the sixth plane's hours by multiplying 673,900 by .68, getting 458,300 man-hours.

THE FINANCIAL DRAIN   After the airplane is delivered, you receive final payment. But this occurs months after you paid for most of the labor and materials that went into it. This puts quite a drain on your financial resources. Depending upon the terms of the agreement made with the customer, you may be able to get some relief in the form of partial payments as certain stages of the airplane's completion are reached. You may not, therefore, have to stand all of the financial drain of carrying the airplanes and their parts in process. Considering that you pay for some material and labor up to two years before you deliver the airplane, partial payments give you considerable relief from what would otherwise be a serious situation. Also, the advance partial payments, being based on prices before renegotiation, are sometimes liberal enough to pay most of your bills as you go along. Although unlikely, it is even possible that at the end of the contract, instead of receiving a final payment, the manufacturer may owe money to the government because its partial payments, in total, exceed the renegotiated price for the completed airplane.

Actually, the learning curve itself makes a far more serious problem of financial drain than does mere long lead time by itself. Here's how it works. We'll continue to use the 32 airplane contract example and we'll leave out the possibility of progress payments in order to show how the drain operates.

We expect the 32 airplanes to average **about** 393,000 direct man-hours. At $4 an hour the direct labor cost per airplane will come close to $1.6 million. Let us assume that the contract price is $7 million per airplane and that that amount includes a prospective $3 million for bought materials and components, and $2 million to pay for costs other than direct labor.

The first airplane will actually require 1.2 million direct labor man-hours, costing $4.8 million. Furthermore, the company has to pay $3 million for components and also has $2 million of other costs, making this first airplane's cost come to $9.8 million. Selling it for $7 million leaves the company $2.8 million in the red. Airplane number 2 will require 720,000 man-hours costing $2.88 million, and again the company incurs an additional cost of $5 million, bringing airplane number 2's cost to $7.88 million. The company is out $880,000 on this airplane. By now the company has had to finance the operation to the tune of $3.68 million.

The important point to see is that these two airplanes have been finished, delivered, and fully paid for, yet you have spent $3.5 million more than you have taken in. This financial drain is over and above the problems created by long lead times on expensive items in process. It is, in fact, usually much worse than our example shows because the company has had to finance the big inventory of work in process (except as progress payments may have been received) of partly made airplanes which will not be finished for several more months.

This drain continues for some time and mounts higher before it starts to shrink. Figure 9-6 shows how it would work in our example. All figures, except the airplane number, are given in thousands.

FIGURE 9-6

COST OF EACH AIRPLANE, THOUSANDS

AIR-PLANE NUMBER	DIRECT LABOR MAN-HOURS	COST OF DIRECT LABOR	PLUS $2,000 OTHER COSTS	PLUS $3,000 COM-PONENTS COSTS	PROFIT ON THIS AIRPLANE	ACCUMU-LATED PROFIT
1	1,200	$4,800	$6,800	$9,800	−$2,800	−$2,800
2	720	2,880	4,880	7,880	− 880	− 3,680
3	608	2,432	4,432	7,432	− 432	− 4,112
4	544	2,176	4,176	7,176	− 176	− 4,288
5	502	2,008	4,008	7,008	− 8	− 4,296
6	470·	1,880	3,880	6,880	+ 120	− 4,176
7	446	1,784	3,784	6,784	+ 216	− 3,960
8	425	1,700	3,700	6,700	+ 300	− 3,660
9	408	1,632	3,632	6,632	+ 368	− 3,292
10	394	1,576	3,576	6,576	+ 424	− 2,868
11	381	1,524	3,524	6,524	+ 476	− 2,392
12	371	1,484	3,484	6,484	+ 516	− 1,876
13	361	1,444	3,444	6,444	+ 554	− 1,322
14	352	1,408	3,408	6,408	+ 592	− 730
15	344	1,376	3,376	6,376	+ 624	− 106
16	335	1,340	3,340	6,340	+ 660	+ 554

You will have to deliver your sixteenth airplane on a contract for 32 before you break even! Also, notice that at one point you will be over $4 million behind.

You might think that you could avoid all this trouble by having a contract with the customer that pays more for the first units delivered. That is not often done. You'd have a more complicated contract than ever and you would still have to figure on the learning curve.

But you can lessen the financial drain of a large contract by cutting it into segments or even separate contracts and repricing each new segment. This doesn't solve the problem completely because the price *per airplane* on the first contract is based on the *average cost* of the airplanes contracted for in this first contract. By the time the first contract is completed the individual airplane cost has worked down to a point considerably below this average. In fact, the last airplane made on the first contract should have cost the airplane manufacturer only 68 per cent of the average cost.

This new low *unit* cost is the *starting point* for determination of the price on the next contract. Costs will work farther down during the progress of the next contract. The new contract price will be based on the *average costs of the next group of airplanes,* and will not include the costs of the airplanes produced on the first contract. The manufacturer will again experience a period of financial drain because the first planes delivered on the new contract will cost him more than he gets paid until he gets about halfway through his contract.

USES AND LIMITATIONS OF LEARNING CURVES

Learning curves are used in the airplane industry for pricing, for deciding to make or buy component parts of airplanes, for forecasting man-power requirements, and for scheduling, designing, production, and deliveries.

Learning curves can be used by industries other than the aircraft and electronics industry. Other industries do, of course, recognize, expect, and plan for lower costs as the quantities of items produced increase. Nearly all of the change, however, is expected very soon after production starts. This is to be expected because most companies are not learning, with new models, to produce wholly new products. You don't have "complete forgetting."

This makes a problem because, as you start in on the new model, you don't know quite how far you are starting along the curve. Is the amount of remembering equivalent to your having already made 100 products or only 50? If you say 50, you expect average costs to go down by 20 per cent after you have produced 50 new items. But if you say 100, then you won't expect to get average costs down 20 per cent until you have turned out 100 of the new model.

In automobile companies the remembering is surely the equivalent of having already turned out some big quantity, say 500,000. If this is the proper number, then automobile companies should expect to reduce direct labor man-hours per car by 20 per cent only after they have made 500,000 of a new model, not after 2, 4, or 8.

Another reason for not using the learning curve idea in many companies is the attitude of organized labor. The difficulty is that the learning curve tells us that we should be able to lower production costs forever although at a slower and slower rate. Yet in large-scale production where we find the volume that lets the learning curve operate, we also find production lines. Once such lines are set up, the unions strongly resist changing the jobs along the lines in any way that lets the line turn out more work. Furthermore, dealer and customer demand for new models is high right at the beginning.

These two conditions, labor resistance and high early demand, both work to defeat the normal operation of the curve. The high first demand for products makes management do everything that it can to hurry along the early part of the curve and to get production up immediately. The resistance to change also causes management to put more effort into working out, before the line starts, many details that would normally come later were it free to make further changes. The effect is to speed up the operation of the early part of the learning curve. Union resistance also slows down putting in additional improvements later so that the continuing reduction that the curve expects later does not occur.

One company making frequent new models (which are much like old ones) sets this rule for starting up new lines: It schedules production at 50 per cent of standard for the first four days, 75 per cent of standard for the next four days, and 100 per cent thereafter. While this is hardly the learning curve the way airplane companies use it, it is a recognition of the idea. Although these adjustments are arbitrary, the company finds that they are much more realistic than expecting top production immediately, and yet they do bring production up fast. The Mattel Company, a toy manufacturer which discards old and makes new products every year, reports that even old workers shifted to new jobs always go through a learning curve in every new assignment. There seems to be little transferability of skill in assembly work. They start slowly on new jobs and then pick up speed.

Industries other than the aircraft and electronics have not, however, really used the learning curve idea. That is, they do not seem to expect efficiency to increase forever although at a declining rate.

Learning curves are not automatic. You can't just sit back and have them do your work for you. Most of the improvements that reduce costs, particularly after the early stages, are accomplished only if management continually tries to cut costs. Without such continuing effort costs will not keep on going down. They might, in fact, go up.

Also the rate of efficiency increase will not always be the 80 per cent curve. Where operations are largely mechanical, being performed by machines, you'll find a slower rate of improvement. Doubling the quantity produced may cut costs by only 5 to 10 per cent—not 20 per cent. If, on the other hand, most of your man-hours go into assembly (assembly being less mechanized than parts manufacture) you'll get bigger gains. In the aircraft industry three-quarters of the direct labor is in assembly so it can reach the 20 per cent labor cost reduction curve.

Several years ago Raymond Jordan of General Electric's Aircraft Engine Division made a study of the operation of learning curves. He reported that if 75 per cent of your assembly costs are assembly labor and 25 per cent machine labor, you should use an 80 per cent curve. But if you have 50 per cent assembly labor and 50 per cent machine labor, an 85 per cent curve would be appropriate. A 90 per cent curve is proper to use if you have 25 per cent assembly labor and 75 per cent machine labor.[4] Clair Blair, consulting industrial engineer, offers the following bench marks: Machining—use a 90 to 95 per cent curve. Short cycle bench assembly work—85 to 90 per cent. Equipment maintenance—75 to 80 per cent.[5]

You also change the learning curve if you change your purchasing practices. If you buy products instead of make them, what you really do is to farm out part of your labor load to the vendor company. If you make instead of buy, you bring in part of the vendor company's labor load. But buying either more or less than you used to buy changes your own inside labor load. If you buy more outside, naturally your direct labor man-hours go down. But the cost of purchased items goes up.

Design changes also affect the curve. Design changes interrupt your ways of doing things and temporarily increase costs. Design changes may also change the labor content inherent in the product.

Changes in indirect labor also affect the curve. The learning curve has to do with *direct labor*. It predicts the amount of *direct* labor needed to make future products. But you can often get greater output from direct labor by using more supervision. Supervision is indirect labor and does not show in the direct labor figures. Similarly, putting many engineers and tool designers to work to try to improve and mechanize jobs increases

[4] For more on this see Raymond B. Jordan, "Learning How to Use the Learning Curve," *National Accounting Association Bulletin,* January, 1958, p. 27.
[5] See Clair Blair, "A Primer on Learning Curves," *Factory,* April, 1966, p. 80.

direct labor output. They increase the mechanization and reduce direct labor man-hours. But the cost of making the gain is in indirect labor, not direct.

In applying the idea of the learning curve to industries other than aircraft and its related industries, it is important to see that they probably can't divide their production into lots—getting a higher price for their first units and less for units produced later. They usually follow a fixed price policy which would increase the early financial drain. Actually, companies sometimes do get high prices for their first products. Then price reductions are made. This operates in a way quite similar to segmentized government contracts.

Learning curves sometimes reverse their direction near the end of a contract and costs go up instead of down. This doesn't invalidate the concept, however, because it only shows the effect of phasing out the contract. Efforts to reduce costs are stopped and job improvement men are transferred to other newer contracts. No new tooling is installed and perhaps some of the best workers are transferred to other jobs. On individual contracts, learning curves aren't effective on the last units produced.

Besides this, there is some tendency for the curves to level out as the contract moves into thousands of units. This is because you get no more effect from job learning by people. Normal turnover whittles away at your experienced worker force and newcomers must be added. The average effectiveness of the work force therefore levels out.

THE LEARNING CURVE AS CAUSE AND EFFECT
In spite of the fact that the learning curve works in the aircraft industry, no one should think of it in a too mechanistic or hard and fast way. To use it you have to know what the proper starting figures are and what per cent reduction to use.

But more serious food for thought is that perhaps the curve is both cause and effect. You believe in the curve, you set prices based on it, and you set schedules based on it. Then, as operations go along, if they match the expectations, you think that all is well. But if costs are higher you leave no stone unturned to get down to the curve figures. This is good.

However, if costs are down to the curve figure you view it as proper and surely do not exert quite so much effort toward further reduction. Possibly you could, early in the game, get costs down below the curve and then keep going down from there. Having the curve to look at as a goal may well keep you from doing as well as you ought just because you regard that accomplishment as good.

Our point isn't so much to object to the curve as a useful tool as it is to point out that, in part, it works because people make it work.

STUDY MATERIALS

9-1 You find that several of your customers place orders and then delay deliveries. This forces you to store finished products which costs you money in extra handling and ties up your money and storage space. What should you do about this?

9-2 When bidding for long-term contracts, such as ship building or large engineering projects, can you hedge against labor and material cost changes? How?

9-3 To check on inside costs, the purchasing agent has got bids on several items that you expected to make yourself. Several bids are below your own estimators' estimates. As manager, you suspect that these bids are from hungry vendors who are quoting prices that are under their full costs (variable costs plus some but not all of the overhead) but you nonetheless decide to look into the accuracy of your internal estimates.

You find that a good many of your high estimates come from one estimator who is relatively new in your company. Most of the other high estimates were made by another new man who used to be a government buyer on military contracts. His estimates are as likely to be low as high and they average out about right.

What should you do in these two cases? Do high and low estimates that average out hurt you? Should you accept the bids from the outside companies?

9-4 What part does cost estimating play in companies manufacturing to stock? If you say that you are bound to stay within certain cost limits dictated by sales prices, what does this limitation do to your estimating procedures?

9-5 The First Flight Airplane Company has asked you to submit an estimate to the Federal government for 50 small airplanes. They will weigh 10,000 pounds and the first airplane will probably require 35 man-hours of work per pound. Labor is at $3.75 per hour. Other costs than labor are $430,000 per airplane. Use an 80 per cent labor cost reduction curve.

1 Find the average cost of these airplanes.

2 Find the total cost of all airplanes.

3 Find the cost of the last airplane.

4 At a selling price of $875,000 each, what will be the peak financial drain?

5 After how many airplanes will the company be out of the red?

9-6 Continuing on from problem 9-5: Suppose that you are part way through your first contract for 50 airplanes and are negotiating for a second contract for 25 more.

   How many direct labor man-hours will you need, on the average, for these 25 airplanes? What will the price be if First Flight is to recover its labor cost plus $5,750,000 of other costs plus 7 per cent of the total costs?

9-7 Suppose that you have to plan manpower requirements for the 50 airplanes referred to in problem 9-5. For this problem we will simplify and say that the total airplane is made as follows and that you are concerned with manning the following work positions:

	WORK POSITIONS
Final assembly made from:	4
Wings	2
Fuselage	2
Empennage	1
Wings made from:	
Wing parts	6
Fuselage made from:	
Forward section	2
Middle section	2
Empennage (tail assembly) made from:	
Empennage parts	9
Forward fuselage made from:	
Parts	5
Middle fuselage made from:	
Parts	7

   For the first airplane you should hire enough men so that one work position represents four weeks work. Also, for the first airplane you will need to have 50 men to man each work station.

   For parts making, just concern yourself with the total manpower requirements without concerning yourself about how the labor is divided among parts. Do not concern yourself about any individual parts taking longer than the time shown above. Do not allow, either, for any dead time for items going into stock and then being withdrawn. Also, for simplicity, assume a five-day workweek with no holidays.

1 Lay out a schedule showing when each activity starts and stops for the first airplane, which is to be finished on Friday, June 1, workday number 762. (Assume one-shift, eight-hour a day operation.) Since we do not have before us a conversion calendar, for converting workdays to calendar days, you may leave your schedule in terms of workdays.

2 Assume that the 80 per cent learning curve operates but that you don't want to increase the delivery rate, at least not for the first 20 airplanes. This means that, as the curve operates, you will need fewer men. By the time that the twentieth airplane is finished, how many men will you have had to transfer to other work?

3 Assume that you are willing to have the learning curve work to speed up deliveries instead of cutting down on manpower. When will airplane number 20 be finished? Let the learning curve as it works at final assembly be your con-

trolling point. Naturally, by the time final assembly occurs, all earlier work is farther along on the curve and so could send components along faster than are needed. Assume, however, that you transfer men out of such departments and, by cutting down on the work crew size, you keep components coming to final assembly only as fast as it can handle it.

4   On what airplane will each work station be working on the day that airplane 20 is finished?

5   By workday 885 how long will it take for items to pass through the various work stations? If you let the final assembly needs set the pace for all other work stations, how many men will you need at each work station?

chapter ten

AUTHORITY TO MAKE

Authority to manufacture deals with *how* to make products and *what, when,* and *how many* to make. In this book we call the authority concerning *how* to make things and perform operations "processing" authority. It is discussed in Chapter 11.

The right to *go ahead* and make products, the subject of this chapter, we call "producing" authority. Producing authority gives permission and requires compliance. Without it, the plant may not produce, but with it, it must proceed. Producing authority is one-time authority and allows the factory to make only the products listed. No other products, not even more of the same kind, may be made without more authorizations.

There are a few manufacturing situations where the standardization and volume of products are so great that you don't see much evidence of either producing authority or processing authority. Whole plants, for example, are devoted to making cement, gasoline, or paper for newspapers. About all the producing authority they need is a weekly output figure. Usually, however, even these plants make several varieties of products so that they need to be told what is wanted.

SOURCES OF PRODUCING AUTHORITY

Because of the need to make only products which will sell, no products should be made without specific authorization. Factory departments get their authorizations from the production control department but the production control department isn't the starting point of authority to produce. Its grants of authority usually come to it in the form of master schedules or production programs both of which evolve from forecasts which in turn usually come from the sales department.

Sometimes, however, master schedules are just the summation of sales orders and don't grow out of forecasts. And in some companies, those which carry thousands of different products in stock, control is exercised by setting limits to the investment in classes of finished products inventories. When this method is used the finished stock control department becomes the source of authority to production control. Besides these main sources, production control receives occasional repair

orders, experimental orders, etc., from the superintendent, the engineering department, or others.

TYPICAL PROCEDURES

We said earlier that companies manufacturing to stock have to forecast
sales so that they will know what to tell the factory to make. Before we
get into the details of how to make production schedules from forecasts
we might describe in a general way how a few companies do this.

The practice of the Frigidaire division of General Motors is typical.
New models of most of its stove and refrigerator lines are brought out
annually. In the early fall of each year, Frigidaire makes a forecast, which
it calls a "program" for the following year. This program shows by month
the quantity expected to be sold of each model during the coming year.
It is used as the basis for tooling up and for making longtime materials
purchase commitments.

The program is also used for making production schedules for the
first four months of the new model's production. Then, as the months go
by, at each month's end, the inventories of finished products, their recent
sales, and their near future sales prospects are reviewed by the sales
department and by the production control department. Also reviewed are
the schedules already set up for the coming three months. If need be,
these schedules are revised and the figures for the new fourth month
ahead are firmed up and added.

United States Rubber Company, in its tire manufacture, uses a similar procedure. Its sales department makes up a sales estimate for the
year ahead and as months go by keeps it 12 months ahead by extending
it to cover additional months. The forecast is reviewed monthly by the
company's executive committee on which the sales, production coordinating, and the production control departments are represented. The production control department is given an opportunity to analyze the plant
capacity requirements of the forecast and to suggest changes before the
committee approves it. Production schedules are then made up, keeping
in mind both the sales needs and the need for the plant to operate
effectively.

The Detroit division of TRW makes automotive parts. It forecasts its
sales for three months ahead and extends this forecast quarterly. Thus in
August, it forecasts its monthly sales for October, November, and December. January, is not, however, added on in September. Instead, January,
February, and March are all added in November. TRW also has a more

tentative general forecast which is projected by quarters for six quarters ahead and which is always kept that far ahead by adding a new quarter every three months. This general forecast is sent to the company's home office for approval, after which it is used for production schedule making.

The forecast of Crane Company, manufacturer of plumbing supplies, takes the form of a sales budget for the year ahead. It is subdivided to show the expected sales of each major classification of products in dollars. This budget has to be in dollars because there are too many individual items to show separately. After the approval of the sales budget, dollar amounts are worked out for each of the company's plants. Only then are they converted (by the plant's production control department) into individual products and quantities. The production control department in each plant develops detailed schedules for from one to three months ahead depending on the product. Subsequent schedules are made up monthly, but as the year goes along, the quantities are more dependent on sales and current inventories than on the original budget.

McCulloch Motors Company, maker of chain saws, starts with what it calls "advanced planning." Advanced planning includes everything related to forecasting. The sales department makes a tentative forecast. After initial approval by management, the forecast's capital expenditure and other financial requirements are investigated. The capital expenditure and working capital needs of the forecast are compared to the money the company has, will have, or can get. Then the forecast is again reviewed by management, after which, changed or unchanged, it becomes the approved forecast. At McCulloch the forecasts are largely in dollar volume terms. After their approval, production control converts them into products, quantities, and, with the help of industrial engineering, tools and machines needed.

Armstrong Cork has its commodity sales managers prepare forecasts for their lines a year ahead. A committee consisting of the controller, treasurer, economist, and production planning manager puts the commodity line forecasts together and develops an overall forecast. Production planning then breaks it down into individual products, develops seasonal demand curves, and tries to balance the opposing forces of fluctuating demand and leveled production as it develops production schedules.

The reader may, however, wonder at the need of some companies, when forecasting, to use only dollar figures for classes of products. It is the variety that forces them to do this. The Doehler-Jarvis division of National Lead is not a giant division, yet look at the list below of what it makes. Doehler-Jarvis does not make the products listed, only some of the parts for them. Most of the parts are die castings.

PRODUCT CLASS	INDUSTRY GROUP	PERCENTAGE OF SALES IN ONE YEAR
1	Automotive parts	64
2	Household appliances —vacuum cleaners, floor polishers, sewing machines, washing machines, irons, ironers, mixers, dishwashers, driers, juicers, radios, television sets, phonographs, cooking utensils, refrigerators and ranges	7
3	Office, store, and factory appliances —adding machines, calculators, typewriters, dictaphones, pencil sharpeners, postage meters, check writers, changemakers, wire recorders, parking meters, staplers, watchman signal and alarm systems, and fire extinguishers	4
4	Defense items	4
5	Power tools, chain saws, farm machinery, lawn mowers	3
6	Miscellaneous —electrical parts, fans, meters, motors, drills, and tools. Airplane parts, railroad equipment, outboard motors, gasoline, pump and service station equipment. Cameras, projectors, binoculars, toys, microscopes, guns, fishing tackle, scales, clocks, cutlery, razors, cigarette lighters, dispensers, recording machines, neckties, flashlights, medical and dental appliances, and textile parts	18
		100

APPROVED FORECASTS

As our company examples show, production control departments often help make out master schedules and production programs. While forecasts are still in their tentative stage, the production control staff goes over them to see if the factory can do the work they call for. They check to see how the forecast will affect production, whether it calls for extreme ups and downs and whether it calls for more than the plant can produce. They report what they find to top level executives together with suggestions for modifying the forecast if the factory can't meet its demands while operating economically.

Top men need to know, before deciding, if the recommendations call for cutting back sales forecasts because of production limitations. Since doing this would tend to drive customers to competitors (during out-of-stock periods) the decision as to what to do should be made by high-up executives.

Prospective sales losses, however, are not the only considerations. Possibly the factory can meet the forecast only by following costly practices such as building up inventories, buying more outside, buying more machines, or hiring more men to meet peak production needs.

The object is to level forecasts to the point where an optimal balance is achieved between the costs of changing production levels and the costs of carrying inventories. Neither holding production constant and allowing all the expected sales fluctuations to be reflected in the inventory position nor allowing production to go up and down with all the sales fluctuations will produce the lowest total cost.

During schedule-making meetings, production control men and production men should not let themselves be outtalked by sales and engineering representatives. Sometimes the sales department talks them into accepting forecasts which result in irregular operations which will be wasteful. Or sales and engineering together talk production men into accepting difficult and costly designs without enough objection. Important though sales are, sales considerations shouldn't dominate schedule making so much that costs get pushed into the background.

MAKING SCHEDULES FROM APPROVED FORECASTS

An approved sales forecast is really a "desired shipping schedule." It shows the products you would like to make and ship each month. And when you don't carry finished products inventories or where such inventories are only a few days' supply, as is true of automobiles, agricultural machinery, tractors, etc., a desired shipping schedule is almost the same as a desired schedule for the assembly operations in manufacturing. Sometimes it is so used.

The first step in translating a desired shipping schedule into an actual assembly schedule is to compute the plant capacity needed to meet the desired shipping schedule as it stands. Maybe the plant can meet it without difficulty, and if so, it can become the actual assembly schedule.

MAN–HOURS AS A MEASURE OF PLANT CAPACITY   To check a sales forecast against plant capacity, most companies calculate the capacity needed in terms of direct labor man-hours. You would get the total man-hours needed by multiplying, for each product, its direct labor man-hours per unit by the number of units wanted. Next you would sum up the various products' requirements and get the work load.

APPORTIONING WORK LOADS TO MONTHS   We are getting along too fast, though. You can't just multiply a product's direct labor man-hours by the number of products and add up to get a month's total, because many of these man-hours have to be applied several weeks or months before the products are finished. Probably, only the hours needed for assembly itself will be done in the finishing month (and even some of these

Preliminary Master Schedule

Date _____

Customer	Product Number	Shop Order No.	Quantity	Shipped to Date	On Hand	Balance On Order	June	July	August	Sept.	Oct.	Nov.	Dec.
X Company	X 297	743	10,000	3,000	700	7,000	1,500	1,500	2,000	1,300	----	-----	-----
Y Company	X 297	817	17,000	0	0	17,000	500	2,500	4,000	4,000	4,000	1,000	1,000
X Company	X 301	522	40,000	5,000	1,000	35,000	8,000	---	8,000	-----	8,009	-----	8,000 (2,000)

Department Load

Date _____

Customer	Assembly or Part No.	Shop Order No.	Man Hours per Unit	June Units	June Hours	July Units	July Hours	August Units	August Hours	September Units	September Hours
X Company	X 297	743	0.50	1,500	750	1,500	750	2,000	1,000	1,300	650
Y Company	X 297	817	0.50	500	250	2,500	1,250	4,000	2,000	4,000	2,000
X Company	X 301	522	0.25	8,000	2,000	0	0	8,000	2,000	0	0

Final Master Schedule

Date _____

Customer	Product Number	Shop Order No.	Quantity	Shipped to date	On Hand	Balance on Order	June	July	Aug.	Sept.	Oct.	Nov.	Dec.
X Company	X 297	743	10,000	3,000	700	7,000	1,500	3,500	0	1,300	etc.		
Y Company	X 297	817	17,000	0	0	17,000	1,000	3,000	3,000	4,000	etc.		
X Company	X 301	522	40,000	5,000	1,000	35,000	8,000	0	8,000	0	etc.		

Manufacturing Schedule

Date _____
Dept. _____
Week of _____

Part No.	Shop Order No.	Total Pieces for Week	Monday Day	Monday To Date	Tuesday Day	Tuesday To Date	Wednesday Day	Wednesday To Date	Thursday Day	Thursday To Date	Friday Day	Friday To Date	Saturday Day	Saturday To Date
X 297 743		400	80	80	80	160	80	240	80	320	80	400	----	----
X 297 817		250	100	100	100	200	50	250	--	---	--	---	----	-----
X 301 522		1,000	100	100	100	200	200	400	300	700	300	1,000		

FIGURE 10-1 Development of a manufacturing schedule from a preliminary forecast. Note the need to see what load a preliminary forecast puts on the factory before a final schedule is agreed upon.

assembly man-hours will be applied in the month before on products finished early in the month). You need to assign the required man-hours to the months when the men will do the work.

Roughly, this is the procedure (to simplify the illustration we have assumed that all assembly man-hours will be applied in the month in which the product is completed): First, multiply the quantities scheduled for assembly, let us say, in February, by the man-hours required to assemble each product. Next, multiply the man-hours required for subassemblies and parts for each product by its quantity. Allocate these man-hours to January, December, or even November, depending on when the work is likely to be done.

To get any one month's total man-hours, add the final assembly hours for that month's finished products plus a goodly share of the man-hours for subassemblies and parts for the following month's products, plus a smaller share of the hours for parts for the second following month's products plus a few hours for parts for the third following month's products.

OTHER FACTORS AFFECTING THE WORK LOAD   The totals we have just arrived at for each month still won't be the plant's full work load, however. You have to add more man-hours to cover making repair parts and accessories, and for all the minor kinds of manufacturing that we talked about in Chapter 3. Maybe these additions will increase the first total by as much as 20 per cent. Of course you don't as yet know exactly what and how many extras you will need but you know from past experience about how many man-hours to allow for them.

Also we have said nothing about several other factors you need to consider. You will need to make an adjustment to allow for the absences of men, their vacations, the loss of production with new men, and so on.

Nor are all months alike. You must pay attention to how many work-days there are in each month. A 30-day month can have either four or five Saturdays and Sundays. This means that you may have 20, 21, or 22 workdays. Also you need to pay attention to the workdays lost because of holidays and other known closed-down periods. In our example on the following pages, we allowed for losing the Friday after Thanksgiving and the whole last week in December for annual inventory taking.

OTHER MEASURES OF PLANT CAPACITY   In some companies a forecast's prospective manpower requirements is not a good measure of its capacity needs. When this is so you have to try to find some other better measure so that you can compare the forecast's requirements with what the factory can do. Maybe you can use weight, such as pounds or tons. Still other measures are the dollar value of products shown in the forecast, their machine hours, and their labor cost.

Dollar-value figures are often satisfactory measures of the volume of work if the ratio of material to labor cost is about the same for most products and if prices are stable. Yet, in the textile industry, for example, dollar figures are quite inappropriate because some kinds of cloth can be run through looms as much as seven times faster than certain other kinds of cloth on the same looms. Loom hours is a much better measure of plant capacity.

Often machine hours is of limited use as a measuring unit of plant capacity. Particularly this is true if there is much manual work because the manual work requirements don't show in either the work load or the capacity figures. Labor cost, as a measure of plant capacity, is also generally not as good as man-hours, although it is used extensively in the shoe industry.

General Electric, in some plants, uses "equivalent standard products" (ESPs) as a measure of work load and of capacity. ESPs are calculated as follows: you have products A, B, and C. In total it takes 17.3 processing

Section			January	February	March	April	May (Number of)
			21	20	23	21	21
1	**Desired Shipping Schedule**						
	Product						
	A						1500
	B		12000	9000	8000	8000	8500
	C				2000	3000	4000
	D						
	E			2000	10000	7000	1000
2	**Man-Hours Required by Desired Shipping Schedule**	Man-Hours Per 100					
	Product						
	A	1050					15750
	B	300	36000	27000	24000	24000	24000
	C	560			7800	11700	15600
	D	390		4400	22000	15400	2200
	E	220					
	Total		36000	31400	53800	51100	57550
3	**Man-Hours Required for Assembly (20 Per Cent of Total) Shown in Shipping Month**						
	Product						
	A						3150
	B		7200	5400	4800	4800	4800
	C				1560	2340	3120
	D			880	4400	3080	440
	E						
	Total		7200	6280	10760	10220	11510
4	**Man-Hours Required for Parts Manufacture (80 Per Cent of Total) Shown in Month Before Shipping Month****						
	Product						
	A					12600	16800
	B		21600	19200	19200	19200	36000
	C						8960
	D			6240	9360	12480	12480
	E		3520	17600	12320	1760	
	Total		25120	43040	40880	46040	74240
5	**Total Man-Hours Required in Each Month to Make the Items on the Desired Shipping Schedule**		32320	49320	51640	56260	85750
	Add 25 Per Cent Additional Time for Making Extra Parts and Accessories		8080	12330	12910	14065	21438
	Grand Total Man-Hours Required		40400	61650	64550	70325	107188
	Number of Employees Required for Operations on a Normal Eight Hour Day or Five Days a Week		240	385	351	419	638

*The Factory is to be Closed the Friday After Thanksgiving and During the last Week in December for Annual Invent-
**Eighty Per Cent of January Man-Hour Requirements are Moved into December in This Example.

FIGURE 10-2 An analysis of the capacity requirements of a proposed shipping schedule. Shown above is a hypothetical example of a forecast of shipments for a year ahead. In practice, such a long-range forecast would show the prospective schedule for all major items produced. The example is confined to five products in order to illustrate the method of translating the forecast into a projection of the man-hours and men required. The first section shows the desired shipping schedule month by month for the five items. Substantial seasonal variation in sales, as would occur in agricultural implements, is indicated. Section 2 shows the translation of quantities into a common unit, in this case man-hours. The man-hour totals for individual months

June Work Days	July	August	September	October	November*	December*	Total
22	22	23	21	21	21	17	
2000	3000	2500	1500	500			11000
15000	18000	24000	24000	24000	20000	15000	185000
2000	5000	7000	7000	4000	1000	1000	27000
4000	9000	15000	15000	9000	4000	2000	67000
							20000
21000	31500	26250	15750	5250			115500
45000	54000	72000	72000	72000	60000	45000	555000
11200	28000	39200	39200	22400	5600	5600	151200
15600	35100	58500	58500	35100	15600	7800	261300
							44000
92800	148600	195950	185450	134750	81200	58400	1127000
4200	6300	5250	3150	1050			23100
9000	10800	14400	14400	14400	12000	9000	111000
2240	5600	7840	7840	4480	1120	1120	30240
3120	7020	11700	11700	7020	3120	1560	52260
							8800
18560	29720	39190	37090	26950	16240	11680	225400
25200	21000	12600	4200				92400
43200	57600	57600	57600	48000	36000	28800	444000
22400	31360	31360	17920	4480	4480		120960
28080	46800	46800	28080	12480	6240		209040
							35200
118880	156760	148360	107800	64960	46720	28800	901600
137440	186480	187550	144890	91910	62960	40480	1127000
343360	46620	46888	36223	22978	15740	10120	281750
171800	233100	234437	181113	114887	78700	50600	1408750
976	1324	1274	1078	684	468	372	
ory Taking.							

reveal the wide fluctuation in demand. Sections 3 and 4 are further steps in the direction of determining exactly what the load will be each month. The extra hours needed for the manufacture of repair service parts and collateral parts are added in section 5 and the grand total of manpower requirements is obtained. In the last step, the conversion to number of employees, it is necessary to consider the number of workdays in each month. After the load of work is expressed in terms of employees required (or tons per day or other appropriate measures), the job of adjusting the plan to level out peaks and valleys in production can begin. The results of such a leveling process are shown in figure 10-5.

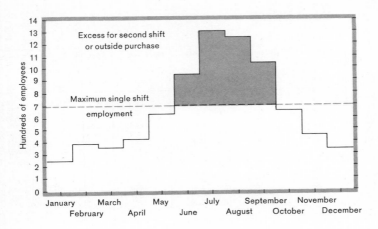

FIGURE 10-3   A graphic presentation of the extreme fluctuations in numbers of employees needed month by month to manufacture the products called for in figure 10-2. It is computed on the basis of all employees working an eight-hour day for a five-day week. The horizontal line drawn across the chart at the 700-employee mark represents the maximum number that the plant can employ on one shift. The capacity required for the tentative schedule is, during the peak period, nearly double the maximum that the plant can supply.

hours to make one unit of A, 16.4 hours to make one B, and 24.0 hours to make one C. Call B 100. One A unit takes as much time as 1.06 B units. One C unit equals 1.47 B units. Suppose that the schedule calls for 35 of A, 10 of B, and 50 of C. Multiply 35 × 1.06, add 10 × 1.00 plus 50 × 1.47, get 37 + 10 + 73.5 = 120.5 equivalent B units. Since a B unit takes 16.4 hours you need 1,975 processing hours to do the work.

You might think that it would be quicker to multiply units by hours and get total hours directly but sometimes it is simpler to express a plant's capacity as its ability to turn out a certain number of B units.

If you can express work loads in two or three ways and can do it without spending much time and money getting the figures, it is a good idea to use both or all such measures rather than just one. This gives you a better idea of how your prospective load and the capacity compare since no one measure reflects perfectly either the work load or the capacity.

PRODUCT MIX IRREGULARITIES   So far, our discussion of translating a forecast into its capacity requirements has paid no attention to the product mix and the possibility that you will end up with unlike loads in different departments. Actually, this omission is usually unimportant in master schedule making. So long as the total plant load stays within reason the normal product mix will load all departments more or less equally. This is because you have, in the past, made your departments the right size so that they all work about the same hours all the time. Each department's capacity handles its normal load while working the same hours as other departments. Variations in the product mix will compensate fairly well so far as departmental loads are concerned.

But if there are bottleneck departments or if the product mix shifts a good bit, it is well to calculate individual department loads. You may need more men or machines than usual in some spots at the same time that other departments will have to go on short hours. Actually, production control pays much more attention to the specific man-hour requirements of different departments and work centers than we have just said. This is, however, more because of its job of manpower planning (see Chapter 15) than because schedule making requires it.

CAPACITY FLEXIBILITY   When converting a desired shipping schedule into an actual production schedule, don't regard the plant's capacity as fixed. You can change it in several ways. You can change the hours of work per day, the days of work per week, the number of employees, the number of shifts, the amount of work subcontracted outside, and the number of machines used. Some of these alternatives cost considerable money. Increasing the number of shifts, working overtime, and buying new machines are all costly. Yet, overtime may well be less costly than hiring more men for a short time. New employees surely cost you $300 or more each before they produce well on the job and then there are more costs if you have to lay them off. Unemployment taxes are high for companies with high turnover, and besides this, unions go after high supplemental unemployment benefits in such companies.

MAKING THE MASTER SCHEDULE   When you have converted a desired schedule into its man-hour requirements (or into whatever capacity measure you use), it is ready for comparison with the factory's capacity. Usually the first comparison will show that the desired schedule calls for too many production irregularities. If so, the next job is to smooth them out as much as possible. You can do this by moving part of the production from peak months into earlier months. Of course, this means building up inventories, so you can't go very far with this idea. There is also the possibility of persuading customers to buy earlier, in the normally slack periods. Sometimes you can induce them to buy earlier by advertising and price cuts. Or maybe you can induce your dealers to lay in their stocks earlier.

After smoothing the desired schedule as much as you can by planning

Section		Man-Hours Per 100	January 21	February 20	March 23	April 21	May Number of 21
1	**Revised Assembly Schedule** Product						
	A				500	1000	1500
	B		12000	12000	12000	12000	12000
	C					500	1000
	D		1000	1000	2000	3000	4000
	E		2000	4000	10000	4000	
2	**Man-Hours Required for Revised Assembly Schedule** Product						
	A	1050			5250	10500	15750
	B	300	36000	36000	36000	36000	36000
	C	560				2800	5600
	D	390	3900	3900	7800	11700	15600
	E	220	4400	8800	22000	8800	
	Total		44300	48700	71050	69800	72950
3	**Man-Hours Required for Assembly (20 Per Cent of Total) Shown in Assembly Month** Product						
	A				1050	2100	3150
	B		7200	7200	7200	7200	7200
	C					560	1120
	D		780	780	1560	2340	3120
	E		880	1760	4400	1760	
	Total		8860	9740	14210	13960	14590
4	**Man-Hours Required for Three-Fourths of Parts Making Operations (60 Per Cent of Total Hours) Shown in Month Before** Product						
	A			3150	6300	9450	12600
	B		21600	21600	21600	21600	27000
	C				1680	3360	6720
	D		2340	4680	7020	9360	11700
	E		4400	1760			
	Total		29220	42630	41880	43770	58020
5	**Man-Hours Required for One-Fourth of Parts Making Operations (20 Per Cent of Total Hours) Shown in Second Month** Product						
	A		1050	2100	3150	4200	4200
	B		7200	7200	7200	9000	9000
	C			560	1120	2240	4480
	D		1560	2340	3120	3900	6240
	E		4400	1760			
	Total		14210	13960	14590	19340	23920
6	Total Man-Hours Each Month		52290	66330	70680	77070	96530
	25 Per Cent for Extras		13073	16582	17670	19268	24132
	Grand Total Man-Hours Required		65363	82912	88350	96338	120662
	Number of Employees (40 Hr Wk)		389	518	480	573	718
	Suggested Days Per Week		4	5	5	5	5
	Suggested Employment		500	500	500	600	700
	Man-Hours Available		68000	80000	92000	100800	117600
	Excess Man-Hours Needed		-	-	-	-	-
	Number of Employees Needed. (If excess Man-Hours are Provided by a Second Shift)						

*The Factory is to be Closed the Friday After Thanksgiving and During the Last Week in December for Annual Inventory
**Sixty Per Cent of January Man-Hour Requirements are Moved into December and Twenty Per Cent of January and

FIGURE 10-4   A work sheet on which one possibility of moving work hours ahead is considered in an attempt to produce the desired shipping schedule shown in figure 10-2. In section 1 the originally proposed shipping quantities have been shifted forward a little to reduce the peaks first called for. Sections 2 and 3 show the total man-hours

June Work Days 22	July 22	August 23	September 21	October 21	November* 21	December* 17	Total
2000	2000	2000	1200	500	300		11000
15000	15000	15000	20000	20000	20000	20000	185000
2000	4000	6500	6500	3500	1500	1500	27000
5000	8000	13000	13000	10000	4500	2500	67000
							20000
21000	21000	21000	12600	5250	3130		115500
45000	45000	45000	60000	60000	60000	60000	555000
11200	22400	36400	36400	19600	8400	8400	151200
19500	31200	50700	50700	39000	17550	9750	261300
							44000
96700	119600	153100	159700	123850	89100	78150	1127000
4200	4200	4200	2520	1050	630		23100
9000	9000	9000	12000	12000	12000	12000	110000
2240	4480	7280	7280	3920	1680	1680	30240
3900	6240	10140	10140	7800	3510	1950	52260
							8800
19340	23920	30620	31940	24770	17820	15630	225400
Assembly Month**							
12600	12600	7560	3150	1890			69300
27000	27000	36000	36000	36000	36000	21600	333000
13440	21840	21840	11760	5040	5040		90720
18720	30420	30420	23400	10530	5850	2340	156780
					880	1760	8800.
71760	91860	95820	74310	53460	46890	26580	676200
Before Assembly Month**							
4200	2520	1050	630				23100
9000	12000	12000	12000	12000	7200	7200	111000
7280	7280	3920	1680	1680			30240
10140	10140	7800	3510	1950	780	780	52260
					880	1760	8800
30620	31940	24770	17820	15630	8860	9740	225400
121720	147720	151210	124070	93860	73570	51950	1127000
30430	36930	37803	31017	23465	18392	12988	281750
152150	184650	189013	155087	117325	91962	64938	1408750
864	1049	1027	923	698	547	477	
6	6	6	6	5	5	5	
700	700	700	700	700	550	500	
145600	140000	151200	140000	117600	92400	68000	
6500	4500	3800	15000	-	-	-	
31	225	176	75				

Taking.
February Requirements are Moved into November and December Respectively in This Example.

required and the assembly hours shown in the month of assembly. Parts-production hours (in sections 4 and 5) have been spread over the two months preceding assembly. Section 6 shows the total man-hours required and converts them into manpower requirements to show the employment needed to meet the schedule.

to carry inventories, the next thing is to figure out how to meet the remaining irregularities by changing the factory's capacity. As we suggested above, you can change the work hours per day, the days per week, and lastly, the number of employees. See how much of the work load irregularity you can take care of by such changes. Set up a table like the one in figure 10-4. If these changes (first, carrying inventories and, second, changing the manhours worked) don't smooth out production enough you'll have to turn to still other alternatives. Maybe you'll have to send a good many more orders outside. Or perhaps permanent expansion, with new machines and a larger work force, is the answer.

While trying to minimize the total cost of production and inventory costs by such changes, keep the emphasis on the overall capacity of the desired schedule and of the plant. But once the overall picture is under control you need to turn to specifics. Any adjustment you make in total figures must finally work down to specific changes in the proposed production of individual products. For major products, you have to look over each of these prospective individual changes before you bed down the schedule. You'll have to decide which items to cut (or raise), how many, and for what month. You are working around now from a desired shipping schedule to a master production schedule. Your proposed schedule should show, for each month, all planned changes in employment, in work hours, and in the volume of work that may have to be contracted for on the outside.

INTERNATIONAL HARVESTER EXAMPLE   To illustrate how all of this is done, we have shown in figures 10-2 to 10-5 how International Harvester figures its capacity requirements using the method we have been describing (product names and quantities are hypothetical). Figure 10-2 shows the calculation, and 10-3 shows, in chart form, how extreme are the fluctuations in manpower called for by our example. We set the seasonal peak high intentionally so that we could emphasize the possibilities of smoothing out production. Finally, on pages 203 and 204, we show how the high and low points were largely smoothed out. In our example, in figure 10-4, we didn't plan to buy any new machines but if we had, this should be shown too.

Compare figures 10-3 and 10-5 which show how the forecast can be met in spite of the big seasonal peak in demand. The proposed schedule, charted in figure 10-5, spreads the work by moving some production into slack months before the peak. It also calls for changing the number of days of work per week and changing the number of men on the payroll. We didn't quite take care of the summer peak load though. During the summer the plant will have to work overtime or buy more items outside.

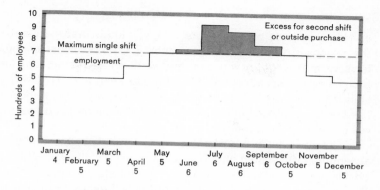

FIGURE 10-5 A graphic presentation of the smoothed-out plan of operations for producing the products indicated in figure 10-4. This plan calls for a minimum employment of 500 employees and a maximum of 700. The workweek also varies from a four-day week in January to a six-day week for the June–September period. The shaded area above the 700-employee mark from June to September represents the employment equivalent of the work that must be contracted for on the outside or provided for by the addition of a second shift, if the program is to be met. Reference to figure 10-3 shows the extent to which employment was leveled and compares it to the demands of the originally proposed shipping schedule.

Although employment is not completely regularized, it is a big improvement over the operations indicated in figure 10-3. Production is spread more evenly, and it is done without building up inventories very much.

Section 1 of figure 10-4 is the proposed revised assembly schedule. Section 2 translates the quantities of all products into the common unit, man-hours. Sections 3, 4, and 5 show the particular months in which the man-hours must be worked. In section 6 the total man-hours needed for each month are summed up, the requirements for repair and collateral parts are added, and the necessary number of employees working a 40-hour week is calculated.

The line "Number of employees (40-hour week)" in section 6 of figure 10-4 indicates that we would need 389 men in January but in July we would have to go up to 1,049 men, nearly three times as many. But by going on a four-day week in January, and a six-day week in the summer, we can produce the schedule with a workforce of 500 in January, and just over 700 in July. True, even with 200 extra men, we will have to work some overtime in the summer. But only in July and August will we have to go to a 10-hour day or buy more on the outside.

Figures 10-2 and 10-4 show how International Harvester makes up master schedules. It is also the way many other companies do it. When you get as far as we have gone in figure 10-4, you know that the plant can handle the proposed schedule and you know just about what changes you will have to make. When you give this work sheet to the top men to show them how the schedule can be met, you need also to give them a chart showing how inventories will go up and down (we didn't work this out here, but the inventory buildup in our example is not large) and how much money will be tied up each month.

The next move is up to top management. Is the tentative schedule acceptable? Or should the forecast be cut? Or should some other action be taken? If so, then you have to recalculate everything. Probably your first attempt to make a schedule out of a forecast won't be perfect and you may have to redo it a time or two. But finally you get it to the point where management approves it. *At this point it is a master schedule, not an approved forecast.* And even though it will probably be changed several times before the factory gets the products out, it now constitutes authority to production control to go ahead and get production started.

TYPES OF MASTER SCHEDULES

"Master schedule" means different things in different companies. Commonly, the term refers to the overall schedule received by production control covering everything that the plant is to produce in a given period of time. This is the kind of master schedule we have been talking about so far in this chapter. A second use of the term refers to the master plan for manufacturing an individual complex product. The master schedule, in this case, is an overall time schedule indicating when certain major parts of the work on a large project are to be completed. It sets the target dates on which to base the production schedules for parts and subassembly manufacture. This second use of the term "master schedule" is discussed in Chapter 21, where, to avoid confusion, we have called it a "master plan."

SALES ORDER LOADS AS MASTER SCHEDULES   Although we have been talking about master schedules as being based on forecasts, in some companies they are based directly on sales orders rather than on forecasts. Companies doing engineering-type jobs, such as Otis Elevator, work directly to sales orders, yet they set up master schedules. They keep records of the work load represented by jobs already received and set delivery promise dates for new orders according to the time when delivery can be made. This requires their knowing the load of work ahead of individual departments—the engineering department and every manufacturing department. If any phase of contract will be held up because it has to

IBM

PREPARATION OF FORM

1. Indicate the adapters (maximum of one per adapter position) by marking an "X" in the applicable adapter position block (normally beginning in adapter position 1).

2. Complete the supplemental code information. When more than two adapters from Category 1 or one from Category 2 are ordered, enter 2 in the applicable block ("Channel 1 or 2") if this adapter is associated with the second channel interface (#1860), otherwise 1 must be entered here. Enter the adapter category type (1, or 2) in the category type block. Enter Z in the synchronous clock selector block unless either 7692, 7693, 2931, or 2932 is specified for this adapter position; if one of these features is specified, this supplementary code specifies whether the adapter interface, the dual interface or both are to be clocked by the synchronous clock feature. Enter 1 if clocking the adapter interface, only; enter 2 if clocking the dual interface, only; enter 3 if clocking both the adapter interface and the dual interface.

3. Indicate the features by marking an "X" in the applicable adapter position block.

4. (D) = Domestic only.
   (W) = WTC only.

BRANCH OFFICE No._____

PLANT ORDER No._____

SYSTEM TYPE_____SYSTEM No._____

CUSTOMER NAME_____

DATE PREPARED_____

SALESMAN'S SIGNATURE_____

SYSTEMS ENGINEERING
MANAGER'S SIGNATURE_____

ADAPTOR POSITION				SUPPLEMENTAL CODE
4	3	2	1	
		1	1	CHANNEL 1 OR 2
				CATEGORY TYPE (1, 2)
Z		Z		SYNCHRONOUS CLOCK SELECTOR
Z	Z	Z	Z	CONSTANT
Z	Z	Z	Z	CONSTANT

ADAPTER	
4633 — IBM TEL. ADAPTER	(D)
4645 — IBM TERM. ADAPTER — TYPE I	
4646 — IBM TERM. ADAPTER — TYPE I	
4648 — IBM TERM. ADAPTER — TYPE II	
4656 — IBM TERM. ADAPTER — TYPE III	
4657 — IBM TERM. ADAPTER — TYPE III	(D)
5500 — PARALLEL DATA ADAPTER	
7695 — SYNC. DATA ADAPTER — TYPE I	(D)
7696 — SYNC. DATA ADAPTER — TYPE I	
7860 — TEL. ADAPTER — TYPE I	(D)
7861 — TEL. ADAPTER — TYPE I	(D)
7862 — TEL. ADAPTER — TYPE I	(D)
7885 — TEL. ADAPTER — TYPE II	(D)
2794 — TEL. ADAPTER — W T C	(W)
7697 — SYNC. DATA ADAPTER — TYPE II	(D)
7698 — SYNC. DATA ADAPTER — TYPE II	
7699 — SYNC. DATA ADAPTER — TYPE II	(D)
(RESERVED)	

ADAPTOR POSITION				FEATURES	
4	3	2	1		
				3855 — EXPANSION FEATURE	
				1302 — AUTO-CALL	(D)
				4636 — IBM LINE ADAPTER	
				4637 — IBM LINE ADAPTER	
				1303 — AUTO-CALL	(D)
				3461 — DUAL COMM. INTERFACE	(D)
				3462 — DUAL COMM. INTERFACE	
				4703 — INTERNAL CLOCK	
				5501 — PARALLEL DATA TIME OUT	
				5505 — PARALLEL DATA EXTENSION 1	
				5505 — PARALLEL DATA EXTENSION 2	
				5505 — PARALLEL DATA EXTENSION 3	
				5505 — PARALLEL DATA EXTENSION 4	
				2798 — SELECTIVE SPEED — 50 BPS	(W)
				2862 — SELECTIVE SPEED — 75 BPS	(W)
				9060 — EBCDIC CODE	
				9061 — ASCII CODE	
				9062 — SIX BIT TRANSCODE	
				9070 — EBCDIC DUAL CODE	
				9071 — ASCII DUAL CODE	
				9072 — SIX BIT TRANSCODE DUAL CODE	
				9700 — TRANSPARENCY	
				9701 — TRANSPARENCY	
				1314 — AUTO CALL	(D)
				7477 — STATION SELECTION	
				3463 — DUAL COMM. INTERFACE	(D)
				3464 — DUAL COMM. INTERFACE	
				3465 — DUAL COMM. INTERFACE	(D)
				7692 — SYNCHRONOUS CLOCK (1200BPS)	
				7693 — SYNCHRONOUS CLOCK (2400BPS)	
				2931 — SYNCHRONOUS CLOCK (600BPS)	(W)
				2932 — SYNCHRONOUS CLOCK (2000BPS)	(W)
				(RESERVED)	
				(RESERVED)	

120-1379-3

1 — PLANT

FIGURE 10-6   Abstract of sales order. (International Business Machines Corp.)

be done in an overloaded department, the whole order will have to be given a more distant delivery date.

In this type of company the master schedule is the composite plan for completing the contracts on order. New master schedules of this type generally are made out monthly. They extend into the future for as far as orders are booked.

Sales orders and their accompanying drawings are direct sources of authority to manufacture. Copies of sales orders, or abstracts of the important information from them, are made out in the sales or order department and sent to engineering, production control, cost accounting, and other departments. Such abstracts of sales orders and drawings only authorize production to be planned and do not authorize production to start. Only copies of sales orders themselves authorize production. The copies of the sales orders describe the products wanted, the quantity, the tests the product is to undergo, the delivery date, and extra parts needed for future repairs; in general, they verify the abstract and furnish more details.

Sales orders are usually for special products, and being special each order requires new processing authority. Production control, therefore, must get processing instructions from the engineering department before going ahead. The sales order itself, along with drawings and processing instructions, may come to production control from engineering rather than directly from sales. Sales orders are direct authority to assemble finished products as well as to use parts from stock. And they are authority to make any parts needed, or to buy required parts and materials.

Sales orders for special products are generally sent to production control whenever they are ready. They are not held by sales and sent in bunches or all at one time such as on the first day of each month. Sales orders show wanted delivery dates which are set only after considering the factory's existing work load and the load they add.

MAKING MACHINERY IN LOTS   Manufacturers of certain other products requiring long "make" times use still other kinds of master schedules. Long manufacturing times must be allowed whenever some of the parts require it. Most of the products sold by manufacturers of locomotives, road grading equipment, lathes, and other factory machines are standard or near standard. Because they are costly they are made in lots rather than singly or to separate orders. But you can't always wait to start the manufacture of a lot of such machines until you have orders for a complete lot on hand. You have to start to make them before you have sales orders for them all. (Often it is helpful to make them in standard lots or multiples of standard lots, such as 25, 50, 75; or 12, 24, 36. Doing this simplifies ordering parts because they too can be ordered in standard lots.)

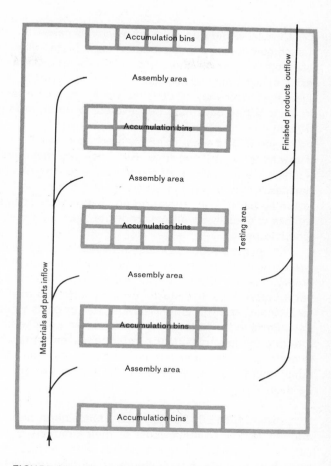

FIGURE 10-7   One manufacturer of varied assembled products has the assembly floor arranged as shown in the diagram above. At any given time, each assembly area is
devoted to one type of product, the parts for which have
been accumulated in, let us say, the bins on the right-hand
side. Parts are accumulated for future products in the bins
along the left of the area. These parts come from stock,
purchase, or manufacture, as the case may be, and are put
into the bins as soon as they are ready. When the assembly
of one product is completed, the area is used for the next
product, whose parts should be on hand in the bins on the
left. While assembly progresses, the bins on the right are
used to accumulate parts for the next product. Parts are
always brought in at the same end of the area and the
assemblies progress toward the opposite end. Upon completion they are given an operating test, packed, and crated
for shipment.

Curiously, the quantities of machines called for on master schedules in such companies are often determined by the allocation of space on the assembly or erection floor. Often the assembly department is set up as a series of assembly bays such as the one depicted in figure 10-7. At any given time each bay is devoted wholly to the assembly of one type of product. Other bays may be devoted to other products or to the same product.

If you had 10 such assembly areas, you could assemble up to 10 kinds of machines at any one time. But since you make more than 10 kinds of machines, some will be off the schedule for months at a time. More popular items may be on the schedule all the time and take up one or more assembly bays for months on end. The master schedule in such circumstances is actually an allocation of the available assembly area during the schedule period.

The master schedule must of necessity cover several months, not just one or two, since it takes several months to get all the parts made. Obviously it is necessary, too, to accumulate the *total* quantity of nearly all parts before assembly starts. Exceptions to this might be parts which can be attached after assembly is under way or parts whose production rate is slow. Parts in the latter category can often be scheduled to be finished by the time the assembly floor needs them even if the whole lot of such parts is not ready when unit number one is to be assembled. So long as additional quantities are received as fast as they are needed, assembly will not be delayed.

ROLLING MASTER SCHEDULES Machinery makers sometimes have enough volume to make most of their products continuously. If so, they can use a "rolling" master schedule which differs from master schedules for products made in lots. Where assembled products are made month in and month out, these schedules project the factory's production ahead for a fixed period. The master schedule is a list of all of the finished products to be assembled during a given number of months ahead. Five months is common but companies having long manufacturing cycles use longer periods and those with short cycles, shorter periods. Figure 10-8 shows how GM's Electro-motive division, which makes diesel-electric locomotives, does it (the figures are hypothetical). Electro-motive's manufacturing cycle is so long that its schedule is projected eleven months ahead. In Figure 10-8 there are two sets of figures for near-future months. These represent half months. Breaking the near months into half months allows for closer control.

At the end of each month, Electro-motive adds a new future month so that the schedule always covers 11 months ahead. Each of the 11 months

Date: March 31

Model Number	Product	April		May		June		July	Aug.	Sept.	Oct.	Nov.	Dec.	Jan.	Total
		11	11	11	10	10	10	14	21	21	23	19	22	21	
225	1500 HP T6	8	12	7	12	7	7	15	20	15	18	23	27	20	191
226	1500 HP T7	5	3	6	1	6	6	4	7	12	14	8	9	14	95
227	1500 HP T18	3	3	3	2	2	2	3	5	5	5				33
228	2250 HP R - Pass	3	3	3	2	3	3	3	5	5	6	5	5	5	51
229	2250 HP S Pass				1										1
262	1500 HP ST 6B			3	2	2	1			4	4	4	4	4	28
263	1500 HP ST 6E	1	2				2	2	3						10
260	1600 HP SP 2	1	3	1	1										6
238	1500 HP Un 4	5	5	4	4	4			5		5		8		40
231	1500 HP Un 4b	1	1	1	1	2	6	9	9	12	13	14	17	8	94

FIGURE 10-8   A "rolling" master schedule for ten months ahead.

covered is shown separately. Slight revisions are made in the schedules for each of the months covered every time a new month is added. Thus, the June schedule, when first added to the August-May schedule, is likely to be changed a little when it appears as a part of the September-July schedule, and again when it comes out as part of the October-August schedule.

Many machinery manufacturers use rolling master schedules similar to that of Electro-motive. Most, however, use a 5- or 6-month period, not 11 months.

SEMIANNUAL MASTER SCHEDULES Machinery makers who make extensive lines of products usually don't sell enough of any of them to make them continuously and so have to make them in lots. A slightly different kind of master schedule fits their needs better. Their master schedules are pushed into the future less often but in bigger jumps, perhaps six-month jumps. Thus, in March they are producing on a master schedule which originally covered January–June. They also already have on hand a master schedule for July–December. No other schedule will be issued until perhaps August when the schedule for January–June of the following year will be issued.

Master schedules adding several months at one time make it easier to plan both assembly and parts manufacture when products are on the schedule sometimes and off the schedule at other times. Particularly in parts making, the quantities made in single lots can be more economically planned when you learn several months' schedules all at once.

Here's how this advantage operates. Suppose that a product lot is to be made (assembled) during September, October, and November. This product has not been on the schedule for several months and will not again be made for several more months after this lot is finished.

Using six-month schedules, you learn about the whole lot at once. You can make parts in quantities to suit the whole assembly lot. This would have been different if you had used a rolling schedule and added one month at a time. In April, you would learn about the products to be assembled in September. You would make up shop orders and start to produce all long lead time parts for September assemblies—making enough for September products only. In May, you learn about October. You have to make another set of shop orders and start new small lots of parts through. The same thing happens again in November. If you had learned about all three months at once you could have combined many of the parts orders.

Actually this difficulty need not be bad. Products newly coming onto the schedule in September are known to be October and November possibilities. You ought to be able to get advance information about their probable October and November quantities so that parts can be provided at the most economical cost.

Master schedules adding 6 months at a time are less flexible than those adding one month, because you must decide what you are going to make farther ahead. In August, you have to decide what you will make through June of the next year—not because you need 10 months in order to get June's products out on time but because you need 5 months in order to get January's products out.

FLEXIBILITY OF MASTER SCHEDULES   Master schedules should be firm and not subject to change for a period into the future at least equal to the manufacturing time. You can, of course, change schedules for products already being made but because it is expensive it should not be done often. It is less costly to *cut* scheduled quantities than to *increase* them. You can, in February, reduce the quantities of products that you will assemble in March. You can cut parts orders. But you can't decide in February that you will assemble more products in March. It is just too late to get the parts.

Actually master schedules should be firm for a period longer than the manufacturing time. If they are firm, you can make parts in bigger lots, quantities that cover several months' needs. This is important because ordinarily you save money by making one large lot of a part rather than several small ones. This is particularly important whenever you have products that you assemble at the rate of one or two a week and keep on doing it for several months.

Even companies making engineering type products find that their schedules, based though they are on orders already booked, are not altogether firm. One big reason is order cancellations. When your customers' business slides off, they cancel orders or want them held back. You have to cooperate or lose their business in the future. Most orders don't get canceled but some do and cancellations disrupt schedules.

Rush orders are another reason why your schedules won't stay firm. You always handle at least a few rush orders from good customers and that upsets schedules too. Master schedules, of course, can be set at less than capacity, leaving the balance of the capacity open for rush orders. If you set schedules this way a reasonable number of rush orders will cause no trouble.

Design changes also sometimes upset schedules. Some such changes are so important that you have to change products in process even though they are already half-made. This always makes extra work and upsets the schedules.

The manufacturing department's own failure to perform perfectly also causes a certain amount of schedule changing. Every month ends with some leftovers, uncompleted jobs supposed to have been finished. Sometimes the incomplete jobs mean lost production, no other jobs having been completed in their place. In other cases, a start has already been made on some of the new month's work. Usually there is a mixture; some old jobs have not been completed and some new ones have been started ahead. In any case, the schedule for the new month always has to be changed so that it continues on from the point where last month left off, not where last month was supposed to have left off.

When large-volume products are being made all of the time, the new month's schedule may or may not have to catch up the last month's discrepancies. If parts production runs behind schedule but assembly does not, the shortages must be made up. But if the number of finished products also falls behind you may not have to make up the parts shortages. It depends on whether management wants the lost finished products made up.

Makers of specially made equipment have a cushion that gives them flexibility. Link-Belt division of FMC Corporation reserves part of its capacity, when making master schedules, for what it calls "merchandise" orders. These are orders for repair items that are carried in stock or they are for small fabricated stock items. Orders for merchandise items give flexibility because in any short period of time they can be pushed aside or stepped up in order to keep the work load even.

Customers buying on blanket contracts can also help make vendor companies' manufacturing schedules more firm by giving them their delivery schedules ahead. Releases for deliveries against blanket contracts should be firm for from two to four months ahead, and besides this the customer should supply tentative figures for an additional three months. Each month both the firm and tentative releases should be extended another month. Don't, however, count too heavily on this giving you a firm schedule. Customers' "firm" releases are often changed, and when a big customer says "Change," you change.

Firm master schedules are, for nearly all companies, unrealized ideals, whether you manufacture to stock or to customers' orders. If you make to stock, you have to change schedules every time sales don't follow the forecast closely. If you sell to customers' orders, you have to move delivery dates forward or backward, raise or lower quantities, change designs or do whatever the customers demand. Not always can you do everything the customer wants, but you have to try to suit him the best you can.

PRODUCTION PROGRAMS

In continuous manufacturing the overall production plans for, say, 3 to 12 months ahead are called production "programs," "budgets," "quotas," or even "forecasts." Production programs differ from master schedules in that they are in general terms only and show, for all but the nearest month or two, only totals for classes or types of products. In contrast, most master schedules show specific items and quantities for several months ahead.

Production programs, for the period 3 to 12 months ahead, confer authority to place purchase orders for materials or even to buy machines. You have to place orders for raw materials before you know exactly what you are going to make because you buy such big quantities that you can't wait to place orders at the last minute. In February, Goodyear doesn't know just how many tires at each size it will make in June but it has to buy rubber and nylon cord anyway. And it does know that it will be making tires in June and about how many tires in total. Programs do not, however, confer authority to go ahead with making the products.

When using production programs, authority to manufacture is issued to production control only a few weeks before the items covered are to be made. This authority comes in the form of a "release" or an "authorization" of a segment of the production program. Until the release is given, the production control department is not allowed to order products made even though it knows that the items and quantities on the new release will, in the main, be the same as those in other recent releases.

Production program releases are *lists of items and quantities* wanted.

They constitute producing authority for all items listed. A release may cover only one week and may be issued only two or three weeks ahead of production. Often it covers one month and is for the second month ahead. Ideally, between release dates, no other orders are sent to production control. None, that is, except for the usual few rush orders, and even rush orders are usually not for different products, but are mostly quantity changes.

Releases authorize both assembly and parts manufacture or materials preparation. Except for very small items, you don't prepare materials ahead nor do you make up parts and stock them ahead of production. You set the rate of materials preparation and parts production to match their use.

Nearly all items covered on one program release appear again on the next release. Successive releases differ from each other largely in the quantities of individual items ordered. The quantities change continually in response to sales and inventory needs and as customers buying on blanket contracts change their orders.

But how do such companies get by with issuing releases such a short time before production? They can do it because the manufacturing cycle time is short. In most continuous or nearly continuous manufacturing, the factory is tooled up to make products and parts in a matter of hours or days once they are started.

Program releases nearly always differ some from what the original program called for in the period. This is to be expected because you are never able to do a perfect forecasting job months in advance. Actually, however, you can't make very much change in the *totals for classes or types* of products because materials from suppliers are coming in at the rate planned earlier when the purchase commitments were made. But for most individual products the quantities are set exactly for the first time only when the release is given. They were never figured out specifically before that.

Production program releases are usually made up by the finished products inventory control department and sent to the production control department. Some companies, however, make most of their products on long-range contracts for large customers. No finished stocks are kept. Products are made to fill the customer's shipment schedules. In this case, *production control gets delivery schedules from the customers* and makes up factory schedules to suit. Production control decides when to start making products so that they can be delivered to suit the customer's schedule.

You may wonder how you can place purchase orders for materials needed for distant months from the information given on a program which shows only overall quantities for class of products. You can do this successfully because many of the items in a product class use the same raw materials or even the same manufactured parts or assemblies. Goodyear can order rubber and nylon cord months ahead even if it doesn't yet know exactly how many of each size tire it will make in any one month. An electric stove manufacturer doesn't need to know in June exactly how many of each type of stove he will make in November. Stoves taking four burners may have them on the left, right, rear, or divided two on the left and two on the right. All he needs to know for order placing is about how many four-burner stoves he will make in November. In fact, he doesn't even need to know specifically about four-burner stoves. If past sales patterns remain relatively constant, the number of burners and/or the number of four-burner stoves can be estimated.

Purchase orders placed before production schedules are made firm may be only verbal. Thus, a stove manufacturer may tell a clock manufacturer that it will buy from him all its clocks (or a certain percentage of them) for next year's stoves. And the customer tells the vendor how many stoves he thinks he will sell during the year. Formal contracts and delivery schedules come later. The vendor can tool up with confidence that he will get a contract before the actual contract comes through. Of course, he doesn't know just how many clocks he will sell but that is only because his customer doesn't know either.

Some purchased items requiring a long lead time are affected by changes in the product mix. For example, you wouldn't know with any degree of accuracy six months ahead the number of stoves requiring deep-well cookers. You might have to give the manufacturers of the deep-well cooker units that go into your stoves orders that stipulate certain maximum and minimum quantities.

FINISHED PRODUCTS INVENTORY CONTROL AS A SOURCE OF PRODUCING AUTHORITY

Companies making the thousands of items to stock, such as manufacturers of electrical accessories, plumbing fittings, nuts and bolts, and pharmaceuticals, confine their forecasts, except for very important items, to dollars or tonnage figures for classes of products.

Manufacturing is largely a matter of replenishing the stocks of products as they run low. The stocks that you have to replenish include what you have in warehouses all over the country as well as what you have in the factory's finished stock warehouse.

But if you only order replenishments when you need more, your production will follow every up and down of sales and you will get irregular operations. So you forecast and level off production as we have described

FIGURE 10-9

| MONTH | SALES | | PRODUCTION | | |
	MONTHLY	YEAR TO DATE	MONTHLY	YEAR TO DATE	INVENTORY
December	. . .	. . .	. . .	. . .	50
January	50	50	50	50	50
February	50	100	50	100	50
March	70	170	50	150	30
April	40	210	50	200	40
May	30	240	50	250	60
June	20	260	50	300	90
July	30	290	60	360	120
August	50	340	60	420	130
September	90	430	60	480	100
October	100	530	60	540	60
November	90	620	60	600	30
December	40	660	60	660	50

earlier. The only difference is that you deal only in dollar forecasts, not individual product unit forecasts.

Figure 10-9 illustrates how this might be done. Our figures cover a whole year. Many companies don't project their figures that far ahead. Figure 10-10 shows, in a chart, the information from figure 10-9. Notice that, in our example, we have smoothed out production very well indeed, but our peak inventory is nearly three times the normal inventory. Probably that is too much inventory. You would probably choose to vary production a little more and hold down the big inventory in the summer.

Figure 10-9 could be your plan for any main product expressed in units or it could be dollar figures for a class of products. You probably would want to make up such a separate projection for each of your main products but not for the thousands of minor products. If figure 10-9 were for a main product, the monthly production figures shown (after approval from the top men) would be the production schedule.

But when you plan in dollar figures for classes of products how do you finally decide how many of each individual item to make? It works like this. Customers' orders come in to an order department. The order department works very closely with the finished products stock control staff. This staff has the records of what you have on hand and on order. It issues orders for the shipment of all items which can be shipped from stock.

Whenever the stock of any item runs low, the finished products control staff makes up orders for more. But so far we haven't made any use

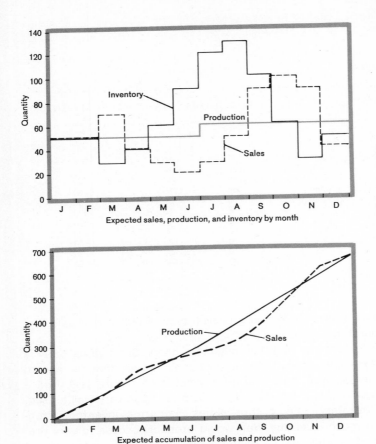

FIGURE 10-10

of our forecast and schedule. Here's how they fit in. The total dollar value of all orders made out each month for individual items in each class has to total up to just about the amount shown in the monthly production column of figure 10-9, not much more, not much less. In June and July in our example, sales are low. You don't really need to order much from the factory so far as replacing low stocks is concerned. But you go ahead and order anyway knowing that your inventory will go up. Our approved forecast and master schedule make us do this. Later, in September and October, you fill your big sales peaks partly out of stock.

It is up to the inventory control group to decide which items to stockpile in June and July. These people have to be careful. If they stock up too heavily on some items, they may go over the approved inventory invest-ment limit and they will have to go light on something else. Yet they are not supposed to keep ordering little quantities of the same items every few days because that runs up production costs. They must send the factory reasonably sized orders.

For items whose ordering is controlled by an inventory control depart-ment, production control gets its authority from that department, not from the approved forecast, nor from approved production schedules for classes of products. The authority reaches production control either as lists of products wanted or as individual product manufacturing requisitions. Lists, when used, usually come once a week and show separately the items and quantities wanted. When individual manufacturing requisitions are used, a separate requisition is made for each item. They are usually sent daily to production control and are not held for once-a-week delivery.

Orders received from the finished stock control group, whether indi-vidual manufacturing requisitions or weekly lists, are orders asking that manufacture be *started*. Orders starting into the plant together will be finished at different times, depending upon their manufacturing times. This is in contrast with master schedules which specify the week or month in which the items ordered are to be *finished*. With master schedules, it is up to production control to start some orders ahead of others. With stock control ordering, it is up to the stock control department to ask sooner for things that take a long time to make.

Requisitions for assembled products are *direct* authority to assemble products and *indirect* authority *to produce the necessary parts*. Products assembled to stock are often assembled largely from parts already made up. In some companies, production control need not await specific assem-bly orders in order to keep an ample supply of regularly used parts. Pro-duction control has permanent authority to maintain an ample supply of such parts whether you buy them or make them yourself. This differs from the arrangement used when you work directly to sales orders. In this situation many of the parts must be made especially for the order and the *sales orders* authorize their manufacture.

STUDY MATERIALS

10-1 What is the relationship between forecasting and scheduling? Does either one affect the other? How does the nature of the product affect the interrelation-ships? What time periods are involved in each?

10-2   What advantages and disadvantages are inherent in flexible schedules? Does flexible scheduling mean that you can be less accurate in your scheduling technique?

10-3   In the International Harvester example on page 202 a revised schedule was offered which called for 500 men in January and 700 in July and August. How could it be that you could put on 200 extra men? What problems of machines would you run into and how would you solve them?

10-4   The forecasters at the Worthington Company have come up with a forecast of 900,000 units of its product A for next year. You have been assigned the job of working out a production program. The expected seasonal pattern in sales is as follows:

MONTH	PERCENTAGE OF AVERAGE MONTH	NUMBER OF POSSIBLE WORKDAYS
January	40	23
February	50	20
March	80	23
April	120	22
May	140	21
June	110	22
July	80	23
August	60	21
September	100	22
October	130	22
November	160	21
December	130	23

You will start on January 1 with an inventory of 200,000 units and, in order to take care of unusual sales demands, should plan not to let the inventory get below about 100,000 units. Top production in regular work hours (40-hour week) is 20,000 units a week using 80 men. Product A has a value of $5 each and it costs $1.25 to carry a unit in stock a year. Overtime production costs 25 cents a unit extra.

The plant closes down for vacation the last half of July; closes down one day for New Year's day, Memorial day, Fourth of July, Labor day, and Thanksgiving day; and closes down two days for Christmas. These are deductions from the possible workdays given above.

Plan your production and inventory levels. How much will your peak inventory investment be? The average inventory in units and in dollars? How many men will your plan call for month by month and how many hours a week will they work?

10-5   Assume that you are asked to determine the program for producing small tractors at the National Farm Equipment Company for next year. This year, through August, your company has sold 20,000 tractors of this type. Sales through August normally account for 80 per cent of your full year's sales. September,

October, November, and December sales are usually 6, 6, 5, and 3 per cent, respectively, of the year's sales. Sales of the three types of tractors you make have been as follows in recent years:

PERIOD	SMALL TYPE	MEDIUM TYPE	LARGE TYPE	TOTAL
This year (8 months' total)	20,000	11,000	6,000	37,000
Last year	24,000	15,000	11,000	50,000
Two years ago	20,000	13,000	12,000	45,000
Three years ago	12,000	12,000	10,000	34,000

Monthly sales and production of small tractors this year have been:

MONTH	SALES	PRODUCTION*
January	500	2,000
February	500	2,000
March	2,000	2,500
April	4,500	2,500
May	5,000	2,500
June	3,000	2,000
July	3,000	2,000
August	1,500	1,500

*Inventory of 3,000 tractors on hand Jan. 1.

Your sales are almost wholly to farmers, although a few are sold to owners of golf courses, real estate development companies, municipalities, etc. You estimate that farm income next year will be 15 per cent above this year. The Kansas City plant is the only plant in which you produce small tractors, and it is devoted wholly to them. Each small tractor requires 125 man-hours of work (direct and indirect hours combined) to produce. Assume that all labor hours fluctuate directly with production. You may neglect absenteeism, productivity ratios, and such matters. Also, for simplicity, assume that all the man-hours are put into the tractor during the month it is produced.

1 What is your forecast of sales of small tractors for next year?

2 Suppose that 3,000 tractors a month is your top possible production; make out a production program for next year. Show sales, production, and inventories by month. End up the year with the same inventory that you had at the start. Here are various cost figures that you need to keep in mind:

  a It costs $25 a month to carry a tractor in inventory.

  b Running out of stock causes losses of $100 per tractor. You also lose any sales which you cannot fill immediately, and you cannot carry negative balances over into following periods.

  c You may produce at any of the following levels, but production costs vary as shown, depending on the level of production (do not plan to produce quantities that fall between those given below):

QUANTITY	COST PER TRACTOR
3,000	$ 700
2,700	725
2,400	775
2,100	850
1,800	950
1,500	1,100
1,200	1,300

3 What will be the average cost per tractor according to your program? (Be sure to include inventory carrying costs and out-of-stock costs.)

4 Assuming that your men work 173 hours a month in all months, how many men will you need each month?

10-6 The Big Bar Company, manufacturers of candy bars, is planning its production schedule for 197–. The program is to be built around sales estimates, as follows:

MONTHLY SALES FOR 197–, IN CARTONS

January	2,500	July	2,000
February	2,000	August	2,500
March	2,500	September	3,000
April	3,000	October	4,000
May	3,000	November	4,500
June	2,500	December	5,000

Plan a workable production schedule in detail, observing these limitations:

1 The opening inventory on January 1 will be 1,000 cartons.

2 At no time in the year can the inventory fall below 1,000 cartons.

3 Maximum inventory at any time is limited by a 3,500-carton warehouse capacity.

4 Candy is perishable and cannot be stored for longer than one month. (Cartons placed in the warehouse one month must be removed the next.)

5 Production, storage, and sales are continuous processes. (As a given month's production is gradually being finished and put into the warehouse, cartons for that month's sales are simultaneously being removed from the warehouse.)

6 Manufacturing facilities limit the production in any month to 4,000 cartons.

7 Labor relations require that in no month should production fall below 2,500.

8 For smooth operations, changes in the production schedule from month to month should conform as far as possible to two principles:
   a Production should remain on a given level for as many months as possible—scale of operations should not fluctuate every month.
   b Transition from one level of production to another should be made as gradual as possible—avoid large fluctuations from one month to another.

chapter eleven

EARLY PLANNING—
ENGINEERING ASPECTS

"Planning" means getting ready to make products. Getting ready the first time is "original" planning while doing it over again is "repetitive" or "routine" planning. In this and the following chapter we will deal with original planning. Repetitive planning will be taken up in Chapter 18.

A word here about terminology. Deciding *when* to do things is part of planning. But this is always called *scheduling, not planning*. Scheduling, except master scheduling, is always a production control job. Scheduling will be discussed in Chapter 20.

ORIGINAL PLANNING   Original planning deals with how products are to be made; out of what materials, how much materials, what operations to perform, and what machines and tools to use. It is the *processing authority* we spoke of in Chapter 10. It takes the form of master bills of materials, master route sheets, engineering drawings, specifications, and possibly other processing instructions. In large companies, except for drawings, these records are all kept on computer tapes. Processing authority is restrictive, since, when you prescribe certain ways for making products, you rule out other ways. It is continuing authority until it is superseded. You don't have to get new processing authority for repeat orders.

Original planning deals also with machinery needs, particularly when you are tooling up for volume production. If you need new equipment, original planners decide what equipment, propose its purchase, and after getting approval, see that it is bought and installed.

Planners usually have a voice in product design in that designers usually consult them at times about how to design products for economical production. Planners, in turn, ought now and then to consult with foremen about how best to make products. They don't always do this, however, and when they don't they sometimes specify uneconomical methods. Planners should spend some of their time in the factory getting firsthand acquaintance with how things are done in the shop.

Processing authority can be almost permanent although in practice it is only semipermanent because products and processes change all of the time. Consequently many processing instructions die a natural death because the operations they cover are no longer done. At the same time you have to keep issuing new instructions for all the new operations that come along. So, although you can find cases where certain processing instructions stay in effect for years, processing instructions as a whole are only semipermanent.

PROCESSING AUTHORITY IN CONTINUOUS PRODUCTION   Processing authority in continuous production is often eliminated completely by the design of the machines or is covered in the initial instructions to manufacture. For example, you don't need any processing authority in the factory for forming an automobile fender. The forming dies in a press do the job, and they are designed to do it exactly right. All that the operators do is put a sheet of steel into the press and push electrical control buttons.

When the need for processing authority (in continuous production) has not been eliminated by machine design it is almost always exercised by the engineering department which issues detailed specifications covering materials, processes, tools, and methods of assembly. You rarely leave those decisions up to either production control or to the foremen. If the assembly process is one of mixing ingredients so that they become inseparable, processing specifications are always used. The laboratory, often a part of the engineering department, sets up specifications which the factory must follow.

In many cases of this type, a chemical or physical change in the material takes place. You mix certain materials and then heat them as a final operation. All rubber products and all baked goods, as well as many other food products, go through mixing and heating processes. Sometimes, as in paint manufacture, all you do is to mix the materials. In all of these cases you have to use the proper mixing formula. You have to measure out exact quantities of each ingredient and the processes have to be closely watched and controlled. Sometimes the raw materials aren't of quite the right consistency and this would make some of your own end-product come out off-standard. To catch such variations you have to make frequent checks. When you find that the raw materials you are working with will cause trouble, the laboratory gives you changed formulas to use temporarily to compensate for the raw materials variations. Engineering or laboratory specifications cover all phases of such "assembly" work.

The engineering department, in continuous manufacture of metal products, always issues instructions telling workers how to do difficult assembly work. Included are instructions covering the way the man is to do the work and the tests the products must pass. Parts manufacture is also covered by specifications, although with automatic machines you need fewer instructions. Remember the automobile fender example? The dies and presses used are special purpose machines. With them the workers need almost no processing instructions.

But you do need specifications for operations that are not fully automatic and for inspection tests. These should be written out in detail and kept in loose-leaf books at the operation so that the worker can refer to them at any time.

WHO DOES ORIGINAL PLANNING?   Original planning is, in large companies, usually done by the engineering department. There the work is done in a section called "planning," "process engineering," "production engineering," "manufacturing engineering," "methods and standards," or "industrial engineering." But this isn't always so. At the Cincinnati Milling Machine Company, the planning department is in the production control department. The same is true at Allis-Chalmers and the Teletype division of the American Telephone and Telegraph Company. In these companies design engineers design the product but production control's planning department engineers decide how to make it.

Sometimes planners work for neither the engineering nor the production control department. At Frigidaire, product drawings go to the manufacturing department, which decides how to make products. Even the tool designers work for manufacturing. Beside doing design work they place tool orders both for tools made inside and for tools bought outside. The master mechanic, who is in charge of this work, does all of the negotiating of contracts with machine tool builders and with tool shops.

The production planning department in General Electric's Appliance division makes out its master route sheets. But before it does, the proposed final design is sent to the "master mechanic" (plant superintendent) who looks it over. His foreman will have to do the work so he makes the final decision as to how to make the item. The planner's process sheets are only tentative until he approves them. Following his approval the production planning department makes out the final process sheets.

No matter where the planners are located, whether in engineering, production control, or manufacturing, large planning departments are usually organized along product lines, meaning that separate groups specialize in separate product lines. In addition, there are usually several process specialists, such as one for welding, one for forging, and one for heat treating. Product line planners consult the process specialists. On unusual jobs, the foreman, too, is consulted because his men will finally have to do the work.

EARLY PLANNING
In a very real sense, you could say that planning for a job really starts when a new idea is first presented. Whenever you talk about new products

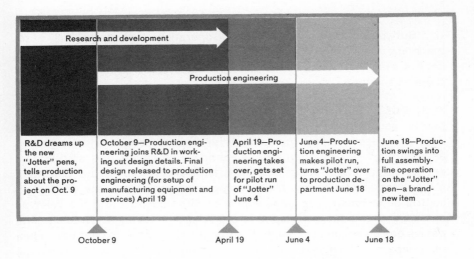

Research and development				
Production engineering				
R&D dreams up the new "Jotter" pens, tells production about the project on Oct. 9	October 9—Production engineering joins R&D in working out design details. Final design released to production engineering (for setup of manufacturing equipment and services) April 19	April 19—Production engineering takes over, gets set for pilot run of "Jotter" June 4	June 4—Production engineering makes pilot run, turns "Jotter" over to production department June 18	June 18—Production swings into full assembly-line operation on the "Jotter" pen—a brand-new item

October 9   April 19   June 4   June 18

FIGURE 11-1   Timetable for new products, research to production, at Parker Pen Co· (Parker Pen Co.)

you get into talking about their design and cost right away. Of course, everything is very tentative at first but you consider different ways of making products and rule out some while the product is still in only rough sketch form.

None of this early thinking—before there is a product, or a design, or a request to bid—is, however, called planning. Planning, in the usual sense, starts when someone says, "Go ahead, we are going to make a product more or less along these lines and in this quantity."

Some companies think of planning as a two-stage affair and set up both a *preplanning* and a *planning* department. Long before starting to make a product, machines to make it must be ordered so they can be installed and ready to go when production is to start. Someone has to decide way ahead what new machines are going to be needed and has to order them. Some companies call the department that does this the preplanning department.

Both the Cincinnati Milling Machine Company and North American Rockwell have such preplanning departments. At North American Rockwell this department helps estimate and bid for new contracts by determining what new machines, tooling, and jigs and fixtures will be needed if a proposed contract is obtained. Preplanning decides, at least for the time being, where the components come from—whether they are made, bought, or furnished by the customer. Immediately after a contract is obtained, the preplanning department orders the required new production equipment. An additional duty is to alert the purchasing department, telling it to get bids on and even to order all materials and purchased components which take a long time to get.

McCulloch Motors, a medium-sized company making chain saws, has engineering make a "prerelease" of a tentative product's design. It goes to an "advanced planning" department which plans the factory's tooling and figures the product's prospective cost. After advanced planning comes up with a tentative cost, McCulloch makes a market survey to see whether or not the product should be developed. If the product is approved, the company's planning department (not the advanced planning department) goes ahead and gets machines and tooling.

Automobile companies do a more thorough job of preplanning than do most other companies. They carry on all of the activities we have described above and also make up scale models, full-sized "mock-ups," and even working prototypes of the cars of the future. Their lead times are so long that some preplanning is done years before a car gets into production.

Preplanning often has to order machines and equipment to make a product before the product's design is fully settled. Foundry patterns, dies, and other tooling are also ordered before designing is complete. Of course, ordering tooling so early means taking calculated risks of loss from change. Yet, on balance, the time saved in getting into production early is worth more than the costs of changing some of the orders.

MATERIALS

What materials should be used to make products? Consumers rarely give much thought to materials, but just as houses can be made out of wood, brick, stone, or other materials, so can industrial products be made out of different materials. A garden hose may be made of rubber or plastic, a skillet may be steel, copper, or aluminum, a trim part of a car might be a zinc die casting, a steel stamping, or made of brass or aluminum. The gears in an automobile timer used to be made of steel. Today some of them are made of nylon.

Which material should be used? Obviously, the one which will cost the least yet do the job well. Yet saying this helps very little because no one material has every advantage and no disadvantage. Steel is strong and cheap but it is hard to machine. Brass and aluminum cost more per pound but can be machined faster and at less cost. Plastics are usually easily formed and look better where colors count but some plastics are brittle when cold and soft when hot. Whichever material you choose gives you some advantages and some disadvantages.

To make the choice more difficult you have to contend with different costs per pound for raw materials and different resale values of the scrap chips you make. Also raw material prices fluctuate. In the late 1950s copper prices fell one-third. Meanwhile steel prices went up. One day's answer might also be the next day's best answer but when prices change very much you need to recalculate to be sure of your choice. Bethlehem Steel even changes the way it makes steel depending on the prices of pig iron and steel scrap. When steel scrap is high, Bethlehem uses more pig iron to make steel than when scrap is lower priced. (Steel made in open hearth furnaces can be charged with any combination of pig iron and scrap. Scrap in most cases makes up from 40 to 60 per cent of the total charge.)

A further complication is volume since proper manufacturing methods depend upon the volume to be made. For small volumes, you probably should choose easily worked materials even if the materials themselves are costly since you save on processing costs. Harder to work materials are usually costly to process unless the volume justifies your buying special tooling which handles difficult materials easily.

There isn't room in a production control book for very much attention to materials, important though they are. Almost always engineering, not the production control department, decides which material to use. For most items, the designer decides. But sometimes, on minor items, the draftsman who makes the drawings decides.

DRAWINGS

Engineering drawings convey design information to production control and to the factory. They show physical dimensions, tolerances, shapes, and contours which the product is to have. Sometimes this isn't enough. The factory may also need written instructions or specifications giving it additional information about how to perform operations, tests that will be required, and similar things that can't be shown on a drawing.

In the early stages of a product's development, drawings may be mere sketches or schematic drawings. They show the way the product is to work but they don't show the individual parts which will be designed later.

Customers ordering machinery and equipment sometimes send drawings and parts lists along with their orders. If they do, you usually need to have your engineering department redo them to get part names, identification numbers, tooling, and other details changed to conform to your plant

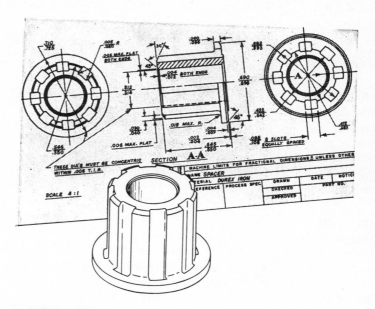

FIGURE 11-2   Drawing of spacer, pictured in the foreground. (General Motors Corp.)

usage. Maybe you will also need to change some minor items to items that are standard in your plant. The master bill should conform to your plant practices as much as possible.

Making drawings is an important part of the work of making new products. Complex products require thousands of drafting hours. This drafting has to be scheduled and the required drawings completed by deadline dates if production is to be started on time. And, just like production itself, you may get into binds when too much work comes along. In order to get out the drawings for a high-priority job you may have to take draftsmen off other projects, work them overtime, or send some work outside.

Many companies are using computers to take over part of their drafting work. Computers, for example, can draw contour lines if you give them the formulas for the lines you want. Computers can actually make drawings or you can have them project a drawing onto a viewing scope for study and analysis. When projected on a scope, the designer can, with an electronic pencil, draw in new lines or erase old ones, as he sees fit. The computer will adjust its memory accordingly and reproduce the newly drawn lines in place of those first projected. It will also smooth out minor irregularities that hand-drawn lines may contain.

Such sophisticated computers are, however, expensive. Low-cost models won't do this, so computers haven't replaced draftsmen yet.

PROCESS DRAWINGS   Drawings of parts show what they look like after they are made. Factory employees usually need no other drawings, even though the part has not—at their operation—taken on its finished shape. Sometimes, however, certain parts and certain operations are so difficult that operators need working drawings (also called "process" drawings or "setup" drawings). They show the operator how to set up the job on his machine and how the part should look before and after his operation.

DRAWINGS IN CATALOGS   Customers who buy machines need a parts catalog for ordering repair parts. Customers may also need a manual telling them how to run the machine and how to repair it. Drawings showing parts and the way they fit together (as in figure 11-3) are often included in the catalogs and manuals to help the customer repair the machine and order replacement parts. Sometimes the parts are spread out as a display and photographed. Part numbers are put on the illustration for accurate ordering.

GROUP DRAWINGS   If the parts of an assembled product are few in number, they can all be shown separately on the drawing for the product itself. Almost always, though, there are too many parts for this to be done. When the parts of a product or subassembly are all shown on one drawing, it is often called a "group" drawing.

DRAWINGS AS ROUTE SHEETS   Parts drawings and master route sheets can sometimes be combined. The operations and all other information required to make the part are listed in one corner of the drawing. In the space alongside the list on the master drawing, blank spaces are provided for filling in information about specific orders—quantities, dates, order number, etc. When an order is to be made, copies of the drawing are reproduced and the blank spaces are filled in on the copies.

ECONOMIZING ON THE COST OF MAKING DRAWINGS   Drawings don't have to be made in expensive ways. They don't have to be hand-drawn pictures. Simple symbols can be used for certain parts. An electric switch or threads on a screw can be indicated by symbols. Nor do parts have to be drawn to scale. The size of a screw can be shown by writing in its dimensions on a standardized outline drawing of a screw. The standardized outline is not, itself, to scale. Of course, the user of the drawing must know

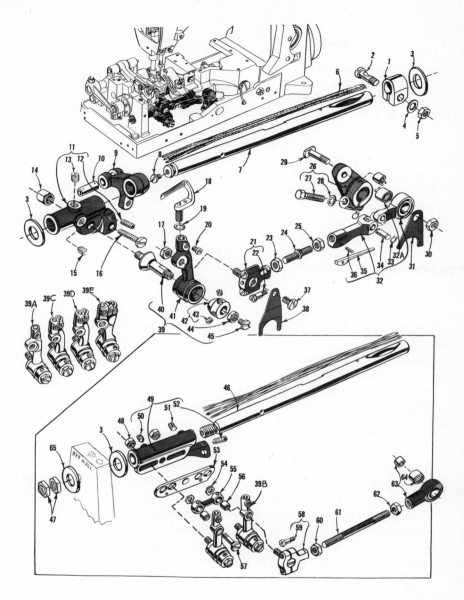

FIGURE 11-3 An unusual type of catalog showing parts and part numbers to aid customers in accurately ordering repair parts. The dark parts of the drawing at the lower left indicate the part of the whole machine (a sewing machine) covered by the particular page. At the upper left is a similar diagram in which the dark parts, those covered on the page, are shown in their relation to other close-by parts. In the middle of the page are shown the parts themselves in an exploded view which, however, shows them in their approximate relation to each other. Numbers are supplied to facilitate ready reference to the adjoining page, on which the item name and specific part number are shown for every part. (Union Special Machine Co.)

the symbols and must know to read the dimensions rather than measure them on the drawing.

Besides using symbols, drawing time can be cut by using transparent cutout guides. These enable draftsmen to make symbols (such as for a pump, a motor, or other such components) quickly. Lettering guides for hand lettering also improve the quality of lettering but they aren't very fast. Adhesive overlays are also timesavers. It is possible to print up drawings for standard parts, and even notes, tabulations, or other information can be typed onto transparent paper with adhesive on the back. They can be put on drawings wherever needed. Typed adhesives also save hand-lettering time.

Actual pictures also save time. Occasionally working models of a product are made before the drawings. When this is done, the parts can be photographed before assembly and the photographs can be mounted on drawing sheets. Dimensions, part numbers, and instructions should be added just as for regular drawings. Photographs can also be used to make new drawings from old ones when they get dirty and worn.

DRAWING CHANGES   Although changes and improvements in a product's design go on continually, rarely is it necessary to redraw big drawings completely. The changes can be made on the drawing and given letters to identify them. A note in the corner of the drawing tells what each change was and when it took effect. Normally, drawing changes affect only future production and not products already in process. Yet if a change is to correct some serious defect, it could be made effective immediately even to spending extra money to change products already half-made.

DRAWING RELEASE   It is important to control the release of drawings to the production control department and to the factory. Commonly, for new products, there will be periodic meetings of a committee which includes representatives from engineering, tooling, production control, purchasing, and manufacturing. This committee will decide such matters as which parts to make and which to buy and, as the drawings near completion, their release date. On that date all of these departments will get copies of all drawings pertinent to their work.

DRAWING FILING AND RETRIEVAL   Most companies have thousands of drawings with more coming in every day. Not only must they be filed but they must be indexed so that they can be found. Indexes need to be by part description, part number, drawing number, and filing location. Computers can keep such indexes up to date with little trouble.

You also have to keep a record of the various bills of materials on which every part appears. If a part appears on several assembly drawings, all of these drawing numbers should be listed in the index. Also put in the index the date when the drawing becomes effective and, if it is a replacement, the number of the drawing it supersedes. In fact, show all pertinent information about drawings.

All original drawings are filed in the engineering department. An extra set of copies is kept in the production control department. Still another set may be kept in the inspection department. Whenever a production order is issued, extra copies of the drawings for use in the shop are made by the engineering department. This is done on production control's order. Production control sends the copies to the appropriate manufacturing departments along with orders to produce.

Be sure to get back all used shop copies of drawings after production is complete so that they can be destroyed. Otherwise there is always the danger that they, rather than revised drawings, may be used for future orders.

Electronic equipment has been revolutionizing the handling of drawings in recent years. A growing practice is to photograph a drawing onto a negative less than 1 inch square. This negative is then inserted into an "aperture" card. As figure 11-4 shows, an aperture card is a tabulating card that goes into a card file. The file of cards is the company's file of drawings (except that the original drawing is probably kept in reserve). The card itself, being a regular tabulating card in all other respects, contains all of the necessary information enabling a computer to find the card when it wants it.

FIGURE 11-4 An aperture card showing a drawing of a part.

When there is need to use the drawing, the computer can locate it and do whatever you want done. It will blow it up and show it on a viewing scope, or it will make enlarged copies in the number required. Or, if you want, it will show the drawing on scopes at different locations, say one in the engineering office, one in production control, and perhaps one out in the factory's assembly department. When you have this kind of equipment you can eliminate the files of drawings that inspection and production control used to have to keep.

This electronic revolution in drawing handling hasn't occurred everywhere due to its cost. The electronic equipment to handle drawings this way is quite costly, so older, less mechanized methods will no doubt continue in use in many places for a long time.

TOLERANCES

When an engineer sets a dimension of a part at 1 inch, he doesn't really expect you to be able to make the part exactly that size (measured to, say, the nearest ten-thousandth of an inch), no more, no less. He knows that nothing can be perfect. When factory employees make the parts and try to make the dimension exactly 1 inch, they will miss it by a little. Tolerances set limits to the variation from perfect that will be acceptable. Usually you accept parts that are within one or two thousandths of an inch.

Engineers are in a dilemma as far as tolerances are concerned. As a general rule, the more exact the measurement and the more perfect that you insist that a part be, the better the product will work. But it will be more costly. If you allow considerable variation, the parts will cost less to make but the product won't work quite so well and will wear out a little sooner.

What we have said is well and good as a *generalization* but *only* as a generalization. Lots of times perfect parts don't work any better than imperfect parts. Think of the dialing part of your telephone. Suppose that some of the holes that you put your finger in to dial a number were $\frac{1}{16}$ inch smaller or larger than others. Would it matter? Or think of the handle on an egg beater. Suppose that one side of the handle is $\frac{1}{16}$ inch thicker than the other, or suppose it is a little "out of round." Or suppose that a bicycle handle bar is $\frac{1}{8}$ inch longer on one side than the other. In none of these cases does it really matter to the user of the product because the imperfect part will work just as well as the perfect part. Probably the customer would never know the difference.

The point we are making is that things don't always have to be perfect. Engineers *can* be overfussy and set too close tolerances, thus running up the cost. Of course, good design engineers know all about tight tolerances hiking costs and about not setting them overtight.

Actually, engineers have no sure rule to guide them in tolerance setting. They often just set them good and tight, particularly for mating or wearing parts, then the product will be sure to work. Of course, tight tolerances do increase costs, but the engineers figure that the factory can hold close tolerances without much extra cost if it tries. Engineers expect foremen to complain about the tolerances being too tight because foremen always complain about all but the loosest tolerances.

Probably, on the whole, the engineers dismiss the complaints too lightly. Tight tolerances do increase costs in spite of the factory's attempts to hold them down. Planners should watch for and try to weed out overexacting tolerances. By "weeding out" we mean to try to get the engineering department to relax those that seem to everyone else to be too tight.

Where working metal parts must fit together, you can't make them exactly the same size or they will bind and not work freely. A shaft going through a bearing needs to have a "clearance" of perhaps .002 inch. You might specify that the shaft's size should be $.998 + .000, - .001$ inch, meaning that it is acceptable if it is between .998 and .997 inch in diameter. And you might specify that the bearing should be $1.000 + .001, - .000$ inch. No acceptable bearing would be less than 1.000 inch and no acceptable shaft over .998. The largest acceptable bearing would be 1.001 inches and the smallest acceptable shaft .997 inch. If the smallest shaft and the largest bearing were put together, there would be .004 inch of "play." But there would be only .002 inch of clearance between the largest shaft and the smallest bearing. The mating of extremes would be rare. Most assemblies would have about .003 inch of play. If you wanted less clearance you'd have to hold to closer tolerances when making the parts.

Engineers have difficult problems in tolerance setting which sometimes make their specifications appear to foremen to be too tight. In "gear-chains," where one gear turns another and it turns another, and so on, a little looseness on each one makes the whole system very loose. A little extra play between shafts and bearings holding the gears loosens up everything. Too much looseness decreases efficiency and makes the parts wear out faster. To avoid this, engineers have to specify close tolerances between each pair of gears.

A cam shaft illustrates another problem in tolerance setting. A certain distance is allowed from one end of the shaft to the first cam. Then you allow for its thickness, then an in-between space of specified width, then another cam, etc. Each dimension has maximum and minimum dimensions. If each dimension happens to be the maximum allowed, the whole shaft is too long. The tolerances on individual dimensions may have to be kept close to be sure that the over-all length stays within limits. On the other hand, it is highly improbable that every in-between dimension will be either the maximum or minimum. Engineers often set the total tolerance as the square root of the sum of all the individual tolerances.

Some engineers set "line-to-line" tolerances. In the shaft and bearing example we used above, the shaft might be set at .999 ± .001 inch and the bearing at 1.001 ± .001 inches. The largest acceptable shaft and the smallest bearing would both be 1.000 inch. Each would be acceptable but they wouldn't fit together because they need a little play in order to fit together. Of course, if one shaft will not go in a bearing the assembler can put it aside and try another. But such selective assembly is somewhat costly.

TOTAL DIFFERENCE TOLERANCES   Engineers, of course, know all about these troubles and have tried to set up guides. One of the most promising ideas is to have the engineer specify the "TD," or "total difference," between mating parts. The dimensions of two mating parts can be set to allow no clearance whatever. Then the TD can be specified. The manufacturing departments can "spend" the TD any way they wish.

Using the TD idea, a shaft and a bearing hole might each be specified to be 1 inch in diameter. Assume a TD of .002 inch. The shaft could be 1.000 inch and the bearing hole 1.002 inches. Or the shaft could be .998 inch and the bearing hole 1.000 inch. Either is all right, either works, but putting a .998 inch shaft into a 1.002 inch hole is not acceptable because the TD would be .004 inch.

BLOCK TOLERANCES   "Block" tolerances often cause unnecessary and unintended trouble. All drawings have a block in the lower right corner. The block is a space containing information about the drawing. It shows the drawing number, what the product is, who made the drawing, etc. Commonly, it says, "all tolerances not otherwise marked are to be ±.005 inch." Sometimes it specifies surface finishes by similar general instructions. Or it may say, in the block, that all corners must have a certain curvature.

Block instructions are often both costly and ridiculous. Allis-Chalmers once received an order for truck frames 30 feet long—with a tolerance (a block tolerance) of ±.005 inch! Minor temperature changes would make it expand or contract more than that.

CHANGING SPECIFICATIONS TO SUIT TOOLING   Tolerances should always be checked carefully during pilot runs and during early production. You will always have to change a few of them, and not always because they were not made out right. Sometimes your new tooling is a little off and that makes the product off a little. When this happens it may be cheaper to change the drawings and specifications than to correct the tooling. Suppose, for example, that the die that forms a hole in an automobile instrument panel where a clock is to go makes the hole just a little too large. If the mounting brackets on the clock will fit anyway or will fit after they are changed a little, the die that makes oversize holes can still be used. But if you decide to go ahead and use the die as it is, you have to change the specification for the size of the holes.

You might even have to change the specification for the mating parts (in this case the mounting for the clock) so that they will match up with the offsize parts. Often, this doesn't cost anything since it is just as easy to make the mounting to fit into the oversized hole as into holes as originally specified. This might not be so, however, if the mounting too had to be made with special tools.

Of course, whenever such changes are made, the drawings must be changed and the customer's approval obtained. During the time while you are getting the customer's approval, you probably won't have to hold up production. Production control can be given the right to approve, temporarily, using "offprint" parts. Or if corrective operations are needed to get the parts to fit, production control can approve that work being done.

TOOL PLANNING

Chapters 8 and 9 on Estimating describe most of the work of planning for new tooling. Estimators and planners should work together if any unusual tooling is likely to be needed. Planners should be consulted early because they know production methods. Also, when the go ahead is given to tool up for a product or a special job, the planners, not the estimators, have to order the tooling. If the exact tooling needed has not already been decided, the planner must decide. He orders all special tools from the tool engineering department.

Before the tool engineering department designs new tools and has them made, it checks the company's supply of special tools. Sometimes old tools can be used or can be easily changed. Sometimes old tools can be used if a part's design is changed a little. The tool designer, planner, and product designer may all have to get together and decide the matter.

You should try to design the tooling used to make experimental models so that it can be used later in actual production. Or, if this can't be done, study the tooling used for experimentals. How did it work? Where did it not work well? Design new tooling, particularly large jigs, only after you have tried to learn all that you can from your experience with experimentals.

Tooling is very expensive. Most large companies own millions of dollars' worth of tooling. Because it is so costly, new tooling costs should be carefully estimated before approval to buy additional tooling is given. Look into every possibility of using, cannibalizing, or reworking old tooling so that it can be used before spending money for new tooling. Also, take care of the tooling you already own. Keep records of its whereabouts, its repair costs, etc.

Because special tools are more costly than standard tools, use standard tools (drills, taps, reamers, grinding wheels, etc.) wherever you can. Some time ago Chrysler's Airtemp division found that 50 per cent of its tooling was specials. By questioning the need for specials more fully, Airtemp cut new specials to 5 per cent. In Airtemp's work, specials rarely paid their way.

Certain types of tools usually need to be special. Jigs, fixtures, dies, cutters, forming tools, and magazine feeds are usually special for particular jobs. Some gages also need to be special, but plug, ring, snap, and thread gages are usually standard.

To permit fast operations, machines need to have loading and clamping accessories to hold materials. This makes them easy and fast to operate. They should be durable so that they won't break down often. And they should be "error-proof" so that the worker can't load parts in a wrong position. Machines should be designed so that wearing parts can be easily replaced. And cutting tools should be made out of carbides or long-wearing metal. Cutting tools should be set into the machine so that they will have proper lubrication, run cool, and remove the chips.

You should also make molds for molded parts with multiple cavities. Make patterns for molds out of metal (except for short runs). Design the parts you are making so that they will fit semiautomatic presses and transfer machines. Put automatic feeds and ejectors on high production punches and dies. Design them so that they use raw material effectively. And design them so that they do their work in such a way as to avoid extra operations later.

In some companies, production control authorizes the release of orders to make tools. This is consistent with its responsibilities for meeting schedules. But tools that take a long time to get must be ordered before production control gets its schedule. These have to be ordered earlier, probably by the preplanning department. Tooling for new models of automobiles, for example, must often be ordered a year or more ahead. Production control couldn't order tooling that far ahead because none of its authorizations reach that far into the future. Replacement tools for current models are ordered five months before their expected need. Production control has nothing to do with these orders either. Some of this tooling is made in the company's own tool-making departments. If it comes from outside, the lead time is usually longer.

Be sure to put all stages of tool making on a schedule if you want to be sure that the tooling will be ready on time. It isn't always done this way—but it ought to be. When it isn't, too often tooling doesn't get made on time. Dates should be set (by the preplanning or the production control department) for the completion of new tool designs, for getting bids, for placing orders, and for getting delivery. Progress reports, at least monthly, should be made on the status of tooling for new projects.

Your regular production control department usually does not expedite tooling. Yet if it sits back and expects tooling to be finished on schedule it is frequently disappointed. Production control had better ask questions about the progress of tooling manufacture. Even with this precaution, new tooling often is not ready when it should be. At the beginning of a long run, production control may have to improvise and juggle schedules or get foremen to manage to get along without some of the special tooling for a little while. Sometimes tool designers make only one set of tooling when, for your volume, you need two sets. Again, you may have to improvise temporarily.

MAKE OR BUY

Large companies, even giant companies, usually spend more than half of their income buying materials and products from other companies. General Motors spends 45 per cent, Chrysler 60 per cent, and Ford 57 per cent of its income for bought items. These companies and all other giant companies buy from thousands of vendors.

Should you make or should you buy is an eternal question. A company can be a purely merchandising company—buying completed products and selling them unchanged. Or a company may do nothing but package products. Or it can buy parts and assemble them. Or a company can make its products complete—making its own parts and assembling them. It can even make "raw materials" (steel sheets, bars, etc.).

In general, it pays to *make* the things you are well equipped to do and to *make* the things you know most about. And it pays to *buy* things foreign to your operations. Not very many companies using paint, for example, should make it. It would be the same with ball bearings. But if you spend over $50,000 a year buying an item, maybe you should look into buying equipment and learning how to make the item. And if you spend millions buying any kind of item, you may be able to set up a plant and make it cheaper than you can buy it, even if it is different from your usual business. It helps to think of purchased items as "outside manufacture." Thinking of them this way reminds you to look into your vendors' costs even if you don't decide to change to making their products yourself.

Some companies make part of their needs and buy the rest on the same items. Why split orders like that? One good reason is to keep your inside department on its toes. When inside manufacturing doesn't have to face competition, it grows inefficient. Buying a portion of what you need gives you a check on your inside costs. It also gives you an outside source if anything goes wrong inside. It also supplies bargaining table ammunition. Wage increase demands are not pressed so hard when the company can show that items can be bought cheaper than made.

Making parts means that you operate a bigger company and this takes more investment and more managerial ability. You need enough capital, you need steady business, and you need management capable of directing large and diverse operations. By making your own parts you get control of your supply source, regulate quality, and get to do your own research.

It doesn't always pay to make instead of buy even with large volume. When you buy you get the benefit of your supplier's research without having to bear much of its costs. You can buy parts below cost in depressions and in temporary slack periods, and you can buy parts at less than your inside making cost in many cases when the vendor company is very efficient, particularly if it is large and has great volume. Automobile companies, big as they are, don't make their own tires because the tire industry is both efficient and competitive. Ford once made its own tires for a few years but it cost more than buying them so it stopped. A. O. Smith, Eaton, Yale and Towne, Timken Roller Bearing, TRW, Dana, and other auto parts makers still sell big volumes to automobile companies.

ITEMS NOT IN THE COMPANY'S USUAL LINE OF BUSINESS For most items, there is no question whether you make or buy. Most radio manufacturers, for example, buy all their tubes, transistors, and diodes because they are not in these businesses. Besides these items are probably all covered by patents. Radio manufacturers probably also buy all their screws, nuts, bolts, wire, and sheet metal, since they are not in any of those businesses. On the other hand, they are probably equipped to make tuning dials and condensers. They could make or buy them or make some kinds and buy others.

A company without a foundry will buy its castings. Companies with foundries usually make some but not all of their castings. They may make only small steel castings. If so, then brass, aluminum, and iron castings are bought. Large steel castings or steel castings of unusual shape or contour would also be bought. A company with automatic screw machines will make most of its small parts. But a company with metal stamping machines, for example, would substitute stampings for castings in many places and would make its own stampings.

Companies often make some items and buy other kindred items at the same time. A survey made a few years ago by *Steel* magazine of over 300 companies using metal stampings showed that 50 per cent of them both made *and* bought. Twenty per cent bought all their stampings, 30 per cent made all theirs. Since there are over 2,000 competing stamping companies in the country, it is very likely that some of the outsiders can beat a company's inside costs on some of the items it makes. Buying some stampings would seem to be advisable for most companies.

AUTHORITY TO MAKE MAKE–BUY DECISIONS   Most make-or-buy decisions are made the first time you make a product. Some companies, once the design of a new product is set, hold a make-buy meeting with production control presiding. At this meeting you have make-buy cost figures and you decide, item by item, to make or buy. And, in most cases, the decision is permanent but it doesn't have to be—particularly when it is almost a tossup of which is better.

On minor items, the planning department, not the engineering department, decides whether to make or buy. If you buy, however, the design or product engineer usually specifies the brand or quality. But not everyone does it alike. At International Business Machines Corporation, the tool engineering department decides. On big items, it is best to let a committee decide; include members from manufacturing, engineering, purchasing, cost, and production control. If the decision is a close one, get cost estimates for inside manufacture and for outside purchase. And don't give up too easily. If the item is something that you can buy cheaper than you can make it, buckle down to work and learn how to make it at lower cost. Try, too, not to buy if you have to buy it from your competitor.

If making means buying new machines, the top administration has to give approval because of the money that the machines cost. Also buying machines commits you more certainly to making the item on into the future since you can't easily change back to buying unless you can use the new machines for something else.

TEMPORARY CHANGES IN MAKE–BUY POLICIES   Sometimes you make today and buy tomorrow. When this happens the production control department is a principal party to the decisions. When business gets so good that you can't handle it all, some items have to go outside. The make-buy decision—as far as individual items are concerned—is a matter of priority. Which items go out first? Which last? The reverse happens when business gets bad. Which come back first? Which last? You may have to pull in items ordinarily bought in order to keep the plant busy. It pays you to pull in such business even if your costs including overhead are a little above purchased costs because overhead costs go on whether you bring the order in or not.

Shifting production in and out of the plant to even out production has bad points. Vendors can't stay in business on a feast or famine basis. If you are a large company, you ought to keep sending outside vendors at least some business even during periods of low production lest they go out of business and not be available in the future. On the other hand, you can't carry this idea too far. If times really get bad, you will have to paddle your own canoe and let others paddle theirs.

Another difficulty turns up if the vendor will need special tooling to make the items you want to order outside. If so, it is usually cheaper to lend your tooling to him rather than have him make up his own special tooling for a small order. But, unless you have two sets of tooling, you won't be able to make any of the items yourself while your tooling it out on loan. If you want to make part of your needs and buy the rest, at the same time, you need duplicate tooling. Unless you have it perhaps you should make and not buy the item.

If most of the parts (but not all of them) of a product are bought outside, it may pay to send the rest out too. Then if the complete product doesn't work, there are fewer quality arguments. When a vendor makes the whole thing, instead of just some of the parts, you can hold him fully accountable for the product's performance.

Occasionally a company adds products or takes on new lines to round out its sales line. New items or parts for new items that would mean buying new machines should be bought until you are sure that the item is a permanent addition to your line of products. Later you can decide to manufacture parts bought outside.

CONTRACTING OUT INDIVIDUAL OPERATIONS The question of making or buying a part generally means making it complete, not just performing one or two operations. Most companies do all of the operations on a part or none of them. Occasionally, however, companies perform the first operations, send the material out to have the next operations performed, and then bring it back and finish the work in their own factories. In metalworking industries, for example, it is not uncommon for companies to send out products for electroplating, particularly for tricky plating, such as silver plating on aluminum. Heat treating may also be done by an outside company. Overflow work on any operation is often contracted for on the outside.

Decisions to send a temporary excess work outside are usually one-time decisions. New approval is needed to keep on sending work out. But if you are buying instead of making parts because you don't have, inside your company, the technical ability or machines to do the work, you don't need approval to send out that work.

REVIEW OF MAKE–BUY PRACTICES You ought, periodically, to re-examine your make-buy decisions. The proper decision often changes if your volume goes up or down. Competitive conditions change buying prices. Or your inside manufacturing cost is not as low as you expected it to be. Or the outside source, which quoted such a low price when anxious to get business, raises the price when its business picks up. Most companies do re-examine decisions to buy but they don't re-examine decisions to make as often.

If you decide to buy, you have, once in a while, the further decision of whether to buy domestically or to import the item. This is particularly true in the case of cameras, watches, and electronics and sometimes in pharmaceuticals and chemicals.

MINIATURIZATION

Miniaturization means making things smaller. Space is at a premium in a "walkie-talkie," a telephone receiver, a hearing aid, a space missile, and electronics in general. Because so much care must be taken and parts have to fit so perfectly, miniature products usually cost more at first than big products. Later, as production problems are solved, in some cases they become less costly because they use less material and require less processing. Sometimes, however, their cost never does get down to what bigger items can be made for. Often too, miniaturization magnifies repair problems.

Today miniaturization has been carried so far that the terms sub-miniaturization and microminiaturization are common. Transistors and other semiconductors are sometimes incorporated into tiny electrical circuits all of which have been laminated onto thin plastic wafers $\frac{1}{16}$ inch square more or less in size. Such extreme miniaturization is possible partly because such minute components take very little electrical power and so they don't heat up as bigger components often do. The basic materials out of which subminiature components are made are now so pure that they have long operating lives without failure. The electrical circuits of which they are a part have stability and durability. This allows the use of printed circuit components as opposed to only printed wiring in miniature circuits.

In mechanical and electromechanical components, however, the problems of subminiature assembly and repair are quite severe. A mere speck of dust is often enough to impair the performance of the item. The use of air-conditioned "white rooms" is a necessity for the manufacture of many electromechanical missile components.

Further and further miniaturization, a constant goal in electronics, is responsible for frequent design changes which in turn make production control in electronics quite difficult. Miniaturization is, however, much more a design problem than it is a planning problem. Production control work is influenced by it only as it causes changes in parts and how they are made. These changes make more production control work.

STUDY MATERIALS

11-1   Your company makes stampings and castings and also machines them according to customer specifications. Because of the current profit squeeze the general manager has appointed you to be chairman of a committee to consider the materials used. What factors should your committee consider in its work?

11-2   The Hodges Manufacturing Company ordered a sprocket wheel for a conveyor to replace one which wore out. It was ordered by telephone from the Minneapolis Conveyor Company, the maker of the conveyor. Since the sprocket wheel was for an old model, it was made to order and rushed to the Hodges company, but it didn't fit. The resulting delay was serious to the Hodges company and highly embarrassing to the Minneapolis Conveyor Company. There had been occasions before when parts supplied did not fit, but none with such serious consequences.

An investigation showed that the sprocket wheel which didn't fit was made exactly according to the drawing used for the job but the sprocket which failed and its mating parts turned out to be different from that shown on the drawing. Exactly what happened was never clear, since the installation had been made years before. Apparently the shop had made a few changes in design and either had not had the drawing changed or had made the changes on their working copy without telling the engineering department. The shop copy was, of course, no longer available. Or possibly a different sprocket wheel and mating parts were put in at the installation. Or perhaps the customer had requested a change which was carried out and not put on the drawing.

Recommend a procedure to prevent such occurrences in the future. Suppose that in the above situation it was found that there were two sets of drawings and that the product had been made according to the original set, which was revised almost immediately, the old set having been canceled and destroyed. How would you provide against such changes giving you trouble in the future?

11-3 Should you make or buy the following items?

	ITEM		
	BUSHING, STEEL	STUD, STEEL, THREADED	STUD, STEEL, SOLID
Quantity needed	40,000	15,000	24,000
Material costs	$460	$185	$275
Direct labor hours	360	900	220
Lowest vendor's bid price per unit	$0.062	$0.122	$0.033

The following data were obtained from the cost accounting department concerning internal shop production:

Direct labor cost per hour $3.40
Variable overhead rate per direct labor hour 3.25
Fixed overhead rate per direct labor hour (based on 2,000 hours per year) 1.60

Variable overhead includes all overhead costs which vary with production. Fixed overhead goes on continually even if there is no production.

1 What would your decision be
   a If you are low on orders and are operating short hours?
   b If you were operating 40 hours a week even without these orders? (You don't, however, need to assume that these jobs will require overtime operation.)

2 Are there any other factors that might influence your decision?

11-4 When you buy instead of make parts you would seem to incur extra transportation costs and extra packing costs, have to carry more inventory, and be out of stock more often than you would be if you made the items yourself. How therefore can it ever be wise to buy instead of make?

11-5 An automobile company placed a trial order with the Sturdee Nut and Bolt Company for some screws of large size and off-standard-pitch threads which were difficult to make on the equipment available. The company managed to solve the production difficulties in a satisfactory way and was prepared to offer to make them for 13 cents per 100 screws.

On his arrival at the automobile company, the Sturdee salesman was ushered into the office of the buyer. He told the buyer that his company had had some difficulties making the screws but had worked them out and was prepared to bid for larger quantities. The buyer excused himself, went into an adjacent office, and called up his own factory department, which had been trying to make the screws. The conversation was audible through the partition, and the salesman learned that the automobile company's own department had had a great deal of difficulty with the screw and that it would probably cost from 35 to 40 cents per 100 to make them inside the company. When the buyer returned to discuss the proposition with the salesman, he was offered a bid of 26 cents per 100 (price not having been discussed before), and the contract was signed on that basis.

Aside from the matter of overhearing the conversation, what is the likelihood that you can make parts in the company cheaper than you can buy them? Why make any parts? Are there any advantages in making a portion of the company's needs and buying the rest outside? If you went to a vendor plant and asked to see how they did something, would they show you? Is the production control department concerned in the question of making or buying parts?

11-6   You are to consider making or buying a part using the following information. There is a 90 per cent probability of selling 5,000, 75 per cent of selling 15,000, and 40 per cent of selling 30,000.

You can buy these parts as follows (and the seller will allow you to cumulate multiple orders for price purposes):

0–5,000	$3.00 each
5,001–10,000	2.00 each
10,001–15,000	1.50 each
15,001 and over	1.25 each

To make them you would have to put $5,000 into tooling and $1.30 into manufacturing cost per unit. Or you could go more automatic at $15,000 for tooling and 50 cents for manufacturing cost per unit.

What should you do?

PLANNING—
ENGINEERING ASPECTS

DESIGN FOR PRODUCTION
Design engineers are responsible both for "functional design," designing a product that works, and "style design," designing a product that looks good. But they should not forget "manufacturing design," designing a product that can be made economically. Low manufacturing cost needs to be one of their objectives.

FREEDOM OF PLANNERS TO DECIDE MINOR DESIGN DETAILS Although designers should be quite cost-conscious, production planners can be even more so. And although the *first* job of planners is to figure out some way to make a product or part at reasonable cost, their *second* job, and almost as important, is to figure out the most economical way to make it. Sometimes the least costly way will require a part to be redesigned in minor ways, so planners, not designers, should finally decide the exact details of how parts are to be made.

General Electric, in its appliance division, gives production planning full authority to redesign parts wherever it will cut production costs. Before designs go to production planning they go to a "preproduction" man, an engineer who "finalizes" the design of new products so far as performance goes. It is his job to "debug" the product and to make sure that it works. His redesigning concentrates on changes to make products or parts work better.

Then the product is turned over to production planning. Planning has authority to make further design changes for economical production. It can, for example, decide to "dip-solder" a part to make electrical connections secure. The designer may have thought that all connections would be soldered separately by operators with soldering irons. Production planning can spot-weld instead of rivet or can specify that either is acceptable depending on which equipment is busy and which is not. Or production planning can add a lug (or "boss") to a casting so that it can be clamped onto a machine. Or planning can put a hole in a part to fit over a "spotting" pin on a machine so that it can more quickly be put into exact position. Or a part may need a notch cut in it to allow a wire to get past it when it is in the finished assembly.

Planners should watch for too high quality. Ideally, a product should

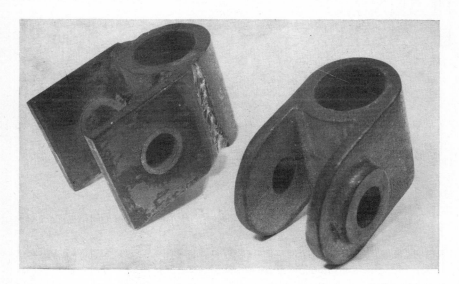

FIGURE 12-1 A plow swivel made as a malleable casting and by fabricating four pieces together by welding. A good router must know alternate methods such as these and select the one which serves the purpose and is the most economical. (Malleable Founders Society.)

be like the one-horse shay that went to pieces all at once. Parts don't need to outlive the product. One company found that some parts in one of its products would last for 80 years, whereas other parts would wear out in 3 years. The company decided to save money by cutting the quality of the 80-year parts.

The engineering department, where design engineers work, is the custodian of quality and sometimes engineers get to thinking that quality is all that counts. There is a tendency to build too much quality into products, particularly new products. A part should be good enough to do its work *but no better* because high quality and high costs usually go together. Chevrolet quality and Cadillac quality ought to be different. If a planner finds high and costly quality where less will do, he should suggest lowering it.

The planner should also always be watching for opportunities to eliminate costly processes. He may find that certain tolerances are too close and can safely be relaxed or that costly finishes can be eliminated. He may find it cheaper in machining or grinding to remove the bulk of the excess metal in a rough machine or rough-grinding operation and add a separate finishing operation, rather than to try to remove the excess metal all in one operation to get a fine finish. Possibly you can take heavier cuts of metal

FIGURE 12-2 An example of a change from a fabricated part to a casting, with result-ing savings in cost. The item is a "Soundhead" used in a Bell and Howell moving-picture projector. It was originally made by welding 33 separate pieces together to form the part shown at the left in each picture. Forty-five operations were required. All of the parts were purchased. It was changed to a die casting weighing $3\frac{1}{2}$ pounds less and having a better appearance. Manufacturing operations were reduced to 21, and the four inspections originally needed were reduced to one. The standard cost of the piece was reduced 27 per cent as a result of the change. Production control, purchasing, and stock record keeping were all reduced materially. (Bell and Howell Co.)

off the item and so reduce machining time and costs if you change the machine and put in a stronger feed rack. Or if your machine chatters when you try a heavy cut maybe you can substitute broad-nosed tools or better-designed cutters along with more rigid fixtures and arbors and, again, do the work fast at low cost.

Sometimes, planners find that changing the sequence in which parts are combined into different subassemblies helps. For example, should an automobile door be fastened to the body before the body is fastened to the chassis? Or should it be put on after the body has been attached to the chassis? Sometimes, out on the production line, one method is better than the other. On regular Ford cars the steering column is put on the chassis before the body is put on but on Ford Thunderbirds the steering column is put on the chassis after the body. Planners should be allowed to decide which way to do it. In case of doubt, designers, planners, industrial engineers, and foreman should get together and decide.

CHOOSING MANUFACTURING METHODS   Figures 12-3 and 12-4 show how Western Electric engineers tackled the job of deciding how to make a small "collar" (a small metal ring) used in telephones. They considered three ways of making the collar from metal strips and three ways of making it from bar stock. They also made cost estimates for three different volumes. As happened in this example, the method that is most economical for one volume may well not be the best for another. In this example, as it turns out, for small volumes, the collar should be made from stamped strips.

Suppose that you want to know how many of an item you would have to make to pay for a more expensive tooling method but which will lower the costs at high volumes. You should start by writing out the cost formulas for each method. In the Western Electric example, you would get the following six formulas. In these formulas, TC represents the total costs and the subscript refers to the method under consideration. P is the production quantity in thousands.

$$TC_1 = \$888.08 + \$6.64P$$
$$TC_2 = \$1,016.16 + \$1.52P$$
$$TC_3 = \$1,676.16 + \$.75P$$
$$TC_4 = \$143.40 + \$73.71P$$
$$TC_5 = \$676.36 + \$15.17P$$
$$TC_6 = \$892.52 + \$11.27P$$

To find out which method to use for various volumes, first set P at 1 unit. Method 4, with a TC of \$217.11, is much the lowest. Then test method 4 against every other method in turn to find the crossover point where the

FIGURE 12-3 An analysis of the costs of producing a "collar" (a small metal ring) by three variations of punch press methods, each requiring a different investment in tools. Method 1 assumes a small annual requirement which will be met by running one lot each quarter. The method figured is to use a one-at-a-time punch and die and raw materials in strip form with a hand feed. Method 2 represents a change to the use of an automatic feed roll, making the collar from a coil of material. Method 3 represents the continued use of the automatic feed from coiled stock and a three-at-a-time punch and die. This type of cost comparison should be carried out before routing is decided. For quantities other than those computed here, you can use the formulas shown on page 248 to find which method would be most economical.

OPERATION	METHOD 1	METHOD 2	METHOD 3
Perforate and blank, etc.			
One at a time, 6,200 per hour, hourly labor $3.30	x		
One at a time, 6,700 per hour, hourly labor $3.51	....	x	
Three at a time, 20,500 per hour, hourly labor $3.51	....	....	x
Setup, hourly rate (all methods), $3.51			
Labor and load per thousand			
(load = 200% of labor)	$ 1.60	$ 1.57	$ 0.51
2.1 lb. material per thousand at $0.45 per lb.			
less scrap 1.38 lb. at $0.135	0.75		
2.04 lb. material per thousand at $0.44 per lb.			
less scrap 1.32 lb. at $0.135	....	0.71	
1.84 lb material per thousand at $0.42 per lb.			
less scrap 1.12 lb. at $0.135	....	....	0.61
Total cost	900.00	1,440.00	2,430.00
Four setups per year, 1½ hours each at $5.27	21.06		
Twelve setups per year, 2 hours each at $7.02	....	84.24	84.24
Knurl and chamfer, 1,300 per hour			
Hourly labor $3.30			
Setup, hourly rate $3.51			
Labor and load per thousand	7.61		
4 setups per year, 1½ hours each at $5.27	21.06		
Tool cost	390.00		
Total labor, load, and material per thousand	9.92	2.27	1.12
Tool cost plus setup cost per year	1,332.12	1,524.24	2,514.24
Total cost to make 3,000 parts	1,362.00	1,531.08	2,517.61
Total cost to make 100,000 parts	2,328.12	1,752.24	2,626.74
Total cost to make 500,000 parts	6,312.12	2,664.24	2,926.74

other method becomes more economical. This is done by setting the two formulas equal to each other and solving for P. To test method 4 against 1: $143.40 + 73.71P = 888.08 + 6.64P$, $67.07P = 744.68$, and $P = 11.1$. The two methods cost the same for 11,100 units. Method 4 costs less for lower volumes and method 1 is less costly for higher volumes. Similar calculations reveal that the crossover points are: method 2—12.1 thousand; method 3—21.0 thousand; method 5—9.1 thousand; method 6—12.0 thousand. Method 4 is, therefore, the most economical way to make small quan-

FIGURE 12-4   An analysis of the costs of producing by screw machine methods the "collar" referred to in fig. 12-3. Method 4 refers to doing the work on a hand screw machine, method 5 is figured for using an automatic screw machine, and method 6 contemplates using an automatic screw machine in which two parts are machined at a time.

OPERATION	METHOD 4	METHOD 5	METHOD 6
Screw machine			
Hand feed, 1 at a time, 200 per hour, hourly labor $3.30	x		
Automatic feed, 1 at a time, 750 per hour, hourly labor $3.51	. . . .	x	
Automatic feed, 2 at a time, 1,280 per hour, hourly labor $3.51	. . . .	. . . .	x
Setup, hourly rate (all methods), $3.51			
Labor and load per thousand (load = 200% of labor)	$ 49.50	$ 14.17	$ 8.24
2.15 lb. material per thousand at $0.57 lb. less scrap 1.17 lb. at $0.135	1.06	1.06	1.06
Tool cost	. . . .	480.00	720.00
Four setups per year, 1½ hours each at $5.27	21.06		
Twelve setups per year, 3 hours each at $10.53	. . . .	126.36	
Twelve setups per year, 5 hours each at $17.55	. . . .	. . . .	210.60
Knurl and chamfer			
Arbor press, 150 per hour, hourly labor $3.00	x		
Punch press, 1,300 per hour, hourly labor $3.30	. . . .	x	x
Setup, hourly rate (all methods), $3.51			
Labor and load per thousand	60.00	7.61	7.61
Tool cost	180.00	345.00	345.00
4 setups per year, 1 hour each at $3.51	14.04		
12 setups per year, 1½ hours each at $5.27	. . . .	63.18	63.18
Total labor, load, and material per thousand	110.56	22.75	16.90
Tool cost plus setup cost per year	215.10	1,014.54	1,338.78
Total cost to make 3,000 parts	546.80	1,082.80	1,389.50
Total cost to make 100,000 parts	11,271.60	3,290.04	3,029.28
Total cost to make 500,000 parts	55,497.60	12,392.04	9,790.28

tities of these collars and it continues to be the best way up to 9,100 units after which it gives way to method 5.

Method 5 is then compared to the remaining methods (1, 2, 3, and 6). The next lowest crossover point is at 24,800 units when method 1 becomes superior. Method 1 in turn gives way almost immediately, at 25,000 units, to method 2. Method 2 should in turn be replaced by method 3 only if very high volumes are in prospect since the crossover point is 857,000 units. For volumes over 857,000 units method 3 would be the best.

If you were planning for high-volume production, say 1 million collars, you ought to raise a question about design stability. You need to have some assurance that the item's design won't change before you reach 857,000 units. Should it change sooner you won't get all of your tooling cost back.

Figure 12-5 shows the cost-volume relationships among the six manufacturing methods under consideration. It shows that, for all volumes of production, method 1 is cheaper than method 6, so method 6 can be dropped from further consideration.

Each of the remaining five methods each has a "domain" or range of production volume where it produces the lowest production costs, so the proper method to choose is dependent on the prospective volume. Probably, however, method 1 should not be included in the alternatives to be considered since its domain (24,800 to 25,000 units) is so small. The choice ought to be among 4, 5, 2, and 3.

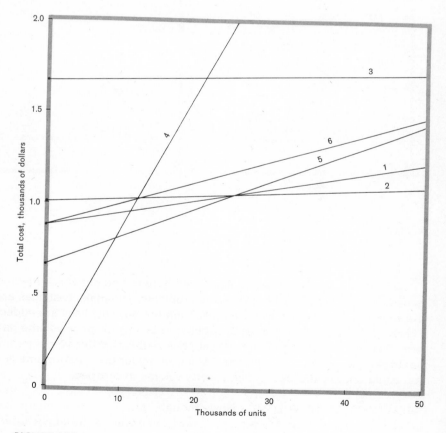

FIGURE 12-5

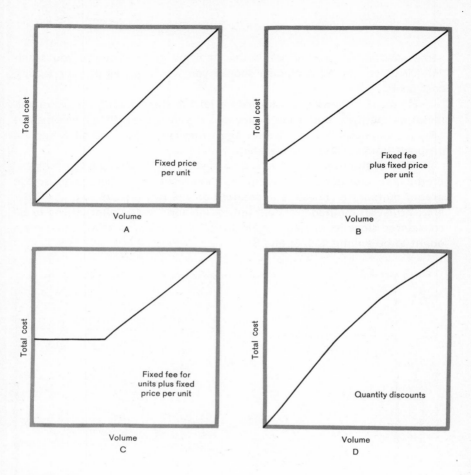

FIGURE 12-6

The kind of analysis that we have used here to find out which method to use can also be applied to make-buy problems. The make cost lines are drawn in just as we did in our example. Then the buy cost lines are added. There would be a buy line for each supplier reflecting his price-volume pattern. Figure 12-6 illustrates four typical price patterns. After you superimposed the buy patterns on the chart along with your own cost-volume line you could choose the best action for the volume in prospect.

THE PROBLEM OF VOLUME   How, though, can you know about volume that lies way off in the future? Actually, you can't know about future sales volumes but you still have to give your planner some kind of a figure even if it is only your best guess. You have to use the best figure you can get after forecasting by one of the methods that we described in Chapter 6.

You don't always have to do this job yourself. Whenever you are tooling up for a big customer's continuing order he will often want to decide his own processing method because he will end up paying for the tooling. If you decide the method and buy the tooling, you put its cost into your selling price. So sometimes he pays you separately for the tooling and owns it himself. In foundry work the customer usually owns the patterns used to make his castings. Whenever the customer buys his own tooling he, not the vendor, has to make the kind of calculation we have just gone through.

MULTI–PLANT DESIGN PROBLEMS

It is just as true in multi-plant operations as it is in single plants, that the proper way to make anything depends on the number to be made. But in multi-plant operations the proper method depends on how many you are going to make *in each plant,* not on the total volume.

Each plant should be given some freedom to develop its own tooling to suit its equipment and methods. This means that an item made in several plants will be made with different kinds of tooling. And this in turn may mean minor design differences to suit each plant's methods. Such changes, if they don't alter the product much, should be allowed, usually without being approved by the home office engineering staff.

One automobile accessory supplier had considerable difficulty on this score until individual plants were given leeway. Its home office in Detroit negotiated contracts with the big three auto companies and settled matters of design and price. The supplier's plants around the country ship to automobile assembly plants in their territories. But they get their drawings showing product design from Detroit.

The designs were not suitable, though, for the individual plants' tooling. When all minor design change details had to be cleared back through Detroit at the car company's home office, delays were too great. Now these little changes are cleared directly and quickly with the customer's plant in the same territory.

Another trouble to watch out for is design changes during contract negotiations. In our automobile part example, the two home offices (the automobile company's home office and the supplier company's home office) discuss and agree on designs, copies of which go to the supplier's plants so that they can start to make tooling. Then, sometimes, the customer changes the design and tells the supplier company. All too often the supplier company's home office forgets to tell all the plants until final drawings come through. By then the individual plant is all tooled up wrong, thus losing both time and money. It is easy to say that these things shouldn't happen but they do unless you watch carefully to prevent them.

STANDARD PARTS

Planners should watch for unusual sizes of nuts, bolts, and threads. Designers sometimes specify nuts and bolts which are supposed to be standard but which are not carried in stock, either by their own company or by nut and bolt manufacturers. They take longer to get and sometimes cost more than more popular sizes. Wherever possible, standard sizes carried in stock should be used.

Not only should standard parts be used but nonstandard parts should be made standard where possible. Automobile manufacturers are notable exponents of "dualizing." Dualizing means that parts performing the same function in different lines of cars are designed so that they are the same. Thus Chevrolet windshields and Cadillac windshields are identical and are in fact, interchangeable. And far more then half of Ford's Mustang and Falcon car parts are identical.

Opportunities for dualizing exist in most products made from parts. In particular, de luxe items, such as TV sets, electric irons, lawnmowers, automobiles, and others, are largely identical to economy models except for trim and decoration.

Dualizing saves money since it reduces variety and increases the quantities of the limited kinds of parts made. Yet it doesn't occur unless designers work toward it all the time. Small companies, in particular, often fail to see its possibilities and so make every product in their lines wholly different when there is no need for every part to be unique.

As a rule, planners should make products with standard parts (and here we mean standard in the industry) because they are readily available and because they are usually cheaper. Products and parts should be made standard in other ways too. Inlet holes or outlet holes for pipes, tubing, or wire need to be of standard size with standard threads. Mounting brackets and mounting positions as on electric motors, fans, and pumps need to be standard.

Don't be a slave, though, to using standard parts. A standard part isn't always the perfect part for a job. Maybe it isn't the right size, maybe it isn't strong enough, maybe it won't wear well enough, or maybe it is too good. Ball bearings for bicycle wheels don't have to be as good as those in electric motors. Unless a standard part is almost perfect for the job, a

FIGURE 12-7 None of these aluminum parts is standard; yet it paid to make them all special because no standard part would do the work.

special part may be worth its extra cost. In fact, if the volume is great enough, special parts may cost no more than standard parts. It is also often possible to standardize parts within a company even though the parts are special so far as other companies are concerned.

Standard parts are usually economical in manufacturing and have an added advantage that they make it easier for the customer to repair his product. But the perfect part for the job, even if nonstandard, may be so much better suited that you should use it.

Some companies use nonstandard parts intentionally to capture the repair parts business. Customers can't get replacement parts elsewhere.

You make money selling repair parts and you make sure that the customer gets the right part. Some companies go so far as to show parts in their repair parts catalog only by the company's identification number—even for standard parts. This helps the customer get the right part for a particular use. But it may cost the company his good will if, after waiting for an item to come from the factory, he discovers it is a standard item.

We have talked about standard parts as if using them were merely a matter of deciding. Actually, it is hard for designers and planners to standardize. Today's new product may have parts that could be identical to those used in another product but the designer may not realize it, and the planner might miss it too. You can't expect a designer to remember every part of every product; nor can he spend all his time checking to see if a bolt or bearing he specifies has ever been used before (although the company's standardization manual will tell him in most cases). Young designers (and planners, too), in particular, just can't be familiar enough with everything you make to see every chance to standardize.

You would hope though to do better than in one company where a standardization program found a steel washer listed in different bills of material as a washer, ring, bushing, collet, grommet, and spacer. The company found that, in one instance, one single kind of steel washer had over a dozen numbers! Imagine the waste in ordering and stocking this washer so many places. Worse yet, the Federal government found one ball bearing with 239 different numbers! It also found that 4,500 supposedly different oil seals were actually only 879 different items.

Sometimes cannibalization is a reason for standardization. Cannibalization means taking good parts out of worn out or obsolete products and putting them back into parts stock. Guns, airplanes, and other materiel of the Army, Navy, and Air Force can be repaired using parts from discarded equipment if the parts are standard.

PREFERRED NUMBERS

One of the problems in standardizing a series of parts is to determine how many parts there should be in a given range and what the relationships between them should be. If you made nails, for example, and decided that the smallest would be $\frac{1}{2}$ inch long and the largest would be 6 inches long, you would next have to decide how many in-between sizes you should make. Then you would still have to decide what the in-between sizes should be.

Once you have decided the limits and the number of in-between sizes you can then set up an arithmetic, a geometric, or some other progression to tell you what in-between sizes to make. Commercial machine screws, for example, have a standard incremental increase of $\frac{1}{8}$ inch within the range of lengths from $\frac{1}{4}$ to 1 inch, and increments of $\frac{1}{4}$ inch for lengths from 1 to 4 inches. The sizes of standard resistors and capacitors used in electronic circuits, however, tend to follow a geometric increase.

The amount of the increase between steps for a geometric series can be determined from the following formula:

$$I = \sqrt[n]{\frac{L}{S}}$$

where I = value of the incremental multiplier
   n = number of desired steps
   L = largest value desired in the range under consideration
   S = smallest value in the range

If, for example, you want to start with 1 and increase to 100 in 10 steps, then

$$I = \sqrt[10]{\frac{100}{1}} = 1.585$$

Each size will need to be approximately 1.59 times the next lower size. Your sizes would be 1, 1.5, 2.5, 4.0, 6.5, 10, 15, 25, 40, 65, and 100.

It may be of interest to note that our musical scale is based on a geometric progression of numbers. The vibration ratios from note to note on the scale go up with an interval multiplier equal to the twelfth root of 2. (The pitch doubles in an octave, and a piano, for example, has seven white and five black keys per octave.)

STANDARD VERSUS INTERCHANGEABLE PARTS

We have been talking about standard parts more or less as if "standard" parts and "interchangeable" parts were the same, but they aren't quite the same. Standard parts are always interchangeable but interchangeable parts are standard in only a limited sense.

An automobile headlight bulb is standard. So are storage batteries, spark plugs, tires, electric fuses, nuts, and bolts. They are made in many types and sizes but each type or size is used many places, by many companies.

By contrast, a door on a Coldspot refrigerator is interchangeable but not standard—not standard in the usual sense. It will fit any Coldspot refrigerator of the same model but not any other make of refrigerator. It is special—not standard, so far as other manufacturers are concerned.

Interchangeable parts do not have to be hand fitted into assemblies. If a company making pistols can make the frames and triggers of a model so exactly alike that any trigger, chosen from a lot of triggers, fits into any frame, chosen from a lot of frames, the parts are said to be interchangeable. They are standard in the sense that they must be almost exactly alike. But they are not called "standard" parts unless they go into different products. The windshields made for Oldsmobile cars are so exactly alike that any windshield made for Oldsmobiles will fit into any Oldsmobile of the model for which it is made. They are interchangeable. But they are special, not standard. They will fit no car but an Oldsmobile and only certain Oldsmobile models.

Interchangeability is a must. The day has passed when parts were hand fitted. And except where extremely close fits are needed, interchangeability is not costly. Today's machines and men can easily produce metal parts within tolerances of one- to two-thousandths of an inch. For most purposes that is close enough. Closer fits can also be obtained, if need be, but they are more costly. Design engineers, planners, production controllers, customers, all expect interchangeability.

Interchangeability is sometimes harder to achieve than it is supposed to be. If you buy parts made to your specification from two manufacturers you may find that although both meet your specification, they are not quite alike and may not be wholly interchangeable. Some suppliers will make part sizes as large as the tolerance allows. Others will make them on the low side. If your tolerances happen to be too large this may keep the parts from being fully interchangeable.

Sometimes, too, such things as electronic tubes are interchangeable functionally but not physically. Different makers make the mounts a little different and they end up not fitting the same sockets. This is particularly annoying if you buy tubes from several manufacturers. And, bothersome as this is in original manufacturing, it is worse for repair parts. You buy a repair part only to find that it would do the work if it would fit but it doesn't fit and so isn't interchangeable. Fortunately, in the case of tubes, they have largely given way to transistors whose electrical lead wires obviate this particular difficulty.

SUBASSEMBLIES

The least costly way to put products together is to make final assemblies out of *subassemblies, not directly out of parts*. The same is true for major assemblies. Make them, in turn, out of minor subassemblies instead of parts directly. Have your planners try to keep as much work away from final assembly as possible. Try also not to put in electrical, hydraulic, or pneumatic systems during final assembly. Wires and pipes are hard to put into a house after the walls are plastered. They are almost as hard to put into machinery at final assembly.

Keeping work away from final assembly makes sure that the pieces go in the right order. You can't put a valve in an automobile engine after it is assembled. It has to go in earlier. Nor can you put an automobile speedometer together piece by piece into the dashboard.

Keeping work away from final assembly also shortens assembly time. You can be putting together any number of different subassemblies at the same time. If an automobile engine were put together after the block was attached to the chassis, then the electrical generator assembled, and the carburetor and the fuel pump after that, assembly time would be endless.

Keeping work away from final assembly keeps workers from getting in each other's way. And it also permits employees to specialize on one thing and allows them to work at places conveniently arranged with tools and accessories for the job they are doing. Also, you can individually test the subassemblies to see if they work, something that you can't do if you put them together as they are fastened to the product during final assembly.

As we said earlier, an engineer making up drawings can't foresee every subassembly possibility but his first idea of subassemblies covers most of the possibilities. Planners laying out the project usually discover a few more. And once production starts, foremen and industrial engineers may figure out still other ways to combine parts into different subassemblies more economically. Don't pass up anyone's suggestions here.

Also try to keep your records right with practice. Suppose that you expected to have a certain set of parts put together as a subassembly at one work station. But the men in the shop find that it works better to put certain of the parts on as part of a later assembling operation. You send the collection of parts out to the first station where they assemble most of them and send the others along with the subassembly to the next station. Try to keep up with these changes. Send parts to the work station when they are actually assembled, not somewhere else. You'll save lost motion and lost parts.

Production control rarely decides how parts shall be put into subassemblies. But production control's work is greatly affected by them particularly in the case of standard subassemblies. Standard subassemblies (sometimes called "basics" and described in Chapter 7) are often manufactured in quantities shown in approved forecasts of basics and not in quantities tied directly to final assembly needs. Production control may set the quantities of standard subassemblies to be made. Basics may be made in standard lot sizes and carried in stock as if they were standard parts.

On big engineering projects you have another kind of subassembly matter with which to deal. These big products are shipped out "knocked down" in sections, probably in different freight cars and even at different times. Engineering will have to specify how you separate sections, which items go with each section, as well as how the sections should be crated, packed, or shipped.

MAKE BY LOT OR CONTINUOUSLY?

You can make products that have a continuing sale in lots or you can make them continuously. When made in lots, a large number are processed together. You put them into stock from which you draw them to fill sales or assembly orders from day to day. When the supply runs low, process another lot. Or you can make products continuously, 100 a day, 1,000 a day, or whatever number will take care of sales.

When final assembly is by lots, subassembly and parts manufacture is practically always by lots too. But where final assembly is continuous the question of making subassemblies and parts in lots or continuously nearly always comes up. Often, deciding is no problem. If the quantities are small or if the processing time is short, you make parts in lots. This is one extreme. At the other extreme—enormous quantities or reasonably large quantities of items which require many hours of processing—you should almost always go to continuous manufacturing. But you don't always have either very small or very large quantities. There are many in-between cases. Quantities are not small nor yet large. Neither manufacturing method is clearly superior.

The pros and cons of lot (or intermittent) and continuous manufacture were discussed in Chapter 2. We don't need to repeat them here. But the discussion there was more about assembling—*final assembly* in particular—than it was about making subassemblies and parts. The pros and cons of making *subassemblies* and *parts* in lots or continuously are a little different. You have to consider each subassembly and part separately. A given rate of usage will justify continuous production of one item but not of another. Since the mathematics involved in calculating the optional economic lot size are closely related to the determination of optimal order quantities in inventory control, a discussion of the calculations needed to find out which way is best is deferred until Chapters 16 and 17.

Anything made continuously—subassemblies or parts—has its own production line with its own machines. They are wholly devoted to its manufacture. Subassembly work, like final assembly, is often manual work, done with portable hand tools. They are relatively inexpensive. You can put assemblies together continuously without putting much money into equipment. So you can get the gains from continuous assembly (in both final assembly and in subassembly manufacture) without spending much more money on machines than you would have to spend anyway if you assembled in lots. You do not have to have enormous volume nor do your products all have to be alike in order to make continuous manufacture pay.

ASSEMBLIES—BY LOT OR CONTINUOUSLY? Assemblies, particularly final assemblies (complete products), are usually costly, easily damaged, and may be bulky. They are expensive to carry in stock. As we said earlier, making them continuously keeps carrying costs low.

However, making them continuously presents problems. First, they need to have their own assembly area and facilities. Second, each assembly line needs its own work crew. Third, each man in the group must have an equal work assignment—equal, that is, in time—and that assignment must be equal, in time, to the production rate. If you plan to assemble one product every twenty seconds, each worker needs to have a little less than twenty seconds of work *per unit*. If any operation takes five times that long, that operation needs five workers, each working on every fifth unit. On the other hand, if any of the men along the line have less than a twenty-second assignment, you'll never see it. They'll just move slower and it will look as though they too have a twenty-second assignment. You just lose part of the time of everyone who has less than a twenty-second assignment.

Similarly, if your line turns out one unit every four hours, each worker's assignment needs to be about four hours long. This is a very long work assignment. The worker needs to remember his whole assignment or should have some very lengthy written instructions for reference. If the production rate is one unit per four hours and some workers have very much less than four hours' work on each one, you will have to fill in part of their day with other work. Of course, a line turning out one unit every four hours is very unusual but not unknown. Most lines turn out one product every few minutes.

Subassembly production and final assembly must be very dependable. If either stops long all subassembly and parts production lines also stop. But, as we said earlier, you can avoid most of these stoppages by carrying small banks of subassemblies which will tide over final assembly for short periods of stoppages.

You don't always make subassemblies continuously. Particularly if they are small and not too expensive, you are likely to make them in lots. If this is the case, you must be sure that a new lot comes into stock before the old lot gets used up. If a lot gets delayed in production for any reason, the next thing you know is that you are out of stock. Consequently, down goes the assembly line.

Stoppages from shortages of items made in lots are, of course, rare because you set their production schedules so that they will be finished well ahead of when you will need them. Normally, you finish parts lots far enough ahead so that you will have to put them into finished parts stores several days before you need them. From this stock room you "call them out" or withdraw them from stock and take them to the assembly line well ahead of their need. Any out-of-stock items not noticed earlier are dis-covered then.

JOB SPECIALIZATION VERSUS JOB ENLARGEMENT   We have spoken as if you had only two choices in making subassemblies, in lots or con-tinuously. Actually, there are two more choices within the framework of continuous production. These we might call job specialization and job enlargement. You can cut the work up into small assignments and have one man do a small set of tasks on every product that comes along. Possibly each man's job will take only 1 minute and the line will turn out 60 units an hour. This is job specialization.

Or you can cut the job up less finely and give each man, say, 10 minutes work on each product. This would be job enlargement. A product would then be assembled complete by 6 men, each with one doing 10 min-utes of work on it. To get 60 units an hour, you'd need 10 teams of 6 men each.

Specialization lets men become extremely skillful but the work isn't quite so interesting. Some men find it quite boring to install lower left-front door hinges on automobile bodies day in and day out. The gains in productivity and worker satisfactions through job enlargement programs at IBM and Non-Linear Systems, Inc. (a relatively small West Coast elec-tronics producer), have received considerable publicity but their example has not been followed by too many firms as yet. Possibly this is because a 10-minute job may not be much more interesting than a 1-minute job.

MAKING PARTS CONTINUOUSLY OR IN LOTS   Making *parts* continu-ously or in lots differs from making assemblies continuously or in lots. Parts made continuously need machines that are usually special, fast, and costly. It takes high volume to keep them busy enough to keep costs down. And the machines, when idle, can't be used for other things because they are special. *It takes a higher volume to justify making parts continuously than to assemble continuously.*

You will, therefore, often find final assemblies and most of the sub-assemblies put together continuously while parts are made in lots. But subassemblies, which are "several generations removed" from final assem-bly, are a little more likely to be made in lots. By several generations removed we mean a subassembly that goes into another subassembly that is a part of another subassembly and so on. But even subassemblies several generations removed from final assembly are often made continuously. Commutators that go on armatures that go in electrical generators that go into automobiles are made continuously. So are the armatures. So are the generators. And so are the automobiles.

The high cost of parts production lines and the low cost of continuous assembly lines is not the only reason for making parts in lots when assembly is continuous. Manufacturing parts or assemblies in lots require more inventory in process, much more, than does continuous manufacture. Assemblies, in particular, tie up more money per unit than do parts. So it is important to keep down the inventory of assemblies. Assemblies are also more bulky. Their inventory needs are kept down to conserve storage space.

Parts, individually, represent less money tied up. And their space requirements are less. So keeping down the inventory of parts in process is not quite as important as it is for assemblies. Manufacturing by lots is, therefore, more feasible.

Lot manufacture is better for small quantities, but setup costs are a bad feature. You can hold setup costs down only if setups can be made quickly. In regular job lot work setups are always different because the jobs are different. Sometimes, though, you have repetitive lots and have to make the same setups over and over again. Better have your tool designers design tooling that can be put on and taken off machines quickly so that your setup costs will be held down.

One method used to make parts in repetitive lots is called "cycling" (see page 711). Cycling means using a machine for an operation on a lot of one part, then changing to an operation on another part, then to another, and so on for perhaps several days. Then the whole cycle repeats itself. Another lot of the first part gets the same operation as the first lot. Following it comes another lot of the second part, then the third part, and so on. Every few days the cycle repeats. Cycling allows manufacturing by lots with a minimum of production control paper work. But it is feasible only if you can keep setup costs down.

OVERLAPPED VERSUS GAPPED OPERATIONS   Actually, manufacture by lots does not have to (although it usually does) increase the inventory very much. You can "overlap" successive operations. Overlapping operations means starting operation 2 on the first parts finished by operation 1 before the whole lot is finished. For small lots, operations are rarely overlapped. They are "gapped." Every item in a lot is finished on an operation before the first item in the lot goes into the next operation. The "gap" is the time between operations when no work is being done on the lot. And this is, of course, what causes the extra inventory. With large lots, this would be wastefully slow and would make very large inventories of work in process. You'd probably go into overlapping to keep it down.

With overlapping, parts coming from operation 1 go into a "live bank" from which they are drawn and processed through operation 2. Parts coming from operation 2 go into a bank that supplies operation 3. Probably the operations take different amounts of time. If operation 2 is slower than operation 1, you can start it immediately, as soon as the first part comes through from operation 1. But if operation 2 is faster, you can't start it until a bank is built up, otherwise operation 2 will catch up to the output of operation 1 and will have to wait.

Production control has to set schedules so that no fast operation ever starts so soon that it catches up with a preceding slow one. If it is desirable to overlap the operations, then production control must plan the size of the banks.

The decision to make continuously or in lots is often so important that the company's top executives make the decision. So much money is involved that engineering, production control, and the superintendent may not be allowed to decide. In fact, normally, production control would not be consulted even on minor decisions about making continuously or by lot. Engineering and the superintendent make most decisions where little money is involved.

PLANNING PRODUCTION LINES   Line production, whether assembly or parts manufacture, has to be engineered. How many units an hour do you want to get off the line? Suppose that we talk about an assembly line and that we want to get 20 assemblies per hour. That means 1 unit every 3 minutes. And suppose that it takes 150 man-minutes to do the whole assembly job. You'll have to have 50 work stations along the line where 50 men will each do a 3-minute task. Allow, say, 10 feet along the line for each man and you find that you will need 500 feet of work space along the conveyor. Your industrial engineers will have to cut up the total assembly job into 3-minute tasks. This may not be easy, particularly when you remember that they have to do it before the line is set up and before the jobs are ever done.

But if you set up your line in the way we have just described, you'll be disappointed. It almost certainly will not produce 20 units an hour. It won't produce that many because men won't always get their 3-minute jobs done in 3 minutes. True, sometimes men will do their tasks in less time, but *the short and long performance times will not and can not average out.*

If man number 1 takes 4 minutes on a product, man number 2 has to wait 1 minute to get it. Then he does his work in 3 minutes but man number 3 now has to wait 1 minute and so on down the line. It is of no help for man number 1 to turn out his next unit in 2 minutes. If he does, he'll just have to wait a minute until man number 2 finishes his 3-minute job on the delayed product.

Now, picture your 50-man line with an occasional delay here or there, each impossible to make up and each ultimately causing delay to everyone, and you will see why our line will not turn out 20 units per hour. All of the reasons for line delays can never be eliminated. Not only do men work at irregular paces, but parts don't always fit, tools make trouble, and parts aren't always available exactly when needed. Besides, men are sometimes absent so that some work stations will be manned by inexperienced men who cause occasional hold-ups.

Can you escape the cumulative effects of delays? Yes, but only by carrying small banks of products between operations, and that multiplies the investment in inventories, increases materials handling costs, and increases space requirements. This is a dilemma that you must contend with in any kind of line work. In later chapters we shall examine various measures of performance that can be calculated from mathematical models or through simulation techniques so that we will be able to predict line performance under various conditions.

SPECIALIZED PARTS–MAKING DEPARTMENTS

Parts are usually made in shops where similar *machines* are grouped together into departments doing certain work. You don't have to go all the way over to continuous production, however, if you want to set up departments to make certain *parts* and those only. In fact, this is common among companies making a considerable variety (variety mostly in minor details) of fairly standard products, made mostly to stock. Gears, for example, can be made in a gear shop, bearings in another kind of shop. Each shop is a little job shop with complete equipment including, if need be, its own electroplating equipment as well as all the machines it needs.

National Cash Register, A. B. Dick, Western Electric's Teletype, General Motors' Electro-motive, Burroughs, and many more make a good many of their heavy-use parts in such departments.

Production control can be much simplified by this arrangement. First of all, you use standard costs for pricing the parts and so don't have to collect manufacturing costs for each lot of product. Nor do you have to make up complete shop orders showing individual operations. Just give the foreman a book of master route sheets.

All that you have to do to get parts made is to send him a list of which items and how many are needed. He turns to his route sheet file, finds out what materials to use, and checks which operations his men should do. And he goes ahead and gets the parts made with no checking or reporting to production control about the progress of lots from operation to operation.

STUDY MATERIALS

12-1 1 Suppose that you make, among other things, scissors for use around the house (but not including such things as tin cutting shears). Would the idea of preferred numbers be of any help to you?

2 Suppose that you make asphalt tile for basement floor covering. Would the preferred numbers idea be useful? Discuss.

12-2 Suppose that you have several generations of subassemblies (a part goes into a minor subassembly, which goes into a bigger assembly, which goes into a major assembly, which goes into the final product). And suppose that final assembly is continuous. What are the pros and cons of making the earlier generations of subassemblies continuously as against making them in lots? What happens to inventories? To production costs?

12-3 Simpson Machine Shop's planner is asked to decide whether to change from an iron casting to a stamping for a carburetor part. Some 12,000 per year have been used in the past, and the future volume for several years is expected to be at least this high.

Castings have been costing 20 cents each, after which machining costing 8 cents is necessary. Two per cent of the castings are scrapped after machining. Present tools and the foundry pattern cost $300 several years ago and are now fully depreciated although they will probably be usable for several more years.

Changing to a stamping will cost $2,500 for dies and new tooling which will last 10 years. Scrap is expected to be so low that you can neglect it in this calculation. Money is worth 25 per cent to the company. Material will be 6 cents per stamping. Because of some welding, labor will cost 8 cents each.

Should Simpson change to a stamping? Should it change if the new dies and tooling will produce only 72,000 units before they are worn out?

12-4 You are the planner at McCann Metals and have been asked if forgings or castings should be used for part number 124. Either will do the job satisfactorily so cost is your only consideration.

Part 124, if made from a steel casting, will have a gross weight of 9 lb. and can be bought locally and in any quantity for $5 each. If made from a forging it will have a gross weight of $10\frac{1}{2}$ lb. and cost $2.80 plus 17 cents freight. The finished part number 124 will weigh 7 lb. in either case, and steel scrap brings $20 a ton.

Since you have been using castings, going to forgings will cost $1,500 for changed jigs, fixtures, and drawings. This cost must be absorbed in the first year.

Forgings are priced at $2.80 only if bought in lots of 600 or more; smaller orders are priced $3.08 per forging. There is no such limitation for castings.

Can you justify using forgings if 500 will be needed next year? 1,000? At what point does it pay to change?

12-5 One of Sanborn Company's items, a rocker base, now a brass casting, is used at the rate of 11,000 per year and probably will continue to be used at this rate. Machining it costs $3 per 100 pieces, material costs $8.09 per 100. Overhead in the machine shop is 150 per cent of direct labor. The present tools are fully depreciated on Sanborn's books.

It is possible to make the rocker base from a zinc die casting but the die would cost $600. Material would be $3.49 less per 100 pieces than the cost of brass castings. Machining labor would also be reduced by $1.27 per 100 pieces.

How long will it take to absorb the cost of the new dies?

MASTER PROCESSING INSTRUCTIONS

MASTER BILLS OF MATERIAL

A master bill of material is a list of parts of an assembled product. It shows the name of the complete product, its identification number, and the component parts, identified by name and number. Shown also are the quantities of each part needed to make one complete product. The list also shows whether an item is an assembly or a piece part. Assemblies are listed as if they were individual parts. They have their own master bills of material which show their parts.

Usually master bills also show the source of each part—whether the company buys it, makes it itself and carries it in stock, makes it itself to special order, or whether it is furnished by the customer. It shows drawing numbers, casting numbers, and pattern numbers wherever they apply. For bought items, it shows trade names and the vendor's identification number wherever the item comes from only one source. It is well, however, to avoid trade names and vendor numbers if possible because doing this would require changing bills of material if the item were bought from another supplier.

We have previously talked about basics and sets of parts. Both need their own master bills of material. They appear on master bills for end products as single items. In fact your end product bill may be largely a listing of special subassemblies, basics, and sets of parts. This is largely so at the Cincinnati Milling Machine Company. CMM makes five sizes and three styles of dual milling machines (15 varieties in all). For these there is one parts list of items common to them all. Besides the common list, it takes 207 other parts sets to make the whole line. Of these, 109 are needed to make one single kind of machine. All of these lists of sets of parts are handled just like master bills for subassemblies.

There are differences of opinion about how to handle "use" items. Use items are paint, solder, grease, nails, tacks, cotter pins, washers, rivets, and sometimes, wire. Some companies don't show these items on master bills of material. Others list them because doing so helps them to know that they need the item.

Stewart-Warner lists even as little as 2 inches of wire solder on its bills of material for radios. So does King-Seeley when it makes dashboard instruments for Chrysler. It lists every part, washer, wire, solder, tape, and

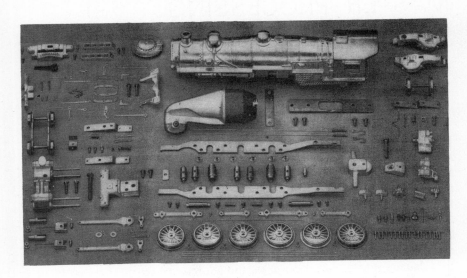

FIGURE 13-1 The master bill of materials lists the various parts and the numbers of each required to make one product. The picture above shows the 200 parts of a small-scale model locomotive. One hundred ten different parts are required, including the motor, which is itself a subassembly made from many parts. The master bill would list all of the different items pictured above, except perhaps standard washers and screws, and would show the number of each required for one engine. (Varney Scale Models.)

paint. You need to list all the parts, too, if the bill is to be used as an assembly instruction sheet so that assemblers will know to put the minor part into the assembly. If, however, you don't use bills of material as assembly instructions, these items could be kept on hand all the time at the assembly floor as "free issue" items. You wouldn't need to calculate their needs from bills of material, nor to issue them directly against assembly orders. So little of any of them is needed for one assembled product that the cost of the item per unit of product need hardly be shown in the cost records. Such items can be handled more easily by charging them to overhead accounts.

Master bills of material don't authorize anything to be produced. That is done by production programs, assembly orders, and master schedules. Assembly orders are actually bills of material, copied from master bills but with the order number, quantity, and scheduled completion date added. Assembly orders are *order* bills of material and constitute one kind of directive to authorizing production.

Simple assembled products sometimes have no master bill of materials other than the parts list shown on their drawings. Most products are, however, too complicated for this. Their final assembly drawings show and list the assemblies and parts needed.

In all but the smallest companies master bills are transferred to tabulating cards and computer tapes, and all future bills are printed by

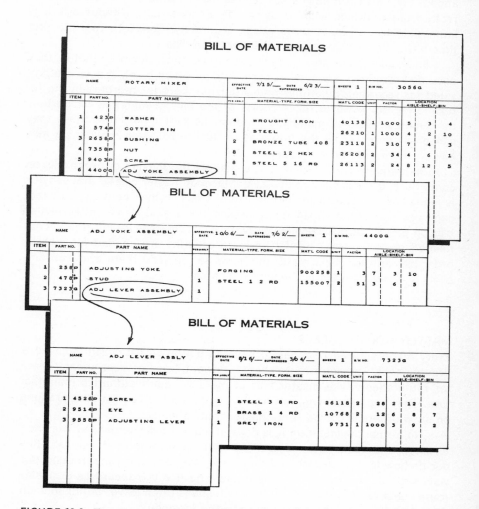

FIGURE 13-2   Three related bills of materials show the basis for progressive analysis of subassembly requirements arising from an order for an assembled product. The lesser subassemblies do not need to be analyzed or planned for at any stage where the stock status indicates that there are sufficient subassemblies on hand to cover the order. (Sperry Rand Corp.)

computers. Master bills for complex producers cover thousands of items, sometimes running to over 100 computer pages.

Master bills of material ought always to be drawn up before making the first order for an assembled product whether or not you expect repeat orders for the product. In large companies, master bills are always made ahead, but small companies sometimes make products the first time directly from drawings without using bills of materials. Without bills it is impossible to anticipate parts needs accurately. Consequently, the first time a product is made there are likely to be delays.

Small companies sometimes keep no file of master bills; that is, they have no permanent file copy of parts lists on which blank spaces are provided for recording quantities and order numbers for reorders in the future. They do, however, have copies of the bills of materials which they developed when they made the product the first time. From these they can easily copy off all the information they need when making up new bills for reorders of old products.

In companies so small as not to handle the making of order bills on computers, there is need to design the form of master bills so that copying is made easy, thus avoiding errors. Order bills can then be made as direct copies by Xerox or other similar processes. It is a good idea to make master bills on printed forms which have several extra columns for information not needed on the master itself. The extra columns are needed for making order bills and for checking off the items as you send them to the order's parts accumulation bin in the assembly area.

MASTER ROUTE SHEETS

Every manufactured part has to have its operation list which is called a "route sheet," "master route sheet," "layout," or "process sheet." Master route sheets, like master bills of material, don't authorize manufacture. They are processing, not producing, authority. The list of operations on shop orders is copied from master route sheets.

No formal original routing is done in many small companies. The shop foremen and their better operators work directly from drawings. They decide how to do the work and then do it. You can do original routing this way, write down how the item is made, and use this record as a master route sheet in the future. Even large job shops often leave routing in such departments as steel fabricating up to the foremen.

Making up shop orders for repeat orders is sometimes referred to as routing. We have called this "routine" or "repetitive" routing. For repeat orders, you don't have to do any of the original routing work over again. All that you have to do is to copy the master and add figures relating to the new order.

A master route sheet for a part shows its identification number, the identification number of the product of which it is a part, and if there is one, its drawing number. Specification numbers are shown for all operations covered by specifications. The master route sheet also shows the kind and amount of raw material needed to make one part.

Operations are listed in sequence by operation name and department in which the work is done. Operations are described in only one or two words. This may seem overbrief but it is usually enough because drawings furnish the rest of the needed information. Many companies also list the machines used for each operation. Some companies list, too, the machines' speeds and feeds, the job setup time, each operation's hourly output, all special tools, machine attachments, gages, and other necessary job accessories. But you don't need to list standard tools and gages because plenty of them are supposed always to be available.

Some companies show, on route sheets, the labor grade for the employee who is to do the work. If the operation is a machine job, you don't need to do this because the machine sets the worker class. On bench or assembly work, however, you may want to show the labor grade. Inspection operations are usually listed along with other operations. Listed also are test and specification numbers as well as the identification numbers for special testing equipment.

Most companies not only describe operations by name but give them operation numbers as well. The National Cash Register Company has a number for practically every operation in the plant. Any specific operation number—on any route sheet—always means the same operation.

A very different system, used by most companies, numbers the operations on every route sheet as 1, 2, 3, etc. Operation 1 on one route sheet has nothing to do with operation 1 on another. Each is merely the first thing done to the item concerned. If extra operations are added later they are numbered $2a$, $3a$, etc. Other companies, using the same idea, number the operations 10, 20, etc. Extra operations, added later, go in as 11, 21, etc.

If a part is normally made in standard lots, the standard lot size is shown on the master route sheet. Some companies show the job setup and teardown time for each operation and the operating time per 100 units. Such times are not always applicable, however, because you may need to make only a partial setup if the previous job setup can be used in part. The same thing may happen to teardown time. If the following job can use part of the setup it doesn't have to be completely taken down.

The extent to which you list details relating to operations on the route sheet depends somewhat on the degree to which production control is centralized. If your control is relatively decentralized, such items as tool and gage requirements are likely to be omitted from the list. Minor operations are also omitted from the list when they are characteristically done along with a listed operation. Deburring or cleaning operations, for example, are common but you won't find them listed too often since adequate capacity is available and the products will be deburred or cleaned as a matter of course after the operation.

Planners set the sequence of operations as they plan them. Occasionally, but not ordinarily, there can be variations in the sequence of operations. If there are two alternative routes or sequences which the material can follow, the planner might list them both on the operations list.

PROPER ROUTING WHEN VOLUME CHANGES

We have said that the best way to make anything depends on how many you are going to make. Usually you don't really know how many you will make but a decision is still necessary. If you are manufacturing to order, you know the size of the order. But you may get repeat orders. When you can't count on repeat orders probably you had better choose the best method for the quantity on only the first order. If, later, you get repeat orders you end up using a costly small-quantity method for a large quantity of products.

The same problem comes up when you manufacture stock items. We talked, in Chapter 7, about forecasting and how you can try to get a reasonable figure. But there are many times when you feel quite doubtful about the future volume so you tool up only for low volume. Tooling up for high volume, which may never come, is too risky. You just have to take calculated risks. If you are wrong, you still did the best thing considering what you knew at the time.

The point to raising this matter here is not that you can get out of the dilemma but that you don't have to be stuck forever with a wrong decision if you did make one. If volume goes way above expectation and seems likely to stay high, you can change your method to suit the new prospective future volume. But, and here is another point, production control and not engineering knows about repeat orders and volume changes. If volume goes up in a big way production control should raise, with engineering, the question of changing. Of course, having already tooled up for one volume affects the new decision. Possibly the volume prospects in the future will not justify scrapping the present tooling. Whether they do or not, though, a fresh decision should be made.

PRODUCTION CONTROL ADDING OPERATIONS

We have said that the planning department does original routing and we have noted that the planning department sometimes is not a part of production control. If it is not, the production control department should have authority to make minor additions to the operation list. For example, you may need to add a washing operation, or a cleaning or a deburring operation, to an operation list where your planners had not originally thought it was needed. (This question would not arise in some companies because they never list these particular operations anyway.) Such additions are not important enough to make a lot of work sending them through channels and doing paper work. They may even be temporary. When things in the shop straighten out you can cut out the extra operation.

But if it is a permanent thing and if it is your custom to list the kind of operation added, the master operation list should be changed too. It should always be a correct list and entering these extra operations in on it makes sure that they will be performed the next time the item is made and also insures that their added costs are charged to the product.

ASSEMBLY INSTRUCTIONS

Production control does not make out assembly instructions. In continuous manufacture, production control has nothing to do with them. But in job lot assembly, as in parts manufacture, production control is the forwarding agent for assembling instructions.

Assembling instructions are relatively simple in continuous assembly. The work is cut up into short work assignments and each man quickly learns his work. Of course, a great deal of industrial engineering effort goes into making the work simple. This is done before production starts and the men are given thorough instructions the first few times they perform their work. Probably you won't have to give them any other instructions.

But it is different when assemblies are made in lots instead of continuously. Then assembly workers work on different jobs every few days. You have to tell them, for each new lot, how they are to put its parts together. Drawings of assemblies may be all that they'll need but a drawing isn't much of an assembly instruction. You just don't explain on a drawing how everything goes together and in what order.

Bills of material can sometimes do it, although this is uncommon. If you want to have bills of material serve as assembling instructions, you will have to use indentations. List major assemblies along the left side of the page. Below the name of each assembly, list (and indent) the names of all lesser subassemblies and parts that go directly into the major assembly as piece parts. List the parts of subassemblies below the name of the subassembly into which they go. Indent them one step more. If there are several generations of subassemblies, use several indentations.

This system of indenting can serve as an assembly instruction. Start with the last assembly listed near the bottom of the bill. Look for the items with the greatest indentation that are listed together. They are the parts that make up the subassembly listed above them. That subassembly, together with other subassemblies and piece parts with the same amount of indentation on the list, goes to make up a larger assembly, and so on.

But, of course, merely listing the items that make an assembly isn't really much more of an assembly instruction than are most drawings. Neither the regular drawings nor bills of material listing the parts of subassemblies are very helpful when things are hard to put together. You'll need special drawings and written instructions from the engineering department for the hard to assemble products.

Another way to tell assemblers how to do their work is to use a sample of the assembly as an instruction. Assemble one unit of the product

FIGURE 13-3 Westinghouse Electric finds that verbal instructions put onto tape recordings boost efficiency as much as 100 per cent and cut down on mistakes. (Westinghouse Electric Co.)

FIGURE 13-4 Mistakes in assembly work are reduced to a minimum when assembly workers both see and hear instructions covering how to do their work. (Sony Corporation of America.)

carefully and slowly with foreman and engineers helping and giving instructions. Then keep the sample (and maybe half-assembled samples as well) at the workplace so workers can refer to it as they put other units together.

Makers of intricate and delicate apparatus sometimes develop quite sophisticated assembly instructions. Assemblers may have a viewing scope in front of them on which successive slides illustrating successive steps are shown. These can be further supplemented by voice tape recordings explaining how to do each part of the work. The engineering department develops all such instructions and production control calls them out and puts them into use whenever they are needed.

ELECTRICAL BILLS OF MATERIALS

Electrical wires are usually not listed on regular bills of material. Wires are different from other parts and need to be specified by kind of wire, type of covering, and length and kinds of attaching connectors. You need to supplement regular bills of material with wire bills.

In addition, you may wish to put other electrical parts on separate bills of material. Ordinarily you buy such electrical items and each one may be a rather complicated component itself. Keeping them apart from regular mechanical parts saves some possible confusion.

ELECTRICAL WIRE

Mechanical products are usually electrically operated and have wiring systems. Most of them have several systems and the wiring is often very complex. An official of an airplane company making small military airplanes (which have wing spans of only 30 to 40 feet) said that each of his company's airplanes contained over 6,000 pieces of wire, which in total comes to 20 miles of wire! Of course, this example is extreme.

FIGURE 13-5 An indented bill of materials isn't much of an instruction. Imagine trying to put together any of the aircraft parts in this picture with only an indented bill of materials to guide you. (North American Rockwell Co.)

Even an automobile uses some 2 miles of wire, 700 feet of which is strung around in circuits, the rest being used to wind coils. Buicks use 34 light bulbs and 12 motors which require a generator that generates 650 watts of electricity. Dodge cars contain 200 electrical assemblies. Radios, television sets, stoves, refrigerators, vacuum cleaners, and desk calculators all contain many pieces of wire besides the wire in electric motors.

WIRE BUNDLES OR CABLES   Drawings usually don't show the exact way a wire threads its way from one terminal point to another. Nor do they show the length of wires. Wires are indicated only as lines connecting terminal points. But when you make a product you have to use a certain kind of wire and you have to put it in exactly the right place. Look at figure 13-6. It gives you an idea of wiring complexities and shows a little of the wiring that goes into an airplane. Note the bundles of wires or cable assemblies. Each individual wire has to be exactly right and it has to have the right kind of terminal connector on each end. It has to thread its way from

Mechanical Handling Systems, Inc.

FIGURE 13-6 Making up wiring harnesses on a merry-go-round assembly line. (Mechanical Handling Systems, Inc.)

one terminal to the other and has to connect to the right terminal. It may have to be bound into a cable and anchored along the way so it doesn't flop around and get caught on moving parts. When there are hundreds of wires going hither and yon, you have to know which is which. Finally, every wire has to be fastened (often soldered) on at each end.

Many companies make up prototypes and working models of new products. If you do this, it gives you a chance to figure out some of the wiring problems as you go along. Put in the kind of wire the electronic engineers specify and wire up the product wire by wire. Try to group the wires so that wherever several follow the same path for any distance they can be tied together into bundles or cables. Some wires run the full length of the cable, others come in partway along or go off before the end. Or one cable splits into smaller cables or joins up with others to make larger ones.

Then take the wires out of the prototype product. Take care to keep them in sets or bundles, called wiring "harnesses." You can then use each harness taken from the prototype as a model for duplicates needed in regular products. Stretch out the original harness against a piece of plywood and mark the start and end points for each wire on the board. Print on the board itself the kind of wire each is and what kind of terminal connections it needs. Drive nails into the board along each side of the cable to make a channel for the wires. Then take out the original cable. Your board shows just how to make up more harnesses for future products. It shows the starting and stopping points for each wire (and so sets its length), the kind of wire, and the kind of terminal connection.

Figure 13-7 shows wiring harness assembly boards set up in a factory. In this instance a number of duplicate boards have been made up and put on a merry-go-round-type conveyor for fast, high volume, low cost production of wire harnesses.

WIRE IDENTIFICATION   Wire identification is a headache. Wires are of so many kinds and they look so much alike. Furthermore, several pieces of the same kind of wire may go into a bundle. They are of different length, each piece of wire has to connect specific points, and each one has to have its own kind of terminal connection.

Wire coverings can be color coded—in solid colors or alternate stripes of different colors. Too many colors become confusing, however. One electronics company uses a color code with different combinations; another has 110! Imagine, a wire bundle with twenty-five different colored wires in it. Imagine that it is your job to attach the gray and white striped wire one place, the lavender and white another, and the black and white striped wire in still another place! If the wires are the least bit dirty, you can't tell them apart. Also, suppose you make assemblies using wires for half a

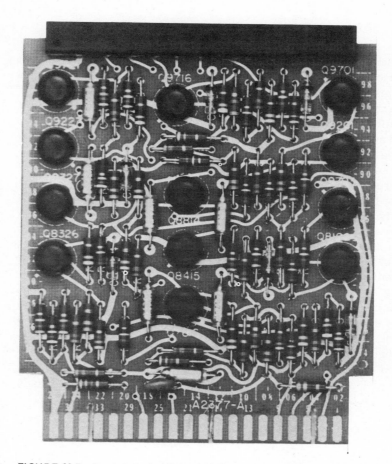

FIGURE 13-7   A printed circuit board. Notice the way the transistors and diodes are attached. Notice also the plug-in electrical connections at the bottom. This component plugs into another unit much as a lamp plugs into a wall socket. (Raytheon Co.)

dozen other electronic companies each with different color codes! The problem of stocking all of these different wires and of getting the right kinds into each product would be indeed difficult.

The United States government is a large buyer of electronic products. It has tried, without complete success, to standardize color codes. It has tried to use standard colors to connect certain standard parts and to show the kind of electrical current carried. For example, in military radios, red wires are used for direct-current high-voltage supply lines, green are control grid wires, brown are filament leads, and red and white striped wires are the direct-current supply to the screen grids. Screen grid connections themselves are orange. Standardizing the colors helps cut repair costs. You can identify wires at the ends of a bundle without cutting open the full length of the bundle (provided they are not so nearly alike as the striped wires in our earlier example).

Some companies use white covered wire and print code numbers onto it. The number is printed every few inches so that short pieces are always numbered and it isn't always necessary to open up any cable for more than a few inches to search for wire numbers distant from wire ends.

Wire *numbers* don't codify the wire. Instead they identify pieces of wire as parts. When you start to make a lot of a certain harness, you start with one of the wires. Get out the coil of the right kind of wire and cut off to length as many wires as you need. Then print the wire part number on each piece of wire. A harness may contain several pieces of wire of the same kind, but each piece will have its own wire number.

Wire harnesses have their own wire bills of materials showing the kind of wire, identification, length, types of terminals, and harness board to use.

Wiring is responsible for many small changes on engineering drawings and causes considerable extra production control work. This is because you are always finding better pathways for wires, figuring out better electrical connections or better protective wire coatings, etc. Or perhaps the wire engineer figured that you could run a wire through the frame at one place only to find that the hydraulics man has already run a tube through that opening and there isn't additional room for wires. Every change means changing production control's bills of materials and route sheets.

PRINTED CIRCUITS
Printed circuits replacing wiring of the ordinary kind are quite common in the electronics industry. They cost much less and are more compact than ordinary wiring circuits, and wiring errors are almost impossible. There is, however, still need for a significant amount of conventional wire and cables to interconnect the subunits or the completed units. Figure 13-8 shows a printed circuit. The lines on the sheet of material are thin metal. They carry the electric current instead of wires.

To make a printed circuit, you first draw up a wiring circuit diagram showing lines drawn from one terminal point to another. Don't, however, cross the lines. Then make up a metal plate of the diagram. The plate is just like the metal plates used in printing books. Using the plate and an ordinary printing press, the circuit diagram can be printed on paper just as a book is printed.

The printing is actually done, however, on a sheet of copper coated

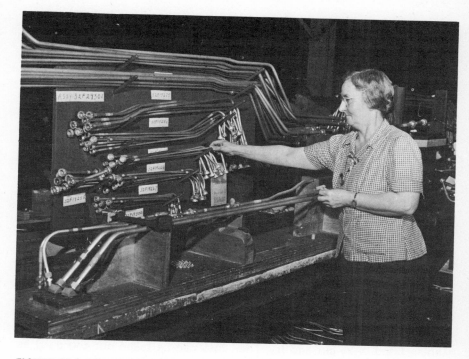

FIGURE 13-8 Pipes and tubing have to be made in many shapes and sizes and are used in most assembled products.

plastic material (copper coated on the printed side only). The copper coat is very thin. After printing, the plastic sheet is dipped into an acid which eats the copper off the plastic—except where it is protected by the ink from the printing. Next, the ink is washed off and there is the circuit, neat and perfect, in lines of thin copper bonded to the plastic.

Terminals, switches, wires, sockets, etc., can then be attached. Usually they are mounted on the other side of the plastic sheet. Small holes are drilled through the plastic right at the ends of the copper lines underneath. Then wires or studs are pushed through the holes and soldered onto the copper lines. They don't even have to be soldered individually; they can be done all at once by "dip soldering." The under side of the panel having the copper circuit attached to it is dipped in molten solder, and when it is taken out the connections will all be soldered.

Printed circuits change both the manufacturing and the production control procedures. Both are simplified. Printed circuits are usually a late rather than an early design feature. First engineering models are usually made with conventional wiring, then they are changed to printing. Original designs can, however, call for printed circuits.

PIPES AND TUBING

Because mechanical products may have built-in lubrication, hydraulic systems, liquid cooling systems, or even exhaust pipes, they contain systems of pipes, tubing, or flexible hose. An F111 fighter airplane contains over 2,000 pieces of tubing. Automobiles and refrigerators contain from 50 to 100 feet of tubing.

Other products need fuel lines or oxygen lines. Like wiring, you can't put pipes and tubing into the product during final assembly any more than you can put plumbing in a house after the walls are plastered and floors laid. Also, like wiring, designers don't try to foresee the exact pathway of each pipe and its every turn and bend. But drawings do show all connections, valves, pumps, meters, and so on. They also show the kind and size of pipe and tubing.

Although pipes and tubing are not bundled together into harnesses like wires, their exact bends are often developed in the same way as we described for wires. The first product can be assembled with the pipes and tubing fitted in by cut and try. Then they can be taken out and used as samples. Or, if they don't have to be bent in unusual ways, their measurements can be taken and specifications covering their preparation can be written.

Usually there is no pipe or tubing bill of materials. Instead, pieces of tubing are listed as parts of particular subassemblies just as are other parts. Each piece of pipe or tubing may have its own drawing. Often the original pipe, bent to a shape that fits, is used as a template or master. New pieces of pipe are cut and the ends threaded. Then, in the case of rigid tubing, they are bent to shape (to match the template) in a special pipe shop. The pipe shop's production orders may say to make and bend pieces of pipe like the sample.

If this is not practicable, you can give the pipe shop dummy products or mock-ups. Pipes can be bent to fit them, thus cutting down on bending and fitting during assembly.

Thin, long-length tubing is not always bent into shape in the pipe shop. Nor is flexible hose. Neither would hold its shape, and as they are easily bent to fit they are fastened to rigid parts of the product during assembly. Each piece must, however, be cut to length and the ends must be threaded or otherwise prepared for assembly in a pipe or tubing shop.

Usually production control must treat pipe and tubing much as other parts. But, like wire, there are usually many minor changes during the early days of making a product. When better pathways are found to route pipe from one point to another, or get it out of the way of moving parts, changes are made. Other changes are made whenever pipe can be put in during subassembly instead of final assembly.

PLANNING IN REPAIR SHOPS

Earlier we said that transportation equipment repair shops had difficult production control problems. The most extreme of these is airplane repair so we will use this type of repair as the example. Repairing other kinds of complex products, when done on a large scale, has many of the same problems.

Airplanes are repaired whenever something gets out of order, when improvements have to be installed, or when the plane is brought in on a scheduled basis. Certain types of overhaul are made at specified periods, depending on the number of hours that the airplane has flown. Just when these repairs are to be made depends, in the case of commercial airplanes, on governmental regulations and on company policies. Certain kinds of minor overhaul must be done frequently. Major overhaul is less frequent.

Repairs of airplanes (and to some extent of trucks, taxicabs, railroad engines, and many kinds of factory machines) are hard to plan. You need to plan the product's use so that it is not 1,000 miles away when its turn for repair comes. But you can't schedule crashes, wrecks, or breakdowns. And even on products overhauled on a scheduled basis, you don't know exactly what each individual product needs until you take it apart. So you can't plan repair activities very well because you never know how much work an item will require.

You can, however, use mathematical probability to forecast the expected occurrence of major repair categories and expected repair time. Such forecasting depends of course on your having past experience with such repairs and on your having good records of the required maintenance work.

Briefly stated airplanes are repaired in the following way. We will use the procedure employed by the Bureau of Weapons at its Alameda, California, airplane repair base. Most Air Force repair bases and other Navy bases use similar methods.

PLANNING FOR FUTURE REPAIRS   Airplane repair really starts long before any actual repair work starts. Like original manufacture, it needs some far-ahead planning and is started when the manufacturer of the airplane starts to make it on a production basis.

On every new model (or "configuration") of airplane, an "E and E" (Examination and Evaluation) group from the Navy's repair shop goes to the manufacturer's plant. There the men go over, with the manufacturer's men, every item on the bill of material. At this time E and E decides, for *every* part, where it will get the part for future repair purposes, whether to make or buy it. Repair shops must follow this decision except in emergencies. Normally, if the manufacturer will stock the item, the decision will be to buy it from him rather than to make it.

Back at its own home base E and E also does an actual pilot overhaul of every new type of airplane just to see what will have to be done when such airplanes come in for repair. Doing this right away lets E and E see both the airplane in production in its manufacturer's plant and how to handle its repair when later it comes to the repair base for overhaul.

At this time E and E makes up routings (operation lists) for parts that it will some day have to make at the base. These routings differ, though, from those of the original manufacturer because the work will have to be done on the machines that the repair base has or will have. In most cases the machines the base has are not identical to those the manufacturer uses. And, as we will discuss later, repair parts do not always have to be identical to the originals; they only have to do the same work. Consequently, the routings are often different from those of the original manufacturer.

These E and E routings are not routings as we use the term elsewhere in this book. They do not show lists of operations needed to repair a part. All that they show is the list of departments that will work on a part. This is hardly routing in the usual sense but it is about all that you can do. Picture yourself, for example, trying to make a list of the operations needed to repair a door that doesn't fit just right, or trying to list the operations needed to fix up the pilot's cockpit so that it looks new and shiny.

Out of these initial overhauls, you get more than just a forewarning of problems. You get full sets of computer cards or if you prefer, computer tapes. First, you get a master deck of subassemblies and parts cards. In case your repair parts will be different from the originals, the cards or tapes will refer to parts as you will make them, not to how the original manufacturer made them.

You will also get sets of routing cards, one card for each department which will work on repairs, or, where it is feasible, a card for every operation on a part. These too will describe your own method of rework in all cases where it differs from the original manufacturer's methods. You will also get to punch up move cards and even to punch "day factors" into the operation cards. Day factors are lead times between operations. We talk about lead times in Chapter 18.

Having prepared all of these tabulating cards ahead allows E and E to be ready when any type of airplane comes in for repair. Shop orders covering each part's repair can be made up quickly for all parts needing repair. Normally a shop order covering the repair of a part will be made out listing *all* of the operations that it *might* need. Operations *not* needed are marked out (and the unnecessary move orders are canceled) so that, as the order goes to the shop, it lists only the operations actually needed on the particular part. Both a traveling copy of the shop order and prepared move orders go into an envelope that goes with the item. Move orders, filled in and returned after each move of the item to the next operation, serve as work progress reports.

POOLED PARTS   Repairing airplanes can be simplified considerably by using "pooled" parts. Pooled parts are carried in stock but only in small quantities and on a rotating basis. Parts removed from an airplane are repaired and not put back into the same airplane but rather are put into the part's pooled stock. Long before the part is repaired you could, if you wished, withdraw a new or repaired part from the pooled stock and put it on the airplane being repaired.

Pooling the stock of any part frees parts repair schedules from the reassembly schedule for any particular airplane and speeds up the reassembly. There are times when the repair cycle time for a part is longer than the time you want to wait to get it. Pooling takes care too of the situations when a part is irreparable and a new one will have to be made or bought, either of which would take a long time.

Pooling parts has its bad features. You don't carry spare airplane wings in small spaces. And a single wing may cost hundreds of thousands of dollars. Also, there are quite a few kinds of airplanes, each needing its own pooled parts. And, in the case of wings, you need lefts and rights. Furthermore the government repairs airplanes at several repair bases—not just one.

Admittedly, most pooled parts are less bulky and less costly than airplane wings but you can see that with the thousands of parts you might want to pool, you could easily tie up many millions of dollars in pooled repair parts.

The Navy in its airplane repair shops deals with some 25,000 items (made up of 300,000 or so "bits and pieces") so it doesn't try to pool very many parts, nor does the Air Force with its even bigger repair problems.

E and E decides, during its pilot disassembly of each new configuration of airplane, which parts and subassemblies to pool and which not to pool. You have probably recognized by now that the term pooled parts means just about the same as stocked parts. You carry these items in stock. It differs from our ordinary idea of stocked parts, however, in that many or all of the items in stock are repaired or rebuilt rather than being new.

ACTUAL REPAIR   Upon arrival at the base for repairs, an airplane goes to the E and E center. E and E "inducts" every incoming airplane. Before disassembling it, E and E men try out all of the systems on the ship to see if they work. One after the other, they try out every electrical circuit, every hydraulic line, and every mechanical system.

This helps them decide on the "depth" of repair needed. However, they end up planning for repairs far beyond just fixing up the things that don't work. Just as a garage mechanic can get some idea of how much overhauling your car needs by his driving it around the block, so the E and E men get an idea of an airplane's needed repairs from their systems tryouts.

E and E has available the airplane manufacturer's original bill of materials but not his tooling nor his operation lists for making parts. In the case of old airplane models, E and E might actually have some of the manufacturer's original wing jigs. Remember, though, that the Government repairs airplanes in many locations. Besides Alameda, the Navy also repairs its airplanes at Pensacola, San Diego, Norfolk, and in other locations. The Air Force too has several repair bases. The original manufacturer never did have enough sets of tooling to send to so many places. Furthermore, the various bases do not all have the same kinds of machines that he had and so couldn't use his tooling anyway.

E and E's check-over of the airplane gives it enough information to decide the major repairs needed. It then classifies the repairs and estimates roughly the shop load (the number of man-hours) represented by the work. Next, after comparing to the shop's existing load, it sets schedules for completion of the repairs. It is up to E and E not to overaccept (overload) the shop.

E and E's induction takes place before any disassembly. Out of the induction come instructions covering the general pattern of the repairs. Also, E and E orders immediately any long lead time items which will have to be bought or made.

When you disassemble, you must decide if it should be done completely in one place or in many special disassembly shops. The problems are similar to assembly. Our general rule in assembly is to subassemble as much as possible. Keep work away from the final assembly line. For disassembly, too, it is probably best, as soon as the volume begins to amount to anything, to disassemble first into major components, and then to disassemble them in special areas where you have men who know each component best.

After the first disassembly, which separates the ship's main parts, most repair bases send the big sections of the plane to a series of second shakedown areas, one for the wings, one for landing gear, and so on.

There the further disassembly allows E and E to look at hidden things and to get at the whole depth of overhaul.

During disassembly, care should be taken not to make unnecessary reassembly work. Don't, for example, disassemble sets of parts which you can inspect while assembled and which prove not to need repair. Don't untie bundles of wires any more than necessary. Also, don't disassemble delicate instruments in general disassembly areas.

As the airplane is disassembled a decision is made on the amount of repair needed for each part. Some parts are beyond repair and have to be replaced. If they are stocked parts, they can be withdrawn from stock; otherwise you'll have to plan to buy or make them. Many wearing parts— those that need replacing in nearly every airplane—are stocked so replacement parts are available. For other parts, it is easier for the base to make them than it is to get them from the part's original manufacturer.

Some parts, such as those made of rubber, have a limited shelf life and so have to be made or bought as the need arises rather than carried in stock. This make-buy decision was made earlier, of course, by E and E in its original analysis of how to repair the airplane when it was first made.

"Made" repair parts (those made at the base) often are different in form from the parts they replace. They must replace the old part functionally but they don't have to look like it. A new part replacing a steel casting might be made out of welded angle iron or aluminum or it might be machined out of a solid piece of metal.

Disassembled products whose parts have been repaired are usually reassembled largely in one spot. You have to collect together all of the parts at the time when you need them. If any part is missing when its turn comes to be assembled, this may be a serious matter. Occasionally you can put the missing part on later but in other cases everything must stop. This is particularly serious if, after disassembly, you find that you need a bought part that takes a long time to get. You could easily have a dozen or more nearly finished airplanes sitting around waiting for parts.

QUALITY STANDARDS FOR REPAIR WORK

Have you ever thought that the repair bill for fixing your automobile was too high? Or that you'd rather the garageman would do things less perfectly and at less cost? This is the perennial repair problem: how much repairing to do and how well to do it.

Not only is this question pertinent to deciding what things to repair but it also extends down into many of the individual operations. Left to themselves, men doing repair work (who are usually skilled craftsmen who take pride in their work) will usually spend too much time doing things too perfectly. They will file and fit and shine the parts until they are perfect. But you can't afford all of this "spit and polish."

Nor can you escape this dilemma by having regularly set standards. First of all, standards won't help you answer the question of *what* to repair. Do you, for example, want a small scratch on your automobile fender repainted? Or do you want a minor dent straightened out? You just have to decide each case on its own merits.

But suppose that you have decided that repairs are needed. Picture yourself with a dented fender to be straightened out. How many man-hours should it take to straighten it out? You can hardly have regular time standards to cover this job. About the only way to tell how long it should take is to have an experienced man look at it and make an estimate. This gives you a standard of a sort for this particular job. Probably this is better than having no standard at all because it will put a limit on the time day-workers can spend on the job. And if you want to pay repair men on piece-work, an estimated standard is fairly satisfactory. But if you put the men on piecework, you'll need to inspect their work carefully to see that they do it well enough. Your problem is directly reversed from your being concerned lest they spend too much time to your being concerned lest they spend too little time.

Actually it is very difficult to write specifications covering the quality of repair work to be done. Picture yourself trying to describe the quality you expect when the job is to remove rust or corrosion. Or try describing smoothness or polish. Remember, too, that you, the specification writer, want to ask for the least amount of shininess that will suffice. Also there are questions of the extent of repairs that you want when they don't help functionally. For example, a new coat of paint in the cockpit of an airplane won't help it fly. Should you spend money for it?

REPAIR OR REPLACE?
Another problem in repair and overhaul work is whether or not to repair or replace parts. As you inspect and disassemble products in need of repair you will come to assemblies and to any number of parts which need considerable repair. Should you spend the money repairing them or just throw them away and replace them with new items?

You may ask, "What's the problem?" Do whichever is the less costly. Sometimes this answer is a good answer. But so often you can't tell for sure. You don't know exactly what the repairs will cost and after you do them the repaired part often isn't quite as good as a new part. You may even want to consider the shop's work load before you decide. If the shop needs work, repair the parts instead of buying new ones.

A comparison between airplane repair costs at the Navy's Norfolk, Virginia, and its Alameda, California, repair bases once showed that Norfolk's costs were higher. Investigation showed that Norfolk spent less for labor and more for bought parts than Alameda. It would be hard to say which is better as a general practice but this illustrates the problem.

STUDY MATERIALS

13-1 You have been asked to evaluate a suggestion submitted by an employee that minor items be omitted from bills of materials and stocked as open inventory on the production floor. What factors would you deem to be important in this suggestion evaluation?

13-2 What advantages or disadvantages are associated with detailed, centralized routing relative to a system wherein the majority of routing is left up to the individual foremen?

13-3 While investigating possible routing changes in connection with a proposed volume increase, two points of view have arisen. One group argues that all costs connected with the present method—planning costs, training costs, tools, and fixtures—are sunk costs and should be ignored in future planning. They say that the only important matters are the costs associated with the new method and the expected payback. The other camp argues that all costs must be recovered in the long run and any unrecovered costs from the old method must be charged against the proposed methods change. How do you resolve this argument?

13-4 The assembly department foreman says that, particularly with his newer men, there is some anxiety that maybe they are not putting assemblies together in the quickest and easiest way. He suggests that on the material list, with which the assemblers are thoroughly familiar, you should print a list of the assembly operations.

How would you answer that suggestion?

13-5 To what extent can repair operations be planned? What are the major problem areas in planning repair operations and how do these differ from planning production operations?

13-6 At the present time you are making five parts for product A on general purpose machines at a total cost of $20, for one of each part.

Product A, which uses these parts, is selling at the rate of 1,000 per month. It seems unlikely that its volume will go up. There is a .95 probability that this volume will hold up for a year, .80 for a second year, and .70 for a third year. Lower volumes seem more certain.

Should you put in tooling attachments at a cost of $10,000 if they will reduce the cost of making the five parts to $19? (The tooling is durable and should easily last for three years although because it would be special, it would have little or no ultimate salvage value.)

Should you put in new machines costing $300,000 if they will reduce costs to $12? (These machines will, at the end of three years, be worth 50 per cent of the cost.)

13-7   The Merriweather Stamping Machine Company makes a variety of stamping machines for use with dies for stamping sheet metal. It is economical to manufacture them in lots rather than singly, and accordingly manufacture is to stock. Most of the time there are sales orders for all the machines in a lot by the time it is finished.

The company finds, however, that its customers frequently want certain variations in their machines. These ordinarily involve minor attachments to the machine, but occasionally they affect the design of a major part of the machine. It has been the custom to disassemble the finished machine to whatever extent is necessary and reassemble it according to the customer's order. The usual accessories are kept in stock so that reassembly can take place immediately. If the parts needed are not in stock, rush shortage orders are made out and the parts are made as quickly as possible.

At the time this practice was instituted there was sufficient demand for the company's product so that the customer bought it in its standard form and ordered his accessories as extras. The disassembly and reassembly with the special parts was usually altogether at his expense. Competition soon made it necessary for the Merriweather company to make these changes at its own expense. Changes, of at least minor proportions, were necessary on almost every unit sold. The practice of completing the assembly and later disassembling and reassembling it was wasteful of both money and time.

What problems were responsible for most of the trouble? Should you quote a standard price for the product and yet give the customer a product designed to suit him? Outline a procedure for correcting the difficulty.

chapter fourteen

IDENTIFICATION SYSTEMS AND CALENDARS

IDENTIFICATION SYSTEMS

When you carry thousands of items in raw materials stock and more thousands of parts and end products in finished stock, you just have to have an orderly identification system. Word descriptions are totally inadequate. Look at this one, for example:

> Generator: standard signal for testing radio receivers, carriers, freq range 16 KC to 50 MC power supply, 115–230 V, 40–60 cyc, compen elect. voltage reg with max. input of 140w; General Radio, Type 805C.

Sometimes you need even more words to describe an item completely yet set it apart positively from all other similar items. Admittedly though, you don't find many that are longer than our example and most are much shorter.

Long word descriptions are awkward. Just change or leave out one word in a description and you will soon be confusing one item with another. With word descriptions it is easy to make errors. Number systems aren't perfect either, but they are shorter and that alone helps cut errors. All companies except the smallest supplement full word descriptions of items with identification numbers.

Identifications can be wholly numerical or can use both letters and numbers. Using letters with numbers shortens the identification because you have twenty-four of them (leaving out I and O) to serve as digits instead of 10. Letters can also help identify an item. (When you use letters to help the memory it is called a mnemonic system.) "SL," for example, can mean "sleeves," "SC," "screws," and so on. Maybe, though, you'll need three letters so that you won't mix up screws and scales. But even then you might still mix up screws and screens. You don't have to have the letters to do the whole job however. You can use numerals and identifications several digits long. Most companies don't use letters very much in their numbering, often preferring all numerals and no letters.

Your complete identification system has to cover raw materials, semi-processed materials, and finished products. Also, you must provide for the physical identification of materials and generally for supplies, patterns, tools, dies, jigs, fixtures, and perhaps gages and minor machine attachments.

SETS OF NUMBERS   An ideal system would both *identify* and *classify* all present items and it should have enough extra numbers in each class to take care of future items. And the numbers should be brief. You want a system that classifies items so that all users will have an idea of what each item is from its identification number. It should make numbers easy to remember and it should help in cost accounting. A perfect system would also be capable of indefinite expansion in every major and minor classification. The system should be all-inclusive so that all kinds of items are covered, yet individual item identification numbers must be different. Each item should have a short, unique identification.

Most companies use number systems that assign numbers in such a way that the number indicates the nature of the item. Groups of numbers are assigned to items that are alike in some way. Numbers are really two-part numbers. The left section of the number, the first two or three digits of a longer number, is coded. For example, all numbers from 33,000 to 33,999 might refer to tank types of vacuum cleaners for *home* use, while the 34,000 to 34,999 numbers might cover similar items for tank type vacuum cleaners for *industrial* use. Other series of numbers would cover upright vacuum cleaners and cleaners for other uses.

The last three digits may be assigned consecutively or may represent a further application of codification: 33,100 to 33,199 might, for example, be assigned to parts of the *motor unit* in a home use cleaner. Similar numbers in the 34,000 series (34,100 to 34,199) could cover parts for *motors* for industrial tank type cleaners.

Sometimes, certain round numbers are reserved for whole assemblies. The motor itself would be 33,100 or 34,100, while its parts would be numbered 33,101 to 33,199 and 34,101 to 34,199 respectively. The tank unit, as a whole, might be 33,200 or 34,200, while its parts would be numbered 33,201 to 33,299 and 34,201 to 34,299 respectively. Prefixes (letters or numbers), separated from the rest of the number by a dash, are sometimes used to represent models or types.

If you use number groups for groups of products and also set up your manufacturing departments on a product basis, the numbers will even tell you the department where the item is made. Classified numbers can also be designed to show the order of assembly of parts.

The examples given above for vacuum cleaners are actually much oversimplified. Numbers are often ten to fifteen digits long; consider, for example, the number 1600-A 024504 11284. This number shows that the part goes into product number 1600. The A shows that it is also for the first one produced of product 1600. The 024504 shows that it is part of subassembly number 4. Product 1600 has 10 subassemblies which are numbered 024501 to 024510. The 11284 is the individual piece part number.

This number is one from actual use. In this numbering system, a block of 200 numbers (from 11278 to 11478) is used for the piece parts for product 1600.

The Armed Forces of the United States government carry millions of items in stock. It is almost impossible for them to develop one single orderly classification system. Very long numbers are required. Consider, for example, this number: 2426 6625-186-1399-24555A. It is almost impossibly long. But go back to page 293 to the word description of the generator. Would you prefer to use that description and not this number? This is the number that belongs to that description. The number, long though it is, seems to be better than all the words. You couldn't even get all the words on one tabulating card. You would need three cards.

NUMBER INDEXES   Users of identification systems should know your code system. So you must make up a master list showing product groups and their code numbers. But this is not enough for the people who deal with individual items. They need to know what the right-hand part of the index means too and for this they need an index. You'll need a cross reference file—one list in order of identification number, another with items arranged alphabetically by item description, and a third consisting of a file of products and assemblies with their parts listed.

Large companies sometimes don't cross-index every item. At General Motors' Electro-motive division, the alphabetical parts file is kept *only* for whole products, main parts, and main subassemblies. It is too much work to keep a complete alphabetical file (which would not be used often) for 50,000 items. There is, of course, a file listing items in part number order. (A computer could, however, make up an alphabetical file if it were needed.)

DRAWING NUMBERS AS PART NUMBERS   Products and parts usually have engineering drawings which have to be numbered. You can make the drawing number do double duty by serving also as the part number. Some companies code their drawings by size. Drawings $8\frac{1}{2}$ inches $\times$ 11 inches in size are A drawings, 17 inches $\times$ 22 inches are B, 22 inches $\times$ 34 inches are C. The letter showing a drawing's size becomes part of its identification number. It is a prefix followed by four or five numerals, assigned consecutively as new drawings are made up. Using the drawing's size as part of its number helps locate it in the drawers where the drawings are filed. Incidentally, the drawing number reflects how new or how old it is.

UNCODED SYSTEMS   Small companies sometimes don't try very hard to develop a classified identification system. They just add new numbers for new items and do not use number sets in any classified way. You'd have to use an index book all the time to find out what the numbers meant, but other than this the system is flexible and easy to operate.

DIFFICULTIES WITH CODES

Coded systems assign *groups of numbers* to parts of a single assembled product. The first several places (often the first four places) of the identification number may be the finished product number. These first digits are identical for all parts of the same assembled product, while the right-hand digits are different for each part.

Coded systems have a built-in conflict that is hard to reconcile. You want to give *related* items similar numbers. The difficulty is that items are related or are similar to each other in different ways. Yet your code can recognize only one basis of similarity.

If you base the code on the *use* of the items, all the parts of one product are assigned similar numbers. But if you do this, you will find that you are assigning unlike numbers to items that are alike in other ways. Roller bearings, for example, would have numbers related to their specific use. If you had twenty-five kinds of roller bearings your code based on use would assign them unlike numbers.

Common use parts, those used in several products, also make trouble. If you number them in one product's series, their numbers are out of series for the other products in which they are used. You might set up a separate series of numbers for common parts. But this is not a perfect solution because of changes made in the course of time. Single use parts may become common parts and common parts may be discontinued in one or several products and may become single use parts. If all common parts were numbered in a separate series their part number would have to change when they became single use parts. So would single use parts that become common use parts.

Design changes also make trouble. You may need some new numbers for new parts in a number series where all the numbers have been used up. Then you have to set up a new unrelated series. Even as simple a classification as one for drawings based on their size is affected by changes. Revisions in drawings may cause their size and thus their classification to change, even though the same item is shown.

The static nature of coded systems is also a handicap, and the more changes you have, the more problems this makes. Of necessity you set up your system at a particular time to cover existing needs. Your code is therefore set. It is static, whereas products change continually. You add, remove, or change parts or add or cut out complete products and product lines. Your orderly system is bound to be upset. To some extent you can anticipate changes of this sort and reserve spare number blocks in the original code, but in time they, too, are exhausted. After that, you have to give additional new items numbers unrelated to their proper classification.

Your code misses the mark if people don't understand it and if they don't know something about the item when they see its number. The whole purpose of a code is to convey, through a number, to all who use it, some idea of the nature of the item. Out-of-series numbers don't convey such meanings unless users of the system learn the exceptions. But when out-of-series numbers become too numerous, the system does not carry out its purpose. Users of the numbers will forget some of the exceptions and the system won't help much. Setting up a supplementary index system will help, but if, in the long run, you have too many exceptions you will have to overhaul the system. Overhauling it is, however, a very big job.

In multi-plant companies, identification systems are usually only plant-wide or, at most, divisionwide. Billion dollar companies never would have enough numbers to put all their divisions on one system.

FINISHED PARTS IDENTIFICATION

Many companies use a part's drawing number as its part number. However, this works only if finished parts have drawings. For other parts, a coded system can be used. You have several choices as to which base for similarity to use. You can use the *use* of the part or its *type, size,* or *color*. When identifying raw material, the kind of material from which the item is made provides another base. For raw materials, the *kind of material* is the most commonly used basis of setting identification numbers.

The significant basis of similarity of finished parts is their *nature* or *use* rather than the material of which they are made. Consequently, you don't try to set their number classifications to reflect the materials from which they are made. Gears, for example, could have similar numbers because they are similar in *nature*. You could reserve a block of numbers for gears. Then set apart subgroups of numbers for spur gears, helical gears, and bevel gears. Within each subclass could be further subclasses to show diameter, number of teeth, tooth shape, diametrical pitch, and so on. Figure 1-3, on page 4, gives you a little idea of the problem.

More likely, however, gears would be numbered according to their *use*. When numbered this way they take numbers in the series of the products into which they go.

A system based on what gears are *made of* would give completely different numbers to steel and nylon gears. But it would give similar numbers to nylon gears and nylon panels for mounting electrical controls. This seems less logical for finished parts than to use a number series showing their *use*.

In codes based on use, the identification number of single use parts not covered by separate drawings often includes the assembled product number as part of the symbol. Either numbers or letters can be used. RC14-1, for example, might be the identification for part of an automatic record changer, model 14. Other parts would be RC14-2, RC14-3, etc.

Occasionally certain small, inexpensive parts (the "use" items referred to on page 269) are not shown on bills of materials and are not given code numbers. Nails, tacks, washers, and possibly screws, nuts, bolts, rivets, etc., may be omitted for simplicity's sake. Just consider them as supplies and always keep an ample stock of them. It is hardly necessary to keep stock record cards for such items because they can be reordered by description. But if their use is irregular you may have to give them numbers and list them on bills of material so that you can calculate how many your assembly orders will need.

MAKING PARTS BEFORE NUMBERS ARE ASSIGNED

You don't assign part numbers until design is complete. Normally this requirement does not cause trouble because you finish the design before you start production. But sometimes you just can't wait that long to start manufacture on hurry-up jobs.

You can, if you must, start manufacture using a preliminary drawing (or just a sketch) so far as design is concerned. (Of course, you may have to change the design before it is finished—this is a risk you run.) If you do start to manufacture before you even have part numbers, you can identify shop orders for parts by the product's assembly order number or the sales department's contract number. Or you can just make up some new numbers to identify parts temporarily until the official identification number is decided. Then the whole temporary number system can be replaced with the regular number.

PARTS NUMBERS FOR EXPERIMENTAL MODELS

Parts of experimental products need identification numbers. But you should not give them regular numbers because the design is not finally set—in fact, the product may never get beyond the experimental stage.

Most experimental models are, however, forerunners of models that do go into production. For that reason it is a good idea, even though not mandatory, to give their parts the numbers they will have if the product does go into production. This reduces renumbering later. You can put the model number or just the letter XP in front of every part number. Later when you go into production, you can drop the prefix and use the rest of the number in the regular way.

SEMIFINISHED PARTS IDENTIFICATION

Parts in process need identification in job lot work but not, as a rule, in continuous production. When the same things are made day after day in limited variety, everyone knows what the partly made items are just by looking at them. But items made only now and then need identification. A tote pan of steel pieces doesn't tell you what they are.

Materials in process nearly always carry the number they will have as finished parts. In job lot work they are invariably accompanied by a traveling copy of the shop order which provides full identification. If there are several tote pans of material to an order, each pan has a tag identifying it as part of the order.

In job lot work, orders do not move fast through the shop. Waits between operations may last for days. Even though you may have large temporary storage areas frequently, so much in-process material is stored that the areas are full and overflowing. Orders are sometimes stacked on top of one another. You can lose orders even though each one has its identification tag. You just don't know what is in a tote pan, two layers back and one layer down. Proper identification alone is not enough; orderly storage of jobs is also necessary.

Batch manufacturing also requires materials in process to be identified. In the rubber industry, for example, batches (weighing perhaps 1,000 pounds) of rubber, carbon black, and other ingredients are masticated and mixed into a consistent mass. But rubber companies use many different mixtures so they need to identify each batch. They use a system that applies only to batches.

In the next operation, cotton, rayon, or nylon fabric is coated with the rubber mixture. This time the product, instead of being in batches, is in the form of rolls of coated material which have to be identified by an individual system. The system used is like that used for raw materials in that it is based on the material's composition and form rather than on its use or type. Since the form of the material is changed substantially several times, it is necessary that it be identified throughout.

RAW MATERIALS IDENTIFICATION

Nearly always you will find it best to number raw materials according to the *material* from which they are made. You can also code them to show chemical content or physical properties. SAE 1040 steel, for example, is a coded number. The SAE means that it is a standard of the Society of Automotive Engineers. The 1 shows it to be carbon steel. The 0 shows that it contains no other metal. The 40 shows that it contains 0.40 per cent carbon. SAE 2340 steel is nickel steel. The 2 shows that it contains nickel. The 3 shows that it contains 3 per cent nickel. The 40, as in 1040, shows the carbon content. If the first number were 5, instead of 3, it would be chromium steel, 7 would be tungsten steel, etc.

Four digits are not enough to identify many items. Most companies use much longer numbers. The International Business Machines Corporation uses a nine digit system to identify raw materials and supply items. The first two numbers on the left show the kind of material or the type of supplies. The third digit indicates the form or shape. The next three places show the chemical composition, while the last three show the size of the item. Here is how IBM's system works:

First two digits:

Metallic materials

01   Aluminum
02   Unassigned
03   Copper, brass, bronze
04   Unassigned
05   Iron
06   Steel—carbon
07   Steel—alloy, except tool and
       N. E.
08   Steel—tool
09   Steel—national emergency
10   Unassigned
11   Unassigned
12   Magnesium
13   Unassigned
14   Zinc
15   Unclassified metallic
       materials

Nonmetallic materials

16   Unassigned
17   Card stock
18   Unassigned
19   Laminated insulating
       material
20   Insulated wire
21   Unassigned
22   Paper, except card stock
23   Plastics
24   Unassigned
25   Rubber
26   Unassigned
27   Wood
28   Unassigned
29   Unclassified nonmetallic
       materials

Supply materials

30   Abrasives
31   Acids, chemicals

32 Unassigned
33 Belting—hose
34 Brushes—brooms
35 Building material
36 Unassigned
37 Candy, soft drinks, tobacco
38 Conduit—pipe, fittings
39 Contains
etc.
77 Small tools—carbides

78 Stationery supplies
80 Technical and medical
      supplies
81 Textiles, fiber
82 Unassigned
83 Waste material
84 Wearing apparel
85 Wooden articles
86 Unassigned
etc.

Third digit:

Form or shape

0 Special forms   Castings, forgings, and special extruded shapes, identified by part number.

1 Round   A solid round section having a continuous periphery and furnished in straight lengths, excluding wire.

2 Square   A solid square section with four equal sides and four equal angles, furnished in straight lengths, excluding wire.

3 Hexagonal   A solid hexagonal section with six equal sides and six equal angles, furnished in straight lengths.

4 Strip sheet   A solid rectangular section up to and including 0.249 inch in thickness. Widths up to 24 inches will be designated as strip, 24 inches and over as sheet.

5 Flat   A solid rectangular section 0.250 inch and over in thickness in any width.

6 Tubing   A hollow section having a continuous periphery, either seamless or welded, including piping.

7 Wire   Flat or round wire and cable, not covered.

8 Powder   Metal in powdered form.

9 Misc. forms   Commercial shapes such as angles, channels, etc. Also any form not otherwise classified.

The remaining six places of the code, showing chemical composition and size, are too lengthy for us to show here. They are, of course, covered in the company's master code book.

International Harvester uses a system similar to that of IBM. At IH the first three digits tell the nature of the item, the first two being broad general classes. The third digit is a finer breakdown. Here is the IH system:

First two digits:

Broad classes

00 Pig iron
01 Steel, manufactured
02 Steel, purchased
03 Tubing and pipe, steel
04 Nonferrous metals
05 Scrap
06 Lumber
07 Duck and canvas
08 Unassigned
09 Rubber and rubberized raw
    material
10 Axles and parts purchased
11 Allied equipment
12 Bearings antifriction
13 Bearings friction
14 Belts and belting

15 Bodies, cabs, frames, etc.

Third digit: (subdivision of class 15
used here for illustration)

150 All bodies, cabs, frames
151 Bodies, cabs, motor truck
    hoists
152 Other allied equipment for
    motor truck hoists
153 Frames and frame parts
    purchased
154 Seats, seat cushions, seat
    frames
155 Bumpers
156 Fenders
157 Doors
158 Shock absorbers
159 All other

Several more digits following the first three are required to identify each item fully. At IH, as in most companies, the first three digits of every number are also the account numbers used by the accounting department. In the accounting department, account number 156, for example, shows the value of all fenders (of all kinds) on hand.

Not all purchased items are raw materials; many are finished parts or products. They go into final products without your doing any processing on them yourself. Such items are generally identified in your *finished parts numbering series*—not in your raw materials series. Of course, if the item is a standard catalog item with the vendor, he thinks of it in terms of his number. Your purchasing people would have to order it using *his* number on the purchase order. But after you get it, you use your own number for it.

Occasionally this makes a little trouble. Warner-Swasey lathes, for example, sometimes are powered by Bodine Electric Company motors. Companies using Warner-Swasey lathes sometimes order new motors directly from Bodine but use Warner-Swasey's part number for the motor. Bodine must find out from Warner-Swasey which motor is wanted.

Government contract work sometimes complicates your numbering system. On some contracts the government buys and furnishes many items to you. Sometimes the items are the same as items you stock regularly for your regular jobs. The government, though, will usually insist that you keep the supply it sends you apart from your other stock. Also you will have to identify the parts sent by its number, not yours. For some items you will have the same parts stocked two places and under two different numbers.

All of this extra work may, however, not be as wasteful as it seems because the government-furnished items may not be truly like your regular stock. They may have been manufactured to different performance specifications and may have undergone much more rigid testing than regular products go through. They may also have come from a different supplier whose product reliability record is excellent.

Some companies making products for the government occasionally buy their standard parts from someone else. But they renumber the item and list it as a specially made item and price it for repair purposes at the price of a special. Probably this is sometimes done with private customers but it is harder to detect on the tremendously complex defense items the government buys. Needless to say, customers think less of the seller if they detect this practice. It is not a way to develop good customer relations.

SUPPLIES IDENTIFICATION

Supply items differ from most raw materials. You use up supply items within the company without their going into products for sale. Many of them, such as grinding wheels or wheels for your industrial trucks, are finished products. Many supply materials—lumber, glass, paint—are used by the maintenance department. Others, such as lubricating or cutting oils, tool steel, and grinding wheels, are used by manufacturing departments. In addition, solder, glue, and paint are used up a little here and a little there in the product itself.

Because there are many kinds of supplies, you may need a more complex identification system for them than for materials going into products. Most supplies have trade names and vendor catalog numbers. You can identify tool steel, for example, by its SAE specification number. Lumber, paint, roofing materials, electric wire, electric fixtures, and plumbing fixtures used by the maintenance department can also be referred to by their commonly used trade names.

Many companies, particularly small companies, never set up an identification system for supplies. Instead, they order by trade name or by description. Occasionally no official inventory of them is carried. The maintenance department and the toolroom foremen order whatever supplies they need, and as soon as the items come in they charge out all of them as if they had used them all, even though the materials will last for several months. No stock record cards are kept. Handling supplies this way does not produce the most accurate cost records and probably results in wasteful use of materials, but it avoids the use of an identification system and it saves record keeping.

Nondrawing items (items having no engineering drawing) used in the product itself need numbers, perhaps in a number group just for such items. Then bills of material can specify exactly what you want. Without numbers, you'd have to describe such items on bills of material in words. This would be too cumbersome.

PHYSICAL IDENTIFICATION OF MATERIALS
Most materials are not self-identifying. Even an old hand can't tell just by looking what most of your raw materials are or what half-made products in process are going to be made into. You have to mark or tag them to show what they are. This is particularly important in job lot work where you have so many different jobs.

There are several ways that you can identify materials: (1) put mark-

FIGURE 14-1   Orbit Valve Company uses a scotch-tape type of adhesive to identify bar stock and tubing. (Orbit Valve Co.)

ings on the item so that it carries its own identification; (2) fasten a tag to the item; (3) attach a tag to the container in which the item is put; (4) put a tag on the storage bin or location in the case of stored materials. Most of the time the identification is attached to the bin or container, since this way one tag identifies the whole stock.

Metal parts and printed materials, such as pages for a book or textile fabrics, may have their part numbers molded, stamped, etched, dyed, or painted on. You can do this whenever the marks won't be removed by later processes but not if the marking weakens the product or mars its appearance. In the food products industries, machinery parts can't be stamped or etched lest food particles catch in the roughened surface.

Steel bars and sheet metal are often identified by colored stripes painted on the end or edge of their piles. Metal castings can have their numbers embossed on them when they are made or the numbers can be painted on later. In foundries it is necessary for all patterns and core boxes to carry identification tags while in use.

For materials in process, identification is relatively simple as long as the tags or "travelers" (copies of the work order) remain on the container. Occasionally they get lost and you have to figure out what the half-made parts are. Sometimes you even have to use chemical or physical tests (such as spark tests) to find out the material used in the unidentified items.

Probably your hardest identification problems arise in customer repair service. The customer sends in a worn or broken piece and asks for another to replace it. Often, particularly on old products, he tells you nothing about the catalog number of the part or even the number of the product into which it fits. He just sends you the worn part. Even if the part originally carried an identification, it is often gone. The part may be so worn that it is hard to figure out what it is. The receiving clerk may have to search a good while before he finds an old employee who recognizes the item.

NUMBERS AS "COVER–UPS"
Television companies have trouble with men stealing popular-sized transistors and other parts. There is a ready market outside where employees can sell what they can pilfer. One way to hold this down is to intentionally put wrong identification numbers on the popular items. This isn't a perfect solution to the problem since some of your employees will have to know the right number but it cuts out some of the pilfering.

Eastman Kodak has another problem. Some of its mixing formulas for emulsions on film, for example, are secret. In the mixing operations the men mix materials by number and do not know the name of the material involved. Perhaps Eastman would use numbers regardless, but by using numbers no one learns the secret formulas. Eastman even goes so far as to put wrongly calibrated thermometers in rooms where temperature is held at certain levels for processing purposes. These precautions protect Eastman against men quitting and taking company secrets elsewhere.

INDENT SYSTEMS

Airplane and space missile companies use a double numbering system. First, there is the regular numbering system for all products and parts just as you find in other industries. Besides this they have a second method called an "indent," "indenture," or "index" system. Although indent numbers have advantages which could be helpful in other industries, their use so far seems to have spread only to the electronics industry.

Airplane companies use indent numbers in scheduling the manufacture of parts and assemblies *made in lots. Throughout our discussion, every time that we refer to using indent numbers for scheduling we are speaking of parts and subassemblies made in lots, not those made continuously.* Most parts and many assemblies are made in lots and not continuously. Most airplane companies send several thousand new shop orders covering the production of parts and subassemblies in lots out to the shop every week.

The length of time it takes to make an airplane makes a problem. You want some parts soon, yet other parts are not needed until next year. Making up schedules so that things arrive when you want them is a very difficult task. And with ordinary scheduling procedures it would become impossibly difficult when you started to change designs, quantities, and product finishing schedules.

Indent numbers show how each part enters the airplane and how long it takes to make it. This tells when you will have to have it finished and from that you can figure out when to start each item's manufacture.

The scheduling department releases shop orders to the factory on a group basis. Indent numbers tell them which to release every week. The shop orders, which are made up considerably in advance, are held until the scheduling department issues the group releases. How these releases are made is explained in Chapter 20. Here we are concerned with the indent numbers themselves.

Every major and every minor subassembly and each individual piece part has an indent number. It tells you:

1 the *stage of assembly* where parts enter into the airplane

2 the *form* in which parts enter the plane, whether directly as parts or as component parts of assemblies or subassemblies

3 the *manufacturing time* required to make parts and to put together assemblies and subassemblies for all parts and assemblies

Notice that different parts with different identification numbers sometimes have the same indent number. They would be the same if they were components of the same assembly and if the manufacturing cycle time for the parts were identical.

Roughly here is how Lockheed's indent system works. It is a three-digit number, the first digit being set off from the other two digits by a dash. The first digit, the one on the left, shows how the item enters the completed airplane:

1 A part entering final assembly as a detail
2 Engine
3 Empennage (tail assembly)
4 Rear fuselage
5 Wing
6 Front fuselage
etc.

The second digit shows how a part enters the assembly:

1-0 as a detail
2-0 the engine itself
3-0 the empennage itself
4-0 the rear fuselage itself
etc.
3-1 parts entering the empennage as details
3-2 subassemblies going directly into the empennage
3-3 parts going into subassemblies going into the empennage
3-4 sub-subassemblies
etc.

The third digit covers the manufacturing time required (the manufacturing "span") to make parts:

3-11 parts entering the empennage as details and which can be made in one week
3-12 parts entering the empennage as details but which take two weeks to make
etc.

Without certain arbitrary rules indent numbers cannot convey all the information they are supposed to.

1 All lots of *parts* must be completed and in stock at *least three* weeks before the first part in the lot is needed for assembly.

2 All lots of *assemblies* must be completed and in stock at least *one and one-half* weeks before the first one is used.

3 *Parts* lots are given fixed "make spans" or manufacturing times stated in weeks *up to nine weeks*, depending on the item. Only unusual items are allowed more.

4 *Assembly* lots *must* be assembled in *one week*.

5 Assemblies cannot be made in lots for more than two "generations."

Having parts and assemblies ready well before they are needed provides a "cushion." It gives a little extra time to get delayed orders into stock. During this time, of course, extreme pressure is put forth to get late orders finished. Having things in stock ahead also gives time to "call out" the stock, that is, to withdraw it from the store room and to take it to its appropriate location in the assembly department.

The arbitrary one week make-span for assemblies may seem unreasonable. Certainly some assemblies take more man-hours to put together than others but this causes no trouble. It is taken care of by assigning more men to jobs requiring many man-hours. Doing this takes care of most cases. But if it is still impossible to put together an assembly in a week, it might better go on a continuous basis and not be made in lots. The *final assembly* of an airplane could not, for example, be completed in one week, nor could the final assembly of most of its major component assemblies. They are, therefore, made continuously.

Before explaining the fifth rule above, it may be well to give examples to show how indent numbers show lead time. First example: a 3-11 part is a piece part which takes one week to make and which is used directly in the empennage as a piece part. And how does the number 3-11 tell us all of this? The "3" shows that it is a part of the empennage. The first "1" shows that it goes into the empennage as a piece part. The second "1" shows that it takes one week to make a lot of that part. Next, how can we use this number to show lead time for scheduling purposes? Rule one requires a time cushion of three weeks for piece parts. That means that any lot of 3-11 parts must be finished and in stock three weeks before the first item of the lot goes into the empennage of the airplane. Since it takes one week to make a lot of the part, any order to make a lot of this part must, therefore, be started into manufacture *four* weeks before the first item is to be used.

Second example: a 3-34 part is a piece part of a subassembly going into the empennage. It takes four weeks to make a lot of the parts. This part needs to start into manufacturing *nine and one-half* weeks before the first subassembly goes into the empennage. We arrive at nine and one-half weeks as follows: *Subassemblies* need *to be in stock* one and one-half weeks before the first one is needed (rule two). One week is needed *to put together the subassemblies* (rule four). So assembly must start two and one-half weeks before even the first subassembly is needed for putting into the final assembly. The *parts* need *to be finished* three weeks before that (rule one) so the lot of 3-34 parts must be finished five and one-half weeks ahead. Since it takes four weeks *to make the lot of parts* it must be started at least nine and one-half weeks ahead.

One may wonder at the seeming liberal time allowances between the completion of making parts or subassemblies and their use. We said above that this is for safety and for call out time. With thousands of orders in process some are bound to fail to get done in time. In the airplane industry the *progress of orders through operations is not checked by the central production control department.* Orders are checked only when they should be complete. The foremen are expected to meet the completion dates set. *Foremen who don't, don't stay foremen!* In the case of the relatively few items which do not get completed on time, expediting is started immediately. Because ample time has been provided between making and using parts and assemblies the expediting can be effective. Only a very small proportion of orders finally is delinquent. They, of course, can be vitally important, hence the emphasis on getting shop orders out in time.

The make-spans provided for most parts are "fat." The lots can, by reducing the dead time between operations, be made in much less than the time allowed. This gives the manufacturing departments considerable leeway. Usually they can shuffle orders about and still have no trouble meeting the wanted job completion dates.

Sometimes PERT mathematical systems (as described in Chapter 21) are used to determine the critical items on the schedule. PERT/Cost can also be used to decide cost-time trade-offs when it is desirable to shorten a time schedule.

Lot sizes ordinarily are not varied. They are set by the planning department at quantities to cover the number of parts or subassemblies needed to make a fixed number of airplanes. Maybe this number is the number of airplanes that will be made in a two-month period. Of course, as the learning curve operates, the number of airplanes produced in two months increases. *Don't change the lot size though.* True, the lots will no longer keep final assembly going for two months but all that you have to do is to order standard lots more often.

Earlier, the explanation of rule five concerning generations was postponed. Now we come back to it. *A generation is a stage of assembly.* The fuselage of an airplane is a major assembly—it is one generation. The front part of the fuselage is assembled by itself before it becomes part of the whole fuselage. It is a second generation. The instrument panel, another generation, goes into the forward fuselage as a unit. On the panel are various instruments and dials. They are themselves assemblies before they are put into the panel and are another generation. Some products are made up of assemblies which contain other assemblies which contain still other assemblies, etc., up to eight or nine generations.

Rule five states that assemblies shall not be made in *lots* for more than two generations. There may be eight or nine generations of assemblies but all but the first two *must be made continuously—not in lots*. Lockheed, whose system we have been describing, does not make in lots subassemblies which go into other assemblies, also made in *lots*, etc. With so many generations some things would have to start long, long before the item gets into the airplane. Stocks of made up subassemblies would be large and design changes, if made, would have to be made on substantial stocks of components already in subassembly form. Hence the rule concerning production by lots for two generations only.

Going back a moment to indent systems, all airplane companies use indent systems but no two are exactly alike. They differ in the makespans and the cushions normally carried. Most of them do not try to have the indent number show the generation of subassembly when there are several generations.

SIMPLIFIED CALENDARS

In scheduling, you have to set dates when things start and stop, or at least the dates by which work is to be finished. You must convert workdays into calendar days. A 16-workday task, started into production sometime during Tuesday, August 16, should be finished sometime during Thursday, September 8, 23 calendar days later. Your 16 workdays become 23 calendar days.

When thousands of parts need to be made for a product, you have to coordinate their manufacturing schedules. Each must get done at the right time. Thousands of dates for completing operations must be set. Because our regular calendar is cumbersome and contains irregularities, many companies use simplified calendars. Simplified calendars are of four kinds: (1) numbered days within a calendar year; (2) numbered weeks within a calendar year; (3) "13-month" years; and (4) thousand-day calendars.

Before discussing simplified calendars perhaps we should mention that you can show production periods with a shortened regular calendar which will take up only four columns on your tabulating card.

Use only the last digit of the year, two digits for the month, and one digit for the part of the month. Thus, 8093 is the third work period in September, 1968. The 8 tells you that it is 1968. The 09 is September and the

3 is the third period in the month. Adel Division of General Metals Corporation uses this method and divides each month into 10-day periods. At Adel the above date would be in the last third of September. The middle third of June, 1968, would be 8062.

NUMBERED DAYS

Some companies, such as Burroughs Corporation, maker of office machines, number the workdays in each year and then use these day numbers instead of regular calendar dates for all inside scheduling.

A minor reason for using workday or workweek calendars is that they save columns on tabulating cards. Workweek numbers are two or three digits long. Regular dates take four columns. If both start and finish dates go on the card, it saves columns for each date. Cards can take only so much information. Sometimes it is almost impossible to get everything on them. Saving columns on tabulating cards can be important.

NUMBERED WEEKS

Many companies, such as International Business Machines, number the weeks of the year from 1 to 52. Week number 1 is the first week of the year but if January 1 comes on a Wednesday, week number 1 starts Monday, December 30. Some, but not all, companies add another digit, 1 to 5, to show the days of the week (or up to 7 if Saturdays and Sundays are possible workdays). Day number 12-3 is Wednesday of the twelfth week of the year.

Week numbers are easier to use in scheduling than calendar dates. A 16-day task (assuming a 5-day workweek) takes 3 weeks and 1 day. If it starts during day 16-4, it should finish during day 19-5. Of course, the schedules must allow for holidays if there are any within the workweeks concerned. July 4th, if it comes on a workday, cuts out one day in week number 27.

Some companies do not add a third digit to show the day of the week. They schedule work only to the nearest week. However, for many companies this is not close enough.

"THIRTEEN—MONTH" YEARS

National Cash Register uses a 13-month year. The year is divided into 13 four-week periods. Like the numbered workweeks, each period begins on a Monday. Days are numbered like workweeks, except that they go up to 20. Also, like workweeks, there is a day or two at the beginning or end of each year that goes with the year before or after.

Thirteen-month periods have advantages in scheduling total work loads. Except for holidays within the week, every period has 20 regular workdays. You can expect the same output in all periods. With regular calendars, February and March production totals have to be different just because of the different number of workdays. In fact, March's *daily* production could even be lower than February's yet its total higher because of the extra days.

Thirteen-month periods do not save columns on tabulating cards but, compared to regular dates, they don't lose anything either. With regular calendars, November 24 would require four tabulating card columns. It would be punched as 1124. With 13-month periods it would be, say, the fifteenth day of the twelfth period. So it would be punched 1215.

Thirteen-month periods have advantages in accounting. We won't discuss them here but we might note that having periods identical in length makes it easy to set budgets for comparing periods.

THOUSAND–DAY CALENDARS
Thousand-day calendars are used throughout the airplane industry and by some other companies. Thousand-day calendars can start at any time. The first workday is day 000. Future workdays are numbered consecutively from 001 to 999. Usually there are about 250 workdays in a year so the calendar lasts for about four years. Then the numbers start in again at 000. Reusing numbers causes no trouble because four years go by before they are reused.

Only regular workdays are numbered. Saturdays, Sundays, holidays, and other known nonworkdays (as, for example, the days you know you will lose if the plant closes down for two weeks of summer vacation) are omitted. Of course, if heavy work loads cause work on Saturdays or other nonworkdays those days are extra. Mostly, however, you do not work Saturdays unless operations are behind schedule. If this is the case, the extra day needs no number because the work done then was supposed to have been done on a regular numbered day that is already past.

Thousand-day calendars are especially helpful in the airplane industry (or any industry) where it takes a long time to make products and where thousands of activities need to be coordinated. Some of the activities take place a year or more apart. Giant airplanes often are more than a year in the making. Part of the planning must be done as much as two years before the airplane is finished. You get rid of any possible confusion over identical dates in different years.

Airplane factories may issue to the plant more than 10,000 shop orders to make parts *every week*. Preparing these orders is an enormous task. Ordinarily you make them out several weeks before you issue them so that there will be no "hitches" about their being available on time. When you make them out, put the start and finish date on every order—but use workday numbers not regular calendar dates. This is a big advantage if the schedule is changed before they are issued to the shop or even after the shop orders are handed out to the shop.

But how does this help if the schedule is changed? It helps because all you do to shift a whole schedule is to change the tie-in of workday numbers with actual calendar dates. In the case of airplanes, you don't have to change the dates on the thousands of orders ready for the shop and in the shop. Suppose that you have to move back to July 1 a contract originally scheduled to start on June 1. All that you have to do is to assign the original June 1 workday to July 1. If June 1 was originally workday 150, July 1 would have been, say, workday 170. After the change, July 1 becomes workday 150 and some still later date becomes workday 170.

You can also reassign workday numbers when orders get behind schedule so much that they are rescheduled rather than brought back to the original schedule. If, over a period of time, production falls a week behind schedule, and if you don't have to catch up to the old schedule, just reassign the day numbers.

Reassigning workday numbers changes the whole future tie-in as well as the present. If July 1 shifts from 170 to 150, it goes down twenty numbers. So does August 1, September 1, and every future regular calendar day. If August 1 and September 1 had been 214 and 235, they go down twenty numbers and become 194 and 215.

Notice what this does to shop orders. It holds them back so that the parts and subassemblies are held back. They won't be finished on the old schedule and so won't arrive in finished parts stock a month too soon. Yet none of the thousands of dates (workday numbers) on the orders need to be changed.

Similarly, if the *rate of production is increased*, products originally intended to be made during one period must be made sooner. Suppose that June 1 was day number 150 but that you want to increase production. Just make it become day number 160. Now all the work originally scheduled for the middle of June is due to be completed on the first. Parts and components schedules are automatically moved up if the workday calendar is moved. If July 1 used to be day 170, making it day number 178 means that things have to be done eight workdays sooner than before the change, and still you don't have to change any dates on the shop orders.

DISADVANTAGES OF SIMPLIFIED CALENDARS

So far simplified calendars sound good, but they have some disadvantages which usually are not serious. The disadvantages are usually more pronounced with thousand-day calendars than with the others. They extend over a longer period and are less like regular calendars.

The first disadvantage is that you have to print up coded calendars showing actual dates and their numerical equivalent. Everyone in the organization having anything to do with scheduling or meeting schedules has to have a calendar showing actual dates and their workday equivalents. And if you reassign the day numbers you have to destroy all of the old calendars and substitute new ones.

A second disadvantage is that sometimes you have to reinterpret workday numbers back to actual dates (although this is easy to do when everyone has a conversion calendar in front of him). If today is day number

SHOP CALENDAR

Calendar Day / Work Day Number	SUNDAY	MONDAY	TUESDAY	WEDNESDAY	THURSDAY	FRIDAY	SATURDAY
	JANUARY						
Calendar Day / Work Day Number		1	2 / **1**	3 / **2**	4 / **3**	5 / **4**	6
Calendar Day / Work Day Number	7	8 / **5**	9 / **6**	10 / **7**	11 / **8**	12 / **9**	13
Calendar Day / Work Day Number	14	15 / **10**	16 / **11**	17 / **12**	18 / **13**	19 / **14**	20
Calendar Day / Work Day Number	21	22 / **15**	23 / **16**	24 / **17**	25 / **18**	26 / **19**	27
					FEBRUARY		
Calendar Day / Work Day Number	28	29 / **20**	30 / **21**	31 / **22**	1 / **23**	2 / **24**	3
Calendar Day / Work Day Number	4	5 / **25**	6 / **26**	7 / **27**	8 / **28**	9 / **29**	10

FIGURE 14-2 Matching workday numbers against calendar dates. (International Business Machines Corp.)

179 and certain things must be done by day number 226 that doesn't mean as much to most of us as saying that it has to be done by August 20. And, of course, all outside contacts, such as setting delivery dates for things that we buy, have to carry actual dates. Our workday number is meaningless to outsiders.

The third disadvantage applies only to numbered weeks and 13-month years, not to thousand-day calendars. Both week numbers and 13-month years have to allow for the year being 365 days not 364. A year is 52 weeks or 13 four-week periods *plus one day*. Also every four years one must allow for February 29. The extra days finally add up to seven. All that you need to do is, when the extras come to seven days, to have a 53-week year or one five-week period along with 12 normal four-week periods.

A fourth disadvantage of simplified calendars is the trouble that you get into if you work days you hadn't planned as workdays. As we said earlier this is usually not serious. Planned nonworkdays usually become workdays only so that work behind schedule can catch up.

A fifth disadvantage of simplified calendars is perhaps more a limitation to an advantage than it is a disadvantage. Workday numbers work best when the whole factory or whole section is working on one contract. Then everything is tied to the same workday schedule. A sign, changed daily, can be hung in each department showing the current day number. It applies to all work being done. If day numbers are reassigned, the change affects everything alike. *But if you have many or even several different contracts* and if day numbers change on some contracts and not on others, you run into trouble. Every day has several workday numbers, one for each contract. July 1 might be day 192 on one contract, day 211 on another, and day 220 on still another contract.

Actually, North American Rockwell has just this situation and it still uses the workday calendar. From the ceiling of each department hangs a sign listing some five or six contract numbers and the workday number for the current date for each contract. Obviously this trouble would be worse if you had many rather than few contracts.

STUDY MATERIALS

14-1 "Classified identification systems are superior to other systems." Discuss this statement.

14-2 The Ace Corporation's engineering design department frequently releases drawings for parts ahead of those for complete assemblies. These drawings are not identified to show what assemblies they will be used on. The drawings cannot be identified at that time, according to the design department, because it does not know exactly how the assembly will be made up, what parts will be sub-assembled, or how many parts there will be, and it therefore does not know what numbers to assign. Numbers are assigned after the assembly design is complete.

The purpose of releasing drawings ahead is to permit parts manufacture to get under way in order to speed up the whole project's completion. In the Ace company the engineering department tells production control how many of each of these advanced drawing parts to make up. The production control department has raised an objection to making parts for which no identification number has been set, because of the likelihood that identification of such parts when finished would be difficult. The production control department suggests that blocks of numbers be reserved for the parts for each anticipated sub-assembly and that numbers be assigned as the parts are designed. The design engineering department claims that that will not solve the problem since there might not be enough numbers saved to cover the parts of a subassembly. Furthermore, the subassemblies finally decided upon would often be different from those anticipated during the parts design work.

Should all parts bear numbers which classify them as parts of a particular subassembly of a particular product? Even if the parts are unnumbered, should that cause any difficulty in their identification? Should parts drawings be released and parts made before the final design of the product is complete? In the case above, where has the authority to produce come from? Should the production control department authorize the production of the parts in the situation above?

14-3   At times the Brass & Bronze Bushing and Bearing Company has had difficulty because of unidentified tote boxes of partially made bearings. The situation sometimes arises from identification tags getting lost, but more frequently it is caused by machine operators. Most of the machines are almost altogether automatic, and the operator has little to do but fill the feed hopper and remove the tote boxes filled with products. The boxes are placed below the machine, and the products as they leave the machine slide down a chute and accumulate in the tote box. A machine operator "operates" several machines. Besides handling the material he gages the material and resets machines if they get out of adjustment. Some of the machines must be stopped when a new supply of parts is put into the hopper, and some must be stopped to remove the finished work.

Idle machine time reduces the operator's bonus, so he lets the tote box below the machine get full almost to overflowing before he removes it. A job may come to his workplace in 10 tote boxes, each one containing an identification tag. Because the boxes are overloaded, the order leaves in 8 tote boxes and the operator destroys the 2 extra tags. Truckers sometimes empty part of the material from the overloaded boxes into empty tote boxes so that they can stack them one on top of the other on their trucks. Thus the order may arrive at the next operation in 11 boxes but with 8 tags. Even if the trucker does not rearrange the material, the machine operator at the next operation may not want to handle such heavy boxes (overfull boxes weigh up to 125 pounds) and so may send the order away from his operation in 12 or more boxes, some of which are unidentified.

Do all tote boxes need to be individually identified? (Remember that many kinds of partially fabricated bushings look alike and that the trucker piles 15 or 20 boxes containing several orders on one truck.) Is the lack of positive identification serious? Recommend a procedure to eliminate the difficulty.

14-4 The stock control supervisor of the Evergreen Garden Equipment Company has called your attention to the fact that in several cases he has ordered replacement nuts, bolts, and such items from manufacturers of the equipment used in the plant, only to find them to be standard items. He pointed out that vendor catalogs did not indicate that the items were standard but gave the equipment user only the item catalog number. Not only is the price much higher when a few items are bought this way, but equipment repair is unduly delayed at times.

The company manufactures a line of power lawn mowers, hedge clippers, and similar items. The stock control supervisor's objections to vendor practices caused the company to do a little thinking about its own practices as a vendor. In the past it has followed exactly the same practice as that objected to in another company by the stock control supervisor.

You are appointed as a one-man committee to investigate the desirability of continuing your present practice. Marshal the arguments for and against the continuation of the present company practice. Would your answer be any different if you made radial drills sold to industrial buyers?

14-5 National Cash Register has for many years used a "13-month" calendar. Burroughs Corporation does not use such a calendar. Actually, the use of 13-month calendars is rare. Is NCR off the track? Should Burroughs and other companies adopt the NCR method?

chapter fifteen

MANPOWER PLANNING

So far in our discussion of production control, we have assumed that the factory will have the men required to turn out the production wanted. But having the right number of men doesn't just happen. Someone has to decide exactly how many men are needed and for what kind of work and when they will be needed. Someone has to decide how many will be needed at each work center and how many indirect workers will be needed and what kinds. The personnel department and the factory departments need this information in full detail for several weeks ahead so that they can get more men if they need them or to plan for orderly reductions in the workforce.

Detailed manpower planning (sometimes called manpower "loading") helps you budget and plan your workforce. And where your labor contract guarantees full weeks of work or a given number of weeks in a year to your men, it helps you to live up to your labor contract.

Some companies do no more planning than to check overall work loads with the total number of men available. One Los Angeles electronics plant with 1,000 employees accepts $2.5 million worth of work a month. This is the only manpower loading it does. It knows that its 1,000 employees can turn out this volume of work. This kind of planning provides too rough a measure to use for real manpower planning or for budget making for individual departments. Differences in the product mix from month to month would make overloads in some places and underloads in other places but they would not be revealed ahead of time by such rough loading.

The Link-Belt division of FMC Corporation in its Chicago plant also does not do detailed manpower planning. The personnel department watches the order backlog and tells the foremen if the backlog is going up or down. The foremen then plan their own staff needs. Weatherhead Company in Cleveland estimates manpower requirements by using a past experience ratio of sales dollars per man-hour for each department. TRW, in its automotive division, translates sales into overall direct labor man-hour requirements at the rate of $27 per hour. Its procedure for determining department loads is like Weatherhead's.

So far as manning the plant is concerned, you might think that planning wouldn't have to be done in detail when business is stable because your present workforce handled yesterday's production, is handling today's, and will handle tomorrow's. Actually, this might be true and the

DEPARTMENT	REPORT NO.	REPORT TITLE	PAGE 2
Planning	P-350(March)	Manpower Requirements for March	OF 3

MARCH
MANPOWER BREAKDOWN

Section	Total Std. Hours	% Perf.	Total Act. Hours	% Ind. To Dir.	Total Ind. Hours	Total Dir & Ind. Hrs.	7% Lost Hours	Total Dir. Ind. & Lost Hrs.	18% Payroll Manpower
601-1	2013	90%	2237	114%	2291	4528	341	4869	26.5
-2	8039	90%	8932	33%	2642	11574	871	12445	67.6
-2(RLC)	(171)		(171)			(171)	(13)	(184)	(1.0)RLC
603-10(RLC)	(9412)		(9412)			(9412)	(708)	(10120)	(55.0)RLC
-10	8280	74%	11189	45%	7916	19105	1438	20543	111.6
-11	5578	74%	7537	34%	1878	9415	709	10124	55.0
-12	3789	77%	4921	34%	1271	6192	463	6658	36.2
-13	4260	80%	5325	46%	1979	7304	550	7854	42.7
-14	3096	82%	3776	35%	1278	5054	380	5434	29.5
-15	830	80%	1038	15%	122	1160	87	1247	6.8
609(RLC)	(684)		(684)			(684)	(52)	(736)	(4.0)RLC
609	1280	67%	1910		667	2577	194	2771	15.1
610	2497	60%	4162	79%	1979	6141	462	6603	35.9
611-30	3526	90%	3918	28%	999	4917	370	5287	28.7
-31	6575	79%	8323	25%	1652	9975	751	10725	58.3
-32	1145	85%	1347	170%	1951	3298	248	3546	19.3
-33	1152	97%	1188	33%	381	1569	118	1687	9.2
-34	3448	80%	4310	15%	520	4830	364	5194	28.2
-35	1298	90%	1442	21%	277	1719	129	1848	10.0
-36	616	67%	919	63%	386	1305	98	1403	7.6
-39	1437	70%	2053	33%	476	2529	190	271y	14.8
615	3434	40%	8585	88%	3029	11614	874	12488	67.9
659-41	4025	73%	5514	34%	1366	6880	518	7398	40.2
-42	1370	95%	1442	21%	289	1731	130	1861	10.1
-43	10308	90%	11453	9%	928	12381	932	13313	72.4
	77996	77%	101521	39%	34277	135798	10217	146015	793.6
RLC Unmeas.	(10267)		(10267)			(10267)	(773)	(11040)	(60.0)
	88263		111788			146065	10990	157055	853.6

FIGURE 15-1   Manpower forecast sheet as used by McCulloch Motors Corp. (McCulloch Motors Corp.)

lack of planning during periods of steady production might not make much trouble. But few plants produce steadily very long. Almost always the total volume goes up or down and the product mix varies. The number of men needed in different departments keeps changing so you really ought to keep recalculating your manpower needs. If you don't your foremen will probably get the work out all right but you'll never know whether they did it with the right number of men or with too many men. You can be reasonably sure that if there is no calculation of how many men you need, there will be too many men on the payroll.

Piecework and departmental efficiency ratings operate reasonably well as controls for *direct* labor even if you don't forecast manpower needs. When work runs low, and if the number of men isn't reduced, men on piecework will run out of work before the day is over and will have to be sent home. Department efficiency ratings will also go down because there is not enough work for the men to do. But these methods don't help much in controlling *indirect* labor in factory departments and in offices. Almost never is any of this indirect work covered by work standards and so it is largely controlled only loosely. The kind of manpower planning we are talking about covers everyone, and helps control even indirect labor costs in all departments.

CONTROL OF MANPOWER IN MULTI–PLANT COMPANIES

Individual plants of multi-plant companies usually set their own operating hours and take care of all of their manpower requirements. They are, however, subject to budgetary control by the home office where a close watch is kept and comparisons made between labor costs in all plants.

If several plants make similar items and if they supply parts for other plants, the home office control may be tighter yet. For example, all automobile companies make out, in their central production offices, monthly car building schedules for all of their assembly plants all over the country. Since production rates per hour are fixed, this amounts to the Detroit offices telling each plant how many hours it will work. Usually, however, the home office's control of work schedules and manpower is not this tight.

PRODUCTION CONTROL'S RESPONSIBILITY
FOR MANPOWER PLANNING

Once master schedules are approved, their manpower needs ought to be calculated specifically for each work center.

As described in Chapter 10, production control nearly always gets the job of preliminary overall checking of the manpower requirements of forecasts and master schedules. Not quite so often does it do the final, detailed job of manpower planning. It used to be that, if manpower planning was done at all, it was almost always done by the personnel department and this is still the way many companies do it. But more companies now assign this work to production control.

At TRW, the production control department each week prepares a "force report." It shows the number of men needed in each department and it *is authority to hire.* Houdaille-Hershey uses the same arrangement. In some companies, however, the production control department only translates the production schedule into general labor requirements and advises the line organization of the prospective needs. The line departments then determine the personnel changes they will make.

Actually manpower planning would seem to be personnel work more than it is production control work. Yet production control gets the job because only it knows what work the factory is going to do. Also production control, when formulating schedules, went through all of the work of figuring out the manpower requirements of the tentative schedules, so it may be better for it just to go on and do the rest of the job.

During final manpower planning, there is one thing you can't do. You can't change the schedule to fit the manpower. You can't boost production in a slack period to keep your men busy, because you are now working on an *approved forecast or master schedule,* which already counts on as much inventory buildup as the company's officials believe that they can afford to carry. The preliminary loading that you did when schedules were tentative showed their manpower requirements and all of the ups and downs. Management reviewed them and ordered changes wherever the ups and downs were too severe. As approved, the master schedule still contains some irregularities, known to management but approved by it because it would take too great an inventory build up to smooth it all out perfectly. These irregularities you must live with.

"Final" planning usually proves to be not altogether final. Master schedules always prove to be less frozen than anyone would like. They are changed in small or large ways even after they are approved and are supposedly fixed. Then you have to do part of the manpower planning work over again.

Even the manpower loads themselves might force a schedule change, although we have just said it shouldn't. This would happen if you had planned to hire more men at certain times to meet the schedule but were unable to find as many men as you needed. Then, of course, you'd have to get along with the number you could get. If a manpower shortage limits your meeting the schedule, you'll either have to accept the limitation and cut the schedule or go on overtime or send more work outside to be done.

Not only does your available manpower sometimes more or less set limits to what you can make; it may be even more important in limiting schedule changes. Schedule changes are almost always short notice affairs. There isn't time to change the workforce very much. Production control is never safe in agreeing to big hurry-up schedule changes unless it checks with foremen to see if they can handle the change manpowerwise.

STANDARD VOLUME IN MANPOWER PLANNING

In Chapter 7, we discussed standard volume in forecasting. Wherever the standard volume idea is used in forecasting sales, it is also used in forecasting the number of men needed. Production lines are tooled up to produce daily quantities in line with the standard volume objective. And manpower needs are determined by the line's requirements.

Having decided the hourly rate of production and the number of men you need, you then take care of minor production variations by changing the work hours, not the number of men. General Motors, for example, plans its manpower so that regular crews handle normal work loads and excess loads (by means of overtime) except when the extra work is substantial and will last a good while. GM uses overtime (up to 2 hours a day plus Saturday work) rather than put on new men unless the new men can be kept on the payroll for at least six months.

FINDING THE DIRECT LABOR LOAD

The first step in finding a schedule's manpower load is to "explode" it into its direct labor manpower requirements. Exploding the schedule is almost always done on computers. The process is one of determining the parts requirements and then the man-hours needed to make and assemble them.

The figure you get is, however, for *standard* man-hours, the number of man-hours needed if men work at "normal" pace. Actually they may work faster or slower. Most of the time "normal" is set low enough that men produce more than standard output. (They are more than "100 per cent efficient.") When this is so you need to convert standard man-hours to expected actual man-hours. Men who work at 125 per cent efficiency do five standard hours' work in four hours. You need, therefore, to find out the typical efficiency rate for each operation so that you can reduce standard hours to expected actual hours.

As an offset, however, to men producing above standard, machines don't run all the time so you don't get eight hours of machine production in eight hours of time. Sometimes the gain from the men's above-standard production and the machine time loss cancel out. If they do you don't need to figure either one. Just plan to get eight standard hours of output in eight hours of a man's time and that is about what you will get.

The next step is to see *when* (in what month) the work has to be performed. Assign each operation's time to the month when the work is to be done. (The process is much the same as that described in Chapter 10 for schedule making but this time it goes into more detail.) Then add up to get each month's total.

Your man-hours total, at this point, is however too low. Remember, your schedule has intentionally been kept on the low side in order to allow room for rush orders. So now you need to add 5 or 10 per cent more into your manpower requirements so that you can handle the rush orders when they come.

Allowing for rush orders in this way keeps your manpower planning from being highly accurate. But you can hit it fairly close. Just go ahead and plan to have a few more men in each department than the scheduled work requires. When the time comes they will be busy because the rush orders will by then have become a reality.

You need also to allow for scrap losses. If you want 100 pieces of a part, you may have to start 105 through production. You'll have to plan manpower time for 105 pieces on the first operations, a little less time for in-between operations, and time for 100 pieces on the last operations.

Also, on long-run jobs, don't forget the learning curve. Not often is the learning curve as important as it is in the airplane industry. But all companies have new products, new models, and new machines that make for inefficient operations for a while. Design changes and schedule changes also cut into your efficiency.

MANPOWER LOADING AND THE LEARNING CURVE

Aircraft companies use the learning curve in all projections of future business levels and in manpower planning. We said that the aircraft companies usually use an 80 per cent curve. This curve is wholly a direct labor man-hours curve.

The learning curve forces the company to make a choice. Does it want to produce aircraft at the more or less ultimate rate as soon as is reasonably possible? If so, there must be a big labor force build-up right away and a later cutting back. But if the choice is to staff up only to later manpower needs, then the first several aircraft on the contract will be slow coming through because each one takes so many man-hours.

Generally the choice is to build manpower high and to try to deliver on a faster schedule. You are not likely to have to lay people off later because it will be months before your labor needs go down much. During this time enough men will quit to reduce the workforce. All you will have to do is hire fewer replacements.

Calculating assembly manpower needs and those for subassembly production and for parts production gets to be quite complicated when you try to do all of it way ahead. You have to deal with operations at different times, such as making parts in November and subassembling them in January for March final assembly, keeping in mind that learning curves are working but at different stages at any one time. By March, parts production employees have been working at their new jobs for five months and some subassemblers have been on their new jobs for two months, whereas final assemblers are just starting. Andrew Vazsonyi has some discussion on these problems in his book on operations research.[1] He shows how aircraft companies do this kind of manpower forecasting by using mathematical formulas.

Nonaircraft companies have to contend with the same problem in a smaller way when they start producing new models on new production lines. Almost always they plan manpower for ultimate needs and get along with lower production during the first few days or weeks. Once new product production gets going well, nonaircraft companies don't expect the learning curve to reduce manpower needs very much. Not only is there worker resistance to change but also new products are so much like old ones that any learning curve effects operate as if you had already made 50,000 or some such large number of the new model products. You would have to produce another 50,000 to cut man-hours 20 per cent. You certainly won't reduce costs 20 per cent as you go from item 1 to item 2, and again as you go to items 4, 8, and so on.

INDIRECT MANPOWER LOADING

Thus far we have talked about finding out how many *direct* production workers are needed. They are usually the bulk of the total workforce and their work load goes up and down directly with production volume. In heavily automated production, however, direct production workers are a smaller fraction of the workforce.

Indirect labor is always a big enough fraction of the workforce to need planning and control. Indirect labor includes all group leaders, material handlers, stock-room employees, inspectors, maintenance men, office workers, and supervisors. In total they may nearly equal the number of direct men employed. Typically, their work load also changes with the ups and downs of production, but it doesn't go up and down proportionally.

Indirect work is so varied that it is hard to budget. It is even hard to talk about because you might be thinking of (1) hourly paid workers in factory departments who do not work on the products (machinery setup

[1] See Andrew Vazsonyi, *Scientific Programming in Business and Industry*, John Wiley & Sons, Inc., New York, 1958, chap. 11.

INDIRECT MANPOWER CONTROL REPORT

DIVISION	MONTH ENDING March					DATE					
	CURRENT MONTH					FORECAST					
STANDARD HOURS	93,412.0					89,450		85,380		89,450	
ADJUSTED STANDARD HOURS	86,304.6					86,400		86,400		86,400	
No PRODUCTIVE EMPLOYEES	589					575		575		575	
DEPT No / NAME OF DEPARTMENT	BUDGET	ACTUAL			OVER OR UNDER	MO. OF April		MO. OF May		MO. OF June	
		TOTAL	SALARY	HOURLY		BUDGET	PLAN	BUDGET	PLAN	BUDGET	PLAN
1 Automatic Screw Machine	6	6	2	4	-	6	6	6	6	6	6
2 Slotters	5	9	1	8	(4)	5	7	5	7	5	7
3 Cold Heading	17	21	5	16	(4)	17	20	17	20	17	20
4 Hot Heading	28	30	5	25	(2)	28	27	28	27	28	27
5 Thread Cutting	8	8	3	5	-	8	8	8	8	8	8
6 Thread Rolling	1	1	1	-	-	1	1	1	1	1	1
7 Heat Treating	3	3	3	-	-	3	3	3	3	3	3
8 Electroplating	12	13	4	9	(1)	12	13	12	13	12	13
9 Cut-off	11	12	3	9	(1)	11	12	11	12	11	12
10 Flame Cutting	2	2	2	-	-	2	2	2	2	2	2
11 Welding	11	13	4	9	(2)	11	12	11	12	11	12
	104	118	33	85	(14)	104	111	104	111	104	111
12 Inspection	12	12	-	12	-	12	12	12	12	12	12
13 Trucking	16	19	2	17	(3)	16	16	16	16	16	16
14 Production Checking	9	14	2	12	(5)	9	10	9	10	9	10
15 Laborers	4	3	-	3	1	4	3	4	3	4	3
16 Machine Repair	66	77	5	72	(11)	66	72	66	72	66	72
17 Receiving	5	5	-	5	-	5	5	5	5	5	5
18 Shipping	33	37	2	35	(4)	33	37	33	37	33	37
19 Packing	18	21	2	19	(3)	18	21	18	21	18	21
20 Stores	16	20	-	20	(4)	16	20	16	20	16	20
21 Supply Stores	4	5	-	5	(1)	4	4	4	4	4	4
22 Toolroom	24	28	9	19	(4)	24	25	24	25	24	25
23 Guards	18	19	11	8	(1)	18	19	18	19	18	19
24 Reception	50	53	4	49	(3)	50	53	50	53	50	53
25 Maintenance	46	52	7	45	(6)	46	51	46	51	46	51
	321	365	44	321	(44)	321	348	321	348	321	348 .

FIGURE 15-2   Use of indirect manpower budgeting based on analysis of the manpower requirements of scheduled production.

men, inspectors), (2) men in service departments (store room, toolroom, maintenance employees), (3) officeworkers, or even (4) supervisors and department heads.

For our purpose it doesn't matter whether you are thinking of one or all of these groups. You would have to tackle the manpower planning job about the same way. Rarely do you have time standards for the work of any of these groups, although once in a while you find companies with standards for a few men in the (1) and (2) groups above.

In order to really forecast your indirect manpower needs you would need to know (1) what tasks need to be done in order to turn out the scheduled production, (2) how long each task should take, and (3) how many times it has to be performed to meet the schedule. All of these requirements give you trouble. They are so hard to work out that many companies don't try to do it.

By this we mean that you have to spend a good bit of time and money to get the figures you need and after you have them they are not very accurate anyway. But granted that controlling indirect labor is hard to do, you ought, nonetheless, to try to control the number of indirect men. All companies try to control indirect labor, although some do it by using only the crudest of yardsticks. Others try to measure the indirect work loads and to budget carefully. Most of the careful budgeters spend more money for controlling and think that they get better results. You want to have the right number of men doing indirect work, not too many nor too few. Besides saving money, indirect labor forecasts help both the personnel department and the factory departments in planning personnel.

Failure to figure out ahead how much indirect labor you will need may interfere with production if you have to expand the workforce. Sometimes it is hard to get men—particularly technical people such as engineers because they are scarce. Even if you need only a few, you should know this ahead of time so that you can try to hire them.

Some companies say that they control the number of indirect men "through supervision." This usually means that they have no standards and really don't know whether they have the right number or not. Usually it also means that they have too many men. If you have too few, you don't get the work out; if you get the work out, you always have at least enough men and you may have too many.

METHODS FOR CONTROLLING INDIRECT LABOR COSTS

THE MEAT AX, SLOW–YIELD METHOD   The meat ax part of this method works when production schedules go down. The slow-yield part operates when schedules go up. Neither is exactly manpower loading or manpower planning but both end up influencing the number of men you employ to get out your work.

The meat ax method is control by edict. If factory production schedules are down 10 per cent, tell department heads to cut indirect costs 5 per cent (or whatever figure you pick). No excuses, cut 5 per cent. Obviously this is·hardly a method of manpower planning but it is a common way of controlling indirect labor costs. In fact it is about the only way you can control indirect costs if you do not do real manpower loading.

Advantages of the meat ax method are simplicity and its own low cost. No one in the production control department (or any other department) spends much time figuring out future loads. You just leave it up to department heads to figure out where to cut.

Cutting by edict is usually a poor way because it makes no attempt to see where and how much cutting is appropriate. It penalizes the most efficient departments by forcing on them an "across-the-board" cut which is too big in their case. By contrast an inefficient department with a good deal of "fat" in it can easily absorb the across-the-board cut. Actually you usually end up cutting by different amounts in different departments, depending on the loudness of the screams of anguish from objecting department heads.

Probably the worst feature of meat ax cutting is that some of the cuts you force are actually wasteful. Maybe you cut off so many material handlers in the factory that direct production men have to wait or do their own trucking or if you cut down on, say, production control, you may not have enough help to get the factory's orders out, and men and work are held up.

Control of indirect labor, is, however, a two-way street. When business is going up you have to put on more indirect people yet you want to do it intelligently. How does edict control handle expansion? You handle it by the slow-yield process. Make it very hard for a department head to add an indirect worker. When he asks permission to hire three men, cut his request to two. And again, pay attention to how insistent he is about needing more men. Look also at the amount of overtime put in by indirect men. If overtime is going up, this is evidence (but not conclusive evidence) that the department really does need more men.

There are several fallacies in the meat ax and the slow-yield methods. Besides those we have mentioned, department heads learn to play the game. If you tell them to cut, they sometimes cut essential services instead of less essential things. Then operations really suffer and they get the cut restored, which is what they wanted from the beginning. Of course, this is a dangerous game for subordinates to play, but top officials can't investigate in every department to see which work continues as before and which work has been cut.

Even screams of anguish become part of the game. If you give in wherever the screams are loud, you soon get loud screams from every department head regardless of his real need. Something similar happens during expansion. A department head needing two men will ask for three, expecting you to cut back the request.

The situation is only made worse by the fact that some department heads "play it straight." Tell them to cut 5 per cent and they follow your orders without much objection even where it is unwise. Or if during expansion they need two men, they ask for two but get only one. They get along with only one more man but the inefficiencies from being short-handed cost the company money.

The meat ax, slow-yield method for controlling indirect labor, common though it is, is clumsy. It probably doesn't actually cost money very often but it saves less than it could because unwise cutting in some spots loses part of its gains. It is giving way to regular manpower planning, which costs more to administer but does the job much better.

THE BITS AND PIECES METHOD   The bits and pieces method means finding out what bits of work have to be done to meet a production schedule, how long each one takes, and how many times each must be done. It is essentially the method used for controlling direct labor in the factory.

Regular factory time study methods can be used to set production standards for some office jobs. Typists, for example, are in some companies paid on a bonus plan (but this is rare). You can put a key-stroke counter on the typewriter or you can count the pages done per day.

But how can such detailed record keeping pay? At first it sounds as if it wouldn't but this idea should not be discarded too quickly. Pitney-Bowes found that in its production control department the best typists turned out three times more than the poor ones. Control methods brought the poor ones up considerably.

Another approach to controlling indirect labor in offices is to use "standard times" for certain work. Several consulting companies have catalogs of standard times for typing a letter, filing a letter, getting a letter out of a file, etc. Their complete catalogs cover most of the things done by office clerks.

Both time study standards and standard times can also be used for some other kinds of indirect work, maintenance, for example. But for most kinds of indirect work these methods are impracticable and almost surely too costly to administer. Picture, for example, trying to decide the effect of a 10 per cent production schedule drop on maintenance. What effect will this decline have on your expenses for painting, roof repairing, or electric light bulb replacement? Or try to picture its effect on the work of the cost accounting, production control, personnel interviewing, or process engineering departments. Or try to see how it will affect the elevator operators in the plant and the drivers of fork lift trucks. It is well-nigh impossible to tell what bits and pieces of work will be changed and how they will affect the man-hours that your men ought to put in.

Yet it is true that production changes do affect the amount of indirect work. Suppose that you have now 250 direct production workers. Then suppose that sales are so good that you boost production and employ 500 direct workers. You can be sure that the number of indirect workers would also have to change. But the bits and pieces method will probably not tell you how many men to add and where to place them.

PROPORTIONAL METHODS WITH STANDARDS McDonnell Douglas Corporation uses a method for controlling indirect that could be characterized as a proportional method employing work standards. McDonnell Douglas has used this method even in offices, including the production control department. In the first stage of this method, employees are given a pack of tabulating cards on which they note the things they do during the course of several days. They make out a card for each kind of work they do.

Analysts then look over the cards and find out what activities are regular duties. Next, the analysts prepare tabulating cards for each activity and give the workers a complete set—a dozen or more little stacks, one stack for each activity.

This starts the second stage of the procedure. Every time a worker starts a job, he notes the starting time on a card for that activity and when he completes the job he writes down his finishing time. This goes on for several weeks, during which time he keeps turning in cards showing where his time goes. Inasmuch as the company knows the production volume, it can work out ratios showing how the amount of time spent on each activity fluctuates with changing production.

With these records McDonnell Douglas can tell how many man-hours were spent on making out purchase requisitions, preparing work orders, or keeping cost records for each week in the period under study. Also, if there was any change in the production level during this time, the analysts can tell how much the work load is affected by changes in factory operating levels.

If you used this method, you would at this point be ready to look at the schedule for near future periods of time. You know what specific tasks have to be done and something of how their total time is affected by production level changes. You could estimate your indirect labor needs. McDonnell Douglas found that at first its estimates were somewhat erratic but nevertheless kept on using cards to record the time for each activity. Before long they had much better records of the changes that production ups and downs make in indirect work. Now, McDonnell Douglas budgets indirect manpower, knowing that the budgets are fairly realistic.

The McDonnell Douglas method contains a weakness which might, at first, be serious. It is based wholly on past experience and tells you only *how long it has been taking* to do things not *how long they ought to take*. Also, whenever you rely on workers, office or factory, to help set up standards covering their own work, you can be sure that they will help set liberal standards. Once started, however, budgets based on loose standards will probably be surpassed often enough to tell you which standards are too loose. You can tighten those that consistently allow more time than is needed.

WORK–SAMPLING   When used for office and other indirect labor jobs, "work-sampling" is similar to the McDonnell Douglas method. Work-sampling is often used in setting standards on factory jobs.

This method involves the observation at random intervals over a period of time of one or more workers. The observer records the activity engaged in by the worker at the time of the observation either by writing it down or by checking it off on a predetermined list. *All* activities observed being done by operators are recorded, whether they are working activities or nonworking activities.

Usually well over 100 observations (several hundred would be better) should be used, but the need for large numbers of observations depends upon the length of elemental times and the variability of these times. Work sampling is particularly good when several workers do the same work because this allows you to get many observations in a short time yet without affecting the validity of the figures. It is important to do the sampling on a random basis so that the sample times more surely approximate the true times of each element of the work being done.

After collecting the observations you can get a good idea of the distribution of the employee's time. If the worker was performing the main parts of his job in 70 per cent of the observations, then that part of the job takes 70 per cent of his day; if he was gaging materials or sharpening tools 5 per cent of his time, then that work takes 5 per cent of his day.

At the end of the period the time study engineers know what the production schedule was and how many man-hours were spent on each kind of activity. But, at this point, they don't know how much change in the man-hour work load a change in the schedule will make. To get some idea, it is necessary to repeat the process two or three times when production levels are different. Then you can figure out how production ups and downs affect each kind of indirect work and how much change will be needed in future periods.

Work-sampling is subject to the same objection mentioned for the McDonnell Douglas method—it tells how much time has been spent on indirect work but doesn't tell how much time should have been spent. Furthermore, if you use work-sampling (or the McDonnell Douglas method) you depend on some one overall measure of production to tell you how much production goes up and down. You will have to use dollars, tons, or perhaps direct labor man-hours. Variations in the product mix are covered up. This will keep your calculations of indirect work loads from being too accurate because product mix variations will affect different kinds of indirect work in unlike ways.

OPTIMUM HOUR METHOD A. O. Smith uses an "optimum hour" method for controlling manpower. It is more a control after the fact than it is a forecast but it also helps in forecasting manpower loads.

To use this method, you find out the most favorable time to produce each product using present methods. Include only direct labor hours. At the end of the month multiply a department's production by the optimum hours for each product and get a total optimum hours of work done. Now, divide by the actual total hours for all workers combined (this total includes indirect workers). Tell your foremen what their ratios are and try to get them to improve them.

Smith found that its ratio was 26 per cent for the first year it used optimum hours. The next year it was 28 per cent. The third year it was up to 30 per cent. Although these gains sound small, A. O. Smith saved $800,000 in the second year and over $2 million the third year. Upon analysis Smith found that the gains came mostly from the cutting of indirect labor expenses by department heads.

COMPARISON CHARTS   TRW uses comparison charts to forecast indirect manpower loads. These charts look directly and only at the total indirect men that have been needed for past schedules. With the charts, you can work out ratios of men to total schedules.

To make such a chart you must first go back into the past. Get a month-by-month record of the man-hours put in on one particular kind of indirect work. Also needed is a month-by-month record of your production. Now you are ready to make up a chart. Put a scale for production across the bottom and a scale for indirect man-hours on the vertical axis. Plot a point representing last month's production and last month's man-hours. Do the same for each of the 24 months for which you have figures.

The points should tend to go up and down with production; the more production, the more man-hours, the less the production, the fewer man-hours. If they don't, you really have had no control at all over indirect in the past. Assuming that indirect man-hours have followed production up and down to some extent, the dots will tend to line up along a sloping line, low on the left and high on the right. You can by inspection draw in a line which shows how much production changes have affected indirect in the past, or you can fit a line by the least squares method.

Now you can forecast your future indirect labor load. See what your future scheduled volume is; read across the bottom scale on your chart to that point. Then go up to the sloping line you drew in and go to the left and read the number of indirect man-hours you will need.

This method is subject to the same weaknesses we have already mentioned for other methods. Your forecast of indirect man-hours will be based on how many man-hours your men have been putting in, not on how much time they should have been putting in. Product mix variations also keep your forecasts from being wholly accurate.

There is an added weakness. We said "get a month-by-month record of the man-hours put in on one particular kind of work." You may not have this record. In such a case, the best that you can do is to set up records so that you can start getting these figures. Then some day in the future you can use this method.

You can make up comparison charts for complete indirect departments or for particular kinds of indirect work, providing only that you have past records for each kind of indirect. You can carry the chart idea into considerably more detail if you so desire. You can make charts for such things as order writing in the production control department.

For some kinds of indirect office help, you need to make an adjustment before making charts. Engineering work, for example, has to be done ahead of production. October's engineering man-hours ought to reflect December's production more than October's or November's production. Whenever this situation comes up, you need to make up comparison charts differently. If you had 1,000 engineering man-hours in December and 10,000 units of products, you should *not* plot a point for December using these two values. Instead, look back to October's engineering man-hours. Suppose you find that 1,200 man-hours were put in in October. Plot the point on your chart for 10,000 units and 1,200 man-hours. You will end up with a line telling you how much engineering time to expect for production two months ahead. And this is just what you should have because today's engineering time is related to tomorrow's products, not today's.

To use this comparison for forecasting engineering man-hour loads, just reverse the process. To find out April's engineering load, look at June's production schedule. Man-hour lead times such as this will not apply to very many indirect classes but when they do you should pay attention to them.

KEEPING MANPOWER LOADS UP TO DATE

So far we have talked about the men you will need to meet tomorrow's schedules. But you always have to change a schedule when it becomes today's schedule. This is because you never quite finish any past schedule exactly as you planned. On the first of the month you start off from where you left off on the last day of the previous month, not from where the schedule said you would start. Most of the time you are about on schedule so the adjustment is minor.

But you'll do a better job of loading if you have foremen report, once or twice a month, the total man-hours called for by jobs in their departments which are as yet incomplete. You will sometimes find that work is not moving along as planned. The work you expected to be finished didn't get done so the excess leftover load has to be added into future loads. It

FIGURE 15-3   Report comparing standard hours of work
done with actual hours taken. (TRW, Inc.)

DEPARTMENT	DAILY FORECAST	LAST DAY ACTUAL	AVERAGE	OVER (UNDER)
1	368	338	368	
2	600	710	685	85
3	828	781	675	(153)
4	563	486	623	60
5	148	155	213	65
6	129	124	127	(2)
7	352	446	326	(26)
8	150	98	151	1
9	383	248	391	8
10	432	376	584	152
	3,953	3,762	4,143	190

doesn't matter, for loading purposes, why work doesn't get done. All that
matters is that undone work becomes part of your future work load. You
must provide the manpower to get it done.

TRW checks up *daily* on its manpower load. Here is its method of controlling within the month: On the 25th of each month a forecast is made of
the standard hours of work that each department should turn out in the
coming month. This total is divided by the number of workdays, giving a
daily budget of standard hours of work that should be done in each day.

Every day the total standard hours of work done is posted (for each
department) alongside the actual hours put in, as are the accumulated
figures from the start of the month. This lets everyone see whether a
department is keeping up or falling behind. Failure to stay within the manpower budgets shows up immediately, thus giving management a chance
to correct bad conditions.

TRANSLATING WORK LOADS INTO MEN

The end product of manpower planning is a list showing how many men
you will need—by department, work center, and job for both direct and
indirect labor—but you are not there yet. After allocating man-hours to
the correct month and summing them up, you have to change man-hours
to man requirements.

It sounds simple. To convert man-hours into men, divide the man-hours needed in a month by the hours that a man works in a month. It would seem that 250 men working an average of 173 hours a month (the normal 40-hour workweek) would do 43,250 man-hours of work in a month. But it doesn't turn out this way.

MONTHS ARE NOT ALIKE They don't all have 173 work hours. February with 28 days has 20 workdays. That comes to 160 work hours. March with 31 days can have as few as 21 workdays (168 work hours), or as many as 23 (184 work hours), or from 5 to 15 per cent more than February. If you want as much production in February as in March, you'll have to put in from 5 to 15 per cent more man-hours per day in February than in March. To convert man-hours into the number of men you need, you have to divide each month's total man-hours requirements by the number of work hours in that month.

MEN ON THE PAYROLL AND MEN ON THE JOB ARE NOT THE SAME THING Attendance is never 100 per cent. For men normal absences are close to 3 per cent, for women nearer to 4 per cent. It will always take about 103 men on the payroll to turn out 100 man-days of work in a day. During the summer, vacations skyrocket absentee rates up to between 15 and 20 per cent. Even 103 or 104 men on the payroll will produce only 85 to 90 man-days of work in a day. It matters not that vacations are authorized absences—they are still absences. Men on vacation are not in the plant making products. The start of hunting season boosts absenteeism in most parts of the country. It is also high when there are severe snowstorms, or influenza or other epidemics.

DO NOT OVERLOOK LABOR TURNOVER Turnover reduces production. You lose production between the time one man leaves and another is hired and put on the job. Then you lose more production time until the new man learns his job. Most factories lose from 2 to 5 per cent of their employees every month. So the production loss from turnover is considerable. Filling vacancies by transferring men from other jobs cuts these losses but does not do away with them. Therefore, the higher your turnover rate, the more men you will need on the payroll to do a given amount of work.

DO NOT OVERLOOK NONPRODUCTIVE TIME BY PRODUCTION WORKERS Lost time waiting for materials, waiting at the toolroom, clean-up time—all cut into the amount of production you will get.

MODEL CHANGES CAUSE LOST PRODUCTION You lose production while difficulties are being ironed out and while employees learn their new jobs. However, as the model year goes along, you should gain just a little more all the time. You should end the year with fewer man-hours per product than at the beginning.

PRODUCTIVITY RATES AFFECT THE NUMBER OF MEN NEEDED   For direct labor, the first man-hours total you get as being needed to meet the schedule is "standard" man-hours. Your total is the total time that your men will take if they just "make out," meaning that they just get to the point where bonuses start. The standards you use are time study standards. If the men do just the standard amount of work—no more, no less— they are regarded as 100 per cent efficient. Almost always they do much better. Whole departments may average 120 per cent efficient. But whatever the usual rate, you must allow for it. If they do produce at 120 per cent efficiency, you'll get six standard hours of work for every five actual hours the men spend on piecework. Don't forget though that such things as hot weather in the summer may cut productivity as much as 10 per cent. Also, you'll lose production if you have to shift men around temporarily from job to job.

WORK QUALITY ALSO AFFECTS PRODUCTIVITY   Consequently, the number of men you'll need to meet a schedule is also affected. Rejects usually are less than 1 per cent of all products turned out. But even so every rejected product means man-hours wasted. Sometimes rejected products can be reworked. Sometimes they must be scrapped. In either case, extra man-hours are required to get out a given quantity of acceptable products.

PAY ATTENTION TO THE SHIFT   Night shift workers turn out, on the average, a little less than day shift men. If you expand your workforce by adding men at night you'll get a little less work per man than from day shift additions. Or if you reduce by cutting off men the output won't go down proportionally.

RELIEF MEN   Over and above regular work crews, relief men are needed on some operations. Many large companies must keep operations moving all the time either because stoppages cost so much for lost labor time or because stoppages would ruin equipment or material. A thirty-minute stoppage of an automobile assembly line probably will idle thousands of men—at a labor cost of 7 cents a minute per man. Besides that, 100 cars would not be produced. A continuous steel rolling mill would be ruined—with hundreds of thousands of dollars loss—if it stopped while rolling steel. Even while it is idle, if it should be running, labor and other costs come to $500 a minute!

All of this leads up to the point. *You have to keep full work crews* on the job all the time. Yet men do need personal time out. Relief men must be ready to step in and take over for any man on the crew. Relief men are part of the regular staff needed. In automobile plants, 5 per cent is a common figure. For every 20 men needed on a line they provide 21. All manpower forecasts must, of course, allow for relief men in its calculation of the number of men needed.

Some states have laws limiting the time that women can be kept steadily on a job without relief. In California rest periods are required. Operations stop during rest periods. You don't need very many extra workers for relief purposes when rest periods are used. But rest periods shorten the workday and may cut your total production. If there are no regular rest periods and if the work must go on, you have to provide relief operators.

FRACTIONAL MEN are often included on full work crews for large machines and sometimes on assembly lines. (Fractional men are also a problem on many indirect labor jobs.) "Fractional" means that a man is needed part time. Fractional men often must act as "whole" men. If you need a man sometimes, he may have to be there all the time. An overhead crane operator is not busy all the time but you have to have him there continually. Two crane operator jobs, each providing enough work to keep a man busy half-time, require two men because you can't combine the jobs.

If you can combine fractional men's jobs into whole men's jobs, it cuts the number of men needed. You can nearly always combine fractional men when machines are automatic. Once the machines are loaded with material, they run by themselves for a good while. Each machine requires a man part time but there is little waste because an operator runs several machines. Of course, he can't be two places at once, so if two machines need him at the same time this won't work. You have to work it out so that their needs dovetail.

Another way to handle fractional men is to have no one on the job for perhaps an hour. Let the work pile up. Then put a man on it. In another hour he has cleaned up the pile, but if he is kept there he will be only half as busy from then on. Instead, take him off the job and give him another assignment until another pile accumulates. Sometimes you can't pile up work, but when you can it takes care of the fractional man problem. Of course, the extra material handling that this piling of work makes offsets part of tne gain from using the man somewhere else in between times.

You have to consider fractional men in manpower planning. It doesn't matter whether they are busy half-time, one-quarter time—or what. If you can't combine the fractions, you will need a man for every fraction. When you make up budgets you probably should combine fractions if there is any chance at all that the department head can work out a solution. Setting his budget this way *makes* him work out combinations of duties. Some companies feel, though, that budgeting the manpower for each function to the nearest whole man is satisfactory since the requirements vary so much.

So far, in our discussion of translating work loads into men, we have discussed factors that reduce production. There are a few factors that increase it. But before discussing them, let's look at the total effect of all of the loss factors working together.

Suppose you start with 173,000 man-hours of work to be done in a month. For the average month that would be full time work for 1,000 employees. But no month is average. Every one is specific. We will use March—a March with five Saturdays and five Sundays—leaving twenty-one workdays. You work eight hours a day, so in this particular March the shop will work 168 hours. You seem to need 1,030 men (173,000 ÷ 168).

But if you need 1,030 men to do the work, you actually need 1,061 men on the payroll because 3 per cent of them will be absent. However, that won't be enough either because of turnover. At least thirty and maybe as many as fifty employees will leave during the month and have to be replaced. Every time a man leaves, you lose production before a new man is hired and until he is producing normally. You may need to keep 1,100 on the payroll to get the work out.

Let us say that you have no model changes coming in March but the sales of some products will be up and others down, so a few employees will have to be transferred from one job to another. Suppose we use a production loss of 1 per cent. That puts you up to 1,111 employees needed to do 173,000 man-hours of work. Your scrap and rework loses another 1 per cent so you now need 1,122 even if there is no problem of relief operators.

Eleven hundred and twenty-two is quite different from the 1,030 men you started with. Actually, maybe you won't need quite that many. You would if there were no offsetting factors and there may be none. But any or all of the following may offset some of the productivity loss at one time or another.

We have already mentioned pieceworkers working at over 100 per cent efficiency as a plus factor. New mechanization, once it is running smoothly, also decreases the number of men needed. If you put in any automatic machines you will need fewer men as soon as the machines are producing as they should. Sometimes, too, your engineers figure out how to improve methods without mechanization. If they do, that increases productivity.

Sometimes, too, customers cancel orders and while this doesn't boost productivity, it has the same effect. It is easier to turn out the remaining work load.

The other factors that sometimes increase productivity are all actually decreases in loss factors. You can cut absenteeism by checking up on the absentees. Maybe you can cut labor turnover by improving labor relations. Or you can increase labor productivity by better supervision, or even improve production control and reduce worker and machine idle time.

Curiously, imminent layoff stimulates production. Companies almost always find that when sales go down and they have to lay off some men, the plant's production does not go down nearly as much as the labor cut would indicate. The remaining employees boost their productivity so much that it partially (or even completely) offsets the fewer workers. Of course, the first laid-off employees are those last hired and they are often the least efficient. That alone would increase the average output per worker but not the total output. The remaining employees, however, perhaps fearing layoff for themselves or wishing to earn as much as they can (when on piecework) before being laid off, produce at record levels. This change in worker productivity will affect the number of men you need.

EQUIVALENT MEN AND ACTUAL MEN

You still do not actually have a plan for manning the plant. What you have found out is how many men you need. But the number you have arrived at so far is only what we might call "equivalent" men.

If your schedule calls for 1,100 equivalent men and that is more than you have, can get, or want to hire, then you can buy more parts outside or have certain operations done outside and you will not need as many men on your own payroll. Suppose that you send out enough work to keep fifty men busy. Now you need only 1,050.

Next you can go to overtime and work, say, six days or 10 hours a day for five days each week. Doing this gives you 200 hours a week from every four men. Without overtime you need five men in order to get 200 hours in a week. Of course, *productivity per hour* slides off a little because of the long hours. Perhaps it would go down 5 per cent. If so, the 200 man-hours of time put in would produce only 190 hours of work done—but that is still more from four men than you get when they work 160 hours in a week. Working a 10-hour day cuts the number of men needed from 1,050 to 885 ($\frac{160}{190}$ of 1,050).

Both the use of overtime and sending work out are methods for reconciling the equivalent men with actual. You can do either or both, and you can treat departments differently—some can go on long hours and others not.

Your problem is a little different if work slacks off. Probably you can bring back all the jobs sent out which you can do yourself. This will boost your own plant's work load. Suppose that you have already done this and have also scheduled extra work to go into inventory up to the limit that you can stand. And suppose that this still leaves you with too little work for your men. Then what?

You are left with two alternatives. Cut the number of men or the hours or both. If your operations require full work crews all you can do is to cut working hours for everybody in the crews. Rarely is cutting hours your only alternative, however, because nearly always you have two or more sets of like equipment. Steel mills can, for example, close down one furnace and leave the others in operation. You can cut off one crew and keep other crews working.

Foundries, meat packing plants, and many others, however, make it a practice to let work load variations work out as variations in the number of hours worked every day.

Which alternative do you choose, cut men or reduce hours? First, read your labor contract. Often it tells you which you have agreed to do and if it does, you must do what it says. In the shoe industry, for example, the contract usually says that you will cut hours and not lay men off. Some contracts call for rotating the men on and off if work declines. In any case, whether the labor contract decides for you or not, you end up having to cut men or hours or both.

Finally, after deciding how much work to send out or to bring back and what your work hours will be in each department, you are ready to complete the manpower planning jobs. Your list of men needed for direct and indirect labor jobs should be reasonably exact, enough so that foremen and the personnel department can use it in their planning and so that accounting can use it in budgets.

STUDY MATERIALS

15-1 A large manufacturing corporation has 12 plants. Six are within a radius of 50 miles of the central staff building while the others are located throughout the Northeastern one-third of the United States. At the present time, all manpower planning is done at the individual plant level with varying degrees of competence.

The central personnel staff has recently been advocating that they should do the corporate manpower planning. What arguments would you raise if you were on the corporate staff? What if you were one of the plant managers?

15-2   After attending a recent seminar, the corporate president has decided that his company could benefit by doing some manpower planning. A three-way battle appears to be looming among personnel, production control, and the line organization as to who is in the best position to accomplish this task. As assistant to the president, what arguments from each would you consider to be valid when recommending where to assign this work?

15-3   After a week's search, the personnel department has been unable to fill a request for a skilled boring-mill operator requested by the line foreman. The one apparently qualified applicant wants $4 an hour whereas your rate for this work is $3.75. Surveys have proved that your rates are in line with others in the area. Should you hire the man and pay him $4? What alternatives do you have? What are the implications of this problem for personnel, production control, and for line management?

15-4   You have been asked to prepare a manpower planning forecast for the next year, by months, for selected groups of employees. Explain in detail what factors you would include in planning for the following occupations: electronics engineers, tool and die makers, and assembly workers.

15-5   Outside research: Examine a group of the Bureau of Labor Statistics publications concerning industry outlooks, geographical area studies, and occupational outlooks. If you were involved in manpower planning for a specific company, of what use would these figures be? To what extent would you have to supplement these figures?

15-6   At the Excelsior Machine Company, you have been given the following list of expected sales of products A, B, C, and D for the coming year. The quantities are shown in the month when the sales department wants you to ship the products. You are to add 20 per cent to the load that you arrive at to cover the making of parts to be sold for repair.

This is all tentative at this stage but the management wants you to come up with a proposal covering how best to meet this desired shipping schedule. You are asked to consider only the factory's direct labor requirements. You need not consider machinery use nor capacity. Nor do you need to calculate the extra costs caused by overtime work.

Normally your plant operates eight hours a day for five days a week. And, normally, one-fourth of the man-hours required to make a product will be put in during the month of shipment. Half of the man-hours will be put in during the month before the product's shipment and the remaining quarter of the man-hours will be put in during the month before that.

In case that your first analysis of the proposal shows that it contains too many production irregularities you may move the making of end products by one month, finishing them during the month *before* shipment (but you may *not* move finishing the product to the month *following* that shown on the desired schedule). You may suggest changing the number of workdays per week or the hours per day.

DESIRED SHIPPING SCHEDULE FOR EXCELSIOR MACHINE COMPANY

PRODUCT	MAN-HOURS PER PRODUCT	JANUARY	FEBRUARY	MARCH	APRIL	MAY	JUNE	JULY	AUGUST	SEPTEMBER	OCTOBER	NOVEMBER	DECEMBER	TOTAL
A	10/12	1,500	2,000	2,500	3,000	4,000	6,000	3,000	2,500	2,500	1,500	1,000	500	30,000
B	15/18	2,000	3,000	5,000	7,000	10,000	9,000	6,000	4,000	2,000	1,000	1,000	1,600	51,600
C	7/8.4	900	1,500	4,000	4,000	5,000	4,000	3,000	6,000	7,000	3,500	2,000	1,000	41,900
D	3/3.6	0	0	3,000	10,000	25,000	35,000	15,000	10,000	5,000	1,000	0	0	104,000
Number of workdays		22	20	22	21	21	22	20	23	21	22	20	16	250

1 How many men will your plan require each month and how many hours a day and days a week will they work?

2 Optional part of problem: You are now asked to tell management (a) what the investment totals will be for each month and (b) what the costs of carrying the inventories your plan will be for the program you have developed. The total factory cost of the products are: A, $64; B, $96; C, $64; D, $48. Raw materials and bought components make up half of this total. The remainder is added as processing progresses. Thus at the end of the month of completion, product A is valued at $64. At the end of the month before it is valued at $56, at the end of the second month before, at $40. You are not concerned with any inventories before that.

   The cost of carrying inventories is 2 per cent each month for the average investment for each month.

15-7 Suppose that your forecast shows the following manpower needs for the next six months:

MONTH	MEN NEEDED
1	100
2	110
3	140
4	120
5	100
6	90

You are asked to decide between overtime and carrying inventories. Overtime costs 50 per cent extra for up to 25 per cent over normal and 100 per cent extra for any still further overtime hours. Overtime work is only 90 per cent as productive as regular hours. It costs 5 per cent a month to carry products. Assume that one man makes one product in one month when working normal hours and that products have a manufactured cost of $1,500.

   Make your recommendation and support it with figures.

chapter sixteen

CONTROLLING INVENTORIES IN ORDER CONTROL

When you "control" inventories you try to maintain enough stock to meet reasonable fluctuations in demand and yet not to build up very large inventories, and not to send out very many small costly reorders for more. Ideally, you try to have new supplies arrive just as the old stocks run out although this is an ideal you cannot achieve perfectly.

INVENTORY CONTROL AS PART OF TOTAL OPERATIONS

Although we are going to discuss inventory control as if it were always best to minimize the overall costs of inventories, this is not always a proper objective. Minimizing the costs of inventories ought sometimes to give way to other considerations.

Several times since World War II there have been steel strikes and you couldn't get steel for months. When a strike is a real possibility you surely should lay in supplies far in excess of normal near-future needs. This would boost inventory costs but because of the possible strike should still be done. In other cases the availability of money may be important. It may be economical to lay in big inventories but if you don't have and can't get the money you'll have to get along with hand-to-mouth buying, even though you recognize that doing this is costly from an inventory point of view.

Price prospects should also affect inventory policies. When it looks as if prices of bought materials or components will go up, you would expect to lay in bigger stocks ahead and conversely you would expect to go to a hand-to-mouth policy if you expected prices to go down. Buying practices ought to be related to price expectations yet such changes are hard to incorporate into narrowly viewed inventory control practices.

Inventories can also serve as substitutes for careful production control. If you are willing to carry somewhat larger inventories you don't have to schedule so carefully nor to have production plans so carefully coordinated. Most companies prefer lower inventories and better production control but this choice can be a policy decision.

There is also the need which we have discussed earlier to build up inventories of finished products in certain situations in order to keep the factory working regularly. Such inventory buildups not only regularize production but also "decouple" production and sales and reduce the need to coordinate them closely. Yet these buildups are uneconomical when judged purely from the inventory control viewpoint.

The inventory policies which we will be discussing from here on represent a "micro" approach to the subject (we mean viewing inventory control narrowly as being concerned solely with minimizing the costs of inventories), but its "macro" aspects, those we have mentioned above, should not be overlooked.

MINIMIZING THE "MICRO" COST OF INVENTORIES

Unless you weigh carefully the costs of acquiring stock (purchase order costs or factory setup costs) against the costs of carrying inventories you aren't likely to minimize your inventory costs. In the case of high-cost items there is a strong tendency to make or buy too many or too much at one time and consequently to have too many or too much on hand for too long. For low-cost items there is a tendency to order or make too few at a time, thus having too many reorders as well as too many stockouts. There is also a tendency to pay too little attention to lead times. Short lead time items tend to be ordered too soon and consequently the material arrives before you need it and you have too much inventory. In the case of long lead time items there is a tendency not to order soon enough, with the result that you have too many stockouts. Proper inventory control minimizes these costs.

Having too much inventory is more or less painless. You don't have trouble with hold-ups from being out of stock of anything. The factory gets long runs of everything and you can always give customers good service. But big inventories are costly to carry, probably too costly for you to afford the luxury. You must try to hold them down, even to the point of running out of stock occasionally.

RAW MATERIALS AND PARTS INVENTORIES

Some products are single pieces and have no parts. Nails, nuts, bolts, castings, sheets of steel, steel bars, extruded aluminum, brass, and steel are examples. So are dinner plates, knives, forks, drinking glasses, and panes of glass. When you make such individual piece products, your inventory problems are simpler than when you make assembled products. You don't have to deal with inventories of parts.

But if you make assembled products you have to find out what component parts and subassemblies are needed and whether they should be bought or made. For bought items you have only to control the incoming stock. And for made items you have to control their inventories when in the form of made items and also the raw materials out of which they are made.

RAW MATERIALS NEEDS

Raw materials inventory control is a little different from parts and subassembly control. More often than for parts, you control raw materials on a general replacement basis rather than tying it in closely with finished products needs. You need fewer kinds of raw materials because you usually make several finished items from a single kind of raw material. So raw materials needs often are really the sum of your needs for several parts. It usually saves clerical work just to stock such materials on a general need basis.

Besides being used several places, you often find that you need more raw material than your products use. This is because of cutting waste. Sheet metal items, for example, have to be cut from rectangular sheets. Products made from leather must be cut from hides. Textile products must be cut out of bolts of cloth. Differences and irregularities in shape make it impossible to avoid scrap. Some materials come in lengths (pipe, lumber, etc.) which don't cut up into even numbers of pieces. Again, a certain amount of waste is unavoidable.

You might call this scrap "cutting" scrap to distinguish it from the rejected products kind of scrap. If you use an inventory control system which requires you to calculate raw materials needs to meet assembly requirements, you must add an allowance for this kind of scrap.

Possibly your cutting scrap may not all be waste. In the shoe industry, for example, the man making tongues for shoes is given *no* leather! He cuts shoe tongues out of the leather waste cuttings left by the cutters of the "uppers" of the shoes. Fisher Body of GM also uses the "offall" from stamping operations. The hole for the glass in an automobile door is a fairly good sized piece of sheet steel when it is punched out. It is used to make smaller steel parts.

In job lot work, someone, at some time, has to figure out the amount of material that you need for an order so that you can write materials requisitions and issue the stock. Usually, production control does this ahead of time, but some companies leave it up to the foreman. When you make parts for special products, you almost have to figure out your raw material requirement ahead of time for every parts order. Otherwise you get caught short if the item takes some unusual kind of material or even a usual kind of material but in an unusual quantity. You need to compute all such requirements ahead, check to see if you need more, and order more if you will be short. Production control, not the foreman, ought to do this ahead of time.

In decentralized production control it is less common for production control to check the adequacy of raw materials stocks and to make up materials requisitions. The foreman of the department where the first production operation is performed figures out what he needs and writes out the requisitions. But even here, if the order calls for unusual material or unusual quantities, you'd better have production control check ahead of time. Otherwise, the first that the stock room knows about your wanting the material is when the man on the job asks for it. Then it is too late to take care of unusual needs quickly. But for usual materials—bar steel, sheet steel—you don't need to do this. You carry enough of them to take care of all normal demands.

When the foreman figures his own needs and writes his own requisitions, there is a tendency to waste material. The foreman (who in turn often leaves it to his department clerk or to the shop worker) often figures his materials requirements hurriedly and carelessly. At best he is likely to be liberal in his estimate of how much raw material he will need. So he withdraws too much and his men use it wastefully. If any material is leftover, the excess lies around in the department on the floor where, soon, it is likely to become complete waste. It gets rusty or trucks run over it and ruin it for any useful purpose. Of course, the foreman can return excess materials to the stock room for credit but he doesn't always do it. Sometimes he uses the excess on another order but doesn't tell you. Then your cost records show wrong figures. Lax control of materials is common in small companies but uncommon in large companies.

BOUGHT FABRICATED ITEMS
Many bought items are actually completed products. Automobile companies buy tires, clocks, radios, roller bearings, spark plugs, and many other items. Those which go into your finished products directly and without further work you probably buy specifically for the assembled items that you know you will make. In Chapter 30 we go into how continuous production manufacturers buy these items.

Job lot manufacturers, too, have to buy such items. Not often do they stock very many of them on a regular basis. These items are too costly and their use is too irregular. The same holds true of "rough stock," which is mostly castings, forgings, stampings, or other partly formed items. These too, in job lot work, you would buy mostly on the basis of the known needs of already on-hand assembly orders.

INVENTORY CONTROL POLICIES

Basically there are only two inventory control philosophies so far as ordering more stock is concerned. The first philosophy is to pay no attention to the past but instead to look only to the future. You figure out, in detail, what you'll need in order to make the products you plan to make and then procure the materials and parts that will be required. We call this the "precalculation" philosophy.

The second philosophy, which we call the "past-history" philosophy, assumes that what you've used in the past you will continue to use in the future. You rely on the record of past use of parts and materials as guides to tell you what you will need in the future. The most common past-history type of control is the maximum-minimum method which we take up on page 360.

You can also combine the precalculation and past history methods and rely in part on future needs as revealed by forecasts and in part on the past being continued into the future.

INVENTORY A B C's

Some companies classify the items they stock into A, B, and C classifications. A items are the "vital few" and C items are the "trivial many."

General Electric started this idea and now you find it frequently. At GE, inventory A B C's were an outgrowth of a study made in its turbine division of the costliness of inventory record keeping. GE found that 67 per cent of the items used up only 5 per cent of the value of materials used. These relatively unimportant items were responsible for most of the inventory control paper work.

At the other extreme, 5 per cent of the items used up 75 per cent of the materials used. These were the important items. In other companies these percentages vary somewhat but you always find that a small number of items are the big money users. Alcoa, for example, found that 4 per cent of its items were responsible for 78 per cent of its material costs. At Frigidaire, 15 per cent of the parts make up 80 per cent of its material costs.

There are the important items. They are A items. They are the heavy

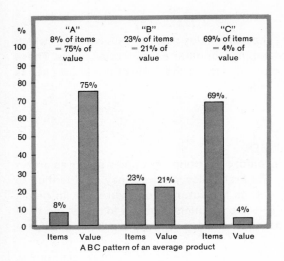

FIGURE 16-1   A B C patterns at General Electric.
(General Electric Co.)

users, the vital few items. *They should get the full record-keeping treatment:*
use the precalculation of needs method for controlling their inventories.
The savings you can make by holding down the investment in A items justifies the cost of the paper work. Buy A items in small quantities several
times a year. Keep protective stocks of A items at the absolute minimum
but be sure to watch the incoming flow of such items and not allow it to
be interrupted. GE tries to carry less than two weeks' supply of A items.

B items are the middle group, the 25 per cent of the items which
cause 20 per cent of the cost. You aren't so fussy about holding B item
inventories at rock bottom figures but you still keep records and issue B
items to operators only in exchange for requisitions. Alcoa makes a practice of buying B items two to four times a year. Maximum-minimum controls based on past usage are appropriate for most B items.

C items are the little things. They are the trivial many. Some C items
in the factory are like paper clips and rubber bands in the office. The
record keeping costs more than it is worth. You should not, for C items,
calculate how much or how many you will need for assembly orders. Instead just keep ample supplies of them on hand all the time. Buy them a
year's supply at a time. Use "bin reserves" (see page 390). Never mind
using requisitions, and don't keep C items in enclosed store rooms. Just
keep them out next to the workmen to use as they need them. In addition

to saving paper work, another big savings from the A B C idea may be the saving in man-hours formerly wasted by men filling out requisitions and waiting at the stock room.

Giving C items short shrift on paper work is not quite all gain. Since you don't know the assembly department's needs of such items you have to carry bigger protective stocks to keep from running out. But since they don't cost much, this isn't important. A second disadvantage is wasteful use. Loosely controlled items are always used wastefully. Frigidaire, for example, expects to lose 2 per cent of all C items, just as normal shrinkage. But again, C items don't cost much. You lose less from loose control than you spend for the paper work you'd have to do to get tight control. In one small division, when it adopted the A B C idea, GE cut postings of numbers to records for C items from 17,000 to 1,500 per year. And using the whole A B C idea let GE's turbine division cut $300,000 out of its inventory.

In order to use A B C inventory control, you have first to analyze your inventory item by item in order to find out which items are A and B and C. Only then can you put A B C policies into effect. And only then you can set up three different procedures for operating the three degrees of control.

A side effect of classifying items into A, B, and C is that orders to make B and C items in your own plant tend to become fill-ins. Your practice of holding stocks of A items very low makes their reorders very sensitive to changes in demand; thus you increase them, decrease them, speed them up, or hold them back. This makes the orders for B and C items that you make yourself take a back seat and get pushed around.

PARTS AND MATERIALS NEEDED, PRECALCULATION METHOD

The precalculation method starts with the finished products manufacturing schedule. From it and using master bills of material you calculate how many of every part and every subassembly you will need. Then see how many of each item you already have on hand and on order and find out how many parts you still have to procure.

You are not ready, however, at this point, to go ahead and buy or make these quantities. True, you need these quantities but you need also to pay attention to economical procurement. Quantity discounts, standard package (such as full barrels or full bundles) prices, freight rates, and your own factory machinery setup costs are all lower per unit when you buy or make fairly big quantities or at least standard lots. When this is so, and where you are going to use the items indefinitely in the future, you should weigh the lower unit costs from ordering large lots or standard lots against the costs of carrying more inventory than you now need. Often you will end up ordering more than your immediate needs call for.

Here is what would probably happen so far as purchased items are concerned. Production control would ask purchasing to buy the quantity to be procured. Purchasing knows whether or not these quantities can be bought at the lowest prices. Whenever other quantities would allow for lower prices, the buyer in the purchasing department would ask production control if it could revise the quantity asked for. This is the point at which production control would weigh the extra inventory carrying costs against lowered unit prices. After considering these factors, production control and purchasing should, together, decide on the actual quantity to buy on a given order.

You should make a similar analysis of the proper quantity to order for items you make yourself. The "economic" lot, the order quantity which will produce the lowest cost, is discussed in Chapter 17. Again, however, you may order more at one time than your near-future needs call for.

For items that you make yourself you next have to determine their raw materials requirements. You already have the list of parts that you are going to make, and using master route sheets, you can calculate the raw materials needed. Again, though, you check this needs list against the supplies already on hand and on order. We talked above about doing this for items bought directly as bought components. And once again, you adjust the quantities you will actually procure up or down a little to take advantage of full packages, quantity prices, or full freight carload rates.

OTHER FACTORS AFFECTING THE QUANTITIES NEEDED   Actually we are ahead of our story in the discussion above because there are several factors not yet discussed that also bear on the quantities needed.

The first of these is the allowance for cutting scrap and for rejects. As we said earlier, when you make items out of paper, cloth, sheet metal, leather, or many other materials, there is of necessity a certain amount of cutting waste. The materials procured must include an allowance for this.

Second, there are rejects. Semifinished or finished parts sometimes have flaws or imperfections and have to be discarded. Enough extras have to be started into production to allow for this attrition and yet produce enough good finished items.

Third is the need to make up extra parts for repair service. In some companies you also need to add in enough extra parts to make up modification kits. These are sets of parts that customers buy to keep on hand to repair their equipment or to bring it up to date.

Fourth is the matter of common parts. Many parts are used in two or more products. It costs less to make all that you need as one big lot rather than as several small lots. So if you need a part in two or three kinds of finished products, you should sum up their total demands and make one big lot.

A fifth matter concerns individual plants of multi-plant companies. You may concentrate making certain items in certain plants, letting one or two plants supply the others. This often happens in the company's home or main plant. It supplies certain parts for all of the other plants, possibly even for foreign plants. So the number of parts that the plant needs to procure is quite different from the totals of its own internal needs. And similarly the sister plants being supplied are freed from making these items themselves. The number of parts they need to make is reduced.

There may be other factors to consider as well but the point is that you need to pay attention to all such needs when you are determining parts and materials needs.

RESERVING MATERIALS FOR KNOWN ORDERS   Whenever your need for any raw materials (except C items) is highly variable, or if one item can be used as a substitute for another item, you will probably be better off not to rely on the usual maximum-minimum kind of past-history controls. You'd better calculate which kind and how much material you will need for your scheduled orders. Then check your stock and order the quantities you need.

To take care of variable demand best, you need a different kind of stock record than is normally used for ordinary maximum-minimum controls. The typical record shows receipts, issues, and on-hand quantities. With such a record, you can't, however, do the best job of preparing for irregular future demand. You will need to add two more sets of data to your stock card (or to your magnetic tape record), one for materials "apportioned" or reserved for particular orders and one for quantities "available." The apportioned column shows the quantity and the order number for which you are reserving or "mortgaging" some of the stock. Later when you issue materials for those orders, you cross off these mortgages.

The Available column is a forecasted On-hand column. It represents what you actually have on hand plus all quantities ordered but not yet on hand, less any quantities allocated or mortgaged for future orders. The available figure tells you how much you will have on hand after everything ordered is received and after all the planned withdrawals are made.

You can actually have a negative balance of available items and yet not be in trouble. If an item can be made in a short time, you can apportion more than you have available until you build up enough demand to give you a sizable order. You can wait, since the order can be processed quickly, until shortly before you really would be out of stock before processing an order.

MATERIALS SHORT LISTS   Materials "short" are materials or parts that you know you will need and which you don't have. Most companies which use short lists use them to show items that the assembly floor already needs or very soon will need. We will talk about this in Chapter 23. Unless you have made serious mistakes, all items on such a short list are already being made in the factory or have been on order for some time.

Using a short list in connection with assembly needing parts right away differs from short lists as used in inventory control. By no means do all companies use short lists in inventory control but those that do usually do it this way: You are making assembled products in lots and you are making products that you make again and again but not steadily all the time. Between lots the product is off the schedule; sometimes for several months at a time. In this situation, many companies don't plan to carry stocks of parts. Instead, they try to make most parts in the quantities called for by the assembly orders. But a few parts are stocked and also since you have made these products before it is likely that you will have some small leftover stocks of most items. So, before ordering new stocks, you check and see what you already have.

After checking to see what you have, you make up a "materials short" list showing all the items and quantities you still need. Actually, we have already said that you always have to make up such lists to tell you what to order, but we didn't call the list a material short list. There is nothing new therefore in this kind of a short list but the name. But you should know of this use and recognize that some companies use it when there is no actual shortage on the assembly floor. The quantities, too, may not jibe wholly with what the assembly floor needs because leftover stocks from previous overruns reduce the quantities of parts that you need to make this time.

Normally you have quite a few items that you stock on a maximum-minimum basis. These do not ordinarily get on materials short lists because their supplies are replenished regularly. Small items, C items, also are not put on shortage lists. Short list items are usually the items you do not stock as a regular thing.

COVERAGE VERSUS ON HAND
Except for immediate use, the effective stock of parts and materials consists of what you already have in bins plus what you have on order. It is true, "on-order" stock is not the same as on-hand stock; yet it is stock

in the sense that it will be on hand by the time you need it. When you order stock you "cover" your needs through some future period.

The advantage of being covered by orders rather than stock on hand is that you have no investment in it and have no expenses in connection with carrying it. Yet you are protected by having your needs taken care of. Admittedly, however, if you are covered largely by on-order quantities rather than on-hand quantities you are in a vulnerable position, because lead times are not wholly dependable.

You do not, however, always need to cover yourself for very far ahead. Except where the economic lot quantity is large, there is no need to order quickly made parts very far ahead. In September, you may know what parts you'll need in January, but if it takes only two or three weeks to manufacture some of these items, there is no need to order them until December. You don't need to cover all of your known future demand.

PAST HISTORY INVENTORY CONTROL METHODS

DOLLAR LIMITS AND CAPITAL TURNOVER RATIOS One of the easiest ways to control inventory investment is to issue an edict telling the inventory controllers that they must keep the total investment below some dollar limit that you set. Normally, when setting dollar limits you would start by reviewing how things worked in the past and how many turnovers you got last year on each kind of inventory. If you used up $100,000 worth of a certain class of material last year and had an average of $20,000 worth on hand, you got five turns of the capital invested and had about 10 weeks' supply on hand all the time. You have to judge last year's performance as good or bad before you can set your new limits. If you think that you had too much on hand most of last year you will probably set the dollar limit at less than $20,000. Other considerations, too, such as the availability of money and future price prospects play a part in where you set the dollar limit.

You can also view the question of the size of inventory investments as a capital allocation problem. Think of inventories not only as dollars invested but also as a potential source of dollars to be released for use elsewhere in the company. If, for example, you have opportunities to invest in capital projects that offer expected rates of return of 25 per cent, you might reduce your inventory investment in order to release money to invest in such projects. It might pay to do this even though the inventory reduction would force you into doing more small order buying, thus boosting inventory unit costs. Or conversely, if other investment opportunities promise low rates of return, you might forego them and allocate even more dollars to inventories. This would allow you to order bigger quantities and save a little on unit costs.

In either case, you would be investigating the question of how many dollars to allocate to inventory. The problem can be solved in the following manner. For every possible level of inventory investment several costs are incurred, such as storage costs, insurance, pilferage, stockouts, deterioration of stock, and obsolescence. At other inventory investment levels these costs come to different totals. You can work out how much it costs for each level of inventory. A rate of return relating savings to incremental changes in inventory investment can then be calculated. This rate of return can then be compared to the prospective rates of other projects to determine how much you can afford to allocate to inventories.

Because dollar limits are easy to apply they are commonly used to control both total inventories and subclasses of inventories. But this may be a costly method. If you set the dollar limit too low you force the frequent ordering of materials and products in small lots. What you save by having a low inventory you may well lose in running out of stock too often or in extra reordering costs, extra setup costs, and higher buying prices per unit stemming from the small orders.

There are also other problems. Suppose, for example, that the needs for some items decline after it is too late to cancel orders for new supplies. When these orders arrive, these items will be overstocked for a while and will use up more than their share of the allowed investment. The only way you can hold the line on the total investment is to understock other items, which means placing too frequent orders for small quantities. It is poor practice to allow your overstock of one item to force you into uneconomical order quantities for other items.

Dollar limits also overlook economic lot sizes. On items where the economic lot is small, dollar limits let you go too high. And if the economic lot is large the overall limits prohibit your making the big lots that produce the lowest costs.

Price changes are also important when dollar limits are used. If prices go up and limits don't go up, the inventory control people have to cut their inventories. They can't carry as much stock. The reverse happens with price decreases. If you don't cut the dollar limit you are loosening up your control and allowing more stock to be carried. It isn't the tightening or loosening that is the bad feature, it is the not knowing about it. You need to watch out for price level changes and adjust dollar limits unless you intend to change the level of inventory that you'll allow.

Changes in the levels of a company's business are also important. If business goes up and the dollar limits aren't changed, you are trying to get more business volume out of the same inventory investment. If your old figure was right, then you can't do this economically. You will run out of stock too often or will have to send out too many little replenishment orders. And again, the reverse happens on downswings. When volume goes down, the old dollar limit is too high and allows too much stock to be carried.

Dollar limits should, however, not be adjusted up and down *proportionally* with sales changes. If business doubles, you need more inventory but not twice as much. Also if business falls to half, you will be cutting too deeply if you cut dollar limits to half.

Dollar limits are about the only kind of overall control that is practicable for whole classes of items. At the same time they are not practicable for individual items except for a few major items. Normally it would be too costly to set dollar limits for each of thousands of items. The most common way, when using dollar limit control, to control individual item investments is to combine dollar limits with time limits. The dollar limit sets the general pattern and this in turn sets the time limit to use for reordering individual items.

TIME LIMITS   Any method of controlling inventory finally has to reach down to specific items whose reorder quantities you have to control. The time limit method will do this for you and it can be tied in with dollar limit control very well. Or you can use time limits without dollar limits. Time limits on inventories are commonly set at from six weeks to two or three months. Companies differ in their practice and they change their limits from time to time if they want to build up or cut down on inventory.

When used with dollar limits, time limits are, in effect, merely another way of expressing the limit in a form that can be applied to individual items. If, for example, you have a limit of $30,000 for brass bearings and bushings, and you use $10,000 worth of these items a month, then you also have a three-month time limit. It doesn't matter which way you express it, as money or time. Probably your inventory will stay close to the $30,000 figure because as you use material, you buy more. The investment will rarely go much below the limit because if you could get by with less you'd have picked a figure lower than $30,000. And it won't go much higher because you won't approve order quantities that push it up.

Time limits are very good for keeping your inventory investment within the specified limit. When you use short time limits, you reduce the chance of loss on inventory from price declines, get rapid turnover of inventory, and cut the risk of obsolescence. You can change time limits readily, and can have different time limits for different types of products.

Against short time limits is the greater possibility of running out of stock whenever an order arrives a little late. Also, short time limits almost completely neglect the savings that you might get through manufacturing or buying in economic lots. You can avoid this objection, however, by making exceptions for items whose acquisition or setup costs are high. Actually, exceptions are not often made so that usually there is a real loss from overlooking economic lots.

Time limits are free from the need to be changed with either price levels or business levels, weaknesses that applied to dollar limit controls. Price level changes do not affect the working of time limits at all. Business level changes do, however, affect the quantities that you order when using time limits, but the change is fairly automatic. As business goes up or down, so do the quantities of items used; this allows you to change the reorder quantity, so the time limit can stay the same but your allowed inventory will fluctuate with the ups and downs of your business.

Although time limits have much to do with reorder quantities, they are not themselves quantities. You have to convert them into quantities, item by item, since a two-month supply of one item might be 1,000 units, but only 50 for another item. If you were working under a two-month limitation, probably you would not order any more than two months' supply for anything. Even so, when the new supply comes in, you'll have over two months' supply of that item because of your safety stock. This won't hurt, though, since other items will be below their maximum.

We have talked about ordering a two months' or a three months' supply as if this were either a fixed or else an easily determined quantity. Actually this quantity is either a little vague or else it takes some work to figure out. If you rely on past usage to tell you what you'll use in the future, the quantity that you should order is a little indefinite.

Some companies figure out reorder quantities (intended to reflect time limit policies) and write them on each stock card or record them on computer tapes. Actually, because of frequent changes, most companies don't do this. Sometimes they let the inventory controller or the computer figure out a new reorder quantity each time that a new order goes out. If you do figure out reorder quantities and write them on stock cards or put them on tapes, you'll need to review them every now and then, particularly during periods of change.

RULE OF THUMB REORDERING PRACTICES

PERIODIC REORDERING   Some companies have their warehouses and stock rooms reorder only once a month, say in the first week of the month. Variations in the need for an item are reflected in changed ordering quantities, not in its being ordered sooner or later than usual. Stock clerks in the warehouses and stock rooms go over their records once a month and order more of everything which is already out of stock or which might run out within the next month. All of the reorders go on a long list made up at this time and, except for emergencies, no other in-between ordering is allowed.

Ordering periodically has the advantage that the purchasing department gets orders all at once rather than a few at a time every day. Purchasing can group orders and cut out making up so many purchase orders. Purchasing can spread out its work load by setting up schedules for orders of classes of products. Certain classes of products might all be ordered in the first week of the month, while other classes are ordered in the second week, the third week, etc.

Periodic reordering boosts inventories somewhat because you have to order, in the specified week of the month, everything that you would want to order any time in the next four weeks because there will be no second chance. Ordering ahead will make items arrive too soon and this will boost the inventory. You can minimize this problem by telling the vendor not to ship right away, but doing this complicates the whole procedure and isn't very practical on run-of-the-mill items. You'll probably end up with somewhat larger inventories than if you allowed reorders to be placed at any time.

STANDARD LOTS   Job lot work is often repetitive in that you often make repeat lots of old products. Some companies make parts for repetitive products in standard lots—maybe 50 or 100 parts in each lot. Or the standard lot may be set at forty-eight or some other number picked because that represents a full carrying rack or tray or pan used in the factory. Making parts in standard lots allows the use of standard route sheets prepared ahead with figures already filled in for the standard lot.

Standard lots for parts are often set at quantities to make a standard lot of assembled products. But parts lots can be standard in themselves regardless of assembly needs.

Standard lot quantities may also be set by manufacturing considerations. GE found that a newly sharpened die on one press job always had to be sharpened before the end of runs up to 50,000 pieces but almost never on runs of 30,000 or less. Sharpening the die meant tearing down the setup and then, after sharpening, setting the job up all over again to finish the run. It cost so much to do this that GE set reorder quantities at 30,000. Now, it sharpens the die after every run and rarely has to stop a run for sharpening and for the extra setup that it would cause.

MAXIMUM–MINIMUM INVENTORY CONTROLS

Maximum-minimum controls are based on the assumption that an item's past history is a reliable indicator as to its future use. Max-min controls are not based on any calculation of the specific needs for future products. Instead, when an item gets down to its reorder point (a figure you have to set for each item separately), you order a new supply. The reorder point is the quantity that you are likely to use up before the new supply comes in plus a safety stock to keep you from running out very often if either (1) you use more than usual after the order is placed and/or (2) it takes more than the usual time to get the new supply in.

When you order, you order a quantity that will raise the stock to its allowed maximum when the new supply arrives. Max-min controls are the kind used mostly for B and C items, not A items. Reordering quantities are determined by time limits or they are set at the economic lot size. In either case they must be set individually for every item you carry, and usually this means 10,000 items or more.

When you use max-min controls, the computer (or the stock record clerk) notices, as it subtracts quantities issued, when each item's stock gets down to the reorder point. It prints up, every day, if you want it that often, a list of all items that got down to or below their reorder points during the day.

If you don't have a computer and have stock record clerks doing the work the job is more difficult. Since you don't want clerks to spend a lot of time writing out descriptions of all of the items they need, you could have them just pull out of the file the stock record cards for all items to

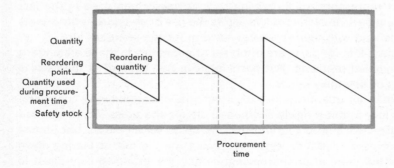

FIGURE 16-2 When use of any item is regular, it is possible to set a "reordering point" which the stock clerk must observe in originating reorders. This point is a quantity representing the quantity ordinarily used between the placement of an order and receipt of the new supply, plus a minimum reserve.

be reordered and send them to the stock control supervisor. But, if the clerk did this, his card file would always have some cards missing.

Some companies have him keep two cards for every item. One is the actual stock record card, the other is a "traveling" or "repeating" requisition card (or "hard card"). It is a separate "order" card for every item. It is kept with the regular stock cards or in a separate file. Reordering is done by writing in the reorder quantity on the order card and sending it to the stock control supervisor. The reorder card tells him what the past reorders have been, how long it has taken to get more, and such information. This card also saves writing out item descriptions for purchasing. After he places the order for more, the buyer in the purchasing department writes in the purchase order number on the order card and returns it to the stock record department. The order card goes back and forth between the two departments every time the item is reordered.

Another variation of the hand method can be used to minimize reordering errors. This is the "two-bin" stockkeeping method. In the stock room, two adjacent bins are used for each item. One bin holds the reorder quantity and the other, the "issue" bin, holds the active inventory, the main quantity of the item. As requisitions are filled the stock clerk issues parts from the issue bin. When this bin becomes empty he sends the traveling card attached to the bin to the inventory controller, and begins to issue stock from the reorder quantity bin. When the new stock arrives, the reorder quantity bin is first replenished to its proper amount and the remaining items are placed in the regular issue bin. The cycle then repeats.

Bausch & Lomb uses still another variation of the bin card arrangement. In each bin a prepunched tabulating card serves as a bin card. When the reorder point is reached the card is pulled out and put into a reporting unit connected to the central computer which immediately starts the reorder procedure. A new prepunched card (on which the computer has revised the reorder point if necessary) is then furnished as the new bin card.

PROJECTIONS OF RECENT USAGE   Today many companies project the near-future usage of items whose use is variable by using a form of weighted average called "exponential smoothing." You start with the actual average use of an item for perhaps the past three months and use this average as your expected use figure for each of the next one or two months ahead, depending on the length of the procurement lead time.

Then when another month goes by you compute a new average by using, say, $\frac{9}{10}$ of the old average plus $\frac{1}{10}$ of the actual use in the month just past. Again you use this new weighted average as your best estimate of the item's use during each of the lead time months. After another month goes by, the process is repeated, thus producing a continually up-dated average.

Some companies carry this idea one step further and analyze the reliability of their forecasts. To do this, you should start by finding the differences, for some 30 or so past periods, between the forecasts and the actual figures that materialized. Then square these differences, divide by the number of cases, and take the square root. The answer is the standard deviation of the past forecasting errors. It can be used to judge the reliability of new forecasts as they apply to the future. (How the standard deviation is used is discussed in more detail in Chapter 21.)

If the standard deviation is 5 and the forecast is 140, then there is a 68 per cent chance that the next month's actual use figure will be between 135 and 145, a 95 per cent chance that it will be between 130 and 150, and a 99 per cent probability that it will be between 125 and 155. These are the three standard deviation limits used on Shewhart control charts (discussed in Chapter 26). They are based on the record of reliability of past forecasts; hence they give you a clue to the reliability of new forecasts.

EFFECTS OF BEING OUT OF STOCK   Relying on past usage as a guide to future needs for materials makes you vulnerable to being misled whenever you run out of stock. Suppose, for example, that an item runs out of stock at the end of January and that you have already ordered a three-month supply (say 300 units), but that it doesn't arrive until the end of March. At the end of April your records show no use of the item in February (you were out of stock), none in March (still out of stock), and only the normal amount, 100 units, in April, so your average for the three months is only 33 or one-third of a normal month's use. If your stock clerk has thousands of items he is very likely to fail to notice that your April consumption of this item (100 units) is approximately normal. He may think that the stock on hand, 200 units, at the end of April is a six-month supply, since it is 6 times 33, the average monthly use for the last three months. In reality it is, of course, only a two-month supply. If it takes two months to get more of the item, it is already time to order more, but the clerk or the computer thinks that there is an overstock and will not make out a reorder. Two months later, on June 1, you will be out of stock again. In this example, having been out of stock causes your underorder.

Overordering can also result from an out-of-stock situation. Suppose that you are out of stock on an item for four or five months; a backlog of demand may pile up. Then when your new supply does come in, you use several months' normal needs in one or two months. Suppose, for example, you are out of stock on an item from October to April. If the demand for it accumulates, then your normal needs for November, December, January, February, March, and April will probably all be filled (provided the new supply is big enough) in April. The February–April three-month average would be way above normal in spite of no stock being issued in February or March. A new replenishment order at the end of April based on the February–April average would call for too much.

Another and slightly different situation (and one much harder to detect by looking at the records) sometimes happens. Suppose that you are out of stock on item X but that item Y is used as a substitute. This is the kind of thing that goes on all the time in retail stores and sometimes it happens in factories. Often when a customer asks for one product and finds it out of stock he buys another. All during the time when X is out of stock, you use an unusual quantity of item Y. This pushes its average use to a high figure, so its reorder quantities go up. Neither the stock record card nor the computer tape gives any indication that part of the demand for item Y is not really demand for item Y at all.

You find this out when item X is back in stock. Then you find that Y is heavily overstocked because its use returns to normal. At Appleton Electric Company, Chicago, this problem has been so serious that the company developed a special inventory card. Appleton added a "demand" column to its stock cards. The demand column shows all issues of products plus all demands for it which could not be filled minus any demands for it as a substitute for other out-of-stock items. With this arrangement you look over the past three months' *demand* for an item rather than its actual use when you project the item's demand into the future.

None of the three situations described above would happen very often, but when you have thousands of items, you don't get a chance to make even a superficial analysis of the situation in each case. With thousands of items, you'll miss cases of this sort and you'll miss them even with computers unless you set up very complex programs.

As a matter of fact, month-to-month demand, particularly for individual finished items, varies enough so that you sometimes have a hard time deciding for sure how much being out of stock influenced the figures on the record. In the case of finished goods, changes in consumer demand cause frequent changes in the sales of individual items. Seasonal variations in use also add to your troubles in interpreting use figures accurately.

TRENDS A different kind of difficulty with rate of usage as a guide to reorder quantities is trends. If usage is creeping up you are always using more stock during the lead time than you used to. And your reorder quantities never cover you as far ahead as you planned. If you don't notice this trend and fail to boost your reorder quantities, you'll suffer chronic shortages. On downswings, the reverse happens. Usage during lead times is less than you expected and reorders cover you farther ahead than they used to. Again, if you don't recognize the situation and change your reorder practices, the normal practices will keep you continually overstocked— and at the very time when you want to cut down.

SAFETY STOCKS

Safety stocks are the reserves you should still have on hand when reorders come in. The cost of carrying such stocks amounts to paying an insurance premium against running out.

The optimum size of a safety stock is where the cost of carrying it is just equal to the expected cost of possible stockout. If you carry more than this much safety stock the inventory carrying costs go up, and since stockouts are fewer, their costs go down but not so fast as carrying costs go up. Conversely, if you carry less than this amount as safety stock, you save a little on inventory carrying costs but not enough to offset the cost increases that result from more frequent stockouts.

With the coming of operations research, formulas have been developed to tell you how big an item's safety stock should be. Yet this particular use of operations research appears to be uncommon. Lamar Lee and Donald Dobler report that mathematical and simulation methods for setting safety stocks have been tried and found wanting in a good many companies. They say:

> In practice very few companies apply the concept [mathematically calculated safety stock sizes] in a formal manner for very many inventory items. Several large corporations once used it on a wide scale for several years, but subsequently abandoned the idea. There appear to be three major reasons why most firms have not yet found it to be a practical operating tool.
>
> The primary reason seems to be the inability of most large firms to determine an accurate stock-out cost. In a given plant the cost associated with a stock shortage of a given item often varies over an extremely wide range. It depends upon the duration of the shortage and a myriad of conditions in the shop which dictate the ease with which workers and facilities can be transferred to other jobs. In most manufacturing operations that are not highly automated these conditions change from day to day.
>
> Secondly, a number of firms have found that for a majority of production inventory items the cost of a stockout under most conditions far exceeds the cost of carrying the safety stock. Therefore they simply compute order points and safety stock values on the premise that they cannot afford to run out of stock.
>
> A final reason—one that causes all businessmen to view quantitative analytical techniques with a skeptical eye—is the fact that a good deal of clerical and

professional time is required to prepare and analyze historical data for each item before the theoretical determination can be made. Such work is currently much more time consuming for the probability approach than is similar work required in implementing an EOQ [Economic Ordering Quantity] system.[1]

If you do not, however, use formulas, you still need to set safety stock sizes. A rule of thumb is to set safety stocks at either one month's supply or the maximum single withdrawal in the last year, whichever is greater. Yet this rule of thumb is probably wasteful in many cases, particularly on short lead time items.

Interestingly, in cases where running out is not a catastrophe you should not carry safety stocks big enough to protect you from ever running out. The bigger the safety stock you carry the more protection you have against running out. *But* as you add units to the safety stock each added unit gives you less and less additional protection against running out. If you carry a big enough stock to keep from running out 90 per cent of the time, you might have to add 25 per cent more inventory to give yourself 95 per cent protection. You'd better run out once in a long time rather than carry so much inventory. Effective expediting will often keep your stockouts down and will shorten those that occur. We don't mean, however, to overlook Lee and Dobler's point that where it is critically important not to run out, you may have to pay the price for near 100 per cent protection.

IRREGULAR USE AND IRREGULAR LEAD TIME   When both the use and lead times of an item are irregular, the mathematics required to calculate the proper safety stock is too complex to be carried through for large numbers of items.

Suppose, for example, that your records tell you that out of 50 reorders of an item, the new supply arrived in one week 4 times, in two weeks 10 times, in three weeks 30 times, in four weeks 4 times, and in five weeks 2 times. Assuming that past supply conditions still hold, if you order only one week before you need more, you will receive the new supply before you run out only 8 per cent of the time. The other 92 per cent of the time you will run out of stock before the new supply arrives. If you order two weeks ahead, you will be out of stock 72 per cent of the time. Ordering three weeks ahead results in your being out of stock only 12 per cent of the time, four weeks protects you 96 per cent of the time, and five weeks gives you full protection.

Now look at what you are doing to the inventory. If you choose 100 per cent protection, you order five weeks ahead. But typically you get orders

[1] Lamar Lee, Jr., and Donald W. Dobler, *Purchasing and Materials Management Text and Cases*, McGraw-Hill Book Company, New York, 1965, p. 217.

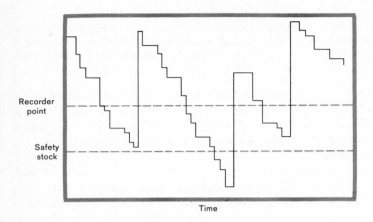

FIGURE 16-3   Example of irregular use of an item.

in three weeks, so, typically, you will be carrying two weeks' inventory forever as a safety stock. If you are satisfied with 88 per cent protection,
order only three weeks ahead. Even though doing this causes you to be
out of stock sometimes, it still results in your averaging to carry some
safety stock inventory because 28 per cent of the time your orders arrive
in less than three weeks.

We are looking at only one side of the picture, however. Usage also
fluctuates. Suppose that your record for the past 100 weeks shows the
following usage:

USE, UNITS	NO. OF WEEKS
0–24	5
25–49	50
50–74	30
75–99	10
100–149	5

Your average usage is about 50 units a week but your weeks are by
no means all average. Sometimes what you think is two weeks' supply is
used up in one week, sometimes it will last for three or four weeks. In 5
per cent of the weeks you used less than half of your average. In 55 per
cent of the weeks you used less than your average usage (which is about
50 units). In 85 per cent of the cases you did not exceed 75 units. But you
went over 75 units in 15 per cent of the weeks.

CALCULATING THE SAFETY STOCK   Although the calculation of the proper sized safety stock is too complex for ordinary use if both use and lead times vary, it is reasonably simple if either one or the other is fixed. If we assume that usage is constant, say at 50 units per week, and if we say that we can arrive at a reasonable cost of stockouts, we can determine the proper safety stock in an example. We will use the variable lead time figures given on page 365. Here is our usage during the reorder period.

LEAD TIME, WEEKS	NUMBER USED	PERCENTAGE OF TIME	ACCUMULATED PERCENTAGE
1	50	8	100
2	100	20	92
3	150	60	72
4	200	8	12
5	250	4	4

We have plotted the accumulated percentage against the quantity used during the lead time in figure 16-4. Figure 16-4 can be called a stockout curve. In order to use it in inventory control you need to know how much it costs to run out of stock, and how much it costs to carry a unit of inventory.

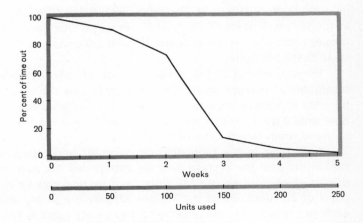

FIGURE 16-4   Stockout probability chart.

To get a reasonable stockout cost figure you might want to consider the lost contribution to fixed charges if a sale or customer is lost because of a stockout. Extra costs may also be incurred through additional ordering costs, extra expediting, and other reasons. If you still feel uneasy about having to put a dollar value on a stockout you can try out two or three different values in your calculations and then decide which to use.

In our example, we will use $100 as the stockout cost and a carrying cost of 5 cents to carry one item for a week. Now we can go ahead with the calculation.

If we set the reorder point at 50 units and reorder when the stock gets down to 50, we will run out of stock 92 per cent of the time, because 92 per cent of the reorders in the past have taken longer than one week to arrive and we use 50 items a week. Our average inventory for the week will be 25 units, which costs $1.25 to carry. Being out of stock 92 per cent of the time costs us: .92 × $100 = $92. The total cost of this policy will be $93.25 per reorder or $93.25 per week.

If we order when we get down to 100 items, our average inventory will be 50 units which we will carry for two weeks and whose cost to carry is $2.50 a week or $5 total. We'll be out of stock 72 per cent of the time, though, before new supplies arrive: .72 × $100 = $72, the cost of stockouts. The total cost now is $77.00 or $35.00 per week.

If we order at 150, the inventory will average 75 units and it will be carried for three weeks with a carrying cost of $3.75 a week for three weeks or a total of $11.25. By ordering at this point, we reduce our stockout cost to .12 × $100 or $12. The total cost is $23.25 or $7.75 per week.

Going on, if we reorder at 200, the inventory will average 100 units and will be carried for four weeks, which will cost $20. The stockout costs will go down to .04 × $100 or $4. The total cost is $24 or $6.00 per week. Ordering at the 250 mark costs $31.25 or $6.25 per week. Our figures tell us that the proper reorder point lies between 200 and 250 units and that probably it is close to the 200 mark.

We started out to talk about the size of safety stocks and are now talking about reorder points. Earlier we said that the reorder point was a quantity which was the total of the expected usage during the reorder lead time plus a quantity (the safety stock) which you really expected to have on hand when reorders arrived.

Returning to the tabulation on page 367 and interpolating, we find that in the past the average time for getting new supplies was 2.74 weeks, during which time we use 137 units. So if we now choose to use a reorder point of 210 units, 73 of the 210 are actually the safety stock. At 5 cents each per week, the cost of carrying this safety stock is $3.65 per week or $189.80 per year.

STUDY MATERIALS

16-1 When should you use dollar limits to inventories?

16-2 From an inventory control point of view, what policies should dominate your thinking in each of the following situations?

1 The stock of sandwiches in a vending machine.
2 Oil in a home heating system tank.
3 The relations between toll booths and cars at the Holland Tunnel between New York and New Jersey.
4 Water in the city's reservoir.
5 Cash in a supermarket cash register at the start of a day.

16-3 Do you need separate control of each subinventory of items stocked at severa points in the same large factory? What problems are involved?

16-4 Do you need separate control of every size package of the same product? What problems are involved?

16-5 Your company is considering using mathematical decision rules to set the size of safety stocks. You are told to gather the necessary data. What data do you want and why?

16-6 The St. Paul Brass Fittings Company has done well at keeping inventories down and turnover up but in some departments setup costs are more than 25 per cent of the payroll. Is this bad? How would you decide?

16-7 The Sunset Manufacturing Company has analyzed its stock-room investment turnover and found it to be considerably below what the management thinks it should be. A quick review of the stock cards showed that a six months' supply of many items was on hand. Very few items had less than two months' supply on hand. The purchasing agent of the company bought the major materials used in the company's products. They were bought on the basis of price forecasts, and it was felt that that practice should be continued. The stocks of items ordered from the cards by the stock card clerk were regarded as excessive. The record clerk ordered replenishment supplies of these items as he saw fit, although he was supposed to order no more than three months' supply on any one reorder. He could, however, use his own judgment as to when to reorder, and if he thought that the demand might increase, he ordered a new supply sooner than he normally would, even when the current stock was ample for the time being. Before he took the job, the shop had been held up frequently for lack of stock. He was quite proud of having solved that difficulty.

Is there a problem here? Since it will all be used in due time, is there any harm in having plenty of stock on hand? Set up a procedure to reduce the inventory without running out of stock.

16-8 The Parts Supply Company is located 500 miles away from the Davis Company. Shipment of electronic tubes, BD649, an item bought in quantity by Davis, is by rail. From three days to one week must be allowed for shipment. In the Parts Supply Company's plant another two weeks is needed to process orders.

The smallest quantity of these tubes that can be produced economically is 5,000 or one-half of a week's usage of the Davis Co. Davis' usage fluctuates, however, between 8,000 and 12,000 per week.

How far ahead should Davis release orders? How big an inventory of this kind of electronic tubes should Davis carry? If you say that you need more data in order to answer, what data? How would you then go about calculating the answers to these questions?

16-9   Your company treasurer says, "Our inventory turnover has always been the lowest in the industry but this year we are going to be tight on capital and will have to keep inventory investment down." The sales manager says, "We can't afford not to give cutomers excellent service and to ship catalog products immediately." The production manager says, "Running out of item L49 might make us close down several important operations."

1   What basic purpose do safety stocks seem to serve in this company?

2   Looking at this record of usage of item L49 what reorder point do you set for it? Why? (It usually takes 2 weeks to get an order in although in the last 10 orders there was one instance where it took 3 weeks.)

USAGE PER WEEK IN UNITS	NUMBER OF WEEKS IN LAST 50
80–89	1
90–99	4
100–109	16
110–119	22
120–129	5
130–139	0
140–149	2

16-10   Your use is 100 bars of 1-inch-diameter steel bars a month (20 workdays). Management tells you to keep a minimum of 10 days supply on hand since there are some irregularities in both the usage and the normal 8-day lead time required to get more bars. If you reorder 125 bars at a time, what will be (1) your expected minimum quantity on hand, (2) the order point, (3) the average inventory? (4) How many times a year would you reorder? (5) What will be the answers to 1, 2, and 3, if slow deliveries double the replenishment lead time?

16-11   Does the reorder point depend on the reorder quantity? Why or why not?

16-12   What is the relationship between reorder quantity, average inventory, and order frequency? Would A B C analysis help in analyzing policy alternatives arising from this relationship?

chapter seventeen

INVENTORY CONTROL (CONTINUED)

INVENTORY FORMULAS

How big an inventory should you carry? In the last chapter we spoke of optimal quantities but only in a general way. We also said that certain costs increase as the size of the inventory increases, and other costs increase when you hold inventories down. Somewhere between these two extremes is a point where the total cost of maintaining the inventory is at a minimum. Formulas can be used to determine this minimum but before examining them a few words of caution are in order.

A formula can produce the right answer only if you put the right figures into it. Here are some of the figures you need to have in order to use formulas in inventory control: future usage, lead time, setup cost (for made items), unit prices for different quantities (for bought items), the probability of obsolescence, cost of storage space, probability that either your rate of use or the lead time will change and so cause you to be out of stock, the costliness of being out of stock, and the interest rate on the money tied up in inventory.

Since you can't get exact figures for most of these factors, it is obvious why objections are often raised to what is sometimes described as an overly quantitative approach to inventory problems. Take, for example, the cost of storage space. If an otherwise unoccupied bin is used for storage of an item, what storage cost should be assigned to the item's inventory? Or what about obsolescence? If an item becomes obsolete its stock may have to be scrapped. Yet when no change occurs there is no obsolescence. So far as individual items are concerned obsolescence usually is an all or nothing situation.

Another objection is the specific nature of formulas or models. Any one model covers one and only one set of related factors. If the situation changes then so does the nature of the formula that you need to use. If you want to cover varied situations you need many formulas. There is also a matter mentioned in the preceding chapter: the extra costs incurred in obtaining the necessary figures for the computations. Without formulas you don't have to get these figures.

These and other objections can often be answered. For example, storage space does cost money and while a single unused bin is free, you would understate your costs if you always assumed free bin space. And although obsolescence is a black and white matter in the case of any single item, it does sometimes happen and in the case of a stock room of thousands of items it can be properly included in the calculations on a probability basis. Admittedly, too, you shouldn't use quantitative inventory controls unless you are prepared to develop enough formulas to do the job properly. And the expense of getting the figures can be judged more or less as any other investment problem. What will it cost to get the figures and what inventory cost savings might result? If the data-gathering costs are high perhaps you really should not use quantitative methods.

Admittedly also the inexactness of the numbers used in formulas is a weakness, yet *these factors do end up affecting costs*. And you must decide on reorder quantities whether you use formulas or not. If you don't use formulas, you have to weigh these factors in your mind. They are surely no more exact in your mental calculations than they are in formulas. So, say quantitative approach advocates, use formulas and get the best answer that you can and then use this answer with discretion if you feel uneasy about some of the numbers you used. And by all means don't forget that if you put a number into a formula that is hardly more than a guess this action does *not* in some subtle way transform the guess into a fact.

Operations research journals contain many examples of formulas by which to minimize inventory costs or to plan inventories for maximum profits under specific circumstances.[1] Because of space limitations we will offer only one example before going on to economic lot sizes. The example given below was developed to help management decide what policy to follow in the case of making up a stock of a Christmas trade item.[2]

The item was a set of three cosmetics packaged together and offered as a special deal for the Christmas trade. If the company didn't make up enough packages ahead, it would either lose sales or have to make up more hurriedly and at extra cost, yet if it made up too many at first some would be left over unsold. These would have to be unpacked and the items later sold separately, and again extra costs would be involved. The following formulas for solving this problem were originally developed by John F. Magee: Let

$$V = \text{the volume of demand}$$
$$f(V) = \text{the probability density function of demand (i.e., distribution of demand during one period)}$$
$$\int_K^\infty f(V)dV = \text{the likelihood of selling an amount } Y \text{ or more during a season}$$

[1] See, in particular, the issues of *Management Science*, the journal of the Institute of Management Science.

[2] This problem is fully described in Robert H. Bock and William K. Holstein (eds.), *Production Planning and Control*, Charles E. Merrill Books, Inc., Columbus, Ohio, 1963, pp. 225–229.

n = the variable cost of making and holding a unit of stock in inventory during the selling period, including the capital charge for inventory investment, etc.

m = the profit per unit sold

L = the cost per unit of not filling an order (loss of good will), over and above the loss of profit

P = the cost of carrying a unit of inventory if unsold by the end of the period

K = the size of the inventory on hand at the beginning of the season

Then the profit earned during the replenishment cycle is given by

$$p = mV - P(K - V) - nK; V \leq K$$
$$= mK - L(V - K) - nK; V > K$$

and the expected profit earned during the replenishment cycle, $E(p)$, is given by

$$E(p) = m \int_0^K Vf(V)dV - nK + mK \int_K^\infty f(V)dV$$

$$-L \int_K^\infty (V - K)f(V)dV - P \int_0^K (K - V)f(V)dV$$

Again, differentiating the expected profit with respect to the inventory on hand at the beginning of the season, K, yields

$$\frac{dE(p)}{dK} = -n + (m + L) - (M + L + P) \int_0^K f(V)dV$$

The maximum profit will be earned when $dE(p)/dK = 0$; that is, when

$$\int_0^K f(V)dV = \frac{m + L - n}{m + L + P}$$

There isn't any one answer to this problem because it depends on how much you lose per unit from making up too few or too many the first time and on how reliable you believe your market forecast to be. This is one of the beauties of formulas; they will give you the appropriate answer for whatever set of figures you put into them. In this example Magee assumed that undershooting would result in cost of $1.75 per package to make up more in a hurry. Unpacking costs of leftovers, if any, would be $1 per package. So, aiming too low would cost $1.75 per package short and aiming too high would cost $1 per package left over.

Magee assumed that the sales forecasts had, in the past, been off as much as 20 per cent in half the number of cases (in one-fourth of the cases they were 20 per cent or more too low, and in one-fourth of the cases they were 20 per cent or more too high) and that in one-fifth of the cases the error was as much as 40 per cent (10 per cent were too low and 10 per cent were too high).

Using these forecast reliability probabilities and considering the fact that it cost more to make up shortages than to rework leftovers, Magee found that the company should make up 10 per cent more packages than the sales forecast called for and that this would result in a greater probable profit than any other policy. Thus his formula told management the optimum choice to make.

ECONOMIC LOTS

When you balance off the savings from making or buying big lots against the cost of carrying bigger inventories, you end up ordering "economic lots." Small lots hold down inventories and all of the costs associated with carrying them. But small lots increase all of the costs associated with reordering. The economic lot (the ELS, for economic lot size, or EOQ, for economic ordering quantity) is the quantity of any item which you need to make or buy at one time to get the lowest possible unit cost. You can express EOQs in units, or dollar values, or as weeks or months of supply.

Quite a few companies recognize the economic lot idea but use only rough approximations and let it go at that. Milwaukee's Falk Company runs a six-month supply of items costing $5 or less, a three-month supply of $5 to $10 items, and a one-month supply of $10 to $50 items. For items over $50, Falk makes parts only to fill the needs of assembly orders. Union Special (sewing machine manufacturer) makes a three-month supply at a time if almost no setup time is needed, a six-month supply for moderate setup cost items, and more for big setup cost items.

Using such rough measures may not be bad since you don't have to hit the most economical quantity exactly. In fact, as figure 17-2 shows, if you produce up to 25 per cent more or less than the ideal quantity, the unit cost isn't affected much because the total cost line is relatively flat in this part of the curve.

Years ago not many companies calculated economic lot sizes because of the calculating work required. But since computers have now made the job simple, many companies use EOQs. The formula for calculating the EOQ is

$$\text{EOQ} = \sqrt{\frac{2 \times \text{number of pieces per year} \times \text{setup cost for one setup}}{\text{cost per piece} \times \text{inventory carrying charge rate}}}$$

In this formula, the setup cost includes the paper work costs of making out an order and the cost per piece includes material, direct labor, and overhead.

The EOQ formula has several assumptions inherent in it. They are:

1 Demand for the item is uniform and constant.

2 The entire lot of the item is received at one time.

3 The number of orders to be written does not exceed the company's ability to write and process them.

4 Dollar limits on inventory are either nonexistent or not exceeded by the quantities ordered.

5 There are no purchase quantity discounts available.

Figure 17-1 shows how the inventory of an item would fluctuate under this set of assumptions.

As we said earlier, there are two sets of costs that concern us, the costs of acquiring stock and the costs of owning it.

In the case of purchased items, the costs of acquisition include all the paper work costs of filling out purchase requisitions, typing purchase orders, filing forms, processing vouchers, writing checks, and similar activities. Besides these, there are the costs of the buyers and the purchasing agent, receiving inspectors, and the stock-room work directly related to putting the material into storage. You can't get very exact figures for placing an order but ordering costs seem to average around $25 to $30 per order in most companies.

In the case of items you make yourself, the costs of acquisition again include paperwork costs. They also include the still larger costs of setting up the factory machines to perform the operations on the lot. These machine setup costs often run up into hundreds of dollars. Most of the costs of acquisition are the same or nearly the same for small or large orders, so their cost per order is almost constant.

The other set of costs that concern us is identical whether we buy

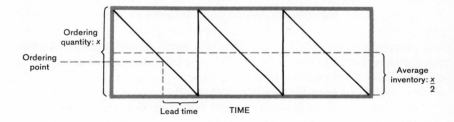

FIGURE 17-1   Inventory fluctuations under EOQ formula assumptions.

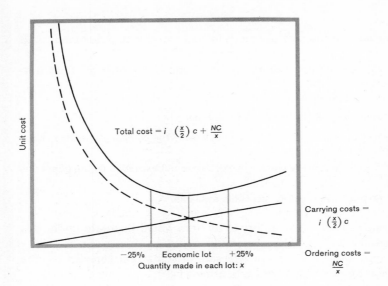

FIGURE 17-2   Cost model for economic order quantity calculation.

or make the item. Carrying costs can be expressed in dollars but they are usually expressed as a percentage of the value of the inventory. They include storage, transportation and material handling, obsolescence, shelf wear, deterioration from rust, mold, or other causes, insurance, property taxes, pilferage, and supplies used in maintaining the inventory, as well as the imputed interest on the money tied up in inventory.

Figure 17-2 shows graphically how inventory costs are related to ordering practices. The per unit costs of acquisition go down as the quantity ordered goes up, as is shown by the downward-sloping line in figure 17-2. Inventory carrying costs, on the other hand, rise linearly with the size of the inventory, as is shown by the rising straight line in figure 17-2. The symbol i is used to represent this carrying charge, while c is the unit cost of the item. (Carrying charges should be calculated on the average inventory investment, which is half of the cost of an economic lot.) The inventory carrying charge rate i in the formulas below would in practice probably be somewhere between 15 and 25 per cent (perhaps 10 per cent for obsolescence, 6 per cent for interest, 5 per cent for shelf wear and deterioration, and 4 per cent for handling, taxes, and insurance).

In figure 17-2 we also see an upper curve which is the total cost per unit for all possible order quantities. This upper curve, which is merely the sum of the two lower curves, is at a minimum where the ordering costs equal the carrying costs. The quantity represented by this low point on the X scale is the EOQ.

This point can be determined graphically or it can be calculated. Since it occurs where ordering costs equal the carrying costs, we can set these two equal to each other and solve the resulting equation. Or we can use differential calculus and take the derivative of the total cost curve, set it equal to zero, and solve the resulting equation.

The latter method is the one usually preferred by mathematicians since it proves the statement that the minimum occurs where the ordering costs equal the carrying costs. The equation for the total cost is

$$TC = i\left(\frac{x}{2}\right)c + \frac{NC}{x}$$

Taking the derivative of this with respect to x gives:

$$\frac{d(TC)}{d(x)} = \frac{ic}{2} - \frac{NC}{x^2}$$

Setting this equal to zero and rearranging terms, we get

$\frac{ic}{2} = \frac{NC}{x^2}$ (If both sides of this equation are multiplied by x, then the equality of the costs is evident.)

Solving for x we obtain

$$x = \sqrt{\frac{2NC}{ic}}$$

This is the EOQ formula as we gave it in text form earlier.

For any given annual usage N, the number of orders written in a year is N/x, where x is the quantity ordered on each order. If we let C be the ordering cost per order, then the total ordering cost per order is CN/x. This is shown graphically in figure 17-2.

An example will show how the formula works. Annual usage: 25,000 pieces. Ordering costs: $100. Cost per piece for each unit: $14. Inventory carrying charge rate: 20 per cent.

$$\begin{aligned}
EOQ &= \sqrt{\frac{2 \times 25,000 \times 100}{14 \times .20}} \\
&= \sqrt{\frac{5,000,000}{2.80}} \\
&= \sqrt{1,785,714} \\
&= 1,336
\end{aligned}$$

You ought to buy this item or to make it in lots of between 1,000 and 1,700 units. It won't matter much where, in between, you set the quantity, because, as we said earlier, the unit cost curve is almost flat for volumes one-quarter larger or smaller than the exact EOQ, 1,336 in this case.

Some companies precompute economic lot answers and plot them on a nomograph. Figure 17-3 shows one developed at Eastman Kodak. Usually, to keep them simple, nomograph makers draw up different nomographs for different interest rates. The Eastman chart is based on a carrying charge of 16 per cent.

To use this nomograph for our example above, you start by locating the ordering cost ($100) on the right scale. Then find the weekly use of the item (500 units) on the inside scale of the left line of the nomograph. Next

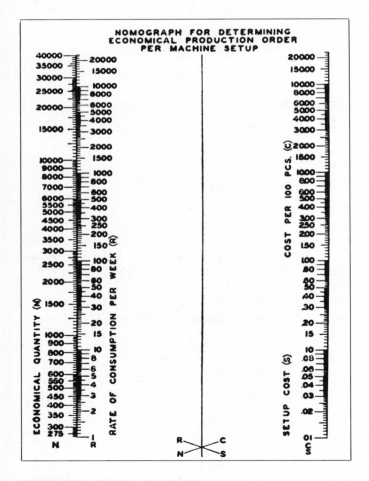

FIGURE 17-3   (Eastman Kodak Co.)

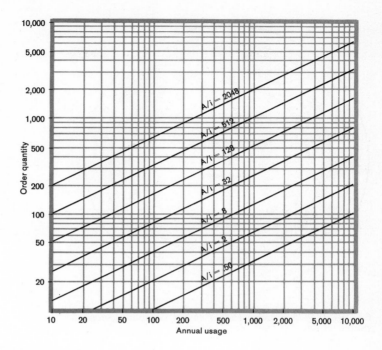

FIGURE 17-4

connect them, noting the point where the line crosses the middle line, point A. Then, find the cost per 100 units ($1,400) on the right scale. Connect it by a straight line to point A and then extend it on to the left scale. Read the economic quantity on the outside scale. It shows 1,500 as the economic lot size.

Using our formula, we got 1,336 as the economic lot size. Using Eastman's nomograph we get 1,500. The difference is caused by the different carrying charge rate (20 per cent in the formula and 16 per cent in Eastman's nomograph).

John F. Magee some years ago developed another kind of chart, shown in figure 17-4, on which you can read off economic ordering quantities from a series of diagonal lines plotted on double logarithmic paper.[3]

In figure 17-4, A is the order cost and i is the annual carrying cost. Use the chart as follows: assume that the cost of placing a purchase order is $10 and that the cost of carrying the item is 20 cents a year. Divide $10

[3] For an explanation see John F. Magee, *Production Planning and Inventory Control*, McGraw-Hill Book Company, New York, 1958, p. 53.

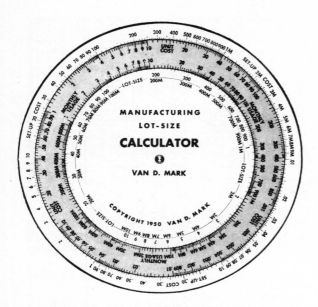

FIGURE 17-5 A circular slide rule for computing economic lot sizes. (Robert Van D. Mark.)

by .20 and get a ratio of 50. On figure 17-4 there is no line for a ratio of 50 but there is one for 32 and another for 128. You can interpolate between these lines by inspection and read off approximate values for a ratio of 50.

We now need to look at our annual usage. Suppose that it is 1,000. Go up the 1,000 line from the bottom to just past the 32 ratio line to where the 50 line would be if it were drawn in. Then go across to the left scale and find the proper order quantity, in this case about 300 units.

Figure 17-5 shows still another way to get the economic ordering quantity. It is a circular slide rule. You rotate a top circular section against the lower, larger circular section and arrive at your answer. This particular slide rule uses a 17 per cent inventory carrying charge rate. Other slide rules could be made using other interest rate charges.

USE OF EOQs WHEN DELIVERY IS NOT INSTANTANEOUS
Now that we have examined the basic order quantity formulation, let us see if we can remove some of the restrictions we placed originally upon the economic order quantity formula.

COMPLETE ORDERS NOT ARRIVING ALL AT ONE TIME   The first restriction we might examine is that the entire lot be received at one time. While this usually is a valid assumption for purchased products, often this is not the case for items which we manufacture ourselves.

Often there is a period of time t_1 when manufacturing, use, and inventory buildup are all occurring at the same time. And there is another time period t_2 when only use and inventory take-down are occurring. The total time t of the cycle is the sum of $t_1 + t_2$. Our inventory model now appears as in figure 17-6.

Since this situation usually occurs when we manufacture the item ourselves, we will refer to the setup cost as S (in place of the ordering cost as C). We will be concerned with the rate at which inventory builds up during period t_1, since this will determine the number of available units at the start of period t_2. The inventory available at the beginning of period t_2 will be equal to

$$x \frac{p - d}{p}$$

where p is the production rate during period t_1, d is the demand or use rate during period t_1, and x is the quantity ordered. (Use is still assumed to be uniform and constant.)

For example, if we manufacture 50 units a day and use 40 units a day, the available inventory at the end of period t_1 will be $.2x$ or 20 per cent of

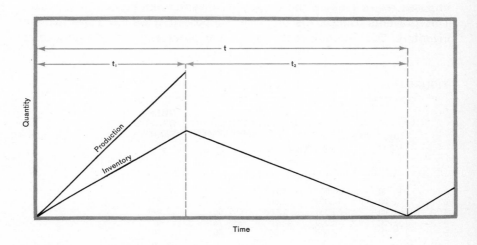

FIGURE 17-6

the lot size ordered (since we used up 80 per cent of the production as fast as it arrived). The average inventory in the whole time period t is one-half of the quantity on hand after the lot is produced. Our new total cost equation then is

$$TC = i\frac{x}{2}\left(\frac{p - d}{p}\right)c + \frac{NS}{x}$$

which can be solved for x by any of the three previously discussed methods. This works out to

$$x = \sqrt{\frac{2NS}{ic}\left(\frac{p}{p - d}\right)}$$

Here x is the EOQ or the ELS, as it is sometimes called when making items in lots yet where arrivals go on simultaneously with usage.

The length of the time periods can then be determined as

$$t_1 = \frac{x}{p}$$

$$t_2 = \frac{x(p - d/d)}{d} = x\frac{p - d}{pd}$$

If the production rate is high relative to the use rate most of the lot will be in inventory when its production finishes because not many items were used during period t_1. The term $(p - d)/p$ will be close to 1 and then figure 17-6 will take on the familiar sawtooth form of figure 17-1.

DOLLAR LIMITS AS THEY RELATE TO EOQs Sometimes management imposes restrictions on the amount of inventory investment it will allow. This prevents using EOQs properly. Suppose that we stock five items in inventory. Our ordering costs are $25 per order and the inventory carry-

FIGURE 17-7

ITEM	COST PER UNIT c	ANNUAL DEMAND N	EOQ x	AVERAGE INVESTMENT $\frac{cx}{2}$	NUMBER OF ORDERS PER YEAR $\frac{N}{x}$
1	$ .50	20,000	3,162	$ 790.50	6.33
2	1.00	10,000	1,581	790.50	6.33
3	1.00	5,000	1,118	559.00	4.47
4	2.50	5,000	707	883.75	7.07
5	2.00	8,000	1,000	1,000.00	8.00
TOTAL				$4,023.75	32.20

FIGURE 17-8

ITEM	NEW AVERAGE INVESTMENT $\dfrac{cx'}{2}$	NEW ORDERING QUANTITY x'	NUMBER OF ORDERS PER YEAR $\dfrac{N}{x'}$
1	$ 589.50	2,358	8.48
2	589.50	1,179	8.48
3	416.70	833	6.00
4	658.80	527	9.49
5	745.50	746	10.72
TOTAL	$3,000.00		43.17

ing charge is 20 per cent per year. Item costs and annual demand are shown in figure 17-7. Also shown are the EOQs for each item, the average dollar investment in each item, and the number of times each item has to be ordered in a year.

The average investment in inventory is $4,023.75. Now suppose that top management decides to hold us down to $3,000 investment in these items of inventory. Where should we make the reduction? All on one or two items or on all proportionally? It works out that the optimal way is to reduce the average investment in all items proportionally until the dollar constraint is met.

Figure 17-8 shows how the new investment in each item is met by reducing it to 3,000/4,023.75 of its former amount. These reduced investments force proportional reductions in ordering quantities and cause an inverse increase in the number of orders per year.

How much will it cost the company to carry out this uneconomical edict? The total annual cost of carrying any inventory is: the average investment times the carrying cost rate plus the ordering cost times the number of orders written. For our unconstrained case (using EOQs) the annual cost would be .20($4,023.75) + $25(32.20) = $1,609.50. For the constrained case (the $3,000 investment limitation) the annual cost would be .20($3,000) + $25(43.17) = $1,679.25.

This reduction in inventory investment of $1,023.75 will cost the company $69.50 per year or 6.8 per cent on the money released. This seems to be a reasonable price to pay for releasing money from inventory. (The extra cost is this small only because, as we said earlier, the cost curve in the vicinity of the EOQ is quite flat. Costs don't go up very much until you depart substantially from the EOQ.)

This relatively small cost of releasing money from investment in inventory explains why monetary policies often override economic lot considerations. You might want to make quantities larger than economic lots during slack periods in order to level out production. Or when you are short of cash, as in our example above, you might want to hold reorder quantities down below economic lot sizes. In either case, as we said earlier, it won't cost much unless you go more than 25 per cent away from the EOQ. And whatever you do you know the price you pay for following other policies and not using economic lot sizes.

Sometimes management doesn't use EOQs because it doesn't realize that production is being carried on in uneconomic lots. One reason for management's failure to appreciate the costliness of short runs is that the setting up of jobs on machines is often done by special setup men whose cost is charged to an overhead account and not to jobs. This is almost always so when you use standard costs. Management doesn't see that total setup costs have been increased because of the many small orders and so does not appreciate the costliness of these small orders. This danger is, however, less important when you purchase in lots (as contrasted with manufacturing in lots in your own plant) because vendors usually charge more for small quantities and cost differences are visible in higher prices.

EFFECTS OF PERIODIC REORDERING   In Chapter 16 we said that companies sometimes reorder on a periodic basis, often on a monthly basis. And we said then that such a practice overlooked the merits of economic lots. We can now test this policy to see how much it costs.

Had we, in our example above, imposed a monthly reordering policy, each of our five items would have been reordered every month so that in a year 60 orders would have had to be written. The order quantity would be $N_n/12$, and the total average inventory investment would be $\sum_{1}^{n} (c_n +$ $N_n/24)$. Figure 17-9 shows the resulting figures.

The cost of maintaining the inventory on a monthly reorder basis would be $.20(\$2,229.17) + \$25(60) = \$1,945.83$.

This tells us that using a monthly reorder policy would cost $336.08 more than using an EOQ policy. Monthly reordering would probably also result in more stockouts than with EOQs because there would be 60 stockout opportunities instead of 32. The stockouts would, however, be short since new supplies come in so often.

Monthly reordering will, however, release $1,794.58 from inventory investment. Yet if this is the only gain, the $336.08 cost, which amounts to 18.7 per cent, is too high.

In practice the choice between periodic reordering and using EOQs

FIGURE 17-9

ITEM	ORDER QUANTITY $\dfrac{N}{12}$	AVERAGE INVESTMENT $\dfrac{cN}{24}$	NUMBER OF ORDERS PER YEAR
1	1,667	$ 416 .67	12
2	833	416 .67	12
3	417	208 .33	12
4	417	520 .83	12
5	667	666 .67	12
TOTAL		$2,229 .17	60

rarely is as clear-cut as we have made it in our example, because of other factors. Maybe bunching orders will save money and make periodic ordering a better practice. And we have already mentioned the possible need to keep the factory busy and the matter of money. Either of these factors may justify practices that are uneconomical when viewed solely from the inventory point of view. The important things to remember are that we are trying to minimize *total* production costs and that the type of analysis we have been illustrating furnishes us information that helps us to make the best decisions.

QUANTITY DISCOUNTS
Suppliers often offer quantity discounts. The bigger the quantity ordered, the lower the price. This means that the unit cost c in our formulas is not always the same number but changes depending on the quantity ordered.

When the vendor quotes different prices for different volume ranges you need first to calculate the EOQ as if the highest unit price (the price for small quantities) were in effect over the entire quantity range. If this EOQ calls for a bigger quantity than the point where a lower price starts, no problem is involved. For example, suppose that a price of $1 per unit applies up to 99 units but for orders of 100 and over the price is 90 cents. If you calculate the EOQ at the $1 price and find it to be 125 units you'd buy 125 units even without the price reduction. The price discount becomes merely a bonus for doing what you would do anyway. You should, of course, recalculate the EOQ using the 90-cent price, but this would only raise the EOQ to a larger figure.

A problem arises, however, when, following this procedure, the EOQ

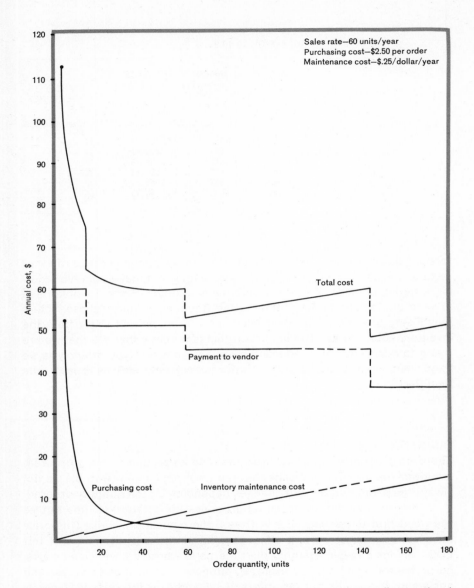

FIGURE 17-10 Cost curve when purchasing with quantity discounts. (International Business Machines Corp.)

falls below the discount point. Suppose that at the 90-cent price the EOQ is 85 units, yet the 90-cent price applies only if you order 100 or more. When situations like this occur you need also to calculate the EOQ for the $1 price and the total cost (including the cost of the bigger average inventory) of ordering 100 units at the 90-cent price. Maybe you will find that it pays to order 100 at 90 cents even though this is more than the 90-cent EOQ of 85 units.

As an aid in solving problems of this kind, tables can be constructed relating the dollar demand of an item to the percentage discount offered and to an EOQ multiplier. If the ratio of the quantity necessary to get the discount to the EOQ is greater than this multiplier, then the discount can be ignored and the original EOQ be used. If it is less than the multiplier, then the EOQ should be raised by using the multiplier to get the ordering quantity. These precomputed tables must be constructed for each different ordering cost and interest carrying charge.

GOVERNMENT–FURNISHED ITEMS

If you make products that go into end products that the Federal government buys you will probably use some items or raw materials furnished by the government.

These make problems. You may be required to keep them apart in special stock rooms. The government may even insist that you post a bond and withdraw its items only on special requisitions. Sometimes this is because the items are valuable and sometimes because they are scarce. Maybe they are both. Government furnished items have their own identification numbers. And you have to keep special records of what you have left and what you have used and what for.

Sometimes the items are identical to your regular stock. You may have to double number them, putting the government's identification on its supplies and your own number on your own stock. Besides, the government will probably want to audit your inventory of its items every now and then. All in all, government furnished items are a bother to handle.

Actually the government has bigger inventory control problems than has any company. Even General Motors or Sears, Roebuck has to control only a few hundred thousand items. But the U.S. Navy alone has to control 3 million items. The government has its problems.

Government furnished items have one great advantage. They are not part of your inventory. You don't have to pay for them nor do you have any investment in them. Perhaps it is only reasonable to expect the government to want you to protect its inventory.

STOCK–ROOM OPERATION

Normally we think of stock rooms as places where you stock and take care of materials and parts, issuing them on demand. Yet look at figure 17-11. Notice that, in a sense, keeping things in bins is all waste. So far as the materials are concerned, stockkeeping is a matter of "pick them up here, put them there, pick them up again, put them somewhere else." The point is that you should try to cut the cost of this service all that you can short of doing it poorly and wastefully. Try to do storekeeping minus the keeping as much as possible. Also, never forget that a stock room is to *serve*. You don't want a neat, well-organized, admirably managed stores department that doesn't *serve*.

Try to cut out all the waste material handling that you can in stock rooms. To cut down on travel, particularly with big items and heavy users, stack them as close to the incoming and outgoing doors as you can. Store items in the original package if you can. Putting things into bins and getting them out again later is all waste. You can cut down this handling by cutting out the bins. Just have shelves and put the material in trays or

FIGURE 17-11   Stored items.

pans that can be taken down and put back, or use rotary bins. They are time savers.

You need to keep records for thousands of items. But this is not the forbidding job it once was because computers can keep all of these records on tapes. Small companies without computers may still need to use files of cards, such as the one shown in figure 17-12. If you do use such cards probably you'll want to use some kind of movable colored plastic tabs or "flags" along the edges of the cards so that you can spot cards whose stock is running low and for other reasons. Flat Kardex drawers of cards are good for this purpose.

C products, those for which you keep the minimum of records, need a little different treatment in the stock room from A and B items. Decide what reorder point you need and then use the "bin reserve" idea described in Chapter 16. Set the reorder quantity apart physically from the rest of the stock of the item. If the item is small, count out the reorder quantity and tie it up in a sack in the bin. Or, if you want, tie up standard quantities in sacks with a tag on each one. When you issue or open a sackful, pull the tag off and send it in to the stock clerk who notes its issue. If the items are stacked, put a cardboard over the bottom two or three layers. Or, if you have enough bins, use two bins. Put the reorder quantity in the right-hand bin. Also try always to use up all old stocks before you start issuing newly received stock. Don't dump new items in on top of old ones.

The point to the bin reserve idea is that you will know it when you dip into the reorder quantity. The stock-room clerk tells the order clerk when he starts using the reorder quantity. The order clerk then orders more. You don't run out of stock yet you keep almost no records.

Some items need protection against "shelf wear." Metal parts need to be coated with oil. You might even have to wrap them in protective paper, or put them in plastic bags or little individual cartons. For better shelf stacking try to standardize these if possible. For items you make yourself you can standardize package sizes but it is harder to do for purchased items.

OPEN STOCK ROOMS An "open" stock room means keeping materials and parts out in the shop next to the men who use them. The men help themselves to whatever they need and it saves writing requisitions and trips to the store room. You find open stocks mostly in assembly work in continuous manufacturing.

Don't mistake, though, about open stock rooms. Don't let assemblers and expediters or even foremen come into regular stock rooms and help themselves. If you let them, they will take what they want and then will sometimes give you a requisition and sometimes not. Letting them do this

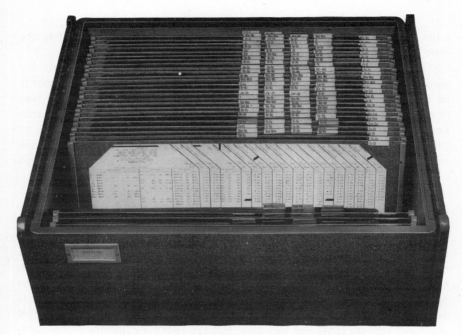

FIGURE 17-12 Some companies use stock record cards of the above type, which are filed in a partially offset vertical position as shown. This arrangement permits the ready selection of any card. It also allows the item number, name, and stock to be visible at all times. (Tallman Robbins and Co., and International Business Machines Corp.)

is sure to result in wasteful material use. They will always take seven when they need six. Then they'll unwrap them all and let them get rusty. Even little items like rivets will be wastefully used. Worst of all they'll use long lead time items, such as roller bearings, and not tell you. Then when you go to use the supply you are supposed to have, it will be gone and maybe you can't get more for months. This is serious so don't let regular stock rooms be "open" in this way. Make enclosed stock rooms out-of-bounds for all non-stock-room employees. Also keep the stock room locked up after hours. Don't allow "midnight expediting" or unofficial "liberating" of parts.

Open stock rooms probably won't reduce your inventories very much because you will usually have to "back-up" most open stocks with stocks in regular enclosed store rooms. The savings are in less handling, not in very much less inventory. The supply that you keep on the shop floor is only part of what you have on hand of any item.

CALLING OUT STOCK   In lot assembly, you need to use accumulation bins. Just before time to start assembly, you "call out" all the parts that you will need. Finished stock-room employees gather the items together and deliver them to the accumulation bin. Depending on your practice, you may or may not withdraw regularly stocked parts needed for the order and put them in the accumulation bin ahead of time. There is an advantage in pulling parts early in that this really amounts to reserving parts for the order. It also lets you draw up a realistic short list.

Some companies do not pull C items for assembly, relying instead on open stocks. Although this saves a certain amount of work it opens the door to mistakes. There will be places where special nuts and bolts are needed but some of them look like regular nuts and bolts. If regulars are kept in open stock the men are more likely to use regulars where they should use specials than if you pull every last nut and bolt especially for the assembly order.

In airplane production, the final assembly is continuous as is the assembly of most big subassemblies. Parts are pulled for several airplanes at a time and taken to the appropriate assembly work stations. There they are used much as open stock. But it isn't open stock in the usual sense because exact numbers of parts are delivered to assemble a certain number (only a few, and maybe only one) of airplanes.

Finished goods stock rooms in airplane and missile manufacture are really stock balancing points. Parts arrive in lots and go out as numerous, frequently small collections of parts for a few airplanes. They come in to the second floor of a two-story stock room. Then, as they are needed, they are pulled and collected together on the first floor in sets or collections as needed by the assembly department.

When assembly is by lot—not continuous—you may choose *not* to send special items, whether bought or made, to the finished parts stock room. Many companies route specials directly to the accumulation bin for that order near the assembly floor. Doing this requires, of course, your putting the accumulation bin number on route tags, shop orders, and purchase orders. Probably you'll want also to put the assembly order number on shop orders and purchase orders for parts. Common parts and parts normally carried in stock are, however, kept in the stock room. You would have to call them out and take them to the accumulation area shortly before assembly starts.

CHARGING STOCK TO ASSEMBLY ORDERS   When you buy or make parts especially for certain assembly orders, should you charge the assembly orders directly with their cost? Or should you charge the items first into your finished parts stock and then back out to assembly orders? You can charge the costs either way regardless of whether you put the items themselves into finished stores and take them out later.

Companies differ on their method of charging. It is surely simpler to charge all special items directly to assembly orders. Some companies prefer, though, to charge them into stores first so that the total value of items moving out of stores to assembly (moving out in a bookkeeping sense) will be the total cost of all materials used.

SURPLUS INVENTORY
Try as you may, you can never avoid having too much inventory of some items. As long as the surpluses are items that you are still using, there isn't much to worry about because time will take care of using any surpluses. You just won't reorder more such items for a while.

But with thousands of items you always have some whose use has virtually stopped or has completely stopped. You'd better dispose of such stocks and the sooner the better. You want to salvage as much of their value as you can, and the possibilities grow less with age. You want to put the money invested in such items back to work again earning something for you.

The best choice is to rework dead items into something similar, thus recovering most of their full value. However, often you cannot do this. You can't rework buggy whips into automobile horns. Probably you'll have to sell old surplus stocks at scrap prices.

No one pays any attention to obsolete stocks unless you make it someone's job. Better make production control or inventory control men responsible for calling your attention to dead stocks. Then be sure that someone decides what to do with the dead items and that he does it.

PHYSICAL INVENTORIES

Probably you should count what you have on hand once a year or more. Don't depend wholly on the "perpetual" inventory, the record that you keep on your record cards or computer tapes, to tell you what you have on hand. With thousands of items and hundreds of thousands of transactions, errors creep in and, here and there, the record is wrong.

Even if you didn't want to count, you may have to. If you borrow money from banks, they will probably want you to count your inventories rather than to rely only on your records. City and state taxes are based on the value of your property—land, buildings, machines, and *inventories*. Tax authorities may not take your word for what you say that you have unless you count once in a while.

The Federal government, too, wants you to be sure that your records are right for income tax purposes. Your income taxes are based on your profits and your profits depend in part on the cost of materials used. And you figure their cost by starting with your inventory investment at the start of a year, plus the cost of what you buy during the year, minus the investment at the end of the year. So Uncle Sam, too, wants to know that your inventory records at the end of the year are right.

Property taxes are sometimes based on the value of inventories as shown by your annual inventory. Companies are not unaware of this. So they run down the inventory to as low a point as possible before they take the annual inventory. This saves counting costs, makes the balance sheet look good (with a low investment in inventory), and, where property taxes are involved, saves taxes because inventories are reported at a low amount.

Actually you don't positively have to count every item that you have even once a year. Not only can you "weigh count" items such as screws (weigh the stock and estimate the count from the weight) but there is also a trend away from counting everything. Companies are finding that counts of sample items (chosen at random) will tell them if all their records are about right. Auditors are willing to accept such evidence, provided their own still smaller check sample proves all right. And if the auditors accept it, so generally will the tax authorities.

Even today, however, many companies close down for a few days at the end of the fiscal year and count everything then. And some companies, for their own purposes, count more often. Usually they do it on a continuing basis (or a "cyclical" basis) by counting one section of the stock room

FIGURE 17-13 It costs more to count thousands of items than it is worth to know exactly how many of everything you have on hand. An estimate of the number of pliers in the bin would, in this case, be sufficient.

at a time, during slack times in the day when stock-room clerks aren't busy, or during evenings or Saturdays. During the course of a year, all items get counted once or twice.

Actually you don't have to count very often to keep your records fairly accurate with regard to short items. If you have less than the stock record card says, you will almost surely, at some time, run out. When you do you get your record corrected at the same time. This is, however, a poor and, sometimes, costly way to correct your records. And it doesn't work on the upper side. It tells you only when you have too few, never too many. You can also set "count points" on your cards. Whenever the stock gets down to this point, count the stock. This way you'll get a check now and then on the accuracy of your records yet not have to count big inventories. On the other hand, don't set the count points so high that you count every time that you reorder. That is too much counting.

Portable magnetic tape recorders are changing annual inventory taking methods in some companies. A checker moves along from bin to bin and calls off the tally and the item identification into his microphone. The tape then goes to tabulating card punchers who make out inventory report cards. From here on everything goes into the computer. This method cuts inventory taking time one-third.

RECEIVING MATERIALS

Materials coming into the plant have to be "received." You have to open up packages, see what the material is, and see if it arrived in good shape. You have to match it against a purchase order and see what quantity arrived and if it is the kind ordered. Receiving clerks need also to find out where to deliver the material—which stock room should get it.

If tricky tests or unusual inspection is required to see if the material passes, you will need to get the laboratory to look over the shipment or, if it is bulk material, a sample.

Normally when you place a purchase order you send a copy to the receiving department to alert the men there. Most companies block off the price (so that it doesn't show) on the receiving department copy lest knowing what things cost give men ideas about thievery.

Some companies even block off the quantity too. Then the receiving clerks have to count what they get. If they know what the count is supposed to be and the packing slip that comes along with the materials says the same thing, the clerks may get careless and not bother to count the quantity in the shipment. Not knowing for sure how many were ordered makes them check more carefully.

You can save paper work by designing the copy of the purchase order sent to receiving to do double duty and serve as a receiving report. Just send enough copies. Then receiving clerks just fill in the quantities received in a few blank spaces and send copies to purchasing, stores, accounting, and production control.

You can also save the time of receiving clerks if you make sure that vendors always put your purchase order number on the packing slip or better yet on the outside of the package. This saves the time of receiving clerks matching up receipts with orders. This is standard practice and rarely causes any trouble.

Material coming in, which was not ordered on a purchase order, makes trouble, however. Someone in your company orders something directly from a vendor by telephone and doesn't go through purchasing. In spite of your rules against anyone doing this, engineers, researchers, and others sometimes do it anyway. When the materials come in, receiving clerks have to go around asking who ordered it, where should it go, and so on. Don't let people order directly. Make them go through purchasing.

PRICING REQUISITIONS

At what price do you charge out materials from the stock room to jobs? At their cost, of course. But when you dig into the matter it proves not easy to do nor is it wholly logical to charge materials out at their actual cost.

There are two problems: (1) can you charge materials at their cost, and (2) do you want to do it? First, however, why is there any difficulty? The trouble is that you receive new supplies before the old stock is all gone but the cost of the new items is different (this is often so on bought items and always so on made items) although the items are alike. When you hand out stock which are you handing out? The oldest stock first? The newest? A mixture?

You have first to settle on your philosophy. Accountants call the alternatives, LIFO, FIFO, average cost, and standard cost. LIFO means that you regard your stock issues as being the last in, first out. FIFO is the reverse. You say that you issue the old stock first (first-in-first-out).

Suppose that you have a stock of 100 items, ten left over from an old stock that cost you $10 each. Fifty came in on another order and cost $12 each. The last forty are the most recently arrived and they cost you $15 each. These differences are extreme but they'll illustrate the point. Your 100 items cost $1,300 (10 × $10 = $100, + 50 × $12 = $600, + 40 × $15 = $600), an average of $13 each.

Now issue twenty-five items. Using LIFO you say that they are all $15 items. So you charge the order using them with $375. But with FIFO you say that ten of the items are $10 items and fifteen are $12 items so the charge is $280. Or you can say that they all cost an average of $13 and so charge them out at $325. Or you can just set a certain cost as expected and use it as standard. This could be $12.50. You'd price the twenty-five issued items at $312.50.

There is also a fifth way to charge them out but accountants don't like this method. You can use the last price. This is not quite the same as LIFO. Suppose that you issue the whole 100. LIFO, FIFO, and average cost will all agree that you issued $1,300 worth of inventory. But, using last cost you'd say $1,500 because that is what they are really worth today.

Accountants don't like this method because it mixes up profits and losses with your store's accounts. Accountants would not object to you setting selling prices as if the parts all cost $15 because there is no particular reason for giving the customer the benefit of your having stocked up before prices went up. But accountants want you to show the difference as a profit on the product rather than as an understatement of inventory investment which is what you'd really end up doing in our example if you issued the whole 100 items at last price. Curiously, accountants do not object to standard costs although it, too, mixes up profits and losses with what you say your inventory is worth.

LIFO and FIFO decisions are important in big companies, so important in fact that the government has rules about them. You must use whatever method you choose for whole classes of products; you can't handle one item one way and another item the other way. And you are not allowed to change your mind about which you use without permission from the government.

Why all of this governmental interest? It is because you get different calculated costs for your products, depending on which inventory charging system you use. And different costs make different profits and profit taxes. So the government is interested. For the most part the differences in the effects of the different methods even out in the long run but it may take a long time.

A minor problem in pricing materials requisitions is the delay—finding out cost figures. If you receive and use bought items right away, you'll have to hold the requisitions until the invoice and freight bills are paid. Only then will you know what they cost. The same is true with the items you make yourself. Unless you use standard costs, you won't know at what price to price out the items until the cost accounting department closes the order and figures the production cost per unit.

STUDY MATERIALS

17-1   Given

Usage 7,000 per month
Purchase price 14 cents each
Ordering costs $11
Normal lead time 8 weeks
Safety stock $\frac{1}{2}$ month's usage or $\frac{1}{4}$ of ordering quantity, whichever is higher
Carrying costs 20 per cent

1   What is the EOQ?
2   What is the annual cost of carrying this inventory?

17-2   In problem 17-1 above what change occurs in the EOQ if carrying costs are 10 per cent instead of 20 per cent? 30 per cent? What do you conclude from these answers about the sensitivity of EOQs to variations in the carrying charge rate?

17-3   In problem 17-1 above what change occurs in the EOQ if usage is cut to half? If it doubles? What do you conclude from these answers about the sensitivity of EOQs to variations in the usage rate?

17-4   In problem 17-1 above how much capital will be released from inventory by an edict to cut the investment 25 per cent? What will be the cost effects of such an edict? What will be the effective interest cost rate to the company for the released capital?

17-5   In problem 17-1 above what will happen to the proper EOQ and to the average investment if next year's volume goes up 10 per cent?

17-6   In problem 17-1 above, if the vendor offers you a 12-cent price if you increase your order size by $\frac{1}{2}$ should you do it? How much would you be willing to increase your order size in order to get a 12-cent price?

17-7   Is it true that in all EOQ diagrams such as that shown in figure 17-2 the EOQ is at the point where the declining sloping curved line crosses the rising straight line? Why or why not?

17-8   You stock storage batteries which have a loss of life of 3 per cent a month from shelf wear. How can you handle this in EOQ calculations?

17-9   What relationships, if any, are there between "materials short" lists and economic lot sizes?

17-10 Would it ever be true that the EOQ curve is *not* relatively flat for volumes of, say, 25 per cent above and below the EOQ? If you say yes, explain how this could be.

17-11 In a year, you use 500 pieces for which you pay $3.10 each, and you have been ordering them 100 at a time. Ordering costs are $25. What is the imputed interest rate?

17-12 Can you put a figure for being out of stock into the EOQ formula? How? Should you want to do this? Why?

17-13 Your company policy on reordering is: if the machine setup cost is $0–9.99, order four months' supply; $10–24.99, six months'; $25 and over, eight months'. in the case of a part with setup costs of $20 and an annual usage of 7,500 units (inventory carrying charges of 25 per cent), how much is this policy costing as compared to the best way?

17-14 Using Magee's ordering chart on page 379, calculate the order quantity for the following cases:

1   Annual usage 2,000 units, setup cost $50, inventory carrying charge rate 20 per cent, value of item $2.50 per unit

2   Annual usage 700 units, cost of placing a purchase order $15, inventory carrying charge rate 25 per cent, value of item $10.00 per unit

3   Annual usage 9,000 units, setup costs $750, inventory carrying charge rate 15 per cent, value of item $25.00 per unit

17-15   Is it proper to put actual purchase or production unit costs on requisitions as their cost? Why or why not? What problems are involved? If you say no, what price do you recommend?

17-16   The Eberbach Foundry has, for some time, taken inventory by sample (counting only certain items). This year they contemplate taking a 100 per cent count of everything. How can you count heavy material?

17-17   The Bill Brown Company uses direct costing. Will its calculations of EOQs be like everyone else's? Why or why not? If you say no, whose kind of calculation gives the proper answer?

17-18   Should you change all of your EOQs if your new labor contract gives everyone a pay raise? Discuss.

17-19   When should you *not* use EOQs? Explain.

17-20   Use a Monte Carlo simulation to test out the relative merits of different inventory policies in the following situation (Monte Carlo methods are described in Chapter 29):

Given

Usage 1,300 per year (250 workdays)

Purchase price $3.00 per unit

Ordering cost $25.00

Carrying cost 20 per cent

Both usage and replenishment lead times are irregular. Here is the record for the last half-year (125 workdays). There were 10 withdrawals and 9 replenishment orders.

WITHDRAWAL QUANTITY	DAYS UNTIL NEXT WITHDRAWAL	REORDER LEAD TIMES IN DAYS
69	12	20
58	19	30
93	8	15
76	12	20
81	17	20
59	10	10
64	7	30
51	7	20
45	19	25
54	14	

Assume that your simulation starts with half of the EOQ on hand as a stock and that the first withdrawal occurs on day number 7. Assume also that there is already outstanding an order for the EOQ and that this was placed 3 days before your simulation starts (day number −3).

1 What is the EOQ?

2 What will be the annual cost of carrying the inventory if there is a penalty of 10 cents per unit per day for being out of stock?

3 What will be the annual cost if there is no penalty for being out of stock?

4 What safety stock should be carried in order for replenishment stocks to arrive in time to avoid stockouts in 95 per cent of the reorders?

5 What effects, if any, will be caused by an executive order limiting ordering quantities to 200? 250? 300?

6 Suppose that it has, in the past, been company policy to carry minimum stocks equal to three months' supply. How much has this policy been costing the company as against your ideal program costs?

chapter eighteen

PLANNING—PRODUCTION CONTROL ASPECTS

We said earlier that production control has to know what the factory can do as well as what products are wanted and how they are made. In Chapter 15 we described how production control uses this information for manpower planning. Now we are interested in how production control uses it to plan the factory's work.

MAKING THE BEST USE OF THE FACILITIES AVAILABLE

Knowing what machines and equipment the factory has is rarely much of a problem. Facilities don't change much from day to day. What you had yesterday you have today and will have tomorrow.

MACHINES But machines, like automobiles, get out of order at times. Not every machine is available for use when you think that it will be available. Also, machines sometimes need repairs even though they haven't actually broken down. You must plan for them to be out of production at times in order for them to be fixed. Also, you get new machines from time to time. Some of them replace old machines. Some are additions. Some are bought especially for certain jobs. So it is that the specific facilities available from day to day change a little. Production control must know what facilities the plant has to work with now or will have by the time an order is to be produced.

Often, too, some machines get more orders than they can handle while other machines don't get enough. Sometimes a job is best done on one machine but can also be done (although at higher cost) on another machine. Production control has to know about such possibilities so that it can smooth out machine loads and meet schedules even if it has to switch some jobs to less efficient machines once in a while.

Smoothing out imbalances between loads on different but similar machines can often be done by using operations research, particularly, linear programming. The problems which can be solved by operations research usually fall into two general classes. The first class, maximizing advantages (or minimizing disadvantages), is called optimization problems. These problems we will treat in the next chapter. The second class has to do with balancing waiting lines or with queuing theory. This class we will take up in the chapters on flow control because it has more pertinence in flow control than in job shop or order control situations.

TOOLING   Tooling is different from machines. Nearly all new orders require at least some special tooling. New special tooling is designed and, in most companies, ordered by the tooling department or by engineering's planning department. Production control finds out about special tooling being needed by seeing it listed on drawings and on the work routing sheets it gets from engineering.

The important thing, from production control's point of view, is that many jobs have to have special tooling and that *you can't count on its being on hand* until you see it. Usually it arrives in time—but usually is far from always. Production control has to check and recheck with purchasing or your own tool making department—whichever is to provide the tooling. Checking doesn't insure that every tool will be ready when it is supposed to be but it helps.

OUTSIDE FACILITIES   When you buy parts you are actually manufacturing with someone else's facilities. Ordinarily you don't think of it this way and don't concern yourself with the vendor's machines or how he makes what he sells to you.

But, on all big orders you are better off if you do take an interest in both his machines and how he makes products. You want to be sure that he can and will *deliver* what you need and on time and that his products will pass your inspection. Sometimes companies promise more than they can fulfill. Send a team of your men from engineering, and perhaps production control too, to the vendor's plant to look over his facilities. See if it is likely that he can fulfill a contract before you give a big one.

Your interest is not wholly a matter of whether or not he can deliver. You also go into cost and price with him. You may even have your engineers help him get his costs down. His costs and his price are not production control's job but when he can deliver is.

HOW LONG DOES IT TAKE TO DO THINGS?

LEAD TIMES   The total time that it takes to get things is called lead time. Earlier we talked about lead time as if you always know how long it will be. But this is not really so. For any item you'll have to look at your stock records and see how long it took to get new supplies in the past.

The trouble is that you find irregularity. No two lead times are alike. Maybe lead times are changing and getting longer or shorter. There is actually a question of whether or not it is worthwhile to try to decide exactly what lead time to use for every one of thousands of items. If you do set lead times and write them on stock cards or put them on tapes, either you have to keep changing them all the time or a good many of them will be wrong at any given time.

There is also a question, in the case of items you make yourself, of how much dead time to allow between operations. Ideally you need allow only enough time to move a lot to the next job. But actually you may have to allow several days, because machines for next operations can't always be free at exactly the right minute and there are also minor delays. The total lead time ends up being made up more of dead time between operations than it does of operating time. If you have your computer make out shop orders, you can set completion dates for individual operations only if you punch "lead time factors" or "day factors" (the amount of time to allow between operations for moving the order and for dead time) into the master operation card for each operation. It is a big job to set all these individual operation lead times and it is still a bigger job to change them to keep them up to date. Some companies (mostly only continuous production companies) do punch lead time factors into their cards and then change them only if they get to be way out of line. Otherwise the cost of changing the recorded lead times costs more than not having them set perfectly all the time.

Look at figure 18-1. It is a monthly report used by the Link-Belt division of FMC Corporation showing lead time for various classes of products. Notice that there is considerable variation. New lists are needed often because the load of orders on hand varies from month to month.

You might expect that long lead times would mean big inventories. But this is true only in a small way. If you have to order in July to get November's materials, the lead time is long but if the items don't come in until the end of October, your inventory need not be very large. By October 1, you will have orders outstanding for what you need in October, November, December, and January. Long lead times mean merely that you will always have several orders outstanding, not that you will have big inventories on hand.

Long lead times do build up inventory a little, though, because they are irregular. A five-month lead time item may arrive in four months or in six months. So, perhaps, you place orders six months ahead in order to be sure. This amounts to your carrying a bigger safety stock to protect yourself against the irregularity. Whenever orders do arrive in four or five months you have more inventory than you'd really like to have.

FIGURE 18-1 Lead time schedule on merchandise items (includes paper-work time).

		INSIDE DEPARTMENTS			
BOUGHT ITEMS THAT WE SELL TO CUSTOMERS	WEEKS	FOUNDRY	WEEKS	MACHINE SHOP	DAYS
Bearings, not L-B. .	3	Bench.	6	Bronze bushings. . . .	5
Belting, canvas. . . .	1	Squeezer.	6	Chain tighteners. . . .	5
Belting, rubber. . . .	4	Small floor work. . .	5	Connecting rods.	15
Bolts, machine	2	Large floor work. . .	5	Cross rods.	12
Brushes, pulley. . . .	2	Machine.	5	Eccentrics.	25
Castings.	4	Sprockets.	4	Gates.	6
Crankshafts.	3	Gears.	3	Gears, cut.	10
Forgings.	3	Pulleys.	5	Jaw clutches.	10
Gears.	4	Rollers.	4	Osc. drives.	25
Pulleys.	4			Pulleys, cast iron. . . .	5
Rivets.	2			Pulleys, large bore. . .	7
Screws, cap and set	2	STEEL SHOP		Reactor levers.	15
Springs.	2			Rollers, not turned. . .	5
V-belt drives.	3	Angles.	5	Segments, wearing. .	10
Wire cloth.	5	Buckets.	7	Shafts.	5
		Flights.	7	Sprockets.	3
		Links.	7	Take-ups.	5
SISTER PLANT ITEMS		Pans	7		
		Slat pulleys.	5		
		Str. face pulleys. . .	5	PROCESSING OF BOUGHT ITEMS	
Bearings.	4	Pulleys, other.	5		
Castings.	6	Slide plates.	6		
Idlers.	5	Take-ups.	4	Flame hardening. . . .	10
Pins and bushings.	8	Yokes.	7	Galvanizing.	10
Speed reducers. . . .	4	Washers.	5	Grinding.	10
Sprockets.	3	Duplex gates.	8	Heat treating.	10
Roller chain.	6			Rolling.	15
Chain, other.	8			Vulcanizing.	10

INDIVIDUAL OPERATIONS TIMES   In all of our discussions up to here, we have assumed that you knew how long operations take on all work you do for yourself. Actually you don't know this until you figure it out. Operations times depend on how fast each machine runs, how much of the time it operates, how much time the worker takes per unit, and how long it takes to set up machines.

And you can't know operation times exactly because rarely do two workers do the same operation at the same rate. How long it takes depends to some extent on who does the work. Even the same worker sometimes works faster at one time than another. You can't foresee all of these variations. Actually, however, these variations don't make much trouble. They tend to be minor and to average out. You can tell pretty well how long operations will take from past experience and by using time study standards.

You can tell almost exactly in one situation found in some companies.

Employees—particularly where the union is strong—sometimes decide how much work they will do. Then they do that much and no more. Anyone who tries to turn out more finds his machine out of adjustment when he comes back from the washroom. Or when he gets ready to set up his machine for the next job he finds that some of his tools are gone.

Nearly always the quantity the men allow each other to turn out is so easily done that everyone can and always does turn out the amount allowed. That makes your scheduling problem easy because you'll always get the quantity that the men set for themselves. This situation is not as common in job lot work as it is in continuous production because every day's jobs are different.

TIME STUDY STANDARDS   Time study standards are the best figures you can get on how long it takes to do work. Most companies have time study standards but some don't. Their main use is often for piecework pay purposes—not for scheduling production. This makes a difference because, not being designed for scheduling, they are not expressed in quite the right way for production control's use.

A time study standard tells the number of products "expected" each hour for pay purposes. Time study's expected and production control's expected output are different. When a factory operator turns out the time study department's expected quantity (sometimes called "normal" production) of output in an hour, he is paid his base rate for it. But this "normal" is actually a quantity that nearly everyone can beat. Everyone who does beat it gets a bonus and nearly all piece workers earn bonuses. Everyone—time study, production control, factory operators, all—expects more production than time study's normal calls for.

This is where time study's expected and production control's expected differ. If time study's standard calls for 100 units an hour, nearly everyone on the job will turn out between 115 to 125 per hour. Production control must expect and plan for the *actual*, perhaps an average of 120, not 100.

We don't need to belabor this point because it is easy to estimate what production control should expect. All you need to know is the time study standard and the average rate of bonus. Men who earn a 25 per cent bonus get it because they turn out 125 per cent of standard output. When time study standards say 40 per hour, production control has to plan for 50. When the standards call for 200 per hour, production control has to expect 250.

STANDARD DATA STANDARDS   Some companies set production standards using "standard data." This method differs from regular time study in that it does not use stop watches or numerous observations of the job.

There are two kinds of standard data. William Gomberg once called them microscopic and macroscopic. Both use catalogs of standard times for small parts of jobs. The catalogs are based on thousands of very detailed time studies. The basic times can be filed on computer tapes or in catalogs. Briefly, here is how standard data are used.

In the microscopic method your catalog gives you standard times for such things as "move hand," "turn hand," "grasp object," and so on. Times for moving the hand depend on the distance. To set a time standard you list a man's movements, find the times in the catalog, and add them up.

Macroscopic methods use longer parts of jobs. On a drill press job you would have a time for "change drill bit" and perhaps a time for "drill hole." These parts of the job ("elements" in time study language) occur on all jobs on the drill press and (1) take the same time, or (2) the time they take varies in a predictable way. In either case you can set up a formula which will give you time standards for new jobs without taking new time studies.

Standards set from standard data are used by production control in exactly the same way as those set by taking time studies. As before, if the standard calls for forty per hour and if the men usually make 25 per cent bonus, then production control must plan for fifty, not forty.

PAST EXPERIENCE　Although most companies have time standards, not all do. Then production control must estimate operation times as best it can. Sometimes it figures operation times by knowing how fast the machine runs and the number of machine revolutions needed. In other cases where the work is largely by hand, or if the rate of output is controlled by the worker, past experience on similar work is usually the best guide.

Using past experience, as a method, sounds better than it is because most companies without standards are also without records of how long past operations took. When there are neither standards nor records, production control probably will be quite liberal and will allow lots of time. Remember, though, being liberal here does not mean being lax about costs. Production control's time allowance ought to be neither a piece rate nor a budget. It is merely production control's guide for scheduling. If you are going to use it either as a piece rate or a budget, then you ought to talk it over with the foremen and the time study department so the estimate can be made as good as possible.

MACHINES AND MACHINE TIME　To get the machine time that you need for performing an operation on an order it would seem that you could just multiply the machine time for making one unit by the number of parts on the order and get the total required machine time for each operation. You do start by doing this. But several things combine to make this useful only as a starting figure so far as machine time is concerned.

First, there is scrap. We've said that you can't tell ahead exactly how many of the pieces you start into production will still be in a lot for its later operations. Rarely is the loss great, so this is not much of a problem but it is sometimes. If, for example, you make small machined iron parts from sand castings, you may very well have to cast 110 pieces for every 100 finished pieces you finally get. You will have to allow machining time for 110 pieces for the first operation or two.

Second, there is scrap's cousin rework. Items rejected along the way can often be reworked and made acceptable but *reworking time on machines is all extra*. It might even be different operations. If you get a dimension too small, maybe you will have to weld more metal on and then grind and machine it to proper size. If you can, you ought to keep rework operations out of your regular shop and do it in a special rework shop. But maybe you don't have the machines to do it.

The trouble is that the pieces to be reworked come back from the

FIGURE 18-2 An automatic card reader located in the shop. New variable data to be reported are dialed in to the central computer by the operator. (Woodward Governor Company.)

inspector after you have finished the lot and have torn down the tooling setup. To do the rework, you have to set the job up all over again and for just a few pieces. Not only is this very costly but it also kills machine time.

Third is machine "downtime," the time taken by machine setup and takedown time, tool sharpening, breakdowns, and personal time of the operator away from the machine. Add to these the time lost from tool shortages, jobs not being ready on time, and power failures. You'll do well if these time losses use up as little as 20 per cent of the machine's time. Most companies find that they eat up 30 per cent of their possible machine time and in some companies it runs up to 40 per cent. And still worse, machine downtime from these reasons is irregular so far as individual machines are concerned. Die setup time on presses, for example, is particularly unpredictable.

Fourth is worker productivity. Think of some job that you do regularly. Does it always take you the same length of time to do? No. And it is the same with factory machine operators. Sometimes they get work done faster than at other times. When a man machining iron castings finds that some of them have hard spots, he can still get the work done but it will take him longer than usual.

The total effect of these kinds of delays and irregularities is to reduce the machine time that you actually have available. This doesn't affect individual orders or their production schedules very much. All that happens is that you take on only as much work as you can do in the reduced hours of work that you really get. Don't, however, schedule operations for individual jobs to follow one another on a tight schedule. Once in a while the delay will happen to your tightly scheduled order and then you will have to reschedule it. Instead, just allow for some dead time between operations on an order. Then if it is delayed a little anywhere, you won't have to reschedule. If you want to be sure to get an order by a certain date, try to start it into production a little sooner than less urgent orders. Starting it sooner gives you time to absorb a few delays with no harm being done.

HOW MUCH TIME TO ALLOW FOR INTERRUPTIONS
Production control needs to know about how much machine downtime to count on, and not just for machines in total but for each type of machine because some kinds are idle more than others. Machine downtime is like automobile trouble. It is unpredictable, yet at least a little trouble is bound to occur once in a while. You don't know exactly when, where, or how much trouble to expect, yet when making a schedule you must try to allow for it. About all that production control can do is to assume that the aver-

age amount of time lost in the past will be lost in the future and load the machine or shop to the expected capacity that will actually be available.

You should calculate overall plant loads, expecting losses to occur. Don't expect the factory to turn out 100 per cent of its theoretical capacity. *But schedule individual orders with no allowance for delays.* Why? Because most individual orders will not be delayed. Of course, some will. Yet, if you schedule individual orders to allow for a certain amount of lost time, those that don't get delayed will be ready for their next operations ahead of schedule.

SETUP TIME   Setting up a machine means getting it ready to produce. Setup time is one kind of idle time because machines don't run while they are being set up. Clamps and holding devices to hold material in place during machining must be attached to the machine. Tools and other accessories must be fastened into place. Then everything must be adjusted just so. A trial piece or two of the product is made to see how they come out. Then there are final adjustments and you are ready to go. Production control must know how long it takes to set up machines.

Setup time usually includes teardown time too. You have to take off the tooling from the previous job before you can set up for the next one. This sometimes makes problems because teardown time is the teardown time for whatever previous job that happened to be on the machine. Teardown time bears no relation to how long it takes to set up the next job. Usually teardown time is short so usually it doesn't matter what previous job is being torn down. You can, however, sometimes schedule jobs in sequence so that part of a previous job's setup can be used for the next job. When this can be done, setup time and costs are reduced.

ALLOWING FOR SETUP TIME   Setup time is sometimes short compared to running time. When it is, you can neglect it in scheduling because it loses so little production. More often, though, setting up machines takes up enough time that you have to allow for it. Sometimes it takes longer to set up for a job than to run it. Teardown and setup time combined often cost companies over 10 per cent of their direct labor payroll. It is expensive both in wages and lost machine time. Setting up automatic screw machines sometimes takes six hours or more. Setups don't have to take that long, however, to justify your paying attention to them.

Production control needs to know how much time in each case so it can know when production will start. In most companies the time study department sets time standards for setups so production control does know how long they will take. But when there are no standards production control has to rely on past experience and estimate setup times.

COMBINING SETUP AND RUNNING TIME   One time study department practice makes problems for production control. The time study department sometimes combines setting up and running the machine into one standard—rather than having two standards, one for setting up and another for running the machine. It does this mostly when setup times are short compared to the time for running jobs of average size.

Here's a typical case: setups (including teardown) take 10 minutes. Once set up, it takes 100 minutes to turn out 100 pieces. You can set two standards: (1) 10 minutes for every setup and (2) 100 minutes for turning out 100 pieces. Doing it this way makes no problem for production control.

The trouble comes when both setup time and machine operating time are combined into one rate—and time study men do sometimes combine the rates this way. They put the two standards together on a proportional basis and end up with only one standard.

To do this the time study man needs to know the typical length of run. Suppose the typical order is for 50 pieces. The combined standard is set as follows: for one setup, 10 minutes; for turning out 50 pieces, 50 minutes; add them and you have 60 minutes allowed to set up the job and run a typical size order. For 50 pieces you give 60 minutes' pay. Put it on a "per 100" basis and you have 120 minutes' pay per 100 pieces.

So far this makes no trouble. But when you use the standard to schedule an order for 200 pieces you find that the standard allows 240 minutes. Forgetting for the moment that the man may work faster than standard and earn a bonus, let's look just at the standard. Had setup and operating not been combined you would say that setting up was a 10-minute job and turning out 200 pieces was a 200-minute job, making 210 minutes in all—not 240 minutes. Combining the two into one standard gives production control an incorrect figure for scheduling.

It works just as poorly on small orders. Suppose you had several orders for 10 pieces. Ten such orders really require 200 minutes (100 minutes for 10 setups plus 100 minutes for turning out 100 pieces) but the combined standard allows 120 minutes for 100 pieces. So long as orders average out those differences don't matter much but they do matter if things don't average out to 50. Production control can do its work better if it has separate standards for setting up and running the machines.

ALLOWANCES FOR SCRAP
The production control department should know the expected "attrition" or reject rate on all operations, although reject rates aren't often recorded in writing. The orders that production control gets call for certain quan-

tities of *finished* items. Finished quantities are targets. During manufacture some (rarely very many) pieces will be damaged or will not measure up to specification. The quantity shrinks as the items go through process. Some rejects can be repaired but others have to be scrapped. So you must start more pieces into production than you really want as finished parts.

How much extra to allow for throwouts you'll have to guess at, relying largely on past experience. Fortunately, failure to hit the finished parts mark exactly is usually not serious, even when the product is special and parts are not to be stocked. The customer often wants some extra parts for possible future repair needs, and since that quantity is flexible it provides some leeway. And even if the customer's order is not for assembled products but for separate pieces, he usually accepts and pays for whatever quantity is finished, provided that it is somewhere near the quantity he ordered.[1] There isn't any point in his refusing to accept a quantity slightly different from what he ordered because your quotation price will always include the anticipated cost of scrap and possible overruns. On the other hand, the vendor should not make it a habit to ship you 10 per cent extra every time just to boost his sales (a practice of one company).

The scrap allowance isn't much of a problem to production control when you make standard products assembled from a stock of parts. Parts orders are always replenishment orders. All that happens if you have an underrun or overrun is that you move the next reorder date up or back a little. Customers' orders are sometimes similar in that they are repeat orders. Again, underruns and overruns merely change the timing (and maybe the quantities too) of reorders.

But on special products the matter of scrap allowances is more important. If you are making a freight car unloader, a drawbridge over a river, or some other large product, you don't want any extra parts. Extras are waste, yet you can't be short on the order for *any* part, not even one. If you are short, you must make up the shortage. As a rule, on big costly parts of products of this type, you make *no allowance for scrap*. You want only a few pieces of such parts, so you start the exact quantity you want. You know that a part may be rejected in process but you take that chance. If the worst happens and a part is rejected you repair or replace it. It is cheaper to do that occasionally than to have waste from very many overruns.

LETTING ITEMS PASS "JUST THIS ONCE"   Scrap allowances usually don't have to be as large as they ought to be if quality standards were

---

[1] Purchase contracts sometimes provide that the customer will accept, at the agreed unit price, quantities up to 10 per cent over or 10 per cent under the quantity ordered as fulfilling the contract.

stringently enforced. What happens is this. The company's management insists on very little inventory of parts being carried. It wants parts, whether they are made or bought, to arrive at the assembly floor just before they are needed.

All of this is well and good. But what happens when an order of parts or a good many items in an order are held up? Because of the small reserve supply, you are in desperate need for the parts at the assembly floor. You either pass the parts or assembly stops. (This weakness is not so great, however, in order control as it is in continuous manufacturing using flow control.)

If you are dealing with an order which is held up because it contains too many defectives, you can inspect every piece. Just throw out the bad pieces and use the good ones. But if, say, 20 pieces out of 50 have been rejected, you can't finish 50 assembled products with only 30 of some one part. You must get the 20 rejects fixed up quickly or make up a new order for 20 more and rush it through production.

But what actually happens in many cases is that the rejected parts are accepted and used as they stand. The engineering department (or, on costly items, a "materials review board") gives its approval to use the items as they are "just this once" so that assembly won't stop. When rejects are handled this way, production control doesn't have to allow so liberally for scrap. When it happens with purchased parts, you usually send the vendor a letter telling him to mend his ways—a letter to which he pays little attention. If it happens to parts made inside, you try to improve future quality so that this won't happen again. Management's policy of low inventory gets everyone into such a desperate situation that it ends up with relaxed quality standards.

In one sense this kind of situation is illogical. The very existence of a materials review board makes one wonder whether the standards are too tight. Substandard items should not be passed by an inspector, an engineer, or a materials review board if the product's performance will suffer. But if substandard items are allowed to pass in emergencies and the product still works maybe the standards are too tight. This point should not be pursued too far, however. Sometimes in allowing rejected material to be used the board permits its use in only limited ways where it is very unlikely to cause trouble. Or the board may allow it to be used only if certain corrective operations are done on it.

Actually we don't need to picture the occasional passing of substandard items as being very bad. Many quality standards have to do with the way an item looks or with imperfections of other kinds that have nothing to do with how it works. Relaxing these standards once in a while probably doesn't hurt much. Or maybe the relaxed standard relates to an item's

---

AUTHORIZATION OF SUBSTITUTE MATERIAL

Date	Purchase Order No.		Part No.	

Models Affected			Serial No.	
Name of Part			Quantity	

Material Spec. on Dwg. & Routing		

Material Spec. Suggested

Material Spec. Authorized

Material is to be Segregated Thru Oper. # _____   Or Routing Dated _____

Reason For Segregation

Signed _____

Special Processing Required

Reason For Request

Requested By		Date	
Manufacturing Approval		Date	
Metallurgical Approval		Date	
Engineering Approval		Date	

FIGURE 18-3   Occasionally it is necessary to substitute another material for the kind ordinarily used. Such substitutions are generally permitted only with specific written approval and are limited to the instance at hand.

probable performance under unusual and unlikely conditions. If the windshield defroster on a Chevrolet, made and sold in New Orleans, didn't work perfectly probably it wouldn't matter. Not very many defrosters on cars sold in New Orleans will ever be used anyway.

DESIGN CHANGES

Products are always being improved. Improvements help sell products and insure jobs. But improvement is change—design change—and design changes mean extra work for everyone. Most employees dislike them for that reason. Design changes, so far as production control is concerned, always are changes in the design of products soon to be in production or, indeed, already in production. Changes in design of products still on the draftsman's board usually don't matter very much to production control. Sometimes, though, they eat up your normal lead time for planning or even for buying materials.

A stable design during production is very desirable from the factory's

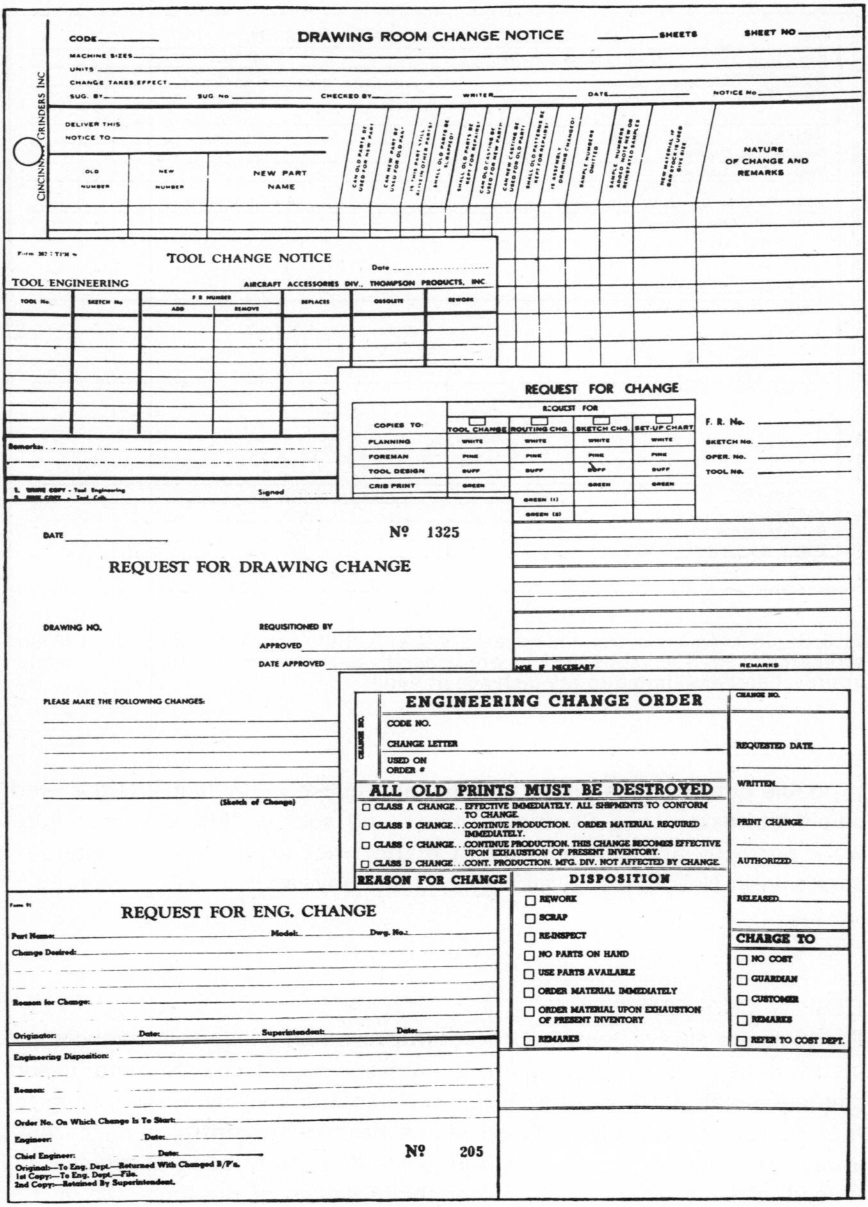

FIGURE 18-4 In spite of the desire to freeze design while production goes on, at least some design changes go on all the time. The above design change forms are varied to suit each company's need.

point of view because changes after production starts are so costly. You should never change as much as in one company where the production control head said, "We can hardly get the engineering department to stand still long enough on design to let us make the product."

If you are going to avoid confusion and waste, you will have to develop an orderly procedure for handling design changes. In big companies, design changes are numerous (averaging several hundred changes per month in many companies) and each change means revising several records (the drawing record index, master bills of material, master route sheets, stock room arrangements, storage bin numbers, parts numbers in customers' catalogs, and so on). Without an orderly procedure you'll soon have the records and the computer tapes all mixed up.

Actually you don't have to change drawings and records for quite all the minor changes. Almost always you do, but suppose that a certain customer wants a few minor variations on his products. Go ahead and make them. But if you don't adopt the changes on your regular products, leave your records alone. You can draw a penciled sketch showing this one customer's variations and file it with the sales order.

In the engineering department, changes mean revised drawings. It is better to make the change on the old drawing if possible but sometimes old drawings have to be canceled and new ones, with new numbers, have to be made. Changing the old drawing keeps drawings up to date and furnishes you a record of all design changes.

In some companies, Allis-Chalmers for one, if a newly designed (and quite different) part can replace the old one functionally without affecting other parts, the old drawing is revised and the old identification number kept. Only if the new part is not fully interchangeable is a new drawing made and a new number assigned. This avoids changing identification numbers of parts and saves a lot of record changing.

DESIGN CHANGE COMMITTEES   We have said that design changes are good. They keep your product up to date so they keep you in business. But they do cost money and so should not be made indiscriminately. Design men should not have full authority to make changes. The chief engineer or, for important changes, a committee should look them over. The review committee should include representatives of production control, engineering, materials control, and perhaps sales and other departments, such as the patent department and customer repair service department. Look into the overall effects of a change before approving it and setting its effective date.

Fred V. Gardner tells of one company where 1,047 engineering changes on one single big order cost $440,000 not counting clerical costs nor the enormous disruption to manufacturing operations. Gardner said that most of the changes were made by quality steeped engineers who listened to every salesman's complaint (and everyone else's) and redesigned parts to take care of every complaint with no thought of cost. Engineering change review committees can stop this kind of waste. On the other hand, many engineering changes on new products are minor, such as running a wire cable in a different location. Not all changes are costly.

Of course, a change review committee needs to know what losses will occur if it approves a change. It is a good idea to have engineering issue "engineering change intention" notices to production control and inventory control. They can check the orders in progress and the stocks of parts on hand to see what making the change will cost in scrap and rework. On small changes you wouldn't need to bother the committee. Just let production control decide when the change should be made. On big changes, the committee should decide. Maybe you should require the engineer to prove that the change is worth its cost. The committee's decision goes back to the inventory control department which issues the change notice telling of the change, its effective date, and what to do with orders in process and parts on hand.

Once in a while, you'll even have to talk over design changes with the union. Sometimes a man files a grievance about his job that causes the design to be changed. Or if a design change alters the men's jobs the union may block its introduction.

RESISTANCE BY ENGINEERS TO DESIGN CHANGE Designs can be too frozen. Engineers sometimes don't want to change. They like to think that they did a good job and receive suggestions for improvements as criticisms of their work. Actually, no design, particularly a first one, should be regarded as more than a designer's best first thought.

Later, when you start to make the product, your designer should go out on the production floor and watch it being made in order to see what changes in design would improve it or make it less costly to manufacture. Suggestions for design improvement from foremen and others should be welcomed; in fact, the making of those suggestions should be part of a foreman's work and accepting suggestions a part of the designer's work.

WHEN TO CHANGE We said above that you should weigh the costs against the need for making engineering changes. You need to ask quite a few questions. How important is the change? Is it a change of necessity or a change of convenience? Can your workers handle the new design? How much cost can you stand? How many parts are there on hand? What happens to them? How costly is it to scrap them? To rework them? How many partly made items are now in process? How far along are they? What happens to them and what will it cost? How many tools, dies, jigs, fixtures, patterns, and gages will be thrown out? At what cost? What will new ones cost? Are any new machines needed? How much do they cost? How long will it take to get them? When can you get the new dies and other tooling that you'll need?

There is also the question of parts in combination when changes affect several parts. You may want to change some parts right now but others have to wait. Deciding just when to change can get to be quite involved.

You probably can think of still other questions besides the above. The answers help the design change committee decide whether to approve a change or not and to set effective dates for those approved. Quick changes always cost more than delayed changes because quick changes make the scrap and rework. Given time, you can use up existing stocks. Because of this only the really important changes should get early effective dates. Changes to correct basic weaknesses in the product would be considered this important and so might changes incorporating important new discoveries. Even here, though, you will probably have to go on with the old design for a while on long lead time purchased items because you can't get any parts of the new design for weeks or months. You might want ever so much to change sooner but you can't do it.

Many big companies end up classifying changes. Changes in class A mean that you should use up the old design parts on hand or in process but that more should not be made. B changes mean to scrap or rework all old design parts. C changes are like B except that you send change lists out to your dealers telling them to change over. D changes go further and call for making changes in products already sold. Not often do you get C or D changes.

In fact, most changes are not so important that they call for scrapping what you have on hand or have already started to make. But you can quit making any more with the old design. When the last of the old is used up you start to use the new. Along an assembly line, you figure out ahead which item will use the last one of the old design. Then you "zero in" the new design (meaning that you start to use it) from this point on. You make the new design effective as of that product.

Some industries are fortunate in being able to make changes whenever they want to. Revolutionary innovations don't come every day. You don't have to redesign cash registers or taxicab meters weekly, monthly, or even annually. Companies making these products can make changes when they like. They can also, like automobile companies, hold up on changes until several collect, and then put them all into effect at one time. If enough changes are made at one time, automobile companies say that they have a new model. Production control in these companies has fewer day-to-day changes to contend with.

Holding back on changes and then sending several through at once (perhaps once a week) saves quite a bit of computer time. Computers will sort out the old cards which have to be replaced by new ones, and computers will update their tapes all automatically. It costs a good bit less to group the changes and make them several at a time once a week than to make changes one by one.

Changes in design after production is *planned* are expensive because so many prepared directives have to be changed or redone. But changes after production has *started* are still more expensive. You have to change all the shop directives and schedules and it has to be done quickly. Worse yet, finished or partially made parts and subassemblies have to be reworked. And remember, the rework is all extra cost caused by the change.

Engineering change costs can be brought to management's attention by charging their costs to engineering change orders. Seeing the cost of changes separately will cause management to think twice about allowing frequent changes.

Some companies are so anxious to put the latest improvements into their products or to get into production on big jobs that they "telescope" design and manufacture. They start making things before they are fully designed. Engineering issues preliminary drawings and temporary specifications. Of course, doing this means many changes and higher costs. But you do get the products out sooner and they incorporate the latest improvements. Airplanes and missiles take so long to make, however, that even with telescoping design and manufacture, they are always a little obsolete by the time they are finished.

ENGINEERING–PRODUCTION CONTROL LIAISON   When making products where you know that you will have to make many engineering changes, you ought to appoint a production control man to do liaison work in the engineering department on prospective changes. He can be told of probable changes before they are spelled out in detail and before they are submitted to the change committee. This gives production control advance notice (and, possibly, he can get new drawings marked up to show the probable change) so that it can hold back on producing any more old parts and not start any more into production until it gets the new design. If the change is a change on a new item, production control may be able to hold up on tool orders and on purchase orders that are already out. Your men won't have to redo so many things when the change order itself comes through.

Liaison between engineering and production control can work both ways. The aircraft and missile industry has special liaison engineers from the engineering department who spend time in the factory and with production control. So do many automotive parts suppliers. Particularly for new products, it pays to have a coordinating engineer who handles all the little changes that you have to make when you start to make a new product. When things have to be done a little differently from what the original design says, the liaison engineer fixes the item so it will work and sees that all drawings and records of drawings are changed. The liaison engineer fixes up the trouble first and corrects the records afterwards, thus speeding up production.

Design changes often affect purchased items. They change the vendor's drawings and tooling. Often a representative of the customer company needs to go to the vendor plant to see that its old drawings are replaced with new ones and to see that all changes are clearly understood. On major government projects where subcontracting is common, some companies maintain an employee in a "drawing change center" in the vendor plant for that purpose.

You find similar practices all the time where one company makes large quantities of items for another company. The customer company gives the vendor company advance warning of coming changes (even if it is still vague about details). The vendor then starts to make parts on only a hand-to-mouth basis. The vendor probably doesn't know quite which parts to make (the old or the new) when a change is coming. Meanwhile production must go on. The vendor can only hope that he won't get stuck with very many obsolete parts when the change order finally comes through.

FIELD REPORTS ON DESIGN Companies making engineering projects often seem to overlook desirable changes. Equipment for electricity generating plants must be installed on the job but it is made in factories. The factory's field representatives install it or oversee its installation. They also stay with it until it is operating satisfactorily.

Frequently, the field installation men make certain changes on the product as received from the factory as a matter of course because past experience shows that they are required. Perhaps they have had trouble before with certain valves or other details. Yet somehow their knowledge that the factory's design will not perform well does not get back to the factory. The same mistakes are repeated on the next job, again leaving it up to the fieldmen to make the usual changes.

The factory's designers never seem to find out that they ought to make these changes. Organizational weaknesses are partially responsible for this situation. Field erection men often work for the sales department, not the factory. Or one division of the company has fieldmen but another doesn't. So the fieldmen of one division have to service another division's products. Information from the field on minor details simply doesn't filter back.

One large radio manufacturer used a poorly designed tuner on its radios. It gave so much trouble that the company's dealers were given an allowance to cover the cost of replacing them with a better tuner free to the customer. Thousands were replaced in a two-year period before the factory designers corrected it.

Design changes caused by customer demand cost money just as do changes initiated by the company. If they are costly changes, and if they are made at his request, the customer should pay for them, but the costs of small changes are usually absorbed by the vendor. Actually, you never really get all of the costs of changes back from the customer, even if he does pay for some of the costs. You end up having to absorb costs of overtime, of getting back on schedule after the upsets caused by the change, of trial runs with the new tooling, and of lost time. Changes are particularly difficult with purchased parts, what with correspondence, time to get new drawings, and so on.

MAKING A DESIGN CHANGE   Although you have to experience the commotion caused by changes to appreciate it, perhaps a description would help. Here's what happens at one company which makes dashboards and dashboard instruments for one of Detroit's big three. The buyer's engineering department wants to make a change. It goes to its own purchasing department which calls the supplier's sales department. The sales department sends a man to the buyer's plant (30 miles away) to discuss the change. During the discussion the change is agreed upon.

Sales submits the change to the supplier's engineering department and makes out an engineering project requisition asking it to design the change and to tell sales what it will cost. After getting the estimate, sales (except on small changes) gets management approval for the change (regardless of whether the seller or the buyer is to pay for it). Then engineering makes up working drawings.

Now it begins to affect production control. Sales asks production control what parts it has on hand and on order. Engineering sends production control a proposed engineering change notice telling production control to slow down on making more parts because a change is coming.

Sales now goes back to the buyer's purchasing department and they settle on approximate costs, who pays for the change, and its approximate effective date. After engineering has revised the drawings, they go to the cost department for a final cost estimate which sales uses in its final negotiation with the buyer of the cost of the change.

After agreement by the customer, sales releases the change for production. Copies of the release go to manufacturing, production control, and purchasing which, with engineering, see if tooling changes in either the vendor's plant or in the buyer's plant are needed. After doing this, schedules are set for putting the change into effect.

If new tools are used, the first parts made go to the auto company right away for preproduction approval before going ahead. The buyer accepts them, tells the vendor's department to go ahead, and sales tells production control that it can produce.

Any number of considerations can complicate the procedure. Sometimes they are important, sometimes not. For example, how about repair parts for car owners? Will this change affect service? Is the new part interchangeable with the old or must the old part be kept in stock? (If it is not interchangeable, the supplier will have to keep old tooling in the morgue and, from time to time, produce old parts for up to seven years.)

Will the change destandardize a part formerly used several places so that in the future it will be a small quantity (and high cost) item? What will be the most economical way to produce the new item? Will the machines and the layout change?

How about handling the new item? Will we need different tote pans, trays, or racks? How about its breakability? How will it be packed for shipment? Will different cartons be needed?

Does purchased material change? If wire insulation is changed, does the present source sell such wire or must the supplier find a new source? Are any operations changed? Will new job rates be needed? Are patents involved, either for the part of for machines used? It is small wonder we say that unimportant changes should not be made all the time.

STUDY MATERIALS

18-1   Your union is rather strong and your pieceworkers keep in line by not earning too much on jobs where the piece rate is loose. In the punch press department they usually finish work by 2:00 or 2:30 and make no pretense of working on till

3:00 when they go home. (Workers who earn more than the groups' self-set ceiling must contribute their excess earnings to the union's flower fund for the sick.)

You are getting swamped with orders and want more output. How can you get it? Could you do it with one order if not for many? How can you correct this problem in the future?

18-2 In the women's clothing industry, dress manufacturers cut cloth for exactly the number of dresses ordered. Then any faulty dresses which can't be repaired become shortages on the order to the customer (and are not replaced).

Isn't this a good practice for all companies to use? What problems would it make in the dress industry? In other industries?

18-3 If the normal scrap loss on the milling operation is 7 per cent, on the following slotting operation it is 8 per cent, and on the following drilling operation it is 4 per cent, how many castings should the scheduler start into production in order to expect to get 180 finished pieces? Suppose that the operator actually spoils 11 per cent on the milling operation, how many pieces are you likely to end up with? If the order needs the 180 pieces and you hold it up until you can start a replacement lot through milling, how many should the replacement lot contain?

18-4 Your normal scrap losses for four successive operations are 2 per cent, 6 per cent, 10 per cent, and 20 per cent. How many should you start through in order to finish with 1,000 pieces? How much machine time will you need on each machine if operation times are 4, 2, 7, and 4 minutes, respectively?

18-5 Suppose that, in problem 18-4 above, you were able to reduce the loss for operations 3 and 4 each by half, what would your answer then be?

18-6 You need 200 pieces and extras are waste. Probabilities of scrap losses are as follows:

NUMBER SCRAPPED	PROBABILITY
0	.00
1	.05
2	.12
3	.20
4	.22
5	.17
6	.10
7	.06
8	.04
9	.03
10	.01

Pieces are worth $50 each and it costs $100 to set up the machines again to make up any shortages. How many pieces should you start into production? (In this calculation, you may omit the possibility of having to scrap replacement parts.)

18-7 The new scheduler has found that the production operators, being on piece-work, turn out work in less than standard time. Here are last month's records of five workers.

WORKER	HOURS SPENT ON JOBS WITHOUT STANDARDS	HOURS SPENT ON JOBS WITH STANDARDS	STANDARD HOURS OF WORK TURNED OUT
A	23	145	172
B	5	163	203
C	16	152	169
D	8	120	152
E	11	149	167

1 How much work should the scheduler expect week by week from these men in the future?

2 What problems are there for him to contend with?

18-8 A new job has had a time standard set at 15 minutes per unit on a grinder. Using the information from problem 18-7 above, how many units per hour do you schedule? How much time will you allow for 44 units?

18-9 Here are figures for a new part which will take five operations:

OPERATION NUMBER	SETUP TIME (MINUTES)	STANDARD OPERATION TIME PER UNIT (MINUTES)	OPERATOR EFFICIENCY	PERCENTAGE OF TIME OPERATOR WORKS ON STANDARD WORK	SCRAP PERCENTAGE
1	10	6	110	100	10
2	20	12	140	90	none
3	50	20	130	100	15
4	40	15	115	80	5
5	20	10	105	90	none

The time between operations is 40 minutes after an operation is complete until the next one starts, but setup can start before the lot arrives. You are to aim for 100 finished items.

How many hours will it take to get this lot out?

18-10 Jake Lassiter had been foreman of the machine shop at the Frederick Lubricating Equipment Company for 25 years. During the 1950s when the company was small, most parts made in his department were made from drawings. Lassiter or his machinists decided what operations to perform as they went along. When the company grew in the 1960s it expanded and put work routing on a more formal basis. Operation lists were set by engineers in the engineering department.

Some time later Lassiter sent through a requisition for the purchase of a set of drawing filing drawers. He explained his request by pointing out that his set of drawings were not in very good shape as a result of his having no file for them. The chief engineer did not know that Lassiter was keeping used drawings. Lassiter explained that he needed them because he made his penciled changes on these copies whenever he made a product. He said that most of the time he could make the product as called for by the drawings and the operation lists issued to him, but that occasionally he found it necessary to change the design somewhat or to use other operations than those listed. It was, therefore, convenient for him to keep his old drawings.

How many poor practices are evident here? What procedures should be used? Justify your answer in such a way that it can be used to explain things to Jake Lassiter.

18-11   When parts are redesigned, the engineering department of the Blumberg Company makes up new drawings and sets their effective date. Before it sets the date, the stock record department is checked to determine the size of stocks on hand. The effective date of the change is set at a time when the stock will be at a low point.

Even with this precaution, substantial losses from scrapped parts have occurred in several cases. In some instances, large stocks which existed in the company's warehouses around the nation had to be scrapped. In other cases, the supply of an item ran low earlier than expected and was reordered by the stock record clerk just before the design change became effective. In one case, a rejected lot of parts in process was reworked and arrived in stock only to be scrapped because the change-over had taken place.

What were the faults in the existing procedure? Develop a procedure which will keep scrap losses of this sort at a minimum. Are there any situations where design change should be made effective immediately regardless of scrap loss?

chapter nineteen

LINEAR PROGRAMMING

Linear programming is perhaps the most important of all operations research techniques, so far as production control is concerned. We will explain it in two stages: first, graphically and, second, by the simplex method using matrices (also called algorithms, tableaus, and iterations). In practice, linear programming problems are usually quite complex, but we can illustrate the method with simple examples.

GRAPHIC SOLUTIONS

EXAMPLE 1   We will assume that we make screws, of which we are concerned with two kinds called A and B. They are large-sized screws and we make a profit on type A of 3 cents each and on type B of 4 cents each. Both types are made complete in two operations, one operation on an automatic screw machine and the other on a slotter. Each unit of type A takes two minutes of screw machine time and five minutes of slotter time. Type B takes three minutes of screw machine time and two minutes of slotter time. Each machine has 3,600 minutes of operating time available in a week. The problem: find the quantity of A and B which will earn us the most money. (We need more of these screws than we ourselves will be able to make, hence there is no problem of not wanting all that we can make. But since we pay more for the screws we buy outside, we want to make all we can inside.)

We have plotted all of the possible production combinations in figure 19-1. Figure 19-1 shows two lines, one for the use of the automatic screw machines and one for the slotters. Product A takes two minutes of screw machine time and product B takes three minutes. If we devoted the screw machine time wholly to making A, we would get 1,800 A items; if we devoted it wholly to B we would get 1,200 B items. Or we could divide the screw machine time and produce some A items and some B items. For every 3 A items we cut off we can produce 2 B items. In figure 19-1 the two extreme points are connected by a line showing every possible combination of A and B and how many of each we can turn out.

The values on the line labeled "Screw Machine Use" show the maximum quantities of the various combinations of A and B that can be produced of the screw machines. Actually, any combination of A and B that either lies on the line or to the left and below it can be made. If, however,

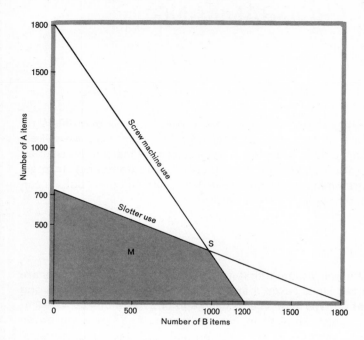

FIGURE 19-1

we choose a combination to the left and below the line, say 1,000 of prodduct A (requiring 2,000 minutes of screw machine time) and 500 of product B (requiring 1,500 minutes), we will not use up all of the screw machine time. There will be 100 minutes of slack screw machine time available in the week.

Next we draw in on figure 19-1 a similar limit line for slotter use (5 minutes of time to make one unit of A or 2 minutes for one of B).

The two lines now on the chart are "parameters" or limits beyond which we can't go because we have used up all of the machines' time. We can produce any combination of products in area M but not beyond. This area is called the solution space because all feasible solutions to our problem lie within the area or on its boundaries. Where the two lines cross, at point S, we keep both machines busy. Just looking at the chart shows that the numerical value of point S is about where product A = 330 and B = 980 (A is actually 327 and B is 982).

Our final object is not, however, to keep the machines busy but to make the greatest possible profit. Introducing the profit idea throws a third element into our problem. If we made all products A and nothing else, we would make 720 of them. At 3 cents each the profits would be $21.60. Or, if we made all B's, we would make 1,200. At 4 cents each the profit would come to $48.00. If we made 327 A's and 982 B's we would make $49.09. This is the greatest possible profit, so our optimal program is to make 327 A's and 982 B's.

It would seem by inspection that point S would be the point of greatest profit but you can't tell for sure without figuring it out. Point S would not be the point of greatest profit if, for example, product A produced a profit of 20 cents each and product B a profit of 1 cent each. If that were the case figure 19-1 would be the same, but for greatest profits it would be better to cut out B altogether and make 720 of A.

As it happens, the optimal solution to linear programming problems almost always will occur at one of the corner points of the solution space. This is because all of the constraints or boundary conditions and the function to be optimized are linear. They are straight lines. (If any factor involved is nonlinear then linear programming cannot be used. For these other cases "nonlinear programming" or "integer programming" may be appropriate. Integer programming is used where the solution space consists of discrete points rather than a continuous region.)

To show that an optimal solution almost always occurs at a corner point, think of every possible combination of making A and B items, as having a profit attached to it. (Obviously, at the origin where no production takes place, the profit is zero but any other feasible solution will generate a profit.) If we now connect together all points having the same profit, we will get a diagonal line and there will be a different (although parallel) diagonal line for every possible profit. For clarity, only some of the possible profit lines have been drawn in on figure 19-2. The dotted lines show the profit possibilities for different production combinations, considering that we earn 3 cents on each unit of product A and 4 cents on product B.

For other profit margins such as 20 cents for A and 1 cent for B, the slopes of the lines would be different. But no matter what the slope of the profit lines, the one having the highest profit will almost always pass through a corner point.

We have said that the highest profit will "almost always" be at a corner point. Actually it is always a corner point and only a corner except for one situation (quite uncommon) where this is not so. This occurs when the slope of the profit line is identical to that of one of the constraint lines which encloses the optimal solution. In such a case every value on that constraint line enclosing the solution space is a possible solution. Suppose, for example, that the profit margin on product A was 2 cents and that on product B was 3 cents. In that case the maximum profit of $36 could be

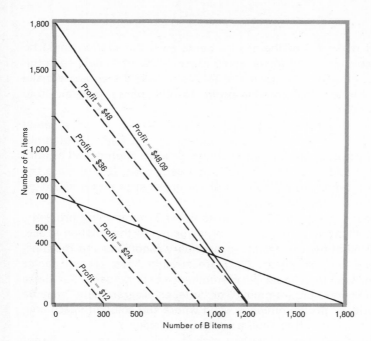

FIGURE 19-2

achieved by (1) producing 327 units of product A and 982 units of product B, (2) producing only 1,200 units of product B and no A's, or (3) producing any other combination where you reduce A's at the rate of 3 for every 2 B's added.

This situation, where there are many feasible solutions to a problem, is rare. Not only that, if it occurs, it is usually unimportant since it doesn't matter which of the feasible solutions you use. (It becomes important in complex examples using the simplex method where it causes a problem called "degeneracy" which we will discuss later.)

EXAMPLE 2   Charts are too complicated for any but the simplest linear programming examples but we will present graphically one more example, this one with four limiting constraints instead of two. This time we will assume that we operate a factory making refrigerators and freezers but, to keep the problem within bounds, we will assume that we will make only one model of each.

The main operations in the factory to be considered are: (1) making compressors, (2) stamping out the metal parts, and (3) assembly. Refrigerators and freezers are assembled on separate lines which can operate at the same time. The refrigerator line has a limit of 400 a day, the freezer line has a limit of 250 a day, and neither one is affected by the operation of the other. Compressors for both products are made in one department, whose production can be divided between the two. The top production for freezer compressors is 350 if no refrigerators are made, but if freezers are cut out, 600 compressors for refrigerators can be made. The stamping department, too, makes stampings for both products and can mix them up. Top production is stampings for 500 of either refrigerators or freezers, or 500 total divided in any way between the two.

Refrigerators yield a profit of $40 each, freezers $50. The problem is to find out how many of each to produce in order to make the most money.

In figure 19-3 we have drawn in all of the parameters. The shaded area M represents the feasible solution space. At point A we make 250 freezers and nothing else. Freezer assembly limitations keep us from making any more freezers. But there is nothing to keep us from also making some refrigerators. In figure 19-3, this is shown by line AB. We can keep on making 250 freezers *and* up to 172 refrigerators, point B on figure 19-3.

From point B on, we'll have to cut down on freezers if we want more refrigerators because our compressor capacity limits us. From B to C we cut freezers down at the rate of $\frac{7}{12}$ freezer cut off for every refrigerator

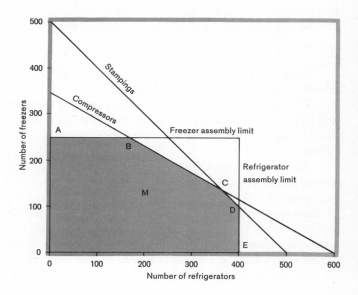

FIGURE 19-3

added until the sum of freezers and refrigerators equals 500, point C. At point C we can produce 140 freezers and 360 refrigerators.

From point C on, because of stamping department limitations, as we increase refrigerator production, we have to cut off one freezer for every one refrigerator up to point D. At point D we have reached our limit of 400 refrigerators. And although we are still making 100 freezers there is no chance to make more refrigerators by cutting off more freezers because 400 is all the refrigerators that we can assemble.

So much for the possibilities but how about making the most profit? Because all relationships are linear, the greatest profit, barring degeneracy, will occur at one of our corner points—A, B, C, D, or E. Here's how it works out:

	FREEZERS		REFRIGERATORS		
POINT	NUMBER	PROFIT	NUMBER	PROFIT	TOTAL PROFIT
A	250	$12,500	0	0	$12,500
B	250	12,500	172	$6,880	19,380
C	140	7,000	360	14,400	21,400
D	100	5,000	400	16,000	21,000
E	0	0	400	16,000	16,000

We should produce 140 freezers and 360 refrigerators, point C on our chart. Doing this will yield the greatest profit, $21,400.

Our second graphic example turns out not to be very different from the first one after all. It turns out that the assembly department limitations in neither department is a limiting factor at the point of greatest profit.

Having a model such as this of our operations not only lets us calculate the most profitable product mix but also has other advantages. For instance, we can see that further investment to increase assembly capacity is useless. On the other hand, extra stamping or compressor capacity would change the maximum profit point. With our model we could see easily how much effect any such changes would have and we could decide whether it would be profitable to invest money in more capacity in either or both departments. And, of course if we did add to our stamping and compressor capacity this might make it desirable also to reopen the question of adding to assembly capacity.

THE SIMPLEX METHOD USING MATRICES

Real-life problems almost never deal with only two or three constraints. Sometimes hundreds of limitations must be considered. For these complex problems the simplex method of linear programming can be used. Computers can solve even these tremendously complicated problems quite readily.

Although the simplex method uses formulas it is in essence the same as the graphic solution and is a step-by-step process. It searches first for a feasible solution at a corner point. Then, after it finds such a feasible solution, the simplex method searches for a better solution. Having found a better solution the method searches for a still better solution, on and on until it finally arrives at the best solution to the problem.

We will continue to use our refrigerator-freezer problem to illustrate the simplex method, after which we will go through a more complex example.

The first step is to define the solution space in terms of the constraints. Since all feasible solutions lie on, or to the left of and below, the boundary line, the constraints can be expressed as a series of inequalities rather than a series of equations. We will let R be the number of refrigerators and F the number of freezers:

$$\begin{array}{lr} \text{Stamping capacity:} & R + F \le 500 \\ \text{Compressor capacity:} & \frac{7}{12}R + F \le 350 \\ \text{Freezer assembly capacity:} & F \le 250 \\ \text{Refrigerator assembly capacity:} & R \le 400 \\ & R,F \ge 0 \end{array}$$

This last expression, $R,F \ge 0$, is called the nonnegative constraint. It closes the solution space so that the meaningless case of negative production is eliminated. It will not enter into our calculations.

Besides these expressions, we need one more equation, the one for the function that we want to optimize or maximize. In this case we want to maximize profits and our equation for doing this is

$$\text{Max } P = 40R + 50F$$

Our problem is now totally defined.

Since we want to investigate the boundary conditions, the inequalities must be converted to equalities. To do this, "slack variables" must be introduced. "Slack" is the difference between any feasible solution point and a given constraint. The ideal solution to our problem might not use up every bit of capacity of every kind of department that we have. Any such idle capacity is slack. Since we don't know, as we set up the problem, if there will be any slack nor if so, where it will be, we have to provide, in our formula, for the possibility of slack in every department concerned.

Since the possible slack is different from every point in the solution space to each of the four department capacity constraint lines, we have to introduce four slack variables into the problem. (In general, you need one slack variable for each constraint.) Our slack variables will be S_1, S_2, S_3, and S_4 and our new set of conditions now reads:

$$\text{Stamping capacity:} \quad R + F + S_1 = 500$$
$$\text{Compressor capacity:} \quad \tfrac{7}{12}R + F + S_2 = 350$$
$$\text{Freezer assembly capacity:} \quad F + S_3 = 250$$
$$\text{Refrigerator assembly capacity:} \quad R + S_4 = 400$$

We next restate our equations and put them into a form where every variable (every symbol in the above four equations) appears in each equation. Variables that do not apply to the equation have a zero coefficient.

$$R + F + S_1 + 0S_2 + 0S_3 + 0S_4 = 500$$
$$\tfrac{7}{12}R + F + 0S_1 + S_2 + 0S_3 + 0S_4 = 350$$
$$0R + F + 0S_1 + 0S_2 + S_3 + 0S_4 = 250$$
$$R + 0F + 0S_1 + 0S_2 + 0S_3 + S_4 = 400$$
$$\text{Max } P = 40R + 50F + 0S_1 + 0S_2 + 0S_3 + 0S_4$$

In practice we would go directly from our original equations to the matrix form below. The intermediate steps described above are only to aid in the explanation. Notice that zero coefficients have also been assigned to the slack variables in the equation for the optimum function since they contribute nothing to the profit.

To form the matrix, we merely list the coefficients associated with each variable in sequence below it. Where, in our equations above, no coefficient is shown, the coefficient is 1, hence the 1's in the matrix below. The constraints or limits are listed in the Quantity column in matrix 1. The coefficients in the optimum equation for the function to be maximized are listed at the head of the table under the appropriate factors. The Program and the Profit columns and base rows I and II will be explained presently.

MATRIX 1

PROGRAM	PROFIT	QUANTITY	R 40	F 50	S_1 0	S_2 0	S_3 0	S_4 0
S_1	0	500	1	1	1	0	0	0
S_2	0	350	$\tfrac{7}{12}$	1	0	1	0	0
S_3	0	250	0	1	0	0	1	0
S_4	0	400	1	0	0	0	0	1
Base row I			0	0	0	0	0	0
Base row II		0	−40	−50	0	0	0	0

When the problem is written in the form given above, there will always be within the matrix a submatrix which is a unity matrix. We have enclosed it here with a dashed line. The unity matrix always has the same number of rows as columns and has a diagonal line of 1's with all other numbers being 0's. The unity submatrix always appears below the slack variables.

In the simplex method, the unity matrix is the starting point for a solution and since this is so the slack variables are listed in order in the Program column. Essentially this means that we start our solution to the problem by assuming that the several production departments make no products at all. Listed in the Profit column are the corresponding profits. Since we earn no profits when the production departments are idle, these profit figures are all 0's.

Return now to matrix 1. In base row I is listed for each variable the profit that we will make using this program. Since at this point we have all slack variables on which no profit is earned, this row is, in matrix 1, all 0's. Base row II we will explain a little later. Here we can say that in matrix 1, the numbers in base row II are the same as the numbers at the top of the columns but with minus signs before them. Also at this point, pay no attention to the boxed-in column and the boxed-in row. These boxes are used as part of the process of developing matrix 2 from matrix 1.

The position that we are now in (as if we had an idle factory) corresponds to starting to check the corner points of the solution space in figure 19-3 at the origin. One may wonder why the solution starts off at the point of no production and no profit. This is because the simplex method has to start with a feasible solution and at the beginning of the calculation this is the only solution known to be feasible. The simplex method then moves on from this poor solution to the optimum solution in a series of steps.

We are now ready to try to improve our program. We start by looking at base row II. Whenever we find a minus number there, it means that we are losing money by not producing the product identified at the top of the column. And the biggest minus number that we find is 50 in the F column, for freezers. We are losing more money per unit by not producing freezers than by not producing any other product. Column F, then, becomes the "key" column. This is indicated in matrix 1 by boxing it in.

Since at this point it appears to be desirable to produce as many freezers as possible, we divide the numbers in the quantity column by their corresponding numbers in our key column. Thus:

$$500 \div 1 = 500$$
$$350 \div 1 = 350$$
$$250 \div 1 = 250$$
$$400 \div 0 = \infty$$

These figures tell us that we can make enough stampings for 500 freezers a day and enough compressors for 350 a day, but we can assemble only 250 freezers a day. So the best we can do is to produce 250 freezers. Doing this uses up all the available slack S_3 in the freezer assembly department. A tentative production program of producing 250 freezers (and nothing else) is therefore the first revision in our program as we start to go step by step toward the optimum solution. In terms of our graphical solution, this corresponds to our beginning to walk around the boundary of the solution space toward point C. At this point we are at point A.

Before we go on to trying to improve this program, however, we have to adjust the other parts of our matrix to show all of the effects of making 250 freezers a day. We have to do this because making parts for freezers takes up part of the slack in the stamping and compressor departments.

First of all we replace the S_3 in the Program column with F. This, the old S_3 row, is called the key row and so is blocked in in matrix 1. Replacing S_3 with F means that the slack time in the freezer assembly department has been wholly replaced by time spent making freezers. Next, the profit per freezer (50) is put into the Profit column in place of zero profits from our first program, which called for no production.

Next we go on to changing the other numbers on old line S_3. To make the other changes we use the number where the key column and the key row cross. This number, 1 in our example, is called the key number, and since it is 1, the other numbers on old line S_3 remain unchanged. (We will show in a moment what happens when the key number is not 1.) The new line F will become part of matrix 2.

Now we have to reduce the other slack variables in the stamping and compressor departments because of the time it takes to make the compressors and stampings for our 250 freezers. Essentially this process is one of subtracting the equation of the key row from the S_1 row (for stampings) and then from the S_2 row (for compressors) since work has to be done in each of these departments. The S_4 row does not need adjusting here since it represents refrigerator assembly and is not affected by our having decided to make freezers instead of nothing. The zero in the F column on the S_4 line tells us this.

To get the new values for a new S_1 row, the calculation is

$$500 - 250 = 250$$
$$1 - 0 = 1$$
$$1 - 1 = 0$$
$$1 - 0 = 1$$
$$0 - 0 = 0$$
$$0 - 1 = -1$$
$$0 - 0 = 0$$

and new row S_1 becomes

$$S_1 \quad 0 \quad 250 \quad 1 \quad 0 \quad 1 \quad 0 \quad -1 \quad 0$$

The same process is repeated for row S_2, which now becomes

$$S_2 \quad 0 \quad 100 \quad \tfrac{7}{12} \quad 0 \quad 0 \quad 1 \quad -1 \quad 0$$

We are now ready to write matrix 2. F has replaced S_3 in the program and F's profits per unit have been inserted in that column. We also have new figures in rows S_1 and S_2. S_4 is unchanged from matrix 1. (As in matrix 1, do not, at this point pay any attention to the boxes drawn around the R column and the S_2 row. They were put in after matrix 2 was complete and are part of the procedure for developing matrix 3.)

MATRIX 2

PROGRAM	PROFITS	QUANTITY	R 40	F 50	S_1 0	S_2 0	S_3 0	S_4 0
S_1	0	250	1	0	1	0	−1	0
S_2	0	100	$\tfrac{7}{12}$	0	0	1	−1	0
F	50	250	0	1	0	0	1	0
S_4	0	400	1	0	0	0	0	1
Base row I			0	50	0	0	50	0
Base row II		$12,500	−40	0	0	0	50	0

To calculate base row I, we multiply the savings in each row by the numbers in each column and then total these by columns. Since there is only one row that contributes savings the answers to our multiplications for that row become base row I. For the F row the answers are:

$$50 \times 250 = 12,500$$
$$50 \times 0 = 0$$
$$50 \times 1 = 50$$
$$50 \times 0 = 0$$
$$50 \times 0 = 0$$
$$50 \times 1 = 50$$
$$50 \times 0 = 0$$

Base row II is calculated as before. (Place a minus sign before every column head value and add it algebraically to the number in the same column in base row I.)

The next iteration, which will produce matrix 3, is now performed by repeating the entire process. The biggest minus in base row II in matrix 2 is in the R column which is therefore the key column; hence the line blocking in the R column. When the numbers in this column are divided into the number in the Quantity column on the same row, we find that the lowest answer is $100 \div \frac{7}{12} = 172$ in the S_2 row. Thé S_2 row is thus established as the key row, so it is blocked in. Seven-twelfths is our new key number.

Matrix 3 tells us that a higher profit results from adding 172 refrigerators to the program. Making 172 refrigerators will use up all of the slack time, S_2, in the compressor department. Then we run into a limiting constraint, the compressor slack time which will all be used up when we make 250 freezers and 172 refrigerators. This corresponds to point B on the graphical solution. Notice that the base row I figure in the Profits column corresponds to the profits made at point B on the graphical plot. (Again the blocked-in column and row in matrix 3 are not really part of matrix 3, but have to do with changing matrix 3 to matrix 4.)

MATRIX 3

PROGRAM	PROFITS	QUANTITY	R 40	F 50	S_1 0	S_2 0	S_3 0	S_4 0
S_1	0	78	0	0	1	−1.72	+.72	0
R	40	172	1	0	0	1.72	−1.72	0
F	50	250	0	1	0	0	1	0
S_4	0	228	0	0	0	−1.72	+1.72	1
Base row I			40	50	0	68.8	−18.8	0
Base row II		$19,390	0	0	0	68.8	−18.8	0

Matrix 3 still shows a minus in base row II in the S_3 column. Repeating our former procedure we find that S_1 is the new key row. This tells us that there are still some more profits to be made if we trade off an increase in slack in freezer assembly for a decrease in slack in stamping capacity. Following the simplex method through to matrix 4 we arrive at the optimum solution to our problem.

Base row II in matrix 4 contains no negative values. This means that there are no other, more profitable solutions. Our final solution is to make

MATRIX 4

PROGRAM	PROFITS	QUANTITY	R 40	F 50	S_1 0	S_2 0	S_3 0	S_4 0
S_3	0	110	0	0	1.39	−2.49	1	0
R	40	360	1	0	2.49	−2.56	0	0
F	50	140	0	1	−1.39	+2.49	0	0
S_4	0	40	0	0	−2.49	+2.56	0	1
Base row I			40	50	30.10	22.10	0	0
Base row II		$21,400	0	0	30.10	22.10	0	0

360 refrigerators and 140 freezers for a total profit of $21,400. This corresponds to point C on the graphical solution. The solution also states that there are 110 spare units of freezer assembly capacity and 40 spare units of refrigerator assembly capacity. Further interpretation of what final matrices show will be given after the next example.

This somewhat lengthy explanation of our simple problem relates the workings of the simplex method to the graphical method. Obviously, in this case the graphical method is considerably easier. But as we increase the number of variables and constraints, graphical techniques quickly become impractical and the worth of the simplex method is evident. Try to imagine what a problem involving 7 variables and 10 constraints would look like graphically. In the first place you would need a ten-dimensional space. This becomes hard to picture, since we normally only think in terms of three dimensions.

EXAMPLE 3. Here we will work out an example trying to find the best product mix using the simplex method and we will set the problem up exactly the same way you would do it for big problems with many variables.[1] Although the procedure is the same as before, it will again be considered in some detail because of the added complexity.

We will make two products, A and B. Both products require machine 1 for their first operation. Product A requires two hours per thousand pieces and product B five hours per thousand. Product A requires a second operation which can be done on machine 2 during regular work hours or during overtime or it can be done on one other machine. This second operation takes three hours per thousand if done on machine 2 or four hours if done on the other machine. No other operations are required.

[1] This example is adapted from one used by H. B. Maynard and Associates, Pittsburgh, in their seminars on linear programming and inventory management.

Product B also requires a second operation. It takes eight hours per thousand on machine 2 or ten hours on the other machine. And again no other operations are required.

We have available 1,000 hours of time on machine 1, 600 on machine 2, 200 of possible overtime on machine 2, and 800 hours on the other machine. Profit margins, per thousand products, are as follows: Product A, made using machine 2 during regular hours $850, using overtime on machine 2, $600, or using the other machine $700; product B using machine 2 during regular hours $1,600, using overtime on machine 2, $1,400, or using the other machine $1,300.

The problem: Find out how many of each product to make per hour and by what method to make the most profit.

We are going to consider 1,000 products as the unit in all of our computations. We'll compute everything using 1 in place of 1,000 and then, at the end, translate the answers back into individual units. For simplicity too, we are going to consider overtime on machine 2 as if it were another machine with different costs. We'll call it machine 3. Our "other" machine then becomes machine 4.

Now we are ready to put all of this into a table. Figure 19-4 shows the relationships:

FIGURE 19-4

OPERATION	MACHINE	HOURS PER UNIT OF PRODUCT						HOURS AVAILABLE
		PRODUCT A			PRODUCT B			
1	1	2	2	2	5	5	5	1,000
2	2	3			8			600
2	3		3			8		200
2	4			4			10	800
Profit margin per unit of product		$850	$600	$700	$1,600	$1,400	$1,300	

Notice that there are three columns each for products A and B. These separate columns represent different ways to make the products.

Although our next step in the simplex method is to recast figure 19-4 into something a little different, it might be well to point out that we could set up equations for each machine's uses, equations that are similar to those used in earlier examples. Before we do that, however, notice that we can think of our two products, each made three possible ways, as if they were six products.

Instead of saying, product A made by method 1, product A made by method 2, product A made by method 3, product B made by method 1, and so on, we can say, products 1, 2, 3, 4, 5, and 6. This is a convenience in the simplex method so we do it. Our six possibilities become P_1, P_2, P_3, P_4, P_5, and P_6.

As in example 2, again we have to set up our equations to provide for the possibility of slack time on each machine. (Another way of describing slack time is to think of it as time devoted to making imaginary products. P_7 will be the imaginary products on machine 1, P_8 on machine 2, P_9 on 3, and P_{10} on 4.) Now we can set up our equations.

Our equations are:

machine 1
I $1,000 = 1P_7 + 0P_8 + 0P_9 + 0P_{10} + 2P_1 + 2P_2 + 2P_3 + 5P_4 + 5P_5 + 5P_6$

machine 2
II $600 = 0P_7 + 1P_8 + 0P_9 + 0P_{10} + 3P_1 + 0P_2 + 0P_3 + 8P_4 + 0P_5 + 0P_6$

machine 3
III $200 = 0P_7 + 0P_8 + 1P_9 + 0P_{10} + 0P_1 + 3P_2 + 0P_3 + 0P_4 + 8P_5 + 0P_6$

machine 4
IV $800 = 0P_7 + 0P_8 + 0P_9 + 1P_{10} + 0P_1 + 0P_2 + 4P_3 + 0P_4 + 0P_5 + 10P_6$

We also need to set up the equation for profits, the function we want to maximize.

V $\text{Profits} = 0P_7 + 0P_8 + 0P_9 + 0P_{10} + 850P_1 + 600P_2 + 700P_3 + 1,600P_4 + 1,400P_5 + 1,300P_6$

Now we are ready to set up the first of the series of matrices for solving the problem. The column of hours available has been headed P_0 in this matrix to conform to common practice. We have also listed the slack factors before the real products. There is no significance to whether they are listed before or after the real products; either may be listed first.

MATRIX 1

PRO-GRAM	PROFIT PER UNIT	P_0	P_7 0	P_8 0	P_9 0	P_{10} 0	P_1 $850	P_2 $600	P_3 $700	P_4 $1,600	P_5 $1,400	P_6 $1,300
P_7	0	1,000	1	0	0	0	2	2	2	5	5	5
P_8	0	600	0	1	0	0	3	0	0	8	0	0
P_9	0	200	0	0	1	0	0	3	0	0	8	0
P_{10}	0	800	0	0	0	1	0	0	4	0	0	10
Base row I			0	0	0	0	0	0	0	0	0	0
Base row II		0	0	0	0	0	−850	−600	−700	−1,600	−1,400	−1,300

Although we will not go through all of the calculation of successive matrices in this example, we will follow it through up to matrix 2 so that the method already illustrated in example 2 is clear as it applies to this more complex problem.

The biggest minus in base row II is 1,600 in the P_4 column so it is the key column. On the P_7 row we divide the 1,000 in column P_0 by the 5 in the P_4 column and get 200. On the P_8 row, 600 divided by 8 gives 75. So 75 is the most P_4's that can be made. The P_8 row is the key row and 8 is the key number.

Now we replace the old program for the key row with the new at the left and divide all numbers in the key row by 8, getting:

P_4 1,600   75   0 $\frac{1}{8}$ 0   0 $\frac{3}{8}$ 0   0   1   0   0

This will be the new second line in matrix 2.

But product P_4 requires machine time on two machines. If we make 75 units they will use up part of the time now shown as available for making P_7's. So the next step is to scale down the P_7 program. We have to get a new P_7 row. Each number in the P_7 row is changed using the following formula.

$$\text{Old value} - \left(\begin{array}{c} \text{corresponding key} \\ \text{row number} \end{array} \times \frac{\begin{array}{c} \text{corresponding key} \\ \text{column number} \end{array}}{\text{key number}} \right) = \text{new value}$$

Here's how it works. We will get a new row 1. To start with it is:

P_7 0   1,000   1   0   0   0   2   2   2   5   5   5

Each number, beginning with the 1,000, has to be figured out for matrix 2 as follows:

$$1,000 - [600 \times \tfrac{5}{8}] = 1,000 - 375 = 625$$
$$1 - [0 \times \tfrac{5}{8}] = 1 - 0 = 1$$
$$0 - [1 \times \tfrac{5}{8}] = 0 - \tfrac{5}{8} = -\tfrac{5}{8}$$
$$0 - [0 \times \tfrac{5}{8}] = 0 - 0 = 0$$
$$0 - [0 \times \tfrac{5}{8}] = 0 - 0 = 0$$
$$2 - [3 \times \tfrac{5}{8}] = 2 - \tfrac{15}{8} = \tfrac{1}{8}$$
$$2 - [0 \times \tfrac{5}{8}] = 2 - 0 = 2$$
$$2 - [0 \times \tfrac{5}{8}] = 2 - 0 = 2$$
$$5 - [8 \times \tfrac{5}{8}] = 5 - 5 = 0$$
$$5 - [0 \times \tfrac{5}{8}] = 5 - 0 = 5$$
$$5 - [0 \times \tfrac{5}{8}] = 5 - 0 = 5$$

So we arrive at a revised P_7 row as

P_7 0   625   1 $-\frac{5}{8}$ 0   0 $\frac{1}{8}$ 2   2   0   5   5

We revise rows 3 and 4 in the same fashion and arrive at the following partial matrix (as it happens there are no changes at all in rows 3 and 4).

P_7	0	625	1	$-\frac{5}{8}$	0	0	$\frac{1}{8}$	2	2	0	5	5
P_4	1,600	75	0	$\frac{1}{8}$	0	0	$\frac{3}{8}$	0	0	1	0	0
P_9	0	200	0	0	1	0	0	3	0	0	8	0
P_{10}	0	800	0	0	0	1	0	0	4	0	0	10

We have also to adjust base rows I and II. We get base row I by multiplying the quantity in each block times the profit per unit. Starting in column P_7, the first row shows a 1. *Looking to the left* (not to the column heading), we find that the profit per unit is 0 so $1 \times 0 = 0$ the profit from making one P_7. Below the 1 in column P_7 is a 0. 0 products $\times$ 1,600 = 0. The other two figures in the P_7 column are also 0 so the column total is 0.

But in column P_8 we have some numbers that do not come out zero. $-\frac{5}{8} \times 0 = 0$, $\frac{1}{8} \times 1{,}600 = 200$, $0 \times 0 = 0$, $0 \times 0 = 0$; total 200. We repeat the process for all columns. Here are the computations that produce base row I (including the two we have just made):

COLUMN

P_7	$1 \times 0 + 0 + 0 + 0 = 0$
P_8	$-\frac{5}{8} \times 0 + \frac{1}{8} \times 1{,}600 + 0 + 0 = 200$
P_9	$0 + 0 + 1 \times 0 + 0 = 0$
P_{10}	$0 + 0 + 0 + 1 \times 0 = 0$
P_1	$\frac{1}{8} \times 0 + \frac{3}{8} \times 1{,}600 + 0 + 0 = 600$
P_2	$2 \times 0 + 0 + 3 \times 0 + 0 = 0$
P_3	$2 \times 0 + 0 + 0 + 4 \times 0 = 0$
P_4	$0 + 1 \times 1{,}600 + 0 + 0 = 1{,}600$
P_5	$5 \times 0 + 0 + 8 \times 0 + 0 = 0$
P_6	$5 \times 0 + 0 + 0 + 10 \times 0 = 0$

These answers are base row I and are listed horizontally as

0   200   0   0   600   0   0   1,600   0   0

Next, to get base row II, we subtract, column by column, the per unit profit figure at the top of each column from the corresponding column number in base row I. Here is base row II.

$120,000   0   200   0   0   −250   −600   −700   0   −1,400   −1,300

The $120,000 figure that appears near the left of base row II for the first time is the profits we make from following the proposed program, in this case making 75 units P_4 at $1,600 each and making nothing else. Now we can complete making matrix 2 which is as follows:

MATRIX 2

PRO-GRAM	PROFIT PER UNIT	P_0	P_7 0	P_8 0	P_9 0	P_{10} 0	P_1 $850	P_2 $600	P_3 $700	P_4 $1,600	P_5 $1,400	P_6 $1,300
P_7	0	625	1	$-\frac{5}{8}$	0	0	$\frac{1}{8}$	2	2	0	5	5
P_4	1,600	75	0	$\frac{1}{8}$	0	0	$\frac{3}{8}$	0	0	1	0	0
P_9	0	200	0	0	1	0	0	3	0	0	8	0
P_{10}	0	800	0	0	0	1	0	0	4	0	0	10
Base row I			0	200	0	0	600	0	0	1,600	0	0
Base row II		$120,000	0	200	0	0	−250	−600	−700	0	−1,400	−1,300

Since the method is now familiar, we will just show the remaining matrices instead of calculating them here. This problem is interesting in that it takes seven iterations to arrive finally at the optimum solution. This is because it happens that we should *not* make the items that have the highest profit *per unit* because they use up so much machine time. The simplex method always has you first try to make all that you can of the highest profit item not already in the program. In our example this guide did not produce the most profitable program at first.

MATRIX 3

PRO-GRAM	PROFIT PER UNIT	P_0	P_7	P_8	P_9	P_{10}	P_1	P_2	P_3	P_4	P_5	P_6
			0	0	0	0	$850	$600	$700	$1,600	$1,400	$1,300
P_7	0	500	1	$-\frac{5}{8}$	$-\frac{5}{8}$	0	$\frac{1}{8}$	$\frac{1}{8}$	2	0	0	5
P_4	1,600	75	0	$\frac{1}{8}$	0	0	$\frac{3}{8}$	0	0	1	0	0
P_5	1,400	25	0	0	$\frac{1}{8}$	0	0	$\frac{3}{8}$	0	0	1	0
P_{10}	0	800	0	0	0	1	0	0	4	0	0	10
Base row I			0	200	175	0	600	525	0	1,600	1,400	0
Base row II		$155,000	0	200	175	0	−250	−75	−700	0	0	−1,300

MATRIX 4

PRO-GRAM	PROFIT PER UNIT	P_0	P_7	P_8	P_9	P_{10}	P_1	P_2	P_3	P_4	P_5	P_6
			0	0	0	0	$850	$600	$700	$1,600	$1,400	$1,300
P_7	0	100	1	$-\frac{5}{8}$	$-\frac{5}{8}$	$-\frac{1}{2}$	$\frac{1}{8}$	$\frac{1}{8}$	0	0	0	0
P_4	1,600	75	0	$\frac{1}{8}$	0	0	$\frac{3}{8}$	0	0	1	0	0
P_5	1,400	25	0	0	$\frac{1}{8}$	0	0	$\frac{3}{8}$	0	0	1	0
P_6	1,300	80	0	0	0	$\frac{1}{10}$	0	0	$\frac{2}{5}$	0	0	1
Base row I			0	200	175	130	600	525	520	1,600	1,400	1,300
Base row II		$259,000	0	200	175	130	−250	−75	−180	0	0	0

MATRIX 5

PRO-GRAM	PROFIT PER UNIT	P_0	P_7	P_8	P_9	P_{10}	P_1	P_2	P_3	P_4	P_5	P_6
			0	0	0	0	$850	$600	$700	$1,600	$1,400	$1,300
P_7	0	75	1	$-\frac{2}{3}$	$-\frac{5}{8}$	$-\frac{1}{2}$	0	$\frac{1}{8}$	0	$-\frac{1}{3}$	0	0
P_1	850	200	0	$\frac{1}{3}$	0	0	1	0	0	$\frac{8}{3}$	0	0
P_5	1,400	25	0	0	$\frac{1}{8}$	0	0	$\frac{3}{8}$	0	0	1	0
P_6	1,300	80	0	0	0	$\frac{1}{10}$	0	0	$\frac{2}{5}$	0	0	1
Base row I			0	283	175	130	850	525	520	2,267	1,400	1,300
Base row II		$309,000	0	283	175	130	0	−75	−180	667	0	0

MATRIX 6

PRO-GRAM	PROFIT PER UNIT	P_0	P_7	P_8	P_9	P_{10}	P_1	P_2	P_3	P_4	P_5	P_6
			0	0	0	0	$850	$600	$700	$1,600	$1,400	$1,300
P_7	0	75	1	$-\frac{2}{3}$	$-\frac{5}{8}$	$-\frac{1}{2}$	0	$\frac{1}{8}$	0	$-\frac{1}{3}$	0	0
P_1	850	200	0	$\frac{1}{3}$	0	1	1	0	0	$\frac{8}{3}$	0	0
P_5	1,400	25	0	0	$\frac{1}{8}$	0	0	$\frac{3}{8}$	0	0	1	0
P_3	700	200	0	0	0	$\frac{1}{4}$	0	0	1	0	0	$\frac{5}{2}$
Base row I			0	283	175	175	850	525	700	2,267	1,400	1,345
Base row II		$345,000	0	283	175	175	0	−75	0	667	0	450

MATRIX 7

PRO-GRAM	PROFIT PER UNIT	P_0	P_7	P_8	P_9	P_{10}	P_1	P_2	P_3	P_4	P_5	P_6
			0	0	0	0	$850	$600	$700	$1,600	$1,400	$1,300
P_7	0	67	1	$-\frac{2}{3}$	$-\frac{2}{3}$	$-\frac{1}{2}$	0	0	0	$-\frac{1}{3}$	$-\frac{1}{3}$	0
P_1	850	200	0	$\frac{1}{3}$	0	0	1	0	0	$\frac{8}{3}$	0	0
P_2	600	67	0	0	$\frac{1}{3}$	0	0	1	0	0	$\frac{8}{3}$	0
P_3	700	200	0	0	0	$\frac{1}{4}$	0	0	1	0	0	$\frac{5}{2}$
Base row I			0	283	200	175	850	600	700	2,267	1,600	1,750
Base row II		$350,000	0	283	200	175	0	0	0	667	200	450

On page 428 we spoke of degeneracy as making a problem when using the simplex method. Degeneracy occurs when two or more choices are equal. Suppose that, in example 3, the P_4 column had a 5 and a 3 where it now has a 5 and an 8. In that case, $1,000 \div 5 = 200$ and $600 \div 3 = 200$. This would make the choices equal; you wouldn't know whether the P_7 or the P_8 row was the key row.

To solve this problem look for the 1 in the first of the two rows concerned. It is in the P_7 column. Divide this 1 by the key number, which is 5, and get $\frac{1}{5}$. Next divide the other key number, 3, into the number in its row in the P_7 column. This number is 0 and $0 \div 3 = 0$. The smaller answer is your choice. It would be the P_8 row. You would now go on with the simplex method, clearing out row P_8 and putting P_4 products in their place.

Returning to example 3, matrix 7 contains no minuses in base row II and therefore it shows the optimal solution. We should make 200 of item P_1, 67 of P_2, and 200 of P_3. Our best solution to this problem will leave a little time left over on machine 1, as is indicated by P_7 still being in the program and having a value of 67. This means that machine 1 will be idle 67 hours.

We are now ready to rephrase the answer back into terms of our original problem. P_1 = product A, made on machines 1 and 2 during regular work hours. P_2 = also product A and also made on machines 1 and 2 except that machine 2's time used is overtime hours. P_3 = still product A, made on machine 1 and the "other" machine. P_4, P_5, and P_6, the three ways to make product B, are not in our program. This tells us that it pays best to make no product B's at all. We need also to translate the units (we used 1,000 as one unit in the computations) back to their original terms.

Here is our program.

PRODUCT	METHOD	PIECES	PROFIT PER PIECE	TOTAL PROFIT
A	Machines 1 and 2	200,000	$ .85	$170,000
A	Machines 1 and 2 overtime	66,667	.60	40,000
A	Machine 1 and "other" machine	200,000	.70	140,000
	Total profit			$350,000

INTERPRETATION OF MATRIX 7   The obvious objective of the simplex method is to tell us the best program. But there are by-product values that can be most helpful to managerial decision making. Matrix 7 tells us much more than the best program.

It tells us (base line II) that, if we should want to do so, it will cost us $667 to make 1,000 P_4 items, $200 for 1,000 P_5's, and $450 for 1,000 P_6's. It will cost us these sums in the sense that giving up other items would lose these sums in excess of the profits that P_4, P_5, or P_6 would produce.

If we decide that we must make some B products to round out the line, we should do it by the P_5 process because then each 1,000 B items will cause a net loss of only $200 on the A items cut out.

Matrix 7 tells us further that if we do this we will have to cut off 8 units of P_2 for every 3 added units P_5 that we will get. And since there are only 67 units of P_2, the most that we can increase P_5 at the expense of P_2 is $67 \div 8 = 8\frac{3}{8} \times 3 = 25\frac{1}{8}$ (25 actually; the extra $\frac{1}{8}$ in the answer comes from having rounded $66\frac{2}{3}$ to 67); the $-\frac{1}{3}$ in column P_5 tells us that for every 3 items P_5 we added we would increase the idle time to P_7 (machine 1) by one hour.

If, in spite of their being more costly, we were to want still more than 25 B items, we should turn next to P_6 not to P_4 because the loss would be less.

The 283, 200, and 175 in base line II for P_8, P_9, and P_{10} tell us how much more we can afford to spend per unit on machines in order to make more of products P_1, P_2, and P_3. We could afford to pay $283 per 1,000 for more regular hours on machine 2 (this is the P_8 process). Also the $\frac{1}{3}$ tells us that we'll get 333 pieces per added hour. The $-\frac{2}{3}$ tells us that for every 1,000 added of product A made this way, we'll cut machine 1's idle time (which is P_7) by two hours.

This is enough explanation to show you how meaningful matrix 7 is when interpreted in a way to help managerial decision making. Don't overlook this knowledge since, often, there are outside reasons which keep you from using the best solution to a problem. The simplex method tells you considerable about the costliness of other courses of action.

EXAMPLE 4.   All of the problems that we have dealt with up until now in linear programming have been maximization problems. It is also possible to solve minimization problems by the same technique. This would be the case where we were trying to minimize costs. With one minor exception, the iterations of the matrix are the same as before. The exception arises in setting up the first matrix.

Suppose we manufacture two products, X and Y. Because of sales commitments, we must make at least 50 units of X per week and at least 20 units of Y per week. Our plant capacity is either 200 units of X per week or 100 units of Y or any linear combination of the two. The employees have a guaranteed minimum of work hours per week during which they can produce either 150 units of X or 80 units of Y or any linear combination of the two. X units cost $4 and Y units cost $6 to make. The problem is to minimize the expense of operations.

The problem is shown graphically in figure 19-5. Notice that the solution space does not touch the origin, so that the origin cannot be used as a starting place. In this case we wish to find the minimal cost line that passes through a corner point. In our example, this can easily be determined graphically to be point C, with a total cost of $520.

If we write the equations for the problem, they are:

Capacity limit	$X + 2Y \leq 200$
Sales commitments	$X \geq 50$
	$Y \geq 20$
Guaranteed workweek	$8X + 15Y \geq 1,200$
	$\text{Min } C = 4X + 6Y$

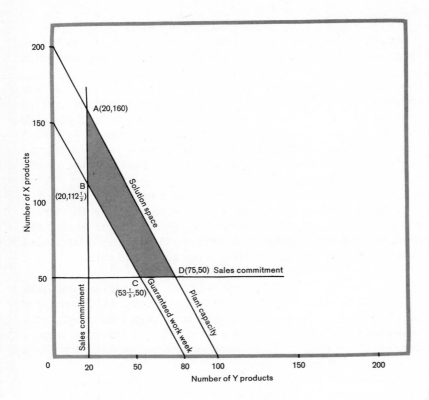

FIGURE 19-5

These equations can be converted to equalities by adding slack variables. Notice, however, that in the last three constraints the slack variables have negative signs attached to them because the variables must exceed or equal some quantity rather than be less than or equal to it. Thus if we start with all the slack variables in our program, we do not have a unity matrix. This corresponds to what was said about the graphical solution.

To circumvent this problem we introduce dummy variables. *Dummy variables are not the same as slack variables.* Slack variables have a physical interpretation; they represent unused capacity. Dummy variables are strictly computational devices and must not appear in any final solution program. To insure this, we assign an arbitrarily high cost to them in our minimizing function. This cost should be at least 10 times higher than any real cost. Here we will assign a cost of $100 to each dummy variable. The dummy variables have positive signs attached.

Our first matrix then is:

MATRIX 1

PROGRAM	SAV-INGS	QUAN-TITY	X 4	Y 6	S_1 0	S_2 0	S_3 0	S_4 0	D_1 100	D_2 100	D_3 100
S_1	0	200	1	2	1	0	0	0	0	0	0
D_1	100	50	1	0	0	-1	0	0	1	0	0
D_2	100	20	0	1	0	0	-1	0	0	1	0
D_3	100	1,200	8	15	0	0	0	-1	0	0	1
Base row I		900		1,600	0	-100	-100	-100	100	100	100
Base row II	$127,000	896		1,594	0	-100	-100	-100	0	0	0

The starting program consists of the first slack variable and the three dummy variables. Because of this, base row I has the indicated values rather than all 0's as in the start of our other example. When a function is to be minimized, we select the largest *positive* value in base row II to indicate our key column. The key row is selected as before. All other computational procedures are also as before.

To keep from being repetitive, only the final matrix (the fifth) is shown below. Notice that in *minimizing* a function, we stop when all values in base row II are zero or negative. The cost of the final program is $520.

MATRIX 5

PROGRAM	SAV-INGS	QUAN-TITY	X 4	Y 6	S_1 0	S_2 0	S_3 0	S_4 0	D_1 100	D_2 100	D_3 100
S_1	0	$43\frac{2}{3}$	0	0	1	$-\frac{1}{8}$	0	$\frac{1}{120}$	$\frac{1}{15}$	0	$-\frac{2}{15}$
S_3	0	$33\frac{1}{3}$	0	0	0	$\frac{8}{15}$	1	$-\frac{1}{15}$	$-\frac{8}{15}$	0	$\frac{1}{15}$
Y	6	$53\frac{1}{3}$	0	1	0	$\frac{8}{15}$	0	$-\frac{1}{15}$	$-\frac{8}{15}$	-1	$\frac{1}{15}$
X	4	50	1	0	0	-1	0	0	1	0	0
Base row I			4	6	0	$-\frac{4}{5}$	0	$-\frac{2}{5}$	$\frac{4}{5}$	0	$\frac{2}{5}$
Base row II	$520		0	0	0	$-\frac{4}{5}$	0	$-\frac{2}{5}$	$-99\frac{1}{5}$	-100	$-99\frac{2}{5}$

In cases where rounding fractional numbers would introduce serious errors, integer programming should be used. This technique is not included in this text. Descriptions of it can be found, along with those of nonlinear and dynamic programming, in some of the books devoted solely to quantitative methods.[2]

STUDY MATERIALS

19-1   What types of problems can linear programming solve? What limitations must be placed on the formulation of the problem? What kinds of information can you get from linear program problem solutions?

19-2   Outside research: Examine several of the journals that are quantitatively oriented such as *Management Science*, The *Journal of the Operations Research Society*, or the *Journal of the Institute of Industrial Engineers* and report on the applications of linear programming that you find. Evaluate the assumptions you find made in the formulation of the models.

19-3   Feline Fancies, Inc., is introducing two new brands of canned food for cats, Tuna Supreme and Turkey Supreme. The canning line can turn out 4,000 cans per week of either or both products in any combination. Processing facilities are, however, limited to 2,500 cans for each product. Vegetable meal is used in both products but Turkey Supreme takes twice as much per can as does Tuna Supreme. One week's capacity of meal is limited to 3,000 cans of Turkey Supreme, or 6,000 cans of Tuna Supreme, or equivalent combinations of the two. Besides these ingredients a vitamin fortifier is used. Its available quantity is limited to 3,500 cans of Turkey or 4,500 cans of Tuna.

Expected profits are 5 cents a can for Turkey and 4 cents a can for Tuna. Assuming that you can sell all that you can produce on these facilities, what quantity of each product will you make?

19-4   The Hershey Company's machine shop has a problem of scheduling three parts to three bottleneck machines. The problem is how to schedule the making of suspension bars, side plates, and hangers on the lathes, millers, and grinders. Other jobs and other operations on these parts and other machines are not involved. The time available on these machines is: lathes, 180 hours; millers, 360 hours; and grinders, 400 hours.

Each of the three parts can be made in alternative ways. The table shows the time, in hours per 100, that it takes to do the operations. Column 1, for Suspension Bars, shows, for example, that 100 units will take 3 hours on lathes, 4 hours on millers, and 3 hours on grinders. Column 2 shows an alternative method. By transferring more work to the lathes, the milling and grinding time will be reduced. Lathe time per 100 will be 8 hours, miller time 2 hours, and grinder time 2 hours. Or (method 3) by transferring more to grinders the milling operation is cut out. Lathe time is 8 hours and grinding time 6 hours.

Side plates and hangers each can be made two ways, as shown in the table.

[2] See, for example, Charles R. Carr and Charles W. Howe, *Introduction to Quantitative Decision Procedures in Management and Economics*, McGraw-Hill Book Company, New York, 1964.

	SUSPENSION BAR			SIDE PLATE		HANGER		HOURS AVAILABLE
	1	2	3	1	2	1	2	
Lathes	3	8	8	2		4	6	180
Millers	4	2		6	6	4	2	360
Grinders	3	2	6	6	12	10	1	400

Hershey uses more of these parts than it can make and buys its excess needs outside. Outside costs are, however, higher. Making suspension bars inside saves $6 each for those made by method 1, $7 by method 2, and $12 by method 3. Side plates made inside save $4 each if made by method 1 and $14 by method 2. Hangers made inside save $3 and $7, respectively.

In order to save the most money possible, how many of each part should Hershey make for itself and by what method?

19-5   In problem 19-4 suppose that you could, by sending orders for other products outside, release 100 additional hours of lathe time, but at a cost of $200. Should you do this or not? If you do, how much money will you make or lose?

19-6   In problem 19-4 suppose that a supplier quotes you new lower prices for making side plates at $2 each less than his old price. At the same time, outside prices for suspension bars go up $1 a unit. Now what change in your program do you make?

19-7   Would you, considering only the jobs in problem 19-4, recommend buying a new lathe (it would add 80 hours of capacity) if it were to be used only for these particular parts, if its operating costs including depreciation came to $3 an hour?

19-8   Hot Fuels, Inc., makes three racing fuels called Flash, Super Flash, and Mega Flash. Flash, Super, and Mega contain 80, 60, and 40 per cent, respectively, of the same high-octane gasoline. Other volatile chemicals make up the balances.

Hot Fuels has a contract with a refiner to order 300 gallons of the high-octane gasoline per week. And it has contracts with nearby racing clubs to sell at least 100 gallons of Flash, 200 of Super, and 200 of Mega a week.

There are four production and material handling employees (and you are unable to hire any more) who are guaranteed a 40-hour week. They can turn out 800 gallons of Flash, or 640 of Super, or 400 of Mega, or any linear combination thereof. Production and handling costs are 60 cents per gallon for Flash, 80 cents for Super, and $1.00 for Mega.

Set up the model and solve it for the least-cost solution. What variables are involved and what does your solution tell you with respect to each?

chapter twenty

SCHEDULING

Scheduling means setting the time when work is to be done. In production control work, this usually means setting expected starting times for operations. Scheduling is not a matter of determining how long a job will take. When you find that operation 3 on order number M-239 will take 15 hours of stamping press time, this is just a measure of the work load; it is not a schedule. But when you say that press number 7 will start on operation 3 on order number M-239 at 9 A.M. on March 5, you have scheduled it. Scheduling also implies deciding ahead of time. We don't say that you have scheduled a job if you decided to put it on a machine only five minutes before you started the job.

Scheduling can deal with both orders and machines. When you have a plan that shows, for an order, its expected start and stop time for each operation you have an *order schedule*. When you have a plan for a machine showing the expected start and stop times for operations on orders you have a *machine schedule*. Normally, in order control, you don't have to make up machine schedules but can just let machines handle the orders that come in the sequence of their arrival. You may resort to machine scheduling if certain machines begin to get behind because unusual changes in the product mix throw unusual work loads on them.

LOADS AND SCHEDULES

LOAD RECORDS The "load" of work ahead of a machine, group of machines, or department is simply the amount of work ahead of it. You don't have to plan a load in order to have one. And if you can avoid keeping load records of work ahead of machines or machine centers, by all means do so and save the record-keeping costs. On the other hand, maybe you have to figure out department and machine loads for manpower forecasting. If you do, it costs no more to use such records for controlling production too.

Not often will you have to spend much money on loading, because so long as your total schedule is reasonable, most department and most machine schedules will be reasonable. They will load themselves. And if you do find it necessary to calculate machine loads, your computer will do it at low cost.

Load records are most helpful when business is good or bad, not in between. When business is good they help you to know where bottlenecks occur and they also help you to avoid trouble by warning you when you will need to work overtime, or to buy more outside, or to quote more distant promise dates, or reduce incoming orders by quoting higher prices. They help when business is bad by telling you ahead when and where you'll have to cut.

Usually you talk about the load in terms of hours, days, or weeks of work ahead of the machine. And usually, but not always, you keep load records in terms of machine hours. Machine hours of work ahead is, of course, the best measure of a department's load if the department does only machine work. Florsheim Shoe, on the other hand, keeps its leather-cutting department load record in terms of the total piecework value of the orders ahead. Link-Belt division of FMC Corporation, in its Chicago plant, uses the dollar value of the orders ahead as the measure of the load.

Any of these measures (piecework value, dollar value, or hours or days of work ahead) is only a rough measure of the load, but probably any of them is good enough to help you set promise dates for new orders and to help you plan department work hours.

Notice that, when you talk about the load in terms of time, this presupposes that you have some idea of how long it will take to do each individual job. Also, you need to allow for normal machine dead time. So you need to know also about typical machine downtime and use ratios.

Figures 20-1 and 20-2 show load reports comparing the capacity avail-

MACHINE LOAD ANALYSIS								
Dept No.	Group No.	Number of Machs.	Load Week	Capacity Hours	Part Number	Order Number	Load Hours	Variance Hours
10	4	14	43	384:0				
			43		120615	11074	:2	
			43		123457	11354	14:4	
			43		123459	12054	18:0	
			43		123500	12064	28:0	
			43		123601	12074	18:0	
			43		123652	12084	70:0	
			43		123666	12094	120:0	
			43		123701	12104	63:0	
			43		123702	12114	3:0	
			43		123704	12124	7:5	
			43		123705	12134	12:0	
			43		123801	12144	35:0	
			43		123802	12154	10:0	
			43		123840	12164	5:9	
				384:0			405:0	21:0CR
40	102	13	42	384:0				
			42		120618	8014	135:0	
			42		120819	8024	198:0	
			42		121019	8034	56:0	

FIGURE 20-1 A detailed load record of the specific orders ahead of machine groups. (International Business Machines Corp.)

MACHINE TOOL LOAD SUMMARY

MACHINE SHOP A

DEPT. NO.	GRP. NO.	DESCRIPTION	NO. OF MACHS.	EFFIC'Y	WK.	CAPACITY	LOAD	AVAILABLE CAPACITY	OVER- LOAD
1	1	BENCH MILLS	5	85%	1	136.0	130.0	6.0	
					2	170.0	160.0	10.0	
					3	170.0	165.5	4.5	
					4	170.0	179.0		9.0
					5	170.0	162.3	7.7	
					6	170.0	185.1		15.1
					7	170.0	150.0	20.0	
					8	170.0	162.8	7.2	
						1326.0*	1294.7*	55.4*	24.1*
1	3	SMALL HORZ MILLS	8	80%	1	204.8	198.0	6.8	
					2	256.0	250.0	6.0	
					3	256.0	251.9	4.1	
					4	256.0	269.5		13.5
					5	256.0	256.0		
					6	256.0	240.0	16.0	
					7	256.0	263.0		7.0
					8	256.0	248.0	8.0	
						1996.8*	1976.4*	40.9*	20.5*
1	5	MED HORZ MILLS	7	80%	1	179.2	178.1	1.1	
					2	224.0	221.0	3.0	
					3	224.0	222.0	2.0	
					4	224.0	225.6		1.6
					5	224.0	218.4	5.6	
					6	224.0	221.0	3.0	
					7	224.0	226.8		2.8
					8	224.0	223.0	1.0	
						1747.2*	1735.9*	15.7*	4.4*
1	7	LGE HORZ MILLS	6	80%	1	153.6	149.2	4.4	
					2	192.0	193.2		1.2
					3	192.0	194.1		2.1
					4	192.0	191.5	.5	
					5	192.0	187.2	4.8	
					6	192.0	191.0	1.0	
					7	192.0	193.2		1.2
					8	192.0	190.0	2.0	
						1497.6*	1489.4*	12.7*	4.5*

FIGURE 20-2 A machine load summary for various machine groups showing their loads ahead week by week for the next eight weeks. Notice the column "Efficiency." This shows the department's normal machine use ratio. "80%" means that you can count on getting four hours work done in five hours of time and that the loads shown recognize this. (International Business Machines Corp.)

able to the load assigned for each week. The 384.0 in figure 20-1 is the total expected number of machine work hours that the company expects to get in one week from its 14 machines. It appears that the plant works a 40-hour week and, on those machines, achieves a use ratio of about 69 per cent.

Some companies distinguish between a department's or a machine's "dead" and "live" loads. Dead loads are production orders planned for but whose production hasn't yet started. Live loads are jobs already released and coming through the plant although perhaps not yet in the department. You will also find that some companies refer to their "load board." A load board is some kind of visual chart of the load. We will talk about load boards later.

LOADS VERSUS SCHEDULES   Machine loads and schedules are nearly, although not quite, the same. As we said earlier, a machine load says that you have 10 days of work lined up ahead for it. But a schedule says that a job starts on Tuesday at 11 A.M. You can make a schedule easily from a work load record but the load record is not itself a schedule.

DAILY PRODUCTION REPORT

DATE_____

PART NO.	ORDER NO.	OPERATION NO.	DEPT.	Sft	MACHINE CODE	MACHINE NO.	CLOCK NO.	PCS. PRODUCED	ACTUAL HOURS	STANDARD HOURS
8 6 7 3 P	1 7 1 4	3 0	5 4	2	5 3	2 4	4 2 2 4	2 7.0	8.0	8 5
		4 0	5 7	1	2 0	8 1	7 3 1 0	2 6.0	7.5	7 8
		4 0	5 7	2	2 0	8 1	7 4 0 8	2 8.0	8.0	8 4
	(9 0 0 3)	5 0	5 7	1	8 1	1 0 0	7 5 1 6	4 6.0	8.0	9 2
		5 0	5 7	2	8 1	1 0 0	7 2 0 6	2 2.0	6.0	6 0
							Hot job—no apprentices			
		6 0	5 7	1	2 1	1 3 8	(6 2 1 4)	1 4.0	8.0	3 7
		6 0	5 7	2	2 1	1 3 8	7 1 7 3	3 0.0	8.0	8 0
	(9 0 1 1)	7 0	5 7	1	2 1	1 2 2	7 0 3 2 *set up*		1.5	1 5
		7 0	5 7	1	2 1	1 2 2	7 0 3 2	6 0.0	6.5	6 0
		7 0	5 7	2	2 1	1 2 2	7 2 1 6	8 0.0	7.8	8 0
		8 0	5 7	1	2 1	1 3 0	7 2 0 0	1 7.0	8.0	8 5
		8 0	5 7	1	2 1	1 3 2	7 0 4 1	1 6.5	8.0	8 2
		8 0	5 7	2	2 1	1 3 0	7 5 4 0	1 3.5	6.5	6 7
		8 0	5 7	2	2 1	1 3 2	7 5 5 5	1 8.0	8.0	9 0

FIGURE 20-3 You'll need reports of work done in order to know when you can schedule the next jobs. Once you get such reports, your computer can easily run off reports such as this one. Someone has looked this report over and has marked unusual situations. (Sperry Rand Corp.)

The load is a running balance figure. Every time a new job is issued, you add in the load it imposes. Every time a job is finished, you subtract its load. The remainder tells you always how much work you have ahead. Actually most companies don't subtract the time for jobs done. Instead, they just have their computer run off new load totals every few days or even every day. They pay no attention to jobs done, only to those yet to be done. Look again at figures 20-1 and 20-2. You can get new load reports like these as often as you want from the computer at very little cost. So it is hardly worthwhile to bother calculating new load totals by subtracting the times for jobs done. Just make new lists of jobs still to be done.

KEEPING LOAD RECORDS UP TO DATE   When you figure a department's load, you are rarely "loading" work to the department in a discretionary sense. You aren't assigning work to that department as a choice against another department. The operations that the jobs call for set the departments; all that you do is to find out the load.

Normally you don't load individual machines—just departments or groups of similar machines. But if you have only one or two of some bottleneck machines you could keep individual records of their loads.

One minor matter. Always add and subtract the load in the same units. If you add in new jobs on the basis of the machine hours that a man would take working at standard pace, then when jobs are completed, subtract their standard hours, not their actual.

But if your men work at 125 per cent, they will do five hours' work in four hours. If you add in each job's standard hours your load record includes five, not four, hours and the same thing happens for all the jobs. Your total is inflated. Don't forget this when using the load for scheduling. Of course, you can add in the four hours that you expect the man to take instead of five. Then your record of work ahead of a machine is more realistic. Be sure, though, to subtract four hours when the job is done, not five, the standard time, nor three and one-half or four and one-half if the man took either of these amounts of time.

Remember, too, that, as we said in Chapter 15, you can sometimes forget this whole matter of incentive pace. Just figure your loads at standard times. True, the men will beat these times when they perform the operation but you may not end up getting any more than standard production because delays and machine downtime will eat up about as much time as incentive workers save.

If you use computers to run off machine load reports, you probably are actually assuming that the delays will offset pieceworker extra output because all loads are stated in terms of standard hours of work ahead of machines. Computers run these lists from tapes which usually have a record of each operation's standard time, but not its expected actual time. If delays don't offset the extra output from pieceworkers, then the computed load is not altogether right.

OTHER USES OF LOADS   You can also plan machine overhaul depending on loads. On heavily loaded machines let all except urgent repairs go. You might even run such machines until they break down and hope that they won't break down until the peak is past. Machines, just like automobiles, sometimes run a long time after they begin to need repairs before they actually stop.

Heavy machine loads at some machine centers or machine groups sometimes make it necessary for you to look for alternative methods. Suppose that your automatic screw machines are overloaded but that *single* screw machines are not. Go back to the product orders and look to see which items you can do on single screw machines. Making them on single screw machines costs more but you balance your loads among machines, get the work out, and maybe still beat outside purchase costs.

Some companies with similar alternative possibilities don't bother with loading. They just leave it up to the foreman to make such shifts. This is probably too loose a system of control because the alternative method often costs more. You don't want foremen making very many such decisions without your knowledge.

SCHEDULING POLICIES
Before we go into scheduling orders and machines, we ought to talk about scheduling policies. Some policy decisions, such as whether to build up inventory in slack periods or lay off workers, are made when master schedules are made up, but there are other policies which relate to scheduling individual orders.

OPERATION WANTED DATES   There is a question, for example, concerning the planning of individual operation start and stop times. Should you schedule, for each order and for each operation, both its start and stop times? Or just the start time? Or just the finishing time? Or just deadline dates, indicating that you don't care when the work is done so long as it is done before the deadline or "due done" date? Obviously the answer to all of these questions is to do as little scheduling work as you can while still getting out the work. So the answer has to depend on whether simple procedures will get the work out.

Setting due done (or "wanted") dates for individual operations is a simple way to schedule. These are merely dates by which you want to have the operations finished. To set them, start with the wanted finish date for an order and subtract an appropriate time for the last operation as well as a time allowance for the dead time between the last two operations. This gives you the wanted completion date for the next to the last operation. Next, subtract its time and a between-operations dead-time allowance and get a due done date for the next earlier operation. Keep on doing this for every operation until you get due done dates for them all.

Actually, if you subtract in the way we have just suggested, you will make more work out of this job than you need to. Companies relying on wanted dates as schedules usually do not subtract *actual* operation times and realistic between-operation time allowances. Instead they use some kind of rule of thumb, often one week per operation. The week is intended to cover the time the operation will take plus the dead time between operations. No one bothers, for scheduling purposes, to figure out whether the operation will take four hours or two days.

This is a somewhat careless way of scheduling but it is simple. Since most operations don't take very long the lead times set this way are usually longer than they need to be. The wanted dates for operations early in an order's processing are really very soft. Little harm is done if they aren't met. This is, however, a bad feature. People get careless about meeting these dates and consequently occasionally you get caught short. Also this method starts orders through production before they really need to start and results in too much inventory in process.

Furthermore, using the one-week-per-operation method gives you no assurance that your machines will be able to handle the work. You assume that, because the master schedule was approved only after its overall requirements were found to be reasonable, subsidiary segments of the total load can also be handled. Consequently you don't go through the work of comparing the work load generated by orders against the capacity of departments or work centers to handle it.

This assumption is usually valid. Almost always your machines will be able to handle their individual loads without any trouble. But if you have any bottleneck machines you may want to check their individual machine loads and even to make up machine schedules for each of them. This applies only, however, during busy periods. Whenever business is a little slow you don't need to check individual machine loads nor to make up any machine schedules because foremen are looking for work. Most jobs come through production in good time using order scheduling only.

You should not, however, carry relaxed schedule making so far as do some small companies. Some of them hardly have a fixed schedule for as far ahead as one week. Sometimes they leave most of the scheduling to foremen, who, being "practical shop men," are likely to do their scheduling on the backs of old envelopes. Often the real schedule can be found only in the scheduler's head, which leaves everyone else at a disadvantage. This type of scheduling amounts to no more than responding to a foreman's hurry-up call "We're almost out of $\frac{1}{2}$-inch machine screws"—or simply waiting for orders to arrive and then investigating whether there is enough stock on hand to go ahead.

LABOR CONTRACT PROVISIONS

Another scheduling policy matter relates to labor contracts. Today's labor contracts usually provide that men must be told ahead of time if there will be a work shortage. If you don't have work for men who report in the morning, you can send them home but you'll have to give them four hours' pay in lieu of notice. Better be sure that individual machines have at least four hours of work ahead.

Overtime is another problem. Men must be warned ahead that you are going to ask them to work overtime or they will be free to refuse to stay. So, if overtime is needed, production control should warn foremen so that they can tell their men ahead.

SHORT WORK SCHEDULES

Short work schedules, necessary when you don't have enough work to keep everyone busy for a full day, bring up another scheduling policy question. What should you do, cut work hours for everybody? Or lay off some men and keep others on regular hours? Answers may be written into the labor contract and if so, the contract provisions are binding, but whether they are or not it is probably not production control's job to provide answers. But it is production control's job to schedule work in line with the answers.

Commonly, in job lot work, you just let differing work loads work themselves out without trying to even things out. If some machines have only five or six hours of work a day, you let the men who operate them go home when they have finished the jobs requiring those machines. If other machines have bigger loads, their operators work longer.

In scheduling when work is slack, you need to pay attention, too, to the load for the week as well as for the day. If you are likely to have 32 hours of work for a machine for a week, you probably ought to work five short days instead of four long days. This is because some of the jobs won't come in from other departments until Thursday afternoon. If you worked four regular days, these jobs would have to lie idle until Monday. But if you worked five short days you could go ahead and do these operations on Friday.

Sometimes you have to pay attention to the need for full work crews. You find this commonly in continuous and in batch manufacturing and less commonly in job lot work. If you have to have full work crews on any operations, then reduced production means fewer working hours, not fewer men.

PERIOD-END PILEUPS

Still another matter is the "period-end pileup." Assembly schedules list products to be assembled month by month, or possibly week by week, never (except in continuous production) day by day. Since you start every period where you left off the old period (the point is that you are *not* starting from scratch) you would expect that the scheduled products would be finished steadily throughout the period.

But it doesn't work like this. If you tell a foreman to get out a quantity of certain products in a month, you may get them out steadily, a few every day, but the chances are that you will get half of the whole month's products in the last few days. You will wonder what his men could have been doing for the first three weeks, they got out so little, and how they managed to do so much in the last few days.

What happens is that delays on products made early in the month don't seem important. Maybe the shop is short a few parts that can be attached later. The men go ahead and assemble products complete except for the missing parts. As the month end nears, the foreman puts on all the pressure he can to get the missing parts so that he can report the products as complete before the month runs out.

So, in production control work with order control, you are very likely to get a good bit of a period's scheduled output late in the period. This is not because assembly doesn't start soon enough to let some units come through early (their assembly should have started during the period before) but because foremen are like you and me—they let things go until the last minute. Actually the pressure to clear products out at the end of a period is probably good. Without it, some orders would be even slower coming through.

Parts production schedules tend to be like assembly schedules in this respect. But the problem doesn't get a chance to become quite so serious because you usually set wanted dates for completing individual operations, and since these are different for every order and for every operation, there is no "period" within which foremen try to get whole groups of operations completed.

We should not, however, present the period-end problem as wholly one of the foreman's making. Production control, itself, has to contend with similar problems in its own paper work. Each month starts out serenely. Then schedule and other changes come along which force production control to change detailed plans and deadlines but without any alteration in the month's schedule. By the week before the month's end there are many behind-schedule orders, and production control is frantic trying to keep production up to the original end dates. By Herculean efforts on everyone's part most of the delayed orders are finished and the equivalent of half or more of the month's output is pushed out the door in the last few days. Then calm settles down for a week or two until the pressure starts to build up toward the next month's end.

If you don't like period-end pileups, what can you do about them? This is where policy comes in. The simplest thing is to change your policy and to schedule for shorter periods. Set assembly quantities for half-months or weeks instead of months. This makes more scheduling work but it cuts period-end pileups into more frequent, smaller quantities. In continuous production, scheduling periods are broken down into days or even hours but you should not have to go this far in order control.

Your problem is not always period-end pileups. If work is slack your trouble may be the direct opposite: products arrive in the shipping room too soon. You certainly don't want products lying around in the shipping room very long; so your problem may be to hold back production so that products won't be shipped too soon.

Alcoa at Los Angeles used to have still another problem. Items would get to the shipping room in good time, and the customer would want delivery. But because orders had to clear through Alcoa's home office in Pittsburgh, Pennsylvania, shipping instructions were often delayed and orders that the customer was waiting for were needlessly late in reaching him. It is unfortunate when your procedure forces you to give poor service.

END OF SHIFT PSYCHOLOGY

Something akin to period-end pileups occurs at the close of each shift. There is a tendency for a man working on a job which ought to end half an hour before the end of the shift to prolong it so that it ends with the shift. This is less likely to happen when the man is on piecework or when the job is largely machine work than when it is a daywork and largely manual job.

To some extent this is offset by a similar tendency to hurry up on a job that normally would finish half an hour after the end of the shift. Probably, however, the tendencies to slow down and to hurry up don't work with the same strength so that there is a net loss in production. If so, scheduling needs to allow for such losses.

ORDER SCHEDULING

As we said earlier, order scheduling for parts is a matter of setting operation dates by successive subtractions of operation and between-operation times back from the wanted completion date. Some companies don't do this, however, but instead just put the wanted completion date for the last operation on the order and send it out to the factory department which will perform the first operation. This is usually a poor kind of control because no one ever knows whether an order is behind schedule until after its final wanted completion date passes.

You can make this method work reasonably well, though, by making foremen always work on low order numbers first. The order number is regarded as a sequence or priority number; foremen must work off low-numbered orders before high-numbered orders.

This procedure results in short-cycle orders coming through long before you need them. Suppose you order, in February, parts for June's assemblies. Some items will take only a few days to make but because they have February order numbers, they will get pushed through and arrive in stock in March, only to lie there until June. Or suppose you get down to the month of April and find some short-cycle February orders still not out. Your foremen will put them ahead of long-cycle orders for July's and August's parts although possibly they shouldn't. Instead the foreman probably should move the long-cycle parts along.

GAPPED AND OVERLAPPED SCHEDULING (SOMETIMES CALLED GAP PHASING AND LAP PHASING)

We have been talking about "gapped" scheduling, meaning that you complete operation 1 on the whole lot and move the lot to operation 2. Then you perform operation 2 on the whole lot and move it on to operation 3, and so on. Usually there is considerable time or a "gap" between operations. Figure 20-4 shows how gapped scheduling works. Example A shows the time schedule for a five-operation part, with the order made complete in 15 days. White areas are dead time. Shaded areas are operation times.

Gapped schedules almost always have a good bit of "fat" in them because there is lots of dead time between operations. You can shorten

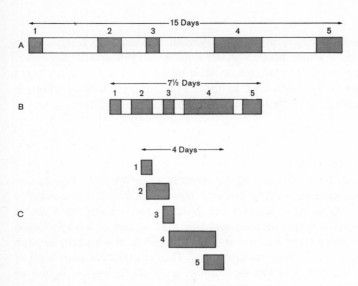

FIGURE 20-4   Gapped and overlapped scheduling.

the cycle time for such orders just by cutting down on the between-operations dead time. Example B in figure 20-4 shows how you could cut our example down to $7\frac{1}{2}$ days.

You may want to speed up the order still more. If so you can go to "overlapped" schedules for a further time saving. Overlapping means performing operation 2 on the first units finished on operation 1 before the whole order has had operation 1 done on it. Then the first products finished at operation 2, go on to 3 before all the units are finished on operation 2, and so on. Example C in figure 20-4 shows how this could work.

In figure 20-4 notice that, although the sum of the operation times is $5\frac{1}{2}$ days, you could get the order out in 4 days. This is because "operation time" here means the time to perform the operation on the whole lot, and not just on one unit. You should be careful, however, when overlapping, not to start a fast operation too soon after starting a slow preceding operation. In example C, operation 5 could not start until most items were out of operation 4; otherwise operation 5 would catch up with 4.

RUSH ORDERS

Rush orders can be given priority by putting early wanted dates on them. But a surer way is to label them "rush" and to print the orders on colored paper so that everyone knows them for what they are—rush orders. Men working on jobs that you don't schedule, such as inspection, will then know which orders are rush. Sometimes orders already in process become rush either because they get behind or for some other reason. If this happens you can make them into rush orders by clipping "rush" or "special rush" tags onto the traveler copy of the order.

Rush orders have a habit of growing in number. During busy periods there may be so many such orders that other orders get pushed back. In time they too become rush. You may end up having different degrees of rush. One company calls its orders "stock," "rush," and "breakdown." Another puts different colored tags on. Blue means "rush," yellow means "special rush," and red means "we mean it." In any case, the idea is that these jobs should be kept moving and that everyone should know this.

One of the most annoying rush orders is the kind which results when customers change their minds about orders already started—particularly when they want to change designs. The job is in midstream. Drawings have been made. Tooling is half prepared. Then the customer tells you to hold everything and you do. Then he gets the change all straightened out and tells you to go ahead, *but he still wants you to meet the first promise date!* Not only that, but he will probably want to see a sample of the changed product before he lets you go ahead and he *still* wants you to meet the original promise date!

When trying to find places to save time on rush orders, don't overlook the shipping room. Typically, delivery promises anticipate that orders will take a week or so to be packed and crated. You can usually save almost all of this time if you have to.

Normally, a reasonable number of rush jobs does not delay other orders much and so does not cost very much to process quickly. Remember, when we talked about making up master schedules, we said to underschedule your capacity 5 per cent or so to save room for rush orders. If you do this, then you can meet your regular schedules and the rush orders too. Also, if rush orders begin to pile up, you can work overtime and increase your output so that other orders don't get held up.

Production control decides which orders are rush and which are not rush *only* for parts orders and possibly for stocked items. But whose rush order comes first among jobs being made for outside customers, someone else decides, probably sales. This becomes a problem when several customers each say that their need is urgent. There seems to be no perfect way of deciding which are really the more urgent, but you can get a tip-off from several little things. How much expediting effort has each customer put into getting his order soon? How did the order come in? In the regular mail? Or telephone or telegram? How does the customer want it shipped? The cheapest way? Or air express? If you can't rush every-one's order these tip-offs will help you decide whose order to put first.

Here's a trick that customers use once in a while to get quick delivery. They cancel the order. Faced with this, the vendor tells the customer that the job is almost finished and will be delivered in the next few days. The customer won't let the cancellation stand, of course, since he is likely to be billed for a cancellation charge if his order really is nearly finished and besides he doesn't really want to cancel his order; all that he wants is to get it quickly. What usually happens is that the vendor rushes the job through.

Rush assembly orders for only one or two of a product need special attention too. You can't schedule them ahead (you don't have such orders very far ahead of the date when the customer wants delivery). Honeywell's Micro-switch division has so many of these that it has set up a special little nonscheduled assembly department just to handle them. This is probably a better solution to the problem than trying to put such orders through the regular assembly shop.

ADVANCED RELEASE OF PARTS ORDERS TO FACTORY

Makers of very complex products usually schedule parts and subassembly making in the way we described earlier, i.e., releasing orders to the factory only shortly before the work should start. The order release date is determined by the date the item will be needed and by the time it will take to make it.

This method holds down inventories of materials in process but it makes you vulnerable to delays. If any part gets held up very long there is trouble because the time span for making the part has very little fat in it.

Makers of very complex parts sometimes find that it is better to release parts orders and subassembly orders earlier (considerably before the work needs to start and perhaps as soon as the orders are made out) to the factory. Admittedly this allows parts to be started into production earlier than need be. And this increases the inventory in process but it cuts down on the harm done by delays in production. Most parts orders can suffer short delays without preventing their completion on time. On complex products this is a very worthwhile advantage.

A second worthwhile gain from releasing parts orders early is that production department foremen can plan their own shop work assign-ments better. They can use their men and their machines to best advantage.

This practice of the early releasing of orders to the factory is one reason why airplane and electronics companies have so many orders in process all of the time and why they have such a big problem of dispatching in their producing departments.

The disadvantage, however, of increasing the inventory of jobs in process is serious and is a costly price to pay for the above advantages.

Philips Company, the large Dutch electronics maker, at its plant in Huisen, Netherlands, has adapted the PERT technique to this problem.[1] A complete PERT network covering all shop operations on big projects is made up when the project is first sent to the factory. Thereafter the progress of all jobs on all projects is checked weekly for each manufacturing department. So are present and future shop work loads. Prospective bottlenecks and remaining lead times show up very clearly. Jobs now lagging or those having tight critical paths through future operations are given special attention. Philips reports that its PERT shop control has reduced the time for two-year projects by one-fourth and at the same time has reduced inventories by the same amount. The number of late production orders has been reduced even more.

INDENT SYSTEMS IN SCHEDULING

In Chapter 14, we described a typical indent system used by airplane and missile companies and said that we would describe later how indents were used in scheduling.

Most parts are made in lots and not continuously. In an airplane factory, lot sizes are set at quantities sufficient to make a certain number of airplanes, with no attempt to make them in economical lots. If the lot is twenty airplanes, the lot size for most parts will be set at the quantities needed to make twenty airplanes. In a few cases, though, the quantities could be for more or fewer airplanes.

Parts, in all large airplane factories, are made in large parts-making departments which do *not* specialize by kind of airplane. Thus parts for large jets, for small fighter planes, and for missiles are all made in a single large parts-making department. Altogether some 5,000 to 10,000 shop orders a week may go to the parts department.

Shop orders are all prepared on computers which are under the direction of the production control department. And since lead times are long, the shop orders for parts can be, and are, prepared way ahead—except that they bear no start and stop dates. They contain all the information that the shop will need *except* for scheduled dates. These almost wholly prepared shop orders are forwarded to the shop, where they are filed.

[1] PERT analyses are described in Chapter 21.

Shop orders are made up also for all subassemblies that are made in lots and are forwarded to subassembly shops. They too show no dates.

Every order shows the part or subassembly identification number, the product or contract it is for, *and its indent number*. Remember that indent numbers show, in coded form, the item's "make span" (manufacturing lead time) as well as the stage of assembly where it enters the airplane. Remember, too, that different· parts can have the same indent number.

The undated shop orders for parts and subassembly lots are filed by sales contract number in the shop where the work will be done. Within each sales contract file, shop orders are further filed by indent number.

The next move comes from the master scheduling department. Months ahead, it releases a schedule for the next twenty airplanes on a given contract. As soon as it sets the assembly schedule, the master scheduling department lists the dates when certain indent number items should start and finish production.

Figure 20-5 shows such a list as used at North American Rockwell (the figures have been changed). It shows the start dates for all shop orders whose production is authorized by the release. Notice that it does not release shop orders individually, but by indent number. *All* shop orders with the indent numbers shown are *released* for production by means of this one sheet of paper.

All are also *scheduled*. North American Rockwell uses a thousand-day calendar so that the dates shown are thousand-day dates. But, you may say, the shop orders do not yet have any date shown on them. True, but each shop's own production control department now takes all the released shop orders out of its file and adds the thousand-day dates shown on the master schedule release. In this way every individual shop order is scheduled.

Releases are issued several weeks before the start dates that they set for orders. This gives the shop a good bit of latitude in arranging its manpower load and in scheduling departmental work hours. It also lets the shop push orders in ahead if others are held up and then reverse the process when the cause for a hold-up is removed.

No progress reports are made to central production control of individual operations performance. Foremen are expected to get orders out. This doesn't mean, of course, that jobs do all get done on time. With thousands of orders in process at all times, work progress reports are confined to weekly reports of *how many* orders are behind, classified by how far they are behind. Also how many old behind-schedule orders have been cleared up and how many new additions there are to the list of jobs now behind are listed. Expediters are given copies of such lists and they work with foremen trying to hurry along the laggards.

CONTRACT: AF-14801 (NA-172)
MODEL: F-86E
SCHEDULING —Dept. 68

DETAIL PARTS MASTER INDEX
SCHEDULE

Date: 4-26
Replaces: 3-14-
Page: 4 of 9

INDENT NUMBER	APR	MAY				JUNE			JULY		AUG.		SEPT.		OCTOBER			NOVEMBER			
	27	4	11	18	25	1	15	29	13	27	10	24	7	21	5	19	26	2	9	16	23
	335	340	345	350	355	360	365	370	375	380	385	390	395	400	405	410	415	420	425	430	435
1-0A				37							38A							38B			
1-1A			37							38A							38B				
1-2A		37							38A							38B					42/391
1-3A							38A							38B					42/39A		
1-4A						38A						38B							42/39A		
1-5A					38A						38B				42/39A						39B
1-6A			38A							38B				42/39A						39B	
1-7A	38A							38B					42/39A				39B				
2-0A													37		38A						
2-1A												37		38A							38B
2-2A											37		38A							38B	
2-3A									37			38A					38B				
2-4A								37			38A					38B					
2-5A							37		38A					38B					42/39A		
2-6A						37		38A						38B					42/39A		
2-7A				37		38A						38B					42/39A				
3-0A						37								38A					38B		
3-1A				37									38A						38B		
3-2A			37								38A						38B				
3-3A		37							38A						38B					39A	
3-4A	37							38A						38B					42/39A		
3-5A						38A						38B					42/39A				
3-6A				38A							38B					42/39A					39B
3-7A			38A						38B					42/39A				39B			

FIGURE 20-5 Use of indent numbers to set start dates for whole groups of prepared shop orders. Such a release is given every two weeks. (Our page is but one of several pages in a release.) Both calendar dates and workday dates are at the top. Along the left side are the indent numbers. The numbers in the body of the table are the sales order numbers.

Indent systems work quite well as methods for scheduling large groups of orders and of releasing them to the shop. The whole system, based as it is on fairly arbitrary (and fairly liberal) make spans, tends *not* to provide a tight control of shop loads and of work in process. Under pressure, probably both the make spans and the amount of inventory in process could be cut materially. On the other hand, any tighter method of control would, when you consider that there could be 40,000 or more shop orders in process all the time, be a costly operation.

A weakness of indent systems is that they treat every part as being unique. Common parts that are used several places in an airplane normally are not (except for rivets and similar items) summed up into a single demand figure. Each specific use is figured and the number needed are manufactured as if the part itself were unique. The complications introduced by trying to bring together such demands, considering that they may well be needed at different times, limit the value of summing up the various demands for common parts.

SET–OVERS

Some companies, apart from airplanes, missile, and electronics, use "set-overs" (discussed more fully in Chapter 31), an adaptation of the indent system idea, in their scheduling. They use arbitrary make-spans of perhaps 30 days for assembly and 30 days for fabrication of parts. Besides this they allow, say, two weeks for packing and shipping.

The set-over idea starts with the orders to make assemblies. A certain number of assembled products is to be finished every month. The due date for finishing all of the parts is then advanced, or "set over," one month, thus establishing due dates for finishing the parts orders. Both quantities and schedules for parts making are wholly dependent on the assembly floor's needs in the following month. The set-over idea in no way interferes with long lead time items being started early because it is wholly concerned with finishing due dates. Starting dates naturally have to be set over far enough ahead to allow time for the manufacturing cycle.

Set-over scheduling probably should not be used often because it does not, as a policy, pay enough attention to economic lots. Economic lots sometimes are greater than final assembly's one-month needs. A lesser weakness is that it often gets parts finished too soon, resulting in finished parts lying around for a good part of a month.

SCHEDULING THE REPAIR OF PARTS IN MACHINE AND EQUIPMENT OVERHAUL

In Chapter 13 we talked about repairing airplanes. The government's airplane repair bases follow a scheduling practice for repairing airplane parts that is similar to the practice we have just been talking about.

When they disassemble an airplane, these government bases send out work orders right away to repair the parts which are to be repaired. This is similar to the practices we have just been describing. But, and this is different, they put operation wanted completion dates on them according to the time it will take to fix the parts, *not according to when they will be needed.*

This means that some orders will say that a required part is wanted by, say, September 1, when really it is not wanted until December. At first, this sounds foolish but it isn't foolish because preparing the repair orders this way allows them to be prepared on the computer. Operation times and between-operation times can be punched into master decks of tabulating cards or put on tapes. The schedulers don't have to try to guess when all the other parts being repaired will be ready for reassembly (which is the real wanted date).

Normally this practice (getting parts ready too soon) would be unwise because it would boost inventory. This is not so, however, in the case of parts being repaired because they lie around somewhere during the whole time between disassembly and reassembly anyway. It doesn't matter, from the inventory point of view, where they wait—whether in unrepaired stock or in repaired stock. One bad feature is that foremen see fictitious wanted dates on their shop orders. Foremen tend to be careless enough in meeting genuine wanted dates, and you hate to educate them into disbelieving all wanted dates.

STUDY MATERIALS

20-1 What is the difference between order scheduling and machine scheduling? Do you have to do either one? Both? Where could you easily do without either one? Explain.

20-2 Machine load records are *not* kept in many situations. When would this be wise as not being worth their cost? Should they really be *machine* load records or should they be *man* load records?

20-3 Are machine loads and schedules the same thing? If they are different, where should each be used?

20-4 You have just received a rush order for 50 of part A73. This part is made complete in two operations done on two adjacent machines. Instead of processing them all through operation 1 as a lot and then through operation 2 you plan to pass each piece directly from operation 1 to operation 2. Operation times vary as follows:

| MINUTES | OPERATION (PERCENTAGE OF CASES) | |
	1	2
6	5	0
7	20	5
8	50	10
9	20	20
10	5	30
11	0	20
12	0	10
13	0	5

Using Monte Carlo simulation (described in Chapter 29), find out how long it will take to get this order out. What percentage of the worker's time on operation 2 will be wasted? What percentage on operation 1?

20-5   Suppose that you are the scheduler in the following situation. The item requires 3 operations; setup times are 25, 45, and 15 minutes respectively. Machine operation times are 10, 12, and 6 minutes respectively. Scrap losses on each operation are 0, 2, and 4 per cent. For a lot of 200 pieces:

1   How many items should you start into production?

2   What is the least time (using gapped scheduling) to finish the order? (Allow 1 hour between operations for moving materials to the next operation.)

3   In order to start operations 2 and 3 as soon as the order arrives there, how many minutes after you start to set up operation 1 will you have to start setting up for operations 2 and 3?

4   Using overlapped scheduling what are your answers to questions 1 and 2? (Do not, however, start operation 2 until it can operate steadily; do not have it wait 2 minutes each for items from operation 1.) You may also cut the transportation delay to 20 minutes when you use overlapped scheduling.

5   At 50 cents per trip carrying products from machine to machine how much extra in transportation costs will overlapping cost as against gapped operations (where only two trips are required)?

20-6   Part number 127B requires the following operations and has from past experience produced the following information:

OPERATION	SETUP TIME, HOURS	STANDARD OPERATION TIME PER PIECE, MINUTES	PIECEWORK OPERATOR EFFICIENCY	SCRAP PERCENTAGE
1	.5	4	133	25
2	1.3	9	120	None
3	.6	2	100	30
4	.3	4	115	10

For an order of 200:

1 How many pieces do you start into each operation?

2 Using overlapped scheduling how many minutes after you start to set up operation 1 should you start to set up operations 2, 3, and 4? (Do not start slow operations until a big enough bank has been built up to let them complete the order in one uninterrupted run.)

3 When will the order be finished?

20-7 Machines A, B, and C characteristically lose .3, .7, and .2 hour each daily for maintenance. Besides, frequent rush orders have in the past taken up .5 hour each on these machines. In planning work it is necessary to allow for such orders. Operators on these machines are usually 110, 135, and 120 per cent efficient respectively.

How many hours will it take for an order to be produced which calls for 20, 15, and 25 standard hours of work on each machine respectively? (The department works 8 hours a day.)

20-8 You are the scheduler at the Kilbourne Company and are to work out a schedule assigning work to five turret lathes keeping in mind the wanted dates for orders as well as minimizing setups.

You are to make up a schedule for March, which has 23 workdays. March 1 is Wednesday. Your five turret lathes work three shifts daily. Of the seven orders that you have, five have definite wanted dates but the other two are stock orders not needed for a good while. In your solution, you may neglect setup time, allowing no time for it. The orders are:

ORDER NUMBER	NUMBER OF SHIFTS	WANTED FINISHING DATE
1	50	March 8
2	40	March 13
3	15	March 16
4	65	March 23
5	100	March 31
6	100	No hurry
7	47	No hurry

20-9 One of the automobile parts produced by Anshen Auto Parts Company is made on a four-spindle multiple drilling machine. Present volume (200 pieces per day) keeps five such machines busy for two shifts (at 87.5 per cent utilization). The element breakdown and times are:

ELEMENT		MINUTES
1	Clear and load jig	3.0
2	Drill four large holes (first spindle)	4.0
3	Spotface four large holes (second spindle)	2.5
4	Drill six small holes (third spindle)	4.0
5	Remove from jig	0.5
6	Tap six small holes (fourth spindle)	4.8
7	Deburr six tapped holes (first spindle)	1.8
8	Put piece away and get another	0.4
	Total cycle time	21.0

Element 3 must be done after element 2 but not necessarily at once. Similarly element 6 must follow 4, and 7 must follow 6. Anshen has been asked to step production up to 240 pieces a day but does not want to operate the present machines any more hours because the plant is completely closed down on the third shift and Saturday and Sunday work costs overtime.

Since the present drilling machines can be used for other work, the company is considering using other machines in order to get the extra production on this job. Anshen's engineers have found that it has five small, single-spindle bench drill presses which could be used. They drill, spotface, tap, or deburr only one hole at a time. Loading and unloading these drills takes 1 minute less than on the four-spindle multiple driller.

How many multiple drillers can you free while still turning out 240 pieces per day in two shifts?

20-10   A customer has asked the Kokomo Company, machine tool builders, for a quick answer on when you can deliver a new machine that he wants to buy.

You find that the machine the customer wants uses largely standard parts of which you have an ample supply. Nearly all of the nonstandard parts you can "rob" from other orders in process.

Five large parts, however, you will have to get especially for the order. Part 627 is a gray iron casting which will require 5 shifts in the foundry, 3 shifts on milling machines, and 5 shifts on drill presses. Part 702, a forging, will take 3 shifts of forge time, 3 shifts on lathes, 5 shifts on grinding machines, and 4 shifts on drill presses. Part 619, also a casting, will take 8 shifts in the foundry, 4 shifts on milling machines, 7 shifts on drill presses, and 5 shifts on grinding machines.

Part 648 is bought outside and will take 5 weeks to get; part 722, also bought outside, will take 6 weeks to get. Part 627 goes into a subassembly which must be test-operated. Subassembling and test operation, together, take 5 shifts. Final assembly, testing, painting, and crating take 20 shifts. You operate 2 shifts a day 5 days a week.

You have the following number of machines with which to do this work: in the foundry, 8; forge, 5; millers, 5; lathes, 6; drills, 9; grinders, 4. The present backlog of work ahead of each kind of machine is (in shifts): foundry, 96; forge, 170; millers, 200; lathes, 180; drills, 450; grinders, 160.

In the normal course of events, without overlapping operations, and without displacing orders already on hand, when can you deliver the machine if these parts are all that hold you back? What is the soonest you could deliver if you pushed other orders aside (and started on these bottleneck parts immediately) but did not work overtime or send any more work out? Do not overlap operations.

chapter twenty-one

PROJECT SCHEDULES, PERT

COORDINATING SCHEDULES FOR BIG PROJECTS

In Chapter 10 we called the master schedule for a large, complex project a "master plan" in order to avoid confusion with master schedules that cover the factory's whole output. Now we want to discuss such master plans.

Master plans can be based on any of several different general patterns. Figures 21-1 to 21-5 show five such patterns for setting schedules

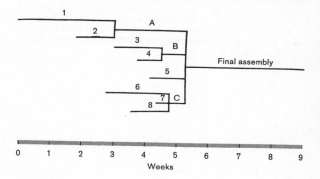

FIGURE 21-1 Diagram showing the assembly of eight parts into subassemblies, A, B, and C, respectively, and their final assembly into a complete product. The scale shows the time that each part of the work takes.

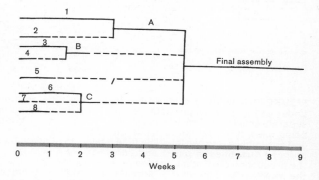

FIGURE 21-2 This diagram shows all parts being made as soon as possible regardless of the time when they will be needed.

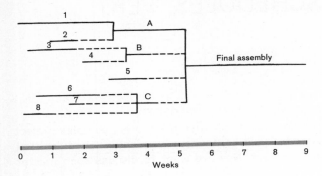

FIGURE 21-3 In this diagram the time taken to produce part 1, subassembly A, and the final assembly sets the time when other parts must be finished. Other parts and subassemblies are produced at any convenient time, it being necessary only that they be done in time to be used in assembly. This diagram more nearly represents the usual situation in manufacturing than does either figure 21-1 or figure 21-2.

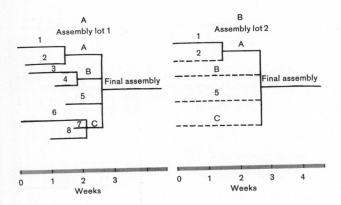

FIGURE 21-4 Often it is desirable to get the final assembly under way as soon as possible, yet without rushing numerous separate small lots of parts through production. In the example being used, it is possible to divide the requirements of part 1 and assembly A into two lots. The time it takes to produce these reduced quantities of part 1 and subassembly A is ample for the production of all other needed parts and subassemblies for the whole order. This method permits the first final assemblies to be ready in about three weeks instead of five and one-half weeks as shown in figures 21-1, 21-2, and 21-3. Later, the balance of part 1 and subassembly A can be made and the balance of the order assembled.

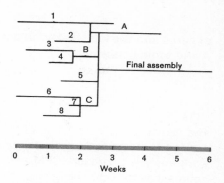

FIGURE 21-5 A condensation of the overall time required to finish an assembly order by overlapping operations. As soon as the first parts come from the last operation, the assembly of subassembly A's can start. The first finished products thus become available in less than three weeks, and the order is completed in approximately six weeks.

for making up subassemblies and parts for big projects. The process shown in figure 21-1 is similar to using gapped schedules for parts. You plan to finish making all of every part before you start to subassemble any of them. And you finish the whole lot of each subassembly before you start the final assembly of the first finished product.

The method shown in figure 21-2 is like the airplane overhaul method. As soon as the orders for parts and subassemblies are prepared they are sent to the factory which goes to work on them right away.

Figure 21-3 shows an in-between situation. You make up parts and subassemblies orders right away and issue them, then put wanted dates on them and let the shop go ahead with the work whenever it is convenient, just so long as it gets the products made by the wanted date.

Figure 21-4 shows how you could set up a schedule if you wanted a few units of assembled products quite soon. You'd start the final assembly of the first product in less than three weeks after the first parts were started. In our other example, final assembly would start early in the sixth week.

Figure 21-5 shows how you could telescope the time even a little more by overlapping the assembly of assembly A with final assembly. The production of part 1 is also overlapped to some extent. This method has the advantage over the method in figure 21-5 in that you still start final assembly in less than three weeks but you do not cut apart the production of part 1 into two lots. It stays in one lot. The same applies to subassembly A and to final assembly.

CPM AND PERT

The planning and scheduling of the thousands of separate work activities needed for large-scale projects can best be handled by a systems or network analysis approach. CPM and PERT are two closely related systems approaches for scheduling such projects.

The Critical Path Method (CPM) was first developed by the E. I. Du Pont Company in the late 1950s in connection with the scheduling of plant construction. The Program Evaluation Review Technique (PERT) was developed about the same time by the U.S. Navy and Booz, Allen & Hamilton, a management consulting firm, for the scheduling of the Navy's Polaris missile project. Both CPM and PERT schedule in terms of time. PERT/COST, which we take up later, an outgrowth of PERT, adds the cost dimension and cost-time trade-offs.

There are also several other systems having various code names (such

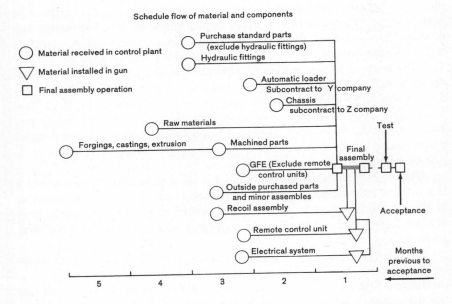

FIGURE 21-6   Assembly diagram showing lead time needed to make an anti-aircraft gun.

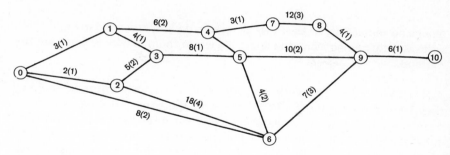

FIGURE 21-7

as LOB for Line of Balance or NMT for Network Management Technique), but they are all variations on the same theme. We shall first describe the PERT system since it embodies all the features of CPM and the other methods.

The common element in all of these systems is the determination of the "critical path" through the network. The critical path is the particular sequence of operations which takes longer than any other sequence. The whole project cannot be finished in less time. Other sequences of operations are said to contain "slack" (or extra time). They can either be started later or they will have extra time at one or more places during processing. But all activities in the critical path have to be completed on schedule if the overall project is to be completed on time.

The PERT system deals with all activities (not just those in the critical path) and the time they take and their sequential relationships.

The relationships of all subparts of a total system can be shown graphically or in tabular form. We start with the graphic representation in figure 21-7. PERT diagrams are made up of circles and connecting lines. The lines represent "activities" or operations, while the circles represent "events" or the finish of activities. Figure 21-7 shows how you might depict the sequence of factory operations: machine, grind, and test. The numbers in the circles indicate the required sequence; thus the activity culminating in event 1 must be finished before starting the activity which culminates in event 2. The arrowheads in our diagram are left off regular PERT diagrams since the event numbers are sufficient to indicate sequences. As we have shown it, low numbers always go before high numbers although you could reverse this practice and have the low numbers be the last events.

In PERT diagrams the lengths of the lines for activities are of no significance. Instead, time is indicated by writing in operation times, alongside the activity lines. PERT diagrams do not, as we did in figure 21-7, write activity names along the lines. We wrote them in only to illustrate the method.

ACTIVITY TIMES   The CPM and PERT ideas usually differ in the way they show time. Under the CPM idea, only the expected time is used for each activity. But most people using PERT set three time values for every activity: first, an optimistic time, or the shortest expected time of completion of an activity; second, the most likely time; and third, a pessimistic time, or a time that would rarely be exceeded for the completion of an activity.

Next, these three times are averaged together on a weighted basis to obtain the "expected" time of completion of the activity. In order not to allow the unlikely optimistic or pessimistic times to influence the expected time unduly, the most likely time is, in the calculation, given a weight of 4 and each extreme a weight of 1. Hence this formula:

$$t_e = \tfrac{1}{6}(a + 4m + b)$$

where t_e = the expected time
a = the optimistic time
m = the most likely time
b = the pessimistic time

From this point on, in all further PERT analyses, the t_e value is used as the time the activity is expected to take. The original "most likely" time no longer enters into any calculations.

So far as PERT diagrams are concerned, three times are usually written in along the lines. These could be, for example, 7, 9, 12, which would be intended to show the optimistic, most likely, and pessimistic times. Or they can be written 2, 9, 3, to show the same thing, the 2 and 3 being the amount of time difference between the most likely time and the optimistic and pessimistic times, respectively. But, if the times are written 5(2), as they are in figure 21-7, then the 5 is the calculated t_e and the 2 is the "variance" which is needed in some of the later PERT calculations. It is obtained as follows:

$$v = \left(\frac{b - a}{6}\right)^2$$

The symbols a and b are as before, and v is the variance associated with the activity's t_e.

Some people object to the use of weighted average time estimates and say that they are no better than single times. Part of the objection is to introducing pessimistic time estimates because of the built-in alibi they provide. When expected times are not met, the man responsible says,

"Well, I told you it might take that long." Some people feel that it is better to stick to "most likely" times and have everyone try hard to meet them.

PERT ANALYSIS PROCEDURE PERT analyses try to answer several questions. First, what is the shortest expected time in which we can expect to complete the whole project? Second, what variability is associated with this time? How certain is it that the project will be done in the expected time, and what are the reasonable short and long variations from this time? Third, are there any activities which must be watched carefully in order to meet the expected completion time?

To answer these questions we must use several new terms:

T_E = the longest possible summation of times, t_e, that it takes to arrive at a given event. This time is the earliest time that a following activity can start.

T_L = the latest time an activity can start and still remain on schedule.

Slack = $T_L - T_E$ or the leeway we have in scheduling an activity.

We can illustrate these relationships by using the example shown in figure 21-7. The activity time figures are for days.

We first calculate the T_E for each event. This is the sum of the expected times for all activities up to that event. (The variance numbers in figure 21-7 are not involved in this calculation.)

Whenever an event can be reached by two or more paths the largest summation of t_e times is used as its T_E. Event 6, for example, can be reached directly from event 0 with a T_E of 8. But going from 0 to 2 to 6 comes to 20 days. 0-2-3-5-6 takes 19 days. So does 0-1-3-5-6. 0-1-4-5-6 takes 15. The greatest T_E, 20 days, is the one for path 0-2-6 so it becomes the T_E for event 6.

We need also to get T_L figures for each event. To get them we work backwards from the project's finish date. Here, the *lowest* number for each event becomes its T_L. (This is in contrast to the T_E calculation where the *highest* T_E is used.) The critical path (indicated by the heavy lines in figure 21-7) tells us that the last activity can't, at best, be finished until 34 days have passed. Working backwards, we subtract and find that event 9 must be reached in 28 days. From event 9 backwards we have to check through several paths. 10-9-5, for example, shows that event 5 must finish by day 17, so event 5's T_E becomes 17.

Whenever the T_L and the T_E figures for an event differ, there is slack in the activity chain. Figure 21-8 shows all of these figures for our example.

As we said earlier, slack shown for an event means that we have a

FIGURE 21-8

EVENT	T_E	T_L	SLACK
0	0	0	0
1	3	3	0
2	2	3	1
3	7	9	2
4	9	9	0
5	15	17	2
6	20	21	1
7	12	12	0
8	24	24	0
9	28	28	0
10	34	34	0

little leeway in when to start and finish the activity leading up to it. Thus in our example, event 5 would normally be reached in 15 days but if it takes 17 days to get that far, this will be all right, because the critical path will not be affected. (Slack never occurs for activities in the critical path, but only for activities not in the critical path.)

Interestingly, it is theoretically possible for all pathways to become equal to each other and hence to become critical paths. This would occur if you could reduce the time of all lengthy activities by putting in more resources. You can build a house in a few days if you put lots of men on the parts of the work that normally take a long time and if you carry on many differing activities at the same time.

Rarely, if ever, would this pay, yet this possibility is one of the advantages of PERT. It tells you the critical path and the total time. If you want to shorten the time by pouring in resources to hurry along the lengthy activities in this path, you know which activities to concentrate on. And if you are able to shorten the original critical path, you can then see if this then makes another path become a new critical path.

Usually the possibilities of shortening the critical path time are quite limited because of costs. It just doesn't pay to build a house in a few days even though you could do it. Furthermore you can't always assign more resources to an activity even if you want to. Available operating time on one machine, for example, often cannot be substituted for needed time on another machine because the machines are unlike. Nor can you always shift men around freely. Their skill limitations as well as union rules prevent your using electricians to lay brick.

VARIABILITY   Up to here we have made no use of the variability figures shown in figure 21-7. Variability figures give us an idea of how far off
our expected times might be.

To use the variability figures we start up adding up the variances for
the activities along the critical path. In our example, these come to 9 days.
This tells us that if every activity takes its maximum time the whole project will take 34 + 9 days, or 43 days. Or if every activity is finished in its
minimum time the project will be done in 34 − 9, or 25 days. (Should there
be two critical paths of equal length, we would, in this calculation, use the
one with the greatest variation.)

Such extremes are virtually impossible, however, because some variations will be on the high side and others on the low side. They might even
offset exactly allowing the project to finish in 34 days. The PERT system
assumes that the actual time T will be the sum of the expected activity
times and that the possible variations in time will be distributed above and
below this time according to normal curve variations.

In order to follow through with this idea we need to compute the
standard deviation of the variances. (This is the same standard deviation
which we mentioned briefly in Chapter 16.) We obtain the standard deviation by taking the square root of the sum of the variances, 9 in our case,
giving us a standard deviation of 3. In normal distributions, the arithmetic
mean ± 1 standard deviation (usually indicated by the Greek letter sigma,
σ) sets a range between which 68 per cent of the cases fall. Plus or minus
2 σ sets limits within which 95 per cent of the cases fall, and ± 3 σ includes
over 99 per cent of all cases. In our example the most likely actual completion date for the project is 34 days but, as we know, it may well take
less or more time. There is a 68 per cent probability that it will be done in
from 31 to 37 days (34 ± 3), 95 per cent probability that it will be completed between 28 and 40 days, and it is virtually certain that it will be
finished between 25 and 43 days.

The type of analysis we have just been describing should be confined
only to cases where there are a good many activities in the activity path.
This is because calculations of probability are not themselves very reliable
when they are based on a small number of instances.

EVALUATING PERT   PERT has proved to be a useful tool yet it has
its limitations. On the positive side, it provides us with a means of analyzing
complex networks which could not otherwise be conveniently done, if
indeed they could be done at all. Also today a PERT analysis of the activities involved in the project is required by the U.S. Department of Defense
on all major defense contracts.

PERT limitations stem largely from its cost and from possible errors.

Not that PERT costs so much but even so it isn't worth any cost at all on familiar work. Subdivision house builders know how long it takes to build a house, and electric utility companies know how long it takes to build a power plant. In such cases PERT should not be used. PERT is most helpful for unfamiliar projects which require estimates based on uncertain knowledge.

Errors when using PERT are most common in making estimates of the time that activities will take. Errors are also sometimes made in the network "configuration" (as occurs when the expected sequence of activities proves not to be correct).

In a study of PERT operations, researchers K. R. MacCrimmon and C. A. Rayavec found that estimates of activity times were sometimes off as much as 30 per cent and that variance figures were off as much as 15 per cent.[1] These were extremes, however. Total times in both total times and in variances were rarely so far off, because errors tend to offset each other. In MacCrimmon and Rayavec's study the errors proved to be in the 5 to 10 per cent range.

Three sources of error caused most of the trouble: (1) human error in estimating the three time values used in PERT, (2) the assumption of the normal curve distribution of actual possible times as differing from the expected times, and (3) the weakness of the formula in representing actual relationships. Actual relationships between activities are often considerably more complex, as for example, when one activity ought to be finished before another starts, yet under pressure it can be finished after the next one starts. Nor do formulas recognize that the time an activity takes is dependent on the resources poured in. A task requiring 100 hours can take $2\frac{1}{2}$ weeks if only one man works on it, but it can be done in 10 hours if 10 men work on it.

MacCrimmon and Rayavec also found that the total times for projects (the sums of the T_Es) were biased on the optimistic side. Also, the standard deviations of the variances were not very reliable. Moreover, errors were greater whenever there were several paths which had few activities in common with the critical path yet which took almost as much time as the critical path. This introduced errors into the probability calculations which then produced erroneous probability projections.

PERT/COST

PERT/COST deals with the cost of projects and with their cost-versus-time trade-off possibilities. PERT/COST shows how much time can be saved if

---

[1] K. R. MacCrimmon and C. A. Rayavec, "An Analytical Study of PERT Assumptions," *Operations Research*, 1964, vol. 12, pp. 16–37.

certain activities are, at greater cost, speeded up. Management can then decide if the time gain is worth its cost.

In order to judge the value of time saved versus its cost, we need to relate each time estimate (the pessimistic, expected, and optimistic times) to its cost. If an activity is finished in minimum time, it would seem that it ought to cost less because it may not have taken many man-hours. At the other extreme, if an activity drags on and is finished in its pessimistic time, it would seem surely to be running up considerably more cost. Each time estimate, therefore, ought to have its own probable cost.

Actually the cost of an activity or of a chain of activities often does not work out the way we have just suggested at all. Short activity times resulting from their consuming less labor than expected are rare. The shortest times actually often cost the most. The work is got out quickly only by putting more men on the job, by working overtime, by flying in materials by air freight, and by using poorly adapted machinery (on account of the ideal machines being busy) to get work done. Almost always you pay a price for hurry-up work.

In figuring cost-time trade-offs PERT/COST assumes a linear relationship (meaning that the cost of saving three days is three times the cost of saving one day).

MONEY–TIME TRADE–OFFS   We can illustrate PERT/COST using money-time trade-offs by using an example of preparing a service manual to accompany certain electronic equipment. We are going to set down five questions to answer:

1   How long it will take to produce the manual?

2   What will it cost?

3   How much will it cost if we cut four weeks off this expected time?

4   Supposing that speed is urgent, what is the shortest possible time to prepare the manual?

5   What will it cost to prepare the manual on this hurry-up basis?

Figure 21-9 shows the information we need. Figure 21-11 is a PERT network diagram of this data.

Although our real interest in figure 21-9 is in the costs of activities, we have first to work out the usual PERT data. Figure 21-10 shows the necessary figures.

The critical path, as we can quickly figure out from figure 21-11, is

FIGURE 21-9

ACTIVITY		MAX. TIME (WEEKS)	MIN. COST	MIN. TIME (WEEKS)	MAX. COST	SEQUENCE
A	Preliminary schematic drawings	2	$150	1	$200	0–1
B	Preliminary artwork	3	90	1	190	1–4
C	First draft of text	3	500	2	700	0–2
D	Edit first draft of text	2	150	1	180	2–3
E	Preliminary layouts	2	100	1	120	3–4
F	Index and parts lists	4	620	3	750	3–5
G	Revise text	5	750	4	900	3–6
H	Final artwork	3	560	2	680	4–5
I	Preliminary page layouts	4	650	3	800	4–6
J	Check schematic, parts lists, and artwork, with equipment	2	90	1	180	5–6
K	Check through test procedures	5	200	4	300	5–7
L	Final layout	4	240	3	320	6–7
M	Release manual	3	80	2	150	7–8

0, 2, 3, 4, 5, 6, 7, 8, and takes 19 weeks. (The critical path is shown by the heavy line in figure 20-11.) The activities in this path are C, D, E, H, J, L, and M. The total minimum expected cost for the whole project is $4,180. This is the project's expected cost if we don't spend any extra money for speeding up activities.

The next step is to calculate the cost per week of possible time saved

FIGURE 21-10

EVENT	T_E	T_L	SLACK
0	0	0	0
1	2	4	2
2	3	3	0
3	5	5	0
4	7	7	0
5	10	10	0
6	12	12	0
7	16	16	0
8	19	19	0

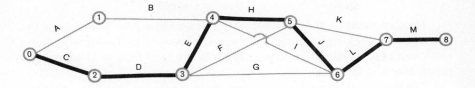

FIGURE 21-11

for each activity. This can be expressed as:

$$\frac{\text{Maximum cost} - \text{minimum cost}}{\text{Maximum time} - \text{minimum time}} = \frac{c_{max} - c_{min}}{t_{max} - t_{min}}$$

ACTIVITY	COST PER WEEK SAVED	NUMBER OF WEEKS THAT COULD BE SAVED
A	$50 \div 1 = 50$	1
B	$100 \div 2 = 50$	2
C*	$200 \div 1 = 200$	1
D*	$30 \div 1 = 30$	1
E*	$20 \div 1 = 20$	1
F	$130 \div 1 = 130$	1
G	$150 \div 1 = 150$	1
H*	$120 \div 1 = 120$	1
I	$150 \div 1 = 150$	1
J*	$90 \div 1 = 90$	1
K	$100 \div 1 = 100$	1
L*	$80 \div 1 = 80$	1
M*	$70 \div 1 = 70$	1

* Activities in the critical path.

Our starting point is to look only at the activities in the critical path (the starred activities) and to search out the least costly starred activity as a place to save time. It proves to be activity E which can be reduced from 2 weeks to 1 at a cost of $20. If we make this change it will reduce the critical path to 18 weeks and raise our costs to $4,200.

It would seem now that the next step would be to follow this up by reducing D (the next lowest cost way of saving time) 1 week at a cost of $30. Perhaps this is proper, yet not necessarily so because we may now have changed our network enough to have a new critical path, and some other lesser cost penalty for saving time may have become available. Upon investigation we find that the reduction in the time for E brings activity F into the critical path.

Now we examine the activities in the new critical path and choose the one where a week saved costs the least. It proves to be D where saving a week costs $30. Making this change reduces the total time to 17 weeks and raises the cost to $4,230.

Continuing this method we find that there are eight possibilities altogether for saving time. Here is the complete list:

TIME, WEEKS	COST	COST OF SAVING ONE WEEK	ACTIVITIES ON CRITICAL PATH
19	$4,180		C, D, E, H, J, L, M
		$20	
18	4,200		C, D, E, F, H, J, L, M
		30	
17	4,230		A, B, C, D, E, F, H, J, L, M
		70	
16	4,300		A, B, C, D, E, F, H, J, L, M
		80	
15	4,380		A, B, C, D, E, F, H, J, K, L, M
		190	
14	4,570		All activities
		250	
13	4,820		All activities
		550	
12	5,370		All activities

We can now answer the five questions we posed above. First, the most economical time is 19 weeks and, second, this will cost $4,180. Third, to reduce the time 4 weeks will raise the project's cost by $200 to $4,180. Fourth, if time is everything and money doesn't count, we can get the work done in 12 weeks and, fifth, this will cost $5,370. This cost figure is $100 less than the total we would have if we speeded up every activity. (We don't need to speed up every activity because even with a 12-week deadline, there is still slack time available for activity B and speeding it up would not reduce the total time any so this need not be done.)

Although management didn't ask to see the figures for all eight of the possible results of buying time reduction, it is easy for a computer to show all of the possibilities. Seeing them, management might make a choice other than one of the three that we have been talking about. Furthermore, computers can rerun this kind of analysis week by week as a project moves along so that management can get a fresh, up-to-the-minute look at changes if decisions are indicated.

LINE OF BALANCE CHARTS

"Line of balance" (LOB) charts constitute still another way to depict actual production and to compare it to planned production. By showing accumulated production against accumulated planned production, LOB charts make it easy to see if we are falling behind (or getting ahead). And if we are falling behind, LOB charts tell us if we are falling farther behind, just maintaining ground, or catching up. LOB charts are most often used for long-run items where production of a lot extends over several weeks or months and for products made from several or many components. For short-run items, the extra work involved is rarely justified.

To make a line of balance chart, we first construct a cumulative output versus time chart as shown in figure 21-12. We need such a chart for each item or component under consideration. Both the cumulative actual and the cumulative scheduled output are plotted.

Let us suppose that the production of our first item, component A, was scheduled ahead for 10 weeks. We are now at the end of week number 7 and find the following:

	SCHEDULE		ACTUAL PRODUCTION	
WEEK	WEEKLY	CUMULATED	WEEKLY	CUMULATED
1	72	72	60	60
2	90	162	85	145
3	112	274	130	275
4	140	414	145	420
5	140	554	150	570
6	140	694	70	640
7	140	834	90	730
8	140	974		
9	140	1,114		
10	86	1,200		

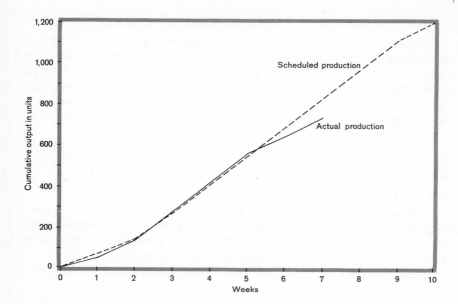

FIGURE 21-12

Figure 21-12 shows the cumulated schedule for the whole 10 weeks and the actual production for the first 7 weeks. It shows that we have fallen considerably behind in the last 2 weeks. (The low production expected in the early weeks was scheduled that way to allow for start-up problems while the low production in week number 10 is to allow for cleaning up rework items.)

Assuming that we have made similar charts for each component and that there are 10 components in all, we are now ready to construct the LOB chart as shown in figure 21-13. The LOB chart shows, as of the close of week number 7, the situation for each component.

Because some components are not needed in assembly as soon as other components, the scheduled quantities of each to be completed shows as a stepped-down staircase line in figure 21-13. This stepped-down line which shows the cumulated scheduled quantities is called the "line of balance." The vertical bars for each component show, for each one, whether it is up to its schedule or not. Lagging parts show up very clearly. In our example, parts A, D, E, and I are behind schedule. Other parts are up to schedule or are ahead.

Although we have said that we need to make up cumulative schedule versus production charts before making up the LOB chart this is not man-

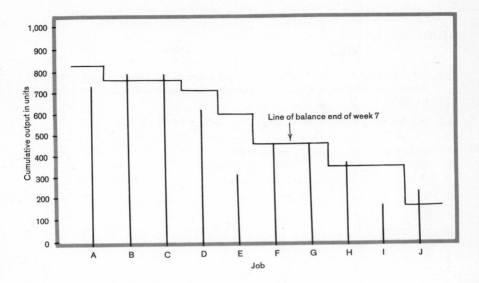

FIGURE 21-13   Line of balance chart.

datory. We could have made the LOB chart directly from cumulative data. Often, however, companies using LOB do make up the cumulative charts for each major component because such charts show trends. Figure 21-12, for example, shows that job A output lagged a little at the start, then picked up and was actually a little ahead of schedule until the machine breakdown in week number 6. And it shows that we need higher than originally scheduled production in the remaining weeks in order to catch up.

STUDY MATERIALS

21-1 In what ways is critical path scheduling superior to using Gantt charts? Are Gantt charts better in any cases? Explain. (Gantt charts are described in Chapter 25.)

21-2 The following information covers part of a large PERT diagram:

STARTING EVENT	FOLLOWING EVENT	EXPECTED TIME IN WEEKS
A	C	11
A	D	6
B	D	5
C	E	7
C	F	5
D	F	9
D	G	10
D	H	12
E	F	2
F	H	8
F	I	12
G	H	4
H	I	8

What is the critical path and how many weeks will it take to complete this work?

21-3 Suppose that, in problem 21-2, you could shorten AC to 6, CE to 5, DF to 6, DH to 10, and GH to 4; which of these changes, if any, would affect the critical path? How long will the work then take? If there is a new critical path, what is it?

21-4 Suppose that, in problem 21-2, you had variances as follows:

ACTIVITY	VARIANCE IN WEEKS
AC	4
AD	3
BD	3
CE	2
CF	1
DF	3
DG	4
DH	5
EF	1
FH	3
FI	6
GH	1
HI	1

What are the time limits within which there is a 95 per cent chance of the work being completed? What are the extreme times that might possibly occur according to the figures in our problem?

21-5 Suppose that, in problem 21-2, you could, by putting on extra workers, shorten the times for the activities at the following extra costs:

ACTIVITY	POSSIBLE TIME REDUCTION	COST *PER WEEK* GAINED
AC	2	$100
AD	2	400
BD	1	300
CE	3	200
CF	1	100
DF	1	300
DG	3	300
DH	2	500
EF	0	
FH	1	200
FI	3	100
GH	0	
HI	1	300

1 If you wanted to save all of the time possible, regardless of cost, where would you shorten the activity time? What would your new critical path be? How long would it take? How much would it cost?

2 Supposing that you could spend up to $1,000 to save time, what would be your answers to the questions in 1?

21-6 Your company is going to market a new product and has the following information about the preparatory work. In the case of activity costs, it is assumed that the minimum time can be achieved only on a rush job basis, hence minimum time costs are greater than expected time costs.

ACTIVITY	EVENT SEQUENCE	EXPECTED TIME IN WEEKS	EXPECTED COSTS	MINIMUM TIME IN WEEKS	COSTS ON RUSH JOB BASIS
Design product	1–2	5	$750	3	$ 900
Design package	1–3	4	500	3	600
Equipment specifications	1–4	2	100	1	200
Advertising layout	1–5	6	900	3	2,100
Order product materials	2–6	3	300	2	350
Test market product	2–7	4	500	2	1,350
Equipment make ready	4–6	2	250	1	440
Order package materials	3–6	3	100	2	150
Test market package	3–8	3	480	1	960
Prepare advertising materials	5–9	4	440	3	550
Fabricate product	6–7	3	240	2	360
Fabricate package	6–8	2	160	1	280
Check advertising copy	9–8	1	100	1	100
Package product	7–8	2	160	1	280
Distribute product	8–10	3	300	2	450
Place advertisements	8–10	3	390	3	390

1 If costs are critical and must be kept down, what is the critical path and how long will it take?

2 When *could* you start the activity "Equipment make ready"? When would you *have* to start it? How much slack is there here?

3 If you want the work done in 12 weeks and are willing to pay the costs, how much extra will it cost? What will be the critical path?

21-7 In a PERT diagram, event 1 is followed by events 2 and 3; 2 is followed by 4 and 5; 3 by 6; 4 and 5 by 6; and 6 by 7. This is a manufactured product of which 50 are to be made. Activities take the following number of hours per unit. 1-2, 1.25; 1-3, 2.75; 2-4, 6.00; 2-5, 1.0; 3-6, 5.50; 4-6, 3.30; 5-6, 2.00; 6-7, 5.00.

Suppose that you can't move more men around so that if you need a fraction of a man for an activity, you need a whole man.

1 How many men will you need at each work station? How many hours a week will be wasted at each work station?

2 If labor costs $3.50 an hour, how much can you afford to spend on job improvement work if you can cut any or all the operation times by 20 per cent? (Since you anticipate making a second order of 50 units you need to recover only half of your job improvement cost out of this order.)

21-8 Listed below are the scheduled and actual cumulative production figures for five critical parts:

END OF WEEK	NUMBER SCHEDULED, PART					NUMBER PRODUCED, PART				
	A	B	C	D	E	A	B	C	D	E
1	10	5	4	0	0	5	4	4	2	0
2	30	10	8	8	0	27	14	8	9	0
3	40	30	16	15	10	30	34	12	13	2
4	40	50	32	21	20	35	42	12	22	12
5	40	70	64	26	30	40	54	58	29	22
6	40	90	70	30	40					
7	40	95	70	33	50					
8	40	100	70	35	50					

What is the line of balance at the end of the fifth week? What other information useful to production scheduling could be derived from the above data?

21-9 Could the line of balance technique be combined with the critical path method of scheduling? What benefits, if any, would be derived from such a plan? Would the addition of a line of balance to a PERT diagram appear to be a costly additional feature?

chapter twenty-two

OPERATIONS RESEARCH IN MACHINE SCHEDULING

You don't always have to schedule machines, and of course, if you don't have to, you shouldn't do it. You don't need, for example, to schedule them when you are short of jobs. If a machine is not heavily loaded, all jobs using it will be done, since otherwise the machine will be idle.

But, if you have any bottleneck machines, you may want to allocate their time (schedule the machines) so that high-priority orders will be done first. You can use Gantt charts (described on page 581) or some variation of Gantt charts. Or you can use some kind of listing of orders ahead of bottleneck machines. Or you can have the computer run off lists showing when each order will start and stop. Probably you would apply one or more of the dispatching rules that we talk about on page 561.

You could even just let the orders stay as a pile of orders, putting the most urgent ones on top. This is not as bad a way to allocate machine hours as it sounds because as we said when machines aren't overloaded all of the orders can and probably will come through on time. True, this method doesn't tell you when given jobs will start and stop but all you have to do to change the order of running jobs on machines is to change the sequence of the orders in the piles. And even then most machines will finish their work or even run out of work most days.

Machine scheduling can't be disposed of so easily, however, because the usual situation is to have enough or too much work for your machines to handle quickly. Jobs queue up and the production control staff has to direct their release from the machine queues. In Chapters 20 and 24 we discuss dispatching rules for releasing orders. In Chapter 20, we refrained, however, from discussing operations research methods for assigning jobs to machines. These we take up here.

TRANSPORTATION METHOD

The "transportation method," a simplified version of linear programming, is one such operations research technique.[1]

---

[1] The name "transportation method" comes from its original use in solving transportation problems designed to minimize freight costs when scattered customers are supplied with products from several warehouses in different locations.

In order to use the transportation method in machine scheduling, several conditions must be met: inputs must equal outputs (the number of pieces the machines will produce must equal what you want), all units produced must be interchangeable (any machine must be able to produce any piece although probably at different costs), the relationships must be linear (more machine hours mean proportionally more production), and it must cost nothing extra to split orders and produce some units on one machine and other units on another machine. (This means that unit costs are the same regardless of volume. It also means that job setup costs don't count.)

Although these restrictions rule out the use of the transportation method in many cases, there are still other cases when it can be used.

To show how the transportation method works we will follow a problem through. We will assume four machines A, B, C, and D and five jobs 1, 2, 3, 4, and 5. Any machine can do any job although at different unit costs. Figure 22-1 shows our starting information. In figure 22-1 the numbers in the body of the table are the costs (in cents per unit) for producing products on each machine. The right-hand column shows the quantity of each item wanted and the bottom line shows how many each machine can turn out. These totals, on the right and at the bottom, are our "constraints" or limiting quantities.

Our problem is to allocate the jobs to machines in the most economical way. To get the answer by the transportation method, we start by drawing up a format resembling a bowling score sheet as in matrix 1. Tentative scheduled quantities go into the big boxes and their costs go into the little corner boxes.

We start toward the final solution by arbitrarily parceling out the

FIGURE 22-1

JOB	MACHINE				PIECES REQUIRED
	A	B	C	D	
1	100	105	95	97	100
2	80	78	80	82	150
3	87	92	97	103	200
4	92	86	84	90	150
5	105	110	107	115	300
Machine capacity	400	100	200	200	900

orders to the first machines listed. This is called the "northwest corner" solution method because it starts in the upper left. In our case, job 1 calls for 100 pieces and since all of them can be produced on machine A, we put 100 into block A1. Machine A can also handle the 150 units needed for job 2, so we put 150 into block A2. Machine A can also handle 150 of the units needed for job 3, so we put 150 into A3.

This completes machine A's load, so the remaining 50 units of job 3 go to machine B and we put 50 in B3. To fill out B's capacity, we assign it 50 units of job 4, hence a 50 in block B4. The remaining 100 units of job 4 go to block C4. Then 100 units of job 5 take up the rest of C's capacity in C5 and the remaining 200 of job 5 go to D5.

It remains only to put the unit costs for each block having an assignment into the little corner spaces and matrix 1 is complete. We have a feasible solution in that all orders are assigned and all machines are fully loaded.

At this point we are not particularly interested in the cost of this first trial allocation of jobs to machines. Actually, it is $860.50. Although in our

MATRIX 1

JOB	MACHINE				PIECES REQUIRED
	A	B	C	D	
1	100 100				100
2	80 150				150
3	87 150	92 50			200
4		86 50	84 100		150
5			107 100	115 200	300
Machine capacity	400	100	200	200	900

example we could tell by looking at our original set of cost figures that we probably don't yet have an optimal solution, we couldn't tell this by inspection for a large matrix such as we might have for a large machine shop. We need a procedure which will tell us for sure if and where we can improve. The transportation method provides such a procedure.

From this point on there are several methods for solving transportation problems. Of them we will present four: the rim value method, Vogel's approximation method (VAM), and two "index" methods.

RIM VALUE METHOD

The rim value method starts from matrix 1 and uses only the corner cost figures for the blocks having assignments. Using them we construct a set of imputed cost figures, one for each open block, that will lead us to a less costly allocation of jobs to machines, if there is one. The rim value procedure is a little difficult to describe although it is simple to use and can be worked out in less time than other methods and in much less time than it takes us to describe it.

From matrix 1 we get the cost figures for each block having an assignment. These costs go into the body of matrix 2. The rim values in matrix 2 we have to calculate. (At this stage of the calculation we pay no attention to the original cost values for the blocks without production allocations. We don't even put them into the matrix.)

It takes several steps of calculating to get the rim values. We will call

MATRIX 2

| JOB | MACHINE | | | | RIM |
	A	B	C	D	
1	100				0
2	80				−20
3	87	92			−13
4		86	84		−19
5			107	115	+ 4
Rim	100	105	103	111	

the rim values across the bottom rim A, rim B, etc., and those along the right, rim 1, rim 2, etc. These values come from a step-by-step procedure which goes as follows:

Step 1a   Establish rim A value:
Rim A is the same number as that in block AI, so rim A = 100.

Step 2a   Establish rim 1 value:
The rule in establishing rim values is that the number in a block must be the sum of its column and row rim values.
Rim 1 is 100 = 100 + rim 1, so rim 1 = 0.

Step 2b   Establish rim 2 value:
Using the rule given in step 2a,
80 = 100 + rim 2, so rim 2 = −20.

Step 2c   Establish rim 3 value:
87 = 100 + rim 3, so rim 3 = −13

Steps 2d and 2e   Establish rims 4 and 5 values:
Since there are no values in the A4 and A5 blocks, rims 4 and 5 cannot yet be established.

Step 1b   Establish rim B value:
Continuing to use the rule given in 2a,
92 = rim B + (−13), so rim B = 105

Step 2d   Establish rim 4 value:
86 = 105 + rim 4, so rim 4 = −19

Step 1c   Establish rim C value:
84 = rim C + (−19), so rim C = 103

Step 2e   Establish rim 5 value:
107 = 103 + rim 5, so rim 5 = +4

Step 1d   Establish rim D value:
115 = rim D + (+4), so rim D = 111

Having calculated all rim values, we are now ready to calculate the imputed cost values for all open blocks, those having no assignments. We continue to apply the rule of step 2a. Each block number is the sum of its rim column and rim row values.

B1:	105 + 0	= 105	C3:	103 − 13	= 90
C1:	103 + 0	= 103	D3:	111 − 13	= 98
D1:	111 + 0	= 111	A4:	100 − 19	= 81
B2:	105 − 20	= 85	D4:	111 − 19	= 92
C2:	103 − 20	= 83	A5:	100 + 4	= 104
D2:	111 − 20	= 91	B5:	105 + 4	= 109

We now construct matrix 3, which shows: our first trial assignments; actual costs in the corner boxes for all blocks with assignments; and imputed costs in all other corner boxes. For the moment, we pay no attention to the x's in the body of matrix 3. They are the last thing we do with matrix 3 and lead to matrix 4.

Next, using these imputed block cost figures, and comparing them to the original actual costs for each block, we calculate the "opportunity costs" of possible job assignments other than those arbitrarily chosen first. By "opportunity cost" we mean the extra cost we are incurring by not using the most economical set of assignments.

In figure 22-2, the AC columns list the actual cost figures for each block, the IC columns are the imputed cost figures, and the OC columns are the opportunity costs, the differences between the other two figures.

In figure 22-2 every minus OC figure tells us one place where costs can be reduced. There are only six such blocks, B2, C1, C2, D1, D2, and D4. If we can shift production to any or all of those blocks, costs will be reduced. Shifting production to good blocks is a one-block-at-a-time matter. We cannot shift to all open minus blocks in one step.

We start with the block showing the greatest loss, 14 cents, in D1. For every unit that we transfer to D1, we save 14 cents. Since all of job 1 is now

MATRIX 3

JOB	A	B	C	D	RIM
	MACHINE				
1	$-x$│100 100	│105	│103	│111 $+X$	0
2	│80 150	│85	│83	│91	−20
3	$+x$│87 150	$-x$│92 50	│90	│98	−13
4	│81	$+x$│86 50	$-x$│84 100	│92	−19
5	│104	│109	$+x$│107 100	$-x$│115 200	+4
Rim	100	105	103	111	

FIGURE 22-2

JOB	MACHINE											
	A			B			C			D		
	AC	IC	OC	AC	IC	OC	AC	IC	OC	AC	IC	OC
1	100	100	0	105	105	0	95	103	−8	97	111	−14
2	80	80	0	78	85	−7	80	83	−3	82	91	−9
3	87	87	0	92	92	0	97	90	+7	103	98	+5
4	92	81	+11	86	86	0	84	84	0	90	92	−2
5	105	104	+1	110	109	+1	107	107	0	115	115	0

assigned to machine A, production for D1 can come only from A1. So we set about making such a transfer. A problem comes up, however, because machine D is already loaded up with job 5. So to transfer work from A1 to D1 we have to make room on machine D by transferring an equal number of units away from machine D. They can go from D5 to C5. But then C4 has to be reduced an equal amount because C is already loaded. This will push job 4 units from C4 to B4. This causes some of job 3 units to move from B3 to A3.

We now have a complete cycle; block D1 is used and the whole system is again in balance. We save 14 cents for every unit we can move. And how many units can we move? Fifty, because 50 is the smallest quantity in any of the blocks (B3) from which production will be taken.

Referring back now to matrix 3, the $-x$'s and $+x$'s in the blocks indicate the changed assignments we made above. As we go from matrix 3 to matrix 4, the assigned quantities are reduced in all $-x$ blocks and increased in all $+x$ blocks. The large X stands for the quantity to be reassigned, 50 in this case.

One might ask why all of the shifting was confined, except for D1, to blocks with assignments? This is the way the rim value method works. It fills only one empty block per iteration; this time it was D1. All other changes are shifts among blocks already having assignments.

We won't go through the details from here on but will show the remaining five matrices needed to arrive at the optimal machine assign-

MATRIX 4

JOB	A	B	C	D	RIM
1	$-x$ | 100 50	91	89	$+x$ | 97 50	0
2	80 150	71	69	77	−20
3	87 200	78	76	84	−13
4	95	86 100	84 50	92	−5
5	118 $+X$	109	107 150	$-x$ | 115 150	+18
Rim	100	91	89	97	

MACHINE (header spanning A–D)

MATRIX 5

JOB	A	B	C	D	RIM
1	87	91	89	97 100	0
2	$-x$ | 80 150	84	82	90 $+X$	−7
3	87 200	91	89	97	0
4	82	86 100	84 50	92	−5
5	$+x$ | 105 50	109	107 150	$-x$ | 115 100	+18
Rim	87	91	89	97	

MACHINE (header spanning A–D)

MATRIX 6

JOB	MACHINE A	B	C	D	RIM
1	95	93	97	97 \ 100	0
2	$-x$|80 \ 50	78	82 \ $+X$	82 \ 100	−15
3	87 \ 200	85	89	89	−8
4	88	86 \ 100	84 \ 50	90	−7
5	$+x$|105 \ 150	103	$-x$|107 \ 150	107	+10
Rim	95	93	97	97	

MATRIX 7

JOB	MACHINE A	B	C	D	RIM
1	93	97	95	97 \ 100	0
2	78	82 \ $+X$	$-x$|80 \ 50	82 \ 100	−15
3	87 \ 200	91	89	91	−6
4	82	$-x$|86 \ 100	$+x$|84 \ 50	86	−11
5	105 \ 200	109	107 \ 100	109	+12
Rim	93	97	95	97	

MATRIX 8

| JOB | MACHINE | | | | RIM |
	A	B	C	D	
1	91	95	93	97 100	0
2	76	80 50	78	82 100	−15
3	87 200	91	89	93	−4
4	82	86 50	84 100	88	−9
5	105 200	109	107 100	111	+14
Rim	91	95	93	97	

ment. As before, the $-x$'s and $+x$'s shown in the matrices are the last things to go in as the process moves toward the next iteration, and they tell us the blocks being changed. And also, as before, X, the number of units transferred, is the smallest quantity found in any block that is reduced.

Matrix 8 shows the final and optimal assignment. We know that this is the best possible solution because there is now no block whose imputed cost is greater than the block's actual cost. (This comparison does not show in matrix 8 but is determined by comparing its imputed block costs with the actual costs given in figure 22-1.) Our final assignment is:

JOB	PIECES	MACHINE	COST
1	100	D	$ 97
2	50	B	40
2	100	D	82
3	200	A	174
4	50	B	43
4	100	C	84
5	200	A	210
5	100	C	107
Total cost			$837

VOGEL'S APPROXIMATION METHOD

Vogel's approximation method (VAM) is another method for solving transportation problems. It is perhaps the quickest of all methods to work out but, as the name suggests, it gives only approximate solutions and may miss providing the very best solution. We will continue to use the problem given on page 494.

As before, the starting VAM matrix lists machines across the top and jobs along the left. At the right and bottom are the requirements. This time, however, the actual block costs are put in every little corner box and not just in boxes which have assignments.

An extra row is provided at the top and an extra column at the right. These show column and row differences which are got as follows: In each column, pick out the two lowest numbers and put their difference in the space above the column in the difference block. Thus in column A the

MATRIX 1

JOB	DIFFERENCE				PIECES REQUIRED	DIFFERENCE
	7	8	4	8		
	MACHINE					
	A	B	C	D		
1	100	105 X	95	97	100	2
2	80	78 100	80	82	150	2
3	87	92 X	97	103	200	5
4	92	86 X	84	90	150	2
5	105	110 X	107	115	300	2
Machine capacity	400	100	200	200	900	

lowest numbers are 80 and 87, and the difference, 7, goes into the block above A. We continue this for each column, getting 8, 4, and 8. Then we follow the same procedure with each row, putting the differences into the last right-hand column. For row 1 the low numbers are 95 and 97, and their difference is 2. The other differences are 2, 5, 2, and 2.

Next we pick out the column or row having the biggest difference. In our example this number is 8 and there are two of them, one each in columns B and D. We use the one having the lowest cost, which is the 78 in the B column. Now we assign as many units to this block, B2, as we can without exceeding the rim conditions. Although job 2 needs 150 pieces, machine B can produce only 100 so 100 goes into block B2 as its assignment. All other blocks in the B column are now marked out (since machine B is fully loaded) and column B is removed from further consideration.

MATRIX 2

JOB	DIFFERENCE				REQUIRED	DIFFERENCE
	$7, \not{12}, \not{8}, 5$	X, X, X, X	$\not{4}, \not{4}, \not{11}, 12$	$\not{8}, \not{8}, \not{7}, 18$		
	MACHINE					
	A	B	C	D		
1	100 X	100 X	95 X	97 100	100	$\not{2}, \not{2}, \not{2}, 2$
2	80 50	78 100	80 X	82 X	150	$\not{0}, \not{0}, X, X$
3	87 200	92 X	97 X	103 X	200	$\not{10}, X, X, X$
4	92 X	86 X	84 150	90 X	150	$\not{6}, \not{6}, \not{6}, X$
5	105 150	110 X	107 50	115 100	300	$\not{2}, \not{2}, \not{2}, 2$
Machine capacity	400	100	200	200	900	

Now we move on to matrix 2. We calculate new difference figures and make a new job assignment just as we did in matrix 1. We see that the B column, however, remains frozen and does not enter into the new calculations.

This time the biggest difference is 10 for row 3 and the lowest cost is 87 in column A. Since machine A can handle all 200 units needed for job 3, we assign all 200 units needed for job 3 to machine A.

Instead of making up a new matrix 3 at this point we will just keep on using matrix 2. We just mark out the old differences and work out a new set and go ahead and make another assignment right on matrix 2. (Actually we could have done this on matrix 1 without making up matrix 2 and we would have done so except for clarifying the explanation.)

The biggest difference is 12 in column A and the lowest cost not yet used in column A is 80 in A2 so we load into A2 all the remaining units needed to complete job 2. There are only 50 units of job 2 left so we assign these 50 to machine A. Now we have job 2 wholly assigned and so we cross out C2 and D2.

Continuing, the 11 in column C is the biggest next new difference and the lowest unused cost is 84 in block C4. So we load C4 up as much as we can by putting in the whole 150 units of job 4 on machine 3. Now we cross out A4 and D4.

On the next set of differences the 18 in column D is the biggest difference and the 97 in block D1 is the lower of the two remaining un-crossed-out cost figures. So we assign the 100 units for job 1 to machine D and cross out A1 and C1. At this point only the 300 units needed for job 5 have not been assigned so they are allocated to the remaining machine open times: 150 to machine A, 50 to C, and 100 to D.

This is the end of the solution to the problem by the VAM. As we said at the start, VAM solutions may not be the optimum but if they are not, they are not far off. Our VAM solution is:

JOB	PIECES	MACHINE	COST
1	100	D	$ 97.00
2	50	A	40.00
2	100	B	78.00
3	200	A	174.00
4	150	C	126.00
5	150	A	157.50
5	50	C	53.50
5	100	D	115.00
Total cost			$841.00

Since we have already obtained the optimum solution by the rim value method we know that its cost is $837; our VAM solution costing $841 is not quite the best. Had we not worked out the rim value method, we would not know if the VAM solution was optimal. When using the VAM it is well to try to improve it by applying the rim value method, using the VAM solution as a starting point rather than the arbitrary northwest corner allocation. In our example it would take two rim value iterations to get from the VAM solution to the optimum solution.

INDEX METHOD

For some shop problems, the simplex method is too long to be practicable. In fact, so are the transportation and assignment methods although they are far simpler than the simplex method. One modification of the transportation method is sometimes referred to as the "index" method. It is a rough kind of transportation method (and a variation of VAM) which unearths about a 95 per cent most perfect solution to problems. It does this quickly at low computing cost and it can be used without a computer. By way of contrast, the simplex method will find the very best solution but is slow when done on desk calculators (computers can, of course, work the simplex method quickly).

Here is an example of how the index method works. Assume that you have five machines and seven jobs to be done. We have other jobs besides these seven but the others can be done on only one machine so they are not considered nor is the time that they take on the various machines.

The orders and the various machines on which they can go are shown below. (The machines are alternatives; only one of those shown is needed for each order.)

ORDER	MACHINE
1	A, B, C, D
2	D, E
3	A, B, C, D
4	A, B, C, D, E
5	C, D, E
6	B, C, D, E
7	B, E

The problem is to find out if we can get all of these jobs done on the machines that we have and in the hours available. If we can we want to know how we can do it in the fewest machine hours. In this problem we assume that the per hour cost of operating all machines is the same. We also do not allow splitting any orders to be run on two or more machines.

FIGURE 22-3

ORDER NUMBER	MACHINE				
	A	B	C	D	E
1	30	34	60	75	
2				90	60
3	60	140	210	150	
4	90	135	112	115	160
5			160	188	210
6		220	70	130	105
7		32			40
Hours available	90	40	200	220	160

Figure 22-3 shows how long it will take to do each job in each of the ways it can be made. The numbers in the body of the table are hours.

If you add up, you will find that if you could get all jobs done on their best machines (and so in the least time) you would need 502 machine hours. But if you had all orders on their worst machines, you'd need 1,005 machine hours. Since you have 710 hours available and certainly several jobs can go on their best machines, it is likely that you can get the work all done without trouble.

The problem is to assign the jobs so as to use the fewest hours (we do not have to pay for unused hours so saving hours saves money). To solve this problem by the index method we set up another table, figure 22-4.

Notice the numbers in the little rectangles in the corners of each space. They are per cent excess figures. Thus for order number 1, the ideal way to make it is on machine A where it would take 30 hours. Machine B would take 34 hours or 13 per cent more time, hence the 13 in the rectangle. Machine C would take 100 per cent extra time. All of the other figures in the little corner boxes are figured the same way.

Now try to load the machines. Look in the column for machine A. It is the best for all of the jobs that can be done on it but we have only 90 hours available. We can run either order 4 or 1 and 3. Since order 4 is a large order, suppose that we tentatively assign all of machine A's time to it. Now try to put the other orders on machines where they have the lowest index. You'll run into trouble and have to change. You can juggle the allocations around by cut-and-try although on this problem you will probably

FIGURE 22-4

ORDER NUMBER	MACHINE				
	A	B	C	D	E
1	⎡0⎤ (30)	⎡13⎤ 34	⎡100⎤ 60	⎡150⎤ 75	
2				⎡50⎤ 90	⎡0⎤ (60)
3	⎡0⎤ (60)	⎡133⎤ 140	⎡250⎤ 210	⎡150⎤ 150	
4	⎡0⎤ 90	⎡50⎤ 135	⎡24⎤ (112)	⎡28⎤ 115	⎡78⎤ 160
5			⎡0⎤ 160	⎡18⎤ (188)	⎡31⎤ 210
6		⎡214⎤ 220	⎡0⎤ (70)	⎡86⎤ 130	⎡50⎤ 105
7		⎡0⎤ (32)			⎡25⎤ 40
Hours available	90	40	200	220	160

arrive at the lineup given below in a matter of a few minutes. Bigger problems of course take more time. Here is the best scheduling solution for our problem:

ORDER	MACHINE	ACTUAL HOURS	EXCESS HOURS
1	A	30	0
2	E	60	0
3	A	60	0
4	C	112	22
5	D	188	28
6	C	70	0
7	B	32	0

This solution gets the work out in 552 machine hours, or only 50 more than the ideal.

Perhaps you wondered how the index method pays attention to the big versus the little orders. It might, for example, pay to shift a little order to a high index machine in order to let a big order save a few points. The index method catches this when you compare the excess hours that different schedules give you. Here, in the final accounting, is the place where size of order as well as degree of efficiency show up. If you put large orders on even slightly inefficient machines, you boost excess hours fast.

The index method does not assure you, in a big problem, that you will finally hit upon the very best combination but, without very much work, it gets up to over 90 per cent of perfection.

Since this method is really a variation of the transportation method and VAM, all the comments made earlier concerning these methods also apply here. The answer obtained by using the index method is about the same as one would obtain by using VAM alone without further refining the solution through the use of the transportation method.

SKF'S METHOD

SKF Bearing Industries, in Philadelphia, has used a somewhat different index method to schedule hundreds of orders each week to 40 machine groups. At SKF most operations can be done on several machines but at different costs. The problem is to perform every operation on the machine that does it at least cost.

This seems simple but often the machines which can do certain jobs at least cost are overloaded. Then some jobs have to be assigned to machines which can do the work but only at a higher cost. The goal is to move orders around to machines that have the time to do the jobs at close to the lowest cost.

SKF makes out a card for every operation to be performed. On the card it lists the different machines that can do the work and the cost of performing the operation each way. Then SKF takes the least costly way as the ideal or base cost and divides each other cost by the ideal cost to get an "index." The index is merely the percentage extra that the second- and third-best ways cost over the ideal.

Each order's card then goes into the queue for its ideal machine. Next each machine's work load is added up. In any case where it exceeds the machine's capacity, some jobs are removed from the queue and put into queues for other machines. The jobs removed are those with low index numbers on other machines. This means that their costs on second-best machines are not much more than on the best machines. Because second-best machines sometimes are also overloaded, a few jobs may have to be moved another time or two until they get to a machine that can handle them, albeit at still higher costs. Each machine ends up with jobs for which it is best or nearly best suited. In its first year of using this procedure SKF saved over $200,000 as compared to its old hit-and-miss method.

MAXIMIZING A FUNCTION USING THE TRANSPORTATION METHOD

Up to now we have been concerned with minimizing costs. But sometimes we work with profit figures instead and these we want to maximize. Can the transportation method be used? Yes, the procedure is the same except for one minor change.

When minimizing costs using the rim value method we searched for the assignment where the actual cost was the greatest amount *below* the imputed cost of not using the assignment. When we want to maximize profits, we search for the assignment where the profit is the greatest amount *above* the imputed profit of not using the assignment.

A similar change occurs when using VAM. We take the difference between the *highest* two profits in each column and row, and select the one with the *greatest difference*. Then we proceed as before.

FLEXIBILITY OF CONSTRAINTS WHEN USING THE TRANSPORTATION METHOD

INPUTS MUST EQUAL OUTPUTS   On page 494, we listed several constraints or requirements for using the transportation method. One of them was that machine capacities and the quantities wanted must be equal. Yet, in real-life situations, not often is this so. We can still use the transportation method, however, by adding "dummy" factors.

We might say that dummy factors represent imaginary machines which make no products or imaginary products made in unused machine time. They are exactly like the slack variables in the simplex method. Mathematically, they convert inequalities into equalities. As in the simplex method, hypothetical and extreme cost figures are assigned to dummy variables to insure that they will not appear in the answer solution.

Suppose that, in our previous example, machine C is out of order so that only machines A, B, and D are available. We now have a production capacity of 700 and a demand of 900. We won't work this problem through

FIGURE 22-5

| JOB | MACHINE | | | | TOTAL REQUIRED |
	A	B	D	DUMMY	
1	100	105	97	0	100
2	80	78	82	0	150
3	87	92	103	0	200
4	92	86	90	0	150
5	105	110	115	0	300
Machine capacity	400	100	200	200	900

to an answer but it can be solved by setting it up as shown in figure 22-5. As in our original matrix on page 494, the figures in the body of figure 22-5 are the costs for each block. (It turns out that we should cut 200 units off job 5.)

Sometimes the inequality is not excess demand over capacity but the reverse, excess capacity over demand. This time a dummy job with zero cost is introduced.

ASSIGNMENTS MUST BE INTERCHANGEABLE   We can also use the transportation method even though not every machine can do every job. If so, we have to block off certain assignments. If, for some reason, job 2 should not go on machine B we just say that if it were done on machine B the cost would be very high, say, $10, instead of its actual 78-cent cost. Because a $10 cost would make it a very uneconomical assignment, it will not appear in any final solution. Similarly if our problem were one of profit maximization we could rule out any particular assignment that can't be made for some good reason, by assigning it a zero profit.

It is possible, therefore, to use the transportation method even if our original constraints, given on page 494, about inputs and outputs needing to be equal are not met. And it can also be used even when jobs are not wholly interchangeable on machines.

RELATIONSHIPS MUST BE LINEAR   The constraint requiring that the cost per unit be the same regardless of volume can now be examined.

Obviously, there are times when unit costs are affected by volume, as when machine setup costs are a factor. Setup cost per unit goes down as the quantity goes up.

We can still handle such situations by the transportation method if we put the setup cost aside as being fixed, treating it later in our thinking. We can then solve the problem working with only variable costs. Another way to handle curvilinear relationships is to break up a factor, such as volume, into segments, and to assume that a linear relationship exists within each limited volume range.

Let us consider, for illustration, a case where the relationships are linear up to where overtime is incurred and then a new higher linear relationship applies.

We will go back to our original problem on page 494, except that we will assume that job 4 has been canceled. And suppose also that two machines, B and C, are down for repairs. We can, however, work both machine A and machine D overtime. Figure 22-6 shows how our first matrix will look. (The costs of overtime listed in figure 22-6 reflect the extra cost of overtime labor *and* of overhead. Overtime labor costs 50 per cent extra but overhead costs nothing extra, so the assumed combined extra costs are 25 per cent.) In figure 22-6, as before, the numbers in the blocks are costs per unit.

FIGURE 22-6

| JOB | MACHINE | | | | QUANTITY REQUIRED |
	A	A (OVERTIME)	D	D (OVERTIME)	
1	100	125	97	121	100
2	80	100	82	102	150
3	87	109	103	129	200
Dummy	0	0	0	0	150
5	105	131	115	144	300
Machine capacity	400	200	200	100	900

Again, because of space limitations, we will not carry through the calculations. The optimal solution to the problem is:

JOB	PIECES	MACHINE	COST
1	100	D	$ 97
2	100	D	82
2	50	A (overtime)	50
3	100	A	87
3	100	A (overtime)	109
5	300	A	315
			$720

With this solution, we don't use any of the 100 units of overtime capacity on D and there are still 50 unused overtime capacity units on A.

HOMOGENEOUS UNITS   In our discussion we have specified machine capacities in terms of pieces, but machine capacity is usually stated in terms of hours whereas job requirements are stated in terms of pieces.

The transportation method cannot be used with nonhomogeneous units. The way to avoid this roadblock is to convert the job requirements from pieces to standard hours by using time study data. Costs can then also be stated in terms of standard hours. And the machine availability is already in terms of hours.

There is still one more hurdle to be overcome. The productivity rates of the machines will vary so that our standard data will refer only to one particular machine. To bring all the data to a common base, a productivity index relating the machines to each other can be developed so that all costs and data will be in terms of standard data per standard machine. After doing this we can solve the problem and then convert the answer back into the number of pieces.

Yet determining the productivity index can be troublesome. If one machine were always twice as productive as another, there would be no problem, but this is rarely the case. On different jobs their relative productivity will vary. If the distribution of relative productivities of the two machines is not too wide, the average relationship will provide an acceptable measure. The solution obtained using this average will not be quite optimal but close to it.

ASSIGNMENT METHOD

In our discussion of the transportation method of assigning jobs we assumed that jobs could be split between machines. Often, however, setup costs are too high to allow this in which case whole jobs have to be assigned to machines. This same problem comes up when you assign jobs to men of varying abilities when some men are good on one or two jobs but not on others.

The assignment method may help here. This method requires a square matrix with the same number of jobs as machines. (If jobs and machines differ in number then we have to introduce dummy machines or dummy jobs. Then if there are extra jobs they don't get assigned and if there are extra machines, they remain idle.)

We will continue to use the same cost figures that we used in other examples. And we will assume that we have five jobs and four machines. The jobs in this case, however, go on and on, so we are concerned only with cost figures and not capacity. Also one job will not be assigned to any of the machines. Matrix 1 shows our starting matrix.

Our first step toward a solution is to look back at the cost figures for each block in figure 22-1. In each column, we find the lowest cost and put a zero in its block in matrix 2. The other blocks in this column show the excess of other block costs. Thus in column A, the lowest cost, 80, is in block A2. Hence the 0 in A2. The costs in A1, A3, A4, and A5 are greater than 80 by 20, 7, 12, and 25, respectively, hence the numbers in column A. Similarly, machine B's lowest cost is in B2 so the column B values become 27, 0, 14, 8, and 32. The figures in column C and D we got the same way. In our example it happens that job 2 costs the least on every machine so we have a row of zeros for job 2. This is pure happenstance and does not affect the calculation in any way. The dummy machine's figures all continue to be zero.

The next step is to draw in vertical and horizontal lines through all

MATRIX 1

JOB	MACHINE				
	A	B	C	D	DUMMY
1	100	105	95	97	0
2	80	78	80	82	0
3	87	92	97	103	0
4	92	86	84	90	0
5	105	110	107	115	0

MATRIX 2

JOB	MACHINE				
	A	B	C	D	DUMMY
1	20	27	15	15	0
2	0	0	0	0	0
3	7	14	17	21	0
4	12	8	4	8	0
5	25	32	27	33	0

rows and columns containing a zero *while using the fewest possible number of lines.* In matrix 2 we can cross out all of the zeros with two lines. Ultimately, when we arrive at the point where it takes the five lines, no matter their direction, to cross out all of the zeros we will have a solution. Five lines are required because our matrix is five columns by five rows.

Having no solution in matrix 2, we proceed to develop matrix 3. In matrix 2, we search for the lowest open number. It proves to be a 4 in block C4. So we subtract 4 from all open numbers to get new numbers for matrix 3. We also *add* this number, 4, to all numbers in blocks where cross-out lines themselves cross, so dummy 2 becomes 4. All other numbers in blocks through which cross-out lines go remain unchanged.

Now we again draw cross-out lines through all 0's while still using the fewest lines possible. This time it takes three cross-out lines, still not five.

MATRIX 3

JOB	MACHINE				
	A	B	C	D	DUMMY
1	16	23	11	11	0
2	0	0	0	0	4
3	3	10	13	17	0
4	8	4	0	4	0
5	21	28	23	29	0

MATRIX 4

JOB	MACHINE				
	A	B	C	D	DUMMY
1	13	20	11	8	0
2	0	0	3	0	7
3	0	7	13	14	0
4	5	1	0	1	0
5	18	25	23	26	0

MATRIX 5

JOB	MACHINE				
	A	B	C	D	DUMMY
1	13	19	11	7	0
2	1	0	4	0	8
3	0	6	13	13	0
4	5	0	0	0	0
5	18	24	23	25	0

MATRIX 6

JOB	MACHINE				
	A	B	C	D	DUMMY
1	13	13	5	1	0
2	7	0	4	0	14
3	0	0	7	7	0
4	11	0	0	0	6
5	18	18	17	19	0

MATRIX 7

| JOB | MACHINE | | | | |
---	A	B	C	D	DUMMY
1	12	12	4	(0)	0
2	7	(0)	4	0	15
3	(0)	0	7	7	1
4	11	0	(0)	0	7
5	17	17	16	18	(0)

So on to matrix 4. Still no solution. Then matrix 5, 6, and finally 7 in which it takes five cross-out lines to mark out all of the 0's.

And what is the solution? A job can go on any machine where a zero shows. Considering that several columns and rows have two or three zeros, how can we tell which job to assign to which machine? Look first to all rows and columns with one zero only. For job 5, the only zero is in dummy 5, so job 5 is assigned to the dummy machine (meaning that job 5 will not be run).

In the machine A column the only zero is in block A3 so A is assigned job 3. Similarly machine C has to get job 4 since the only zero in C column is in C4. Only jobs 1 and 2 and machines B and D are now left. Machine D can do either job but B can do only job 2 so that becomes its assignment, leaving job 1 for machine D. The cost of producing one unit of each of the four products using permanent setups is $3.46 and is less with this set of job assignments than any other combination.

In large problems of this sort, such as you might have for a factory department, there might be several solutions. If this occurs, the several solutions have the same cost and it doesn't matter which is selected.

"REGRET" MATRIXES Sometimes our problem is to maximize some measure of performance rather than to minimize some factor. If the problem is one of maximizing instead of minimizing, you can still use the assignment method but you would have to convert the first matrix into a "regret" matrix. In a regret matrix the numbers you use show losses from not being able to do things the best way. The procedure is like measuring contours of terrain by calling the top of the highest hill the zero reference point and measuring all other points downward from it, rather than measuring upward from a zero reference plane.

MATRIX 1

OPERATOR	JOB			
	301	302	303	304
Smith	10	8	6	4
Green	8	6	5	1
Jones	6	10	7	5
Black	6	10	9	3

First, however, you need to set up the problem as you find it, more or less as if you were at the low point looking up. Suppose that you have four operators and four jobs. Each man can do each job but not equally well. Matrix 1 shows their relative abilities to do each job: 10 is best, 0 is worst. As you see, none of the men can do job 304 very well, whereas three of the men can do job 302 well.

The second step is to set up the regret matrix, matrix 2. You do this by comparing all numbers to the largest number, which, in our case, is 10. In all blocks put in the difference between 10 and the number in matrix 1. Matrix 2 shows these difference numbers.

From here on the solution to the problem follows the usual assignment method. Matrix 3 shows the answer solution.

We see in matrix 3 that Green has only one zero in his row so he gets job 301. Job 303 has only one zero in its column. This is opposite Black's name, so Black gets job 303. Jones is the only one left with a zero for job 302 so he gets it, leaving Smith with 304.

MATRIX 2

OPERATOR	JOB			
	301	302	303	304
Smith	0	2	4	6
Green	2	4	5	9
Jones	4	0	3	5
Black	4	0	1	7

MATRIX 3

OPERATOR	JOB 301	302	303	304
Smith	0	1	2	⓪
Green	⓪	1	1	1
Jones	5	⓪	2	0
Black	5	0	⓪	2

Turning back to our starting matrix in positive form (not the regret matrix) we see that this set of assignments adds up to 31 "skill points" if we could call them that. This is an average of 7.75 points per job and is a higher figure than any other set of assignments in this problem. Notice that this is so even though Smith gets the job he can do least well.

SCHEDULING MAINTENANCE WORK

Maintenance machine repair work is particularly hard to schedule because it is so unpredictable. Sometimes there is too much for the maintenance staff to handle and at other times the men aren't busy. Such a situation is typical of queuing problems whose solutions are best worked out by simulation. We will take up simulation in Chapter 29, where we discuss flow control.

Preventive maintenance is, however, another matter. Good preventive maintenance reduces breakdowns and lost production time. Often breakdown costs are high as when whole lines stop, idling men and machines ahead of and after the breakdown spot. Production is lost, overhead costs are not absorbed, and production workers have to be paid during their wait for work to resume.

But preventive maintenance too costs money. Machines are repaired before it is absolutely necessary. Parts are replaced before they wear out so their remaining useful life is lost. And undoubtedly some of the repairs would not have had to be done at all if things were left alone. Preventive maintenance does not, however, cost money in terms of idle machine time because the repair work itself is usually done during afterwork hours, weekends, or vacations so that there is no lost production time. Only in process industries operating 24 hours a day is production time lost during preventive maintenance repairs.

We are interested in arriving at a balance between the costs of over-maintaining against the breakdown losses which it prevents. To work this out, let us assume a factory with 100 machines, each with its own electronic control system which includes such items as speed regulators, measuring devices, counters, and in a few cases beta-ray radiation gages. We will also assume that, because we have so many machines, we have good records of breakdowns in the past. These show the following pattern of probability of trouble:

MONTHS SINCE LAST REPAIR	PROBABILITY OF BREAKDOWN	CUMULATIVE PROBABILITY
1	.400	.400
2	.015	.415
3	.010	.425
4	.010	.435
5	.012	.447
6	.018	.465
7	.025	.490
8	.037	.527
9	.055	.582
10	.083	.665
11	.130	.795
12	.205	1.000

We also have records covering repair costs. They show that, on the average, a breakdown takes 3 hours to repair whereas preventive repair takes 1 hour. Maintenance labor costs $10 an hour ($5 for labor cost, $5 for overhead). Materials used in breakdown repairs cost $70 but preventive repair jobs use only $10 worth of materials. Machine production time lost costs $50 an hour. So, in total, every breakdown repair costs $250 and every preventive repair costs $70.

Our records show that machines almost never operate for a year without repairs being needed. It appears, too, that a good many repair jobs really don't get the difficulty fixed very well because in 40 per cent of the cases, they need repairs again within a month.

Having a high rate of early failure is similar to a situation sometimes found in regular manufacture. A few faulty or weak performing parts get by inspection and into final products where they make trouble right away.

To combat this, in certain military equipment (and before they are installed) electronic tubes and similar equipment are "aged" by being operated under normal load conditions for, perhaps, 50 hours. Truly defective parts fail during the trial and so never get into final products, thus almost eliminating the high initial failure rate.

In any case in our machinery maintenance example, the records show that a good many repaired machines need repairs again almost immediately. Our problem is to establish a preventive repair policy.

COST OF BREAKDOWN REPAIR POLICY   We will assume that we start with a breakdown repair policy, with no preventive repair at all. Our first step is to calculate the cost of this policy. For this we need the expected average time between breakdowns for which the formula is:

$$T_E = \sum_{n}^{N} T_n(p_n)$$

where T_E = the expected average time between breakdowns
T_n = the time between breakdowns
p_n = the probability of T_n occurring
$n = 1, 2, 3, \ldots, N$
N = the maximum number of months

So we add $1 \times .400 + 2 \times .015 + 3 \times .010$, etc., and get 6.354 months as the average length of time between breakdowns. Repairing 100 machines at $250 per repair costs $25,000 every 6.354 months or $3,933 per month. This is the cost of following a breakdown repair policy.

Expressed in formula form, this becomes

$$C_M = \frac{M(C_r)}{T_E} = \frac{100(\$250)}{6.354} = \$3,933 \text{ per month}$$

where C_M = the cost of maintaining
M = the number of machines
C_r = the cost of a breakdown repair job

COST OF PREVENTIVE REPAIR POLICY   The cost of preventive maintenance is harder to calculate. It is easiest just to assume one policy after another and to calculate the cost of each one.

First we will try the policy of repairing every machine every month. Doing this will entail the costs of 100 repairs plus the breakdown costs of the 40 per cent of the cases that failed within the month. The 100 preventive repairs cost $70 each or a total of $7,000. But this policy would not prevent the 40 breakdown repairs that occur during the month so these, at

$250 each, would cost $10,000. Monthly preventive repairs therefore would cost us $17,000 per month. This is far more than following a breakdown repair policy so we should not go in for monthly preventive repairs.

Expressed in formula form, this becomes

$$
\begin{aligned}
C_{PM} &= M(C_p) + M(p_1)(C_r) \\
&= 100(\$70) + 100(.4)(\$250) \\
&= \$7,000 + \$10,000 \\
&= \$17,000 \text{ per month}
\end{aligned}
$$

where C_{PM} = the cost of preventive maintenance
C_p = the cost of a preventive repair
p_1 = the proportion of machines that will need repair in month 1

Next, we go to a policy of preventive repair every two months. This will cut the cost of preventive repairs by half but at the expense of more breakdowns. Using this policy, there would be 40 breakdowns in the first month plus another $1\frac{1}{2}$ breakdowns in the second month. But besides these 41.5 breakdowns some of the machines repaired during the first month will break down again the second month. Forty per cent of the 40 repaired machines will fail again so they will add 16 more repair jobs. This brings the total number of breakdowns in the two months to 57.5.

The cost of preventive repairs every two months is 100($70) + 57.5($250) or $21,375 for two months or $10,688 per month. Although this is much better than a monthly preventive repair policy, it is still nearly three times as high as breakdown servicing only.

Going into three, four, five months, etc., preventive maintenance policies make the arithmetic become complicated. Figure 22-7 shows in diagram form how many repairs would occur in four months. In figure 22-7 the numbers along the thin lines show the number of machines which needed repairs each month.

It is easier to use a formula to calculate the number of repairs for each possible preventive maintenance policy. The cost per month of any policy is

$$
C_{PM} = \frac{M(C_p) + B_n(C_r)}{n}
$$

where C_{PM} = cost of preventive maintenance
M = number of machines (100 in our example)
C_p = cost per preventive repair ($70 in our example)
B_n = the probable number of breakdown repairs in spite of preventive repairs
C_r = cost per breakdown repair ($250 in our example)
n = the number of months

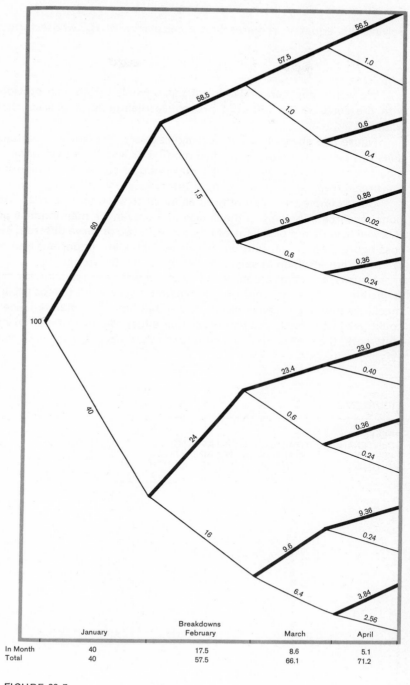

FIGURE 22-7

Solving this equation requires first a calculation of B_n, whose formula is

$$B_n = M \sum_1^n p_n + B_{(n-1)}p_1 + B_{(n-2)}p_2 + B_{(n-3)}p_3 + \cdots + B_1 p_{(n-1)}$$

We won't stop here to work out this formula but its use provides us with the costs of the different preventive maintenance policies that we want.

Figure 22-9 shows how the cost figures vary. Preventive maintenance does not pay if it is done every five months or less. It is best done every nine months where it will save the maximum of some $300 a month over the breakdown repair policy. Longer intervals are less economical.

Our example has been offered as an illustration of now to use operations research in helping in the choice of a preventive maintenance policy. It is well to work out problems of this sort with two or three different sets of cost figures. Then you find out which variables are important and which are not. Your intuition in such matters is frequently wrong.

Usually, in actual practice, the situation will be more complex than it is in our example. We did not, for instance, consider the possibility of machines that need repairs having to wait until the busy maintenance men could get to them. Unless you have men either idle or working on makeshift work, they will sometimes be busy so that machines will have to wait.

FIGURE 22-8

PREVENTIVE MAINTENANCE EVERY N MONTHS	TOTAL EXPECTED BREAKDOWNS IN N MONTHS	AVERAGE BREAKDOWNS PER MONTH	TOTAL MONTHLY COST OF MAINTENANCE
1	40.0	40.00	$17,000
2	57.5	28.75	10,688
3	66.1	22.03	7,842
4	71.2	17.80	6,200
5	75.1	15.02	5,155
6	79.3	13.22	4,471
7	84.6	12.09	4,021
8	92.0	11.50	3,750
9	102.8	11.42	3,633
10	118.8	11.88	3,670
11	143.3	13.03	3,893
12	181.5	15.12	4,365
None		15.74	3,933

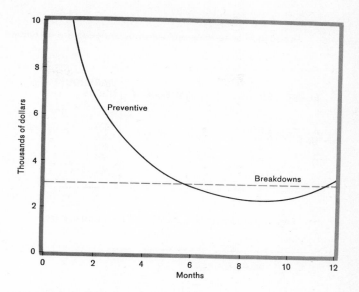

FIGURE 22-9 Costs of preventive and breakdown maintenance policies.

We are not going to add this complication to our example here. But we can say that the costs of breakdown maintenance are probably understated considerably because of this. So, in a lesser way, are the costs of preventive maintenance. It is unlikely, however, that the low point on the preventive maintenance cost curve would be noticeably moved to the left or right because of this circumstance.

STUDY MATERIALS

22-1 The transportation method illustrated in this chapter is a special case of the general linear programming method. As an example of the difference in the ease of solution using the two methods, set up the example in this chapter in the simplex format. Remember that a separate equation is required for each constraint, and that every possible assignment must appear in the cost minimization function.

22-2 The Weller Furniture Company has four plants and four warehouses and must decide from which plant to supply each warehouse with product model 174.

Production schedules and warehouse needs are as follows:

PLANT	PRODUCTION	WAREHOUSE	WAREHOUSE NEEDS
A	1,800	1	600
B	2,400	2	1,400
C	600	3	3,500
D	1,200	4	500
	6,000		6,000

Freight rates between plants and warehouses are:

	WAREHOUSE			
PLANT	1	2	3	4
A	$ 9	$ 8	$12	$10
B	10	10	12	14
C	8	9	11	11
D	10	10	11	12

Allocate each plant's production to the warehouses in such a way as to minimize freight costs.

22-3   Four machines have available time to run four jobs. In the case of two of the machines, A and B, some of the available capacity is on regular shift hours while the remainder is on overtime. The other two machines, C and D, have only regular time hours available. With the exception of job 3 which cannot be run on machine B, any job can be run on any machine, although at cost per piece, in cents, given in the table below.

	MACHINE					
JOB	A	A(ot)	B	B(ot)	C	D
1	5	7	4	6	6	7
2	6	8	5	7	5	3
3	4	5	–	–	8	6
4	7	10	6	8	3	7

Machine capacity in units is:

MACHINE

A	A(ot)	B	B(ot)	C	D
600	100	600	300	400	500

while the number of pieces to be produced are:

JOB

1	2	3	4
300	200	500	1,000

What is the minimal cost at which this set of jobs can be scheduled? (NOTE: In the solution of this problem, you *may* encounter a degenerate condition. That is, one wherein it is impossible to obtain all the rim values by the method described in this chapter. This condition may be alleviated by introducing an incremental quantity, e, into the matrix at any appropriate point, treating it as a real allocation with a cost, so that the process of filling the rim boxes may be finished. At the point where this incremental quantity is the only quantity that is being reallocated, the quantity may be ignored with the resulting allocation being an optimal one. The solution obtained by this process is exact. There are two solutions to this problem.)

22-4   If setup costs were charged, in problem 22-3, as fixed amounts according to the following schedule:

	MACHINE			
	A	B	C	D
Charge	$10	$15	$12	$20

1   Would there be an advantage to choosing one or the other of the solutions obtained above? (It may be noted above that there is greater machine capacity than there is demand for parts.)

2   Would there be any advantage in scheduling all the work on machines A, B, and C and not using D since it has the highest setup charge? How much would the advantage be?

22-5 You own a number of delivery trucks, but some are old and some new, and they are of different makes. Your drivers have strong feelings about getting the one they'd like. In order to minimize their unhappiness with having to use trucks not to their liking, how do you assign them?

	WORKER AND HIS PREFERENCE RANK				
TRUCK	SMITH	JONES	THOMAS	TAYLOR	DAVIS
A	1	1	2	3	2
B	5	3	1	2	3
C	4	2	5	1	1
D	3	5	4	4	4
E	2	4	3	5	5

22-6 Using the index method, how do you assign the following jobs to machines all having the same machine hour cost and all capable of doing any of the jobs but at different rates?

	JOB			
	A	B	C	D
Number of pieces	150	170	250	150

	MACHINE			
	1	2	3	4
Hours available	160	200	240	260

MINUTES PER PIECE ON EACH MACHINE

	MACHINE			
ORDER	1	2	3	4
A	50	60	70	80
B	100	50	60	55
C	75	40	80	50
D	75	50	80	45

1 What is your assignment of jobs to machines?

2 How many machine hours will be unassigned?

3 If it costs $10 per machine hour, what price should each product sell for in order to yield a gross profit margin of 25 per cent over manufacturing costs?

22-7 Your plants can produce the following number of units:

	PLANT			
	A	B	C	D
Quantity	400	500	400	700

Warehouse needs are:

	WAREHOUSE				
	1	2	3	4	5
Quantity	400	500	700	200	200

Transportation costs are:

	PLANT			
WAREHOUSE	A	B	C	D
1	14	15	10	11
2	8	10	14	9
3	13	10	11	12
4	9	14	10	15
5	12	8	8	8

1 Determine the optimum distribution of the product.

2 If plant A could expand its production to 700 units what difference would this make?

3 If factory production costs were A—$20, B—$22, C—$25, and D—$24, what would be the optimum distribution of the product?

22-8   You have 100 machines which cost $10 each to repair on a preventive basis or $80 each to repair if they break down. The probabilities of failure are as follows:

MONTHS IN USE AFTER LAST REPAIR	PROBABILITY OF FAILURE
1	.15
2	.02
3	.02
4	.03
5	.03
6	.04
7	.05
8	.07
9	.10
10	.13
11	.16
12	.20

What repair policy should you follow? If you find that a preventive repair policy is best, what repair cycle should you use and how much per month will this policy save you as against following a breakdown repair policy?

chapter twenty-three

PREPARING FOR PRODUCTION

The end products of production control's preparation work are shop directives of which, in order control, there are many. You have to prepare order "sets" separately for every order. Order sets include all drawings, shop orders, materials requisitions, operation tickets, tool orders, move orders, inspection tickets, material identification tags, and work schedules. Of these items, production control prepares them all except drawings, which it gets from engineering.

For repeat orders, most of this preparatory work is routine because the file for past jobs, whether it is on computer tapes or not, shows how you worked these things out before. If all went well before, you just do again on repeat orders what you did before. Of course, you have to use new order numbers, new quantities, and new schedule dates.

For first-time orders, production control has first to collect information about the job. It has to get drawings from engineering and either work out a list of operations or get a list of operations from engineering.

You'll get disappointing production, however, if you confine yourself, in preparing for production, just to making up the shop's directives even though this is the biggest part of the job. Besides making up forms, you must always check up ahead on the availability of tools, jigs, fixtures, gages, materials, and any other facilities (except those that you always keep plenty of). Anything special, anything the least bit unusual, check up on. It isn't enough to say that it is someone else's job to get these things ready on time (although this may be true). If you don't check up you can be sure that some of these items will not be ready on time and this will hold you up.

Large companies sometimes don't subscribe to what we've just said. And it isn't because they don't appreciate the problem. It is because production control men would be spending all their time checking to see if other people were doing their jobs. Large companies protect themselves by insisting that each department meet schedules. If drawings are supposed to be ready on November 1, they are ready then or engineering has to do some explaining to high officials. If tooling is to be ready, it is the same story. Also purchasing. And foremen who don't meet schedules don't stay foremen. Admittedly top management edicts saying that everyone must meet schedules "or else" don't always produce results but it is usually quite effective and relieves production control of the checking-up job.

ARRANGEMENTS OF BILLS OF MATERIALS We said earlier that the engineering department's drawings should list everything needed to make a product. They are, thus, complete master bills of material. Production control transfers these lists to tabulating cards and then onto computer tapes.

When preparing *order* bills of material you can have the computer run them off listing parts in any sequence you want. You can indent them as we described in Chapter 14, in which case they are helpful as assembly instructions because they show the order of attachment. Actually, indented bills are uncommon since the men or the assembly floor either need no instructions because they already know the assembly sequence or else they need and get other more complete instructions than an indented bill would give them.

In any case, however, a listing of parts in order of attachment is the wrong order for stock issue clerks. Stock-room clerks have to gather together the parts to take out to the assembly floor for the assemblers. They would waste too much time going back two, three, and four times to the same bins to get one, then another, and then still another of an item as it shows up several places on the bill. You can save the time of these men by having the computer run off a list for them arranged in part number order. Then the issue clerks won't have to go time and again to the same bins.

Even listing items in stock number order doesn't do all that the stock-room clerk needs. Probably you can save still more of his time by giving him bills of material or "pickup lists" showing the items in order of stock-room location. You can, of course, prepare such bills on the computer only if you make stock-room bin numbers part of your tape record. Not only will arranging the items on bills this way save the clerk's time but it reduces the errors that he might make. He is less likely to miss items or to get wrong items.

PREPARING SHOP PAPERS

Figure 23-1 is a diagram of a large company's production control procedure. Notice all the shop directives it uses: part drawings, shop traveler orders, material requisitions, identification tags, tool notices, move tickets, inspection and scrap tickets, progress record copies, cost notices, labor tickets, and job envelopes. Some of these are single-copy directives and some are made in several copies.

Not everyone uses quite so many forms as does this company, but most companies do. Try, for example, to cut out one of the forms listed. How, without it, would you convey the information that it conveys?

ASSEMBLY ORDERS   Actually our diagram shows only the paper work for making *parts*. You don't start there, however; you start with assembly orders.

You make an assembly order by taking a master bill of materials and multiplying the quantities of parts needed to make one item by the number you want to make. You also write in the schedule date and the order number. In this text we call this list an "order bill of materials" although you find companies calling it an "assembly order," a "requirements list," a "parts list," and other names.

Order bills are authority to the assembly department to make the products. And, as previously stated, the arrangement of the parts listed may serve as an elementary kind of instruction telling how to put things together. Order bills are also requisitions. You send one copy to the finished goods stock room where it is overall authority to issue the parts listed.

Although an order bill is authority to issue parts, you don't issue parts to the assembly department right away because you make up the bill well ahead of time. Some of the parts will be regularly stocked parts but some are made or bought special for the order. Probably you should physically separate the parts that you can take from stock right away and put them in an accumulation stall reserved for the order. Then you know that you have them and that they won't be used for something else.

You will need an accumulation stall in any case because some parts are being made especially for the order. As the lots of especially made parts begin to arrive, you will need to take them to a temporary storage area reserved for that one order. The accumulation bin is such a temporary storage.

You can save extra handling if you provide these accumulation stalls right next to the assembly floor. Yet in spite of the prospective savings in handling costs, you'd better *not* put accumulation stalls there because expediters and assemblers will surely "rob" your supply and use parts for other orders. You'll be better off to keep the accumulations of parts for assembly orders inside a finished parts stock room.

SHORT LISTS   Some companies use "short" lists here. Earlier we mentioned using short lists in inventory control. Here we are interested in how they are used to speed up the production of items on the list. You would use such a short list like this: Start with a copy of the order bill of materials. Check off all the items you take out of stock and deliver to the accumulation

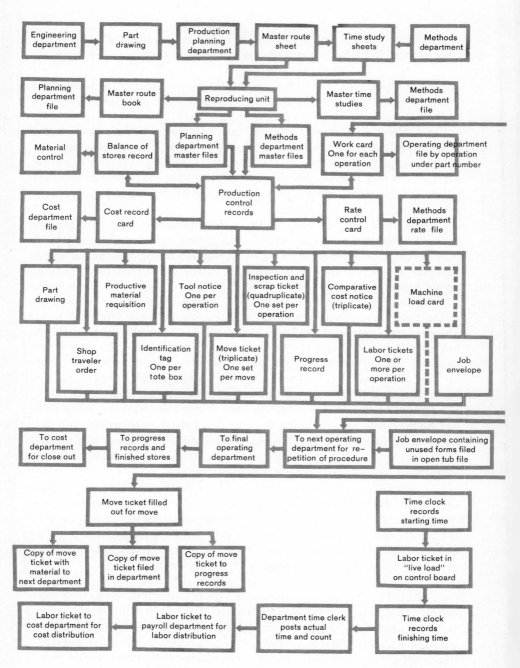

FIGURE 23-1   The production control system of a large com-

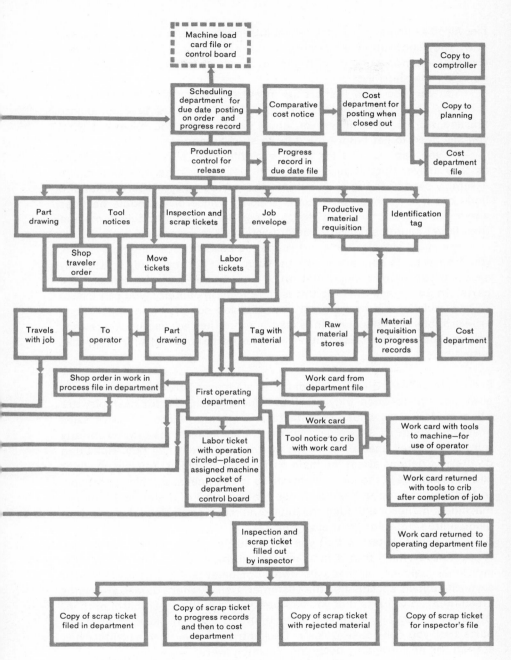

pany. Notice the many forms that need to be prepared.

bin. All other items are "short," meaning, in this case, you don't have them now. They show up in the "short" column. Of course if your production control system is working as it should, you have already ordered all the items on the short list.

You can use such a short list in either (or both) of two ways. Use it simply as a check sheet, checking off the items as they come into finished stores. At all times you know exactly what you have and what you still need to get before the date to start assembly.

Or you can give the list to an expediter who also checks off items as they arrive. But he does more than just that. Some time before the assembly start date, he goes out into the parts making departments and finds out how each order is coming along. Those on schedule he does nothing about. But he keeps after foremen on behind schedule items and tries to get all items delivered before you start to assemble.

You could also use the short list as the basis for ordering parts. If so, you'd have to, in January, make up such a list for, say, July's assembly orders because you'd need that much time to buy or make some of the parts. An advantage of doing this is that, even in January, you can assign an accumulation bin to the order. This lets you put the bin number on all orders to buy or make parts thus insuring that they will end up where they belong. You will have less trouble with losing parts or getting them into wrong bins.

SUPPLEMENTARY BILLS   Bills of material for assembled products are not always complete when they are first issued.. Machines, for example, are often made in lots whose manufacture is started before you have sales orders for them all. Customers buying complex machines often want any number of small special variations on the machines they buy. Not often do these variations affect the main parts of the machine. You can consider all the machines in the lot as identical up to the final assembly operations. In fact, you can, up to this point, use the same bill of materials for all the machines in the lot although the individual machines in the lot will end up being a little different from each other.

The bill of materials that you start with is actually only a partial bill. It covers everything that is the same for all the machines in the lot. Each individual machine will need its own supplementary bill of materials to cover the details specified by the customer. Usually these details are minor attachments and parts that you can put on late in the assembly operation. Often, too, they are standard parts that you keep in stock or they are parts that you can make quickly. Deciding on these after assembly has started will not ordinarily delay the assembly work.

Here's how this works at Cincinnati Milling Machine Co. As the assembly of a lot gets underway, the production control department tells sales what kinds of machines are coming through. Sales then allocates each machine to a specific sales order. A supplementary bill is then made up for each separate machine, listing the specific accessory parts needed for that order. CMM then withdraws stocked parts and makes up a shortage list for items it will have to make or buy. Purchase requisitions or parts manufacturing orders are then made out for the short items.

Occasionally, as we said earlier, you have to make up kits of repair parts of accessories to be sold with the product. Supplementary bills of material can authorize the putting together of such kits. In still other cases, bills are used for special packing materials, cartons, or containers. Foreign shipments invariably require special packing.

FIRST-TIME BILLS OF MATERIALS   You have to pay more attention to bills of material for first-time products than for old ones because they sometimes contain errors or bugs. Normally you catch these things and straighten them out the first time you make a product. The second and third time around you usually have reliable bills of materials.

PURCHASE REQUISITIONS   Whenever you need finished parts which you can't fill from stock, the stock record division originates a request for more. For purchased items, this request takes the form of a purchase "requisition." A purchase requistion asks the purchasing department to buy the item. Purchasing then sends a purchase order to your supplier company. For manufactured items, the request is first a manufacturing requisition and, after approval, a shop order.

REQUISITIONS FOR RAW MATERIALS
In job lot work using order control, you almost always issue materials only in exchange for separate materials requisitions, one for each kind of material. Finished parts, in contrast, you usually issue on the basis of a single bill of materials covering many items.

In form, a raw materials requisition is nearly always a small slip of paper or a tabulating card. Generally, each card authorizes the issue of a specified quantity of a single kind of material for use in making an order of one part. If you need the same materials for different orders, you make up separate requisitions for the materials for each order.

Raw materials requisitions differ from finished parts requisitions in another way. You get your information for calculating the quantity of raw materials needed from the route sheet rather than a bill of materials. Route sheets show the kind and quantity of raw materials needed per unit, whereas bills of materials do not.

Usually the production control department makes out raw materials requisitions well in advance of production. After making them out, it holds them until a short time before the materials are needed. Then they are sent directly to the stock room for filling.

Some companies don't do it this way. They turn the requisitions over to the foreman of the department where the first operation is to be performed and let him send them to the stock room when he needs the material. Still other companies, and they are few and usually small companies, let the foreman figure out what he needs and write out his own requisitions.

Raw materials are often received into the stock room measured in terms of one unit but are issued from it in terms of another. Wire, for example, is bought on a per pound basis but issued in feet. Liquids and powdered materials are bought by the container, drum, or pound and issued by the gallon. Pipe comes by the length and may be issued by the length, but it is used by the foot. You have to consider these matters when writing out requisitions. Not only should you figure requisition quantities in terms of units of use but you have to ask for enough extra footage to cover cutting waste.

Besides showing the information that you need in order to issue material, raw materials requisitions, since they serve other purposes too, show more information. First, you'll have to correct your stock record so you'll need the materials' identification number as well as the quantity issued.

Second, you need to know what you're going to use the material for so that you can charge its value to the order using it. Ordinarily the shop order number is information enough here. But if you are going to use the materials for repair or similar work, you can charge the costs to standing accounts. Third, just to place responsibility, it is well to have the clerk who issues the material initial it. And fourth, the requisition form must provide a space for pricing and cost extension. The stock record clerk gets the unit price from his permanent record for the material and writes it on the requisition so that the accounting department can figure the value of the material issued and adjust its accounts. Or, if you have computerized this work, the computer will make this calculation using data already on tapes.

Figure 23-2 is a requisition form used by J. I. Case. This requisition shows spaces for "rough size" and "finished size." Probably this means that stock-room employees cut pieces of material to be issued out of sheets

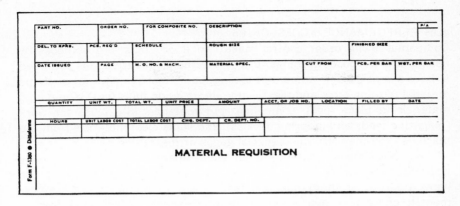

PART NO.		ORDER NO.	FOR COMPOSITE NO.	DESCRIPTION					P/A
DEL. TO RPRS.		PCS. REG'D	SCHEDULE	ROUGH SIZE			FINISHED SIZE		
DATE ISSUED		PAGE	M. O. NO. & MACH.	MATERIAL SPEC.		CUT FROM		PCS. PER BAR	WGT. PER BAR
QUANTITY	UNIT WT.	TOTAL WT.	UNIT PRICE	AMOUNT	ACCT. OR JOB NO.	LOCATION	FILLED BY	DATE	
HOURS	UNIT LABOR COST	TOTAL LABOR COST	CHG. DEPT.	CR. DEPT. NO.					

MATERIAL REQUISITION

Form F-1360 ● Dataforms

FIGURE 23-2   A material requisition card providing spaces for the essential information, including the unit price of the material issued and its total value. This type of requisition card fits computer input units and so can be used both to authorize the issue of materials and as a report of their issue. (J. I. Case Co.)

or lengths of material. You wouldn't have any use for such spaces on most requisitions. It is the same with the spaces on figure 23-2 for bonus, unit labor cost, and total labor cost. Normally you just issue material and would not use all of these spaces but you would if you had to do some work in the stock room on the material before you issued it.

You sometimes cut out requisitions altogether for C items. If you don't want to make them wholly free issue items, you can let the foreman requisition them one package at a time.

Occasionally you find "meal-ticket" requisitions. These are for valuable materials, say gold or silver in the jewelry industry or drugs in the pharmaceutical industry. A worker has a meal-ticket card allowing him to withdraw standard quantities of material. Every time the man withdraws the standard amount, the stock issue clerk punches out one hole on the card. The man is responsible for making a certain quantity of products from his issue of materials. And since the material is valuable, the man is given very little allowance for shrinkage.

CREDIT SLIPS   You'll need also to provide credit slips for materials returned to the stock room for credit. Not often do you have any leftover material but when you do it should go back for credit. Credit slips are like requisitions in form but are made of a colored paper to distinguish them and are never made out ahead because you try always not to withdraw more than you need.

JOB PERFORMANCE ACCESSORIES

Companies using order control make varied products and of necessity use general purpose machines. But to use them for varied jobs you need to have a considerable amount of tooling. Some tooling items cut or shape material (cutting tools and dies), some items guide tools (jigs), some hold materials in place (jigs), some help put materials into place for work (magazine feeds and indexing devices), and some eject materials from the machine. You may also need special gages or measuring devices.

All these tooling items (and for every operation) have to be ready when the time comes. If you use completely detailed route sheets, these items are listed on them making it easy for the production control department to check their availability. If the route sheets do not show the accessories, you assume that nothing unusual is required and so make no check.

MANUFACTURING ORDERS

We have already talked about making order assembly bills and have said that they are authority to assemble products as well as to provide the parts you need to make assembled products. We also said that final assembly was regarded, so far as production control is concerned, as just one big operation. You have to make out only one order to cover all the final assembly activities.

Subassemblies need their own shop orders sometimes and they are always needed if you make them in quantities not tied in directly with your present final assembly orders. You might also want to make out orders for subassemblies even if they are made especially for your present final assembly orders if they are common to several kinds of final assemblies or if you make them ahead and store them. But you don't need separate orders for subassemblies that the foreman of the assembly department makes up especially for one final assembly order and just before final assembly.

Parts are different. Each lot of parts has its own manufacturing order. So you have many parts orders to support one assembly order. But the big difference is that parts orders list, operation by operation, the things that you have to do to make the part. Orders for parts are both instructions and authorizations to perform operations.

Sometimes it helps to be able to tell from the order number just what kind of an order it is. Orders to make assembled products naturally become A orders. The A is a prefix to a regular number. Orders to make parts are often referred to as shop orders. Some companies use a prefix M for orders to make parts special for a particular assembly order. An S prefix means that the part being made is one that you stock. When you finish making S orders they go into stock. M orders you deliver to the assembly order accumulation bin.

Parts orders show the order number, the identification number and description of the part, the quantity to make, the wanted date, the material to be used, the list of operations, and the department in which you do each operation. Most companies also list the kind of machine required for an operation if it is not obvious from the name of the operation. Many companies list the time standard for each job and the total time it will take to process the lot through the operation. Sometimes machine accessories and tools needed for operations are also listed, mostly, though, as we said, only when they are special. Finally, if the parts are for a specific assembly order rather than for stock, you want to show the assembly order's number and its accumulation bin number.

VARIABLE MASTERS   You get all of this information that goes on shop orders from two sources. Most of it (everything that has to do with *how* to make the part) you get from master route sheets. Information relating to the specific order you put on "order" or "variable" masters (a "master" is a form from which you copy). Figure 23-3 shows how Convair division of General Dynamics puts the information on the two kinds of masters.

If you have your procedures computerized, making up shop orders is simple. The computer gets the records of operations and other master routing information from its tape of master routings. Then it gets the specific order information from a current file of specific order data that it keeps receiving for new jobs. By putting the two together the computer can make up and print out new shop orders.

A good many companies still don't do all of this work on computers, however. So to hold down order preparation costs they have to design their master bills of material and master route sheets so that they have certain blank columns for specific order information (such as order number, accumulation bin, dates, and quantities). When making order bills and shop orders, the master is laid down flat and then a "variable master" is laid over the open column parts. The variable master shows all of the information pertinent to the specific order. Then the whole thing is reproduced by Xerox, Thermofax, or some other copying process. After the new orders have been made the master bill or master route sheet goes back into the permanent file and the variable master can be discarded. We will take up this matter of forms duplication more in Chapter 32.

FORM 15895 !

SERIAL NO.	W. O. OR LOT NO.	LOT QUAN.	ADJUST.	SPARES	START 2-1-9	DUE 3-1-9	TOT. QUAN.	PART NUMBER 12-426-72
502645	1102	40			0-27	11-16	40	6-10982-4

PART NAME ANGLE	.750	PART NUMBER 6-10982-4			
MATERIAL BAC 1514-562 24 ST AL AL	SPECIFICATION	E. C. EFFECTIVE D/C C	CHG. LTR. A	TYPED 1-17	PAGE 1 OF 1
	SIZE 8.93" LENGTH		CL 1	ITEM IND. 6-19-5	PER SHIP 2

INSPEC.	QUAN.	OPER. NO.	OPERATION AND TOOL PLANNING	DEPT	MACH. CC	NO.	TOOL SYMBOL	TL CD	TL DEPT	SCHED.	SET UP TIME	UNIT TIME
		10	CUT TO SIZE (1 CUT)	10	11	CC10	PDSE				.23	.0070
		20	IDENTIFY	10	11	QZ					.03	.0010
										T	.26	.0080*
		25	ROCKWELL			TH						
		35	INSPECT & COUNT									
		40	ANODIZE	12	41						-	.0035
		45	INSPECT									
		50	1 GP	12	41						-	.0070
										T	-	.0110*
		55	INSPECT & COUNT									
			STOCK									

9   -TOOL & OPERATION SHOP ORDER ONCANNON FORM 15898

FIGURE 23-3 A master route sheet ready for duplication by the fluid duplicator process. The original sheet from which shop copies are run can serve as a master route sheet for a repeat order by attaching a new variable master to the duplicator so that it blocks off the old individual order information. (General Dynamics Corp.)

COPIES OF ORDERS   It takes quite a few copies of assembly orders and parts orders to fill all of the needs. Usually some of them are designed a little differently from others to allow for recording different information, so each department which gets a copy has to get its own copy. You could print in large type each department's name on its copy but some companies do even more to avoid confusion over which copy goes where: they use different colors of paper. Here is the list used in Sperry-Rand's Remington-Rand division: One copy (ecru) for central production control, copies (green) for each factory department that will work on the order, a traveler copy (buff) to go along with the order, a raw materials requisition copy (salmon), a parts requisition (blue), and a cost department notification (pink).

If you use decentralized control you need to send a copy to each department that will have to work on the product as well as one each to several record-keeping departments. Actually some factory departments need more than one copy. A foundry, for example, may need as many as five copies of foundry orders, one each for the foundry foreman, the casting weigh checker, the pattern storage department, to go with core boxes, and to stay in the planning department.

Department heads receiving copies of shop orders use them as authority and instructions to go ahead and process the order when it arrives in their departments. Production control probably also makes out job tickets (one for every operation) for the men doing production operations although this, if you used decentralized control, is not always done ahead by production control.

Copies of shop orders can do double duty or even triple duty. First, they tell foremen about future jobs. Second, they tell them what work to do and authorize them to do it. Third, they can become reports of what is done. You can have foremen write in the date when they do jobs on their copies of shop orders and return them to production control as reports of work done. All of the double- and triple-duty work that you can get one piece of paper to do saves money.

There is a catch to all this money saving, however. If an order form is to serve all these purposes, you have to put more information on it. You will need on it a rough schedule in the form of due dates or wanted dates for every operation. You might even want to put on the piecework rates for workers. Some companies which pay only by hourly rates show the labor grade for each job.

If you want to use the shop order form for reporting production, you have to design it with extra columns for reporting results of operations (when the operation was done and how many units passed inspection). Provide also columns for showing the actual time taken by workers and reasons for rejection of any items rejected by inspectors. Hardly ever will you need to provide instructions for truckers or materials movers, but if specific storage locations are to be used between operations, you might need to show them. You also might want a column where you can record the exact storage location in a general storage area where the trucker stored an order.

Companies using centralized production control do not always make up large numbers of copies of shop orders for all departments although they may. If they do, the copy that a foreman gets is information only. It is *not* an authorization nor is it the form on which to report work done. Instead the production control department's dispatch offices issue orders to the men to go ahead with operations and the dispatch offices hand out job tickets to the men and get them back when the work is done, and so uses them as reports of work done.

Having dispatch offices do this is a more certain way of getting it done than by leaving it up to foremen. On the other hand, the foreman may be able to plan his work better if he knows ahead what is coming.

With centralized control, using dispatch offices, you don't ordinarily send copies of shop orders to foremen. Of course you still need to make a "traveler" copy of the order. It goes along with the material from operation to operation, but it is only for identification and information to truckers and is not an authorization to perform operations.

JOB TICKETS   If you don't use copies of the shop order to direct and authorize production, you authorize production by means of individual job tickets. Job tickets are individual operation assignments. A shop order may list a dozen or more operations to be performed, but job tickets cover only one operation. Where there are a dozen or more operations to be performed, you make up a job ticket for each operation. These can all be prepared by the computer and so their preparation is relatively easy.

Job tickets are usually tabulating cards so that they can be processed by the computer after the operation is performed. Since job tickets cover the performance of single operations only, usually you make only one copy. On the card you put the description of the part, both by name and by code number, and the quantity to be made. Show also the order number. Unlike the shop orders, job tickets never show drawings and specification numbers. If you need drawings you send them along with the job ticket, or along with the material itself.

The J. I. Case card, shown in figure 23-4, provides for much more

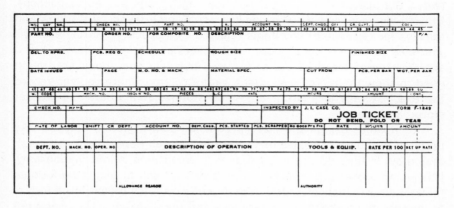

FIGURE 23-4   A job ticket prepared on a card so that it can be used with a computer. This kind of job ticket is usually prepared ahead of time by the computer for the production control department. (J. I. Case Co.)

ORDER NO.	PART NO.	QUANTITY	PART NO.		DRAWING NO.	
5685	4408-E	150	4408-E		LL-663	
DATE ISSUED	DATE WANTED	AUTHORIZED BY	PART NAME			
		HHS	Threaded Screw			
RAW MATERIAL				SIZE		
14/56 COH Steel				1-3/4" RD x 4-1/3		

						HOURS	QUAN. FIN.	EARNINGS
		PRODUCTIVE LABOR CARD						

OPER-ATION	DEPT.	MACHINE	DESCRIPTION OF OPERATION	RATE PER 100	SET-UP RATE	HOURS PER 100	OUT-PUT	DATE COMPLETED
3	3	16-L	Cut Thread	.95	.15	.6		

FIGURE 23-5 A job ticket prepared by the fluid duplicator process. The form pictured here contains all of the information that you normally need on a job ticket. (Ditto, Inc.)

information than you normally put on job tickets. Normally, information on the ticket includes a very short description of the work to be done, perhaps no more than the name of an operation, such as "grind ends." If you have to give any further instructions they go on the accompanying drawing. The drawing is also the proper place to tell the man what you want in the way of size, finish, and tolerance. If you need to give the man instructions beyond size, shape, and dimension, these go into a "specification" in which you write out whatever you can't describe on a drawing.

Most of the time the instructions that you provide for the man tell him what the product is to be like after he does his operation, not how he is to do the operation. You expect that the man can himself produce the results or that he can call on the foreman for help and added instructions if needed. Of course, normally the man really doesn't have much latitude, and isn't likely to go wrong, particularly when you remember that you specify even the tooling that he uses.

Job tickets have a space where the operator signs and reports his production. There should also be a space for the foreman to sign. This is a must if you use piecework because the production reported on the job ticket is used as the basis for determining the man's earnings. And you need to have the foreman verify the output the man claims. If you don't, some of your men will report more work than they did in order to make more money.

SPLITTING ORDERS

Assembly orders sometimes call for such large quantities of a product that it takes weeks to assemble the whole lot. Cincinnati Milling Machine Company, for example, sometimes issues assembly orders for twenty-five or fifty of one kind of milling machine. You can't assemble such lots in a day or two. They tie up a section of the assembly floor for perhaps weeks. A certain number of completed products are finished every week. Of course, you will have to have at least a small supply of all parts on hand before even one product can be finished. Probably you will make most of the parts in single lots and so will have finished the whole lot of each part before any assembly starts.

It is, however, often impractical to manufacture the parts in this way. Some parts are too big and would, if made in single lots ahead of assembly, take up far too much storage space. Besides that, you don't want to tie up so much money for the weeks of time that pass before the assembly lot is completed. Certain parts might even rust before they were used. Furthermore, if you process large orders for parts for one type of product in single lots, you would tie up too much of your parts-making machines for too long a time. You wouldn't have any machine time open, for long periods of time, in which to make parts for other products and that would hold up their assembly schedules. Also, if you tie up one machine with one big order, other orders can't get moved along and so other machines for later operations would be idle.

You get around all these difficulties by breaking up large orders for parts into several smaller orders. Issue these smaller orders on a time schedule that pays attention both to when you will need the parts and also to the machine time requirements to make parts for other assembly orders.

Sometimes you find that some one machine is a bottleneck and that you have to parcel out its time. You can, in such a case, process an order as one large order up to the bottleneck machine and then split it into suborders for this operation and for operations that follow. If you do this, production control will have to make up additional manufacturing orders to cover each section of the order through all operations concerned.

Sometimes you will need to rush at least a few of the parts on an order through to the assembly floor if it runs out before the parts order comes through. You can make the parts order into a "send-ahead" suborder and hurry it through. This costs double set-ups and wastes machine time, of course, so you don't do it unless it is absolutely necessary. Or if you have a short-run shop, you might process the send-ahead lot there on general purpose machines. This too is costly but so is holding up assembly. Notice that using the short-run shop reduces the remaining size of the order going through regular production. This will save you a little machine time on regular machines for the remaining operations.

COMBINING ORDERS

Sometimes you have parts, perhaps for different assemblies, that differ from each other in only minor detail. Often such items are exactly the same through most of their processing, with the difference turning up only in the last two or three operations. You can save considerable set-up cost and time by combining orders for such parts and running them through early operations as single large lots.

Imagine, for example, that you are making the little wheels in your automobile speedometer which record the miles you travel (this part of the speedometer is called an "odometer"). These little wheels can be finished with white numerals on a green background, or yellow numerals on a black background, or in other colors. You can process them all just as if they were identical (as, indeed, they are) up to the painting operation. It is the same with, say, nuts and bolts, which will have a different number of threads per inch. They are alike up to threading. Gear blanks are the same through casting, cleaning, rough grind and early machining operations, and up to cutting teeth. Frequently, too, where parts become lefts and rights, they are alike through early operations. So are parts that end up being a little larger or smaller, as for example screws of slightly different lengths.

Most of the opportunities to combine orders are in beginning operations before parts take on their different forms, although you may find an occasional opportunity to group orders through finishing operations such as painting, washing, degreasing, or electroplating.

You can't group orders all the way through production except, of course, for common parts. Sometimes the savings from grouping orders for beginning operations is great enough that you don't actually group orders at all. Instead you just make out orders for big lots processed up to the differentiating operation. Up to this point the parts are "blanks." Put them into stock and think of them more or less as raw materials to be used for making future orders of the items you make them into. Put them into stock under one raw material number, then withdraw them and make them into lefts and rights or longs and shorts under different numbers.

Production control should know your products well enough to see all the possibilities of grouping orders and should group them whenever possible. You ought, too, to give production control a little leeway here. Let it set quantities for grouped orders high enough to cover near future as well as present needs.

Once in a while you find orders combined for scheduling reasons. Suppose that you have two orders for the same part in process and the first one is delayed. Unless you need the lot badly, just hold it up a little longer until the second order catches up with it, then combine it with the second order and save setups by letting them go through the remaining operations as one big lot.

TOOL ORDERS

Ordinary tools in general use are usually issued to men in exchange for tool tags. The worker decides or finds out from the traveler copy of the shop order what tool he needs; then he goes to the toolroom and asks for it. Each worker has a few tool tags with his clock number on them. One of these he leaves with the toolroom attendant as a record of who has the tool. This common way of handling tools requires no written-out tool orders.

Most companies, however, find that, except for ordinary cutting tools and gages, it is better to use written tools requisitions. You can let the man on the job or the foreman make out written tool orders as they need tools but it is better not to make a practice of this. It costs less to make them out and they are more accurately made out if you prepare tool orders ahead in the production control department or by the computer.

MOVE ORDERS

You can't use conveyors very well with intermittent manufacturing because the orders all follow different paths through the plant. You move materials, therefore, by hand truck or power truck. This means that you have to tell the truckers what material to move and where to take it. Some companies use written "move orders" for this purpose. They make them out ahead, one for each move between operations, the same as with job tickets. Move orders tell what the material is, where it is now, and where it is to go. The form should have on it a space for the trucker to report that he has moved the material; then he can use this same sheet of paper to tell production control that it has been moved and where it is now located.

Many companies don't use prepared move orders and so have to direct truckers in other ways. Usually the traveler copy of the shop order that goes along with the material is enough, since it lists all jobs and shows the department in which each is to be done. Letting the traveler copy become the trucker's instructions does not, however, give you any report that the material has been moved.

Nor does it tell the trucker where to go to find orders ready to move. Probably you will need to set apart departmental pickup and receiving areas. Truckers pick up any orders set in the pickup area and deliver them to the receiving area of the next department. You might think that this would make extra handling but usually it doesn't. Rarely can truckers, even with written move orders, pick up and deliver orders directly from machine to machine. The temporary storage space at the machines is too small. It allows room for only one or two orders so most orders go from machine to temporary storage area to next department temporary storage to machine. You have to do most of the extra handling, written order or no.

MATERIAL IDENTIFICATION TAGS

In intermittent production, with so many different orders, you can't tell what materials are by looking at them. This is true whether they are raw materials, materials in process, or finished parts. A truckload of gears, for example, would obviously be gears, but what gears are they? For what are they to be used? Of what are they made? What further operations do they need? To what order do they apply? And you never learn by experience to identify very many of the parts just by looking at them because tomorrow you work on something different.

You need identification tags to tell you what things are. If you don't have material identified properly you find that your men sometimes mix up materials at the start and make parts out of wrong materials. You might have to throw away the whole order, or worse you might not find it out and go ahead and use the parts, finding out only then that they won't hold up. To avoid trouble you have to identify materials.

Usually, for items in process, all you need is a very short word description, such as "back plate" or "left bracket holder," and the part number and the order number. On the other hand, you have to put both name and numbers on a tag and so long as you have to have a tag on the material or its container, you can put more information on the tag if you want to. Almost always you end up using a tag on which you put the item name, part number, quantity, style, type, dimensions, size of finished product, the finished product's number, and maybe more information.

If the items are big and are not in containers, you might make a tag for every unit and fasten it on or you could even paint information on big items. Usually, though, you find either that marking will be removed or covered over in process, or it costs more to mark it than to fasten on a tag. Possibly, marking the item will mar it. In any case you usually use tags.

Some materials are in liquid, powder, or other unmarkable form. Then you have to put the identification on the container in which the material is stored. Usually small parts in tote pans are identified by tags. If an order fills several containers, you have to make out duplicate tags, one for each container. If the operations are not too numerous, you might also list them, since this helps keep track of things. Production control is responsible for making out the tags required.

The traveler copy of the shop order or route sheet is often put into the material container. This way it is both an identification and an instruction to truckers for moving the material from operation to operation. Travelers are often on letter-size sheets or cardboards, and are put in a transparent envelope to protect them from getting dirty and unusable. You use only one traveler per order though, not one for each tote pan as in the case of tags.

STUDY MATERIALS

23-1   Bill James, a young man in the finished parts stock room of the Radial Drill Company, has to gather together the parts from bins for assembly orders. He quickly discovered that the way the items were listed on the bill of materials bore no relationship to the arrangement of the storeroom. He decided to eliminate some of the work involved by making copies of all bills and rearranging the items in the order in which they were stored, so that he would not have to backtrack with his truck but could go right down his list.

Making up his own master bills was a lot of work the first time, but after several months he accumulated many of them. With his rearranged bills he could gather together parts for orders more quickly than before.

Should Bill be told not to work from bills of his own making? Why?

23-2   The Burdette Machine Company numbers shop orders for parts to replace other parts scrapped in process with the original order number plus a suffix of $\frac{1}{2}$.

What other methods might be used to indicate that the items on replacement orders really belong to another order? What notation, if any, should be put on the original order? On the parts stock card? On the parts short list? What difficulties might arise in changing all the records?

23-3   The B. R. Ragen Gas Engine Company manufactures a line of gas engines and compressors. Master schedules are used, and periodically, individual models are made in lots, depending on sales. The assembly floor can be used for four models of engine at any one time.

Many of the parts used are made in economic lots and carried in stock. Their replenishment is therefore independent of particular assembly orders. Parts short lists are not used. Instead, the items needed for an assembly order are checked against stocks and replenishment orders are issued for parts for which the stock is inadequate. The parts orders do not show the assembly order number and are delivered, upon completion, to the finished stock room. When assembly is to start, the finished goods stockman withdraws the parts needed and delivers them to the assembly floor.

What advantages, if any, does this method have compared to the use of materials short lists and the setting of parts manufacturing quantities in accord with assembly order needs? What disadvantages? In the method described above (which uses no accumulation bins), what would you do with items made or bought specially for an assembly order? Where would they be kept and what records and instructions would be needed to get them to the proper place on the assembly floor at the right time?

23-4 Set up a procedure for changing an order already in process from a regular into a rush order. Remember that not only should the identification that goes along with the order be changed but so should all papers having to do with undone work.

23-5 The Regency Equipment Company has been troubled with high inventories of castings for parts arising out of its experience with scrap during machining operations. The trouble seems to develop because small castings are made several to a mold, in some cases, on very small items, as many as 40 to a mold.

Sometimes an assembly order for 100 machines requires 100 of some small part whose casting is made with 40 to a mold. The reason for 40 cavity molds in this case is that the item used to be a large-volume item. Ordinarily, three molds producing 120 pieces will be made. Occasionally scrap losses exceed the extra 20 and it is necessary to make another mold, i.e., it is necessary to make 40 castings to get perhaps 1 or 2 more. In most cases, however, very few of the 120 pieces are lost, so as a general thing 15 to 18 extra pieces are processed. The problem is not confined to small parts. Sometimes 10 pieces are wanted of parts that come 8 to a mold, and again excess results.

Is it economical to make one or two molds? Can you suggest a way to keep the parts and the castings inventories at reasonable levels? (Remember that redesigning the molds to produce fewer castings per mold costs money for redesign and results in much higher foundry costs per casting.)

23-6 The Avon Parts Company has had only a poor system of tool crib operation and wants to improve upon it. Several problems are to be solved.

1 How can the tool crib be informed of the tool requirements for orders coming up so that it can have the tooling ready when the operation is to be performed?

2 How should standard tools such as drills, taps, and reamers be checked out? Also, if a standard tool checked out to an operator becomes part of a machine setup, how can the operator be cleared of responsibility for it at shift change time without creating a bottleneck at the tool crib window and without tearing down the setup?

3 Should there be "in" and "out" windows at the crib?

4 Should the tool crib handle oil rags, pulley belts, goggles, gloves, and smocks for operators?

5 How about having a grinding wheel in the toolroom so that crib operators can sharpen tools in their spare time?

Give your views on how to handle each of these situations; discuss the pros and cons of your answers and of other ways to handle these problems.

chapter twenty-four

DISPATCHING

We said earlier that production control ought to check up on purchased items, on tooling, on drawings, and on all the facilities which you will need but which you don't already have. This checking up is merely a matter of asking the other departments how the item is coming along, whether or not it will be in on time, and so on.

You don't need to rely on your memory about such things. Keep a "tickler" file. A tickler file is merely a file of reminders in order of date (the date when you want to check up, not the date that something has to be ready). It reminds you, ahead of time, that you'll need an item. Production control usually finds that tickler files pay off and result in its getting more items in on time.

After your check shows that an item is on hand, stamp the shop order to show it. Stamp it "tools available" or "materials available" or "drawings available." Then you will always know which orders are ready to send to the shop.

DEVELOPING A SENSE OF RESPONSIBILITY

Also, try to develop in everyone a sense of responsibility for meeting schedules. You don't want everyone thinking that this is only production control's job. Although it is true that production control sets schedules, it does not make products. They are made by the foreman's men. Particularly in decentralized control, it is good policy to try to get foremen as well as production controllers into thinking that meeting the schedule is everyone's responsibility.

If a foreman doesn't get his work out on schedule, the next foreman will have trouble getting his work done on time. In a way, therefore, each foreman is responsible, not only for schedules in his own department, but also for the schedule as a whole.

Link-Belt division of FMC Corporation has meetings with foremen to go over the progress of orders. Schedules are more likely to be met when foremen see how their work ties in with that of other foremen.

Signode Steel Strapping Company uses no progress reports but holds a twenty-minute meeting every week with every foreman about orders in his department. The production control supervisor goes over every order and its status with them. Particular attention is paid to "fall downs." Signode uses its own variation of a Sched-U-Graph control board so that behind-schedule orders stand out clearly.

Signode reports that these meetings are very effective and that foremen learn to meet their schedules lest they hold up another foreman. Signode's operations are such that foremen of departments normally doing final operations sometimes have to send jobs from their departments to those where previous operations are normally done. If they have been held up in the past by foremen of the early departments and consequently not had enough work for their men to do, they soon "make Christians" out of other foremen by intentionally holding them up when their chance comes.

ACTUAL DISPATCHING
Dispatching is the actual release of orders to producing departments. Here is where production control turns the job over to the factory. In a few companies this is the last production control activity for some time. Foremen see that the work is done and done in time to meet the schedule. Production control again becomes interested only when all of the operations on a job are supposed to be done.

Almost always, however, you'll need a tighter control than this. Rarely can you count on foremen to get out *all* of the orders with so little checking up. You had better get reports of work done operation by operation so that you will know every time that things aren't going along according to schedule.

Very often you'll find that even these "progress" reports aren't enough. You may want to dispatch jobs operation by operation and not all at once. This way production control has to redispatch the order for every operation. It costs more to do it this way but you get much closer control.

Perhaps you should think of getting reports of work done as being part of dispatching too. Certainly you don't want to pass out an order to perform operation 2 on a job and then find that the job isn't ready because operation 1 isn't finished. You need progress reports in order to pass out the next job at the right time.

FIRST OPERATION DISPATCHING   Instructions and authorizations to perform the first operation on orders are different from those for later operations. The foreman of the first department can start on an order whenever he wants, without having to wait until the job comes to him from another department. Instructions for first operations tell him not only what work to do but they tell him the kind and quantity of raw materials to use. Also, he gets (or makes out at this point) both a job ticket covering the work and a materials requisition authorizing the issue of the material.

As mentioned previously, production control usually prepares requisitions ahead and releases them together with the first operation authorization. Job shops and small companies often do not prepare the requisitions ahead, leaving it up to the foreman to figure out what he needs and to write his own requisitions. Other companies have production control prepare requisitions ahead and send them to the stock room where the material is gotten out, measured, cut to size if need be, and made ready for issue when the job is to be done. Stock-room employees then deliver the material to the jobs.

DISPATCHING—DECENTRALIZED CONTROL   In Chapter 4 we said that one kind of control was called centralized and another decentralized. Decentralized control leaves job assignments up to the foreman. Shop papers are, however, prepared in a central production control office. Decentralized control does not do away with the central office. It just shifts some of the work to the foreman.

Decentralized control seems to save a good bit of production control effort in that the production control department doesn't do as much detailed work as it does in centralized control. The saving is not all clear gain, though, because a good bit of what the production control department doesn't do, the foreman has to do.

In decentralized control, foremen need to set up their own departmental production control systems to keep track of orders coming in the future, orders waiting ready to work on, machine loads, and so on. The foreman's own staff will have to check the incoming order area frequently to see what orders have arrived, and will then have to change the job cards from the file of jobs coming to jobs waiting. They will have to keep some sort of file to tell him which jobs should go first and to check on tooling and write out tool requisitions for the tools needed. What all of this amounts to is that a secondary kind of dispatching takes place in the foreman's department.

In the decentralized method, you give the foreman of every department concerned a copy of each shop order. This copy tells him about jobs coming his way and lets him plan his department's work. You give him such shop order copies days or weeks before the jobs will come to him. Notice that the farther ahead you give him the orders, the less tight control the central production control department has over production. But you give the foreman more freedom to run his department efficiently. You run the risk, however, of foremen picking out the easy jobs and paying no attention to dates. The easy jobs come through ahead of schedule while hard jobs lag. You may have to hold back on giving foremen copies of orders very far ahead.

In a sense, you "dispatch" the orders the moment you give out these copies. You give the foreman authority to go ahead. But they are not yet "dispatched" in the sense that the job starts into production right away —they are dispatched only to the extent that the foreman has the right to go ahead when the order arrives in his department without any further authorization from production control.

This holds true even in the first department. You give the foreman of the first department his copy of shop orders days or weeks before he needs to start the job. He also gets the traveler copy of the shop order and the cellophane protector envelope containing the order "set" or order "package" of drawings, materials requizition, job tickets, move orders, inspection tickets, and tote pan identification tags if you have production control make all of these up ahead.

In most companies the central control staff prepares ahead job tickets and inspection tickets for all operations. These can be stapled together and put into the traveler envelope which also contains the traveler copy of the shop order and all drawings. When an operation is to be performed, the department dispatcher pulls off the job ticket for that operation and issues it to the operator. This traveler envelope containing all of the order's papers travels with the order from one department to the next, but once in a department it is usually held in the departmental dispatch office. When an operation is finished, the dispatcher stamps the date on the shop order traveler before sending it on to the next department.

The foreman, in decentralized control, checks up on tooling and has his men get tooling from the toolroom and also sees that it is returned. He also has full charge of which men are given which jobs and which jobs come first and which last—except that he has to get jobs done by the wanted dates.

Normally you get the most economical operation of his own department when you let the foreman decide on work sequences. For example, if one order on a turret lathe is made from 1-inch bar stock, you'll cut down the setup time for the next job if another job calling for 1-inch stock is put in next. Also, sometimes you get fussy jobs or jobs for fussy customers. Foremen can assign such jobs to their more careful workmen. Admittedly, production control's dispatchers should know about such things too but sometimes they don't know, whereas your foremen do.

Square D Company has its industrial engineering department watch for economical sequencing of jobs. Order sets don't go first to foremen. They go first to industrial engineering, where they are held and issued in groups only once a week. Just before releasing them IE goes over them and sets "series runs," meaning that it groups the orders and arranges them in sequence for most economical machine processing.

MEN SELECTING THEIR OWN JOBS   Sometimes when you use decentralized control, orders come into a department and are set down in a receiving area. When a man finishes a job, he comes over to the area, picks out a job he likes, and starts in on it. Under no circumstances should you let men do this. But when you leave it up to the foreman to assign work to his men (as you do in decentralized control), some foremen will be careless and allow this to happen.

What is the objection to this? The objection is that the men will select the easy jobs and the long runs. No one wants to do the fussy jobs, the jobs that they may have trouble with, and the short runs. Particularly if you pay the men on piecework, they will want the long runs because then they can get into the swing of production and make bigger bonuses. It is harder to make bonuses on short runs.

What happens, if you let the men select jobs, is that they pay no attention to schedules. Orders that you want first, if they are unwanted by the men, lie around and get behind schedule, while other orders, the choice ones, come through long before you need or want them.

DISPATCHING—CENTRALIZED CONTROL   In centralized control each specific operation is separately authorized by the production control department. You set up branch offices of the production control department (called "dispatch" offices) in each manufacturing department. You might need two or more men in dispatch offices in large departments. One man can dispatch, at the most, about twenty jobs per hour. Twenty jobs an hour ought to take care of from fifty to seventy-five operators.

Dispatch office employees work for the production control office—not for foremen. You prepare all shop papers centrally (as you do with decentralized control). Then instead of sending them to foremen, send them to your own dispatch offices. There they are held until a man is ready for a job; then the dispatcher gives him his order directly—bypassing the foreman. Actually you could, if you felt that this method did not leave the foreman with enough authority, let him have a voice in the specific assignments of jobs to men. You don't have to freeze him out.

You don't need, with centralized control, to make out very many copies of shop orders because foremen need none at all. Traveler copies of shop orders go with the jobs but they are just for general information or at most are used to direct truckers. Operations are authorized by individual job tickets passed out by the dispatcher. Many companies even use individual move tickets, passed out to truckers by the dispatcher, for all moves of jobs.

In centralized control very few production papers travel along with the job—just a traveler copy of the shop order, drawings, and tote pan identification tags. Job tickets, move orders, tool orders, and special drawings that apply to one operation only—all are sent directly to the dispatch office in the department where they will be used and do not go along with the job. Most of these papers passed out by the dispatcher are prepared ahead in the central office although you could let the dispatcher make them out himself. Cincinnati Milling Machine, for example, has its time checkers (who work for production control) write out job tickets at the job.

TOOL DISPATCHING   Some companies leave it up to the foreman, who usually leaves it up to the operator, to withdraw whatever tooling he needs from the toolroom. Others, Union Special for one, make it part of the dispatcher's job. He knows which jobs he wants to assign next and so he gets whatever tooling will be needed. After operations are performed, he also returns the tooling to the toolroom. This applies, of course, only to special tooling. Every operator has, permanently assigned, certain minor tools for which he is responsible.

One company has the trucker deliver orders to the receiving storage area of a department and then tell the tool crib man that the order is in the department. He writes down the exact storage location on his "transfer ticket" (move order) and takes it, with the inspection copy of the shop order, to the tool crib. Both the inspection copy of the shop order and the regular traveler copy go along with the order in a cellophane envelope.

When the crib man gets the report from the trucker, he gets out the tools shown on the shop order as needed for the next operation and puts them with the order in the storage area. Unusual tools, fixtures, machine attachments, gages, or models are requisitioned by the departmental tool crib from the central toolroom. Tools issued are charged to the order until their return. When they are all ready, the dispatcher is ready to assign the job. Not all companies have the tool crib man deliver tools to the order but many would expect him to "pull" the tools and have them on the tool crib counter ready to issue when the man asks for them.

Ordinarily, tool requisitions for special tools are made out ahead by the production control department. The tool requisitions go along with production orders to the dispatch office where they are held until shortly before the order is to start into production. Then the tool requisitions go to the tool crib, which will get the tools all ready to issue when the operator needs them.

PRODUCT DEPARTMENTS Some companies, making fairly standard assembled products, set up manufacturing departments that make certain parts, rather than do certain operations. Continuous production companies always do this as do some companies in intermittent production. Parts are made in such departments at A. B. Dick, Teletype, Burroughs, and many others. We talked about this kind of department earlier in Chapter 12.

Parts departments can be small or large but in either case there is no "dispatching" in the usual sense. The foreman has a file of routings for all parts that he works on. He sees that each parts lot goes through the operations on his operation list for the part without further instruction and without reporting to anyone when he finishes an operation on a lot.

All that you need to do is to give the foreman lists of parts and quantities wanted. Usually you make parts in lots rather than continuously and so use lot numbers. A. B. Dick uses traveler copies of shop orders which list the operations but the list is only for information. The foreman has authority to make parts and perform all the operations shown on his file copy route sheet. Once he gets an order number telling him what parts to make, he needs no individual operation authorizations. Teletype does not even list operations on its shop orders. Its lot number and traveler (without operation lists) are solely for identification.

NEW JOB DISPATCHING Whatever special tooling you need is used for the first time when you make the first item. It may or may not work. This is a common problem with forming dies and presses, particularly when you work with sheet metal. Normally about all that this means to you is that setup times will take a little longer, but it also means that you aren't sure that you'll get to run the job at all for the present. Once in a while there will be a real hold-up.

You can avoid some of the trouble by planning for a trial setup to see how the tooling fits. Most new tooling ought to be tried out before you plan to use it on an order. This sounds like a good idea and it is. But this makes a different problem for you. Suppose that it fits fine and works well. You don't want to waste the setup. So, quickly get the raw materials out and run the order right away. This means that you have to have the shop order all ready even though you hadn't expected to run the job just yet. When you make an item the second or third time you don't have so much uncertainty.

NONCONTROLLED OPERATIONS Nearly all companies have certain operations that they never "control." First, there are jobs such as washing, cleaning, degreasing, and deburring which always follow after certain regular operations. These operations are sometimes not even listed on route sheets. In a way, you think of them really as the tail end part of the previous operation.

Then there is inspection. You don't schedule a time for inspection when an inspector (a "roving" or "first-piece" inspector) goes around the department checking machine setups and inspecting the first pieces very carefully before telling the man to go ahead. The inspector also checks pieces from time to time while a lot is being processed. This, too, you never put on the route sheet as an operation.

If you use central inspection, after certain operations only, you might show it on the route sheet but ordinarily not. The only inspection that you normally list is the part's final inspection after it is made complete and before it goes into stock. Even the final departmental inspection that you often do before items leave each department is not a listed operation.

A third kind of noncontrolled operation is the heat-treating and electroplating kind. You list these as operations but always leave it up to the foreman to schedule work in his department. This is because there are so many possibilities of combining orders that are unlike in every way except that they need the same heat-treating, or carburizing, or plating. Also, the foreman can work out the most economical sequences of running jobs based on his knowledge of his processes, knowledge that production control doesn't have.

In all these kinds of noncontrolled operations, we don't really mean that they are not controlled, only that they are not controlled by production control. Someone, foremen or the chief inspector, has to see that the work is done.

Most noncontrolled operations are also non-job-ticket operations. You don't make out a job ticket covering the work that an inspector or an electroplater does. A floor inspector does not work on any one shop order for any extended period of time. He does a little on this job, then a little on that job. In heat treating and plating, the operator prepares several jobs for the process, then does other work while the process takes place. Finally he sends the several jobs on their way.

It is well, though, to control all individual controllable jobs with separate job tickets. Allis-Chalmers found that it pays to use job tickets for even a five-minute job. It sounds impossible that this should be economical because it costs at least 10 cents just to prepare a job ticket and costs more yet in wasted time for the operator to ring in and out on the job.

Here's why it pays to have job tickets even on little jobs. If you don't, the man will ring his other job cards wrongly. He'll ring out on his last job before he finishes it and in on his next job after he starts it. Then he'll claim that the non-job-ticket job took all the time in between. So a five-minute job shows on the record as taking fifteen or twenty minutes. For this the company has to pay the man the full time shown at his average hourly earnings. Allis-Chalmers found that it cost too much to police the card ringing and that it cost less to make up short-job job tickets than to handle the situation in any other way.

WORK OF THE CENTRAL OFFICE   No matter whether you use centralized or decentralized control, you have a central production control office. It does most of the production control work we have been talking about for several chapters. It "explodes" assembly orders, makes out all orders, sets all schedules, and makes out most of the other papers.

The central office also keeps track of the progress of jobs. It gets reports of work done and posts them onto "tracer" copies of shop orders so that its records are right up to the minute on where jobs are and which are on schedule and which are not.

As you can see no department except central production control can keep progress records because no one else has to do with the making of the finished item. Each factory department is concerned only with what is done in its own department.

This is why you'll find control "boards" (described in Chapter 25) showing the progress of orders mainly in central production control (if you find them used at all). You can keep the boards centrally yet dispatch jobs quickly because of instant communication via inter-com.

Sometimes, in decentralized control, you find control boards out in producing departments. If you do, they show machine loads, not the progress of orders. They can't show order progress because that requires showing work done in several departments.

DISPATCHING POLICIES
As we have said, dispatching means the releasing of orders to factory departments. But it means more than this. It also means handing out orders to the men who will perform the work.

When a large department, particularly a parts-making department, has thousands of orders in process and thousands more on hand waiting their turn, then deciding which orders go first becomes a big problem. And this is in spite of what we said earlier about using "wanted" operation start and "wanted" operation completion dates as priority guides. When faced with this situation, you need to have dispatching rules or policies covering job priorities.

There are actually many possible such dispatching policies or "queue disciplines" from which to choose. You could let the due date rule and issue orders by due date. This would seem to be the best policy. Yet if you are overloaded and can't meet all due dates then some orders have to wait and you have to make choices. This is where policies come in. (And, of course, if you don't precalculate individual operation due dates you have *only* these policies as guides.)

Among the possible policies are: first-come, first-served; first-come, first-served but with dollar value classes; shortest time for present operation; longest time for present operation; least slack (imminence of due date) in department; least slack in all remaining operations; least average slack time between remaining operations; longest wait up to now (longest wait in the queue); greatest cost penalty if due date is missed; most remaining operations; fewest remaining operations, most work remaining; least work remaining; later passage through overloaded work centers; and later passage through presently idle work centers. Other factors which you sometimes would want to consider are: minimizing setup times for following jobs (some jobs can use half of another job's setup, whereas other jobs can't); the type of customer (you may want to give high priority to the military or to other large customers); or the profitability of the item. And whatever priority rule you adopt for general use, it needs to be supplemented by a policy of "hot jobs first."

Operations researchers, both in industry and in universities, have carried through many simulations on computers to see which policies are best to follow.[1] They regard jobs waiting to be done as being in a series of waiting line queues, one queue ahead of each machine or machine group. Then, on a computer, they apply different dispatching rules on a simulated basis to see which rules get the work through the shop the best, considering the starting backlogs, the expected arrival rates of new jobs, and the expected machine output. Not surprisingly, they have concluded that no one policy is superior to all others. It appears that different factors are important in different circumstances so that no one rule is clearly superior to all others. If any one rule is best it seems to be to always do the shortest jobs first. This policy results in the fewest delayed orders.

The first-come, first-served policy, for example, has the advantage of simplicity, yet this isn't a sufficient recommendation for its exclusive use.

[1] See J. M. Moore and R. C. Wilson, "A Review of Simulation Research in Job Shop Scheduling," *Production & Inventory Management*, Journal of the American Production and Inventory Control Society, January, 1967, pp. 1–10. This article lists 27 references to other articles on this subject. See also William S. Gore, Jr., "Heuristics in Job Shop Scheduling," *Management Science*, vol. 13, no., 3, November, 1966, pp. 167–190; and J. William Gavett, "Three Heuristic Rules for Sequencing Jobs to a Single Production Facility," *Management Science*, vol. 11, no. 8, June, 1965, pp. B166–B176.

A newly arrived job with a long list of further operations might well need to go ahead of another job already on hand which has only one more operation to go. Nor should a big first-come job be allowed to delay many later arriving short jobs.

Nor will the exclusive use of the due date always be wisest. An order with a due date of March 10 and with no other following operations might better give way to another order with a due date of March 14, but with many operations to follow.

Still a different policy, aimed at reducing the investment in inventory, is to give priority to high-dollar-value jobs. Obviously, this will reduce the investment but low-value orders need to be finished too. Also, if several low-value orders are held up while giving way to one high-value order, the investment may not be reduced at all. The sum of the value of the small orders may exceed that of the one big order.

One main reason why companies are interested in dispatching rules is that they would like to turn all of this scheduling and dispatching over to a computer. And computers need rules. Simulation techniques are the only ways to find out which rules are best so this is why the operations researchers have used simulation here. But, as we said, most companies have found that since no one rule is always the best, computers have not wholly solved the difficulties. In some situations, they have, however, improved the performance by following rules found by simulation to be better than other rules.

At Hughes Aircraft, for example, as a result of simulation, each foreman now gets weekly lists telling him the priority of jobs in his department and of those he will get during the week.[2] This lets foremen get out tools and be ready to move hot jobs along fast.

Hughes first checks the manpower requirements of loads. Then after it is sure that the load can be handled, it uses priority according to the average slack time between operations. Jobs with the least average slack time go first. If average slack time is equal on two jobs, then the one with the most remaining operations goes first. Hot orders get a special first priority code.

This is in a department with 1,000 machines grouped into 120 functional work centers (milling, drilling, etc.) and 400 men. There are 2,000 to 3,000 orders in the shop all of the time and their average of seven operations per order requires an average shop cycle time of three to four weeks.

Now that the computer sets priorities, expediting has been reduced 60 per cent; the cycle time has been cut one week with a consequent reduc-

[2] Reported in Michael H. Bulkin, John L. Colley, and Harry W. Steinhoff, Jr., "Load Forecasting, Priority Sequencing, and Simulation in a Job Lot Control System," *Management Science*, October, 1966, vol. 13, no. 2, pp. B29–B51.

tion in inventory in process. Machine idle time has been reduced and jobs finished on time are up 10 per cent. Another plus value is that the foreman's job has been enlarged.

ASSEMBLING NONSTANDARD PRODUCTS

So far as production control is concerned, assembly, the final stage of production for assembled products, is simple compared to the problems it has getting parts made. You don't make out written directions for each assembler and you don't check up on every little thing done. Assembly, so far as production control is concerned, is just one, or at most a few, big operation, not a hundred little operations. Actually, assembly is hundreds of little operations but they don't separately concern production control.

Be sure, though, that parts are ready. You have very little time cushion here. This is in contrast with the time that it takes to make parts. When you make parts, your manufacturing cycle usually has some fat in it. Getting behind schedule is usually not serious because you just cut out some of the dead time. Not so when you get to assembly. Parts not ready delay assembly and most of the time you can't make it up. You end up not finishing the assembly work on schedule and this makes you miss delivery promise dates.

What do you do, though, if the time comes to deliver parts to assembly when they aren't all ready? Probably you'll deliver the parts you have and let assembly start, meanwhile moving heaven and earth to get the late parts before assembly is held up.

Even though production control regards assembly as one large chunk of undifferentiated work, it is still a good idea to check up on its progress. Maybe you won't want to go so far as to get regular progress reports because it is hard to tell how far along you are on assembling a product like, say, a diesel powered ditchdigger. It is a little like building a house: you can look right at it and still not know whether it is 45 or 60 per cent finished. Of course, if you are assembling a half-dozen ditchdiggers, or type A milling machines, you'd want a count of those finished. But for partly done assemblies, better get an estimate from the foremen as to how complete they are. Quite often the last few parts take more than their proportionate share of time to assemble.

We have said earlier that the order bill of materials sent to the assembly department is its authority to go ahead. And we have discussed the need for production control's getting all the parts and subassemblies ready either ahead or at least before they will be needed at the assembly floor.

When you assemble finished products by lots you will probably use one part of the assembly department (or "erection floor") for the order. If it is a small part, you may assemble one product at a time, finishing one before starting the next. More likely you will have enough space to allow you to put two or three together at the same time.

If so, you get a choice of how to do it. Suppose that you have enough space for three at a time. You can use space A for one assembly, space B for another, and space C for the third. Each product is assembled complete where it starts. The method is just the same as when you have room for only one at a time.

PROGRESSIVE ASSEMBLY   Having three spaces, however, lets you use "progressive" assembly. Progressive assembly is most common in companies making standard products in considerable quantity but you can use this method sometime when making more varied products.

Here's how you could use progressive assembly: Divide the whole assembly job into three more or less equal parts. Do the first stage of assembly on one product in space A. Then move it to space B and do the next stage. While this is going on at space B, a second product is getting first stage assembly at space A. When product one finishes its second stage, it goes on to space C for the last of its assembly. At the same time the second product moves from space A to B for its second stage assembly work and a third product starts in at space A. The next step occurs when the first product finishes stage C and moves to the shipping room (assuming that testing it is part of stage C work). The second product moves to space C, the third moves to B, and the fourth starts in at A. This goes on until all products are assembled. As you continue to divide the operation so that each assembler has only a single operation, or just a few simple operations, the process begins to approximate a continuous assembly flow process such as is used in automotive plants.

Assembling this way lets you keep specialized groups or teams of men busy on certain jobs. It also lets you use special equipment better and you can keep it at one location. You can also use scaffolds or assembly jigs that stay put at certain work areas. You don't have to move them around so much.

Having different work areas for different stages of assembly also makes it easier to bring in parts. If you assemble all in one area, you can bring all the parts there ahead and let some of them lie around a good while until they are put into the product. You bring enough of every part to make one product. Later you bring parts for the next product and so on.

You do the same for work areas B and C. Not only do stock clerks have to make up separate parts sets for each unit of product but the men in the different areas help themselves to parts from parts sets of other areas.

This kind of "robbing" of parts sets is sure to occur. You never know where you stand on parts and assemblies when they are held up waiting for parts they are supposed to have already.

Robbery isn't the only danger in having parts lying around. They almost always get kicked and bumped and sometimes run over by trucks. And of course they aren't well protected and so are more likely to rust and deteriorate.

You can cut out part of the trouble by having stock clerks bring out to the assembly floor only what the men need at first, then bring out the parts that they need next, and so on. This means a good bit of checking back and forth between stores and assembly. Or, if you are assembling several of the same product at once, you can go to progressive assembly. Progressive assembly, with different areas for different stages, doesn't solve these problems wholly, but it helps. You cut down the work of stock clerks when they can take several parts sets for stage 1 assembly to area A and parts sets for stage 2 assembly to area B.

You also cut down on robbery because only one crew of workers assembles certain parts. If these men use parts intended for one product for another, they know it and can tell your stockmen that they are short of those parts. You also cut down the waste from extra parts kicking around because you have only a fraction of the total variety at each area.

Progressive assembly makes some problems, however. Probably you will have to assemble the product in some kind of carrying cradle or on some kind of wheeled rack because partly assembled products have to be moved. If you do assemble on a wheeled cradle or rack, you can move the product by towing it to the next area or by overhead crane.

Usually parts of assembled products have to be put together in a certain order. This is pretty well set for products that you have made before. But you ought to give the assembly department foreman some leeway on new products. Also, try to keep as much minor assembly away from final assembly as possible. Subassembling them together first pays off. You won't even have to use up scarce assembly floor space for minor subassemblies. Put them together in side bays near the assembly floor.

If the order is for a very complex product and only one is ordered, the progress of assembly work must be estimated from time to time so it can be compared to the expected progress. If, however, the order is for a number of the same kind of products, a report of completion is made to production control as each one is finished. When the whole order is completed, the shop order is marked completed and returned to production control. This method of reporting is sometimes varied by having the final inspector make out the completion report.

Assembly work is more flexible in one way than is parts making. Suppose that you get behind schedule and want to get caught up. Quite often you can do it by putting more men on the job—just so long as they don't get in each other's way. But not always can you do this. You can get only about so many men into an airplane cockpit at one time so there is a limit. There is also the question of the new men's skill and the availability of tools. But since most assembly work is relatively simple and the tools are hand tools, you can sometimes get out of the "bind" that you are in just by putting on more men.

ASSEMBLING SEMISTANDARD PRODUCTS

We said earlier that semistandard products can have identical bills of material for most of the parts. On the assembly floor you can treat these products as being the same up until the final tasks where you put on different accessories. You can use progressive assembly to advantage because you get to assemble a good many products that are alike most of the way through assembly. You can also use subassemblies better and for the same reasons.

SUBASSEMBLIES

Following the axiom—keep as much assembly work away from final assembly as possible—you want to subassemble even in job lot assembly. You'll end up doing less subassembling than in higher volume work because you won't see as many opportunities and you won't be able to set up special facilities to speed up subassembling. Also, since each job is a little different, you subassemble less because you can't tell just how a subassembly might fit into the final assembly. It is safe to put more parts on at final assembly; then you know that they fit in.

But to the extent that you can subassemble, you should do it. Engineers and planners will have to figure out the possibilities. Production control is affected only in schedule making. It must figure out when subassemblies must be complete, when their assembly must start, and when to finish parts for them.

If, however, you can use "basics," it is another matter. Basics, or standard subassemblies, are assembled either to stock or to a forecast of their needs in the several products using them. As far as final assembly is concerned, a basic is just the same as a standard part. You don't think of its assembly as part of assembling the end product.

STUDY MATERIALS

24-1   Why not simplify the matter of dispatching down to "do the shortest job first"? Would this result in the fewest number of delayed orders? What would happen to long orders? Is this a good policy to adopt?

24-2   In the case described in this chapter concerning the use of job tickets for short operations, would you suggest the same procedure if the workers were paid on a day rate basis instead of on a piece rate basis? What alternative scheduling or dispatching procedures might you use if you had a large number of small jobs?

24-3   Here is a list of operations needed to make a part:

1	Rough cut and thread	7	Degrease
2	Finish machining	8	Deburr
3	Drill cross holes	9	Inspect
4	Degrease	10	Cadmium plate
5	Deburr	11	Final inspect
6	Mill		

1   Is this operation list satisfactory from a production control point of view? If not, what would you add or subtract? Why?

2   Operation 3 could be performed later in the sequence. Should you show this on the list? Should you insist that the shop follow the sequence listed? What if the shop wants to degrease and deburr only once after all machining, should the shop be allowed to change on its own?

3   If in question 1 you said that the machines for the operations should be listed, what is your position if the shop wants to use a different machine?

24-4   In the St. Louis Milling Machine Company, the shop order number is used as a "sequence" number. That is, it serves as a priority numbering system. Parts manufacturing orders are not scheduled by the production control department in any other way. Each foreman is required to process the order having the lowest number ahead of other orders or justify his failure to do so on a daily report. This method is supposed to operate almost automatically to get first orders out first.

Starting with the above procedure, devise modifications to take care of: (1) rush orders for parts, (2) getting a part requiring many operations finished by the same date as a part requiring few operations.

If, in the above situation, you leave gaps in your order numbering system to use for rush orders, what happens to your expected completion dates for other orders when you use your spare numbers for rush orders?

24-5   Write out instructions for operating dispatch offices located in factory departments in the Hammand-Western Company. Specifically tell how to mark orders, or to file them, or to get more information to handle the following situations, also what to do when the situation is either corrected or changed to something else.

Your instructions should tell the dispatcher how to show which orders are now in process and on what machines, which are waiting to be moved, and which are waiting to be inspected. Also show where all orders waiting are and why they are waiting. (Is it just not yet their turn? Or is it a scheduling matter, and you just don't want to work on them yet? Are they held up for lack of tooling? Is the machine down? Are rush orders holding other orders back? Is an order waiting for rejects to be reworked and returned to the lot? Is the lot not all there? Is there no machine operator? Are the tags lost? Are the drawings lost?) Be able to answer questions too about machines: Is an idle machine idle because there is no work for it? Also how will you show rush orders?

You may think also of other things that the dispatcher has to contend with. Tell him how to handle his job.

24-6   The general manager of the Raydall Stove Company made it clear to the production control manager that any sales department demands for rush orders to give service to customers should be taken care of as requested if at all possible. The sales department has since made repeated requests for rush orders of certain accessory apparatus. In carrying out the policy laid down by the general manager, the production control department has been scheduling successive operations on these orders on an overlapping basis, i.e., as soon as a few pieces of product are through operation 1, they are taken to the next workplace and operation 2 is performed even though most of the order has not yet passed through operation 1. Operation 3 is then performed on some of the items as soon as a few units are ready. This process was continued throughout all operations.

The method was quite effective in getting the selected orders out quickly. The process of other orders was interfered with, but their delay was not serious. A more serious problem, however, was the way fast operations were being performed. If operation 3 was a fast operation it was performed on all items ready, but it soon exhausted the supply of parts on which the preceding operation had been finished. The setup was torn down and the machine used for other orders. When some more items on the rush order were ready, it was reset up for the job and run until that supply was exhausted. Sometimes three separate setups were made for each of several of the operations needed to produce a rush order. The policy of giving rush orders top priority in this way resulted in considerably greater setup costs.

Should the production control manager do anything besides carry out the policy? How much concern should and do sales departments generally have for such matters? Will the problem be changed any if the setups are charged to the orders instead of to overhead accounts?

chapter twenty-five

KEEPING PRODUCTION MOVING

PROGRESS REPORTS

Making up orders and passing them out are the easiest parts of production control. Other aspects of the job would be as easy if only the plant would turn out the work as you planned it. On the whole, the plant does carry out the plans, but not in exact detail and this makes trouble.

So, first, your production control system has to provide reports of what *is* done so that you can see where you stand. Or better yet, get reports of jobs *not* done as they were planned. Have foremen send you "behind schedule notices." You can cut out a good many reports just by assuming that no news is good news. This is often referred to as "management by exception."

But whether you use progress reports or lack of progress reports, or both, you need to know what is going on because when things don't go right you have to change orders and schedules. If an order is held up halfway through production, you'll have to change the schedules you made for its remaining operations. Besides that, other orders can now be made sooner so you'll have to change their schedules too.

The dispatch offices are the eyes and ears of centralized production control. Usually we think of their work as passing out orders but they also find out when work is done and when it is not done. Dispatchers get job information in several ways: through returned job tickets, move orders, inspection reports, what they see going on, and what foremen, machine operators, truckers, and inspectors tell them. Dispatchers send in to the central office all of the reports that they get.

Move orders are a source of information as much as are job tickets. You pass them out to truckers, who, after moving the material, sign and return them to the dispatch office. The move orders now tell that the material has been moved and where it is located. Usually it is also a good idea to have included the date that it was moved.

If you don't use move orders you have to find out that material has been moved in other ways. You can have truckers turn in a written memo or have them report all material moves on a blackboard. Some companies just depend on the truckers telling them that they have moved certain orders. Some have truckers turn in, at the close of the day, lists of all materials moved. Still another way is just to assume that material will be moved within a reasonable time after the machine operator finishes his operation. Some of these methods are a little vague and don't keep you right up to date but they are less costly than making out move orders and, unless you have to have exact scheduling, they may work satisfactorily.

Inspection and scrap reports are other kinds of progress reports but of course you don't get them after very many operations because you don't inspect very often. Inspection may be merely routine counting, or it may amount to so much that it is much like a regular operation. If it is, you'll probably plan for it, put it on the list of operations, and make out an inspection ticket. This inspection ticket is not a job ticket—it is not to report the inspector's time. Instead, it is a report of how many items pass, how many are rejected, and why they are rejected. The prepared ticket of course doesn't show these quantities but it shows everything about the order—its number, and so on. All that the inspector does is fill in the quantities and send the various copies of the inspection ticket to production control, the chief inspector, foreman, and perhaps others.

Tags identifying rejected materials are usually not prepared ahead by

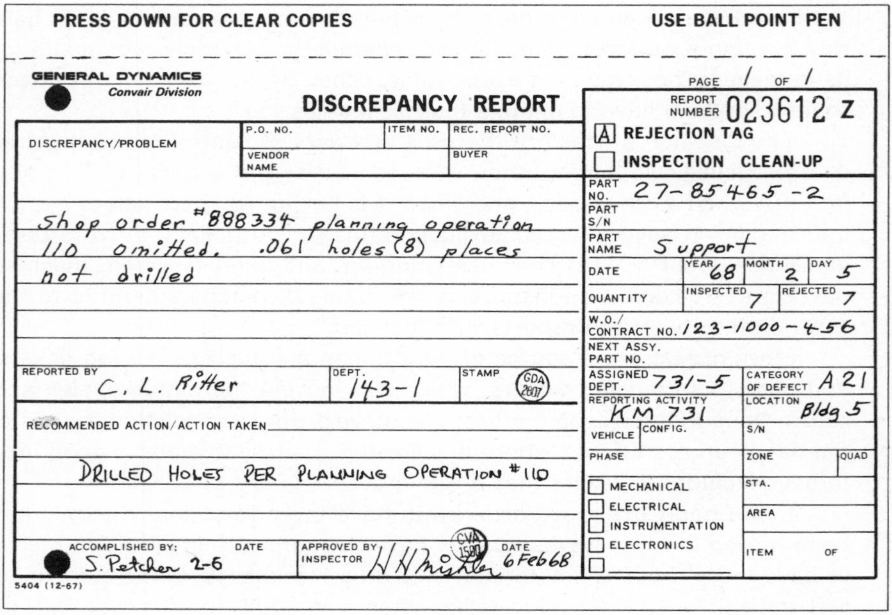

PRESS DOWN FOR CLEAR COPIES USE BALL POINT PEN

GENERAL DYNAMICS
Convair Division

DISCREPANCY REPORT

PAGE 1 OF 1
REPORT NUMBER 023612 Z
[X] REJECTION TAG
[ ] INSPECTION CLEAN-UP

DISCREPANCY/PROBLEM
P.O. NO. | ITEM NO. | REC. REPORT NO.
VENDOR NAME | BUYER

Shop order #888334 planning operation 110 omitted. .061 holes (8) places not drilled

PART NO. 27-85465-2
PART S/N
PART NAME Support
DATE YEAR 68 MONTH 2 DAY 5
QUANTITY INSPECTED 7 REJECTED 7
W.O./CONTRACT NO. 123-1000-456
NEXT ASSY. PART NO.
ASSIGNED DEPT. 731-5 CATEGORY OF DEFECT A21
REPORTING ACTIVITY KM 731 LOCATION Bldg 5
VEHICLE CONFIG. S/N
PHASE ZONE QUAD
STA.
AREA
ITEM OF
[ ] MECHANICAL
[ ] ELECTRICAL
[ ] INSTRUMENTATION
[ ] ELECTRONICS
[ ]

REPORTED BY C. L. Ritter DEPT. 143-1 STAMP GDA 2607

RECOMMENDED ACTION/ACTION TAKEN
DRILLED HOLES PER PLANNING OPERATION #110

ACCOMPLISHED BY: S. Petcher DATE 2-6
APPROVED BY INSPECTOR H H Mishler DATE 6 Feb 68

5404 (12-67)

FIGURE 25-1 A rejection slip describing the reason for rejection and indicating the department responsible as well as the disposition of the rejected material. (General Dynamics Corp.)

FIGURE 25-2   A maintenance worker calling in to the central officer using a telecontrol direct line. Notice the little control box into which he has plugged his phone.

production control. After all, you might have no rejects. The inspector makes out reject identification tags. It is the same with scrap tags and scrap reports covering nonrepairable rejects. These you need in at least triplicate for the various departments. Be sure not only to tag rejects and scrap but to set them aside out of the main flow of work.

Besides the three kinds of written reports (operation tickets, move tickets, and inspection reports), foremen should tell you right away if anything unusual turns up. As long as all goes well, you don't hear from them. But if anything goes wrong, such as an unusual amount of scrap, foremen or inspectors should tell you right away. Unfortunately, you can't count on them telling you in every case but verbal reports are a fourth kind of report of work done.

One Chicago company uses a "dial" system for reporting work done. Dials, similar to telephone dials, are spaced around the plant. When a man gets an order he "dials in" to central production control, giving the order number and operation. When he finishes his operation, he "dials out." This method keeps progress reports in central production control (although it is a decentralized control system) right up to the minute.

Some companies, too, have reporting boxes located at various places in the plant. When an operator starts his job, he puts the job card, which is a prepunched tabulating card, into the reporting box which is electrically connected with the central office. This reports his starting the job to the office. During the operation he keeps the card and then reports in again in this same way when he has finished the job.

Big important key machines are sometimes hooked into the central office in such a way that their production is recorded there on counters. So long as the machines operate, the counters show the output. But if the machines stop, so do the counters and red lights go on. Foremen are quickly sent to the trouble spot to try to clear it up.

Yet, in spite of what we have said at the start of this chapter about the need for progress reports, they can sometimes be done without. If work usually does come through of its own accord and if you do not have very many hold-ups, it may be less costly to endure the few interferences that arise rather than to do all of the reporting needed for control.

At Cincinnati Milling Machine Company no report is made to production control of any individual operation being completed on parts orders. The only report is made when the order is completely finished. Expediters check the location of all orders shortly before they are supposed to be finished. If they find any orders lagging, they push them through. One official says that the system works well with a minimum of paper work because after all what goes into one end of the department has to come out the other end or things will pile up.

PROGRESS REPORTS FOR ASSEMBLY

Progress reports for assembly are usually rather sketchy except as they may be considered reports of products completed. For big items which take a long time, you can, of course, get a report of direct labor hours already put in. Ordinarily this is fairly good as an indication of progress. If half of the expected hours have been put in, the project is probably about half done. You can supplement hours reports by asking the assembly foreman for his estimate of the project's per cent completion.

This method, using man-hours put in as a progress report, works fairly well too for varied assembled products. As long as man-hours are going into assembling varied products, and as long as your men and foremen operate as usual, you are making progress toward completing the products.

In decentralized control you don't get as good nor as many reports of work done as you do with centralized control. Usually, for example, no one tells you that a job has been moved. On the other hand, even in decentralized control, you ought to get some kind of progress report. One way to get it is to have the foreman of each department report it on his copy of the shop order. He then sends it to production control as his report of having done the operation. Or you can have the foreman make out a list every day of jobs completed and moved out of his department.

USE OF PROGRESS REPORTS

Just what do you do with progress reports after you get them? First, and this is their main use, you use them to aid in controlling production. You compare the work done with what was supposed to be done. You can compare just by looking at the report and at the schedule. Wherever what is done and what should have been done differ, you have to decide what to do. Notice, though, that you have to make a comparison between what happened and what was supposed to happen. Progress reports by themselves furnish the basis for comparing but they do not themselves tell you whether or not you are in trouble.

Probably you'll want to post onto your central office copies of shop orders the date and quantity of items that passed inspection. Or if you use control boards, you change them so that they are up to date.

Some of the reports you get tell you that certain jobs are delayed. Then what? First, you have to hold up all plans for future operations on the held-up orders. Also, change the schedules for other orders so that they can be pushed up into the place of held-up orders. Next, start in getting to the seat of the trouble, the cause for the delay. Your report of a hold-up should tell you its cause but it may merely say, "tooling not ready," or "machine broken down," or "man absent," or give some other reason.

A word of caution about investigating why something wasn't done the way originally planned. It pays to let most minor discrepancies go uninvestigated. As we said previously, if you have 195 pieces when your card says that you have 200, don't spend too much time finding out why. Investigating costs more than the value of what you'll find. After all, the discrepancy already lies in the past and you have to live with its results. Put most of your energy on what to do from here on, not on past events.

Not often can the production control department actually remove the cause of trouble, but it can and should tell whoever is responsible for it and should ask for the date that it will be fixed up. Production control should also make reports on delays to higher management so that real pressure will be brought to bear to get rid of the cause for the delay.

Actually your reports of work done (and not done) don't automatically tell you the reasons for differences from schedule unless you make reporting reasons part of your system. All that you get is a report of work done or perhaps a notice of a hold-up if an order is held up. But if an operation is done before you wanted it, or after you wanted it, or the inspector rejected too many items, your report tells you none of these things directly. You just get a report of what was done. You, in production control, have to figure out why the schedule was not met, and you have to see whether the deviation will make you change other schedules or not.

At the moment we are not so much interested in your having to make changes as we are in the fact that when the job is done but not exactly according to schedule, *you*, in production control, have to be aware that something was wrong. And *you* have to find out why. And *you* have to push someone else to get rid of the condition that caused the deviation so that it won't happen again.

You ought to require foremen to notice deviations and to tell you why they happened. Have them make out "trouble" reports covering all serious "fall downs" on the schedule. Production control, in turn, can send summaries of all fall downs to the general manager. He will then know what is going on and is the one who can put real pressure on fixing up trouble spots.

A second use of progress reports is to supply information on the status of orders so that you can answer inquiries from the sale department. In addition, if production is falling short of schedule, production control can tell the sales department. It, in turn, can tell the customer.

A third use of progress reports is for future job estimating. They give you a record of how long operations take, how much scrap to expect, and so on. This helps you do a better job of cost estimating in the future.

Fourth, progress report forms themselves are often passed on to the cost accounting department by production control. Cost records should be a by-product of good production control. Cost accounting needs to find out what materials and labor expenses to charge to shop orders. Job tickets and materials requisitions provide this information. Years ago the mere passing around of the forms themselves made some problems. Materials requisitions usually went directly from the storeroom to cost accounting. But job tickets came in first to production control where, after serving as reports of work done, they were forwarded to cost accounting. Some companies, thinking that this method was too slow for cost accounting, made out job tickets in duplicate so that one could go directly to cost accounting. Today computers update all records so quickly that all departments get immediate information.

Fifth, the payroll department may also need to get information from the job tickets, move orders, and inspection reports that are turned in to production control. Payroll doesn't, however, need this information unless your men are on piecework. If they are on piecework, payroll needs work report information in order to figure the men's pay. If you don't do this work on a computer, you probably will have to let the payroll copy of job tickets do double duty and go on to cost accounting afterwards to fill its needs.

Processing instructions—drawings, specifications, and other job instructions—are ordinarily not used in reporting progress. Usually, though, you want to be sure to get back those prepared specially for any one order after it is finished so that you can destroy them and keep them out of circulation. Of course, you keep a file set. Occasionally, as we said earlier, you have to change drawings a little in order to make them conform to the shop's needs. Don't do this, however, without reporting it and clearing it with engineering. Doing this is not really a part of progress reporting but it is an example of the "feedback" of information from the shop.

Notice that if you plan to make shop orders, job tickets, or any other of your printed forms do double duty, you have to design the form to serve both purposes. This may mean extra spaces, columns, or extra copies of the form.

REPLANNING AND RESCHEDULING

A great deal of the work of the production control department is *replanning* and *rescheduling* after your first plans don't work out. This is normal rather than unusual. Most of the changes are caused by all the little interferences to production that always happen. Fewer, but bigger, changes are caused, however, by changes in customers' orders and by changes in master schedules.

When you make products to customers' orders, you have to expect to change your schedules often because customers change their orders so often. And the fact that you have already started making their products doesn't stop them from wanting you to change. Sometimes they want to change the design, sometimes it is the quantity, sometimes the time of delivery, or maybe they will cancel the order altogether. The burden of making the changes falls heaviest on the production control department, which must revise all the orders affected by the changes.

Companies manufacturing to stock have less of this, largely because your own company has to stand all of the costs. When a customer wants to change, you can often get him to pay its costs, but not so with your own items. When you have to stand the costs yourself, you think twice before you change and you don't allow it without good cause. International Harvester allows changes in its master schedules no more than three times a year. In contrast, Timken Roller Bearing has to make changes in orders already in process almost daily. Changes so often as that multiply the production control costs but Timken has to satisfy its auto company customers.

Production irregularities of the day-to-day type are responsible for a good bit of replanning and rescheduling. Sometimes a man gets a job done before you expected. Then his machine is freed sooner, maybe so soon that the job you'd planned next isn't ready yet so you have to shift things around. More often, however, you are dealing with jobs taking longer than you'd planned and again you have to change schedules. Materials or tools aren't ready, or the tools don't work well, or sub-par material takes longer to work, or other reasons make delays.

In Chapter 18, we discussed one situation where you can just about count on getting exactly so much work, no more, no less. When you use piece rates and where the rates are very loose, workers, afraid that the rates might be cut, set a ceiling on their output. They peg it at a point considerably below what they can do.

From management's point of view, this is most unfortunate because it holds down production and holds down machine use to the worker's ceiling. Unfortunate though it is, it simplifies scheduling. You know how much output you'll get and can plan accordingly. Minor delays during the day don't cut output down any because the men can easily make up the loss in the ample time they have available. You won't find this situation very often.

Material rejected by the inspector also makes some schedule changes. Most of the time you suffer the normal number of rejects and schedule accordingly. But what do you do if an unusual number of items are held up? There are several solutions: (1) scrap the rejects, cut down the quantity

SPARES CHANGE AUTHORIZATION

WORK ORDER_____

SUPPLEMENT_____

DISTRIBUTION:

| SCAS | | CHECKED | | DATE | | WRITTEN | | SHEET | OF | | PAGE | | REL. | CANC. S N. O. S |

EXHIBIT_____ {TO CHANGE ORDER} {TO AMENDMENT} _____TO CONTRACT_____

_____{REVISION TO SPARE PARTS ORDER FOR_____MODEL AIRPLANES} TURRETS

TYPE	ITEM NO.	PART NO.	NOMENCLATURE	UNITS REQ'D.	UNIT PRICE	TOTAL PRICE	NET CHANGE CHARGE	CREDIT	GLM USE ONLY

REQUEST FOR CHANGE

REQUEST FOR

COPIES TO:	TOOL CHANGE	ROUTING CHG.	SKETCH CHG.	SET-UP CHART
PLANNING	WHITE	WHITE	WHITE	WHITE
FOREMAN	PINK	PINK	PINK	PINK
TOOL DESIGN	BUFF	BUFF	BUFF	BUFF
CRIB PRINT	GREEN	GREEN (1)	GREEN	GREEN

PART NUMBER   DESCRIPTION   ISSUER   DATE   DESTINATION   JOB NO.

QUANTITY

YEAR JAN FEB MAR APR MAY JUNE JULY AUG SEP OCT NOV DEC
19

YEAR JAN FEB MAR APR MAY JUNE JULY AUG SEP OCT NOV DEC
19

☐ INCREASE JOB FROM_____PIECE _
☐ DECR___

SCHEDULE CHANGE MEMO

No.
Date
Signed

CUSTOMER		FR No.		PLAN No.		CUST. PART No

TOTAL ORDER	AMOUNT SHIPPED AS OF	CANCELLED AMOUNT INCREASED	BAL DUE	CUST. ORDER No.

YEAR											
SCHEDULE	JAN.	FEB.	MAR.	APR	MAY	JUNE	JULY	AUG.	SEPT.	OCT.	NOV.	DEC.
PRESENT												
CHANGE TO												

CUSTOMER				
TOTAL ORDER				
YEAR				
SCHEDULE				
PRESENT				
CHANGE TO				
CUSTOMER				
TOTAL ORDER				
YEAR				
SCHEDULE				
PRESENT				
CHANGE TO				

MASTER CHANGE RECORD FOLLOW-UP SCHEDULE (15)

DATE_____; MOCK UP SHIP NO_____ DEV. SHIP NO_____ PROD. AIRPLANE NO_____; M. C. R. NO_____

WORK ORDER DATE_____ CLASSIFICATION_____ PARTS TO SERVICE—YES___NO___

CUSTOMER	TITLE		DEPT.		SCHED. DATE	DEPT.		SCHED. DATE

ENGINEERING	P. E. R.		TOOLING	TOOL WRITE-UP	
	A. M. R.			TEMP. TOOLS. DETAILS	
	DEVELOPMENT RELEASE			TEMP. TOOLS. SUB-ASSEM.	
	PRODUCTION RELEASE			INSTAL. TOOLS	
PLANNING	SIZING & RELEASE			PROD. TOOLS. DETAILS	
	EMERG. ORDER RELEASE			PROD. TOOLS. SUB-ASSEM.	
	PURCHASE REQ'N TO PUR.			CHECK BLOCKS	
	PROD. ORDER RELEASE			DROP HAMMER DIES	
	G. F. E. ITEMS			SAMPLE PARTS. TOOLS	
PURCHASING	RAW MAT'L (RECD. IN STORES)			S/C TOOLS	
	PROCUREMENT (RECD. IN STORES)		MFG.	G. L. M. DETAILS	
	S/C PARTS (RECD. IN STORES)			G. L. M. WELD ASSEM.	
	DETAILS SHIP TO S/C			G. L. M. SUB-ASSEM.	

PROGRESS TICKETS

No.	PG.	DATE	No.	PG.	DATE

Remarks: NOTES

Form 1072-9

ITEM NO.	PART NUMBER	DESCRIPTION	PIM	DEPT. RESP.	TOOL NO.	LIST. S/C OR PURCH. REQN. NO.	QUAN.	DATE	PROM. DATE	STOCK ROOM	CONT. POINT	REMARKS
1												
2												
3												
4												
5												
6												

M. C. R. No_____
PAGE ___ OF

FIGURE 25-3 Changes in addition to those made necessary by factory conditions are continually being made. The above forms are used for changing schedules because of processing changes, design changes, spare parts changes, and schedule changes. Changes of these kinds are responsible for a great deal of extra work in the production control department.

on the order to the number that passed inspection, and let this quantity go through as the full order; (2) finish the good parts, scrap the rejects, and make up a replacement order for the quantity lost; (3) finish the good products on schedule, rework the rejects, and finish them later; (4) hold up the good products while as many rejects as possible are reworked and put back with the order; (5) hold up the order, scrap the rejects, and wait for a replacement order to catch up before going ahead with the whole lot. There is even a sixth alternative—the one that we said in Chapter 18 was a poor solution. Tell engineering how desperately the assembly floor needs the parts and get its permission "just this once" to pass the rejects.

In all these choices except numbers 1 and 6, you rework the rejected pieces or replace them. This means making out new orders to cover the repair operations or the replacement order. Production control has to originate these orders and see that the operations are scheduled and performed. Such rework orders also insure that you get a record of their costs. If you send through a replacement order, you can more or less tie it to the original order by numbering it the same as the original order number but with a "$\frac{1}{2}$" or an "A" after the number.

You have to decide about rejects, whether they are repairable or not, and if they are repairable, what repair operations to perform. TRW puts rejects on a "red skid" until it is decided. At TRW, the foreman usually makes the decision. In most companies, however, the decision is made by the engineering department or the inspection department or by both together. This is an important decision on big items where you are making only one or two. If castings are to be repaired by being welded or brazed, special welding rods and special heat treatments may be necessary.

Shifts in the degree of rush among orders are common causes of schedule changes. Usually someone wants orders speeded up rather than slowed down. Not all behind-schedule orders become rush orders because most schedules have some fat in them. But let them be delayed very long and almost all behind-schedule jobs have to become rush jobs. Regular orders become rush orders and rush orders become special rush orders. You have to "bump" nonrush orders to make way for rush jobs. Fortunately rushing orders does not affect most of the details of an order itself. It just changes which orders come first. Sometimes one order is even "robbed" to fill another order with higher priority. This takes care of the rush order but makes you do a lot of replanning and rescheduling of other orders.

Whenever changes in plans are made, you have to change all the production papers. You have to change all operation start and stop times and maybe quantities too on all shop orders, job tickets, and move orders.

And you have to revise all production control boards and charts. In fact, you might find it a good idea to make the changes on charts and boards first, before changing any production papers. Then you can see the overall effects of the change.

GANTT CHARTS

Over 50 years ago, Henry L. Gantt figured out several kinds of charts to use in controlling production. Even though they lack some of the merits of the PERT-type systems, the principles embodied in these charts are still used sometimes. Where Gantt chart scheduling and control are used today, the original hand-drawn charts have usually been replaced by their first cousins, control "boards." Several varieties of these will be discussed later.

A Gantt chart tries to show schedules graphically. You can show how you are going to use machine time, how the operations for orders follow one another, or how your materials supplies compare to their needs.

Besides showing your plans, Gantt charts can show you how you are doing in meeting the plan. Seeing this information graphically enables you to do a good job of replanning when it is necessary.

The scale across the top of all Gantt charts is a time scale showing days or hours These may be "forward-looking" with the left side representing the near future. Or they may use a backward looking calendar, with days numbered backward from the project completion date. The vertical axis of the chart is always a list of the items being charted—machines, orders, materials supplies, or men. Lines indicating the plan and the performance are put in with chalk. Every week they are erased and a new plan for the next week is drawn up.

Although the symbols employed on Gantt charts will vary somewhat among users, the following symbols are fairly standard:

⌐	The start of an activity
⌐	The end of an activity
⌐⌐	Time allotted to an activity
◤⌐	Work actually completed in an activity
16 ⌐	Work load in time or quantity for the activity
128 ⌐	Cumulative work load to date in time or quantity
▷◁	Time allocated for other than productive activities
∨	Time reference point indicating point to which work should have progressed if it were on schedule and point at which charting activity was stopped

When work is behind schedule, letters such as the following are often used to indicate the reason for noncompliance:

A   Operator absent
G   Inexperienced ("green") operator
I   Instructions incomplete or unavailable
M   Material shortage or unavailability
P   Power failure
R   Machine or tool breakdown or scheduled repairs and maintenance
T   Tools or dies unavailable
V̇   Holiday

A typical section of a Gantt chart might appear as shown in figure 25-4. This indicates that the chart was posted to noon on Thursday, January 16. Job number 37 was scheduled to complete 32 parts on this day and to have a total of 128 parts completed by the end of the day. It is, however, running two hours behind schedule because of a material shortage. Job number 44 which was scheduled for eight hours is running an hour ahead of schedule. On machine 3 the job was completed on time and the next job scheduled to begin. Notice that the second machine has a two-hour preventive maintenance period scheduled on Friday morning.

Although considerable information can be gained from Gantt charts, they are by no means a panacea for all scheduling and control problems. They don't indicate the critical sequence of activities as do CPM routines.

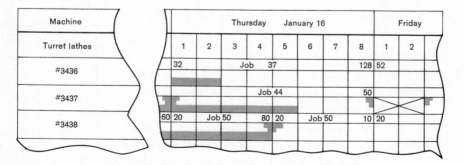

FIGURE 25-4   A section of a Gantt chart.

Also, Gantt charts, like other planning aids, must be kept right up to date if they are to be of any use. They are static, and only show a picture of a situation as of a given moment.

Finally, no planning or control device is a substitute for replanning on a more or less continuous basis. You can draw up charts to show what you are going to do next Monday, Tuesday, and so on. But when Monday and Tuesday come you won't do quite what you planned. Your charts need changing. Some orders are ahead of schedule. That means that all start dates for future orders have to be changed. Other orders get behind. Again you have to change other schedules. Also, because one order gets held up you must fill in other orders in its place. Unless you have some easy system for making corrections, the chart becomes quite messy and confused. It is primarily in ease of change that control boards are superior to hand-drawn charts.

Charts can be helpful when you are trying to get out the last ounce of production. Officials can see at a glance how orders are coming along. Charts can warn management of bottlenecks and give officials time to do something to avoid them. The charts themselves do not, however, indicate the criticalness of the bottleneck. As do any other tools, they have their uses, good features, and limitations. Properly used, they are helpful in getting a job done; improperly used, they can be of no use or actually a hindrance.

MACHINE USE CHARTS

If you had bottleneck machines and wanted to chart their use, you would go about it this way: list the name or numbers of each machine to be charted down the left side of the chart. Each machine is considered separately, with one horizontal line devoted to it. Divide the space across the top into sections for days. Subdivide each daily subdivision into quarter days or hours.

Now you are ready to chart your plan. On the line for the first machine draw a light line across the chart starting at the left of Monday's space and extend it to the right. If this order will tie up the machine until Tuesday noon, extend the line through Monday and halfway through the Tuesday space and end it with a bracket. Write in the order number in small figures above the line so that you will know to what order you have allocated the time.

Now, suppose that there will be no work for this machine on Tuesday afternoon or that the machine will be idle while being set up for its next job which will start Wednesday morning. Fill in the Tuesday afternoon space with the appropriate symbol to tell you this. Then plot the next order showing the time it will take and so on for as far ahead as you have the machine scheduled. Go ahead and do the same for the other machines and you will end up having a chart that shows your planned use of the machines.

To use the chart for control, you must get performance reports and plot them on the chart. Put in a heavy line right below the line representing the planned output. Make it longer or shorter than the time reference line for the plan depending on whether output is up to schedule or not. This works reasonably well for the first day or so, but you'll soon have to change the lines you first had on your chart for the days ahead because you won't be starting them from where your plan said that you would.

ORDER CONTROL CHARTS

You may also want to show your plan for *orders* on a Gantt chart. Charts help you, for example, to see that the orders for separate parts of an assembled product are timed so that all of the parts will be ready on time. The process is the same as for machines except that each line, on the vertical scale, plots the making of one part.

There is one difference, however. If you want to overlap the operations for a part you have to use more lines on the chart. If operation number 2 will start on some of the pieces before operation number 1 has been finished on all pieces, you will have to show operation 2 on the line below the line on which you plot operation 1. When this occurs it may be better to show the planned progress of no more than one order for one part on each chart. Each vertical space can represent an operation, and its plan and its progress alone are shown in that space. Show the second, third, and other operations in successive spaces below each other on the chart.

CONTROL BOARDS

There are quite a few kinds of control boards on the market. Almost all are applications of the Gantt chart idea. Two long time favorites are Produc-trol boards and Sched-U-Graphs. Produc-trol boards use a series of lines of holes and colored pegs. Sched-U-Graphs use cards lined up from left to right in a series of rows from top to bottom. Besides these two forms of boards there are several others. Some clip in little colored squares along lines. Others are magnetic and let you attach colored sections in whatever arrangement you like.

MERITS OF BOARDS

Don't go overboard on boards. They are not the essence of production control and they don't solve all of your problems. Although they are better than charts and can be set up and changed more easily, all that they do is to help you visualize your plans and, as we said earlier, they let the boss see the plans better. Looking at them, he can see at a glance where you are now having trouble *and* where you are likely to have trouble. This is a worthwhile advantage because it's about the only way you can show him, quickly, a picture of overall conditions.

O. A. Smith, in Milwaukee, uses boards to tell everybody how all the big orders are coming along. Every Monday morning production control sets up Sched-U-Graphs showing the status of all major orders. Then it photographs the boards and sends pictures of them to all interested departments. Smith uses various kinds of black and white cross hatching (not colors) to show various situations. They show up better in the pictures.

Boards have several weaknesses. First, they are costly to operate—they are all extra cost. Even their first cost is an item. Since all the board work is extra, it does not replace or save anything else. You still have to have shop orders and to get reports of work done and not done and when things occur.

Second, boards only help you see your plan. Unless you are working at 100 per cent of capacity, you don't really need to see your whole plan. You will have few bottlenecks to worry about. Far from worrying about too much work, you won't have enough work to keep your machines busy. Jobs will come through without any picture on a board. We must admit, however, that even in slack times an assembled product needs *all* its parts and not *all* of them will come through production automatically. If a board will tell you that one or more parts are lagging, it may save an assembly floor hold-up.

Third, you have trouble running off the right side of the board! Suppose that your board has 30 inches of horizontal space and that you use it to show your loads for three weeks.

What do you do for machines scheduled already for four or five weeks ahead? Use another board? Doing this doubles the number of boards that you need. Or do you just not show the fourth or fifth weeks ahead.

Doing this means that you don't have a picture of your tightest spots. Your board shows all the noncritical situations but not the critical situations.

There is also the matter of one week later. After one week, there are still two weeks left on the board. The left-hand third of the board is now blank (last week is past) and the board shows things for two weeks ahead— and that isn't very far. You can get out of this trouble by moving the second and third week cards over into the one, two, and three week spots. But, of course, all this moving of cards is extra work. And besides, you have three weeks on your board only on Monday morning. By Friday you are down to just two weeks.

You can, however, get out of moving all the cards by going round and round. When the left section of the board is empty, use it for the third week ahead, the week you want to add at the right of the board but can't (it was the fourth week ahead when you first set up the board). Two weeks after you first set up the board the middle section will be empty. So put the next week (the fifth week ahead when you originally set up the board) into that section. By this time the current week is in the right section of the board. The board reads a little backwards but makes very little trouble for your men because they get used to it.

Fourth, you have difficulty with boards, too, in the matter of standard or expected hours. Every kind of machine load record has trouble with this so it is not exactly a weakness of boards. The problem is, do you show on the board the hours that the job ticket or shop order says that a job should take or not? They show the standard hours but men making bonuses won't take that long and everyone knows it. If you show standard hours on the board, it does not show a true picture of how long operations will take and how long machines will be busy. But if you try to show how long jobs will most likely take, you have to make a conversion from standard to actual for every job.

Fifth, boards don't even highlight behind-time jobs very well. When you reschedule a delayed job, you show its new schedule on the board but its new schedule could just as well be its original schedule as far as the board tells you. You'll have to have some kind of special flagging device to tell you that order A's schedule is really a revision of an earlier schedule and that it is behind time, whereas order B's schedule is its original schedule.

Sixth, Gantt charts and control boards, to be useful, *must* be kept up to date, not day by day but hour by hour. You must get reports of work done and of new schedules and you must post these to the boards right away. If you don't, boards are worse than useless, they are misleading. They not only *fail to show* you what is going on, they *do show* that something else is going on.

HOOK BOARDS AND POCKET BOARDS

Hook boards and pocket boards have a long history. There isn't much to them. They are much less formal and take much less work to maintain than charts or control boards. In contrast to them, however, they are usually located out in the departments rather than in a central production control office.

Hook boards are large boards on which you put three pairs of hooks for every controlled machine. Hang copies of shop order sheets or job tickets on these hooks. The left pair of hooks holds order sheets or tickets for jobs ahead of the machine. The middle pair is for the job now on the machine. The right-hand pair holds orders finished but not yet taken out of the department. You can even add a fourth pair of hooks to hold the machine's "dead load," orders that will turn up sometime in the future, as distinguished from its "live load," orders already in process or even in the department waiting for the machine. Some companies assign their hooks differently to jobs. Here is one variation: hook 1, this job; hook 2, next job; hook 3, jobs ready; hook 4, jobs waiting.

Pocket boards are the same as hook boards except that you have pockets or shelves for each machine instead of hooks. You use them the same way. They are a little better than hooks because you don't need holes in the papers. You can stack drawings, job tickets, and shop orders all together. You use three or four pockets for each machine, just as with hooks.

Either of these arrangements, hooks or pockets, takes up considerable space, although their first cousin, McCaskey clip boards, takes less. Neither a hook nor a pocket board is a real schedule nor even a machine loading record. They are really "order-of-work" arrangements. They don't show any starting or stopping times for orders ahead of a machine. If you want to know how big a load you have ahead of a machine or when a certain order will be processed, you have to look over the orders ahead and figure it out. This is not a big job, but the point is that hook or pocket boards don't automatically answer these questions. Hook boards and pocket boards are very simple to operate since all that you have to do is to hang up papers, tags, or tickets.

Today you can buy any number of kinds of rotary file arrangements which are particularly well adapted to use in stock record keeping. All that you need do is to set aside separate sections in the file to hold production orders for each machine. The Rotor-File appears to be an improvement, for this purpose, over hook and pocket boards. Other helpful devices include Wheeldex, Rol-dex, Revo-file, Cardineer, Kardex, and other visible card filing systems. They have not, however, made hook and pocket boards obsolete.

STUDY MATERIALS

25-1   How can you tell, during the assembly of a big project, whether the work is up to schedule or not? How can you tell whether or not it is running ahead or behind the cost budget? If it is behind either time-wise or cost-wise, what *can* you do about it? What *should* you do about it?

25-2   The business of the Lindner Products Company has been declining slowly for some time. The company makes assembled products, usually in lots, and makes most of its own parts. Lately considerable difficulty has been encountered at the assembly floor, where operations are being carried on at a reduced pace because of the laying off of the second shift. The difficulty has been caused by the arrival on the assembly floor of parts and subassemblies for orders whose assembly is not yet ready to be started. These parts and subassemblies have overflowed the space available in the storage bins and have been piled around in the assembly area.

What weaknesses in the present procedure permitted the difficulty described to happen? Could it happen if business were good? How can parts be prevented from arriving too soon? How can their arrival at the proper time be assured?

25-3   The Belding Company has found that, on automatic screw machine products, its production control department records are sometimes inaccurate. Belding uses decentralized control and gives shop orders to foremen to assign to their men. When operations are complete, the foremen report this to production control.

The problem is that reports sometimes fail to come in even though the operations are performed. The record shows that an order is behind so expediters chase it down only to find the screw machine operation done and the job piled over in the corner. The foreman is always rather vague about it, claiming that he didn't know it was done.

Further investigation showed that both foreman and men knew full well what the problem was. The screw machine piece rates were so loose that if the men turned in job tickets for all that they did they would make so much money as to bring down the time study men on them with rate cuts—or so the men and the foremen thought. The men did the work all right but they didn't report it at all, even threw away a job ticket now and then rather than send it in.

What, if anything, should production control do about this? Suppose that the union is strong enough to successfully oppose rate adjustments yet won't let the men make too much money. What should production control do?

25-4   The Smith-Benson Engineering Company sales department bid on a job which required a considerable amount of engineering work before it could be produced. The bid was accepted and the order turned over to the engineering department. The engineering department was not quite as busy as usual and turned out all the drawings and parts lists in two weeks instead of the expected five weeks.

Since the customer was anxious for his order, the sales department wanted the job started into production immediately. The head of the production control department objected on the grounds that if this order were pushed ahead, other orders would be delayed. The sales department was unwilling to change the completion dates on any other orders and yet was very anxious to get the new order out quickly. The general manager was asked to decide whether the order should be started immediately without moving back any other promise dates.

Is it usually possible to get "one more order" out in a given length of time when the schedule is supposedly full? If so, how? Who should really know whether another order can be produced without holding up previous orders?

25-5 You own the following equipment:

SIZE	NUMBER OF MACHINES	PRODUCTION CAPACITY PER HOUR (POUNDS OF METAL SHEET) PER MACHINE

SHEET METAL SHEARS

72 inches	4	750
96 inches	2	1,000
120 inches	2	1,100

FORMING AND PUNCH PRESSES

5 tons	5	Forming and punch presses all operate
20 tons	2	30 hours per week.
50 tons	1	
100 tons	1	

Usually after punch press work, the metal has to be cleaned. For this you have 4 tanks, capacity 150 lb. of material per hour per tank.

ARC AND SPOT WELDERS

Arc welder	1	12 pieces per hour
Spot welders		
20 KV	3	750 spots per hour
50 KV	2	600 spots per hour
120 KV	1	600 spots per hour

Final product cleaning and finishing has 14 employees. Painting capacity is limited to 4 men. Each of these men turns out 40 hours of work per week.

As you start the week ending March 12 you find that you have the work load shown in the table below. Work "behind schedule" is *not* included in the scheduled quantities shown for the next three weeks.

The work must all pass through: first the shears, next forming and punch presses, then cleaning, then welding, final cleaning, and finishing and painting.

MACHINE	BEHIND SCHEDULE	WORK SCHEDULED FOR WEEK ENDING		
		MARCH 10	MARCH 17	MARCH 24
72-inch shears	60,000 lb.	48,000 lb.	24,000 lb.	126,000 lb.
96-inch shears	60,000 lb.			128,000 lb.
120-inch shears	37,400 lb.	88,000 lb.	88,000 lb.	35,200 lb.
5-ton presses		200 hours	100 hours	20 hours
20-ton presses	10 hours	16 hours	16 hours	16 hours
50-ton presses				32 hours
100-ton presses	20 hours	40 hours		8 hours
Cleaning tanks	15,000 lb.	12,000 lb.	19,200 lb.	9,600 lb.
Arc welder			16 hours	36 hours
20 KV spot welders	100,000 spots	45,000 spots	162,000 spots	27,000 spots
50 KV spot welders				19,200 spots
120 KV spot welder			19,000 spots	
Cleaning, finishing	860 hours	560 hours	560 hours	168 hours
Painting	114 hours	160 hours	112 hours	128 hours

On Monday morning, March 6, you get the following orders through the mail:

Order No. 4711   Five tons of 96-inch sheets to be cut and formed on 20-ton presses. All tools and dies are in our shop. Shipment required not later than March 30th. (Estimated forming time on presses: 80 hours.)

Order No. 4712   1,248 pieces to be arc welded per accompanying drawing. Shipment to be made in two weeks.

Order No. 4713   100,000 pieces spot welded according to specifications already in our possession. Shipment on earliest possible date. Each piece requires four spots which cannot be made simultaneously—20 KV welder to be used.

1 Draw a Gantt load chart showing the above schedules.

2 If you can, fit into the chart the three new orders without disturbing any of the work already scheduled for the equipment.

3 Now set a delivery promise date for each of the new orders.

25-6 Unless you have a fully worked out procedure to cover changes, they will almost surely make trouble for you because something will be overlooked. Some instructions already issued will be missed and trouble will ensue.

Write up instructions for a procedure which will insure one of the following changes being carried out (pick whichever change you want):

1 Change the quantity on an order.

2 Change the design of a part.

3 Repair a tool.

4 Rework rejected material.

5 Replenish a shortage.

6 Cancel a part use (i.e., that part is still used in some models but is canceled in one model).

chapter twenty-six

QUALITY CONTROL

In previous chapters we have been concerned with quantity scheduling and control. But we not only need the right number of parts, we also need "good" parts. Thus we must not only control quantities, but also the quality of parts that are produced. This is especially important in piecework operations where there is a tendency to sacrifice quality for quantity.

The subject of quality control covers an extensive area and many excellent books have been written on the subject. Here we can consider it only in a limited way. Fortunately, quality control divides itself into two areas, the technology of inspection and the methodology of control. It is this second area that we will focus upon here with only minor mention of the other.

INSPECTION TECHNOLOGY   Inspection technology is concerned with such matters as how the waviness of a surface is measured, or what kinds of gages or equipment are needed to measure the diameter of a shaft to the nearest ten-thousandth of an inch. Other common problems deal with how accurate must the master gages be in order to insure that the inspector's gages are also sufficiently accurate, and how often should the operators' working gages be checked. There are also problems in measuring subjective things such as the proper taste of a blend of tea or the aroma of a perfume. Although there are many technological problems involved in inspection they are rarely pertinent to the work of production control.

CONTROL METHODOLOGY   The methodology of quality control is concerned with such problems as: should all parts be inspected or should we rely on samples? If samples are used, what risks are involved (such as accepting a lot when in fact it contains too many defectives)? Another question is what variation might we tolerate from a machine before we say that it is out of control (and is producing too many off-standard units)? In trying to answer these questions, we will talk about "acceptance sampling" and "statistical quality control charts" for process control.

RESPONSIBILITY FOR QUALITY
Before considering these matters, however, we should note that the largest responsibility for quality rests with operating departments. They make

products which are good enough to pass inspection or which are not good enough to pass. Parts are either good or bad before inspectors see them. A small responsibility does, however, rest with inspection and quality control because by inspection, you can find and throw out bad items, thus improving the outgoing quality. And by quality control, you can help prevent the making of bad products, again improving quality.

ZERO DEFECTS   "Zero defect" programs, which became popular in the mid-1960s, rest on the idea that operating departments are responsible for quality. The zero defects idea started on government missile contracts and then became common in civilian work. These programs are not aimed primarily at better inspection procedures but at instilling in production workers a desire to make products right the first time.

Zero defect programs have come out of the use of statistical procedures in quality control. In the past, using statistical quality control, a certain percentage of defectives, perhaps 1 or 2 per cent, in a lot of items has been thought of as acceptable. Perfection has not been expected because it is almost always so costly to attain. This has been known, recognized, and accepted. Statistical procedures were used to decide how many bad items would be allowed.

Yet it is these few defects that a zero defects program tries to eliminate and *at no extra cost at all.* Such a program tries to impress upon production operatives that even one defective item in a lot is too many. When you have a zero defects program, you reject the whole lot of parts (whether you bought them outside or made them yourself) if you find *even one* defective item in the sample you inspect. After this happens once or twice everyone tries his very best to make products right the first time.

One reason why the adoption of a zero defects program is important in production control work is that it changes the number of extras that need to be made to provide for losing some production to defectives. Fewer extras need to be provided. But a more important reason is that whole lots of products are more likely to be rejected than formerly. This is usually an initial effect. Later on, as the zero defects program becomes effective, fewer lots are rejected because defects are fewer. Production control has to live with the vagaries in rejections caused by zero defects programs.

INSPECTORS' AUTHORITY
In job lot work you find both central and floor inspection. Central inspection is done at an inspection crib where the trucker brings jobs. It occurs after production, maybe during the next workshift, and is inspection either of samples or of every piece. In job lot work, central inspectors usually can

approve or reject individual pieces or whole lots. Central inspection also provides a convenient way of getting production counts and so acts as a check on operator reports of work done. Inspectors don't like this phase of the work but it is a low-cost way of getting a count check.

Most companies confine inspectors' authority to deciding and reporting but some go further and let inspectors decide if rejects are repairable and if so what operations are required. Most often foremen and engineers together decide repair matters.

Floor (or "patrolling" or "roving" or "first piece") inspectors go from machine to machine inspecting the operator's first few pieces after he has set up his machine. If they pass, he goes ahead with the lot. Floor inspectors can hold up starting a job until the setup is right. Usually, floor inspectors do not, in job lot work, have the right to stop a machine that is turning out more than the usual number of off-standard products. Only foremen can do that. This is in contrast with the usual situation in continuous production where inspectors can stop such a machine.

Floor inspection makes fewer production control problems than does central inspection. Being done right at the job and before the operation is performed, it keeps bad products from being made. There is therefore little likelihood of a whole order being rejected. Furthermore, jobs don't have to go to a central inspection area so transportation costs and inventory in process are lower because jobs go more directly through the plant. With central inspection, whole orders are sometimes rejected after an operation has been performed on the whole lot. Replacing such lots makes extra production control work. Sometimes too the slow progress of jobs through the plant makes problems. Jobs have to start into production earlier and be handled more often. And they get lost more often.

Many companies today use quality control charts of the Shewhart type (described later in this chapter) out in the shop at the machines. A roving quality control checker goes from machine to machine making spot checks of quality and keeping the charts up to date. Where this is done and for the machines so checked (usually not all machines are checked this way) the quality control checker replaces the old kind of floor inspector. But since not all factory operations are controlled by charts, some old floor-type inspection must still go on. Almost always, however, control chart inspectors have authority to stop production on a machine that is discovered to be turning out too much bad work.

ACCEPTANCE SAMPLING

Normally inspection to determine whether parts are acceptable or not is carried on at several stages of production. Inspection usually begins with incoming purchased parts or bought raw materials. Manufactured parts are also inspected several times during their manufacture, especially before they enter a costly stage of processing and before they are put away in a stock room.

Interestingly, 100 per cent inspection of parts may not actually give any greater assurance concerning a lot's quality than a well-designed sampling plan (which is usually considerably less costly). This is because, when large lots are involved, inspection of every part is a dull, boring job in which employees find little interest or job satisfaction. They get careless and some parts which ought to be rejected slip by.

Sampling systems, on the other hand, tend to instill a sense of responsibility in the inspector. He knows that the fate of the entire lot rests upon his examination of the sample, so he examines the few pieces in the sample very carefully. Also since fewer pieces are examined, fewer and better trained inspectors can be employed. The end effect is that carefully done inspection of samples by good inspectors is more reliable than 100 per cent inspection by bored low-grade inspectors.

RISKS IN SAMPLING PLANS   Even though sampling plans have much to commend them, they are not the answer to all problems because they entail risks. With proper sampling, however, these risks can be set at whatever level you choose. Risks are of two types: (1) rejecting a lot when, in fact, it is acceptable and (2) accepting a lot when it should be rejected.

A lot is considered acceptable when it has no more than a stated number of defective pieces. If it has more than this number it is rejected. The number chosen as the maximum number of allowable defectives depends upon how serious their effects in use would be and upon the extra cost of producing better work and upon the size of the sample. Having considered these, you set up an inspection "plan," telling inspectors to look at a given number of items (a sample chosen from the whole lot) and accept or reject the lot depending on the number of defectives found in the sample. The matter of risk comes in since by pure happenstance the sample might contain proportionally more, or fewer, defectives than the lot and thus give misleading evidence about the lot's quality.

Suppose, for example, you have a lot of 100 parts and want to accept it if it has 5 or fewer defectives. You take a sample of 10 and find none to be defective. Can you then decide reliably that the lot should pass? Or if 1 of the 10 is defective should you reject the lot? The question is, what risks would you be taking of misjudging the quality of the lot? We won't answer the question here. Detailed plans, and instructions about sample size, number of rejects allowed, and risks are in statistics books.[1]

[1] See, for example, Samuel B. Richmond, *Statistical Analysis*, 2d ed., The Ronald Press Company, New York, 1964.

TYPE I AND TYPE II ERRORS   We might pursue this risk matter a little further, however. We can picture acceptance sampling as a 2 by 2 game in which we have two possible decisions or "strategies," and two "states of nature." The strategies are (1) accept the lot, S_1, or (2) reject it, S_2. The states of nature are (1) that the lot is truly good, N_1, or (2) it is not, N_2. These relationships can be diagrammed as shown in figure 26-1, which shows the four possibilities. The lot may actually be good and the sample may verify this (N_1, S_1), or the lot may be bad but the sample may not show it (N_2, S_1). Then we make a type I mistake and accept a bad lot. Or the lot may actually be bad and the sample may agree (N_2, S_2). But if the lot is good and the sample misleads us, we make a type II mistake and reject it (N_1, S_2). The words "success" and "failure" in figure 26-1 mean that the inspection plan has led us to a true or a false judgment about the lot's quality.

The acceptance sampling plans in statistics books are designed to confine the risks of making both type I and type II errors to whatever levels you care to assume. The more sure you want to be to avoid type I errors, the larger must be the sample (and the inspection costs), or the fewer the rejects allowable (but at the expense of increasing the risks of making type II errors or both).

ATTRIBUTE INSPECTION

Acceptance sampling is usually done on a go–no-go basis. Degrees of acceptability, such as measurements, don't count. The part either passes or is rejected. All that counts is the number passing and failing and the ratio between them. Pass-fail inspection is called attribute inspection. We

FIGURE 26-1

	N_1 (LOT IS GOOD)	N_2 (LOT IS BAD)
S_1 (accept lot)	Success	Failure. Type I error committed.
S_2 (reject lot)	Failure. Type II error committed.	Success

usually think of attributes as dealing with dimensions and whether or not they are within tolerance. But this doesn't have to be so. You can count defects in a coil of steel or bolts of cloth and accept or reject according to the count. Even products relying on subjective standards such as taste and smell can be judged to be good or bad. Attribute inspection is not limited to physical measurements.

SAMPLING PLANS   A sampling "plan" has first to be defined or specified. The simplest kind of plan is one where you inspect one sample only and accept or reject the lot based on its quality. To set up such a plan you must stipulate four requirements or parameters. These are (1) the acceptable quality level (AQL), (2) the producer's risk (α), (3) the lot tolerance percentage defective (LTPD), and (4) the consumer's risk (β).

The AQL is the quality level (say 2 per cent defectives or less) that we want to be accepted almost all of the time. Actually the words "acceptable quality level" are not properly descriptive because, as we shall see, the average quality of the products we accept will not be that good. The AQL is such a high quality level that we want to set up a plan that will rarely make a type II error.

The Greek letter alpha, α, represents the producer's risk, the risk that a type II error will occur and cause a highly acceptable lot to be rejected.

The LTPD is at the other end of the spectrum from the AQL and deals with bad lots. Lots as bad as the LTPD should be rejected by the plan almost all of the time, thus making type I errors rare.

The Greek letter beta, β, represents the consumer's risk, the risk that a type I error will occur and allow a very poor lot to be accepted.

Decisions must be made for each of these four factors and then a plan to implement them can be set up. Suppose that we set α at 5 per cent, β at 10 per cent, the AQL at 0.8 per cent, and the LTPD at 5 per cent. This means that we want a plan which will accept 95 per cent of all lots submitted which contain 0.8 per cent or fewer defectives and which will reject 90 per cent of all lots which contain 5 per cent or more defectives. If many lots of varying quality are submitted the average quality of those accepted will contain about 3 per cent defectives. (As we said above, the term acceptable quality level seems to say that the average quality accepted will be 0.8 per cent whereas this is not so.)

The "plan" that we need in order to implement these restrictions is a statement to the inspector telling him how big a sample to inspect and how many defectives the sample may contain. The mathematics involved in developing plans for any set of restrictions that you may choose to set up are very complex. But you don't have to work out answers. They have all been precomputed and you can look them up in published sampling inspection tables.[2]

A "plan" then ends up specifying for every possible lot size N two numbers: n, the size of the sample, and c, the allowable number of defectives. In our example above, if a lot of 500 items were submitted, a sample of 100 should be inspected and the lot should be accepted if 2, 1, or 0 defectives are found.

OPERATING CHARACTERISTIC CURVES   Each plan has its own "operating characteristic" (OC) curve which is a plot of the probabilities of acceptance of lots of varying quality. Figure 26-2 shows the OC curve for the plan that meets the conditions we have just laid down above. Very good lots, those with few defectives, fall near the left of the chart and have

[2] See Harold F. Dodge and Harry G. Romig, *Sampling Inspection Tables: Single and Double Sampling*, 2d ed., John Wiley & Sons, Inc., New York, 1959. See also MIL-STD-105D, *Military Standard Sampling Procedures and Tables for Sampling by Attributes*, U.S. Department of Defense, 1961.

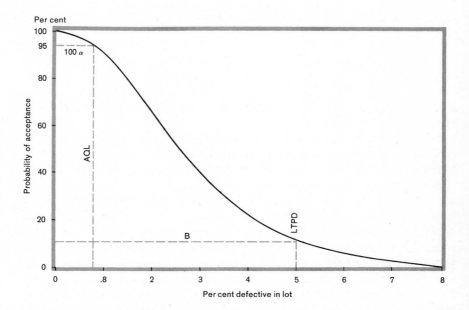

FIGURE 26-2   The OC curve for a sampling plan, with an AQL of 5 per cent and LTPD of 10 per cent, for a lot of 500, using a sample of 100, and accepting the lot if two or fewer defects are found in the sample.

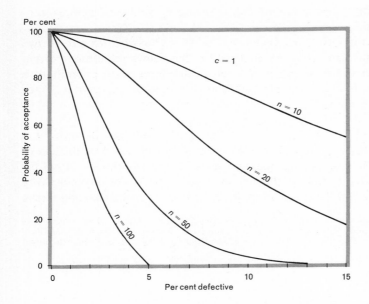

FIGURE 26-3 OC curves for acceptance plans allowing only one reject in the sample. As the sample size increases the plans are much more discriminatory.

a high probability of acceptance. Poor lots are off to the right and have little chance of being accepted.

Looking at figure 26-2 we can see the probability of accepting incoming lots containing any given percentage of defectives. For example, if (although unknown to us) the lot contains 3 per cent defectives, then there is a 42 per cent chance of its passing.

We turn now to sampling plans in general. Figures 26-3 and 26-4 show how, in general, sampling plans relate to each other. In both charts, the bottom scale is an "if" scale just as it was in figure 26-2. If the lot of parts being submitted has a certain percentage of defectives, then the curves above and the vertical scale at the left show the chances it has of passing.

Figure 26-3 shows four OC curves which are progressively tighter. All are for plans that allow 1 reject in the sample ($c = 1$). But the sample sizes vary from 10 to 100 ($n = 10$, etc.). A lot which actually contains 5 per cent defectives will pass almost always with a plan where $c = 1$ and $n = 10$: it will pass most of the time when $c = 1$ and $n = 20$, but it will not

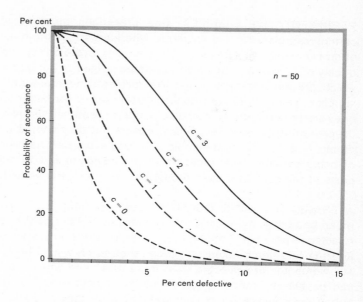

FIGURE 26-4   OC curves for acceptance plans using samples of 50. As the number of rejects allowed goes down the plans are more discriminatory.

pass very often when $n = 50$ and rarely when $n = 100$. (In these charts the sample is assumed to have been taken from an infinitely large lot.)

Figure 26-4, on the other hand, shows the same idea except that n is held constant and c is varied. If you inspect a sample of 50 and allow 3 defects, you are obviously allowing poorer quality to pass than if you set c equal to 2, 1, or 0.

In both charts, we see that the tighter the plan the more surely bad lots will be rejected. This reduces the consumer's risk. Also, implicit in these curves as drawn is a progressively tightened AQL. The AQL tightens up so much, in fact, that the producer's risk may be increased. You may not want these effects and if so, should not use a sample of 50 with a c of 3, 2, 1, or 0. Maybe what you need is a plan where $n = 100$ and $c = 2$ or some other plan.

Sometimes you can hardly devise a plan which incorporates and reconciles everything just as you want it. Perhaps, for example, to get the certainty you want you'd have to inspect quite large samples at higher inspection costs than you are willing to pay. Double or sequential sampling may help here. We discuss them later in this chapter.

REPRESENTATIVE SAMPLES   One precaution must be observed concerning samples. Just as any housewife knows that the quality of a quart of strawberries can't be judged by sampling those on top, neither can the quality of a lot of manufactured parts be judged by sampling those on top which are easy to reach. Just like farmers and merchants, workers or suppliers have been known to stack a tote bin or container so that the bad ones are underneath. To get valid results, acceptance sampling depends on "representative" samples, which means that they should be chosen randomly. In a true random sample each and every part has an equal chance of being selected. This means that the inspector has to dig into various parts of the container even though this may be inconvenient.

AVERAGE OUTGOING QUALITY   Bad incoming lots don't necessarily mean bad outgoing quality. In our example, a 3 per cent bad lot would be rejected 58 per cent of the time. But, if this lot is then 100 per cent inspected and the bad items taken out, those that go on will all be good. Similarly, still worse lots are rejected even more often and when they are, they too can be 100 per cent inspected and the rejects removed. In case all lots submitted average 3 per cent defectives as they come in, the effect of removal of the defectives from rejected lots will, when combined with lots

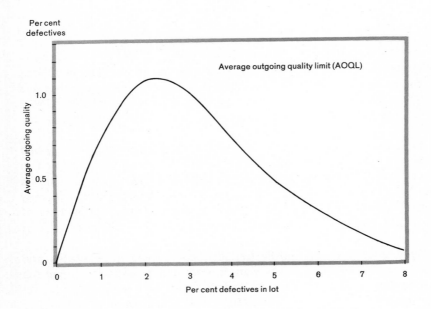

FIGURE 26-5   An AOQ curve.

that passed to start with, result in an average outgoing quality (AOQ) of 1.01 per cent.

Figure 26-5 shows how the AOQ is related to the quality of lots submitted. Up to the quality point where the plan is likely to accept or reject on a 50-50 basis, the AOQ worsens. But from this point on, more lots are rejected and then purged of defectives. So from this point on, the worse the average quality of lots submitted, the better the AOQ (but at a higher and higher inspection cost).

The good part about this procedure is that you know that no matter how bad the incoming lots may be, your plan sets a known limit, the average outgoing quality level (AOQL), to the ratio of defectives allowed. If more than this limit are actually passing through inspection, then your plan is not being followed by the inspectors so you get an automatic check on their work.

DOUBLE AND SEQUENTIAL SAMPLING PLANS

We said that sometimes you would like to have the reliability that large samples provide but don't want to spend so much money on inspection.

Double or sequential sampling may take care of your problem although both have the disadvantage that they make irregular inspection work loads. Both double and sequential samplings use the fact that small samples discriminate very well for lots with either few or many defectives. Only in the middle quality range do you need the added discrimination that large samples provide.

In both double and sequential samplings you start with a small sample but you use two c numbers. In a sample of 25, c_1 might be 0 defects and tell you to accept the lot, and c_2 might be 2 defects and tell you to reject the lot. But if you find 1 defect, you go on to a second sample of 25 more. For the total of 50, c_1 might be 1 and c_2 2. All lots would therefore be accepted or rejected.

If you used sequential sampling, after two samples of 25 each, c_1 might be 1 and c_2 3. Then if you had found 2 defects, you would still be uncertain and go on to a third sample. In rare cases even a fourth sample might be required.

As in the case of single sampling plans, precalculated plans for either double or sequential plans are available embodying whatever parameters you choose.

Some people think that double and sequential samplings are "fairer" than single sampling because they gives borderline lots another chance. This is spurious reasoning, however, because for every set of parameters you make up, the appropriate single, double, and sequential sampling plans are identical in the long run in their ability to sort good lots from bad.

VARIABLE INSPECTION
Variables are quality characteristics which need measuring, so the inspection of variables deals with measurements and their variations. And it is concerned with actual measurements and not just with whether items are within acceptable limits or not.

Being concerned with actual measurements makes the inspection job different. For one thing inspection costs are higher. It is one thing to check a part or diameter with a go–no-go gage that tells whether an item is within tolerance limits or not, but it is another thing to use a micrometer, get the actual measurement, write it down, and then use the data provided in a meaningful way.

When variable inspection is used for already produced lots, it operates much as does acceptance inspection of attributes. OC curves can be used but the vertical scale on the chart is a scale of measurements of the variable instead of a percentage defective scale.

Another difference is that in attribute inspection a part which is too small or too large is rejected. The limits to acceptability have been set and are enforced. But sampling by variables expects and accepts variability. Variable inspection is concerned with discovering when there is *too much* variation and with trying to reduce it. A machine, even when it is in adjustment, will turn out an occasional defective or off measurement part. Variable inspection isn't so much for the purpose of finding and removing such defectives as it is to make sure that they are neither extreme nor occurring too often.

In order to do this, control charts are set up showing limit lines for the largest average measurement allowed and for the smallest average measurement allowed. These "average" figures are the averages of the several measurements taken when the inspector makes his periodic check at the machines. There is little interest in the individual measurements. If one or two individual pieces are too big or too little for acceptance, this doesn't matter so long as the average is OK. Such occasional outsized parts are regarded as normal.

There is, however, interest in the spread between the extreme measurements of the units sampled. This range should be small, and if it is large, the process may be getting out of adjustment even though the average is still within the limits.

Variable inspection is sometimes used with already produced lots.

Compared to attribute inspection, such variable inspection is more costly, takes longer, and requires better-trained inspectors. But there are off-setting gains. For the same level of reliability of inspection, smaller samples can be used. This can be important wherever attribute sampling requires large samples.

In one circumstance, where testing is done to destruction, this is a very important advantage. Testing to destruction means pulling things apart or smashing them down and keeping a record of how much pressure they withstand before failing. In textiles you need to know how strong thread is. Paper and paperbound containers have to have a certain minimum strength. Concrete roads or floors have to have certain load-bearing strengths. Some samples fail soon and some not so soon. Your interest is in the measurements and the average of the measurements.

If you used attribute inspection here, you would just set some limit and test to find how many items stood up to this limit and how many failed first. To get any reliable idea about a lot's quality, you'd have to test a large number of items. But with variable inspection, you test a much smaller sample to destruction and note, for each item, the load it with-stood before failure. Variable inspection gives you far more reliable evidence about a lot's quality, per item inspected, than does attribute inspection.

Not only that, but variable inspection covering factory operations is done right at the machine as products are made. The nature and extent of the defects found often tell you something about how the machine should be reset to correct the trouble.

CONTROL CHARTS FOR VARIABLES

Quality control's greatest contribution comes from preventing the making of defects. As we have implied, this can best be done by using variable inspection right at the machine and keeping up-to-date "control charts" there. These are the Shewhart charts referred to on page 593.

Control charts show whether the machine or process is turning out products that meet tolerances and specifications. If it is not turning out good work, then it needs resetting. And if resetting still doesn't correct the trouble maybe the machine isn't capable of turning out such close tolerance work. You'll have to be satisfied with more defectives than you'd like or else get a better machine.

When using control charts, the quality control inspector stops at each controlled machine, say, every half hour, and measures a small sample of the output, perhaps five units. The average measurement of the five items is plotted on the control chart which has a horizontal time scale so that the inspector can plot a figure for 10:30 A.M., 11:00 A.M., etc. The vertical scale on the chart is a scale of measurements.

The chart also shows limit lines running horizontally across the chart. Whenever the average measurement gets outside the limit zone, the operation is "out of control." Tool wear, for example, usually causes the dimensions of the products being made to drift away from the ideal measurement.

Individual items, of course, always show some variation usually resulting from causes either beyond our control or which can be controlled only at high cost. For example, when several gears have to work together there is usually some "play" or looseness. By costly precise machining the gears can be made so perfectly that the play is eliminated, but doing this almost always costs more than it is worth so we accept the variations that less costly machinery produces.

Sometimes there are process variations due to temperature or humidity changes. For most work these are so small that they are accepted as normal. But sometimes, as in some electronics and missile parts making, parts need to be made to very close tolerances. So we find work done in "clean rooms" where dust is eliminated, and the temperature and humidity are held constant.

Our point is that we try to eliminate variation up to some point but leave the remaining variation up to chance. The part we try to control is considered "assignable" variation. If it occurs we can usually find out why and eliminate the cause.

Control charts assume that the variations in actual measurements above and below the average size will follow the shape of the "normal" curve. And although, unknown to you, this may not be true in a given situation, this assumption is the best that you can make and it usually is a valid assumption.

In a normal curve distribution, the dispersion of the actual measurements above and below the average follows the "normal" or bell-shaped curve. The dispersion is usually expressed in standard deviations. The standard deviation is usually indicated by the Greek letter sigma, σ. We explained this in Chapter 21. There we said that, in a normal curve distribution, the mean ± 1 standard deviation sets limits between which 68 per cent of all measurements fall. Plus or minus 2 standard deviations sets limits between which 95 per cent of the cases fall. And the mean measurement ± 3 standard deviations sets limits between which practically all cases fall (actually 997 out of 1,000 cases fall within these limits). The horizontal control limit lines on control charts which we spoke of above are usually the ± 3 standard deviation limits.

Turning now to quality control in operation. Suppose that the inspector finds that the average measurement of the five sample items that he measures at 11:00 o'clock is outside the 3 σ limits. What has he learned? He has learned that this much off is not a chance variation. Something has happened to the process to change the sizes of products it is turning out. The operation is "out of control."

Often, however, you don't really want to let products be produced even this much (± 3 standard deviations) off the perfect dimension. If so, you can set a limit of 2 standard deviations. But chance alone will result in 32 per cent of the samples yielding average measurements outside the 2 standard deviation limits when actually the process is in control. This means that in 32 per cent of the cases when the average is beyond limits, the process is still in control and really needs no fixing. Yet if you were to use this rule (beyond 2 standard deviations is too much), you'd go ahead and adjust this machine anyway. You would make a type II error.

Control charts are not like acceptance sampling because you can't find precomputed charts in statistics books. You have to make your own.

To start with, you need to find out what the variation is in the products now being turned out by a machine. Suppose that for a certain job on a certain machine you plan to have your inspector measure samples of 4 units every half-hour. Have him measure 10 such samples for the purpose of getting data on which to base the control chart (20 or 30 samples would be better).

You need this first set of figures in order to calculate two other figures, the first of which is the grand average measurement for all 40 items. Second, for each sample of 4, you need to know their measurement range, the difference between the largest and smallest of the 4 items. Next, having gotten these 10 ranges, calculate the average range.

Now you are ready to use the following precomputed table:

NUMBER IN EACH SAMPLE	FACTOR
2	1.88
3	1.02
4	.73
5	.58
6	.48
7	.42
8	.37

Suppose that in our example, the grand average of all 40 measurements was .420 inch and that the average of the 10 ranges was .007 inch. The .420 inch is the mean measurement of the work now being turned out by the machine. Next we refer to our table and find that for sample sizes of 4, the factor is .73. So we multiply the average range of .007 inch by .73 and get .0051 inch. (We will round this off to .005.) The mean plus .005 is the upper control limit and minus .005 is the lower limit. So our control limits are .425 and .415 inch. These are the measurements on the vertical scale from which we draw horizontal lines across the chart to serve as the 3 σ limit lines.

Notice that this process for setting limit lines completely ignores tolerances or allowed deviations. This is because all that we are doing is finding out what the process is now doing. If it happens that the tolerance limits allow more deviation than we are getting, all is well. But if the tolerances are, say, .422 and .418, then the present operation (assuming that it is now correctly set up) is not capable of doing as well as we'd like. There will be a good many parts that are beyond tolerance limits and will have to be rejected. We may have to go to 100 per cent inspection in order to catch and remove the off-standard items. Or we may have to get a new machine capable of doing more precise work. Otherwise we will just have to relax our standard and accept what we are getting.

Process control chart uses are not limited to determining whether processes are in control or not. If, for example, tool wear is slowly causing the sizes of products to change, this will show up as the periodic half-hour checks show the average measurement moving closer to one of the limits. The trend shows that the process will soon be out of control, so we find out that we should really stop and reset the machine now, before things get worse. Or if things aren't yet very bad we can, by watching the trend of the dots, predict how long we can wait before taking action.

It is possible too for several successive dots to be above or below the perfect measurement yet show no directional trend. Should this happen, it is probable that some minor change in the way the machine operates has occurred. Operators on different shifts may use slightly different settings for the same operation, or the raw material in two different supply tanks may not be quite alike. If you draw material alternately from these tanks you get some variation even though the process remains in control. Unless things get worse, no corrective action may be needed.

You may also be interested in the process's variability. If so you can construct control charts for the range with upper and lower limit lines. These are constructed in the same way as are regular control charts dealing with average measurements. Tables showing the precomputed factors to use are in statistics books.

If you were to use charts both for averages and for ranges, you might find that both were out of control at the same time, although either one can be out of control by itself. Tool wear, for example, will usually affect average measurements but not the process variability. Bearing wear, on the other hand, will usually affect variability but not process averages.

Control charts can show good conditions as well as bad. If the process average or the range shows less than normal variation, you should try to find out why and to keep on doing whatever has made it good. Perhaps a worker has modified a jig or has found some other way to improve a job. He should get a suggestion award bonus and his improvement be made standard and new charts drawn up.

CONTROL CHARTS FOR ATTRIBUTES

Earlier we spoke of using attribute inspection in connection with acceptance sampling. And we have just been talking about control charts for variables as if all control charts dealt with variables. This is usually so but attribute control charts can be and sometimes are used.

P–CHARTS   P-charts are one kind of attribute control chart. They are the same as variable control charts except that the vertical scale is a percentage defective scale instead of a measurement scale. Setting up such charts is like setting up variable control charts. You have to first inspect quite a number of samples and find the percent defectives in each, then calculate the standard deviation of the several percentages found, thus allowing you to set control limits. The charts are then used just as are variable control charts.

Although attribute inspection is go–no-go inspection and is therefore easier than measurement inspection, it requires much larger samples both for setting up the charts and for using them. The periodic checks during the day have to be of samples of 50 or more in order to get percentage defective results which have any reliability at all. The sample size should also always be the same regardless of the size of the parent lot otherwise the size of the standard deviation and the control limits would change.

Although attribute control charts tell you when a job is out of control just as do variable control charts, they, in contrast with variable charts, tell you nothing about why. You don't learn whether dimensions are too large or too small or are drifting in one or the other direction. The causes of trouble are harder to find with attribute charts.

C–CHARTS   C-charts are also attribute charts but here you are plotting the ratio of defects of several kinds per unit or per 100 units of product. You might use C-charts, for example, with bolts of cloth. The kinds of defects can be many, knots in the thread, dirty or discolored spots, missing threads, etc. Surface blemishes of all kinds are counted as defects. If they get to be too many, the process is out of control.

In the case of C-charts the sample is a single standard unit, such as 1 yard of cloth.

One difference, however, is that since the defects are independent of each other and are random events, C-charts are based on Poisson distributions. This means that the standard deviation is calculated a little differently. It is the square root of the average number of defects per sample found in the samples used to furnish data for the charts. After the standard deviations are obtained, C-charts are made up and used just as P-charts are.

STUDY MATERIALS

26-1   If you were told to set up a quality control "system" how would you go about it?

26-2   To what type of productive process would the "zero defect" concept appear to be most applicable? How would you go about "selling" it to workers? Does it have application in maintenance work?

26-3   Outside research: Examine the Dodge-Romig tables or MIL-STD-105D and report on the interrelationships of the various components of a quality control system, such as the AQL, LTPD, the consumer's and the producer's risk, the AOQL, the shape of the OC and AOC curves, the sample size, and the acceptable number of defects. Do this for single, double, and sequential sampling plans. Relate your findings to your answer to problem 26-2.

26-4   The specification requires the dimension to be 6.0 inches $\pm.04$ inch. Using a sample of 4 every half-hour gives you the following figures:

	8:30	9:00	9:30	10:00	10:30	11:00	11:30	12:00	12:30	1:00
Sample average	5.96	6.06	5.90	5.94	6.07	6.15	6.11	6.01	6.07	5.86
Sample range	.058	.045	.014	.066	.061	.204	.047	.075	.038	.027

1   Was the operation ever, or is it at 1:00 o'clock, out of control?

2   If it is in control does it seem to be on the way to getting out of control?

The next day the following data were reported

	10:00	10:30	11:00	11:30	12:00
Sample average	6.20	6.08	6.25	6.31	6.33
Sample range	.044	.052	.063	.056	.078

3   Answer again questions 1 and 2.

4   Should the inspector take any action? What action and why?

5   What might cause the effects indicated?

26-5   What is the difference between attribute and variable inspection? Are all situations the one or the other? What difference does it make in the statistical methods whether inspection is attribute or variable?

26-6   Your specification says 4 inches $\pm.02$ inch. Your process reports show an average of .398 inch and a standard deviation of variations of .009 inch. Do these
figures call for any action by anyone? Who? What action?

26-7   On P-charts is there any good reason for a lower limit? Isn't it good to have this
number go to zero? If you say that you should have a lower limit line other than
zero, justify your position.

26-8   Suppose that you are to set up a control chart and get the following figures
while taking 9 sets of 3 measurements for setting up your chart:

.995	.993	.987	.989	1.004	.990	1.009	1.013	.987
.994	.991	.988	1.007	.990	.988	1.008	1.007	.991
.996	.990	.995	.990	.996	.999	1.002	.996	1.011

1   Set up the control chart.

2   The next three sets of measurements are:

1.007	1.001	.998
1.012	.990	1.005
.990	1.012	1.004

Is the operation in control? Is it headed out of control?

chapter twenty-seven

OTHER SHOP PROBLEMS

COUNT PROBLEMS

All companies have a certain amount of trouble with counts of how many items pass through certain operations. Some of these problems come from deliberate misrepresentation by pieceworkers but much of it comes out of the nature of the work and from the fact that men can't always tell what items are by looking at them.

Lost identification tags make part of this trouble. So do tag shortages. Products come to an operation in, say, five tote pans and leave in six, the extra one being untagged. Lefts and rights are troublesome too. They are often alike in almost every detail and are sometimes mistaken one for the other. Repairs and reruns also make trouble. They get counted not at all or they get counted twice. Besides, factory operators sometimes make errors and you get wrong reports. You must, of course, try to have as accurate counts as you can without spending too much time on counting.

Job tickets tell when the man starts and finishes his operation. Some companies also have the inspector write in on the man's ticket how many good pieces he turned out. You don't get such a check after every job, however, because you don't inspect after every job. Nor do you always, even when you do inspect, inspect every piece. Usually the count of pieces turned out is the same as the number on the order so you might think that you wouldn't need to check the man's own count. You do need to check, though, otherwise you won't find out about the losses from a few defectives at each operation that keep eating into the quantity.

You'd expect that job tickets would be pretty good reports of work done, and they are. Yet here is a situation that J. P. Smith Shoe Company ran into where it wasn't so. The men were on piecework and they collected their own job tickets for work done. Job tickets in the shoe industry are tags that the worker pulls off the traveler copy of the order. The men collect tags and turn them in at the end of the pay period as their report of work done. Meanwhile, of course, the work itself has gone on to other operations.

The men, at the end of February, started to save their last tag and report it as part of March's work. Then they held perhaps two March tags and reported them in April, and maybe three or more April tags for the May report. The added hold-back was so little each time as not to be particularly noticeable. Then in May, the men turned in all their tags, holding back none. And the purpose behind it all? To boost May's earnings because vacation pay was calculated at so many hours of pay at the hourly rate earned in May!

Actually, job tickets, if you use an incentive pay plan, are not perfect reports of work done. Unless you police their reports rather carefully, the men will exaggerate the quantities and fail to report scrap. And they will ring the clock wrongly on tightly and loosely timed jobs. On a loose piece rate, they will start another job before they ring out on the last job (the one with the loose rate) so that you won't find out that they got the job done so quickly. Then they'll ring in on a tight rated job after they have started in it, not because they want you to think that they can do that job so quickly but to cover up the extra time left over from the previous job.

A. O. Foote Company once found men turning in time cards two and three weeks, even a month, after they did jobs. This wasn't typical but it happened when the men had several loosely rated jobs one right after the other. They were afraid to turn in the cards right away lest their high earnings reveal the loose rates and lead to cuts. It came to light when time

FIGURE 27-1   Weigh counting is a good quick way to get reasonably accurate counts. (Toledo Scale Corp.)

cards were turned in for several jobs after they had been shipped and whose job orders had been closed in the accounting department.

Naturally, you don't want this situation and the better your time study standards, the less of it you'll have. Also, these matters don't often affect production control very much. They just mean that your actual operating times differ, here and there, from what your record shows. You can control clock misringing pretty well by having the dispatcher do all the card ringing. Just don't have clocks around the plant for the men to ring their own cards. Even then collusion is not unknown.

ASSEMBLY FLOOR SHORTAGES

As a practice, don't deliver assembly parts accumulations to the assembly floor until they are complete. Then there won't be any assembly floor shortages of individual parts. But you can't always wait. There are times when you have to go ahead with assembly and hope to get the missing parts before it is their turn to be attached.

Assembly floor shortages are not always known ahead. You think that you have all the parts or you have them scheduled to arrive before their need, and then you find that they don't arrive or that you just don't have them after all.

Sometimes assembly floor shortages are not because you don't have enough parts but because when you try to put parts together, they don't fit. Parts should never have to be rejected at the assembly floor because they should have been inspected when they were made. But nevertheless parts sometimes don't fit or don't work and have to be rejected no matter that they were passed or got by your earlier inspection. Reports of assembly floor rejects are highly important because you have to replace the parts right away. Even if they are stocked parts, you will have to take more out of stock than you intended. And if they are special you'll have to repair the rejects right away or make some more and do it fast.

Since it is very costly to hold up assembly, you need to pay special attention to shortages at the assembly floor. What can you do about them? First, at the assembly floor itself, "work around the shortage" if you can. Go ahead with assembly work and put on the missing part later.

After you've done as much of this as you can (but don't assemble far enough so that you will have to take the product apart to put in the missing part when it arrives), you have to try something else. Next, if you are still held up, try to push other jobs through. Go ahead and work ahead of schedule on other jobs if their parts are ready. Meanwhile, of course, you are pushing the missing parts along toward the assembly floor as fast as possible. If the delayed parts lot is sizable, it may pay to split it and send ahead a small number of parts, pushing them through the remaining operations as fast as you can so that assembly will not be held up. Later, when the delayed parts for the first order come in, hold back on other jobs and push the delayed products through.

When the assembly floor is desperately in need of parts you don't want to delay them by putting them into finished stock and then having to withdraw them. Send them directly to the assembly floor even though you do, on your books, charge the parts into finished goods and out again.

Be sure, though, to send a notice of the parts order completion to the finished goods stockman so that he will check it off his short list. Otherwise you'll be asking him if the parts are all ready so that assembly can go ahead and he'll say no although they are available.

If the parts are common parts you want only part of the lot to go to the assembly floor directly. You can save trouble here by making out a requisition ahead for the quantity needed by assembly. Attach it to the shop order back in the factory. Then when the lot is finished, deliver to assembly the requisitioned quantity and send the rest of the order and the requisition to the stock room.

COMING OUT EVEN   You need to try to come out even on parts for assembled products. If you are short any parts, you'll have to put through rush orders for ones and twos to get exactly the right amount, and yet you don't want extras because most of them will be waste. Such little orders are so expensive if you put them through the regular operation that you might better make them more or less by hand in the toolroom machine shop in the short-run shop.

You may wonder, though, what goes on sometimes when, after an assembly order is finished, you have quite a stock of leftover parts, some of which were made to the exact number needed. You wonder what improvisation the men put into the products. Sometimes they rob parts from other orders or may just leave out the part. The first that you know about this is when you hear from the customer. Sometimes your records were in error and you had more parts than you knew about. Sometimes rejected parts are replaced by making up more parts. Then somehow the rejected parts get repaired and turn up at the assembly floor after all. In any case, production control should try its best not to end up with a pile of waste parts.

ROBBING ORDERS
Occasionally orders in process are "robbed." Men use the materials intended for one order for another. Sometimes the robbing is done by work-

ers who mistakenly get hold of the wrong materials. More often it is done by workers who have spoiled or lost the regular material and want to avoid criticism. This type of robbery makes a good bit of trouble for production control since the shortage on the robbed order is not reported. Losing the material or even a whole order is bad but almost worse is the fact that you don't know about it for a while. When you find out about it, you have to make out new orders and schedules and do it fast. Unfortunately, too, an order that disappears after operation 5 has to be replaced by an order which has to start in at operation 1. Also, robberies sometimes result in parts being made from the wrong raw material.

Order robbing is not always of the unauthorized type described above. You sometimes do it intentionally but if you do you know about it and so start replacement orders through right away. The sales department comes in with a rush order from a good customer for a product which you are already making for someone else. You just transfer the items over to the new order number and soon have them ready to ship. Of course, doing this makes no end of extra paper work for production control what with different quantities on the orders and with having to start some more items into production to replace the robbery.

Consider, too, the effect on your salesmen and customers. How will the ones that the robbed order was intended for take it? Be careful that you don't end up protecting the salesman who gives the most rash promise dates to customers.

Usually the possibilities of changing partly made items from one order to another late in processing are quite limited because, operation by operation, different end products become more different from each other. But in companies whose end products are more similar, you find a good bit of order robbing, particularly during boom times. A piston ring manufacturer reports that in his company there is a great deal of shuffling of rings between orders as the work goes through the shop. It can be done easily since the flnal operation determines the exact type of rings made. Up to that operation, several types of rings can be made from the castings that are in process. TRW, too, can do this with valves up almost to the last operation.

Actually, authorized parts order robbing is a little like using the "basics" idea. You start parts or products through production not wholly sure to what order they will be assigned. That you end up changing your mind and using the items first intended for one order for another order is not too much a condemnation of robbing. It gives you a great deal of flexibility and lets you fill last-minute orders quickly. It is, however, hard on production control because it has to replace the robbed parts and it must do it quickly or it will be in trouble on the robbed order.

Accumulated sets of parts at the assembly floor are sometimes robbed by men needing parts for an order they are already working on. This makes no end of trouble because it isn't reported and then the next order is short of parts. But don't condemn the assemblers too quickly. What would you expect them to make assembled products out of if some parts are missing? They either stop production or get the parts where they find them. Maybe, if they came and asked you what to do, you would tell them to do the same.

But first you'd like to know why they are short of parts. The men were supposed to have enough parts. Your records said that they had enough. Where did the material go? Possibly the records were wrong but just as likely they were right and yet the parts are still short.

You never get good answers to what happened to missing parts and in one sense you don't care. What you want are parts not explanations. You do want explanations, of course, so as to prevent similar shortages in the future. Actually, many of today's shortages come from yesterday's robberies, from men taking minor parts home, from men spoiling parts during assembly and throwing them away, from parts that just don't fit and so are tossed aside, and from errors in your records. Or you may lose an order this way: it comes into the department and is set on the floor. Other items get piled on top until you don't know what is on the bottom. The order is now lost and you are short the parts. Later, of course, you find the order, probably after you have made up a replacement order. If this happens, better set up a procedure to tell you what is in a pile so this kind of thing won't continue.

Some of these reasons for being short are perfectly legitimate and the men ought to tell you about the losses but they don't. They just solve problems their own way and leave you in the dark about the future problems that they are making for you.

You may also have to contend with parts being robbed from assembled products. A radio company found that when experimental department employees working on Saturday wanted an antenna they just took it from the assembled products ready for shipping. Expediters also make trouble by robbing (if you let them in to the stock room) the finished parts stock room and assembly parts sets. They take parts for today's work from the supplies that you expected to use for tomorrow's products and they don't tell you about it.

But aren't we looking at only one side of the picture? What about the engineers and laboratory technicians who come in to work on Saturday? Don't they need materials sometimes? Yes, they do. You ought to take care of them. If you don't want to keep a stock-room employee on duty you still ought to do something for them. One electronics company keeps a special unlocked stock room for such men so that they can help themselves. There is some loss, of course, but the paper work savings more than offsets it and the technicians are not handicapped by having no materials to work with.

We should note that the problem of how to deal with order robbing is not a job for a computer. This is one of so many parts of production control work that need human attention.

SHRINKAGE

Probably there are good reasons for material shrinking a little in quantity as it goes through most departments. It can happen literally in some companies. Liquids, for example, evaporate. Procter and Gamble finds this to be so in soap manufacture. So do chemical manufacturers and oil refineries. Sometimes there are little things that foremen can do to correct or to hold down even this kind of shrinkage. If so, it is a good idea to set budgets for it and to keep department heads under some pressure to hold it down.

Some companies apply the same idea in a general way to all kinds of materials losses, whether they be scrap, pilferage, or whatever. They charge the foreman with everything that goes into his department and he is given very little allowance for losses whatever their cause. After all, as far as the company is concerned, the materials are gone no matter the reason. Doing this seems to help hold down losses.

PETTY THIEVERY

Unfortunately men will pilfer things, personal property from fellow workers or anything that they can carry home belonging to the company. They seem somehow to think that stealing from a company is not really stealing. A man who takes home a file, screwdriver, micrometer, radio tube, wire, electric soldering iron, or even a package of pencils doesn't think of himself as a thief at all. Such items he thinks are inconsequential. In fact, in the case of small tools, carrying them home may be accidental. Only failure to return them is intentional.

One company, wanting a photograph of large numbers of workers streaming out of the factory, kept the main gate closed long enough to hold up enough men for a good picture. Before the gate was opened, a rumor spread that a gate check was being made for stolen property. Within moments all kinds of things were dropped. After looking over the veritable gold mine of small tools and portable items left, the plant manager said, "We knew that they were robbing us, but not that badly."

Materials, parts, tools, and supplies are all subject to being taken home. Probably you should try to stop it by looking in lunch boxes of men leaving once in a while and by having guards at the gates eye people suspiciously. At Bell and Howell all the men must show open lunch boxes every day when they go home. Eight millimeter moving picture cameras and similar equipment are very tempting.

One electronics company found that it had altogether too many "ham" radio fans on its payroll. It had no end of trouble with disappearing diodes, transistors, condensers, tubes, and the like. It wasn't only the value of the items that made trouble, even worse was running out of stock. Finally it adopted the policy of *giving, free* to the men, any parts that they asked for. This licked the problem. Authorized take-home items didn't amount to much and unauthorized disappearances naturally stopped.

By making a show of policing thievery you prevent most big stealing. Actually, you don't want to catch people stealing because you'd have to fire them but you do want to keep stealing to a minimum. And certainly you want to stop all organized large-scale stealing. Also, there is a lot of sympathy for the underdog. It is hard to escape being a Simon Legree when a million dollar company fires poor Joe Doaks who was caught stealing a 50-cent item.

You might as well face it. Any item having use in the home is doomed to shrinkage. The company will almost surely furnish most of the hand work tools that men have in their basement workshops at home. A few companies let men sign out tools for home use and make it so easy for them to take things home officially that there is no reason to steal. One company even lets the men charge themselves for tools taken home. It reports very low loss since starting this practice.

You have trouble, too, with materials, particularly scrap. Better let men take home small pieces of scrap to work on or sell them at 5- and 10-cent prices in a scrap shop. Until they did this, airplane companies had trouble with plexiglass disappearing. The men took small pieces home to make carvings. Not only that but because of loose production standards the men even did their hobby work on the job just to keep busy.

You need also to watch toolroom employees lest they take home tools and the same warning applies to stock-room employees. They, too, are not above helping themselves. One way that helps is to put the supervisor's desk where he has a good view of his stock room.

Another way is to act as if your stores have value. Take care of them. If the company is careless about material it is small wonder if a man feels that "I might as well take it before it has to be thrown out" or "Since I can use it, I might as well take this old rusty stuff because it will never be used anyway."

EXPEDITERS

There are two kinds of expediters, inside and outside. Outside expediters, working for the purchasing department, call on suppliers in order to try to hurry up the critical items you have purchased. They are outside the province of production control except when one of your customers' outside expediters gets into your plant to annoy you.

Inside expediters go by many names. You'll find them called "followup men," "stock chasers," or even "coordinators" or "schedulers." Expediters are a part of most production control procedures. They are "after-the-fact" planners and should be supplements to production control rather than the main kind of control. They can break bottlenecks but can't prevent them. Actually, production control people, not titled expediters, do a great deal of expediting. So do foremen. A great deal of expediting is sometimes done in companies having no "expediters."

Expediters are trouble shooters; they find lost jobs and push late jobs and orders for items on short lists. They "bird dog" or "father" the fussy and "hot" jobs through production, trying to foresee and eliminate probable delays.

Theoretically, you should not need expediters because your production control system ought to pass out complete enough directions and get back adequate control reports to get production out. Where production control is highly centralized you shouldn't need expediters at all, but because things don't always go right, you may need some. You'll find them in all decentralized systems.

Expediters seem to be particularly helpful on rejected items. Once a lot or a shipment from a vendor gets rejected, it seems that everybody loses interest in it. By the time it shows up on a shortage sheet it is too late to handle it in an economic manner. Every plant seems to have places where rejected lots find resting spots until some wild-eyed expediter, desperately in need of it, unearths it.

Expediters are primarily job pushers. They push orders through the plant faster than they would otherwise go. This applies only to particular orders and not to all orders. Actually, why would you ever need job pushers? All good production control procedures provide a system for pushing rush orders through. Mark rush orders "rush" and make everybody work on rush orders first. But it just doesn't work out that way. If telling someone to do something were the same as having it done, you wouldn't need any expediters. But things don't go as planned, particularly when you are busy, so you need expediters.

Even in centralized control where you get good reports of work done and know pretty well where orders are all the time, an order gets lost once in a while. You'll have to put your expediter on it. Tell him to locate it and find out why it was delayed and try to get it moving again. The expediter in this case is more a job finder than an investigator or pusher. You are only slightly interested in why something happened. What you want is to get the job moving again. If you need a thorough investigation, someone in engineering or an assistant to the superintendent, not the expediter, should make it. After finding the order, the expediter in centralized control need follow it no farther, because the scheduler can see that it is rushed through the remaining operations.

In decentralized control you rely more on expediters. The looser control means more lost and delayed orders. Expediters work for the production control office, but they do their work in all the parts-producing departments. Some companies, Timken, for one, don't have expediters, but they expect foremen to go even into other departments and try to expedite behind-time orders. Most companies would frown on this.

An expediter pushes a job through by first of all finding the order, the material itself, if it is lost. Then it must be moved to the next operation. Small lots the expediter himself may carry or truck to the next operation. Bigger lots are moved by a trucker. Then the expediter gets the scheduler to assign an early time on a specific machine to do the operation. He should try to extract a promise from the foreman—a definite promise and not just a promise to "work on it." This is all that the expediter can do for the moment. But he doesn't forget the order. He keeps checking back from time to time to see that the order does get put on the machine and that the operation gets done. Meanwhile, he arranges for machine times with foremen or schedulers for the remaining operations so that there won't be much between operations dead time. Between operations the expediter sees to it that the material is moved quickly even if he has to move it himself.

Sometimes he finds that there is some reason why a certain operation can't be done on the order. Lack of special tools, for example, might be holding up the job. If he finds that the cause for the delay is something minor, he is supposed to have it taken care of and get the order on its way. Bigger delays he reports to production control. It is part of his job to find out the reason for delay and report what he finds to the control office. Someone there then takes over and tries to get the cause of the hold-up removed. The expediter will, however, keep checking back with the control office periodically to see whether the cause of the delay has been removed.

When expediters are used extensively, you have to watch that they don't push orders too hard because other orders get pushed back. Sometimes at the expediter's urging the foremen will tear down a machine set up for one job to do the rush job and then set up the machine again for the first job. This gets the rush order out all right but at the cost of extra setups. Worse yet, the setups eat up machine time and pyramid the rush order problem.

Foremen usually don't like to see expediters headed their way. No one likes to be rushed, especially by someone not his boss. Besides running up the foremen's expense there is the open question of authority. In most companies the expediter's authority is a little vague. The foreman is supposed to pay attention to the expediter's requests yet not if he asks for costly changes or for overtime work. You never quite know whether he is expediting a job that the president of the company wants hurried along or not. Expediters usually create a certain amount of dissension. Don't write them off, however, because they seem to be necessary evils although some companies manage to get along without them. They are much like Gantt charts and control boards in that they serve best when production is at such levels that regular control procedures tend to break down occasionally.

CONTACTING SUPPLIERS

While it is true that outside expediters belong to purchasing, it is also true that sometimes production control men need to talk to suppliers directly about shipments.

Usually this is done unofficially by telephone. Production control men discuss with the supplier's production control men details of quantities and shipping dates and get it all settled. Then it is all confirmed in writing by the purchasing department writing to the vendor company's sales department.

MATERIALS MOVEMENT

In order control, you have to move materials around from place to place by truck so you have to tell truckers what materials to move and where to move them. In companies using centralized control, truckers usually work for and get their instructions from production control. You can use written-out or computer-prepared move orders but most companies rely on the traveling copy of the shop order to tell the trucker.

If you do use move orders, the truckers will get them from departmental dispatchers just as operators get their job tickets. Like the operator, the trucker signs and returns the move order after he has moved the material.

If you rely on the traveler copy of the shop order to convey instructions to truckers, foremen, inspectors, or dispatchers can just tell truckers verbally what is ready to move. Or you can use departmental pick-up stations. They are locations in which orders ready to be moved are set out for the trucker. He takes all orders placed there to the operation shown on the traveler as the next to be done.

It is a good idea for truckers to report material moves so that the production control department will know that they have been made. Also, truckers usually deliver orders to a receiving area in a department rather than to a machine. This is often a good-sized area of floor space or it may be storage bins where orders coming into the department are temporarily held. Floor spaces and bins are numbered. If the traveler gives you a report of the move he can also write down the exact storage point where he left the order. Moves can then be recorded on the "tracer" copy of the shop order in the production control office or recorded on the computer tape.

Move orders are not commonly used in decentralized control. Foremen have laborers who do all of the moving of material within their departments and on to the next department, although moving orders between departments is sometimes assigned to a plant-wide transportation department.

Big items, those requiring overhead crane service, you might wish to move from one work station to another between shifts. Since it may be a slow process, allowing a half-hour between shifts will give ample time for the move, yet will not idle your whole workforce while the move takes place. If you moved the project (it might be a locomotive) during work hours, no one could work on it while it was being moved and besides they have to stand clear during the move itself.

DRAWING CONTROL

When you have thousands of drawings in your file and more coming every day, filing them and finding them get to be quite a job. Very little of this is production control's job. But production control does have to requisition the drawings the shop needs and to see that they get to the man on the job and are returned after use.

Today many companies use computers to help in drawing control. A drawing is photographed and reduced down to a film perhaps an inch square. This film is inserted into a window hole in a computer tabulating card like the one in figure 11-4. The card itself is punched with the drawing's identification. When you want it, the computer will find it and, on a magnifying and reproducing unit, blow it up and make as many copies as you want and then return the card to the file of drawing aperture cards.

Computerized handling of drawings has not yet, however, replaced older procedures. By no means do all companies have their drawing handling computerized.

Some companies using older methods use "drawing cribs" in the various departments. In each they keep the drawings used regularly in the department. This sounds like a good idea but this makes men have to come to the crib for the drawings and to make a return trip after they are finished with them. The men not only waste time but also they may start their own personal files of drawings and not return them. So you have to have more drawings. Besides, on repeat jobs, the men use their old prints and don't find out about changes.

Before Northrop Aircraft went to computers to help in handling drawings, it found that, what with issuing 2,600 drawings a day, its men took over eight minutes per drawing just getting drawings. And this in spite of the fact that they averaged getting two drawings on each trip to the crib. Northrop then changed to central drawing control and delivered drawings to some 45 delivery points in the plant. Requests came in by phone. Used drawings went into drawing mailboxes around the plant. Northrop cut its use from 26 copies to 18 for jumbo-sized drawings and to 10 of the little one- or two-fold kinds. Northrop figured that this move saved it $160,000 a year, half from savings in lost time of operators and half from cutting down on the number of copies of drawings. Computers have since improved on this gain.

TOOL CONTROL

Large companies have several toolrooms. You find a central tool storeroom, where special and particularly expensive tools that may be needed at different places in the plant are kept. There are also departmental tool storerooms where supplies of tools frequently used in the department are kept. And there are dead storerooms for tooling no longer in use. Departmental tool storerooms are usually too small to store tooling used only occasionally even though it is used nowhere else. The central storeroom keeps such items.

Tooling needs control, just as does raw materials. Don't forget, though, that in thinking of the need to control tools, *serving the shop*, not controlling the tools, comes first. Any system of storing, issuing, inspecting, or maintaining tools should be subservient to serving the shop. And it should serve the shop with little or no delay of production.

Inside the tool crib, you need indexes to tell you where tools are stored —what row, cabinet, shelf, and shelf division. And you need a charge-out system so that you can tell at all times where issued tools are. You ought also to have, in the toolroom, a record card for each kind of item. Such cards show the quantity you have on hand, the number of each item worn out or broken in use, and the replacement quantities ordered and received in the past.

You ought to keep separate record cards for each special tool and each kind of "wearing" tool (cutting tools, grinding wheels, etc.). Show on the card the tool's name, identification number, drawing number, storage location, and amount on hand. Cards for special tools should show the

FIGURE 27-2 Careful storing of tooling makes it last longer and saves the time of issue clerks.

items for which they are used and the machine operation where they are used.

Wearing or "expendable" tools must be reordered and kept in stock just as are regular raw materials. You can show reorder points and quantities on the card. Wearing tools regularly used in the factory are not always returned to the toolroom. When you issue them, just assume that they are used up. Subtract the quantity issued from the card and order more when the stock runs low. It is better, though, to make the men return worn-out expendable tools to the toolroom before you issue any more to them. This holds down wasteful throwing away of halfworn expendable tools.

Be careful, though, when trying for low tool costs. You don't want the men repairing tools and saving tools and finding substitutes. One company found that a tight-fisted tool issue clerk was unintentionally causing these things to the extent that it hurt production. His efforts to save were costing the company far more than he saved.

Be careful too that your tool control procedure doesn't make men waste time. If they will use up one tool and need another or even if the tool will need sharpening before they finish a job, issue two or more at the start. This saves them trips to the toolroom. Don't even let machine operators sharpen their own tools. Their doing it takes their time and their machine's time, and they may do a poor job of it anyway. Save these losses by issuing the man enough tools, and sharpen tools in the toolroom.

Keep a record of tooling and accessories issued, so that you know where everything is all the time and who is using them. Perhaps you can get by with no more record than operators' tool checks. Every time a man withdraws a tool from the toolroom he leaves one of his tool checks at the tool crib in exchange. His tool check has his number on it. Hang it on the hook for the tool issued.

You can also have a more formal tool control procedure. Some companies use written tool requisitions made out and signed by the foreman. Sometimes they are made in triplicate so that the toolroom can keep two files, one showing the tool issued and one showing who has it. The man keeps the third copy. Tool orders are sometimes made out ahead by the production control department.

Chrysler's Airtemp division uses a charge-a-plate (like a credit card). Airtemp's men fill in the tool number that they want on a punched card, then the credit card is used to put his name on it and he gets his tool, and gets charged with it too. Airtemp also issues kits of tools to men who use varied tools. They go in a locked box issued to and charged to individual men.

Getting tools to the job and back is always troublesome. You can do it three ways. First, you can let the man come to the tool crib for the tools he needs. Try to avoid this method because you lose machine time and the man so often has to wait at the tool crib. It is a costly way to do it. You have the advantage, though, that this way the man usually gets exactly the right tool, something that doesn't always happen otherwise.

Second, you can issue complete sets of tools to the men and make them responsible for them. Let the man keep them as long as he is on the job. This is what Airtemp does with its kits of tools. This method works fine for all the tools he uses regularly but won't do for the occasional special tool.

Third, production control can tell the toolroom in advance what tools will be needed and where and when. Toolroom employees can then deliver them and later pick them up and bring them back. This method calls for more planning but for special tools is probably the best.

Inspect all tools on their return to the toolroom to see if they need repair before further use. If they do, repair them before they are put away unless they are special and may not ever be used again. Some companies make factory foremen responsible for tool repair. They write out the repair orders. But most companies make tool inspection and repair a toolroom responsibility.

Make sure, too, that your tool crib men are careful. If they toss tools around carelessly, reprimand them. If they don't improve, get rid of them.

When in use, keep tooling at the job. Portable hand tools, such as nut tighteners, riveters, and soldering irons, are usually kept at the job, not in the toolroom. Extras are, of course, kept in the toolroom. If you let workers keep them in operating departments you can be sure that some tooling will get damaged or become lost. If it can be used in the men's home workshops, you can be sure that some of it will find its way there. Nor is it enough to control the use of tools by shop men. You have to watch the tool crib men themselves.

What should you do with old tooling used for completed jobs? Better store it for a while. Since you won't discard the machines for a good while, you could safely adopt a rule of keeping old tooling no longer than you keep the machine. But that is a maximum. Many special tools can safely be thrown away long before the machine is discarded. Keeping old tooling takes space, you have to keep records of it and its location, and you have to cover it with rust protection coatings.

It costs money to keep old tooling. Is it worthwhile? No pat answer can be given. In many cases the customer owns it. You can't scrap it until he says so. In other cases you have to keep it for several years because you guarantee customers to supply replacement parts for that long. In general, however, probably too much tooling is saved too long.

GAGE CONTROL

Everything said about tools also applies to gages but with one or two exceptions. Gage inspection is perhaps even more important than tool inspection. Also, gages don't wear or get out of adjustment very fast unless they are dropped or mishandled. Some of them, except for their need to be inspected, could stay forever in the shop and never come back to the tool crib.

This doesn't mean that you don't need to inspect gages. On the contrary, since people know that gages are in adjustment most of the time, they come to expect them to be in perfect adjustment all the time. So you need to set up a system of regular gage inspection either at the tool crib or at the jobs. Normally you check gages in use against master gages which are themselves ten times as accurate. But you'll need very precise master gages to check inspectors' gages because their gages are more accurate than the operator's gages. You may have to set up a gage checking laboratory, temperature controlled and dust free, to check inspectors' gages.

SPECIAL PROJECTS

In Chapter 2 we talked about special projects and how their enormous size and complexity made controlling their production very difficult. Projects of this kind are bread and butter items for some companies. They make them all the time although no two are ever alike.

In a way, controlling their production is easier then if they were less complex. You plan and schedule only in an overall way but it is impossible to plan minor details ahead. Probably you can't even make out an exact and complete bill of materials. Nor can you made out exact operation lists. Operation times cannot be determined ahead of time and you can't use time study to set standards on jobs that take days or weeks. PERT-type control can usually help on such special projects.

It is common for the engineering department to want to determine the final design of some parts as you make them. Needless to say, this makes delays at times and you'll end up making a good many costly changes but no one can foresee just how certain work will turn out. The magnitude, the sheer size alone, of some of the parts not only requires outsize machines to make them but gets you into unforeseen difficulties in manufacture.

Engineering, production control, and foremen all have to work together closely on these big jobs. Job instructions from production control are very incomplete and are largely confined to engineering specifications and drawings. You give the drawings and specifications to the foreman and almost tell him to go ahead on his own as far as operations are concerned. Schedules for getting the work out are very loose. They are really only "hoped for" dates, since no one really knows how long it will take to get the project out. Large projects of this sort sometimes take months to complete, so minutes, hours, or days do not matter in scheduling.

Companies having a considerable amount of this sort of work usually divide their main production control department into two main subdepartments. One is the "planning" department and the other is the "scheduling" department. The planning group handles all preliminary work before any scheduling is done and works very closely with the engineering department on getting materials and operating specifications made up. The scheduling group takes over when actual manufacturing schedules are to be made up. It makes up the PERT data and handles all dispatching and control of progress. The practice of subdividing the department this way is common in all companies, but you are almost sure to find it in special project companies.

It is characteristic of most large projects that you want only one or two items, and most orders are one-time affairs. You don't get a chance to learn from experience how to handle every possible situation and so to avoid mistakes in the future. This makes it doubly necessary to have everything worked out as well as you can in advance, although since so much of the work is unique, you have to "make haste slowly."

Wholly different projects are not the rule, however, even among special projects. Whenever new orders for similar items turn up, you can go ahead on a more planned basis. Some of the production difficulties will have been ironed out.

STUDY MATERIALS

27-1   One afternoon the plant guards held a surprise dinner box inspection of workers going home. Upon seeing this, one worker stepped into the office, left his dinner box, and went out empty-handed.

Later the box was found to contain half a dozen spoiled water pump parts. By looking at the last operation performed, the box was easily traced to the guilty man. He, it turned out, had for a long time made a practice of throwing extra spoiled parts into the river on the way home.

You in the production control department have had a good bit of trouble with orders turning up with short counts. What do you do about this?

27-2   The MacBurney Company has had trouble with parts not arriving at the assembly floor. The difficulty has not often been serious but has caused minor delays.

Parts intended for particular assembly orders have been made up and put into the finished parts stock instead of being taken to the accumulation bin. When assembly starts, their absence causes delay because they must be brought from finished stores.

Parts are manufactured on individual manufacturing orders and show the part identification and the identification number of the product they go into. The fact that some or all of these parts are to be used for a particular assembly order is not shown on the order.

Should the assembly order number be put on all manufacturing orders for parts to be used for that assembly order? Do you want parts delivered directly to the accumulation bin? How will you close the parts manufacturing order on your records if the parts go directly to the bin? How will you handle orders where the parts are to be used for two or more assembly orders? How will you handle orders where part of the lot is for an assembly order and the balance for stock?

27-3 At the assembly area, assemblers use parts directly from the adjacent accumulation stalls. Parts that don't fit are tossed aside or back into the supply and other parts are used. By the time the assemblers get down near the end of an order, they are short of parts or have only parts that don't fit. How can you, in production control, handle this situation?

This problem has also extended into the finished parts stock room. The assemblers, needing more of a part, go to the stock room and help themselves. How should this be handled?

27-4 The Waynesboro Furniture factory called the Wheeling Stamping Company to check on its order for 1,000 hinge and catch combinations for card tables. The call was made on the 25th of the month, and shipment had been promised on the 4th of the month following. A check on the progress of the order showed it to be nearly complete with no expediting being required.

On the 8th of the following month the Waynesboro company called again stating that the hinges had not arrived. It asked that they be sent on immediately. A search was made, and it was found that the production control department dispatcher had transferred the hinges from the Waynesboro order to an order for the Pensacola Furniture Company. Shipment to the Pensacola company had been made on the 2d of the month. The hinges originally on the Pensacola order were still in process and would be complete and ready for shipment on the Waynesboro order on the 15th. When asked why he had made this change, the dispatcher explained that the Pensacola order had farther to go, and since it would take several days longer in transit he had arranged to get it finished first.

Under what conditions should material for one order be used for another? What authority should be necessary? Who should be notified? What records should be changed if a transfer is made?

27-5 At the Bronxville Brass Company, order number 742, calling for 100 bushings with oil grooves, was reported to have had the grooves machined on July 8. No report of the following operations being performed was received, and Dick Moran, an expediter, was told to see what was holding it up. Moran went to the department but could not find the order. It seemed to have disappeared completely.

On checking with the dispatchers in the several departments where the order might be, he found that there was another order, number 547, which called for 250 quite similar bushings. This order was completed with 248 good pieces. A further check showed that 23 pieces from order 547 had been scrapped before it arrived in the ring groove machining department. Fourteen had been lost from order 742 when it arrived in that department.

The bushings made on order 547 were still in stock. They had two oil grooves on them and were supposed to be made from a slightly different bronze from that used for order 742. A dozen bushings from the bin were taken to the metallurgist, who said that four of them were made from the material used for order 742.

What causes orders to disappear? What are the possible consequences of situations such as that discussed above? How can they be prevented?

27-6   The Hanover Specialties Company makes a varied line of machine accessories for industrial users. Most of the work is made directly to customers' orders and most of the products are assembled products. Typically, there are several thousand parts orders in process at all times.

On a recent order 100 gears disappeared after passing through the heat-treating process. An extensive search proved fruitless, and a replacement order was rushed through production and used in the assembled product. Two months later the lost gears turned up. They were in a tote box on a skid in the corner of the heat-treating department. Other tote boxes, containing rejected material, had been placed on top of the box containing the gears. The storage area was one where there were always several skids on which were piled tote boxes of material. The skid and box in question were almost impossible to get to. When located, the gears had to be scrapped, since there was no use for them.

Is the above example an extreme situation? What weaknesses in the production control procedure permit such situations to arise? Can you prevent it without an overly detailed system?

27-7   The Simpson Spark Plug Company was somewhat chagrined to learn that its spark plugs were being marketed in the city where the factory was located at a retail price below its factory selling price. A check of dealer records disclosed that Joe's Handy Shop, where the spark plugs were being sold, was not listed as a purchaser. The spark plugs were genuine Simpson plugs and were of first quality. It appeared certain that they were being stolen by workers in the factory. A careful watch was kept of all finished stock, but the leak was not discovered.

Production records disclosed no disappearance of materials in process, yet Joe's Handy Shop continued to sell Simpson plugs at prices under factory costs. All the checking was done without fanfare and was carried on for a whole year. One day an unannounced inspection of empty lunch boxes of workers leaving at the end of the first shift was made. One lunch box was found to contain a substantial number of porcelain parts for spark plugs. Upon being confronted with this evidence, the employee explained the leak. Three employees were involved. Each took home an occasional handful of the completed parts made in his department. The spark plugs were assembled at their homes and sold to Joe's Handy Shop. Spark plug parts were made in very large numbers, and no exact counts were made during processing. Production records were all kept in terms of pounds instead of pieces, and tote boxes of parts were filled reasonably full and then sent on to the next operation. The few scrap pieces produced were thrown into scrap cans at the site of the operation. Generally no check was made on the volume of scrap except for an occasional check to see that it remained within the limits permitted. It was easy for workers to remove a few pieces at a time at any point in the operations without detection.

Can you devise a system to control this situation? Is petty thievery a problem in many companies? Would your system be worth its cost? Should you have regular lunch box inspection?

27-8 At the Ithaca Gun Company, every order for special items is assigned to an expediter who sees it through production. The expediters are somewhat demanding at times. If orders ahead of a special order would tie up all the available machines for several days, they insist on their specials being put ahead of the other orders, even rush orders for regular items temporarily out of stock. They also insist at times that machine setups be torn down and production halted on other orders, to get the specials out faster. The plant superintendent has finally told his foremen never to tear down a setup to put a special order on the machine and to let the specials wait their turn after regular stock rush orders.

What lines of authority should be set up to cover production situations like the above? Who should decide priority among orders? What authority should expediters have? Or should there be any expediters? What kind of procedure do you think would take care of the Ithaca Gun Company's problem?

27-9 The expediter is happy. He got the order through even though it took air express to get some of the parts. As president of the company are you happy? Are you going to do anything? What?

In order to convince the vendor of the urgency of your need, your expediter wants to go to the vendor plants involved. Should you send him? What can he do? Whom will he talk to? Does anyone use outside-of-the-plant expediters? Under what circumstances?

27-10 The Avon Parts Company has had only a poor system of tool crib operation and wants to improve upon it. Several problems are to be solved.

1 How can the tool crib be informed of the tool requirements for orders coming up so that it can have the tooling ready when the operation is to be performed?

2 How should standard tools such as drills, taps, and reamers be checked out? Also, if a standard tool checked out to an operator becomes part of a machine setup, how can the operator be cleared of responsibility for it at shift change time without creating a bottleneck at the tool crib window and without tearing down the setup?

3 Should there be "in" and "out" windows at the crib?

4 Should the tool crib handle oil rags, pulley belts, goggles, gloves, and smocks for operators?

5 How about having a grinding wheel in the toolroom so that crib operators can sharpen tools in their spare time?

Give your views on how to handle each of these situations; discuss the pros and cons of your answers and of other ways to handle these problems.

chapter twenty-eight

BLOCK AND LOAD CONTROL

Some industries are in-between industries. We might call them "semiprocess" industries. They are like continuous production in that all products go through almost exactly the same operations but they differ from continuous production in that products are made in lots or bunches.

Because there is too much variety in the products, these industries do not lend themselves very well to flow control, yet they don't require as much detailed clerical work as does order control. Processing instructions and work routing are simpler because routings are almost always the same and there aren't many processes. But because of minor variations in products you have to send directions to various key points.

Some semiprocess industries have to concern themselves with spoilage. Once raw materials start into production they have to keep on going or be ruined. This is true in most industries using heat or chemical processes and in most food preparation industries. If materials stop very long anywhere in process they are very likely to spoil.

You'll find all kinds of hybrid mixtures of order control and flow control in in-between industries. Two kinds of hybrids are common enough to have names and to be worth describing separately. One is "block" control and the other is "load" control.

BLOCK CONTROL

Before describing the usual kinds of block control we should say that the airplane industry system of releasing orders for making airplane parts is a kind of block control. We said earlier that these orders were released to cover groups of airplanes. This method is not, however, known as block control.

Returning to the more usual kind of block control we find that where products are somewhat varied but all go through the same operations and where the variations have very little effect on processing times, you can simplify plant loading and progress control by using block control. The nub of block control is that you send the factory "blocks" of orders. Students sometimes get to thinking that a "block" is a part or section in a factory. This is not it at all. A "block" of orders is a collection of orders whose work load adds up to, say, one half-day's work. You send orders out to the plant in blocks and only in blocks. You don't send out orders one at a time, nor do you send out a month's work all at one time, nor does the factory get any master schedule of any kind.

Suppose that we say that Monday morning's block is block 69. Some days earlier, you send to the first operating department all of the orders that have been put into block 69. On Monday morning the first department will start to work on block 69 orders. True, there will still be in the department most of last Friday afternoon's block 68 orders not finished but if the work is up to schedule, all of Friday afternoon's block will have been cleared out of the first department by noon Monday and all of block 69 will have been started into production. By Monday afternoon, block 70 will be moving in as orders in block 69 clear out of the first department.

The same thing is going on in all other departments at the same time. Department 2 on Monday morning is clearing out orders in block 67 as block 68 orders come in from department 1. Monday afternoon, block 68 orders are being cleared out as block 69 orders move in from department 1. Department 3 will receive block 69 orders during Tuesday morning and will have them all cleared out by Tuesday evening.

We are, of course, oversimplifying in order to make the pattern of block control clear. You may have thought of several questions, such as whether or not orders actually move so fast through the plant. If your product passes through only five departments will you get finished products in two and one-half days?

The answer *could* be yes, orders do move through each department in a half day, but the answer is almost surely that they will not. You can have all the inventory-in-process around that you want. You can use block control when individual operations take days instead of hours. Monday morning's block 69 can be the block that you clean up the following Monday morning, a week later, when you start on new block 79. Blocks 70 to 78 can be in process somewhere in the department. And the same thing could go on in other departments.

You may also be wondering, first, what good the block idea is and, second, is a block of orders a half-day's work for all departments? To answer the second question first, yes, a block is, in our example, a half-day's work, or close to it, in all departments.

To answer the first question, the block idea does several things. It is a means for sending a given work load to the shop. It is also a method for pushing work through the shop. Every order in a block bears two numbers, its own order number and the block number. Every department is required to clear out blocks *in sequence*. No orders in a new block can be sent on to the next department until *all* lower numbered blocks are cleared out. You cannot start to deliver block 69 orders from department 1 to department 2 until *all* block 68 orders have been sent on. (Should an item be clearly delayed for a good reason, it can be moved back into a later block and a substitute moved up to take its place.)

Because blocks have to be cleared in sequence, there is strong pressure on foremen to clear up every behind-time order. A single item, put aside because it is "fussy" (so the men leave it till the last), will hold up other blocks and bring every department in the plant down on the neck of the responsible foreman. Hence, there is strong pressure to keep all orders moving along.

Our second question was, "How does it happen that a block is a half-day's work for each successive department?" Suppose that the work done in department 2 on any and all orders takes twice as long as the work done in department 1. This makes no problems. The relationship of 2 to 1 is fairly constant. Just have twice as many men or, for machine work, twice as much machine capacity in department 2 as you have in department 1.

Since all products require practically the same operations, you scale the size of departments to the amount of work each has to do. A department having to do half as many man-hours of work on typical orders is only half as big. Departments with more work to do are bigger. A given work load keeps each department busy about the same length of time. A half-day's work for department 1 is also a half-day's work for every other department.

CONTROL POINTS   Foremen having to clear blocks out in sequence gives you, in block control, a certain amount of control over the progress of orders through the plant. It makes foremen push to keep laggard orders moving. When they clear a block, they report it to production control so that production control knows pretty well where orders are all the time.

You can even get a closer check without adding much work by using "control points" within each department. Every item has to pass certain inspections so all that you have to do is to keep a record there of the items that pass through.

If you were making men's suits, each line on a page in the control report book could be for a suit. Each suit in the block would have its own individual suit number. The only work you'd have to do at each control point is to put a check mark on the line for each suit as it passes the control point. You could even note the time of day that it passed.

It is simple enough then, if you want to locate either one unit or a whole order, to call the control points by phone and find out which items have passed through. You'll soon find which is the last point that a given suit has passed. You'll find the item in the next work area.

BLOCK CONTROL IN MEN'S CLOTHING   You find block control used in shoe factories, clothing factories, and once in a while in printing establishments. Here's how it works in making men's suits. The sale of suits to retailers starts several months before the season of consumer demand. You don't actually deliver the suits this early but you make up pictures and samples and have your salesmen take orders. When the orders come in to the factory, production control groups orders for suits by kind of cloth, pattern, suit model, style, and size, so that orders for suits cut from the same cloth will go out to the shop together.

About the only major variation in suits is the need for or lack of patch pockets, pocket flaps, full or part linings, number of buttons, and such details. With only minor changes in a process here and there, every suit will flow through cutting and sewing processes to final pressing and inspection. These minor differences have almost no effect on processing times. And since most of the work is by hand or is done with sewing machines you don't have to worry much about machines change or setup times. Operators can switch from one order to another without losing much time so orders, even for different kinds of suits, can follow each other in a practically steady stream.

But how do the workers find out about all the little differences? After all, minor though they are, you have to tell operators what you want. Kuppenheimer, and its procedure is typical, does it by using the instruction card shown in figure 28-1. A card of this kind is made out new for *each* suit of clothes. It is a combination card that does three things. First, it instructs men on what operations to do. Second, it supplies job tickets for all operations. And, third, it lists all the odds and ends, or "findings" (buttons, zippers, etc.), that each suit needs.

Figure 28-1 is a standard instruction card. It lists *all* of the possible operations that you might have to perform on any suit. Any that don't apply are just marked out and not used. As the cutters (the first operation) cut the suit pieces from bolts of cloth, they put the cut pieces with the "findings" which they draw from stock and send everything on to the sewing department.

A problem in making men's suits is to see that the various parts of a coat—its sleeves, back, and other suit parts—come together at the sewing operations. Kuppenheimer solves this by sewing a little cardboard tag bearing a suit's number on every little cut piece of cloth that will go to make up the suit. Then you get the sleeves for suit number 147 into coat number 147 and not into some other coat.

BLOCK CONTROL IN OTHER INDUSTRIES   You can use block control anywhere that you have products that vary in minor ways if the variation doesn't affect processing time very much. You won't find block control used often outside the clothing and the shoe industry, but you do find the same idea used now and then in other industries.

One large manufacturer of surgical supplies uses the block idea but

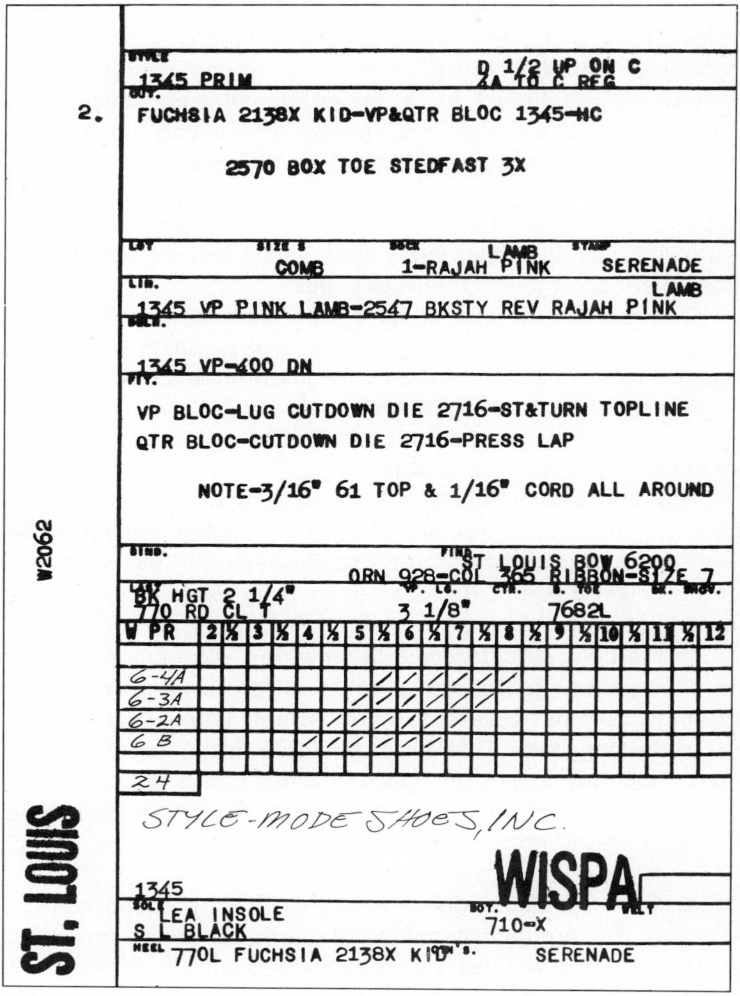
STYLE 1345 PRIM D 1/2 UP ON C 2A TO C REG
QUT. 2. FUCHSIA 2138X KID-VP&QTR BLOC 1345-HC
2570 BOX TOE STEDFAST 3X
LOT SIZES COMB SOCK 1-RAJAH LAMB PINK STAMP SERENADE
LIN. 1345 VP PINK LAMB-2547 BKSTY REV RAJAH LAMB PINK
WELT. 1345 VP-400 DN
FIT. VP BLOC-LUG CUTDOWN DIE 2716-ST&TURN TOPLINE
QTR BLOC-CUTDOWN DIE 2716-PRESS LAP
NOTE-3/16" 61 TOP & 1/16" CORD ALL AROUND
BIND. FIND. ST LOUIS BOW 6200 ORN 928-COL 365 RIBBON-SIZE 7
LAST BK HGT 2 1/4" 770 RD CL T VP. LG. 3 1/8" CTR. B. TOE 7682L SK. SHOV.

W PR	2	½	3	½	4	½	5	½	6	½	7	½	8	½	9	½	10	½	11	½	12
6-4A								/	/	/	/	/	/								
6-3A							/	/	/	/	/	/									
6-2A						/	/	/	/	/	/										
6 B					/	/	/	/	/	/											
24																					

STYLE-MODE SHOES, INC.
WISPA
1345
SOLE LEA INSOLE S L BLACK BOT. 710-X WELT
HEEL 770L FUCHSIA 2138X KID CTN'S. SERENADE
W2062
ST. LOUIS

FIGURE 28-1 Production orders in the women's shoe industry must be designed to cover minor variations in almost identical products. This order, for example, covers the making of six pairs of shoes of different sizes. Most individual production orders are made directly to customers' orders. (Florsheim Shoe Co.)

sets its blocks at one hour's work, not a half day as is common in men's clothing. Mail order houses use a kind of block control, using fifteen minute blocks, in order filling work. Florsheim Shoe, on the other hand, uses a one day block. Whatever your block, you gather together orders whose total requirements add up to your block.

QUANTITY RIGIDITIES   Block control situations dealing with assembled products are often like order control in that you want just so many parts, no more, no less. In fact, block control situations are worse than order control situations. If you underrun on any part you can't make the number of finished products that you'd planned. You'll waste all of the other parts and the costs that have gone into the two or three almost finished products that you can't finish. Every man's suit needs a left sleeve. Without it the rest of the coat is waste. Every shoe needs leather across the toe of the shoe. Every book needs *all* of its pages.

Overruns, too, are wasteful but not so much so. An extra left sleeve or piece of shoe leather or page for a book is waste but it is small waste compared to having to discard almost whole products.

Notice too that parts are not interchangeable as between orders. Having too many pages for a production control book in no way helps you if you are short of pages for a cook book.

How about saving the leftovers and using them the next time you make the same product? Sometimes you can do this but usually not because you never carry stocks of parts. And you never carry parts because so often you never get a rerun. Besides not carrying parts stocks keeps inventory investment down.

In the book industry, you do, however, sometimes store "parts"—in this case pages. Publishers sometimes have printers run off more page sets than they put covers on right at first. Later, covers are put on the rest of the page sets. This doesn't hold down the investment in pages but it does hold down the investment in whole books because the expense of covering them is delayed. And the cost of carrying page sets is less than setting up the printing presses an extra time.

DISPATCHING   Block control is largely first operation control. We have said that the production control department feeds orders to the first department in quantities that match the plant's approximate capacity to produce. But remember, the plant's capacity depends on how many men are employed and the current work hours, whether they are 7 or 8 a day or 40 or 44 hours a week, etc.

No other dispatching, beyond passing out the orders to the first department, is done. Products go from operation to operation and department to department always the same way. All later operations are authorized when the orders are handed out for the first operation.

Rarely, in block control, do you need machine schedules. The product mix variations don't change the work loads on machines very much. Usually, too, production control is not concerned with finishing dates nor with getting products into finished stock. As long as you keep pushing new orders into the first department and as long as no orders or individual items in blocks are allowed to lag, products are bound to arrive in finished stock in about the usual time.

Progress reporting in block control is largely confined to the daily (or even hourly) reports that control points make to production control when blocks clear past these points. Production control will probably post the progress report to each individual order. Doing this lets production control know where all orders are all the time.

PARTS MAKING   Parts for assembled products made where block control is used are almost never made up ahead and stocked. In most cases they could be made up ahead but there is no reason for it. Machine setup times are so small that you can afford to make limited quantities often if the finished products schedule calls for it.

In fact, there is almost no "setup" work as such. It is more a matter of "get ready" and "put away." In the clothing industry, you'd have to get out a bolt of cloth and the patterns to be used. In the shoe industry, you'd have to get out hides of the proper leather and the lasts for the particular style of shoe. In printing, however, it is different. Here you would have to set up the presses and setting them up is a big job.

Making parts ahead would mean that you'd have to keep them all apart because they are not interchangeable. A sleeve for a size 40 coat goes only into a size 40 and besides the fabric has to match. It is the same with shoes and with books. So it ends up being easier just to make parts directly and only to assembly orders. Releases of authority to make finished products are always authority to make parts too. And they are also authority to withdraw from stock all the "findings" (bought accessories) that the order requires. These would be buttons, zippers, buckles, shoelaces, and heels.

LOAD CONTROL

Load control is not a wholly different kind of control from other types. It is a mixture of detailed control over some operations and almost no control at all over other operations. Load control is a matter of schedule making for key machines or primary processing equipment. It is a matter of loading or allocating the time of key machines to individual orders. And it is usually a matter of allocating a few big jobs to the key machines rather than many little jobs.

Big jobs and long runs don't, however, always dominate your schedule making. Many key machines need new schedules daily. A steel rolling mill, for example, takes preheated billets or slabs of steel and rolls them down into long strips of sheet steel. The rolling operation is done by a set of rolling mills costing millions of dollars. The mills operate in unison as one gigantic machine. This rolling is the key operation. The rolling mill line is by no means the only equipment in the plant and rolling steel strips or bars is only one of the operations done but all other operations are subsidiary. The schedule of the unified rolling mill line sets all other schedules. Its production rate is so high that during a day it can turn out all the steel that you want of several kinds and thicknesses. So you need to make up a new schedule for it every day.

The printing industry is another example of load control. R. R. Donnelly, Cuneo Press, and several others print *Life* magazines, Sears, Roebuck catalogs, and telephone books by the millions. Again, a few key pieces of equipment dominate. This time it is the printing presses (which turn out as many as 10,000 magazines, with up to twenty colors, per hour). Their schedules determine all other schedules.

We could list other examples. The essence of load control is, however, apportioning the time of these very few and very expensive machines to orders and in the best sequence for their operation.

The plant's whole operations are geared to these large machines. Their pace sets the pace for all other operations. When deciding what jobs you can and cannot do, you pay almost no attention to any operation or any machine except the big ones. True, there are other operations both before and after key operations but you make sure that their capacity is big enough to handle all that the key machines will turn out. Don't ever hold up a key operation for lack of capacity to handle subsidiary operations. If a minor operation is a bottleneck, expand its capacity.

Often you don't even need to make up schedules for the lesser operations before and after the key one. Let jobs come to the lesser operations in whatever sequence works best for the big machine.

SEPARATION OF ORDERS   Load control products are somewhat varied so you have to keep lots apart. Making books illustrates this need. Ordinarily the processes required to produce one book are the same as those for any other book, but in manufacturing, you have to keep the pages for each book apart.

Other industries which can use load control but which have to keep lots apart include textiles, shoes, paper, rubber, soap, pottery, glass, wire, as well as steel rolling mills. They include some companies which turn out assembled products and others which merely change the form of material without any addition or subtraction of materials.

BATCH MANUFACTURING

Load control is the usual method in batch manufacture. Batch manufacture means that you process materials in batches equal to full loads on primary equipment. Usually the process is one of mixing or heating several ingredients together in large mixers or pressure or heating tanks and vessels.

Enough material is put into the equipment to load it, then the process starts and carries through a pre-set cycle. No products come out of the process until the cycle is complete, at which time you get the whole batch. Each such load is a "batch" and it is always set at the top figure that the primary equipment will handle. This way you get the lowest processing cost per pound. In fact, you may even need to load the equipment full in order for the operation to work right.

Batch manufacturing is not too good a descriptive term for all that goes on because it gets its name from one single very important process that takes place early in processing. Other operations that follow this primary one are not batch operations although they are affected by the batching done in the first process.

They are affected because batch quantities block you into certain quantity patterns. A batch of paint mixture will make a certain number of gallons of paint, never much more and never much less. Suppose that we say 500 gallons. If you want 750 gallons of a certain kind of paint you can't get it because a batch makes 500. So you schedule either 500, which is less than you want, or 1,000 which is more.

Table glass stemware manufacturers have a similar problem. They melt up a "heat" of, say, yellow glass. Perhaps it will make up into 500 goblets. Again, if you want 750, you can't get it without making two heats and wasting half of one heat. Rubber is the same. A batch may be 1,000 pounds which will make 100 tires. If you want 150 tires, you can't get the rubber mixture to come out even.

Actually we are exaggerating the problem because you normally make dozens or hundreds of batches of materials for heavy use items, so cutting off or adding a batch won't make you change your finished quantities very much. Also, you usually want more of the material every day so you can balance out—not that you keep a half heat hot for an extra day but you can overrun on one item on Monday and underrun on it on Tuesday.

You also get flexibility from having several pieces of equipment. Rarely is one piece of equipment so productive as to turn out all of your production. (It is, though, in many steel rolling mills.) Usually you have several batch making machines and, furthermore, they are not all of the same size. You make small batches on small machines and large batches on large machines. This gives you flexibility by letting you, if you don't want much material, make small batches on small machines. Try to avoid this, however, because small batches on small machines cost more per pound to process than large batches on large machines.

The batching operation is actually a material preparation operation. It furnishes the materials for later operations which make specific products out of the prepared materials. Departments performing later operations rarely need to continue using the batch idea. Their work is not in batches and they may well not use load control but instead use a kind of continuous manufacture with flow control.

IDENTIFICATION OF BATCHES   You need tags to identify materials in batch manufacturing because different batches often look alike. You can make the tags in advance and let the foreman use them as needed. You don't need work orders, job tickets, or move orders. Merely make up a list of batches you want. Let the foreman assign batches to individual machines. Usually you'll need to make up new batch lists every day.

You don't need job tickets even if the men work on piece rates because the rates are in a rate book and are usually for the same jobs. And you won't need move orders because there aren't very many kinds of batches and any one kind of batch always goes to the same next department. Your plant-wide truckers move materials by working regular routes.

Whoever—central production control or the foreman—makes out batch schedules for individual machines should pay attention to their economical operation. For example, on rolling mill and calendering operations, don't mix up runs of thick and thin materials. Resetting the rolls often wastes time. Or where color pigments are involved, don't try to run white or transparent materials after black or dark blue. You'll waste too much time trying to clean the equipment. And in spite of the best cleaning job that your men can do on the equipment, the first light-colored material that you run after dark material will have dirty places on it. Run the white through first and you'll have fewer problems. A little light pigment is more readily covered up in the dark material than vice versa.

Or you might do what medicine companies do when making pills. Pills contain only very small although exact amounts of active medicine.

Most of the bulk of a pill is composed of an inactive and inexpensive filler. At the end of a run of one kind of pill it is very important to get every last bit of the concentrated medicine from the first run out of the machine before starting to make the next run of pills. After the end of a run, the companies just make some more pills with filler alone for a few minutes. These pills are, of course, waste but they clean the machine better and at but a fraction of the cost of men stopping the machine and cleaning it.

PROCESSING AUTHORITY

In semiprocess industries, including load control situations and batch manufacturing, processing instructions, work routing, and the forms necessary to instruct workers on *how* to produce are similar to those needed in continuous production. Production control rarely tells the plant *how* to do any operation or even what operations to perform.

The group leader of the work crew at each key operation has a "spec" (specification) book which gives him all the information he needs. Sometimes the spec does no more than describe the *results wanted* from the operation. Sometimes it goes further and tells him *how* he should go about doing the operation. His spec book is generally a loose-leaf book which is kept up to date by the engineering department. Production control and the foreman also have identical spec books.

PRODUCTION AUTHORIZATION RELEASES

In semiprocess industries, the production authorizations coming to production control are usually received in the form of weekly lists of products wanted. The list of products wanted may be called a production "ticket," "release," "order," or some other name. It shows no specific "due dates," although everyone assumes that the items listed will arrive in finished stock shortly after the period to which the list applies.

The list is producing authority only and shows the products to be produced by some main operation, usually assembly. This main operation is the operation from which all planning and scheduling of other operations are determined. Its schedule controls all schedules for operations before it and after it. Production control will have to see that all earlier operations are done far enough ahead to let the controlled operation take place during the schedule period. It is the same with operations that follow. Their schedules also depend on the controlled operation's schedules.

Whenever there are operations following the controlled operation, the products covered by a release do not all arrive in finished stock in the period covered by the release. Products passing through the main operation toward the close of the period (say on Friday) arrive in finished stock a few days after (maybe on the following Wednesday) the end of the period.

In some hybrid control companies, where weekly production releases are used to authorize production, virtually the whole of production, parts preparation, and assembly occurs within the week referred to in the list. Sometimes the operations taking place before the main operation are simple and can be performed rapidly. In other cases the preliminary operations cannot be done far ahead of the main operation because the materials are bulky or may spoil, as in the case of food products. Often, too, operations following the main operation are simple and fast. In these manufacturing situations, nearly all the operations are performed in the same week as the main operation. When this is the case, production authorization release can be made a short time ahead of production.

In most companies the production cycle takes longer, and if the controlled operation is late in the cycle, the release must be passed out to production control farther ahead to allow for planning and performing earlier operations. In many companies, assembly (which operation usually comes late in the processing cycle), of necessity, has to be considered the main controlled operation because the product is nonexistent or nonidentifiable as a product up to that point.

In the manufacture of rubber heels for shoes, for example, the production list would be stated in terms of quantities and types of pairs of heels. Until the "curing" operation (an operation similar to cooking a waffle in a waffle iron), there is no rubber heel. There is just a mass or slab of compounded material which could be made up into any one of a wide variety of types or sizes of rubber heels or even other products.

In companies which make nonassembled products, the main operation can be the first operation instead of one of the last operations. Steel rolling mills, for example, have no assembly operation, and authorizations to produce would probably cover the first operation. In this case, the list could be issued shortly before production started, but if there are several operations after the first one, some time will elapse before the material arrives in the finished goods stock room. You would have, therefore, to issue the list well before you wanted the products delivered to finished stock.

PREPARING PLANT DIRECTIVES

In discussing assembled products made by order control, we said earlier that orders had to be "exploded" by the production control department. Parts needs have to be determined and directives issued covering their manufacture. A similar explosion process is necessary in both block and load control wherever assembled products are concerned. The process is simpler, however, because although you have to do this explosion work over again for every release, it is just doing the same thing over again every time. Each member of the production control staff handles the same part of the job every time. There is no problem of determining operations or their sequence. These, as in continuous production with flow control, are the same for all products.

The list of products to be made is received by the head of the production control department, and immediately one member of the staff makes out operating schedules for the controlled operation. With this schedule as a guide, the other members of the production control staff make out the directions needed (assuming the controlled operation is assembly) to get the component parts made. Each member of the department is responsible for a certain part. He knows the lead time required to get his component part ready in time to meet the assembly schedule and prepares directives for his materials preparation departments.

In making automobile tires, the "curing" or cooking operation after the tire is assembled is the main operation for production orders received by production control. Its schedule is made out first. The assembly operation, called tire "building," immediately precedes the curing operation and its schedule is made out next to suit the needs of the curing schedule. The schedule for tire building is in turn the guide for production control staff members who are responsible for seeing that the material to be assembled into the tires is prepared. One man sees that the proper amount of rubber compound is mixed and made into treads, the wearing surface of the tire. Another staff member sees that rayon or nylon fabric is coated with rubber compound and cut into strips ready for the building operation. Still another man is responsible for the preparation of the bead or rim of the tire, and so on. Each staff member, using the permanent data on file in the production control department, figures out how many units of his materials are needed and arranges to have them prepared.

This preparatory work is often quite similar to that required in order control in intermittent production, for it often goes beyond just making out lists of prepared materials that you want. Production control may have, for example, to figure out the raw material requirements, although this is often done by a separate materials control department working directly from the release list of products wanted.

Other preparatory work may be checking on the availability of minor equipment and on miscellaneous purchased items. In the shoe industry, for example, you may have to check to see if the accessories are ready ("lasts" on which shoes are made, heels, laces, buckles, and the like).

Everything that you have to check on has to be on hand before production orders are released to the first department.

Another different feature that you find in some load control situations is that in the early processing operations, you prepare materials in different form and in different units from the unit of product into which the material later goes. Often the early operations make materials in "runs," "batches," or "heats." This makes an extra operation in the work of production control. You have to convert the products you plan to make in later operations into their batch requirements so that you can then schedule batch making. This makes little trouble, however, because each member of the production control department staff specializes on one phase of the whole task. He knows all of the conversion ratios by heart.

In the case of the automobile tires example which we used above, after the tire-building schedule is made up, the production control staff member responsible for tire treads would first order the required quantity of rubber mixture to be prepared. The mixing of materials is done in batches of fixed weight, so the mixed material is ordered as a certain number of batches of each kind of material needed to make the tires scheduled.

But before making up the batch order list, the production control staff man in charge of making batch mixing schedules adds together the requirements for each kind of material needed for the several sizes of the same kind of tire. He also waits until he gets similar lists of batches needed from the men who schedule rubber hose, belts, heels, and other products. Then he combines requirements for similar batches and makes up schedules for the machines that mix the batches. He also breaks down his orders into their new material ingredients and orders them.

Very few plant directives (only lists of batches or of quantities of parts or products to make) are issued in semiprocess industries of the kind we have been talking about. Raw materials for first operations are usually withdrawn from an open storeroom next to the first operations. Requisitions are rarely used. Some companies make out daily materials withdrawal reports for stock record purposes. On large products, you won't need such lists since production schedules themselves are sufficient to tell how much material has been used. The production control department rarely has to figure out raw materials requirements in these companies. Both figuring out the requirements and buying them are handled by a materials control department, acting on the authority of a quarterly estimate of future production.

Continuing our example of tire making, the assembly operation is done in departments having many identical machines, except that with a little adjustment they can be used to make different sizes of tires. Each week

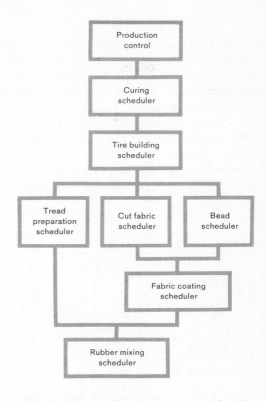

FIGURE 28-2 In the manufacture of automobile tires, the curing operation is the "controlled" operation. The production order
received covers all tires to be cured in the
period of the release. After this schedule is set,
the tire building (assembling) schedule is
worked out. The tire building in turn is used by
the schedulers for tread preparation, fabric
cutting, and bead preparation. The fabric
coating scheduler gets his information concerning requirements from the fabric cutting
and bead schedulers. The rubber mixing
scheduler sets his schedules after getting
requirements lists from the tread preparation
and fabric coating schedulers. At each stage
the proper lead time is allowed so that the
schedule for the following operation can be
carried out.

the tire building departments get from production control a list of how
many machines to use during the following week for each size tire.

Tags are used for exact control of each day's quantities. Each day production control gives the foreman tags, one for every tire his men are to

make that day. He passes them out to his men as their job assignments. Tags, used this way, act to control overruns and underruns. If the foreman uses up the tags, and doesn't run over, he will hit the schedule on the head. Also, he won't overuse or underuse prepared materials coming into his department.

Using tags as precise instruction allows some flexibility to be put into the day-to-day production assignments. The foreman can transfer work from one machine to another if one is ahead and another behind schedule. Failures to meet scheduled production are revealed by the extra tags left over. If you want to make up the lost production, add the leftover tags to

DAILY SCHEDULE 12 MID. TO 12 MID.				SMALL TRUCKS						DATE Wed. 2-16-	
TIRE SIZE	TICKET	GREEN TIRE INV.	TOTAL TIRES TO BE BUILT	BUILDERS				CURE SCHED.	MACHINE NUMBERS	TIE-IN	BUILDERS
				4	1	2	3				2-17
700x20 GHY 10p		400	265	4	4	6	4		65-15-12-8-11-14	H97S4	
700x20 GLRQ 8p		406	24	1	idle	1	idle		22	H97S3	12
900x16 GBKY 8p		211	36	1	1	1	1		67		36
700x20 GBRGQ 8p		404	0	Follow 750x17 GBTY 10p							0
750x17 GBTY 10p		436	20	1	idle	idle	1		62	H97S4	C00
750x20 GHY 10p		413	631	14	14	13	14		27-25-17-16-28-18-20 29-26-23-24-10-32-19		
750x20 GLHY 10p		414	24	1	idle	idle	1		13	H97S4	24
750x20 GLRQ 8p		415	44	1	1	1	1		68	H97S3	40
750x20 GPLQ 10p		409	0						21	H230	0
750x20 TGHY 10p		411	48	1	1	1	1		21	H97S4	48
750x24 GBRGQ 8p		406	0						22	H97S3	12
825x18 GBY 8p		439	20	1	idle	1	idle		66	H97S3	20
825x20 CLBY 8p		421	30	1	idle	1	1		64	H97S3	40
825x20 GBY 12p		420	80	3	2	2	2		69-70		
825x20 GLRQ 12p		433	0						60		20
825x20 GPLQ 12p		427	36	1	1	1	1		61		40
825x20 GLRY 8p		432	0						63	H97S3	10
825x20 TGBY 10p		431	44	1	1	1	1		59	H97S4	40
825x20 GBTY 8p			30	1	1	1	idle		60		0
825x20 GXY 10p		442	30	1	1	1	idle		63		20
825x20 GBN 10p		430	0						60	H97S3	30
650x20 GHY 8p		503	150	1	2	2	1		53-56 135357		
700x17 GCY 6p		505	25				1		31		100
700x17 GBY 8p		504	40	1	1				55		50
700x17 TGY 8p		506	40			1	1		53		60
700x18 GBY 8p		507	40	idle	1	1			54		40
700x18 TGY 8p		531	20				1		54		20
700x20 GBY 8p		508	220	3	3	3	2		52-549-31		
750x17 GBY 8p		515	140	1	2	2	2		57-46		
*750x17 TGBY 8p		516	20	1					46		20
750x20 GBY 8p		512	100	1	1	1	1		43		
825x16 GBY 8p		518	0	Follow 10p							0
900x16 GLBY 8p		520	216	3	3	3	3		48-47-50	A97	
900x16 GKY 8p		625	0						48	A91	0
700x15 GAB3Y 6p		601	250	3	3	3	3		42-45-51		
700x16 TGABBY 8p		605	80	1	1	1	1		58		80
700x16 GABY 6p		604	680	7	7	7	7		40-36-37-38-35-39-34		

FIGURE 28-3 In departments where there are very many machines to be allocated to a somewhat limited variety of products, it may be possible to assign certain machines to given products for a week at a time. Sometimes, however, changes in assignments within the week are called for. At the Goodyear Tire and Rubber Company, the production of small truck tires is put on a daily basis, with new tire building schedules being issued daily. (Goodyear Tire and Rubber Co.)

those passed out the next day. If you decide to cancel the orders for the lost production, destroy the old tags and issue only the usual number of tags the next day.

The production control department has a problem in load control with respect to inventory in process which is common in job lot work but less common in continuous manufacture. There is often a decided lack of balance in the productive capacity of the key operation machines or equipment. You have to carry inventories or "banks" of partly fabricated material between jobs where lack of balance exists. You may have to work slower equipment longer hours than fast equipment and to have an inventory of partly fabricated material ahead of fast machines. And you can't escape this problem by putting in equipment that has equal capacity because you use the equipment for different materials. Changes in types and kinds of products change the productive capacity of different machines in unlike ways. If the production capacity of two successive operations is in balance when you are making one product, a shift in sizes will throw them out of balance. This problem is treated in more detail in the following two chapters.

Semiprocess industries are like continuous production industries in that they are high-volume industries. Materials move through production rapidly. If any operation slows down, large quantities of materials pile up quickly. The banks or inventories of goods generally carried between unbalanced operations are primarily capacity balancers and are relatively small. They are not big enough to let one machine work very long unless other operations also keep going. On the other hand, they are often big enough to let operations go on for as much as a day.

You have to control these "between-operations" inventories carefully lest they be too small to keep a fast machine busy when it starts on a run, yet you must keep them down as much as possible because of storage space or storage rack limitations, the possibility of material spoilage, and the need to keep materials moving. You need to check these between-operation banks often to be sure that they are big enough yet not too big. Better have your production control men who are responsible for schedules make daily physical counts or visual checkups on stocks.

IDENTIFYING MATERIAL IN PROCESS

The material identification problem is an important one in load and block control. As in the case of intermittent manufacturing, the materials are usually not self-identifying, particularly in the early stages of manufacture, when the unit being produced is different from the finished unit. Sometimes you can mark the materials themselves as leather, paper, or glass.

In other cases, you can put tags on the material. Where this is not feasible (as in liquids or granulated materials), you can fasten the tags on the container or rack. Usually this identification can be a simple code number, but it is not uncommon to add other descriptive information. If the material is processed in batches or rolls, the identification should tell you the kind and amount of material in the container. The date the material was processed may also be important if old materials need to be used first.

As in order control, usually it is better to prepare tags ahead of time. Large numbers of tags are often required in semiprocess industries because you need one for every container or even for every piece of material. Tags are generally prepared ahead by production control and sent with the schedules to the key operations, where they are fastened to the product after the operation is performed.

In the textile industry, strip operation tags, already referred to, are often used. The tag forms are made as a series of detachable stubs which are printed with blank spaces left where data concerning particular lots of goods may be filled in. A lot number is used to identify each lot of products. At the top of the stub tag, the lot number, quantity, and perhaps the type of material are shown. On each detachable stub the identification is repeated. Each stub bears the name of an operation, printed on, for which it is to be used. These tags serve to identify materials and also serve as job tickets.

In semiprocess industries you need new tags after some of the operations, particularly key operations, because the material is changed in form or goes into containers which hold a different number of units. Maybe the material comes into the operation in rolls and leaves as pieces, or maybe it comes in as pounds and leaves as pieces. Different containers holding more or less than the original containers may be used after the operation is performed.

PROGRESS CONTROL

In load control, the schedules sent out for key operations provide spaces for recording the quantities produced as each run is finished. These schedules are returned at the close of each day to the central office and serve as a report of output. When production falls short of that scheduled, the next day's orders are boosted enough to offset the loss. Or if an overrun occurs, the next day's orders are cut down.

Telephone or inter-coms allow for quick reporting if any trouble comes up during the day. The foreman tells production control right away if trouble comes up or even if it seems likely. It is important that he do this because schedules for other departments have also to be changed if he has trouble. One foreman's 10 o'clock delay may be someone else's 11 o'clock delay.

Departments which have many machines allocated to a few kinds of products also report production daily. We spoke of using tags as work assignments to men. As the operator turns out products, he puts a tag on each one. When he runs out of tags he stops even if his neighbor doing the same work still has some tags. The foreman uses the tags as a control on the total output of the group. Tags are also initialed or stamped to show the worker's clock number so that there is a record of who made the product.

In industries where the stub-tag arrangement is used (clothing and shoes), whole tags are given to the foreman of the first department. He passes out the tags to his workers as their job instructions. After performing the first operation, the operator pulls off the stub for his operation at the bottom end of the ticket and sends the materials with the remainder of the tag on to the next operation. As the other workers perform their operations, they pull off the stubs for their operations (each stub has the name of the operation printed on it).

Each worker saves tag stubs for the jobs he has done during the day and turns them in as his report of work done. His piece rate pay is based on the stubs he turns in. Some companies have the inspector instead of the worker collect and turn in the stubs.

MATERIALS MOVEMENT

Materials move by truck instead of conveyor much more often in load and block control than in flow control. One reason is because the high production machines referred to earlier are often used for several kinds of material each day. A full day's supply of one material may be run off between 8 and 10 A.M. Similar full day's requirements of other materials are produced in short spans of time throughout the day. Some of the items will stay in storage for as much as a day because even though you keep using them all the time, it will be a whole day before the next supply is run off.

Usually you don't get a chance to store such banks on conveyors because if you tie up a conveyor for storage, you can't use it at the same time to move materials. It is expensive to use a conveyor for storage although you do sometimes find conveyors used this way. Generally you end up storing materials on the floor and moving them by power lift trucks.

The second reason for using trucks is because of the lack of balance mentioned previously. You might want not to build up banks anywhere but you must when successive operations don't have equal capacity. Again, conveyors are not very good places to store materials so you move materials by lift truck.

A third reason for using trucks is that the output from key equipment goes to different locations for the next operation. Conveyors are not as well suited to take materials to several locations as are trucks.

Truckers usually work regular routes and are often under the control of the production control department. Movement of materials between departments is by truck, even when inside department movement is by conveyor. The workers in the internal transportation department (the truckers who work for the production control department) do little or no trucking between operations within departments. Their work is always between departments. The truckers receive fewer directions in their work than they do in order control, since most materials follow regular paths through the plant. The trucks usually operate from pickup areas in one department to receiving areas in the next department.

The lack of balance in productive capacity between operations *within* departments sometimes makes necessary considerable moving around of materials within departments. Truckers or materials handlers within the department who work for the foreman handle this work.

STUDY MATERIALS

28-1   How are block and load control alike? How are they different? Under what conditions would each be best to use?

28-2   What are the distinctive features of an operational system suited to the type of control discussed in this chapter? Could these control systems be used in service operations as well as in production operations? Give some examples to support your reasoning.

28-3   Richard Hamer, newly appointed head of the production control department of the Rigney Foundry and Machine Company, was 28 years old. He came to the company after two years of college and had been with the Rigney company ever since. In a factory management magazine he read an article describing the operation of "block" control in the textile industry. It pointed out how scheduling was greatly simplified by assigning orders to "blocks" which moved through successive departments more or less as units. The idea seemed good, and Hamer decided to try it out.

He decided that the logical way of grouping orders was to use the molding department as the basis. A block was set as an amount of work which would keep the molding department busy one-half day. Various jobs were to be assigned to each block. Their total molding time requirements would equal that available in one-half day. Individual orders would show the block number in addition to the order number. The foremen of all departments were to be required to complete all orders in a block before another block would be cleared out of their departments.

What difficulties would probably arise in using this system in the foundry? What would happen in the machine shop (still assuming that block numbers were set to equate molding requirements of orders)? Can any part of the block idea be used in the case above? A requirement of block control is that the production capacities of successive departments be equal. How can that be accomplished in the above case?

28-4   How important is the balance of operations in using load control? Draw a flow diagram for a series of operations such as steelmaking, rolling, and finishing. Indicate the key operations in the system, and the effects of any imbalance in the system.

28-5   In terms of the required information flow, how do block and load control compare with order control? For operations of a comparable size, would the work load on the production control operations be less, or greater, with block or load control as opposed to order control?

28-6   In batch or semicontinuous processing operations, how do the material handling operations differ from those where order control is used? Would one be more likely to find centralized or decentralized material handling control procedures? Would one be likely to find highly automated material handling systems in these operations?

chapter twenty-nine

FLOW CONTROL—I

FLOW CONTROL IS CONTROL OF RATE

In continuous production you find flow control since the factory is essentially one big, single purpose machine geared to turn out a fixed quantity of output per hour. This production rate is set during the early planning stages long before production actually starts.

Continuous production factories turn out tremendous volumes of products yet carry very small quantities of materials in process. Flow control's job is to maintain the *rate* or *flow* of production. You have to try to match the rate of inflow of raw materials and outflow of finished products with the production rate. You never get it done perfectly but this is the goal. Flow production control, therefore, deals with incoming materials delivery schedules and outgoing shipment schedules as well as with inside production rates. Order control, in contrast, is primarily inside control dealing with individual orders and operations.

In flow control, the production control department has to make up many schedules for parts and subassembly making, for incoming materials, and for outgoing products. Whenever things don't go right, almost always you have to change many rather than few schedules.

Sometimes it isn't your own production irregularities that cause trouble. The amounts of materials coming in may be different than planned. Maybe a snowstorm delays trucks and trains or your supplier has a fire, flood, or strike. Or maybe it is your customer. He wants more or less than he originally ordered. And changing your own production schedules is only half the battle. Production control has also to make new schedules for suppliers and change requests to railroads for freight cars and to trucking companies for picking up shipments.

Inside the plant, flow control is also a matter of matching many flow rates. Parts and subassemblies are produced "in parallel," at the same time. To get their schedules synchronized requires centralized control over the schedules of all lines. The central production control office must control the shop's operations; habitual failure by the shop to produce scheduled quantities makes serious problems. Admittedly, however, the manufacturing department's problems do, sometimes, force schedule changes.

Products *flow* past men who work on assembly lines and they *flow* off the end of assembly lines. The line "pulls" on the supplies of parts and subassemblies so they *must flow* into the assembly line at a rate which matches their use. Some parts and subassemblies are, themselves, made by continuous production. If they are, their *rate* must match the assembly line's needs—not necessarily hour by hour or even day by day but week by week. If it takes only six hours (or ten hours) of work on a parts or subassembly line to make enough to keep the final assembly going for eight hours, this is all right. Just work the lines different hours or even a different number of days and use supply banks of parts to balance out production.

Often parts are made in lots and bought items are, of course, always received from suppliers in lots (truckloads or freight carloads). This would seem to make no particular problem. Just schedule their making or their arrival so that the assembly line never runs out.

FIGURE 29-1 Production control's work in flow control is even more behind the scenes than that in order control: (upper left) making up shop orders, (upper right) posting production quantities, (lower left) scheduler who has to have enough products but not too many. Today computers do most of the data posting and record keeping but they aren't up to manual methods when it comes to visual control boards which everyone can see.

FIGURE 29-2 Making automobile wheels. You can't always
design every machine to produce at the hourly rate needed
by the final assembly line. Such a machine as this large
stamping press may have to operate different hours from
that of the assembly line. (Automobile Manufacturers Assoc.)

It isn't nearly this simple, though, because you have to deal with thousands of parts (an automobile contains 13,000 bits and pieces) and subassemblies whose inventory costs would be sky-high if you carried very much
of each one. You *must* keep inventories down and *this* makes no end of
problems. All the time you try never to run out of anything yet have only
the barest minimum on hand. It is the trying to do both at once that makes
many of production control's problems in flow control. You should try,
though, to carry such inventory as you must carry as raw materials or
parts and not as finished products. This holds down the investment.

Variety is another thing that complicates flow control. A chemical plant or a cement plant doesn't have much of this to contend with. But a television factory or an automobile factory has a good bit of variety. They are almost gigantic custom producers. Autos are different colors, they have 6-cylinder or 8-cylinder motors, and they have any number of minor variations in trim and accessories. Buick has twenty-six sets of options and accessory parts and up to ten trims per model. Ford and Chevrolet have so many possible different combinations that they could produce cars all year long without making two cars exactly alike. Production control has to maintain the overall flow, yet within the flow, has to control these minor variations.

PROCESS INDUSTRIES AS A DISTINCT TYPE

We mentioned process industries earlier and said that they are more truly continuous manufacture than are fabricating companies. This group includes those producing liquid, powdered, or granulated material. Petroleum products, paint, chemicals, dyes, carbon black, flour, cement, and even pharmaceuticals are examples. Sometimes these process situations are not separate industries but are the early stages of production in companies carrying on later stages of production, controlled by one of the types already discussed. Examples in which the early stages of production are processes rather than operations include the rubber, glass, pottery, rayon, paper, and steel industries.

These industries have one thing in common. Their raw materials are usually products taken directly from nature and are not themselves semifabricated products. Customers of companies in these industries are almost always other companies which process the material further before it reaches the ultimate consumer. The variety of finished goods is often, but not always, limited.

In controlling production, process industries have one problem which is not often found in fabricating industries. Process industries frequently have to compensate for the variations in the products of nature as they attempt to make standardized end products. It is basically a laboratory job to keep a constant check on the exact physical and chemical characteristics of the raw materials and to order slight changes in mixing formulas or processing temperatures to offset the differences, sometimes slight, found in the raw materials.

Industrial rayon, for example, blends together the wood pulp that it gets in different purchased lots to help compensate for the variations in raw materials bought from different sources and at different times. This is the only way that it can end up making rayon of consistent quality. Goodyear Tire and Rubber does the same with both carbon black and with rubber.

The petroleum refining and chemical industries have used linear programming to help solve problems of this sort. They have varying sets of inputs and sometimes they want varying sets of outputs yet they want to operate in the optimal way allowed by the constraints. Linear programming is well suited to such problems.

FLOAT

Float is an automobile industry term used to describe inventory in process, particularly the products going down an assembly line and any "live banks" of products along the way. A live bank is one continually being built up by one operation while at the same time being used by another.

When you start operations, you have to "float the line" ("fill the pipeline") before any products come off the end of the line. Also, when you stop operations, the finishing end of the line can operate for a while longer then the starting point. You don't always do this at the end of the day or a shift. Instead you just stop where you are unless the operations are of the kind (as in rolling steel into strips) that must be finished once anything is started.

Some companies don't, however, just stop where they are at the end of a day and start in right from there tomorrow. Instead, they run the last products started on down the line. If you do this you'll need, the next day, to bring in the men at the start of the line 15 minutes or so ahead of those at the finishing end of the line in order to float the line again. Most of the time it pays to stop where you are at the end of a day rather than to finish out all of the partly made items.

Float also enters into lead times on bought items. It takes several days for freight cars to travel a few hundred miles. During this time finished parts are on wheels but unavailable for use. All purchase and order lead times need to contain realistic time allowances for transportation float. This problem grows more important in the case of centrally made component assemblies. One plant gets parts from its sister plant but the parts are in transit for, say, 5 to 10 days. Then the component assembling plant sends the components on to the final assembly plant and there is another travel float of 5 to 10 days. Final assembly planners have to get their orders in early and allow for a good bit of travel time float if they want to get products in time.

RATES OF OUTPUT OF PRODUCTION LINES

Most production lines use a good many machines yet the line's output rate depends only *partly* on their output rates because you don't accept machines just as they are. Engineers setting up lines work toward certain output goals. If today's machines won't do the work at the speed you want, and if it isn't too costly, you have your engineers design new machines. If this can't be done, maybe they can put in two or more machines to handle a bottleneck job along a production line. Sometimes, though, the difficulties are too great and you end up letting the speed of certain bottleneck machines set the line's pace.

Here's how the engineers would tackle the job of setting up a line. They start with the quantity of output you want per year, and then convert it to a daily rate. A new automobile plant, for example, would be "sized" more or less as follows: 365 days minus 104 Saturdays and Sundays = 261 days, minus 6 holidays = 255, minus 15 days for inventory and model change = 240, minus 15 days lost at the start of a run getting up to normal = 225 days.

If you want to produce 300,000 cars a year in this plant divide 300,000 by 225 and you find that you will have to make an average of 1,333 cars a day. Divide this by 16 hours (two shifts) and you find that you will need 83 cars per hour. Actually because of seasonal variations in sales, you would probably set up a line that could turn out, say, 100 cars an hour during busy seasons.

Suppose that from past experience you have learned that you ought to divide up the work into assignments of about two minutes per work station and to get 30 cars per hour from the line. Since you need 100 cars an hour you'll have to set up three assembly lines. This will give you 90 cars an hour so you'll have also to work Saturdays during peak seasons.

Next, the engineers will have to "balance" the line, to set it up so that every operation, whether performed by man or machine, is a two-minute (or slightly less) job. Balancing the jobs along the line so that each man has a two-minute job or slightly less is difficult. And you may also have to redesign certain machines so that they can turn out 30 units per hour.

Furthermore, there is the matter of setting the line's speed of movement. Cars need to come down the line with a total space of about 16 feet per car. At two minutes per car this means that the conveyor needs to move along at the rate of 8 feet per minute, regardless of whether it moves continuously or on a stop-and-go basis.

DIFFICULTIES IN LINE BALANCING

It is easy to speak of balancing the line but in actual practice, it is, as we said, a big job to do it. Certain minor bits of operations have to be performed one before the other. You can't, for example, mount a component until its holding fixture has been installed. Nor can you run final tests on a product until it is assembled and in working order.

WORK STANDARDS AND EQUIPMENT CAPACITY RECAP SHEET

PART NAME

PART NUMBER

OPER. NO.	SHEET___ OF___ DEPT.____ GROUP NO.___ NEXT ASSY.___ NEXT DEPT.	CLASSIFICATION CODE	NO. OF MACHS.	OPERN. MINS.	INHER. DELAY	MANPOWER	HOURLY PRODUCTION			STANDARD MINUTES
							BASIC	OPERN. LESS I.D.	EQUIP. CAP. ANAL.	
10	Rough & Finish Broach (Cinn. Combination Broach & Mill)	81-0-002	1	.800	.132	1.0	75	75	75	.932
20	Drill, Chamfer, & Tap Holes (Exept Valve Holes) (NATCO 13 Station Transfer Machine)		1	(AUTOMATIC)		---	69	64.4	64.4	--
22R	Machine Setting Operation #20	81-0-002-8	-	.932	--	1.0	--	--	--	.932
	Repairs After Operation #20 (7.00 mins/pc x 5% occurance)(Cinn. Sing. Sp. Drill Press)	38-0-23	-	.350	--	.38	--	--	--	.350
30	Rough & Finish Bore Valve Holes, Etc. Heald 12 Station Transfer Machine	--	1	(AUTOMATIC)		---	92.3	75.9	75.9	--
40	Machine Setting Operation #30	81-0-002-8	-	.932	--	1.0	--	--	--	.932
	Flush Out All Passages & Cavities (Special Flushing Machine)	04-0-038	1	.785	.147	1.0	81	76.5	76.5	.932
50	Air Test Water Jacket (Special Air Test Machine)	04-0-002	1	.835	.097	1.0	74.0	71.8	71.8	.932
52R	Water Test Leakers (2.16 x 17.4% x 2 = .752) (Water Test Machine)	04-0-196	1	.752	--	.81	30.0	27.8	27.8	.752
55R	Impregnate (Partial) Performed by Foundry Repair	--	-	--	--	---	--	--	--	--
60	Finish Broach Contact Face (Oil Gear Tunnel Broach)	81-0-002	1	.677	.183	.92	90	90	90	.860
63R	Repair - Exhaust Cavities (.718 x 5%)	38-0-23	-	.0359	--	.04	--	--	--	.0359
65R	Repair - Intake Cavities (.718 x 5%)	38-0-23	-	.0359	--	.04	--	--	--	.0359
70	Wash (Industrial Washer)	--	1	(AUTOMATIC)		---	--	--	--	--
80	Final Inspection (Charge to an Acct.)	--	-	--	--	---	--	--	--	--
	Relief Operations 10, 20, 30, 40, 50, & 60 (5.59 mins. x 5.26%)	--	-	.294	.460	.81	--	--	--	.754

	TOTAL STD. MINS./PC.									7.45
	TOTAL STD. HOURS/PC.									.124
	Control Factor = .932 mins./pc. or 64.4 pcs./hr., controlled by									
	Operation #20 (515 pcs. in 480 mins.)									
	Remarks: Reason for revision - converting from preliminary to normal standard									
	Repair allowance high du to high number of porous castings being received;									
	Foundry at present experimenting with core wash to correct									

IMPORTANT: QUANTITIES, DESCRIPTIONS, SEQUENCE OF OPERATIONS., LISTED ABOVE ARE CURRENT FOR LOCATION STUDIED. NOTIFY WORK STANDARDS AND METHODS SECTION OF ANY CHANGES IN OPERATIONS.

DATE_____ BY _____ PART NUMBER _____

FIGURE 29-3 Plan for activities along a cylinder-head production line.

Other constraints are imposed by the location of parts, the type of part or operation, the number of tools the worker uses, and the frequency of change in the tools he uses. For example, it is not practical to have a worker assemble a part on one side of an automobile and then walk around to the other side of the car and assemble another part over there. Similarly one man should not have to handle both greasy engine parts and interior upholstery fittings. Nor do you want a man to spend much time picking up and putting down tools. It may be better to have one worker put several bolts on loosely and another worker finish tightening them, rather than to have each of them use two or three tools to do the complete operation on a smaller number of bolts.

Unless a line is completely automated and designed to produce only a single, or a limited range, of products, it isn't always possible to design the machines for perfect balance. Time, technology, and economics, all may prevent your reaching this goal.

INFLEXIBILITY   Furthermore, even if you could balance a line perfectly you might not want to because then the line becomes one giant special purpose machine and becomes quite inflexible. You can't change to new products nor even make major changes in the existing product, without making a big project out of the change. Probably the existing line will have to be dismantled, redesigned, and rebuilt. Sometimes even minor changes make an entire line obsolete. This is one reason why automobile manufacturers don't change basic engine designs very often. Because engine plants are their most highly automated plants, they change them only infrequently.

Line speeds are also inflexible. If lines run too slowly, men and machines are wastefully used. And when the line moves at its regular speed, you can't speed it up because the men and machines are already busy. Even if you were willing to have men and machines underused, there are times when technological restraints prevent this. Chemical, electrochemical, and heat-treating processes must all be carried on at specific rates with almost no variation. Once the process is started it has to run its course to completion at the established rate or the material will be ruined. In the steel industry, all of the steelmaking activity, the tin-plating and galvanizing lines, and the annealing operations are of this type. A petroleum refinery must also be run as a continuous operation at a given throughput. In these examples the operation must be run at regular speeds or shut down.

In many cases you can get some flexibility by varying the number of hours a line operates. An automobile engine assembling plant can operate anywhere up to 21 full or part shifts per week. But you don't always have this kind of freedom. Blast furnaces, certain oil and chemical processes, and similar operations don't shut down at the end of a shift. Once operating, they have to go on operating continuously, 24 hours a day, 7 days a week.

Still another rigidity concerns scheduling orders. Once jobs or lots of materials start down the line, you can't, except at high cost, change job or material priorities. A large furniture company ran into this after conveyorizing its finishing operations. Salesmen's requests for special rush orders could no longer be taken care of except at high change-over costs. The company finally set aside a small area for processing special orders and retouching furniture before shipment.

In general, the more manual the work, the more flexible is the line's output. In radio and television assembly and in airplane and missile assembly, for example, you can almost always get more output from a line by adding workers, just so they don't get in each other's way. Or you can reduce the output by reducing the number of men. Doing this, however, upsets the old work assignments. Not only do you need to have your men trained to do two or more jobs but you will have to resubdivide the job elements so that you create a few more jobs or cut out a few jobs yet have the remaining jobs about equal to each other in terms of time.

Sometimes you can operate effectively at a reduced rate by leaving some work stations along an assembly line unmanned. Then you can "cascade" the work, much as traffic lights regulate traffic. If the product is not fastened down to a moving conveyor (automobiles and farm tractors are fastened down and keep moving along slowly even while men work on them. Television sets are, however, not fastened down.) Let an operator do one operation on several products and build up a small bank ahead of the next operation. Then have him stop performing the first operation and go over to the next workplace and perform the next operation on the products in the bank. Cascading the work this way gives you a good bit of flexibility in quantities produced.

Or instead of cascading the work, just let each man do two operations in immediate succession. After a man finishes his first operation on a product, he goes with it to the next work station and does that operation too; then he returns to the first work station for the next product. Naturally, you don't send products down the line at the same rate as when you have a full crew.

It is well, within the assembly line itself, to provide little one or two piece supply banks here and there. This lets workers set aside, now and then, a product that needs repairs and to replace it with another from the bank so that production won't be lost. You can provide a few wayside

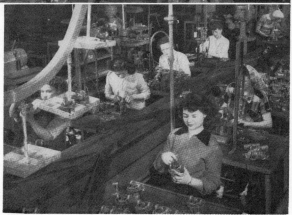

FIGURE 29-4 Automobile engine and carburetor assembly lines. To change the engine line's output you would just change the number of men along the line and have each one do a little more (or less) on each motor. The girls on the carburetor line can, in contrast, let work pile up at workplaces. You could have these workers move from work station to work station if you wanted to change the line's output. (Automobile Manufacturers Assoc.)

storages or even overhead racks. Doing this means that you have not scheduled the line quite so "tightly" and so will have fewer delays, although you have a little higher inventory in process.

Parts production lines, as contrasted with assembly lines, are harder to balance because so many machines have speeds faster or slower than the rate of output you need. Some of the machines need the operator only to load and unload the material. Sometimes, while a machine is performing an operation, you can have the operator run another machine (or possibly more). Doubling up like this (some people call it "machine coupling") may lose a little production if it happens that at any time both machines need the man at the same time. One will have to wait while he takes care of the other. If there is very much of this you will have to balance off the cost of idle machines against the man's idle time if he does not run two machines.

On parts lines, the price of flexibility usually is machine idle time. Consequently, and because of the variation of parts that may be run on each machine, it may not be profitable to use highly specialized equipment. Instead, it is better to use standard machines and equipment. Standard equipment is usually considerably cheaper and doesn't need the extensive debugging that new special machines usually require. Highly specialized equipment usually has a low resale value because nobody else can use it. Often it can be sold only for scrap. In trying to find a compromise between flexibility and low unit operation cost, some companies have turned to machines using modular units such as drilling heads, mounting bases, and transfer equipment which can be assembled into specialized units much in the manner of a child's Tinkertoy set. After a model run, these units can be disassembled and then the components recombined in different ways to make them into new specialized machines.

We spoke earlier of operators' "pegging" their production (limiting their output). In continuous production, both in parts making and in assembly, this problem is sometimes bad. Men do the same work day after day and get used to doing just so much. If you try to increase the output, no matter if you add more machines and more men too, you may have a strike on your hands. Both Ford and Chrysler have had their troubles when they tried to boost the output rate of lines by putting in more machines and men. The amount of work per worker wasn't changed but, to the union, it was a "speed-up" so the men went on strike.

QUANTITATIVE METHODS IN LINE BALANCING

Computers and operations research can be used to solve many line balancing problems. Several kinds of operations research techniques are available. These include simulation, heuristic line balancing, and queuing models.

SIMULATION

Simulation models (sometimes called Monte Carlo methods) start with either make-believe data or past data, dealing with such activities as lengths of production runs for various jobs and different frequencies of arrival at a machine. These figures are used on a pretend basis to generate a simulated record of how operations might work out.

To illustrate simulation we will assume that we are to make continuously a five-operation part. Each operation is done on its own machine but the machine output rates differ a little from each other. Furthermore there is, for each machine, some variation in its operation times.

Past records show that the average operation times for operations A, B, C, D, and E are 1.7, 1.9, 2.0, 2.0, and 1.8 minutes, respectively. The expected deviations of operation times are 0.20, 0.10, 0.15, 0.20, and 0.10 minutes, respectively. The "expected" deviation time here is the same "standard deviation" that we used in Chapter 21 and in Chapter 26.

And, as in the earlier cases, the arithmetic mean ± 1 standard deviation sets a range within which 68 per cent of all values fall, ± 2 standard deviations enclose 95 per cent, and ± 3 standard deviations enclose almost all cases. Operation A's average time is 1.7 minutes and its standard deviation is 0.20 minute. Sixty-eight per cent of the actual operation times are, therefore, between 1.5 and 1.9 minutes; 95 per cent of them are between 1.3 and 2.1 minutes; and almost all are between 1.1 and 2.3 minutes.

Right now we don't use this information but we will shortly.

Returning to the five operation times, operations C and D each take the longest, 2.0 minutes, so we will be limited to 30 units per hour at the most. Almost certainly we will not get this much production because of the variations in operation times of the several jobs. Were it not for variations we could assume that we would get 30 units per hour and that the men and machines for operations A, B, and E would not work quite so hard as C and D.

We can also plan to let the operations ahead of C and D go on steadily for some time and then close them down until the slow operations, C and D, catch up. Meanwhile the A and B machines and men can do other work. In the case of E, a faster operation than D, the problem is reversed. We probably should keep machine E idle and use its operator elsewhere until D builds up a bank, then we could start operation E and let the bank work down.

We are going to use simulation to find out how many units we really can get per hour, considering the variations in operation times.

First we must generate a list of simulated times for operation A on successive units. Then we build up similar lists for B, C, D, and E. After we have such lists we can pretend to do operation A on unit 1, then B, C, etc. Unit 2 follows 1 and 3 follows 2, etc. We can make up a table showing when each operation will start and finish. This we have done in figure 29-5.

The way to construct the simulated operation times is to start with the average time for the operation and to apply an adjustment factor which represents the variability. In the case of operation A, the average operation time is 1.7 minutes. Next, we consult a random number table (such tables are available in statistics books and in computer memories) and find a number. Suppose that our table contains numbers between 1 and 100 and that our number is 54. Next, we refer to a table of areas under the curve in normal distributions. (See Appendix B at the end of the book.) The number 54 is found to be +0.1 standard deviation above the average of 50. Now we can set the simulated time for this particular simulated performance of operation A. It is 1.7 + 0.1(0.20) = 1.72 minutes.

We repeat this process (going on to the next number in the random number table and then calculating a new simulated time) for the performance of operation A on unit 2 and get its simulated time. Then we go on to unit 3, 4, etc. Then we do the same for operations B, C, D, and E.

At this point we have simulated operation times for all five operations. We computed such times for 20 units. In figure 29-5 these are the numbers in the T columns.

Once we get lists such as these we can see how things would work out in practice. Suppose, for example, we planned to put in an assembly line, down which we hoped that one product would move every 2 minutes. Figure 29-5 shows that we can't get one unit every 2 minutes. In figure 29-5 the headed S columns show the time the operation starts, and the F columns show the time it finishes.

In our simulation we got 16 units finished in 41.99 minutes or one each 2.5 minutes, not one each 2.0 minutes as we wanted. This is because whenever any operation takes longer than 2.0 minutes, it stops the line until it is finished, thus holding up all other jobs. Sometimes it happens that more than one operation is slow at the same time. When this happens only the slowest one matters because the slowest one has to finish before anything else can go on.

You can see how this operates by looking at what happens as unit 6 moves through operation A. It starts at 10.56 minutes. While operation A is being performed on unit 6, operation B is being performed on unit 5, C on 4, D on 3, and E on 2. All five operations start at 10.56 and none can start any sooner because that was when operation D was finished on its preceding unit.

As it happens both C and D are slow this time, each taking more than 2.0 minutes. C, taking 2.17 minutes, is the one that matters though

FIGURE 29-5

UNIT	OPERATION TIMES IN MINUTES														
	A			B			C			D			E		
	T	S	F	T	S	F	T	S	F	T	S	F	T	S	F
1	1.73	0	1.73	1.72	2.00	3.72	1.84	4.00	5.84	1.93	6.13	8.06	1.55	8.39	9.94
2	1.75	2.00	3.75	2.13	4.00	6.13	2.26	6.13	8.39	2.17	8.39	10.56	1.97	10.56	12.53
3	1.63	4.00	5.63	1.87	6.13	8.00	1.85	8.39	10.24	2.15	10.56	12.71	1.81	12.73	14.54
4	1.73	6.13	7.84	1.91	8.39	10.30	2.17	10.56	12.73	2.09	12.73	14.82	1.83	14.82	16.65
5	1.64	8.39	10.03	1.92	10.56	12.48	1.76	12.73	14.49	1.67	14.82	16.49	1.81	16.83	18.64
6	1.61	10.56	12.17	1.73	12.73	14.46	1.78	14.82	16.60	2.11	16.83	18.49	1.76	19.17	20.93
7	1.87	12.73	14.60	2.01	14.82	16.83	2.34	16.83	19.17	1.91	19.17	21.08	1.88	21.10	22.98
8	1.85	14.82	16.67	1.82	16.83	18.65	1.93	19.17	21.10	2.07	21.10	23.17	1.63	23.17	24.80
9	1.79	16.83	18.62	1.88	19.17	21.05	1.87	21.10	22.97	2.09	23.17	25.26	1.86	25.26	27.12
10	1.37	19.17	20.50	2.07	21.10	23.17	1.92	23.17	25.09	1.77	25.26	27.03	1.78	27.30	29.08
11	1.81	21.10	22.91	1.99	23.17	25.16	2.04	25.26	27.30	2.05	27.30	29.35	2.07	29.36	31.43
12	1.62	23.17	24.79	1.75	25.26	27.01	2.06	27.30	29.36	2.01	29.36	31.37	1.65	31.43	33.08
13	1.70	25.26	26.96	1.78	27.30	29.08	1.99	29.36	31.35	2.03	31.43	33.46	1.73	33.64	35.37
14	1.79	27.30	29.09	1.84	29.36	31.20	2.21	31.43	33.64	2.33	33.64	35.97	1.76	36.16	37.92
15	1.47	29.36	30.81	1.61	31.43	33.04	1.93	33.64	35.57	1.83	36.16	37.99	1.87	38.16	40.03
16	1.75	31.43	33.18	2.52	33.64	36.16	2.00	36.16	38.16	2.07	38.16	40.23	1.76	40.23	41.99
17	1.71	33.64	35.35	1.69	36.16	37.85	2.00	38.16	40.16	2.05	40.23	42.28	1.87		
18	1.74	36.16	37.90	1.76	38.16	39.92	1.86	40.23	42.09	1.94			1.68		
19	2.02	38.16	40.18	1.94	40.23	42.17	1.90			2.02			1.91		
20	1.53	40.23	41.76	2.05			2.28			1.91			1.71		

since all other operations including D are finished before C finishes at 12.73 minutes. 12.73 minutes then becomes the operation start time for all five operations as the next units move to each work station.

We started out knowing that on the average, the five operations take 1.7, 1.9, 2.0, 2.0, and 1.8 minutes, respectively. Each unit, therefore, ends up having 9.4 minutes of work done on it. Yet our simulation tells us that we will get only 1 unit each 2.5 minutes. For the five operations this comes to 12.50 minutes of machine and man time. Out of this total, 3.1 minutes on 24.8 per cent of the time is idle time.

We won't pursue our simulation any further. We could go on and try "decoupling" successive jobs and provide for balancing banks and small stocks of products between operations and see what improvements we could make. Or we could try out other policies. Simulation would show us the results we'd get. We ought, however, to go through more lengthy simulations than we did here in order for all possible results to have a chance to show up.

USES OF SIMULATION   Simulation techniques can be useful in analyzing both relatively simple systems and highly complex systems. Once a model is constructed, you can try out various sets of input data to see how these changes affect results. You can get systems performance data for a fraction of the time and cost involved in experimenting with a "live" system. Bad proposals can be discarded without having to be tried out in practice.

Simulation models can also be used to find out what is important and what is unimportant. You might find out, for example, that you should carry a good bit of inventory rather than hold inventory down if holding it down would cause very many stockouts. Your intuition might not evaluate stockout costs versus inventory carrying costs properly.

Simulation models can also be used in training men and helping them to understand the interrelationships among factors in a system. "Business games" simulations are of this kind. Introduced in the 1950s, games are now widely used both by universities and by other organizations engaged in management training programs. They allow the compression of a substantial amount of simulated operating experience into a short time.

HEURISTIC LINE BALANCING
Men working along assembly lines each do a small collection of minor tasks. If products go down the line at the rate of one every three minutes, then each man has a collection of minor tasks which take him three minutes or slightly less to perform. If you have 50 men along a line they may be doing 1,000 to 2,000 small bits and pieces of work. Some of the bits and pieces need doing before others. And some take half a minute or so while others take only a few seconds. Gathering the bits and pieces together into a succession of three-minute jobs is a big job.

It is possible to use the simplex method of operations research to develop the very best (most nearly equal) set of work packages for each man. Solving this problem by the simplex method would, however, be such a big job that even a computer would spend a long time arriving at the answers.

But computers can do this job heuristically very quickly. The answers aren't quite the most perfect but they are nearly so. A "heuristic" method is a cut-and-try method. You read into the computer the long list of minor tasks together with the time each one takes and with all of the necessary sequence constraints. Then the computer selects a three-minute set of minor tasks for worker number 1. These particular minor tasks the computer then regards as being disposed of and as not to be assigned again. The computer then goes on, repeating the process for worker number 2, 3, etc., until all bits and pieces of the total work have been assigned.

The computer doesn't always manage to collect together exactly three minutes of work for a man because of the several constraints such as what has to be done first, no handling of dirty and clean parts at the same workplace, and, as on an automobile, no underneath and top tasks for the same man, etc. Also the total time can't exceed three minutes. Probably too, you'll tell the computer not to accept, say, a work package of less than 2.70 minutes without further search to see if another short task can't be added. Most likely quite a few of the work packages won't be exactly three minutes but they will come close.

The reason why heuristically set job packages will miss being the very best is because the computer does not investigate every possible work package. The perfect allocations of every bit and piece of work may mean that tasks initially put into package number 1 or 2, etc., may be better placed a little later. But the computer, having put them into an early assignment, never, in a heuristic process, considers reassigning them to later jobs.

Actually, in heuristic problem solving, the computer goes through the same process that an industrial engineer would use. The advantage of the computer is its speed, particularly if you want to consider the effects of changing constraints a little and so want to try out several alternatives. You might, for example, want to study different line speeds and to consider cutting the work up into two-minute or four-minute assignments. A computer can give you heuristic answers fast. Probably an industrial engineer can still add a few improvements, but the computer does the main work.

QUEUING THEORY

Queuing or "waiting line" theory can tell you about delays to machines, men, or materials that come from imbalances in capacity between successive operations. You can find out how often queues will build up, how long they will last, and how big they will get both on the average and in extreme cases.

Queuing problems, if they are not too difficult, can be mathematically handled. But if several factors work together to produce results, then mathematical solutions become quite complex, and should not be used. Instead, Monte Carlo simulations should be used. Queuing formulas are in statistics books.[1]

[1] See, for example, Thomas L. Saaty, *Elements of Queueing Theory*, McGraw-Hill Book Company, New York, 1961.

To illustrate mathematical solutions to queuing problems we will assume that we have a single service facility with irregular demands being made upon it for its services. Examples of such a demand on a single service facility are: the arrival of patients (where no appointments are involved) at a doctor's office, letters arriving at a clerk's desk, or, in a factory, men coming to a tool crib for tools.

As in the case of simulation you need to know or to assume certain characteristics about the system before you can calculate how it will operate. And you need either real data or assumed data about the system.

ARRIVAL RATE   The first thing you need is the arrival rate. Sometimes one man will arrive at a tool crib 10 seconds after another man has arrived. But in other cases the interval will be 3 minutes. The length of time between arrivals will vary. In order to use queuing models you need to know or to assume an average rate of arrival.

Usually, in queuing situations, the variation in arrival intervals will *not* follow the "normal curve" pattern. Instead, most arrival patterns are Poisson in shape. There are more short time intervals than long ones but a few of the long intervals are long indeed. Figure 29-6 shows the shape of a Poisson curve. It is low on the left, rises quickly to a high level, and then slopes off and extends well to the right. A curve showing the waiting time in line at a bank teller's window would be a Poisson-type curve. Almost never do you get served in 10 seconds. Most often it takes half a minute and still more often, say, a minute. Sometimes, however, it takes 2 minutes, once in a while, 5 minutes, and in rare cases, longer. The most frequent wait would be relatively short, say 1 minute, but there would be occasional much longer waits.

Since queuing models assume a Poisson pattern in arrivals you don't have to supply specific arrival interval data, although the formula does need the average arrival rate and the standard deviation of arrival times. The Poisson curve formula can then tell you the probability of any specific arrival rates other than average. This would work as shown below.

The Poisson curve formula is

$$P_n = \frac{e^{-\lambda}(\lambda)^n}{n!}$$

where P_n = the probability of n arrivals

e = a constant: 2.71828

n = the stated number of arrivals

λ = the average arrivals per unit of time

$n!$ = "factorial" n

Suppose that we say that on the average, 4 men arrive per minute

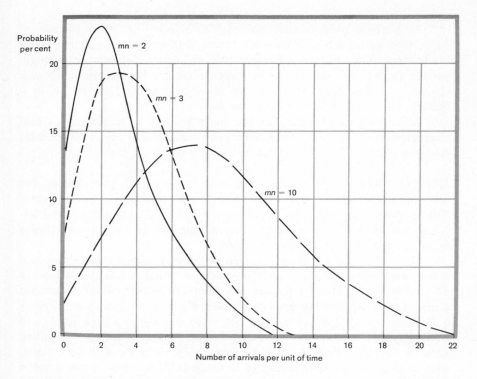

FIGURE 29-6   Poisson distributions of data with differing arithmetic means. (These distributions are not continuous functions; the curves are put in only to aid the eye and to reduce the confusion that would result from using vertical bars.)

and we want to know what are the probabilities that 6 will arrive in any given minute.

$$P_n = \frac{2.71828^{-4}(4)^6}{6!} = \frac{(1/2.71828)^4(4{,}096)}{6 \cdot 5 \cdot 4 \cdot 3 \cdot 2 \cdot 1}$$

$$= \frac{1/54.6(4{,}096)}{720} = \frac{75}{720} = .104$$

There is a 10.4 per cent chance that there will be 6 arrivals in any given minute.

SIZE AND TOTAL POPULATION   In order to work out queuing problems, you need also to know the size of the population, or the group from which the arrivals come. If there are only 10 men in the group and 5 men have already arrived for service, there is less likelihood that a sixth will arrive than if there are 1,000 in the group and 5 have already arrived. Normally, you assume that the whole group is large enough that the arrival of one man won't significantly reduce the chances of another man arriving.

SPACE FOR QUEUES   There are other matters too, such as: is there room for as long a queue as might form? Sometimes in automobile traffic a stoplight backs up traffic beyond the next street back and blocks traffic there. A car washing establishment needs a long driveway so that cars can wait without queuing up out in the street. In a factory along an assembly line, there usually isn't room enough to pile up products between operations, so a queue can't build up. Instead a delay forces operations to close down. In queuing problems we nearly always assume that a queue can build up.

DEFECTIONS   Then there is the question of defections. Do people facing a wait actually wait or do they go away? Sometimes you leave instead of wait, but when you need groceries you have to go through the line to get out, so you get into the queue and wait. Queuing problems usually assume that items in line don't defect.

QUEUE DISCIPLINE   Queuing models usually also assume first-in, first-out discipline. First arrivals are served first.

NUMBER OF SERVICE CHANNELS   A bank has several tellers, a supermarket has several check-out counters, and a toll road has several pay booths. A tool crib usually has two or three attendants. These are "M-channel" systems, where M is the number of parallel service stations. You could also view an assembly line as an M-channel set of service stations but they are in series rather than in parallel. Whenever there are two or more parallel service stations, and unless they are alike, you need rules governing their use, such as "eight items or fewer" for the express check-out cashier at the supermarket, or special toll booths for trucks and buses on the toll road. You may also need rules concerning the possibility of "queue barging" (changing lines and getting ahead of others already there). At traffic lights ambulances go first.

SERVICE TIMES   We need also to know the average service time and the dispersion pattern of service times. The pattern of service times is often just like that of arrival intervals. When it is, a Poisson curve would apply. Unfortunately, however, the Poisson distribution of service times can't be used in the formulas or models because of computational difficulties. Instead, a negative exponential distribution of expected service times is generally used. This means that you assume that the shorter the time, the more common the occurrence of that service time. Longer and longer service times are assumed to occur less and less often. The slight error introduced by using a negative exponential curve instead of a Poisson distribution of service times is usually minor.

SUMMARY   In summary, we can say that queuing models usually assume a Poisson distribution of arrivals from a large population. No limit is put on queue lengths, there are no defections, and service is first-come, first-served. Service time occurs on a negative exponential basis.

OBJECTIVES   There is still one remaining question. What are you trying to maximize? Do you want to keep the service unit busy? Or do you want, instead, to reduce waits by units needing service. A doctor keeps himself busy by scheduling patient arrivals so that if anyone waits, it is the patient, not him. This is good as he sees it but his waiting time is minimized at the cost of patient waiting time. At a hospital emergency receiving station the objective is different. It is to take care of the newly arrived patient fast, cutting his waiting time, even at the expense of a certain amount of lost time by interns who are on hand ready and waiting. And possibly at the expense of other patients in less need of immediate attention.

WAITING LINE EXAMPLE   We are, in an example, going to show how various questions about waiting lines can be answered, and how these answers are calculated. But we are not going to go on to show how much different the input data would have to be to produce other answers which you might want to know about.

The average use ratio of a service facility is the ratio between the rate of arrival of units to be serviced and the rate of service. In our model the Greek letter rho, ρ, is the average use ratio; lambda, λ, is the rate of arrival; and mu, μ, is the rate of service. Therefore,

$$\rho = \frac{\lambda}{\mu}$$

If units arrive at the rate of 40 per day, and the service unit can handle 50 per day then $\rho = 0.80$.

Next, we might ask how much time the service facility will be idle, or stated differently, what is the probability that there will be no units in the system? If ρ is the ratio of use time, then $1 - \rho$ is the ratio of idle time. Since the service facility will be busy 80 per cent of the time, it must be idle 20 per cent of the time. A mathematician would say that the probability of there being no units in the system is: $P = .20$. (Do not confuse this P, standing for probability, with the Greek letter rho, ρ, which we have been using to symbolize the service facility's use ratio.) Put into formula form:

$$P_0 = 1 - \frac{\lambda}{\mu}$$

This same formula can be stated in such a way as to tell us the probability of there being 1 or more units in the system. Expressed this way, the formula becomes:

$$P_n = \left(1 - \frac{\lambda}{\mu}\right)\left(\frac{\lambda}{\mu}\right)^n$$

For 3 units in the system, the calculation is:

$$P_3 = (1 - \tfrac{40}{50})(\tfrac{40}{50})^3 = (.2)(.8)^3 = (.2)(.512) = .102$$

This tells us that there is a .102 probability that there will be 3 units in the system. By itself, however, this figure probably doesn't interest us very much. More likely we'd like to know what is the probability that there will be 3 or fewer units in the system. So we must sum up the probability of there being zero in the system (.200), plus the probability of there being 1 (.160), plus the probability of there being 2 (.128), plus the figure for 3 (.102). Summing these up we find that there is a .590 probability that there will be 3 or fewer units in the system. Conversely, there is a probability of .410 that there will be 4 or more units in the system.

Still another question is: what will be the average number of units in the system? If L is the number of units in the system, then:

$$L = \frac{\lambda}{\mu - \lambda} = \frac{40}{50 - 40} = 4 \text{ units}$$

This result may seem surprising since we just discovered above that there was only a .41 probability of there being four or more units in the queue. It would seem that, if there were less than a 50-50 chance of there being 4 units in the queue, the average number of units in the queue could hardly be 4. Yet the average is 4 because there are occasional long queues which pull the average up.

Or perhaps you are interested in the average numbers of units in the queue itself. Letting L_q be the number of units in the queue, then:

$$L_q = \frac{(\lambda)^2}{\mu(\mu - \lambda)} = \frac{(40)^2}{50(50 - 40)} = 3.2 \text{ units}$$

This figure, too, is surprising. It would seem that if there are, on the average, 4 units in the system, 1 of the 3 units is being serviced and 3 are in the queue. The average is not 3, however, because there is no queue at all during the 16 per cent of the time when there is only 1 unit in the system. So when there are queues, their average length is a little longer than 3.

Another question that we can answer with our formulas is: what is the expected average time that a unit will spend in the system? If we let W be the total time in the system, then

$$W = \frac{1}{\mu - \lambda} = \frac{1}{50 - 40} = 0.1 \text{ day}$$

There may be still other questions that you'd like answered about how the queue would operate. We will calculate only one other answer: What would be the average waiting time for service? Let the waiting time be W_t; then

$$W_t = \frac{\lambda}{\mu(\mu - \lambda)} = \frac{40}{50(50 - 40)} = .08 \text{ day}$$

Although we won't plot the charts to show it, as the system use ratio goes up from 0 to 100 per cent, the number of units in the queue and the waiting time both go up but not at a straight line rate. These lines go up slowly at first and then at an increasing rate.

As we said earlier, as queuing models become complex, the mathematics quickly become very complex. Soon it becomes easier to solve such problems by simulation. Interestingly, Curtis Jones, writing in the Harvard Business Review, said:

> Waiting line theory is in the paradoxical position of being almost useless as a solver of problems, but of great value in understanding them. The assumptions required for the application of waiting line mathematical techniques are almost never valid. Yet the conceptual framework of this theory does provide insights. The insights are particularly useful because they are frequently at odds with our common sense.[2]

In other words, our intuition is often wrong and waiting line theory can help straighten us out.

STUDY MATERIALS

29-1 Contrast the nature of the process and control of the type of operations discussed in this chapter with those discussed in previous chapters. Include such factors as line balance and information flow with respect to both content and work load of the production control department.

29-2 From the characteristics of the flow process systems described in this chapter, what can be inferred about the characteristics of highly automated systems in general? Can these systems be designed to overcome some of the less desirable features?

[2] See Curtis H. Jones, "Keeping Informed," *Harvard Business Review,* September-October, 1966, p. 26.

29-3 Since demand for some of their basic components both in their own end products and as components sold to others has reached a sustained level, the engineers at Interface, Inc., have decided to set up a continuous production facility for the basic parts. One operation on a casting used in the basic hydraulic motor unit is performed on a multiple drill. The drilling operation takes $1\frac{1}{2}$ minutes, with another $\frac{1}{2}$ minute needed for the setup of the casting in the drilling fixture. Unloading and cleaning of the drilled part also requires another $\frac{1}{2}$ minute.

The operation requires a machinist A, whose wage rate is $5 per hour, but the unloading and cleaning operation could also be performed by an apprentice machinist who has a rate of $3 per hour. Machine time is calculated at $10 per hour. Up to six multiple drilling machines, all identical in characteristics, are available, as are a sufficient supply of machinists and apprentices. The desired output rate for this operation is 120 pieces per hour.

Set up the work station so as to minimize the cost of the drilling operation.

29-4 Suppose that, in our example on page 666, operation A had an average time of 2.0 minutes and D had 1.7 minutes. All other basic data are the same. What does this do to the line's output rate? (Appendix A at the end of the book is a random number table and appendix B gives the normal curve distributions that you might need in order to work this out.)

29-6 The following 40 elements and their time values are from a list of thousands of bits of work needed to assemble an automobile. Assume that they constitute a complete assembly job and that you are to group them together into man job assignments. The times are in hundredths of a minute.

ELE-MENT	TIME	MUST PRECEDE	MUST FOLLOW	ELE-MENT	TIME	MUST PRECEDE	MUST FOLLOW
1	.38	25		21	.14	22	
2	.17	25		22	.23		21
3	.24	4	2	23	.38		
4	.13	25	3	24	.13	25	23
5	.12			25	.75	32 and all higher numbers	Many numbers under 25
6	.11	6, 25		26	.08	27	25
7	.17		6	27	.19		26
8	.11	10, 11, 25		28	.33	29	25
9	.29	10, 11		29	.22	25	28
10	.67	12, 25	8, 9	30	.39		25
11	.47	12, 25	8, 9	31	.22		25
12	.42	25	10, 11	32	.53	33, 34, 35, 36	25
13	.28			33	.26		32
14	.34	15, 16, 25		34	.24		32
15	.47	16, 17	14	35	.16		32
16	.64	17	14	36	.11		32
17	.29	18	15, 16	37	.09		25
18	.22		17	38	.43	39	25
19	.73	19, 25		39	.13		38
20	.14	25	19	40	.10		25

The requirement that an element precede or follow another means any time before or after. The one does not have to be done immediately before or after the other.

1   Group the elements into job sets so that you will get one product off the line every 1.5 minutes. How many men will you need? What fraction of their time will be wasted? (Remember that no work package can exceed 1.5 minutes.)

2   Do the same for a production rate of one product per minute.

29-5   How many men should you have in a tool crib to service machinists who arrive at the rate of 20 per hour when it takes an average of 10 minutes each to serve them? Both arrival times and service times are irregular.

The machinists cost you $10 an hour ($5 for themselves and $5 for their idle machine) whereas the tool crib attendants cost $4 an hour. When tool crib men are not serving the men at the issue window, they spend their time cleaning tooling previously returned. This work is regarded as being worth $2 an hour.

Would your answer be any different if $3 an hour truckers instead of the machinists came for and took away the tooling?

chapter thirty

FLOW CONTROL—II

FLOW CONTROL IN MULTI-PLANT COMPANIES

All companies big enough for continuous manufacture have several factories. This means that there will be sister plant relationships, with one or more plants making some items for the others, and that certain production control work and certain purchasing work are done centrally. It also means that certain other parts of production control and purchasing are *not* done centrally. So you have the problem of what should be done centrally and what should be done in each plant.

Automobile assembly is a good example. The Detroit office makes up weekly and daily final assembly schedules for each factory. It also makes up, for each factory, lists of the parts and subassemblies that each plant will need and it sets up schedules for subassembly and parts production or purchase for each plant. It may even set individual plant work hours. And finally, it directs interplant shipments and gives shipping schedules to suppliers. All of this is complicated by the fact that you make four-door cars in all assembly plants but station wagons and convertibles in only some plants.

At first, this sounds like too much home office direction. Isn't it unwise for Detroit to make production schedules for Atlanta, St. Louis, Philadelphia, and Los Angeles? How can Detroit know all of the details of each plant's work? Actually, you want Detroit to do as little as is necessary and you do let individual plant production control departments make up all but their overall schedules.

Yet you need central control to coordinate the shipment of materials that come from the outside, whether from sister plants or other companies. Suppliers may have to ship to a dozen or more of your plants (Ford buys from 800 suppliers who ship 11,000 kinds of parts to sixteen factories) and they need to know the total demand so that they can plan their production. A seat fabric maker, for example, has to plan his runs of each fabric. Also, suppliers are themselves often multi-plant companies and they can divide your total order best among their plants if they get the whole order from one source instead of getting a dozen uncoordinated lists from your dozen factories. And, of course, the supplier might be your own "home" plant. Buick assembles seventeen car models in Flint, Michigan, and supplies many parts for fifteen of these models to all five other Buick plants.

Multi-plant suppliers try to fill your multi-plant needs by shipping to each of your plants from their nearest factory. Young Spring and Wire

Model	Comb.	Plant	Thru Mar.	Apr.	May	June	July	Thru July
43	41	Cincinnati	1	110	250	840	760	1961
	46	"	57	83	130	200	130	600
	47	"	97	333	550	800	584	2364
	48	"	103	207	340	480	350	1480
	49	"	99	201	340	480	350	1470
		TOTAL	357	934	1610	2800	2174	7875
43	41	Philadelphia	8	112	270	890	750	2030
	46	"	60	90	140	200	130	620
	47	"	126	344	580	860	567	2477
	48	"	108	212	350	500	340	1510
	49	"	94	216	350	500	340	1500
		TOTAL	396	974	1690	2950	2127	8137
43	41	San Leandro	8	92	240	880	662	1882
	46	"	51	89	130	200	110	580
	47	"	98	312	520	840	515	2285
	48	"	91	199	330	490	310	1420
	49	"	77	203	330	490	310	1410
		TOTAL	325	895	1550	2900	1907	7577
43	41	Atlanta	3	67	210	670	480	1430
	46	"	37	63	110	160	80	450
	47	"	79	221	460	640	374	1774
	48	"	66	134	290	380	217	1087
	49	"	63	137	290	380	220	1090
		TOTAL	248	622	1360	2230	1371	5831
46R	40	Toledo	2600	850	630	560	495	5135
	42	"	7400	2040	1530	1320	1158	13448
	43	"	4530	-	-	-	-	4530
	43A	"	131	1039	790	680	545	3175
	44	"	3925	-	-	-	-	3925
	44A	"	350	1110	830	710	577	3577
	45	"	1086	214	160	140	115	1715
		TOTAL	20012	5253	3940	3410	2890	35505

FIGURE 30-1 A tentative assembly schedule for each of the plants of a multi-plant company.

Company, maker of automobile seat cushions, for example, makes in Chicago springs for delivery to cars made in Indiana, Illinois, and Wisconsin. Its Chicago factory also ships directly to automobile assembly plants in Detroit. And its Los Angeles plant ships to plants in southern California.

Multi-plant suppliers probably shift orders around more between factories than customer companies shift orders around among their own assembly plants. This is because suppliers feel the effect of their customers' changes as well as their own. If Chrysler in Detroit boosts its seat cushion order a great deal and in a short time, Young boosts its Chicago production, but if its Windsor, Ontario, plant is low on work, Young might make some of the excess needs there and truck them in to Chrysler in Detroit. Young can shift the production around among its plants.

Young can do the same if its own Chicago seat cushion production is interrupted. Windsor's output can be boosted and Detroit's needs partially met by shipping cushions from Windsor. This time it is the supplier's own troubles that caused the shift. In the paragraph above, it was caused by the customer's problems. In either case, production gets shifted around.

It is not production control's job to make everybody like interplant transfers, and such transfers usually are unpopular. Whenever you shift one plant's normal output to another plant for whatever good reason, the managers of the plant from which you took business don't like it because this makes it harder for them to earn a good profit in their own plant. Neither do Chicago employees like it, if you give work (their work as they see it) to Windsor employees, or vice versa.

You might expect that since the transfers probably balance out in the long run no one would feel hurt. More likely, though, everyone feels hurt. Everyone remembers the work he lost but forgets the work that he gained.

POOLED FREIGHT CARS   Multi-plant companies spend so much on freight that possible freight savings sometimes override the continuous idea. Shipments of parts from source factories to assembly plants is sometimes not direct. It may pay to collect parts in a central shipment point, such as Chicago, in order to be able always to ship full cars to West Coast points. The freight savings from using pooled cars and getting full car discounts also makes it worthwhile to ship more than is immediately needed when there is extra space in a car.

LINEAR DECISION RULES   One operations research technique, linear decision rules, sometimes helps in allocation problems of this type. Suppose we consider a case where we produce a product in one factory and distribute it through three regional warehouses. Because of differences in sales, taxes, warehouse costs, and other factors, the cost of carrying inventory in each warehouse differs and so, of course, does the optimal inventory level.

If the inventory carried goes above optimal, this raises the carrying cost per unit used. Yet below this point, the higher the stockout costs. Figure 30-2 shows how these changes are related. We find that we are looking at a chart like the economic ordering quantity charts shown in Chapter 17. The total cost curve is at its low point where the cost of acquisition and the cost of possession curves cross.

Here, however, we are interested in marginal costs as such. Up to the optimum inventory level, point A on figure 30-2, the cost of each added unit carried reduces the total cost of handling the item. But, to the right of point A, if we carry bigger inventories, every added unit raises costs. The marginal cost is the amount of change in the total cost line as items are

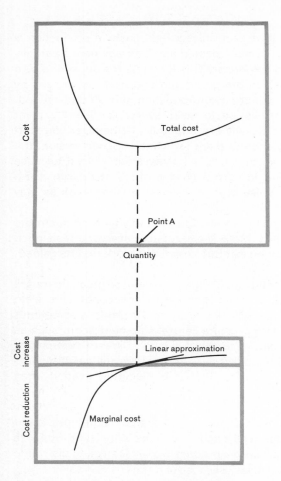

FIGURE 30-2 Total cost curve showing that a linear approximation of marginal cost changes is valid for changes in quantities close to the lowest cost point.

added. This amount of change is shown in the lower part of figure 30-2 as a curved line. At point A the marginal cost line crosses the zero line; in other words, it no longer reduces average costs. Up to this point every added unit reduces costs, but from point A on, every added unit raises costs.

Suppose we say, for example, that for warehouse I the optimum inventory to carry is 100 units at which point it costs us $20 a year to carry each unit. We find that if we carry 101 units it will cost $20.01 each to carry them, or $2,021.01 for the 101 units per year. The extra one unit added $1.01 to the cost. So our marginal cost is $1.01, and the slope of the marginal cost line at point A is +1.01, meaning that for every added unit, costs increase $1.01.

We know from our EOQ analysis that this type of total cost curve is relatively flat near the optimal point. This means that the slope of the incremental change curve is relatively constant. For small changes in volume above and below optimum, the rate of change can be used as if it were constant (at $1 per unit in our example). We have shown this in figure 30-2 by drawing in a straight line which provides us with a linear approximation of the marginal changes in costs in the area near the optimal point.

We should make such calculations for each of the three warehouses. Suppose that we find that the marginal cost for warehouse II is $.90 for a volume of 110 units and for warehouse III it is $1.10 for 130 units. The average marginal cost for the three warehouses combined is $1 per unit but since warehouse II is below average, we should probably carry bigger stocks there. In fact, we should carry all the stock we have there if our assumption that marginal costs don't change is really reliable. But, of course, we know that marginal costs are relatively fixed and our linear approximations are valid only for quantities near the optimal point. Our point is, however, that the proper inventory to carry in any one warehouse is, when the total situation is considered, not necessarily its own optimal quantity. In our example we ought to carry more stock at warehouse II, enough more to bring its marginal cost up to $1.

PROCESSING INSTRUCTIONS

You don't see many instructions telling men how to perform operations in continuous manufacture. You'll almost never see, for example, anyone in the shop having a complete bill of materials. Nor do you find very many instructions covering how to do individual jobs. Often the equipment is special, designed for the job, and all that the men have to do is to operate it. In some cases, such as chemical manufacture, processing instructions come as formulas and specifications covering mixing, heating, electrical treatments, and the times needed for chemical reactions.

In fabricating industries, such as radios, TV sets, and autos, you don't need any day-to-day instructions telling men how to make parts and how to put them together into assemblies. But you do need them, and in great detail, whenever you start to make new products or new models of old products. So many machines are new and nearly all of the men's work assignments are new that it takes two or three weeks to get everyone trained and familiar with the new operating arrangement. After the start period, though, things should go smoothly and employees should not need any more instructions.

On the other hand, electronics products assemblers always have instructions before them in the form of drawings showing which wires they are to connect with which contact points. Sometimes individual assemblers have lengthy assignments (fastening two or three dozen wires into place) so it doesn't hurt for them to be able to look at the drawing now and then. Also, sometimes you have to move men around and the transferred men need the drawings to tell them what to do. Occasionally the actual subassembly is placed where the worker can look at it. This helps if the actual placement of the wires is itself important.

A good deal of engineering effort goes into the "run-in" period. And considerable worker training is often necessary. Burroughs Corporation, for example, assembles its "Sensimatic" office machines continuously but breaks assembly work up into fifteen-minute assembly assignments. Each man has a fifteen-minute job. Every ten assemblers have a group leader who is shown, when a new product is in the prototype stage, how to assemble it and he has to learn how to do it. Later, when production starts, he teaches his ten men how to do their work. From here on, however, the men don't need any further instructions. Automobile companies follow the same practice. Supervisors and key workers learn, while lines are being installed, how to assemble the new product on the new line.

Besides actual instructions to assemblers, the engineers work out ahead the intended size of banks. Naturally these will fluctuate, but the engineers must calculate their maximum and minimum expected sizes. Little items of low value which take up little space may be set at from two or three days' supply on up. But big items, particularly those big in size, you want to keep moving. Plan to carry very few of them. Some companies even intentionally locate machines close together to prevent building up the float. On the other hand, regardless of the kind of item, you should always carry banks after likely trouble spots. Then trouble in the trouble spot won't hold up the following operations. Possibly simulation will also help here.

TRIAL RUNS

New models need new production lines. Usually the new lines use some old and some new equipment so that it is impossible to set up whole new lines and to have try out runs of whole lines while you are still producing old models.

It is still a good idea, though, to try out every new machine and to prove the tooling before you actually plan to start production. You can do this by scheduling a preliminary small run of new model products a month or so ahead. True, they can't be made on any line yet set up. But you can make parts and assemble products using whatever machines are available (some are in the current production line and some are set off to one side waiting to be installed). Turn them on and run off the trial items. You'll have to carry trial items around from machine to machine and you'll have to do this during off hours on the machines already in use. But after the trial run you'll be more sure that the new line will not have serious starting up troubles.

STARTING PRODUCTION

Automobile companies close down operations during model changeover periods, then start up and operate at full capacity as quickly as possible. During the first weeks of producing a new model, the auto companies want top production so that they can take care of the first rush of buying new models and of supplying dealers with floor stocks. This comes at the very time that you also have to solve the difficulties that always go with new lines.

In Chapter 9 we talked about the learning curve and how you become more efficient as you continue making a product. The learning curve doesn't appear to operate very much in automobile making. As we said, this is partly because today's new products and today's ways for doing work are enough like yesterday's so that to a large extent you just pick up on the new model from where you left off on the old. It is as if you had already made 500,000 and have to get to 1 million in order to reduce man-hours by 20 per cent. By no means are you starting from scratch.

We also mentioned that learning curves often don't operate normally because of worker resistance to change. It is particularly important, when a line is started, to tell everyone what the final expected rate is and how much time is allowed to get up to this rate. Usually, doing this keeps you from having anti-speed-up strikes. If you expect 30 products an hour as the final rate, start by saying that you expect 30. Then set schedules for less at first but tell everyone how much you are stepping up the schedules each day during a short "learning period" as the line works up to 30.

Unfortunately you probably will have to sacrifice, during the life of a model run, all possibility of further gains from the learning curve. In the case of our automobile assembly line example, you are not likely ever to get 32 an hour even though you might learn where to cut enough corners to do it later. The men would resist and besides you'd have to rebalance the line because not all jobs would change similarly. Some could be shortened considerably, others not at all.

Rarely do companies, other than automobile companies, close down for change-overs. Makers of TV sets, stoves, refrigerators, washing machines, lawn mowers, typewriters, cameras, and any number of other products bring out new models now and then, sometimes even annually. Usually this means discontinuing making old models. If not, then companies either set up whole new production lines or modify old lines to allow for producing the new models right along with old ones.

If possible, change-overs should be made at low points in production. If you have duplicate lines you can change one line at a time during a transition period. You can even use some of the regular operators to help make the change, thus avoiding laying them off. Sometimes, too, you can minimize production interruptions by doing the actual moving of machines at night or over a week end.

If you discontinue old models it is well to do it during a transition period rather than all at once. Frigidaire, which brings out new models annually, starts in October to produce new model refrigerators but does not stop making old models until the end of December. During the last three months of the year, the scheduled quantity of new models goes up month by month and the production of old models goes down. The new models produced are sent out to dealers so that they will all have floor stocks by the first of January.

Having such a lengthy transition period makes considerable extra work for production control since it must order double sets of parts for three months. But the lengthy transition eases some problems, particularly new tooling problems.

When you are getting hundreds of items of new tooling you can be sure that some of them will not be ready when they are supposed to be and some of them won't work according to plan. It takes time to straighten out all of these minor difficulties.

During this early period, production control should overorder on parts for the least changed new models. Overordering means that you will have more inventory (per unit of product) than you will keep in banks later on after production gets into full swing. Then why do it? You do it so that if you get held up on one model, you can swing over to another and not lose production. True, you'll overrun on the item you change to but you can cut it back later. After you straighten out the trouble on the product currently in difficulty, you will boost its schedules and cut on the overrun product. The point to see is that you have to be prepared to overrun on the items least likely to give you trouble or else you can't do it when you'd like to. It is much better to overrun on one item if another one holds you up than it is to lose production.

The practice of overordering parts for the safe models is not confined to producing old and new models in a transition period. Auto companies too do this although they change over all at once and have no transition period. They have their troubles getting new production lines up to their desired rate so they overstock (a little) on parts for models that are least changed and so least likely to run into production trouble.

Actually, overordering is usually confined to small parts because of investment and storage space limitations. All that you do on the big items is to warn suppliers that you may have to change up or down drastically and in a hurry. The same applies to your inside parts-making departments. You expect them to be fast on their feet and not to hold you up if you have to change schedules.

ROUTING

All product design work, making parts lists, deciding on subassemblies, making operation lists, deciding on machines required, and operator work methods have to be worked out in advance in continuous production. Usually the results of this work are embodied in the design and in the arrangements of machines and in the conveyors used between operations. You might say that the routing has been "conveyorized."

All of these activities are carried on with an eye to economical production. Work routing is much less an independent activity in continuous production than it is in intermittent production. It is tied in closely with product design and machine and process design, and these are never part of production control's work.

Once the engineers have decided on the routing of parts and have gotten the machines needed, it is costly to change. In intermittent production, the last minor routing decisions are often made in the shop. In continuous production, after production starts, you might find that certain changes ought to be made but the shop never acts on its own. The effects are too far-reaching. Other departments or even suppliers or customers may be affected. Even on little changes, engineering must approve. We should not imply, however, that you never change designs or methods once a line is set up because you do. Major changes are rare, however, because they are so costly. It is well to freeze designs for reasonably long periods, perhaps for the model year, on fundamental parts.

AUTHORITY TO PRODUCE COMING TO THE PRODUCTION CONTROL DEPARTMENT

In continuous manufacture using flow control, the production control department usually receives authority in the form of production program releases. In Chapter 10 we said that program releases cover everything that you make in a given period of time and are lists of quantities of finished products wanted. The variety is limited, and the volume of most types of products is large. Releases, in some companies covering a one-week period and in others one month, are given to production control from two to four weeks ahead.

Actually, in most continuous production plants, the production control department probably does *not* get just one single release covering everything to be made. Some of your biggest production items are made on blanket contracts for one or two big customers. Production control often gets releases to make these products directly from the customer's production control department. It has to incorporate these customer release orders into the schedules that it issues to the shop. In a very real sense production control ends up getting releases from several sources and makes up its own overall schedule for shop operations.

In fact, production control has even more authority over making its own overall schedules. Customers' releases sometimes come in very late. Today they ask for products that they want tomorrow. Production control knows that the release is coming and has to guess at the quantities and go ahead and make factory schedules accordingly. This problem is particularly important near the end of a model run when the customer company under-releases to be sure that it doesn't get caught with excess parts. Then it sends you last-minute releases for rush deliveries for a few of various items. The vendor company has to do a lot of scrambling. The effect is to transfer all the guesswork and the risk of getting stuck with overruns or having many extra setups for small runs from the customer company to the vendor company.

Customer releases show the quantity of the item that he wants you to deliver in the period covered by his release and also show the total, the "accumulation" of all releases to date and the accumulation of all deliveries received against earlier releases. Showing accumulation totals makes sure that you furnish enough parts. If you have run under (or over) the release amounts for past periods, or if you are currently running under or over the amounts authorized by current releases, the accumulation figure lets you know just where you stand. There is no confusion about whether last week's underrun is to be dropped or made up or is included in the new release figure.

Customer releases are not very reliable. Normally the customer is supposed to give you a firm release for a matter of three or four weeks ahead and tentative figures for releases up to three months ahead. This he will do. Then he will phone and change his releases any number of times even after you have started production on them.

Automobile companies try to give upholstery fabric makers five months' lead time. Yet orders for cars come in from dealers only one month ahead. The sales department tries to anticipate the details of dealers' orders but there is small wonder that releases given way ahead prove to not be very firm.

Automobile makers make up broad plans for their expected sales volume for months ahead and even set up tentative 90-day sales schedules. The next 30 days are "firmed up" or are definite schedules day by day for each separate day. Actually, there is some shuffling around even in the 30 days' schedules. Within the 30 days, the daily schedules for the first 10 days are supposed to be so firm that shipping schedules are made that far ahead. Makers of refrigerators, stoves, washing machines, and TV sets follow the same practice although their firm daily schedules are sometimes for only one week ahead. Bell and Howell follows this same practice too with motion picture cameras and projectors but it first sets a monthly schedule and then breaks it down into daily schedules.

PURCHASING

Often, in continuous production, enormous quantities of a limited variety of materials are used. Purchasing of heavily used raw materials is based more on market conditions than on production needs for any specific period. The purchasing agent is a major official in the company and can buy materials forward on the basis of his evaluation of market conditions. He knows about how much material you will need from looking at the manufacturing program. He needs no purchase requisitions from the production control department.

Companies in food processing industries (flour milling in particular) using agricultural products as raw material often "hedge" their purchases to protect themselves against loss if prices go down. When they buy raw material which they will own for a good while, they sell a futures contract at the same time. This contract calls for them to deliver at some future time the same quantity of raw materials that they just bought. If during their ownership of the material prices go up so does the value of the raw material they own, but so also does the cost of fulfilling the futures contract. So the company gains on the inventory value but loses on the futures contract. The reverse happens on downswings. The overall effect of hedging is to protect the processor against inventory loss during price downswings but at the cost of foregoing inventory profits on upswings. This frees them to go about their main business and frees them from having to engage in inventory speculation.

Most of the raw materials you buy are, however, not raw materials in the sense that they are just as nature provided them. Most items are someone else's finished products. Particularly is this true with buying items to go into assembled products. You buy enormous quantities of some items and you buy all of the big items on blanket contracts covering your needs for a long time ahead. One purchase order serves to buy your whole commitment for a complete model run.

Commonly you divide the contracts for big items between two or more suppliers buying a certain share of your needs from any one company. Exact quantities are left open and are agreed upon, in purchase contracts, to be a share of whatever you need, although top and bottom limits may be set. Also, deliveries are to be made not all at once but to meet delivery releases as sent from the buyer's production control department to the vendor's production control department.

Usually your volume is so great that there is no loss in unit price from dividing orders among two or three suppliers. Dividing the orders gives you protection from one source being cut off by strike or other reasons. And it keeps competitors on their toes to keep their prices down. On the other hand, capability and dependability are perhaps the most important things of all. Vendors must be *capable* of making your product, making it well enough to pass your inspection and in the quantities you need. And they must be *dependable*. Vendors *must* not hold you up. If they do hold you up two or three times, place your orders elsewhere or make the item yourself.

Coming-in items are so voluminous that you try to schedule them to come in just before you use them in order to cut down on inventories. About the best you can do on this, however, is to arrange for daily deliveries from nearby suppliers. Scheduling deliveries down to the hour is usually cutting it too fine.

Sometimes you can save a good bit on handling by having incoming items shipped in in trays or racks which can be trucked directly to the point of use. This saves costs of loading and unloading freight cars and handling costs both for vendor and purchaser. It doesn't take long to pay

FIGURE 30-3 Automobile frame bank stored out-of-doors. Although these frames will keep production going for only a few days, you would still keep smaller banks of items bought close by. These frames were made in Milwaukee and used in Detroit. (Automobile Manufacturers Assoc.)

for the carrying racks, and the freight costs for returning empty racks don't amount to much.

When you receive 50 or more freight carloads of incoming materials daily, and most continuous production plants run way over this (Ford's River Rouge plant receives over 1,000 freight cars of material every day), you have to schedule freight cars and trucks to arrive at certain times of day so that you can get them unloaded. Try, of course, to schedule them so that the materials can go directly to production lines. Assign certain materials specific times on the freight car unloading platform or truck unloading dock. Then you can plan the work of car unloading crews so that they will be ready to handle particular materials when they arrive.

You might even, at times, just leave materials in freight cars until you need them, then unload them directly to the assembly line. Railroads charge you car rent (demurrage) for failing to unload cars promptly but sometimes you can afford to use a freight car as a warehouse for a few days rather than find space inside the plant and then have to double handle the material.

Sometimes you have more of a problem of keeping things out of the plant than you do of getting them in. Vendors like to deliver ahead of schedule so that their deliveries won't have to be scheduled so closely. Not only do early deliveries run up the inventory, they make extra handling, all of which is waste because you would not have to do it if the new supply arrived when it should. Production control must keep things out of as well as in plants.

The purchasing department sometimes works quite closely with the materials control group in the plant in setting delivery schedules particularly in the case of parts as against raw materials or rough stock. More often, though, the whole matter of scheduling deliveries in is left up to production control or to a materials control group so that purchasing has little to do with deliveries. Vendor schedules must be closely tied in with your own shop schedules, so closely that they are, in fact, merely extensions of shop schedules into vendor plants. Be sure, in all releases, to show current and future quantities for each period and also the accumulation of quantities released in the past and the accumulated deliveries on the contract up to date.

Production control, too, rather than purchasing will make all the arrangements when schedules change in any way. Purchasing is kept informed of all releases, however, and of all incoming products received against blanket contracts. Then it can authorize paying bills and carry through all official and final correspondence.

Placing orders for purchased items and sending out releases to vendors are not enough to insure your getting materials. In fact, with thousands of items coming your way every day you can be sure that some won't arrive without further effort. You need to have follow-up men (expediters) in the purchasing department and in your material planning group.

They watch freight shipment notices and incoming receipt notices, and try to keep any items from lagging. If materials have been shipped but not received, they try to locate trucks and freight cars and to get them moved along. Or if materials haven't been shipped they keep after the vendor and even go to his plant to see what is holding things up. Usually doing this is just to prod him but if he is having trouble making the product and needs engineering help, the expediters will arrange for some of your own engineers to give his men a helping hand.

Not everyone likes the idea of traveling expediters. Once in a while a vendor will welcome him. Frequently he only irritates vendors although you don't care too much about that if he gets the material. Also, it often seems that your expediter is never where he is needed. When you need him in

Pittsburgh, he is in St. Louis. Expediters quite often don't seem to know what the other fellow is doing. A machinery maker shipped a machine to one of automobile's big three. Several days later an expediter, not knowing that it had already been delivered, turned up looking for it. Then one after another, for four more weeks, other expediters turned up looking for the same machine! None of the men knew about the others.

Raw materials used in smaller quantities may be bought differently from those bought in large quantities. You might very well let them be controlled by a materials control group, working from stock cards. Purchase requisitions are sent to the purchasing department when stocks are low and need for the material is indicated. Some of these minor items, in continuous manufacture, include packing containers, cartons, labels, and even freight car dunnage (lumber to hold freight in place).

In flow control, because the inventories carried are so low, suppliers need to be very dependable. Yet dependable as they are, you ought to consider distance. Transportation times are not wholly dependable. When ordering from distant suppliers, it is well to allow perhaps an extra day above expected lead times for every 500 miles of distance. If all goes well you get supplies a little too soon but you won't be disappointed very often.

STUDY MATERIALS

30-1   At a recent executive meeting, Mr. R. T. Samson, the director of purchasing for the Monolith Corp., mentioned a problem he has been having with Mr. R. E. Arrow, the divisional manager of one of the company's assembly divisions. This division, located some 600 miles from the central office, manufactures a range of consumer products from parts of its own manufacture, parts received from sister plants in other divisions, and purchased parts. For corporate control purposes, the division is considered a separate profit center.

   Mr. Samson has set policies stating that all purchasing should be done through the central office for reasons of efficiency, consolidation of orders, and ease in dealing with Monolith's suppliers. Mr. Arrow has consistently ignored many of these since his appointment as divisional manager, claiming that his function is to operate his division as profitably as possible. He argues that as long as he is ordering quantities greater than those necessary to obtain the maximum supplier discount, there is no need to go through central purchasing. Furthermore, he argues that local conditions, of which the central staff may not be aware, often allow him to obtain a better price than he could otherwise get and that he is often subject to requests from local community officials to "buy local" rather than having orders go to outside firms. Mr. Arrow agrees that when small quantities which are not urgently needed are to be ordered, they should go through central purchasing.

As president, what issues and implications do you see arising out of this dispute? What action, if any, should you take?

30-2   How does processing authority operate in flow control of assembled products made from metal products? Explain fully.

30-3   Assembled product manufacturers using assembly lines often go ahead and assemble a product discovered early along the line to be defective in some way. Normally this doesn't sound smart. Under what conditions would it be smart? What do you then do at the end of the line with the faulty product?

30-4   What are linear decision rules? Does the linearity assumption limit their usefulness? Can you foresee any problems that might arise through their use?

30-5   When changing models, is it desirable to shut down the entire period for the change-over? What factors should be considered in shutting down the plant as opposed to a gradual phase-in of the new product line?

30-6   Under what conditions should a company engage in inventory speculation? Are the consequences of success and failure in this type of operation of equal magnitude? Can a company protect itself from unfavorable price variations when entering into long-term contracts with suppliers?

chapter thirty-one

FLOW CONTROL—III

SCHEDULE CHANGES

Continuous production plants probably have more serious problems of replanning and rescheduling than do job lot shops. Usually if anything goes wrong in job lot work, one order at a time is affected. But in continuous production, changes are more far reaching. If customers buy less, more, or different products than you'd counted on, or if upsets occur in your own, your customer's, or your supplier's plant, everything is upset.

For major changes, production control has to redo hundreds of schedules and fast because, above all, the factory must keep on producing, and economically too. Before computers, auto companies needed two weeks to do a complete reschedule job but they never got even this seemingly short time in which to make a change. Schedule changing periods (and they are frequent) are hectic times in continuous production.

SCHEDULE CHANGES TO SUIT THE SHOP

In the automotive kind of continuous manufacture, each individual product assembled has its own list of main parts and accessory parts. Most cars made have already been ordered by a dealer who specifies all the details that he or his customer wants so it is important to try to make the car that way.

However, this is not always possible because in spite of your best planning you won't always have on hand exactly the right combination of accessories and trim to meet the dealer's specification—that is, you don't have them by the time the car is supposed to be made. You have nearly all of the specified items and you have other alternative nonspecified parts but you don't have exactly the full list that the customer wants. Let's say the dealer wants tinted glass for a station wagon. You can make the station wagon, with every detail exactly as specified, except that you have no tinted glass station wagon windshields.

What do you do? Lay all the parts that you do have aside until you get every last one? Should you let the shortage of one part hold up all other parts? Or should you go ahead and change a detail or two so that you can make the car almost as specified? Chrysler used to let the factory make changes on orders for Plymouths. Before long the factory was paying less and less attention to the details specified and changing orders all the time.

Chrysler had to clamp down and not let the factory change the specification in order that the dealer could get the *exact* car he ordered.

Then Chrysler had trouble with hold-ups from lack of the exact accessory or trim item. This put the pressure on the production control department to get *all* the parts and to get them in time. Chrysler ended up with production control being better done but it did cost some money in extra production control work to do it and it boosted inventories a little.

We are exaggerating, though, when we imply that all of the parts might be held up if one detail of trim is missing. Nor do you have to change the details on a dealer's order. Instead, just bring forward into today's assembly schedule a car from tomorrow's schedule for which all the details are available. Push back the order for the car requiring the missing item. All of this changing makes extra production control work but it can be done.

Another thing that you sometimes do when you have to substitute a nonspecified detail is to go ahead with the substitute detail and plan to replace it later with the specified item. This avoids interrupting the line and keeps up production. Sometimes, too, the substitute detail is accepted by the customer. The dealer who ordered the tinted glass may, for example, not yet have a customer for that car so tinted glass is really unimportant. If you go ahead and use a substitute detail, at most you pay a repair cost to make a change. Automobile companies sometimes substitute a wrong color fender if they don't have the right color. Repainting it afterward is the least costly way of handling the shortage of the wanted colors.

On the other hand, this method of handling today's problems makes more problems tomorrow. The unordered detail that was accepted by today's customer was intended for a product tomorrow. Tomorrow you will be short the detail you used today and will have the detail that you wanted today as an extra item. Even the red fender that you used today and painted blue afterward makes trouble tomorrow when you are short one red fender and long one blue fender.

The question is which is the worse of two sins. It is bad practice to let the shop decide what it will make. You'll end up getting too many of some products and not enough of others. But it is also bad (and probably worse) to lose production. If you ought to produce 500 refrigerators or 1,000 cars a day, you ought to get that many.

It is probably worse to get only 450 refrigerators or 900 cars than to get the full number but to have some items with details different from those ordered. Since, most of the time, the sales department is really only guessing what the ultimate consumer wants, it may not be so bad to produce a few items that turn out to be a little different from what it asked for or even what a dealer asked for. If your original order list really did foresee consumer demand exactly, you can correct the overruns and underruns in the next few days. The extra production is not really "unwanted" production, it is merely not wanted this week or it is not exactly what the sales department thinks that some customer will want.

Companies other than automobile companies have this problem too. Something happens that holds up production on one or more parts. What do you do? Of course you try to straighten out the trouble but if this is impossible then the shop wants to change the schedule and overrun some other product (assuming that you either have enough parts to overrun on it or can boost its parts schedules quickly). Should you let shop needs dictate schedule changes of this sort? Usually, yes. Then when the first trouble is straightened out, you can reverse the schedule adjustment. Above all try not to lose the production because many of your costs are the same whether you make the scheduled quantity or some lesser quantity.

Changes of this sort are frequent rather than infrequent and make no end of schedule changing. Such changes reach way back into release schedules given to suppliers. If you run four-door cars because you can't run two-doors, you need seat cushion sets (which you buy) for four-doors and not for two-doors. It is the same with doors, door hinges, latches, and windows. So the suppliers have to scramble and change their schedules so that you can go ahead with your change. Or if a die for a 7-foot refrigerator door goes bad and it will take three days to be repaired, you have to stop producing 7-foot refrigerators. Rather than just lose the production, you switch to 9-foot refrigerators and produce extra quantities of them for three days. Again, production control has to change any number of schedules.

Nor do changes affect all suppliers alike. TRW makes front end suspension spring units for 6-cylinder Plymouth cars but not for 8-cylinder cars. If Plymouth unexpectedly shifts from 6's to 8's TRW goes on short hours. A reverse change puts TRW on overtime.

Sometimes the shop produces minor overruns and underruns without even checking with production control. It alleges that changes of this sort will let it operate at lower cost. Such changes amount to small-scale schedule changes but you must expect them. In fact, if they really do save money you want them. If big changes seem desirable the shop checks with production control to see if the overall supply picture will permit them. Production control would have to check too with other factory departments to see if they have the men to handle the different quantities that come to them because of changed schedules.

It is a curious twist to find that in our biggest companies with the most highly developed engineering, forecasting, and production control procedures, there is a reversion back to the long discarded practice of letting the factory decide, in part, what it will make. If kept within bounds it seems to be economical to let this happen. But as a practice it is dangerous. If permitted at all, a sharp eye should be kept on it at all times so that it does not get out of hand.

LIMITS TO USE OF FLOW CONTROL

Continuous production requires a considerable amount of centralized control, since the work of several departments has to be closely coordinated, but this doesn't mean that you necessarily use flow control throughout all your operations. Actually, most parts are made in repetitive lots instead of continuously. Use flow control wherever you make items continuously but not elsewhere.

ASSEMBLY CONTROL

In job shops, you think of assembly as if it were one big job. In continuous manufacture, you think of assembly more as a series of small jobs because that is the way the work is actually divided up. Workplaces are arranged along side each other in a line.

Since there is some variety in the assembled products that you make, you have to tell the assemblers *which* parts and subassemblies to put into each product that they assemble. Does this car get a 6-cylinder motor or an 8? Does it get a radio or not? We will come back to this later.

The minor variations in the end products of continuous production which make extra production control work are not confined to the auto industry. Refrigerators may be 6 cubic feet, or 7, 8, or 9. They may have flat or curved fronts and may be any one of several colors. You find similar variety in radios, washing machines, electric sweepers, and many other products.

You end up having to control the assembly of *each individual product* made on the final assembly line. You will have to set schedules for parts and subassembly lines so that they produce all the varieties you want. You have to send lists to various key points along the final assembly line telling them which parts and attachments to put on each product. If you don't do this you'll find red automobile bodies on cars with blue wheels or 6-cylinder motors in cars meant to have 8-cylinder motors. Maybe we are exaggerating because the wrong motor probably wouldn't fit, but the point is that parts and subassemblies have to match the rate of complete products in (1) *quantity*, (2) *kind*, and (3) *proper sequence*. If the parts or subassemblies come to the final assembly line on a supply conveyor, the man who loads the supply conveyor has to have a list telling him the quantity, kind, and sequence of parts to load on the conveyor.

You will probably want to make out, for the final assembly line, a list showing, in sequence, every product which is to come down the line. The list shows, for each product, the exact kind of subassembly or part needed for every component which could be different on the various models. Every day you need a new list of this sort, called, in the auto industry, a "car building schedule," "assembly building sequence," or "order-of-run" sheet. These are the daily schedules we spoke of earlier and which are made out up to thirty days ahead.

One automobile company, however, makes up its sequence list as it goes. When an automobile frame is put on the assembly line as the first step in assembly, then, and only then, are the various parts supply lines told what kind it is to be. A computer printout system relays the information to each parts supply point so that it can supply the correct part.

MATCHING PARTS AND SUBASSEMBLIES PRODUCTION WITH FINAL ASSEMBLY NEEDS   Actually, the instructions sent to assemblers to tell them about details of variations of products are a minor part of the job of controlling assembly. Production control's big job is to match assembly rates and parts and subassembly rates.

Several things make matching these rates hard to do. One is that you have to stop one or another of the lines occasionally. And if you stop one, you stop all very quickly. Banks between parts and subassembly lines and final assembly lines give you some protection but in some places for not more than a half hour or so.

Another upsetting factor is parts being rejected either in the parts lines or at the assembly line. If rejections climb you won't be getting enough parts to keep assembly going. Actually, rejects rarely cause you much trouble because having them is so serious that you put a good bit of money into developing equipment that makes parts just right. Besides you inspect parts very carefully as they are made so that only good parts ever get to the assembly line.

A third factor with which production control has to contend is the lack of balance between parts production rate of output and their needs. You can't always design machines that will make parts at exactly the same rate as they are needed on the assembly line. Nor do you want always to do this because many times you can make parts faster than the line needs them. In other cases you can't, without terrific expense, design machines that will turn out parts fast enough. But then you can always buy two machines.

FIGURE 31-1 Supply bank of motors ahead of automobile final assembly line. (Automobile Manufacturers Assoc.)

What can you do about lack of balance? If a parts-making line is slower than assembly needs, you can work it more hours and build up a bank ahead of assembly. If the parts-making line is faster, work it shorter hours. We don't mean to say that you can't handle lack of balance, only that you have a problem of scheduling different work hours for some departments than for others.

Sometimes you run into rather difficult problems from lack of balance between operations in the final assembly line itself. You can't always adjust the speed of machines performing successive operations to a fixed rate. Fast machines can only be run now and then. Let banks of work build up, then run such machines for a while until the banks are processed.

Maybe the trouble is a bottleneck operation which doesn't turn out enough. If it is a hand job, put an extra man on the job to help until the bank of work that has piled up is processed. Then put him on other work until another bank builds up. If the bottleneck is caused by a slow machine, supplement its production from time to time with production from another machine not in the line.

Sometimes certain products take considerable work at bottleneck work stations, whereas others don't. If so, maybe you can mix up the

Automobile Manufacturers Assoc.
FIGURE 31-2 Supply bank of gasoline tanks. (Automobile Manufacturers Assoc.)

products coming down the line so that products that go light on the bottle-neck operation come down the line often enough and at the right time so that no hold-up occurs.

If you use any of the above methods to keep production moving it will mean moving men around and working some machines longer hours than others or even changing production quantities. You can do all of these things but doing them means that production control will have to make up special schedules so that they will all come out right.

SUBASSEMBLIES

In Chapter 12 we said to keep as much assembly work away from the final assembly line as possible. Make final products out of major subassemblies and make major subassemblies out of lesser subassemblies. Final assembly lines are not good places to handle fingernail size parts, nor to try to put in parts that go inside of assemblies. Don't assemble automobile generator commutators at the final assembly line. Put the commutator together as a subassembly. Fasten it to the armature, a bigger assembly. Put the armature into the generator, a still bigger assembly. Then fasten the generator to the motor, a major assembly, and put the motor into the car on the final assembly line.

Notice how, doing this, you would end up having several "genera-

FIGURE 31-3 Automobile engine inspection. (General Motors Corp.)

tions" of subassemblies. At each stage of assembly, you decide whether to assemble continuously or in lots.

If you subassemble continuously, you reduce overall lead time. Your Monday's minor subassemblies go into major assemblies in a day or two. But if you subassemble in lots, they have to lie around longer and so have to be made earlier to meet any given schedule.

Multiply this time saving (as well as inventory investment saving) by eight or nine generations of subassemblies and you can see that you'd have to start to make parts months farther ahead for airplanes (which have many generations of subassemblies) if you made subassemblies in lots than if you made them continuously. What with long lead times to start with and with innumerable design changes (which might obsolesce stocks already made up), you can see why it is of utmost importance to hold down the overall lead times in airplane and missile making. Consequently, in all cases of many generations of subassemblies, aircraft companies make all but the first generation or two by the continuous method.

Lockheed Aircraft uses a two-generation policy (mentioned earlier in connection with indent systems). In our commutator, armature, generator, motor, automobile example, Lockheed would say: "Make commutators in lots if it seems most economical and make armatures that way too if it seems best, but *not* generators, motors, or automobiles. Make them continuously."

You can subassemble continuously even though the final assembly line's need for subassemblies is irregular. For example, you can produce 8-cylinder motors for cars continuously even though they are mixed up with 6's in final assembly.

Other industries, except electronics, which is like aircraft in this respect, do not have critical obsolescence problems but they have minor obsolescence loss possibilities. They also have, in a small way, the lead time problem. Nonaircraft companies too want to cut lead time and inventories so they also try to make subassemblies continuously where several generations are involved.

A bad feature of making several generations of subassemblies all continuously is that you enlarge the number of activities that are tied tightly together. There are bound to be occasional hold-ups here and there. The more activities that you tie tightly together, the more often you will tie up everything because any lengthy delay anywhere holds up everything.

We have mentioned that making continuously is supposed to reduce inventories in process, and so it does, in spite of the need to carry banks. This is because the number of assemblies in a bank is rarely any more than the *least* number that you'd ever carry on hand if you made subassemblies in lots. If you make subassemblies in lots, whenever new lots come in you have considerably more on hand than you keep in continuous production banks. So you end up having more inventory, on the average, if you make subassemblies in lots.

The fact that subassembly lines work some little time ahead of final assembly gives you a chance to work out their own most efficient schedules. Automobile body shops, for example, work about a week ahead of final assembly. This allows them to pick out bodies of the same type and color from the assembly schedules for several days and group them for most economical runs in the body shop.

Production control's job with subassemblies is, at the same time, both simpler and more complex than controlling final assembly. It is simpler in that most subassemblies are of only a few kinds at most. No one auto company makes dozens of kinds of generators. No one subassembly line is as hard to control as the final assembly line. As against this, production control has to control dozens of subassembly lines (for water pumps, generators, carburetors, transmissions, etc.) but only one or two final assembly lines.

Three things are different between controlling final assembly and subassembly lines. First is quantity. Subassembly lines always make larger quantities than the final assembly lines use. The extra quantity takes care of rejects during final assembly and supplies repair service parts for cus-

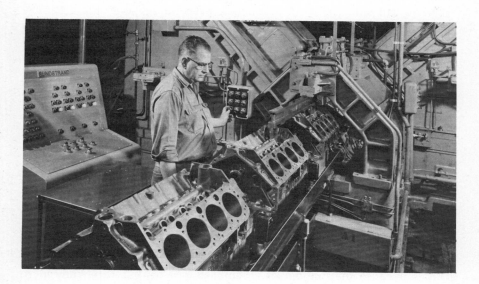

FIGURE 31-4 Engine blocks passing through inspection machine. (General Motors Corp.)

tomers. This also loosens up the tight connection between subassembly production and final assembly needs. The extra needs are a cushion that takes up any sudden change in assembly needs.

When we say that subassembly line quantities must exceed the final assembly line's needs, we mean the final line's need for each particular item. There are a few situations where individual subassembly production is less than final assembly output. One situation is where you have alternative subassemblies. An automobile needs a motor, an 8-cylinder or a 6-cylinder, *but not both*. The output of neither 8's nor 6's will, by itself, be as great as the number of cars made. Another situation is where you have optional subassemblies. Some automobiles have radios, but some don't. Subassembly quantities do not all, individually, have to exceed the quantities of final assemblies turned out.

The second difference between controlling final assembly and subassemblies is one which we mentioned earlier; subassembly production and the need of the final assembly lines *do not* have to match up on an hour-by-hour basis. Nor do they have to match on a day-by-day basis. Subassembly production ought, however, after providing for repairs and rejects, to match assembly line needs on a weekly basis.

Third, the home plant makes some subassemblies for sister plants. Subassembly production at the home plant might bear little resemblance to home plant assembly needs. It is the same in the sister plants. Shipments from the home plant (or other sister plants) allow your own subassembly production to be quite different from your needs.

Notice that these three conditions (subassembly quantities being greater than assembly line needs, the requirement of meeting the final assembly line need only in an overall way, and the need to supply sister plants) make interplant scheduling become quite a job. And they also make you carry more inventory because shipped in items come in bunches and don't always arrive when they should. Plants receiving subassemblies (or parts) from sister plants need to carry more inventories than they would for items they made themselves. Both of these conditions boost the average size of inventories.

PARTS CONTROL

Behind assembly, the showy part of manufacturing, lies the much bigger job of making parts. During assembly, the product takes form. All of the parts are ready; they are the right shape, size, color—and they are ready on time—*but only if production control has done a good job of getting them there.*

Controlling parts production is much like controlling subassemblies except that there are thousands of parts to make or buy and only dozens of subassemblies. The trick is to have them all flowing in to subassembly and to final assembly in streams or in cascades that match their use. And because of there being so many parts, it is more important than ever to keep supply banks down to as low a point as possible. You try not to rely on big inventories to absorb differences in production rates between parts and assemblies.

As in the case of subassemblies, the rate of parts production must more than match the needs of assembly in order to take care of rejects at assembly, repair parts for customers, and, sometimes, sister plant needs. And also, the rate of parts production does not have to be exactly the same hour by hour or even day by day as the need rate because you can work parts production lines different hours or days per week.

COMMON PARTS
Parts and to some extent subassemblies are sometimes used in several places in finished products and also in different models of finished products. Almost always you should total these demands when setting production quantities for parts rather than make up separate runs of the same part for different uses. Naturally, in the case of such common parts, their production rate is matched against their total demand rate, not the demand for any one use.

Suppose, for example, that you make stoves and are figuring out how many burners you will need. And suppose you have assembly orders for 1,000 four-burner stoves and 500 two-burner stoves to be assembled in November. Add the needs together and you find that you need 5,000 burners for the two kinds of stoves. Now, add an allowance for burners for service parts, say 25 per cent (1,250), and you find that you need 6,250 burners for assembly into stoves in November. Then add a little more for burners that might not fit just right and you come up with a figure of 6,300 burners needed for the stoves to be assembled in November.

Common parts are sometimes used several places, not just in two places, so it becomes quite a job to set schedules that will match their production against their several demands. Adel Division of General Metals Corporation (maker of electronics) has some parts that are used in 85 to 90 products. The difficulty of bringing together the demands for common parts is heightened by all the little delays here and there that affect a part's supply or its use or one of its uses.

In fact, sometimes it gets to be so hard to keep up with all of the little changes that it is hardly worth all the record keeping. Instead, you just watch the banks. When they start to go down, boost the rate of production of the part. Airplane and missile companies assemble their products continuously but they do not try to add together every demand for every part into one total and then produce that number of parts. One reason is the time lag. A single part can have several uses. Hence, it may be needed in June for one of its uses, but not until July and September for other of its uses.

If you try to group the demand for common parts with such a demand, you'd do better to add together the June demand for airplanes needing the part early in their assembly to the same part's halfway through demand for airplanes started in March, plus the demand for the same part for nearly finished airplanes started in January. It gets to be a pretty mixed up affair, so much so that you are sometimes better off not to try to bring together all the different demands. Go ahead and make several lots of the part, one lot for each of the several demands, or carry the item on a maximum-minimum basis.

Such extreme difficulties are, however, unusual. In most companies you would do well to sum up the demands for common parts because this lets you make them in larger lots or even to make them continuously. You will have, however, to divide up the production of common parts and send the proper quantities to the several storerooms or assembly work stations where they are used. Also, be sure not to let common parts production get behind because this would hold up production several places, not just one place.

CONTROLLING THE COUNT   Operating schedules for parts made continuously need be only statements of rates per hour and hours per day. Hourly reports of parts started into the line and those finished are usually necessary so that you know if parts are piling up anywhere. Get reports also of quantities passing through key operations and of quantities not passing inspection. Use inter-com systems to get fast reports.

If you use piecework, better establish frequent "count" points to check workers' reported production. One company, finding that it was paying for greater output than it was getting from operators, found the trouble started in its inspection procedure. At the end of each shift, the inspector went over the work of all operators and occasionally rejected a tote pan of products, placing a rejection tag on the pan and separating it from the acceptable products, which were taken to the next operation. What was happening was that the operators on the next shift came in, pulled off the rejection tags, and threw them away. Then they put the pans of products at their workplace to be counted in with their own output.

We have said earlier that you can use balancing banks and unlike work hours to take care of imbalance between successive operations. You have to watch the size of those banks, however, and count them (rough counts will do) every now and then during the course of a day. If there are many banks, it helps to have the materials in standard containers or racks so that you can tell at a glance how many items there are. These quick counts supplement and check the production reports that you get regularly.

It isn't always easy to count the banks, particularly those on conveyors. Some conveyors are not used primarily to move material from one place to another but are really bank balancing conveyors which hold banks of work between unbalanced operations. They are even located inconveniently for counting. Some circulate close to ceiling levels except for loading and take-off points. Also, service conveyors that bring parts to assemblers from stock rooms hold considerable inventory which is hard to count because the conveyors circulate over wide areas and are continually being replenished in the stock room and are continuously depleted by assemblers.

MAKING PARTS IN LOTS   Most parts are not made continuously because the rate of assembly is not sufficient to sustain continuous production of parts. So you make parts in lots, but since you make them in repetitive lots, you don't need to use order control. If you make only a few types of finished products in large quantities, maybe you can lay out a schedule for making the parts in repetitive lots at regular intervals of time. You can "cycle" the time of parts-making machines. This was discussed earlier in connection with economic lots and will be discussed later in this chapter.

This method, in its operation, is quite similar to block control. There are, however, no blocks. The work load represented by the orders issued varies according to near-future end-product needs and is not set apart into equal blocks.

Whether you cycle the making of parts lots or not, you have to set lot sizes. Almost always, you base their quantities directly on assembly floor requirements. Figure out, say three months ahead, the parts requirements for each month's assemblies. Have your computer run off a list of every part that you use, showing the sum of all already calculated demands. Show also the sum of all orders already placed and the projected balances and each item's lead time. This list will tell you if you have to order more of any item to meet your new demands.

Using this list, go ahead and make up shop orders (or purchase requisitions) for the quantities you'll need. *But* these shop orders are not like the ones used in order control. They merely identify the lot and show the quantity. They do not list operations or departments, do not serve as job tickets, have no operation due dates or order completion dates, nor are they used as a basis for collecting costs. They go to the raw materials stock room which delivers the materials to the department where the first operation will be performed. The materials carry identification showing the kind and quantity of finished product they are to be made into.

The foreman of the first department has a permanent file of processing instructions which tells him what operations to perform on every kind of part which might ever go through his department. He sees that the required operations are performed, after which the lot goes to a department's final inspector. The inspector uses the identification form as his inspector's report, and sends it to production control. Then he makes up a new identification tag and sends the lot on to the next department, where the next foreman works from his permanent file of processing instructions.

We have been describing the method used by General Motors' Electro-motive division but it is a fairly common method. It cuts out almost all of the papers needed in order control but it can work only where most lots are repetitive, although quantities vary and the items are not all reordered regularly.

You need, with this system, to have dependable lead times because you hope not to have to push orders through with expediters. Electro-motive uses the order number to push orders through (Electro-motive calls it a "sequence" number). Formen must process low numbered orders before higher numbered orders. Naturally, too, by using this system, you need to get telephone reports if any orders are held up.

When you make parts in repetitive lots there is another way to have some control over their finishing dates yet without doing much paper work. Let each order have an order number and a traveling ticket which shows the assembly period (week or month) during which the parts are to be used in assemblies or subassemblies. Require all factory department schedulers to get such orders finished before the first day of the assembly period.

You may run into trouble with making parts in repetitive lots because several orders for the same part may be in process, but at different stages of completion, at the same time. It is easy, if they get close together, to mix them up, and then you won't know which is which or how many items you have. The likelihood of having such problems is heightened by the fact that you often "overlap" operations (start operation 2 on some units before operation 1 is done on all the units in the lot). One order may be in several departments at once.

SPECIALIZED PARTS–MAKING DEPARTMENTS   We have previously described parts-making departments, meaning small departments devoted to making just certain kinds of parts and making them complete. Burroughs, A. B. Dick, Teletype, and other companies use this method.

Each such department has every kind of equipment that it needs to turn out its parts complete. All that you need to do is to tell the foreman how many and what kind you want. With a minimum of paper work he'll get the production out. He and his men know exactly what operations are required so they go right ahead.

This method of making parts is a little wasteful in its use of equipment because you may need, for example, several little sets of electroplating equipment in several different parts-making departments. It is the same with heat treating and certain machines. The waste comes in having the same kind of machine in a half-dozen departments, none of which use their machines nearly all the time. This waste should be more than offset by the gains from having exactly the equipment that you need exactly where you need it. If the gains are not that great, then, of course, you should not set up parts-making departments this way but should use a job shop method instead.

This specialized department at Burroughs Corporation does more than just make parts. It has set up what it calls the "unit method" of manufacture. A factory department makes subassemblies, making both the parts and putting them together into subassemblies. There is no dodging of responsibility if something doesn't work right.

SET—OVER   "Set-over" (or "set-back") is a term that you hear used sometimes in production control work. As we said in Chapter 20, it refers to making schedules (really setting wanted completion dates) for making parts. Some companies use monthly schedules and show set-overs in months, whereas others utilize weekly schedules and use weekly set-overs.

We'll use an example of a set-over in weeks. Start with the weekly schedule for assembled products. Explode each week's assembly orders into parts and assembly requirements lists, and keep apart the requirements list for each week's assembled products.

Now, go down the list of requirements for assembled products to be made during the week of October 24. Assemblies and parts going directly into the finished product ought to be finished during the week of October 17. You "set them over" one week.

Next, look over the lead times for subassemblies. If they must be finished during the week of October 17, perhaps all of the subassemblies and parts going directly into subassemblies as piece parts ought to be finished during the week of October 3. So set these requirement quantities over into the October 3 column. Repeat the process for subassemblies until everything has been reduced to parts.

You end up having set over all the requirements into earlier periods and so have wanted completion dates for making all subassemblies and all parts. Then you can scan the list up and down for each week to see if there are several demands for any part. If this is the case, they can be grouped and made as one lot.

Set-overs apply largely to making repetitive lots of parts or assemblies. Usually the lot size is wholly dependent on the demand of one week's assembly needs. You can use the same idea on items produced continuously but you don't want such a big set-over then. You don't want all of one week's supply to be finished and ready before the end of the preceding week. The supply banks would be much too big. You could, though, set over parts and assembly requirements (for continuously produced items) a half day or even an hour.

Teletype Corporation uses monthly assembly schedules but uses half months in its set-overs. March assembly parts requirements have to be at the assembly floor by February 15. This leaves the last two weeks of February open to put together subassemblies and to have them ready by March 1. The first two weeks of February are for parts accumulation and for picking parts into sets for assembly, so parts for March's assembly have to be in the parts stock room by January 31. A part needing two months for processing would have to be started by December 1. Its raw material requirements would be set over into November so its ordering would probably have to be set back into October or September.

Adel of General Metals uses a 30-day step-back for each generation of subassembly. Thus, three generations of assemblies mean that parts making has to be set back four months or more. Raw materials ordering is stepped back six months.

Companies using the set-over idea often use quite arbitrary "make-spans." They don't pay much attention, for example, to how much time it takes to put an assembly together. They may allow two weeks. But what happens if you want a large quantity and each assembly takes a good many man-hours? Just put more men on this work, enough so that they get the assemblies made. This is slightly a hit-or-miss method, however, so far as manpower planning is concerned. To make it work you may have to work overtime or hire more people at times, or just be a little overstaffed part of the time.

There is less arbitrariness in the make-spans allowed for parts, although, in practice, they are fairly liberal. More than enough time is allowed. Be careful, though, about being too liberal or items get started into production (or even finished) so early that they boost the inventory.

CYCLING   When continuous production of assembled products is confined to a limited number of types of products, you can sometimes use the parts-making machines in cycles. You process parts in repetitive lots and apportion machine time to different parts in a cycle basis.

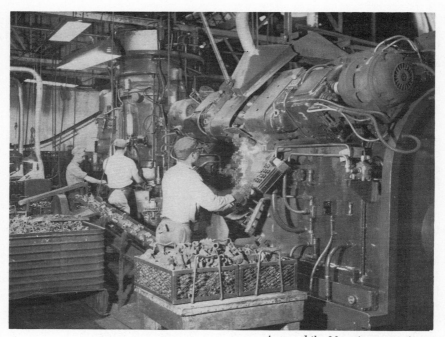

Automobile Manufacturers Assoc.

FIGURE 31-5 Making brake cylinders. This is the kind of machine that you might cycle, using it, during the course of a week, for various products. (Automobile Manufacturers Assoc.)

If assembly requirements call for 500 of a given part per day, you can make them in lots of 2,500 and do it once a week. Suppose that such a lot would keep the machine doing the first operation busy for six hours. This machine will then be free for the balance of the week before another lot of 2,500 of these parts is to be run. When you "cycle" the machine, you allocate six hours of its Monday time every week to performing operation 1 on this part. The rest of the machine's time is allocated to operations on other parts but they should always be the same items and in the same sequence. You cycle other parts-making machines the same way.

It sounds as though it would take considerable planning to dovetail the operations and machines so that you always get new parts supplies on time. This is not usually so, though, because cycling is not a hard and fast arrangement. Parts quantities can shift around and you can even put in new jobs or shift them around among machines in a limited way. All that this will do is to change the work hours each day of some of the cycled machines.

Cycling is usually done for short periods only, a week or less. Cycling in such short periods may, however, be wasteful in machine setup costs because you set up the same jobs over and over again every few days. You can cut this waste, though, by having your tooling designed so that the men can get it on and off machines quickly. This saves setup costs and cuts the machine downtime that eats into your running time. Long period cycles cut setup costs and time but they run up your carrying costs on the bigger banks of parts. Economic lot size calculations can be of considerable use in finding optional cycle times.

With cycling there are no lot numbers and very little paper work. Everyone—operators, truckers, foremen—soon learns what work to do on whatever items come their way without much more than an identification and a record of the count. You probably won't even need schedules for the cycled machines.

LEAD TIMES   As previously noted, lead time is the time that elapses between ordering an item and getting it. In continuous production, you try to work with very small inventories of parts and subassemblies so it is most important to know the lead time for each item that is bought or made.

In a way, this is not quite so important for items made continuously as it is for items made in lots because you get no new supplies of items made by lots for days or even weeks. If you are wrong about lead times, you either get things in too soon and have big inventories, or they come too late and you run out before the next lot comes in.

It is so easy to say "order with the usual lead time in mind" that it sounds simple. Actually lead time varies a great deal, yet you have to finally pick a figure. Also, in continuous manufacture of assembled products, you have thousands of items to order and must try to get *all* of the lead times right.

GM's Buick division has to make up, in its central office, over 10,000 schedules every month just for assembly work alone! How many more schedules its factory production control departments make out for piece parts in Buick's six separate factories Buick has never counted. Our interest here in such schedules is in pointing out the complexities that you get into when you have to deal with lead times for thousands of schedules.

Lead times for items coming in to Buick's main plant vary from 0 to 10 days, the longer times usually applying to items coming from more distant suppliers. In Buick's main plant, some parts take less than a day to make, others up to 30 days, and there is some variation in how long it takes to make each item. It takes from 5 to 8 days to ship home-plant supplied parts to other plants. And in the other plants lead times vary in a similar way.

Notice that these lead times follow one another chain fashion. If you add them all up, the totals at Buick come to as little as 5 days and as much as 58 days. Production control has to know each item's own lead time in order to schedule it properly.

Once you set item lead times, sometimes called "day factors," and punch them into tabulating cards, they tend to stay put because it is such a big job to change them. GM's Electro-motive division, for example, has a special form for requesting a change in approved lead times. It has to be approved by the man in charge of material control.

Punching lead times into cards tends to make them rigid because to change them you have to punch new cards. This is unfortunate because actual lead times move up and down a good bit. If your cards are wrong they will cause you to order too soon or not soon enough.

FINISHED PARTS AND SUBASSEMBLY ISSUE

In continuous production, finished parts and subassemblies are issued in much the same fashion as are raw materials, from open stores or from supply conveyors. Parts made in lots usually go to stock rooms and from there are sent to the assembly line. They may be "called out" and made up into sets which are trucked to assembly work stations where the operator attaches them. Or if they are to be attached at various work stations, such parts might be put in a tray and sent down the assembly line with the main product.

"Service" or delivery conveyors, utilizing pans or hooks, might also be used. The service conveyor circulates, traveling slowly but continually, and passes the men at the assembly line within their reach at work level. Assemblers just reach out and help themselves to what they need. Stockmen load the proper parts onto the service conveyor as it circulates past them in the stock room.

Service conveyors are loop conveyors traveling continually from the stock room to certain work stations along the assembly line. In order never to hold up the men, always have hooks and pans close together on the service conveyor. You never want the assemblers to unload every pan. Move so many full pans past them that no assembler, not even the last one, has to wait for a full pan to get to him. It does no harm for half of the pans to arrive back in the stock room still loaded. This means, of course, that you always have perhaps several hours' supply of parts on such conveyors.

Little items such as transistors or radio parts, subject to being stolen, or fragile items that are easily damaged can be issued from enclosed stock

Automobile Manufacturers Assoc.

FIGURE 31-6   Loading pistons onto a service conveyor which takes them to the engine assembly line. (Automobile Manufacturers Assoc.)

rooms in exchange for requisitions. Hand them out in lots to the worker and hold him responsible for their use. You can use written requisitions or coupon "meal-ticket" requisitions of the kind previously described. Meal-ticket requisitions are punched every time a lot of material is issued as a record of its issue. Occasionally, certain material is kept under lock and the key given to one worker who is responsible for it.

MATERIALS MOVEMENT

In continuous production, production control is rarely concerned with moving materials from job to job or from department to department, for it is generally done by conveyor or possibly by overhead crane. But if you do have to truck materials or parts around, the truckers who haul things *between* departments may belong to production control. Trucking *within* production departments would be under the direction of the foreman.

On the other hand, when you call out parts against an assembly bill of material, the trucker has to know where it goes. Production control has to see that parts get to the assembly line work station where they are needed.

FINISHING OPERATIONS

Continuous production products often end up being a little different from one another or they are packaged in varied ways. You cannot regard products coming off the end of the line as all a part of a flow like water over a dam. Instead, you have to think of end products one by one. Assembled products made continuously are sometimes assigned to specific customers' orders before completion so that you can put in exactly what the customer wants in the way of trim, finish, and accessories.

Tin cans, for example, often have labels lithographed on as they are made. One can factory recently had over 70 label and cover varieties of number 1 cans on its schedule for a two-week period. Soft drink manufacturers frequently bottle several kinds of soft drinks. So do alcoholic beverage makers. Each kind of liquor is put up in several sizes of bottles, and each of these varieties may be marketed under many trade names with as many different labels.

One cereal products company lists over 100 breakfast food items on its printed schedule sheet. Many of these items are the same food items put into different packages. Over 150 items appear on this same company's list of animal feeds, and again packaging and labeling are responsible for most of the variety. A large coffee packer lists 20 items on a list covering grinding and packing instructions for only two kinds of coffee. Whenever you find such situations, it means that production control has to issue rather detailed instructions to men performing the finishing operations.

OUTGOING PRODUCTS

In continuous production, production control is rarely responsible for moving finished products out of the plant. The exception would be where you are making directly to customer releases and have to ship on a tight schedule. The customer wants his products to come in just as he needs them so that he will have little inventory to carry.

You, too, want to carry no finished inventory. So it is up to production control to schedule production so that you get products into the shipping room just before the time when they are supposed to go out. Don't cut this too fine, however. Better carry a small bank. Then you can produce economically yet give the customer good service even if he boosts his releases or wants deliveries pin-pointed by day or hour. Good customer service often outweighs your desire to carry no inventory. This really amounts to your carrying part of your customer's inventory for him but you have to do it.

ANCILLARY PRODUCTS

The high volume achieved by most continuous manufacturers allows them to go into other kinds of manufacturing businesses to supply certain needs if they so desire. Large fruit or vegetable canneries, for example, sometimes make the cans they use. Many companies make cartons, containers, and cloth bags. Most companies using crates make them too. Many companies print their own labels; some companies make their own bottle stoppers.

Ancillary products have one thing in common. They are themselves manufactured products, and they are very different from the main product made. If volume is enough, they may be made in other factories owned by the same company, as when newspapers and book publishers operate paper mills. In most continuous manufacturing plants, the production control department must direct one or more small departments making products which are very different from the main product. Frigidaire, for example, has to make crates, so do National Cash Register and any number of other companies. These companies have to make up schedules for crate making to match the products that they assemble.

STUDY MATERIALS

31-1 What are the major differences, if any, between flow control and assembly control? Is the work load on production control equally affected by such matters as changes in quantity demanded, specification changes, and parts delay under either system? Give examples, if possible, to support your argument.

31-2 In the St. Louis Milling Machine Company, the shop order number is used as a "sequence" number. That is, it serves as a priority numbering system. Parts manufacturing orders are not scheduled by the production control department in any other way. Each foreman is required to process the order having the lowest number ahead of other orders or justify his failure to do so on a daily report. This method is supposed to operate almost automatically to get first orders out first.

Starting with the above procedure, devise modifications to take care of (1) rush orders for parts, (2) getting a part requiring many operations finished by the same date as a part requiring few operations.

If, in the above situation, you leave gaps in your order numbering system to use for rush orders, what happens to your expected completion dates for other orders when you use your spare numbers for rush orders?

31-3   The Polar Bear Refrigerator Company wanted to make the most effective possible use of its machines used in making parts. Accordingly it adopted a "cycling" arrangement whereby certain equipment was used on several jobs during the course of each two days. A set sequence of jobs and regular quantities of parts were turned out each two days. In all, the machines in the cycled group were each used for seven operations.

The objectives of the management (getting a steady flow of parts and full machine utilization) were realized. The management's satisfaction in this accomplishment was somewhat deflated, however, when the records showed that one-quarter of the pay of the men on the cycled machines was paid to them for changing machine setups and that the machines were idle one-quarter of the time while being set up.

What are the values of short cycles? Are the benefits great enough to justify higher setup costs and machine idle time? Is there any way to work on short cycles and not lose considerable money and capacity because of setups?

31-4   Are there any similarities between machine "cycling" and the time limit method for controlling inventories?

31-5   Compare load control with machine cycling. Explain points of similarity and difference.

31-6   The Nuveen Indicator Company is faced with the problem of trying to get certain parts of a gyroscope made on a limited number of machines. These parts are:

   A Case cover
   B Rotor
   C Support
   D Wheel
   E Synchronizer

Nuveen needs 250 each of these units per day. Because of the very close tolerances and the high scrap rate, you need to produce 35 per cent more, or 337 units of each of these parts. Assume that all of this scrap loss occurs after the parts have been made complete. There are certain further operations on these parts but they do not enter into this problem.

The company works six days a week, and three shifts, or $22\frac{1}{2}$ production hours a day. It is possible, in a tight squeeze, to work machines through lunch periods, thus getting up to 24 hours of running time in a day. In this problem you are to neglect the possibility of machinery breakdowns and time for their repair. Also you are not required to allow for any time for moving materials between operations. Your only concern with lot sizes is to produce a two-day supply (and no more than a two-day supply) every two days.

Lay out a program showing how to cycle the production of these items on these machines on a two-day cycle. Each time that you have to set up a machine, allow 10 per cent of the required operating time for a two days' supply of parts as the time for the setup.

How many of each kind of machine will Nuveen need? Show the use of all machines at all times. How long will it take for lots to come through production? What is the best that you can do in the way of getting these parts through quickly if you do not overlap operations? What is the best if you do overlap them?

The following list shows operations, machines, and rate of output:

OPERATIONS LIST AND MACHINE ASSIGNMENT

OPERATION	MACHINE	PIECES PER HOUR
A Case Cover:		
1 Drill 15 holes	Avey drill	62.0
2 Finish face hub	Monarch lathe, 12-inch	20.0
3 Finish turn	Monarch lathe, 12-inch	32.5
4 Form recess	Monarch lathe, 12-inch	67.9
5 Face	Monarch lathe, 12-inch	29.3
6 Bore	Excello Borematic	138.0
B Rotor:		
1 Form	B & O turret lathe	33.1
2 Finish bore	Excello Borematic	138.0
3 Bore beads	Monarch lathe, 12-inch	19.4
4 Finish grind	Landis grinder	89.8
C Support:		
1 Turn	Hardinge lathe	24.0
2 Spot, drill, bore, and ream	Edlund 6-spindle drill	15.6
3 Spot, drill, and tap	Edlund 6-spindle drill	15.6
4 Bore	Excello Borematic	138.0
D Wheel		
1 Form	Monarch lathe, 12-inch	55.2
2 Finish bore	Excello Borematic	138.0
3 Face two sides	Monarch lathe, 12-inch	30.3
4 Mill buckets	Multi miller	14.4
5 Finish grind	Landis grinder	61.3
6 Smooth grind	Landis grinder	82.3
E Synchronizer:		
1 Turn	Monarch lathe, 12-inch	23.4
2 Bore	Monarch lathe, 12-inch	46.3
3 Mill one side	$8\frac{1}{2}$ Gorton mill	54.0
4 Mill other side	$8\frac{1}{2}$ Gorton mill	54.0
5 Spot, drill, and ream	Edlund 1-spindle drill	22.6
6 Drill	Edlund 2-spindle drill	31.2
7 Face	Edlund 4-spindle drill	71.0
8 Counterbore	Edlund 4-spindle drill	27.8

31-7   Should companies engage in the manufacture of ancillary products that are outside their main line of production? The Ford Motor Company, for example, is the only auto maker that supplies some of its own steel needs. Most of the major steelmakers sell a limited range of industrial chemicals as a result of their coke oven operations. What factors would seem to govern a company's entering into ancillary production?

chapter thirty-two

INFORMATION PROCESSING

By now it should be evident that operating a large-scale production control system requires that tremendous amounts of information be processed, analyzed, and acted upon. And it should be equally obvious that production control procedures are not only concerned with producing this mass of information but also with its relevance and timeliness. You can't control production very well when it takes a month to get reports of what goes on. If fact, in many assembly operations, it is hard to control outputs even though it takes only one day to get reports.

Today, flow control operations are often controlled "on-line," meaning that reports are made electronically as the work is done. These reports are made directly to a computer which, because of its tremendous data storage capacity and tremendous speed of handling data, had a significant impact on production control procedures during the 1960s.

One effect was to make "real-time" control feasible. Instead of collecting figures, say for a whole day, and then batch processing them at night all at once in a single run, data reporting and processing go on all the time on a continuous basis. The computer operates on a time sharing basis as it handles such varied work as payroll, cost accounting, inventory control, and purchase invoices. Computers capable of doing this do not, however, come cheaply, and although not everyone uses them, they are becoming more common.

Computers have also opened up the possibilities for using simulation for testing systems designs. Before computers it was almost impossible to carry through complex simulations. Now we can get a better understanding of the reactions and interactions of the various parameters in complex systems. As a result, we are better able to design systems which will react to changes in variables in the way we want. Before installing their computerized seat reservation system, the airlines studied the way they would work by simulating their operations on computers. Then, after some changes were made, the systems were put in.

Even though computers are very helpful in analyzing data, preparing reports, setting inventory levels, and printing job tickets, purchase orders, bills of materials, and the like, they can work only on data made available to them. In order to achieve real-time, on-line control, we need, therefore, to provide for gathering accurate, timely, and relevant data for processing. Not having this constitutes a serious roadblock to operational control.

Not uncommonly you find a company with a sophisticated computer-

FIGURE 32-1   An IBM 360 computer. (International Business Machines Corp.)

controlled inventory system whose primary data are collected on a pencil and paper basis. A department store, for example, may run its inventory system on a computer, when the most automated piece of equipment at the point of sale with respect to information processing is the device for imprinting the data from the customer's charge plate onto the sales slip. The clerk writes up the sales slip, rings up the sale on a cash register, tears off a section of the item ticket, and puts it in the cash register drawer. The sales slips, cash register tapes, and tickets must then be "processed" and their information punched onto tabulating cards or paper tapes so that they can be used by the computer. The possibilities of errors through mishandling and mistranscription are numerous.

What with the usual time lags that occur in translating data to a form intelligible to the computer, and the possible errors introduced into the data, the control of high-volume fashion goods may be considerably less than ideal. Although they are costly, recording cash registers are available which can record all of the sales data necessary for billing and inventory control directly onto punched cards or tapes that can be read by a computer.

Computer applications using integrated systems and on-line reporting can be found in other service industries and in manufacturing concerns. The Southern Railway has a master control system controlling its freight cars and the scheduling of their use. Car movements and uses are reported continuously to Southern's central office. With this up-to-the-minute information, Southern's executives are in a position like that of a military general staff which is always kept informed of the combat readiness of their units.

By the late 1960s all of the leading computer makers had come out with large on-line time-sharing computers for use in controlling shop operations. These systems collect, automatically and continually, in a central control room, reports of jobs finished, inspection reports of rejections, reports of materials moved, jobs ready for work, jobs held up, etc. And they collect information about machine output, breakdowns, tool availability, work quality, etc.

The computer thus monitors what the shop does. It accumulates and records this information and keeps it available for instantaneous retrieval. Upon call it will display information on scopes or print out whatever you want. The computer keeps a record of the status of orders and machines and of all changes in their status. At any time, you can, therefore, see up-to-the-minute records just by pushing the button. And from such records, kept on magnetic tapes, the computer can later compile whatever other reports you may need.

Large, on-line computers can help in so many ways that we can't begin to describe them all. By way of a sample here are a few of the things that they can do automatically:

Originate requests for more inventory; make out reports calling attention to machine downtime, orders behind schedule, production of each shift, or production of each work center.

Make up status reports of the orders in each shop's load, of order progress, of job completion, of machine and man use, etc.

Make comparisons of machine output rates against their standard or budgeted output.

Trigger alarms when off-standard conditions appear either in the quality of work or when machines break down.

Provide a complete intercommunication and paging system.

Compile reports of delays, machine downtime, rejects, etc.

Figure 32-2 is a diagram depicting the kinds of things the computer can do.

The computer itself is, of course, the focal point of the system. It is linked electronically with the several input and output stations around the factory. But the work is done by the central unit. The control room operator can use the monitors, scopes, status displays, and print-outs to initiate

Type of machine response		Initiating control source	Power source	Level number	Level of mechanization
From a variable in the environment	Responds with action	Modifies own action over a wide range of variation	Mechanical (nonmanual)	17	Anticipates action required and adjusts to provide it
				16	Corrects performance while operating
				15	Corrects performance after operating
		Selects from a limited range of possible pre-fixed actions		14	Identifies and selects appropriate set of actions
				13	Segregates or rejects according to measurement
				12	Changes speed, position, direction according to measurement signal
	Responds with signal			11	Records performance
				10	Signals preselected values of measurement (Includes error detection)
				9	Measures characteristic of work
From a control mechanism that directs a predetermined pattern of action	Fixed within the machine			8	Actuated by introduction of work piece or material
				7	Power tool system, remote controlled
				6	Power tool, program control (sequence of fixed functions)
				5	Power tool, fixed cycle (single function)
From man	Variable			4	Power tool, hand control
				3	Powered hand tool
			Manual	2	Hand tool
				1	Hand

FIGURE 32-2

instructions over the inter-com or paging systems. Thus a high degree of control over the workforce, the equipment, and the work floor can be obtained with almost no time lag.

Not all production control systems need an information handling system as comprehensive as the one we have been talking about even though the same functions have to be performed. In a small shop, for example, a good foreman can keep in touch by personal contact. The volume of work is still small enough for him to keep track of things on a pencil and paper basis. But as the scale of operations grows you have to make more use of the various forms of inter-communication systems that permit speedy transmittal of both oral and written information. The information handling system should be appropriate to the scale of operations. In large companies, in particular, skimping on information collection systems and equipment often leads to production inefficiencies, high costs, and delays.

We have mentioned the need for information to be timely and relevant. The feedback part of the system needs to be designed so that continued steady reports of work done come in. But more particularly, the system should report immediately all deviations from standards and plans. The trouble signal flag should go up immediately. Then if there are automatic corrective actions they will be initiated immediately. And if corrective action isn't automatic, then the men who have to straighten things out need to go to work.

Interestingly, much of what today we call automation is really information processing. Figure 32-2 is a schematic classification of the levels of automation developed by James R. Bright.[1] It shows the importance of information processing in controlling actions. Curiously, simple tools need human guidance but sophisticated machines are self-controlled and self-guided by their own mechanisms. The highest-order machines not only process the signals they receive but they even take action *in anticipation* of expected irregularities. Bad products are not only rejected, they aren't even produced in the first place.

In spite of all that we have said, computers haven't wholly displaced slide rules and desk calculators. Small companies can't afford computers so they still use simpler methods. And even in large companies some production control work is neither voluminous enough nor complicated enough to justify using a computer. Sometimes computers handle complete systems when parts of the work should not be computerized. When, for example, the only advantage of a computer is its speed, there is no need to use it on low-volume work. It will probably be less costly to use desk calculators. So desk calculators and slide rules are still with us.

[1] James R. Bright, *Automation and Management*, Harvard University Press, Cambridge, Mass., 1958, p. 45.

COMPUTERS

Electronic computers are of two main kinds, analog and digital. Analog computers might be likened to gigantic slide rules while digital computers are like gigantic adding machines. Analog computers are best for scientific problems involving millions of calculations but they are not well suited to production control work because they are not designed to take in large masses of figures, perform a few calculations, and to turn out thousands of answers. Nor do they have the inherent accuracy of digital computers. Digital computers are better for production control and for most business problems.

Business companies do, however, sometimes use analog as well as digital computers to control production operations. At Great Lakes Steel, for example, both kinds of computers are used for directing the work of its hot strip rolling mill. Data concerning orders are fed into a digital computer. It sorts the orders out and issues them in proper sequence to an analog computer which controls the setting of the mill rolls, the rolling speeds, and other matters relating to the actual rolling.

During rolling, automatic measurements are continually being taken by feedback sensors which tell the analog computer how the operation is going. Should the rolls need adjustments in their settings or if rolling speeds need changing the analog computer makes the corrections.

After rolling, the digital computer comes into play again as coil weights and the number and kinds of defects are reported to it. It also calculates wage data for the rolling crew and makes up billing and shipping instructions for sending the steel to the customers.

It is hard to make any positive statement about computers because there are so many kinds and they are so different. They are, however, electrical, not mechanical. They operate by electricity using pulsating not steady electricity. It is the pulses operating billions of times per second that do the work. These pulses magnetize (or demagnetize or remagnet-

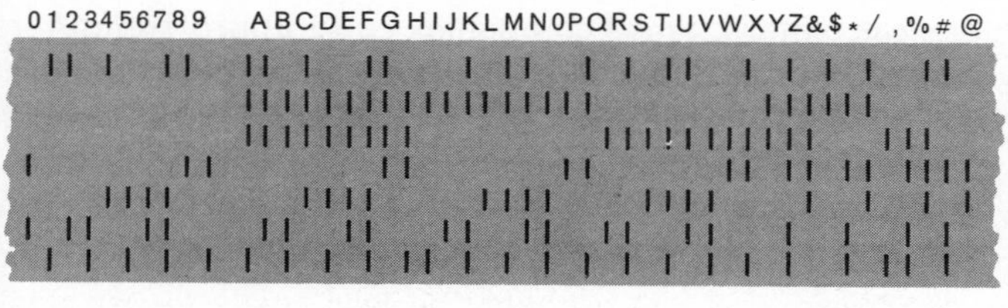

FIGURE 32-3 Diagram of magnetic tape showing how letters and numbers are coded on a magnetic tape.

ize) tiny specs in the machine's memory or on magnetic tapes and thereby allow it to remember, or to do arithmetic calculations. Computers handle letters and words as well as numbers.

You can feed information into computers several ways, although tabulating cards and magnetic tapes, particularly tapes, are the most common ways. Computers can handle cards at rates of from 200 to 900 a minute or tapes at up to 100 inches per second. In appearance, tapes look like plastic typewriter ribbons on reels like moving picture film reels. They are up to half a mile long and one reel holds information equivalent to nearly a half million cards.

Depending on the kind, computers add, subtract, or multiply at more than a billion operations a second. Dividing is perhaps half as fast. Sorting goes at many thousands a second. Printing, up to 1,500 lines a minute. Searching its memory for something it is remembering takes as little as a millionth of a second.

Suppose that we use an example to show how a computer would work in exploding an assembly order. First, you "read in" the master bill of materials. To read it in, you pass the master deck of parts cards or a magnetic tape (onto which the bill of material has already been put in magnetized coded form) through the machine. It will magnetize parts of its memory area and so will retain this information.

Next, read in the master order information. Then tell the machine (by means of a "program") to make up a list of parts and quantities that you will need for the order. The machine will give you this information printed out, or as a deck of newly punched cards, or as a newly magnetized tape, whichever you want. Or, if you prefer, it will just remember this information. Now, read in your stock record and ask the machine (again by using a program) to subtract the needed quantities from what you have on hand and tell you which items you'll have to reorder and how many short your present supply is.

PROGRAMMING   Computers need to be told (by means of cards or tapes), step by step, what to do. Developing the instructions is called "programming" and is a slow and costly procedure. In the early days of computers General Electric spent over 20 man-years of work programming its computer in Louisville to handle making out the payroll for GE employees there. Today programming goes faster but it is still costly. On the good side is that programs never have to be done over again for the same procedure. Once prepared, you can use them over and over again. They can be stored in the computer's memory and automatically called up and put into use whenever you want them either as complete programs or as parts of bigger programs. Also, over the years, computer companies have built up libraries of prepared programs on tapes. For many of your problems, you would not have to develop your own program at all.

Stored programs and subprograms can be kept in the computer's memory and used to control job priorities, the selection of the subroutines to use, and the shifting of data between the computer's big and little memories. Computers have big (but slower in use) memories just to remember things, such as the items on a bill of materials. These memories are usually reels of magnetic tape, or record-like disks. Computers also have a smaller extremely fast working memory which holds the numbers while doing the work. Thus the machine has to remember that it is multiplying, how to multiply, what number is being multiplied, by what number, where each number comes from, and where the answer is to go. The fast memory remembers all of these things while doing the calculating.

Programming has been much simplified since the early days of computers. Standard languages such as FORTRAN, COBOL, and others have been developed to make this work easier. In the early days you even had to tell the machine how to divide and multiply. Now simple symbols set off such processes automatically. These languages are essentially shorthand languages which the machine understands.

LIMITATIONS TO COMPUTER USE IN PRODUCTION CONTROL

Computers are so widely used that you might think that they help everywhere. They do help in most production control situations but not in all. They are costly in rentals ($1,000 to $20,000 a month or more, depending on how much equipment you need) and so they are not worthwhile unless you can keep them busy. But even small companies (under 500 employees) can often keep a medium-sized computer fully occupied if they use it for accounting, sales, and production control.

A computer is most helpful where the product made is complex, when repeat orders occur, where there is some variety, yet where most products are about the same except in minor detail. Great variety complicates the production control problems even with nonmechanical procedures but large numbers of changes are quite hard to handle on computers.

For a completely unique job, one which is new and which will not be repeated, it might not pay to use a computer at all because you'd have to make up all the parts cards and all the operations cards for just the one use. The real gain from using computers comes from the repetitive use of master cards on future repeat orders.

On the other hand, no one would ever think of making an airplane or a ship without using computers in controlling its production. Such products are so complex that human errors in production control could be very costly. Computers cut down errors enough to justify their use even though the master cards are used only once or twice.

There are many little problems to work out when you use computers. Extra allowances for scrap, for example, require that extra quantities be started into production. You'll have to figure out for each item an appropriate multiplier for boosting wanted quantities and you'll have to punch such multipliers into your master cards. Reworking repairable rejected parts is also a complicating factor. Engineering changes concerning parts or operations also complicate the work no end.

Anything which is not repetitive in a predictable way is hard to handle. We don't say that you can't solve these problems, but if they are numerous, they cut down the effectiveness of computers in production control work. Admittedly, though, these complications interfere with the smooth operation of production control no matter whether you use computers or not.

Another limitation is the cards themselves. A tabulating card can contain only 80 (IBM) numerals or letters. It happens that you often find that this isn't nearly as many characters as you'd like to have but this is all of the characters that you can get on a card. In order to get along with this limitation, you shorten everything, particularly words, all that you can. Cut product, part, and operation names to one or two words and use abbreviations. Notice in all of our pictures in this chapter how brief are all work descriptions.

Notice, too, that on worker job tickets the one or two word descriptions of the job are much too brief to serve as real instructions to a man telling him what to do. He will need more instruction somehow. Be sure that your drawings and specifications fill this gap.

We said earlier that you can't use computers in production control unless you have bills of material and parts lists. This is true. But it is also true that it is easy to make up new master bills or order bills, master route sheets, and shop orders once you have these bills of materials and parts lists and get them transferred to cards.

Supposing that you don't have master bills and master operation sheets, then what? You can start by making up a first set of cards from a rough kind of original bill of materials. This lets you make up copies of bills for first round use. Whenever anything isn't right, fix the cards and soon you will have a good set of cards. From here on you can make out reliable bills electronically.

As for master operation cards, don't try to make them all up the first time that you make an item. Let the engineers and the foremen figure out how to do it as they make the first order. Write down how they do it. Then make master cards from this list of operations. These are your master cards for future use.

We have been talking almost wholly about making assembled products. How about making single integral units, such as plumbing fittings or nuts and bolts? Production control in these situations is much like it is in making parts for assembly, but it is usually simpler because not very often is there a positive requirement that you have to have certain exact quantities of anything ready at specific times.

We have talked already about computers not being able to decide about reorders. Another thing that you can't put on computers is the preparation part of production control work. All of the checking up that you have to do on bought materials, facilities, tools, gages, and so on cannot be transferred to computers. Also computers do not solve all types of scheduling problems. Assigning machine times to the most urgent orders still works better when a man does it. And, in spite of the fact that you can set due dates and wanted dates mechanically, even this can sometimes be improved by men. And, of course, computers cannot do the whole job of progress control. It takes men to look over reports of work done and to decide what to do next.

It might seem that computer procedures are very complicated, that tremendous numbers of cards are used, and that there are all kinds of chances for error. To some extent all of these things are true. The original preparation of the permanent file of basic data cards is somewhat expensive. Also, large quantities of cards are used, but since they cost but a small fraction of a cent each, this is not often a critical factor.

As to the complexity, no method of production control can be simple when the problem is complex. Computers do many things that would otherwise have to be done clerically. The checks on accuracy in electronic production control are better than they are where it is not done electronically. Errors with electronic control are fewer than when you use other means.

BASIC CONDITIONS REQUIRED

To use computers successfully in production control, several basic conditions must be met. First, you have to have a share of the operation time on the equipment. This is not a problem in big companies because production control has its own machines. But in small companies, accounting, sales, and other departments share the equipment.

Second, you have to have reasonably complete and accurate basic data. For assembled products and for subassemblies, you must have bills of material and they have to be complete and correct. And for every man-ufactured part you have to have an operation list, operation times for every operation, the kind and quantity of raw materials needed, and lead times. You need also to know expected scrap loss rates during processing for every item manufactured. If you don't have all of this information when you start to use a computer, you'll need to get it.

You really need all of this information anyway, though, in any good system of production control. No *extra* information is required. The point in mentioning it is that electronic production control is exact by its nature, and you have to have exact information, not vague or inexact numbers. Wherever, in production control, you don't have exact numbers, you'll have to get numbers or give up computerizing the work.

Some companies, recognizing this, use data processors for part, but not all, of their production control work. Stock records and materials req-uisitions are, for example, frequently put on tabulating cards and mag-netic tapes. Shop orders are printed by the computer too. But many of these same companies do not try to have computers set schedule dates for operations, nor do they have their computers keep load records of work ahead of machines.

BASIC DATA

Today basic data are usually kept in either of two forms: (1) as a series of holes punched into tabulating cards or (2) as a series of magnetized dots on reels of plastic tape. In some cases, a third method, punched paper tapes, is used. There are advantages and disadvantages to each method, such as cost, processing speed, and accessibility, but these do not concern us here. Punched cards are the most familiar form of data storage so the ensuing discussion will describe a system using this form of basic data storage.

The basic information that you need falls into three categories: (1) *permanent master data*, (2) *variable master data*, and (3) *stock records*. Nor-mally this basic information is first put onto tabulating cards by means of holes punched in a coded arrangement. From the cards it is then trans-ferred to magnetic tapes which are used by the computer for all records and calculations.

Permanent master cards contain information about *products.* *Variable master cards* contain information about *orders*. Each of these two kinds of master records supplies part of the information needed by the computer in order to make other cards or tapes required in controlling production. After being used as the basis for making new single-use records (cards or tapes) for controlling production, permanent master cards go back into the files. Variable master cards are one-time-use cards and need not be kept long. You need new ones for every new order.

Stock records are also necessary for computerized production control and we don't mean just the usual stock record cards. Probably you will want to keep the usual record cards and tapes but you also need to maintain a "stock status" tape. This lets you use the computer to tell you how many parts or how much material you will need and to compare what you

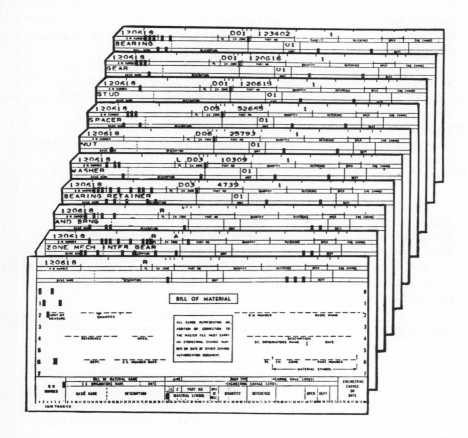

FIGURE 32-4   A group of master parts cards. The first card identifies the subassembly as number 120,618. The next two cards show the subassembly name. The remaining cards are for individual parts. All the parts cards show on the left that they belong to subassembly 120,618. Their own individual part numbers appear in the center of the card. The bearing retainer card, for example, shows its own part number to be 4,739. All parts must have such master cards so that bills of material can be printed and so that operations lists covering their manufacture can be made. (International Business Machines Corp.)

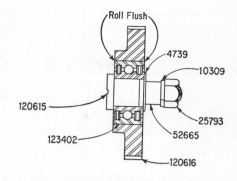

FIGURE 32-5   Drawing of assembly covered by the parts cards shown in figure
32-4. (International Business Machines
Corp.)

need with what you have on hand and on order. The computer can keep
these stock records for you and will record all changes automatically.

PERMANENT MASTER RECORDS

Permanent master records are of two general types: (1) those for products, subassemblies, and parts, and (2) those relating to operations. As
with stock records, usually this information goes first onto tabulating cards
and then onto magnetic tapes. Once on tapes, the cards are only a reserve
file since all calculations are made using the tape. As we said earlier, we
will talk about card and tape files more or less as if they were the same
thing.

   Product master card files contain one tabulating card for each kind of
product that you make. Besides this, you need a second file of master
cards, one containing a card for every *subassembly* and one for every *part*.
Figure 32-4 shows a set of master parts cards for the simple little subassembly shown in figure 32-5.

   Master product cards show little more than their name and identification number. Subassembly and parts master cards show the identification
number of the product to which they belong and the quantity needed for
one finished product, as well as their own individual part name and number. Master parts cards should also show whether you normally buy or
make the parts and, if you make them, the kind and quantity of raw material needed to make one part. Many companies also punch into their master cards the normal lead time that you have to allow for to get more.

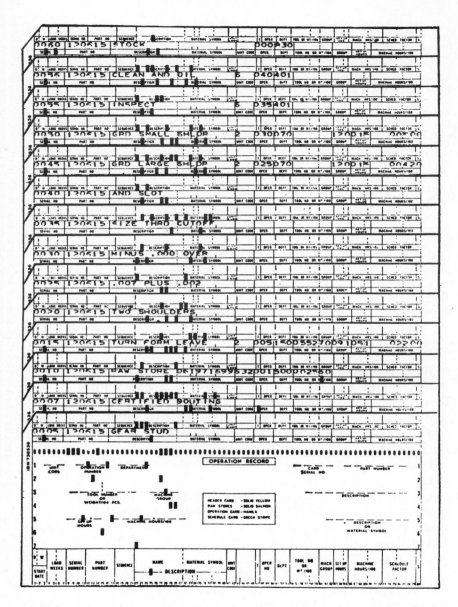

FIGURE 32-6   Master cards for the individual operations required to make stud number 120,615, shown in figure 32-4 as a part of gear and bearing assembly 120,618. There is a card for each operation and one to show the material from which it is made. Several of the cards (serial numbers 0015 to 0040) are for printing the instructions and tolerances for one operation, and one card indicates that the item, when finished, should be put into stock. (International Business Machines Corp.)

Probably you should make a master parts card for every part. Some companies do not make a card for general use items but other companies make separate parts cards for even paint, solder, welding rod and nuts, bolts, rivets, and screws. If you do this you will have quite a few cards for general use items, one for every product that uses each one. If you handle general use items on a B or C basis you don't really have to have parts cards for them because you'll keep them in stock without figuring their assembly needs.

There are two ways that you can file subassembly and parts master cards, either by "decks," "packs," or "sets" in a finished products file, or in one large general file containing cards for all parts of all products. It would seem simpler to file them as sets of cards and this is what most companies do. They usually do the same with data on magnetic tape files.

It is different, though, with raw materials. Almost always you would want to file their cards in general files because not often are they used solely for making one and only one kind of part.

The second general type of permanent master card kept on file is the file of *master operation cards*. Figure 32-6 shows the master operation cards for a gear stud, one of the parts of the subassembly shown in figure 32-5. Figure 32-7 shows the stud itself.

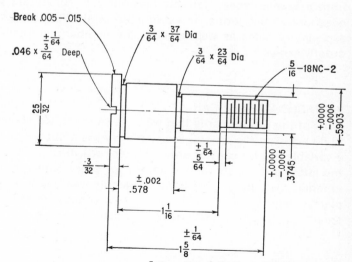

International Business Machines Corp.

FIGURE 32-7   Drawing of the gear stud covered by the operation cards shown in figure 32-6. (International Business Machines Corp.)

You need a master operation card for every operation on every man-ufactured part or subassembly. Such master cards show the operation name, number, department, and the amount of time it takes to process one part through the operation. For operations where parts may be spoiled, the expected loss ratio can also be shown. The card for the first operation may also show the kind and quantity of raw material needed to make one part. Operation cards may also show tool and machine attachment num-bers where they apply.

MASTER BILLS OF MATERIAL AND MASTER OPERATIONS LISTS

Having decks of master cards is not a very useful form in which to have master bills and master operation lists. You need to have printed up copies. These you make simply by passing the master decks through the printer and making as many copies as you like. Figure 13-2 shows parts of several automatically prepared bills of materials. Our sample is drawn up to show how subassemblies appear on bills of materials for products where they are used. Subassemblies are listed just as if they were piece parts, then each subassembly has its own master bill of materials.

This is even simpler with computers since it is so easy to print up lists from magnetic tapes. Not only that but with computers you don't even need preprinted forms; the computer prints titles, column heads, and explanatory notes as well as all of the numbers you need and all in an orderly array.

VARIABLE MASTER CARDS

None of the master cards that we have so far talked about have anything to do with specific orders. Each order needs a specific order card, called a variable master card or order master card. It is called variable because the information it shows is different for every order. It shows the order number, the kind of product, the quantity wanted, and the wanted com-pletion date. You have to make up new variable master cards for every shop order because the variable information changes.

STOCK RECORDS

The ordinary tabulating card is not large enough to serve as a stock record card nor would it be well suited to that use anyhow, since only a limited amount of information can be put on it in punched form. So even though you use a computer in production and inventory control, you may still want to keep visible stock record cards for both raw materials and finished parts. Receipts and disbursements can be recorded on them automatically by facsimile posting procedures.

This is not a must, however. You can let the computer tape record be the only record of inventory status and transactions. Whenever you want a print-out of the inventory of what you have on hand you can get it. On the other hand, a tape is not a very good way for keeping long-term records of all of the inventory ins and outs, details which you might sometime want but which you rarely do want again.

DETERMINING SUBASSEMBLIES AND PARTS REQUIREMENTS

Having decided to make a certain finished product, say a four-transistor portable radio, the first step is to make up a variable master telling how many you want and when. We'll say that we want 100. Now, get out the tapes of master subassemblies and parts for this radio. Put the variable master card and the master subassembly tape into the computer and have it make for you a new deck of parts cards or a new tape showing what you need for the order.

From here on you work only with the newly prepared card deck or tape, and you can put the master tape and the variable master card away. The new deck of cards shows the order number on every card and the quantity of that part needed. If the four transistors that you need are the same kind of transistor, the card for this item in the newly prepared pack of cards shows 400, not 4 and not 100. Using the new cards or tapes, you can print up the assembly order (the order bill of materials).

The new cards are also "requirements" cards. They tell you what items you'll need in order to make 100 radios. At this point the requirements cards include cards only for items that go directly into the final assembly. Even a major assembly has only one card.

Next, have the computer analyze the subassemblies. Essentially what the computer does here is to lay aside all of the requirements cards for individual piece parts and for general use items, and, for the time being, devote itself to subassemblies. It "sweeps" the stock status records for these assemblies, meaning that it checks to see how many of each assembly are on hand and on order that are not already committed to the other orders. Then the computer subtracts the new requirements from any uncommitted stocks of any of these assemblies and makes up a new set of requirements cards; this time requirements means the number we don't have and so will have to make or buy.

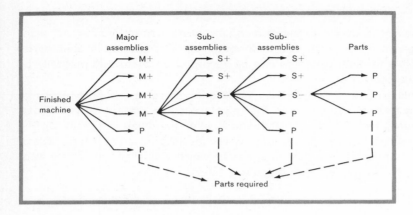

FIGURE 32-8 Schematic diagram of the process of "exploding" orders for completed products into orders for parts making. (International Business Machines Corp.)

The process isn't complete here, however, because we have to repeat these steps for every *assembly* that we have to make or buy. For each assembly, the computer calculates *its* parts and subassembly requirements, compares them to any uncommitted stocks, and produces a list of items still to procure.

Then once again the process is repeated for every *subassembly* and still again, if there are several generations of subassemblies, on down until all requirements are in terms of piece parts or general use items. Figure 32-8 shows schematically how this operates.

Out of all this you get new order cards for every assembly, subassembly, and part that you need to procure. And you get new stock status records showing the new status of every item.

COMMON PARTS

We have already said that it is a good idea to combine your various needs for common parts so that you can make or buy them to best advantage, considering your total demand. We also noted that in some cases, such as aircraft production, the problem of combining demands for common parts gets to be so complicated that they don't do it in every case.

In the electronics industry (as in most industries) it is very important to bring together the needs for common parts such as diodes, condensers, switches, sockets, relays, transistors, microcircuits, and such items. Some

STOCK STATUS SUMMARY

DATE

PART NUMBER	PART DESCRIPTION	SCE	PERIOD	OPENING BALANCE	ACTUAL TRANSACTIONS			PLANNED TRANSACTIONS		
					RECEIVED ⊕	ISSUED ⊖	ON HAND ⊜	REQUIRED ⊕	ON ORDER ⊜	AVAILABLE
27057	CONDENSER	2	125	358			358	185		173
27058	CONDENSER	2	125	175	75		250	325	1000	925
27069	PLATE	1	125	210	50	155	105	75		30
27070	SOCKET	1	125	1755	1205	2885	75	595	1200	680
27075	SOCKET	1	125	1327	1190	1872	645	400		245
27082	SOCKET	1	125	1285	1210	2200	295	425		130–

FIGURE 32-9   Stock on hand and on order. (International Business Machines Corp.)

products (computers, for example) use these items by the thousands in one product. The same item may turn up as a part in a dozen or even a hundred different places in the product.

The problem is this: Each product's deck of master parts cards contains a card for every part. Any part used in two or more products has a card in each product's deck or is listed as a need on each product's tape. When you calculate the needs for one product, you end up with a requirements card for the part for this one end product. Then when you calculate the needs for another product, you get another requirements card for the same item. But at this point you don't know that you have two requirements cards for the same item. You will find this out, though, in the end, when you put *all* the parts requirements cards or tapes together and sort them by part number before making up reorders for parts. This is the last step in the process of finding out what parts to order.

You can escape this whole problem for many parts by using max-min controls for them although this is a little dangerous if their use varies much. Also, it boosts your inventory a little. Actually though you should rarely need to "escape" the problem. Computers can easily handle most such situations.

STOCK STATUS REPORTS

Unless you use a computer, you'll probably never see a "stock status report." They are too costly to make up very often. Yet with computers status reports become the core of the reordering procedure, particularly in repetitive manufacture. Computers can make out status reports at such low cost that many companies run them off weekly or even daily.

A stock status report is a list, item by item, of what you have on hand. But it is a great deal more than just that. You can and usually do have it also show what is on order and the total available. You also show the demand side, how many parts you need for assembly orders already issued, and how much raw material you need for parts orders already planned. And you can show the future demands on a scheduled basis, week by week or month by month. In addition, you can show reorder points and reorder quantities on status reports.

In the process that we described earlier of making requirements cards and then order cards, you would need several stock status reports. They would not, any of them, be complete surveys of every item that you carry but would show the status of certain groups of items. You would need one first when you checked the requirements for major assemblies against their status. This would cover only the assemblies involved. Next, you'd need similar status reports for subassemblies at each stage where you made out new requirements lists. And finally, you'd need a parts stock status report for the last stage described.

Stock status reports by no means replace stock records. Stock status cards are more or less like the last horizontal line on the ordinary stock record card. Status reports are single-use reports. Any time that stock is

STOCK STATUS SUMMARY
HORIZONTAL TIME SERIES
DATE

PART NUMBER	PART DESCRIPTION	SCE	ON HAND	TRANS-ACTION	PERIOD						BALANCE TOTAL
					1	2	3	4	5	6	
27057	CONDENSER	2	1200	BALANCE							1200
				REQUIRED	400	410	420	450	410	420	2510-
				ORDERED			600		600		1200
				AVAIL.	800	390	570	120	310	110-	110-
27058	CONDENSER	2	1500	BALANCE							1500
				REQUIRED	450	480	500	500	510	520	2960-
				ORDERED			2000				2000
				AVAIL.	1050	570	2070	1570	1060	540	540
27069	PLATE	1	15000	BALANCE							15000
				REQUIRED	310	350	400	300	350	300	2010-
				ORDERED				5000			5000
				AVAIL.	14690	14340	13940	18640	18290	17990	17990

FIGURE 32-10   Requirements by time periods. (International Business Machines Corp.)

issued, ordered, received, or apportioned, the old status record is brought up to date, and a new status record is generated immediately. Probably you would have the computer make all of these changes on tapes and not make up status cards at all.

The procedure is a kind of perpetual inventory with no record of past transactions. You can, of course, have the computer keep records of all old status positions and of all changes, but mainly you are interested in where you are now.

REORDERS

Stock status reports are tied in very closely with reordering because they tell you at every stage from major assemblies down to piece parts whether or not your stock covers your demand for an item. This is how you find out that reorders are necessary.

Reordering is, however, one part of the process that you don't trust to the machine. You may want, for example, to reorder more than the demand in order to gain advantages from standard lots or economic lots, or full car shipments. Or you may make subassemblies as basics and not tie their reorders closely to assembly needs. Or you may carry B and C items on a max-min basis and again there is no close tie-in with assembly needs. Or you may order less than the demand, as you probably would on short cycle items whose demand is for products that you'll make several months hence. You may very well calculate today the parts that you'll need for products to be made six months from now. But if they can be made quickly and won't be needed until the end, you don't need to order them made now. Whenever you do reorder, though, and in whatever quantity, you must always make out an order card and its quantity becomes your demand in any further analysis.

You make reorder decisions at each stage of the analysis. Assembly needs set the requirements for major assemblies. But major assembly *reorders* set the requirements for subassemblies. And subassemblies *reorders* set the requirements for lesser subassemblies. The more generations away from final assembly that you get in your calculations, the less directly do final assembly requirements set reorder quantities.

MAKING UP MANUFACTURING ORDERS

To make up manufacturing orders mechanically, you start with a master order card for every item that you are going to make. This card shows the order number, its identification, the quantity wanted, and its wanted completion date. Next, get out the deck of operation master cards for the item. Each of the master cards gives you the operation information that you need.

Put the order card and the operation cards into the computer and it will make you a new set of one-time use operation cards. The computer will multiply the operation time per unit by the number to be made and, for each operation, will punch in the time that it will take to do the operation on the whole order. The deck of master operation cards then goes back into the file.

This new deck of single-use cards now contains all the information about the order and the operations. You can now run off shop orders by passing the cards through the printing machine. Each card will print one line. Figure 32-11 is a shop order for an order of gear studs, the one pictured in figure 32-7. (Remember all of this can be done on magnetic tapes without cards having to be made.)

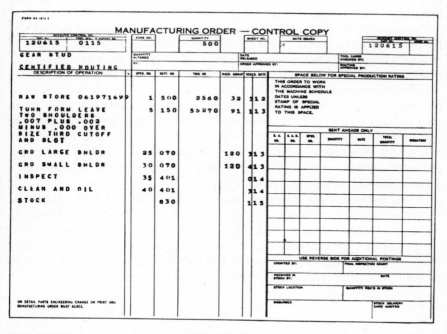

FIGURE 32-11 A manufacturing order for 500 gear studs, showing operations and due dates. This order, including the setting of the schedule due dates for operations, was made up by the computer. The operations listed are those shown on the set of master cards illustrated in figure 32-6. (International Business Machines Corp.)

Some companies use computers to set due dates for every individual operation. To do this you have to start with the operation card for the last operation because it and only it has the wanted completion date for the order punched in it. Have the machine subtract its operating time to get its start time. Then have the machine subtract a standard between-job time allowance to get the finishing time for the next to the last operation. Punch this date into the operation card for the next to the last operation. Repeat the process, operation by operation, and you will work back to a date when the raw material should come out of the stores department and be delivered to the first operation. Once you have dates in all of the operation cards, you can run off shop orders showing the wanted completion date for every operation. Remember, though, that you have been, in this procedure, allowing for standard job times. Men earning bonuses will take less time than you have allowed. Also, remember, your computer can do all of this without cards.

After preparing shop orders, the individual operation cards for all the orders that you have can be sorted by machine group and by week. You can add up their machine time requirements and find the new work load that you are adding to each machine group. Adding this to the loads already ahead of each machine group gives you their full work load. Print this up and you have your machine load record. Again, though, remember that this may not be a very good load record because you have loaded all the jobs in at standard man-hours.

This, as we said earlier, is not a serious criticism to such work load records because normal machine deadtime may offset the gains from bonus workers' extra production. Also, in any case you get a list of jobs ahead of machines. Bullard Company, heavy machinery maker, varies this idea a little by separating out and showing on its weekly load sheet a list of jobs already waiting at each machine center. It calls this list its "Where-is-it?" report.

You can also prepare job tickets for the men from the same individual operation cards, and also prepare move tickets and extra copies of any of them to be filed in shop offices or for other uses.

RESCHEDULING

Whether you make all different products or make the same assembled products continuously, you will have to contend with schedule changes. Computers help here because they will redo your schedules with new dates so much faster than you could do them any other way.

The Electric Boat division of General Dynamics Corporation finds that when it makes submarines, each month-end sees so many changes that it has to change some 3,000 scheduled dates every month. Computers make out all new operation cards with new dates and print up all the new work orders in a few days. Also, automobile companies with computers are able to make schedule changes in days instead of weeks in spite of this requiring the making over of thousands of individual schedules.

FORMS DUPLICATION

Production control has an unusual problem in preparing the factory's directives. You might call it a "double duplication" process. It arises from the need to make up assembly orders and shop orders for parts from two kinds of original information.

With computers this problem no longer exists because computers can do this work automatically. But in companies which have not computerized their production control procedures, this problem still exists. We spoke about it briefly in Chapter 23.

Using assembly orders as an example, we start with the master bill of materials. To make an order bill (an actual assembly order), as we said in Chapter 23, you copy the list of parts and their quantities per unit from the master bill. You also copy the individual order information from the variable master. In some companies the variable master is called a "strip master" because it is a long narrow strip of paper which fills in a blank section of the sheet listing the parts. After multiplying the number of parts per unit by the number of units on the order and filling in these new numbers, the end product of this process is an order bill of materials. Making it from the master bill and the variable master is the first of the two duplications.

We have used an assembly order to illustrate double duplication. You find the same thing when making shop orders for parts. Again you have a master list, this time a list of operations. And again you have a variable master showing individual order information. From these you make up the shop order.

At this point, though, you have only one copy of the order bill or shop order. Now you have to make several copies of *it* for production purposes. This is the second of the two duplications. The trick is to have a procedure which makes orders from masters easily and which then allows further copies of them to be made readily.

With shop orders for parts you may well have to do still more duplicating beyond making copies of the whole order. You need job tickets and materials requisitions too and you need to be able to make them from the same original records with as little extra work as possible. Of course, computers can readily make job tickets for every operation and can also make out requisitions just as easily but we are assuming that you don't have this work on a computer.

Companies without computers used to make multiple copies of order bills and shop orders by fluid duplicators (variations of the old purple transferable ink "ditto" process). Some companies still use this method. The point here is that you have to make up order bills and shop orders on a special kind of paper so that you can make copies from it.

Today, most copying is done by one of the numerous dry electrostatic processes. These dry copy processes produce any number of copies directly from an original. Of these processes, perhaps Xerox is the most common in use today. Electrostatic processes all work in about the same way. A treated blank sheet is sensitized electrostatically to attract black ink dust to an image of the original. Then the black ink dust is heated and adheres permanently to the sheet even after the electrical charge is gone, thus producing a copy of the original.

Xerox machines will copy almost anything whether the original is typing, computer print-outs, or whatever. In some machines the original has to pass through the machine together with the sheet being copied onto. These processes can't copy book pages, but other processes work from copy placed on top of the machine which makes it easy both to make many copies and to copy book pages if you want.

THE FORMS TO BE DUPLICATED

The forms which production control has to make out include bills of materials, manufacturing orders, job tickets, move orders, material identification tags, tool orders, purchase requisitions, and materials requisitions.

The less fully production control is centralized, the fewer are the forms to be duplicated. You need order bills of material and shop orders for parts in any case but in decentralized control, the production control department might not need to prepare move orders, individual job tickets, and materials requisitions. Materials identification tags are also required, but they may be made out in the factory department where the first operation is performed. You usually have to make up many copies of assembly order bills and parts shop orders. Every department concerned ought to get a copy.

The production control department rarely prepares copies of drawings

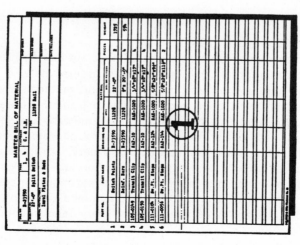

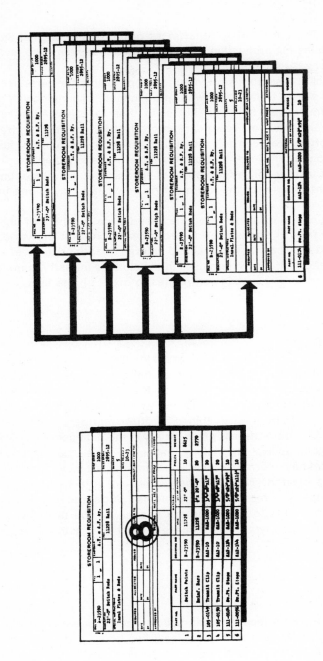

FIGURE 32-12 The way you set up forms to use a fluid duplicator. Form 1 is a master bill of materials. Numbers 2 and 3 are variable masters, which provide individual order information. Number 7 is production control's copy of the order bill of materials (numbers 4, 5, and 6 are for other departments). Number 8 shows a preassembled set of requisitions, which when run through the duplicator and then pulled apart become individual requisitions for each item on the bill. (Ditto, Inc.)

or specifications. The engineering department prepares the original and also makes up copies for production whenever you need them (whenever production control asks for them).

In flow control in assembly work, men at supply points for parts need copies of the run sheets to tell them what products are coming down the line and when. You might, however, not send them a copy of the run sheet at all and rely wholly on Telautograph or electric typewriters wired into the central office. You can tell the supply points, item by item, just what items are coming. In load control, you have to make schedules for key machines but usually only a few copies of such schedules will do, one for production control, one for the key machine crew, and maybe one for the foreman.

In flow, load, and block control you may need large numbers of tags. These tags differ from the tags used in order control in that the variety is not so great and they can be made ahead in large quantities to cover all types needed. In the stub-tag system used in the clothing industry, numerous tags are also used. Production control has to make up the tags.

TAG REPRODUCTION

In some companies large numbers of materials identification tags are used and production control usually gets the job of making most of them. They usually contain enough repetitive information that you print them up or reproduce them mechanically rather than by writing, although often you will have to write or stamp in such things as order numbers and dates.

In order control, where there is great variety in the data going on tags, you can make tags on special tag making machines. These machines are easily set up to print any information that you want and will make whatever number of tags is desired. The tags themselves are attached in chain fashion in long strips. The machines print one line of data at a time with whatever letters, numbers, or fractions are needed. If you need two or more lines of information, you have to pass them through the machine once for each line.

OTHER COMMUNICATION SYSTEMS

The regular company interdepartmental mail service is generally too slow for production control. It usually takes at least two hours and sometimes a full day for mail to get to its destination. Production control has to move faster, so it usually has its own mail service and inter-com systems. Occasionally you will find pneumatic tubes used for sending forms but they are unusual. Inter-com systems are almost always a must and you will often find comprehensive systems of input and output stations linked into the computer. You may also find Telautographs and even teletypewriters electrically connected to the central office.

Company-wide computer connections and teletypewriter connections are often used between distant plants which have to coordinate their work. You can type something in Chicago and have it come out on type-writers in Houston, Boston, or wherever you want it. Or you can have data come into your central computer and have two-way connections with out-lying points. Two-way radios to control plant truckers and maintenance men are common. Television has also found a place in industry, particularly to let you look at hard-to-see places, such as inside furnaces, or to enable you to watch storage yards. Most of these applications do not concern production control.

STUDY MATERIALS

32-1 According to some authorities, the role of middle management will slowly atrophy as a result of computerized total information systems. Using the *total* production control function from the design of the system to the detailed scheduling aspects as an example, does this statement appear to be correct? What aspects of production control appear to be the most vulnerable to computerization? To what extent is the whole process of automation related to mechanized information flow and processing?

32-2 In contrast to the opinion expressed above, others have argued that computers have not had any real impact on production control—they merely do the same job that was done before, only somewhat faster. Considering what has been said in this and previous chapters on the amount and types of production control information that must be processed and transmitted, does this statement appear to be valid for both punch-card systems and computerized systems?

32-3 The Richmond Boiler Company installed a system using tabulating equipment in its production control work. Both job tickets and materials requisitions were prepared ahead on tabulating cards.

Job tickets were issued to the men whenever they started on new jobs, by the department clerk in each factory department. The cards for jobs completed were kept by the men until the end of the day, when all cards were turned in to the clerk. Requisitions for raw materials also were given to the operators by the clerk whenever they were needed. The operators presented the requisitions at the stock room and withdrew the required material. The workers usually kept their job tickets in their pockets and often carried requisitions around for some time before presenting them at the stock room.

As a rule the job tickets came in to the tabulating department folded, creased, and dirty. Sometimes the requisitions were just as bad. It was necessary to make new cards for all of the defaced cards because they would not go through the tabulating machines. The cost of making the extra cards amounted to a sizable sum, and the Richmond company management was concerned about it.

What do companies do in such cases? Are most of them able to eliminate the trouble? If you could not eliminate it without a change in procedure, what change would you recommend?

32-4   Outside research. Examine the changes in technology taking place in a given industry including such matters as new equipment, processes, products, materials, and patterns of management. How will these affect the production control function? Be as specific as possible in your evaluation.

Random Numbers

322	810	756	344	027	658	943	289	965	276
536	990	532	094	539	308	696	080	366	451
439	027	759	272	623	364	407	449	370	694
238	273	941	799	485	587	120	543	918	238
709	739	310	999	272	310	994	017	945	927
692	912	670	037	018	695	518	273	123	943
270	999	075	207	030	043	006	852	957	768
054	579	869	904	033	672	414	850	951	621
834	482	068	703	098	970	174	840	391	543
287	594	981	611	407	697	476	973	687	859
260	572	947	508	195	374	721	198	057	531
747	416	870	169	543	422	617	523	351	152
416	877	332	396	115	728	252	071	748	679
322	654	798	539	181	370	520	532	608	883
002	807	118	786	354	861	141	025	229	731
217	590	735	629	491	869	431	285	371	709
686	359	273	135	133	215	172	626	463	616
584	895	372	641	297	544	156	890	049	784
379	668	206	282	056	196	714	283	184	154
933	051	047	229	685	146	774	114	027	141
755	482	252	990	340	319	396	116	843	317
806	672	856	082	843	918	606	453	942	797
242	601	105	135	187	940	108	406	743	855
593	877	679	400	368	619	920	539	991	799
638	780	709	516	898	433	576	496	837	673
039	302	411	741	996	457	161	875	060	475
322	160	509	153	050	758	933	332	843	475
507	794	941	506	502	258	287	963	896	467
447	300	889	404	761	876	223	032	477	832
547	539	210	854	417	093	145	298	356	455

Cumulated Percentages of Cases in a Normal Distribution from Small to Large, by Tenths of Standard Deviations, above and below the Mean[1]

STANDARD DEVIATIONS	PER CENT	STANDARD DEVIATIONS	PER CENT	STANDARD DEVIATIONS	PER CENT	STANDARD DEVIATIONS	PER CENT
−3.0	.1	−1.4	8.3	+0.2	57.9	+1.7	95.3
−2.9	.2	−1.3	9.9	+0.3	61.7	+1.8	96.2
−2.8	.3	−1.2	11.7	+0.4	65.4	+1.9	96.9
−2.7	.4	−1.1	13.8	+0.5	69.0	+2.0	97.5
−2.6	.6	−1.0	16.1	+0.6	72.4	+2.1	98.0
−2.5	.8	−0.9	18.6	+0.7	75.6	+2.2	98.4
−2.4	1.0	−0.8	21.4	+0.8	78.6	+2.3	98.7
−2.3	1.3	−0.7	24.4	+0.9	81.4	+2.4	99.0
−2.2	1.6	−0.6	27.6	+1.0	83.9	+2.5	99.2
−2.1	2.0	−0.5	31.0	+1.1	86.2	+2.6	99.4
−2.0	2.5	−0.4	34.6	+1.2	88.3	+2.7	99.6
−1.9	3.1	−0.3	38.3	+1.3	90.1	+2.8	99.7
−1.8	3.8	−0.2	42.1	+1.4	91.9	+2.9	99.8
−1.7	4.7	−0.1	46.0	+1.5	93.1	+3.0	99.9
−1.6	5.7	0.0	50.0	+1.6	94.3	+3.1	100.0
−1.5	6.9	+0.1	54.0				

[1] To use random numbers yet get a normal distribution, set blocks of random numbers as equal to the above percentages. Thus random number 001 means −3.0 standard deviations from the mean, number 002 means −2.9 standard deviations. Numbers 039 to 047 mean occurrences between −1.8 and −1.7 standard deviations. Numbers between 580 and 617 mean occurrences beyond +0.2 and up to +0.3 standard deviations above the mean.

Administrative Management: "Control Boards from Pegs to PERT," July, 1963.

Agin, Norman: "A Max-Min Inventory Model," *Management Science*, March, 1966, pp. 517–529.

Amey, L. R.: "Allocation and Utilization of Resources," *Operational Research Quarterly*, June, 1964, pp. 87–100.

Anthony, R. N., and J. S. Hekimian: *Operations Cost Control*, Richard D. Irwin, Inc., Homewood, Ill., 1967.

APICS Dictionary: American Production and Inventory Control Society, Chicago, 1963.

Balas, Egon: "Solution of Large-scale Transportation Problems through Aggregation," *Operations Research*, January–February, 1965, pp. 82–93.

Banerjee, B. P.: "Single Facility Sequencing with Random Execution Times," *Operations Research*, 1965, pp. 358–364.

Barba, B.: "Some Numerical Data for Single-server Queues Involving Deterministic Input Arrangements," *Operational Research Quarterly*, June, 1964, pp. 107–115.

Battersby, Albert: *Network Analysis for Planning and Scheduling*, St Martin's Press, Inc., New York, 1964.

Beckman, M. J.: "Dynamic Programming and Inventory Control," *Operational Research Quarterly*, December, 1964, pp. 389–400.

Beranek, William: "Financial Implications of Lot-size Inventory Models," *Management Science*, April, 1967, pp. B401–B408.

Biegel, John E.: *Production Control*, Prentice-Hall, Inc., Englewood Cliffs, N.J., 1963.

Bock, Robert H., and William K. Holstein (eds.): *Production Planning and Control*, Charles E. Merrill Books, Inc., Columbus, Ohio, 1963.

Bomberger, Earl E.: "A Dynamic Programming Approach to a Lot Size Scheduling Problem," *Management Science*, July, 1966, pp. 778–784.

Bowman, Edward H., and Robert B. Fetter: *Analysis for Production Management*, 3d ed., Richard D. Irwin, Inc., Homewood, Ill., 1967.

Brown, Robert G.: *Smoothing, Forecasting, and Prediction of Discrete Time Series*, Prentice-Hall, Inc., Englewood Cliffs, N.J., 1963.

————: *Decision Rules for Inventory Management*, Holt, Rinehart and Winston, Inc., New York, 1967.

Buchan, Joseph, and Ernest Koenigsberg: *Scientific Inventory Management*, Prentice-Hall, Inc., Englewood Cliffs, N.J., 1963.

Buffa, Elwood S.: *Models for Production and Operations Management*, John Wiley & Sons, Inc., New York, 1963.

————: *Production-Inventory Systems: Planning and Control*, Richard D. Irwin, Inc., Homewood, Ill., 1968.

Bulkin, Michael H., John L. Colley, and Harry W. Steinhoff, Jr.: "Load Forecasting,

Priority Sequencing, and Simulation in a Job Shop Control System," *Management Science*, October, 1966, pp. B29–B51.

Carroll, Phil: *Practical Production and Inventory Control*, McGraw-Hill Book Company, New York, 1966.

Chorafas, Dimitris N.: *Systems and Simulation*, Academic Press Inc., New York, 1965.

Crane, Dwight B., and James R. Crotty: "A Two-stage Forecasting Model: Exponential Smoothing and Multiple Regression," *Management Science*, April, 1967, pp. B501–B507.

Crowther, J. F.: "Rationale for Quantity Discounts," *Harvard Business Review*, March–April, 1964, pp. 121–127.

D'Anna, John P.: *Inventory and Profit*, New York, American Management Association, 1966.

Dantzig, George B.: *Linear Programming and Extensions*, Princeton University Press, Princeton, N.J., 1963.

Dobbie, J. M.: "Forecasting Periodic Trends by Exponential Smoothing," *Operations Research*, November–December, 1963, pp. 908–918.

Easterfield, T. E.: "Optimum Variety," *Operational Research Quarterly*, June, 1964, pp. 71–85.

England, Wilbur D.: *The Purchasing System*, Richard D. Irwin, Inc., Homewood, Ill., 1967.

"Exclusive Survey Shows New Directions in Production and Inventory Control," report on APICS study, *Factory*, October, 1966.

Fabrycky, W. J., and J. Banks: *Procurement and Inventory Systems: Theory and Analysis*, Reinhold Publishing Corporation, New York, 1967.

Feeney, G. J., and C. C. Sherbrooke: "The (S-1,s) Inventory Policy Under Compound Poisson Demand," *Management Science*, January, 1966, pp. 391–411.

Feldman, E F., F. A. Lehrer, and T. L. Ray: "Warehouse Location Under Continuous Economies of Scale," *Management Science*, May, 1966, pp. 670–684.

Fetter, Robert B.: *The Quality Control System*, Richard D. Irwin, Inc., Homewood, Ill., 1967.

Foster, F. G.: "Batched Queuing Processes," *Operations Research*, May, 1964, pp. 441–449.

Frank, O.: "Optimal Order to Serve in Certain Servicing Problems," *Operations Research*, May, 1964, pp. 433–440.

Gallagher, Paul F.: *Project Estimating by Engineering Methods*, Hayden Publishing Company, New York, 1966.

Gavett, J. William: "Three Heuristic Rules for Sequencing Jobs to a Single Production Facility," *Management Science*, June, 1965, pp. B166–B176.

Geisler, M. A.: "A Study of Inventory Theory," *Management Science*, April, 1963, pp. 490–497.

———: "The Sizes of Simulation Samples Required to Compute Certain Inventory

Characteristics with Stated Precision and Confidence," *Management Science*, January, 1964, pp. 261–286.

Giffler, B.: "Mathematical Solution of Parts Requirements Problems," *Management Science*, July, 1965, pp. 847–867.

Glassner, B. J.: "Cycling in the Transportation Problem," *Naval Research Logistics Quarterly*, March, 1964, pp. 43–58.

Gomersall, Earl R.: "The Backlog Syndrome," *Harvard Business Review*, September–October, 1964, pp. 105–115.

Goslin, Lewis N.: *The Product Planning System*, Richard D. Irwin, Inc., Homewood, Ill., 1967.

Greene, James H.: *Operations Planning and Control*, Richard D. Irwin, Inc., Homewood, Ill., 1967.

————: *Production Control*, Richard D. Irwin, Inc., Homewood, Ill., 1965.

Gross, Donald, and Jack L. Ray: "A General Purpose Forecast Simulator," *Management Science*, April, 1965, pp. B119–B135.

Hadley, G., and T. M. Whitin: *Analysis of Inventory Systems*, Prentice-Hall, Inc., Englewood Cliffs, N.J., 1963.

Hanssmann, Fred: *Operations Research in Production and Inventory Control*, John Wiley & Sons, Inc., New York, 1962.

Harris, R. D.: "An Empirical Investigation and Model Proposal for a Jobshop-like Queuing System," Western Management Science Institute (UCLA), July, 1965.

Hartmeyer, Fred C.: *Electronics Industry Cost Estimating Data*, The Ronald Press Company, New York, 1964.

Harty, J. D., G. W. Plossl, and O. W. Wright: *Management of Lot-size Inventories*, Chicago, American Production and Inventory Control Society, September, 1963.

Hirschmann, Winfred B.: "Profit from the Learning Curve," *Harvard Business Review*, January–February, 1964, pp. 125–139.

Hunt, Joseph A.: "Balancing Accuracy and Simplicity in Determining Reorder Points," *Management Science*, December, 1965, pp. B94–B103.

Ignall, E., and Linus Schrage: "Application of the Branch and Bound Technique to Some Flow-shop Scheduling Problems," *Operations Research*, May–June, 1965, pp. 400–412.

Industrial Education Institute: *How to Use the Learning Curve*, Boston, 1965.

International Business Machines Corp., "1440/1311 Bill of Material Processor," Application Description H20-0079-1, Programmer's Manual H20-0151, and Operator's Manual H20-0152, 1965.

Krone, L. H.: "A Note on Economic Lot Sizes for Multi-purpose Equipment," *Management Science*, April, 1964, pp. 461–464.

Lawson. W. H.: "Computer Simulation in Inventory Management," *Systems and Procedures Journal*, June, 1964, pp. 38–40.

Levin, Richard I.: *Quantitative Approaches to Management*, New York, McGraw-Hill Book Company, New York, 1965.

Llewellyn, Robert W.: *Linear Programming*, Holt, Rinehart and Winston, Inc., New York, 1964.

Lomnicki, Z. A.: "A Branch and Bound Algorithm for the Exact Solution of the Three-machine Scheduling Problem," *Operations Research Quarterly*, 1965, pp. 89–100.

Magee, John F., and David M. Boodman: *Production Planning and Inventory Control*, 2d ed., McGraw-Hill Book Company, New York, 1967.

Maxwell, William L.: "The Scheduling of Economic Lot Sizes," *Naval Research Logistics Quarterly*, June, 1964, pp. 72–82.

McGarrah, Robert E.: *Production and Logistics Management*, John Wiley & Sons, Inc., New York, 1963.

Mellor, P.: "A Review of Job-shop Scheduling," *Operations Research Quarterly*, June, 1966, pp. 161–171.

Miller, Robert W.: *Schedule, Cost, and Profit Control with PERT*, McGraw-Hill Book Company, New York, 1963.

Moder, Joseph J.: *Project Management with CPM and PERT*, Reinhold Publishing Corporation, New York, 1964.

Muth, John F., and Gerald L. Thompson (eds.): *Industrial Scheduling*, Prentice-Hall, Inc., Englewood Cliffs, N.J., 1963.

Naddor, Eliezer: *Inventory Systems*, John Wiley & Sons, Inc., New York, 1966.

Palmer, D. S.: "Sequencing Jobs through a Multi-process in the Minimum Total Time—A Quick Method of Obtaining a Near Optimum," *Operations Research Quarterly*, June, 1965, pp. 101–107.

Plossl, G. W., and O. W. Wright: *Production and Inventory Control: Principles and Techniques*, Prentice-Hall, Inc., Englewood Cliffs, N.J., 1967.

Prabhu, N. U.: *Queues and Inventories*, John Wiley & Sons, Inc., New York, 1965.

Presby, J. T., and M. L. Wolfson: "An Algorithm for Solving Job Sequencing Problems," *Management Science*, April, 1967, pp. B454–B464.

Prichard, James E., and Robert H. Eagle: *Modern Inventory Management*, John Wiley & Sons, Inc., New York, 1965.

Production and Inventory Management, Journal of the American Production and Inventory Society, Inc., Chicago (quarterly).

Rago, Louis J.: *Production Analysis and Control*, International Textbook Company, Scranton, Pa., 1963.

di Roccaferrera, Guiseppe M. Ferrero: *Operations Research Models for Business and Industry*, South-Western Publishing Company, Cincinnati, 1964.

Scarf, Herbert E., Dorothy M. Gilford, and Maynard W. Sheely (eds.): *Multistage Inventory Models and Techniques*, Stanford University Press, Stanford, Calif., 1966.

Silver, Edward A.: "A Bayesian Determination of the Reorder Point of a Slow Moving Item," *Operations Research*, November–December, 1965, pp. 989–997.

————: "Some Characteristics of a Special Joint-order Inventory Model," *Operations Research*, March–April, 1965, pp. 319–322.

Smith, Robert M.: *Automated Inventory—Production Control,* Management Services, New York, 1965.

Starr, Martin K.: *Production Management Systems and Synthesis,* Prentice-Hall, Inc., Englewood Cliffs, N.J., 1964.

—— **and D. W. Miller:** *Inventory Control Theory and Practice,* Prentice-Hall, Inc., Englewood Cliffs, N.J., 1962.

Stilian, Gabrial, et al.: *PERT: A New Management Planning and Control Technique,* American Management Association, New York, 1963.

Stocktom, R. Stansbury: *Basic Inventory Systems,* Allyn and Bacon, Inc., Boston, 1965.

Sudderth, W. D.: "Another Formulation of the Inventory Problem," *Operations Research,* May–June, 1965, pp. 504–507.

Szwarc, W.: "The Transportation Problem with Stochastic Demand," *Management Science,* September, 1964, pp. 33–50.

Thomas, A. B.: "Optimizing Multi-stage Production Processes," *Operational Research Quarterly,* June, 1963, pp. 201–213.

Thompson, G. L.: "On the Parts Requirements Problem," *Operations Research,* May–June, 1965, pp. 453–461.

Thompson, Howard E.: "Forecasting Errors, Diversification and Inventory Fluctuations," *Journal of the Academy of Management,* March, 1966, pp. 67–77.

—— **and William Beranek:** "The Efficient Use of an Imperfect Forecast," *Management Science,* November, 1966, pp. 233–243.

Trigg, D. W.: "Monitoring a Forecast System," *Operational Research Quarterly,* September, 1964, pp. 271–274.

Van De Mark, Robert L.: *Production Control Techniques,* Gilson Press, Grand Rapids, Mich., 1964.

Veinott, A. F.: "The Optimal Inventory Policy for Batch Ordering," *Operations Research,* May–June, 1965, pp. 424–432.

Voris, William: *Production Control,* 3d ed., Richard D. Irwin, Inc., Homewood, Ill., 1966.

Wagner, Harvey M.: *Statistical Management of Inventory Systems,* John Wiley & Sons, Inc., New York, 1962.

White, D. J.: "Dynamic Programming and Equipment Resetting Decision Rules," *Operational Research Quarterly,* June, 1964, pp. 133–137.

Whitin, Thomas M.: *Analysis of Inventory Systems,* Prentice-Hall, Inc., Englewood Cliffs, N.J., 1963.

Wilson, F. W. (ed): *Manufacturing Planning and Estimating Handbook,* McGraw-Hill Book Company, New York, 1963.

Wolfe, Harry D.: *Business Forecasting Methods,* Holt, Rinehart and Winston, Inc., New York, 1966.

INDEX